HANDBOOK OF INTERNATIONAL LAW

A concise account of international law by an experienced practitioner, this book explains how states and international organisations, especially the United Nations, make and use international law. The nature of international law and its fundamental concepts and principles are described. The difference and relationship between various areas of international law which are often misunderstood (such as diplomatic and state immunity, and human rights and international humanitarian law) are clearly explained. The essence of new specialist areas of international law relating to the environment, human rights and terrorism is discussed.

Aust's clear and accessible style makes the subject understandable to non-international lawyers, non-lawyers and students. Abundant references are provided to sources and other materials, including authoritative and useful websites.

ANTHONY AUST is a former Deputy Legal Adviser of the Foreign and Commonwealth Office, London. A solicitor, he now practises as a consultant on international law and constitutional law to governments and international organisations, both privately and with the law firm Kendall Freeman of London. He is a visiting professor at the London School of Economics. His publications include *Modern Treaty Law and Practice* (Cambridge University Press, 2002).

HANDBOOK OF
INTERNATIONAL LAW

ANTHONY AUST

London School of Economics and
Kendall Freeman Solicitors

CAMBRIDGE
UNIVERSITY PRESS

CAMBRIDGE UNIVERSITY PRESS
Cambridge, New York, Melbourne, Madrid, Cape Town, Singapore, São Paulo

Cambridge University Press
The Edinburgh Building, Cambridge CB2 2RU, UK

Published in the United States of America by Cambridge University Press, New York

www.cambridge.org
Information on this title: www.cambridge.org/9780521530347

First published 2005

Printed in the United Kingdom at the University Press, Cambridge

A catalogue record for this book is available from the British Library

Library of Congress Cataloguing in Publication data
Aust, Anthony.
Handbook of international law / Anthony Aust. – 1st ed.
p.   cm.
Includes index.
ISBN 0-521-82349-8 (hardback) – ISBN 0-521-53034-2 (pbk.)
1. International law.   I. Title.
KZ3410.A94   2005   341–dc22

ISBN-13   978-0-521-82349-4 hardback
ISBN-10   0-521-82349-8 hardback
ISBN-13   978-0-521-53034-7 paperback
ISBN-10   0-521-53034-2 paperback

For Kirsten

CONTENTS

FOREWORD

Tony Aust has already produced *Modern Treaty Law and Practice* (Cambridge University Press, 2000). This was an exercise in the handbook mode which some scholars profess to dislike, and which most of them certainly neglect. In my own case I confess that his handbook is often to hand, because it is a place to start looking at problems in the law of treaties on an everyday basis. It does not claim to be definitive, but it succeeds in its task of introducing and of providing initial guidance in a clear and well-informed way. Take for example the short discussion on provisional application (*ibid.*, pp. 139–41), an issue of great practical significance as to which there is little or nothing in the older treatises. What he says is clear, well illustrated – one is pointed to difficulties and prominent instances (e.g. the Energy Charter Treaty) – and one is told that the case of provisional application which everyone knows – GATT 1947 – is 'hugely atypical'.

The clear guidance and practical sense of *Modern Treaty Law and Practice* is here repeated on the broader canvas of general international law, an area of equal significance but much less accessible than the law of treaties. These days everyone including taxi-drivers talks about customary international law, although they probably (and wisely) do not use the term. But there is an awareness that an imminent threat is a condition for action in self-defence; that the Security Council can authorise individual states to use force but may be expected to do so in clear language; that crimes against humanity are punishable and might be punished; and that human rights confront state responsibility with consequences for both. Providing guidance in this much broader frame is a challenge. But non-specialists have to start somewhere and this is a good place to start.

Tony Aust brings to the work a sense of humour, of balance and of British practice – but the work is not parochial. Her Majesty's Government has a long tradition (back to the 1880s) of a legal adviser in the Foreign Office, and there has been a consistent pattern of consultation on issues perceived as legal. It can be traced in the United Kingdom Materials on International Law (UKMIL), published in the *British Yearbook of International Law* since 1978 and running now to thousands of pages – but it goes back much further than that. Senior decision-makers tend to say that they like their lawyers 'on tap and not on top' (as one British ambassador to the UN put it). But if one is ever involved in a long-running international dispute it is a fair bet that the government which has had a consistent, legally informed approach is the more likely to prevail, whatever the initial merits may have been. Aust has been a participant in this process from the British side for as long as thirty-five years – a process sometimes affected by forays from Lord Chancellors (as in Suez in 1956) or Attorneys-General (as with Iraq in 2003) but constant and generally consistent. In turn good international law has reinforced sustainable international policy – witness those two occasions where the costs of the alternatives were considerable.

The treatment of the subject is light and sometimes schematic – more detailed issues will require more detailed research. But he covers the ground and gives a good idea of its shape and contours, and this is a valuable service at a time of overspecialisation.

James Crawford
Whewell Professor of International Law
University of Cambridge
28 April 2005

PREFACE

[Q]uotation is a national vice.
Evelyn Waugh, *The Loved One*, 1948, Ch. 9.

The *Oxford English Dictionary* defines a handbook as a short manual or guide; and this book is intended to be a helpful means of finding out about international law. It is meant to be kept, literally, close at hand, so that when one comes across a problem (perhaps a new area of the law or a new concept or term) one can turn first to it and get a quick answer to questions such as: What is the exclusive economic zone? Who is a refugee? What is the legal regime of Antarctica? How are diplomatic and state immunity confused? What is Palestine? Should one prefer an arbitral tribunal to an international court? What is a Chapter VII resolution? My purpose is to explain international law principles and rules in a clear and concise way. I avoid as far as possible theory and speculation.

Although the book can be read as an introduction to the subject, it is designed to meet the need for a practical guide for those concerned with international law, whether on a regular or occasional basis. In the last century a tremendous amount was written on the subject. General works may be intended rather more for the student. Dealing as they do with the history of international law, its doctrines and intellectual problems, such works do not have enough space to set out the law in detail. That is right. Most students of international law, whether undergraduate or postgraduate, will not practise it.

Yet many other people need to know about international law, not only legal advisers to foreign ministries. Therefore another object of this book is to make more people aware of the international law that lies behind so many ordinary activities. Today international law affects almost every human activity. To take one simple example: foreign flights by air are only possible because of an elaborate network of bilateral treaties; and they have been concluded pursuant to a multilateral treaty of 1944 which provides the basic structure for the regulation of international civil aviation.

And when the aircraft crashes, treaties going back to 1929 may limit the compensation received by your family (see pp. 349–51 below).

In recent years treaties providing for the protection of human rights and the environment have become widely known. But there are many other important areas regulated by treaties, some dating back to the nineteenth century, yet they are largely unknown except to the specialist. That the Table of treaties is much longer than the Table of cases merely reflects the fact that treaties now play a much more important role in the day-to-day work of the international lawyer. Today, decisions of international courts and tribunals have a less central role. Similarly, common law practitioners will be familiar with the way legislation, primary and secondary, has increased so much in volume and complexity in the last fifty years that it is now the principal element in their work.

The vital role played by international law is often not obvious even to lawyers, unless they specialise in the subject. Fortunately, in recent years George W. Bush, Saddam Hussein and Slobodan Milosevic have done much to heighten awareness of the law on the use of force, UN sanctions, war crimes and crimes against humanity. Yet even specialists – whether lawyers or not – in areas such as human rights, the environment or the European Union, often do not have a good grounding in international law, even though their fields have been created wholly or largely by treaties. A physicist needs to have advanced mathematics, and no doctor could qualify without a good knowledge of chemistry and biology. Similarly, international civil servants, government officials, NGO staff and other specialists all need to be more familiar with the international law underlying their subject, not just the particular texts that are immediately relevant.

It is a mistake to think that only international courts and tribunals decide disputes about international law. National courts and tribunals still decide most of them. And international law can reach far down into the internal legal order of states, sometimes with unexpected effects. In 1994, a merchant ship belonging to a former communist state was arrested in Scotland at the initiative of the crew who had not been paid for months. Normally the arrest would have been perfectly proper, but, unknown at first to the local court, there was a bilateral treaty between that state and the United Kingdom which prohibited the arrest of merchant vessels for such a purpose.

Although law is always developing, it is a mistake to think that all of it is uncertain. International law develops continually, and has its share of grey areas, but that does not mean that it is always a matter of opinion.

Most of the basic principles and rules are well established. As with the law of each state, the problems faced daily are concerned more with how to apply a rule to the facts. This goes also for most cases before national courts and tribunals. Cases such as *Pinochet* (see pp. 5 and 178 below) are the exception, not the rule.

All practising lawyers know how different the practice of law is from what they learned as a student. It is the same for international law. I have therefore included as much as possible of its practical aspects. This book explains how the law is actually developed and applied by states and international organisations. I was very fortunate to have been a foreign ministry legal adviser for thirty-five years. It gave me an insight into how things are done, and I have put much of my experience into this book. When I have not been able to draw on that experience, or that of former colleagues, I have been able to use my understanding developed during a lifetime of practice. This inevitably gives one an instinctive feel for what is really important; and I have aimed to convey this throughout.

I hope that teachers and students of international law will also find the book of value. There is an increasing awareness of the need to teach international law, and especially how it is developed, within its proper context. That is largely a diplomatic context. One cannot properly appreciate why a treaty or a UN Security Council resolution was drafted in a particular way unless one understands something of the political or diplomatic process that produced it and how problems are eventually solved. That knowledge helps to explain what diplomats and other international negotiators actually do. I have therefore tried to set the law in that context.

This book is not therefore just of interest to diplomats, as is largely the case with *Satow* and similar books. My aim is to cover most areas of international law, not just those that are of particular interest to a diplomat (Denza's excellent and authoritative *Diplomatic Law* is limited to the Vienna Convention on Diplomatic Relations). Nevertheless, I hope the book will be useful to diplomats, who are concerned with many more aspects of international law than may be thought. Even those who work in foreign ministries or embassies with easier access to expert legal advice have a need to understand that advice so that they can act upon it properly and effectively. And there are all too many diplomats with no or little legal knowledge who have to work largely without legal advice, dealing with international legal problems as best they can.

The chapters vary much in length. The longer ones, such as those on the law of the sea, the law of treaties and diplomatic relations, give a fairly detailed treatment of those topics which are at the centre of international law. Other, more specialised topics like human rights and environmental law are dealt with more summarily since they cannot be described in detail in a book of this length (the leading British work on international environmental law has nearly 800 pages). So, those chapters are more in the nature of introductions; the background and concepts are briefly described, and learned sources of information are referred to.

Whenever possible, I have tried to use primary sources: treaties, judgments and authoritative commentaries. But, like others, inevitably I have had to rely also on leading general works like *Oppenheim's International Law* (vol. 1, 9th edn, London, 1992), Shaw's *International Law* (5th edn, Cambridge, 2003) and Brownlie's *Principles of Public International Law* (6th edn, Oxford, 2003), as well as many books on specialist areas.

All chapters have references to books and articles, cases and other materials, which the reader is encouraged to consult. Websites are indispensable today. An up-to-date, online list of websites with links to them (www.asil.org/ilmlinks.htm) is used by the American Society of International Law in compiling its indispensable publication *International Legal Materials*. Shaw's *International Law* also has a useful list of websites. This book does not have a list, but wherever possible the text will mention the relevant sites, including some of the more obscure. But one must always remember that website addresses do sometimes change.

As far as possible, the facts and law are stated as at 31 December 2004, though some later developments were added at the proof stage.

All comments and corrections to aiaust@aol.com, please.

ACKNOWLEDGMENTS

Practitioners and scholars expert in a particular field have been good enough to take time to comment on whole or parts of draft chapters, to point out mistakes and omissions or to provide or suggest material. I must therefore sincerely thank, among others, Roberto Barcella, Alan Boyle, James Crawford, Martin Eaton, Rolf Einer Fife, Malcolm Forster, Martha Haines-Ferrari, Hazel Fox, Richard Gardiner, Philippe Gautier, Christopher Greenwood, Nicholas Grief, Johannes Huber, David Kornbluth, Roderick Liddell, Ruma Mandel, Denzil Millar, Adam Roberts, Julia Schwartz and Elizabeth Wilmshurst. But all opinions and errors are mine.

I must also thank Finola O'Sullivan, and the team at Cambridge University Press. Lastly, I must again thank my wife, Kirsten Kaarre Jensen, for putting up with the demands of writing, as well as reading some of the chapters and making perceptive suggestions from the viewpoint of a former diplomat and non-lawyer.

TABLE OF TREATIES

Where appropriate, a treaty is listed under the name or acronym by which it is commonly known or the subject matter is mentioned first. Today, some multilateral treaties are regularly amended, and therefore the most reliable source for the up-to-date text is an official website.

Multilateral treaties

Bilateral treaties

TABLE OF MOUs

For an explanation of the term 'MOU', see pp. 53–7 below.

Multilateral MOUs

Bilateral MOUs

Although there are many more bilateral than multilateral MOUs, this list is very short since few are published even when they are not confidential.

TABLE OF CASES

GLOSSARY OF LEGAL TERMS

accession	Same effect as ratification (q.v.), but not preceded by signature.
acquis communautaire	See p. 481.
adherence	Shorthand term for consent to be bound (q.v.).
agrément	Formal approval by the receiving state of the appointment of a named person as an ambassador (see p. 120).
comitology	See p. 481.
comity	Principles or rules of politeness, convenience or goodwill observed by governments and courts (see p. 12).
compromis	Special agreement to take a dispute to an international court or tribunal (see p. 438).
consensus	See p. 60.
consent to be bound	To ratify or accede to a treaty (see p. 62).
customary international law	Rules derived from general practice among states together with *opinio juris* (q.v.) (see p. 6).
de facto	Existing as a matter of fact.
de jure	Existing as a matter of law.
domestic law	The internal law of a state (sometimes referred to as 'municipal' or 'national' law).
erga omnes	Valid for all (see p. 10).
estoppel	The principle that a state cannot act inconsistently if it has acquiesced in a particular situation or taken a particular position with respect to it (see p. 9).
ex gratia	Without admission of liability.
exchange of notes	Two or more instruments which constitute either a treaty or an MOU (see p. 54).
exequatur	Formal approval by the receiving state of the appointment of a named person as head of a consular post (see p. 157).

final act	Formal document recording the results of a diplomatic conference, especially one to adopt a multilateral treaty (see p. 61).
full powers	Formal document authorising a person to sign a treaty or do other acts with respect to a treaty (see p. 59).
international law	The body of rules legally binding on states and other subjects of international law (q.v.) in their relations with each other (see p. 2).
international legal personality	Being a person or legal entity to which international law attributes legal rights and obligations, mainly states and international organisations (see p. 198).
intertemporal	The principle that facts must be assessed in the light of the international law at the relevant time, not the law at the time a dispute arises or an issue falls to be decided (see p. 35).
jurisdiction	The right in international law for a state to exercise authority over its nationals and persons and things in its territory, and sometimes abroad (extraterritorial jurisdiction) (see pp. 43 *et seq.*).
jus ad bellum	The law on the use of force (see p. 223).
jus cogens	Peremptory rule of law (see p. 11).
jus in bello	The law of armed conflict (see pp. 251 *et seq.*).
lex ferenda	Law which is being sought to establish.
lex lata	Established law.
lex specialis	A specific legal rule which is an exception to a general rule.
memorandum of understanding	Name given to both treaties and MOUs (see p. 54).
MOU	A non-legally binding international instrument (see pp. 53–7).
non-liquet	See p. 442.
norm	Imprecise term (see p. 9).
opinio juris	General belief by states that a non-treaty rule is legally binding on them (see p. 7).
party	A state which has consented to be bound by a treaty and for which the treaty is in force (see p. 51).
primary legislation	Law made by a legislature (cf. secondary legislation (q.v.)).

private international law	The domestic law dealing with cases with a foreign element (also known as 'conflict of laws') (see p. 1).
ratification	Following signature, the expression of a state's consent to be bound by a treaty (see pp. 63–4).
rebus sic stantibus	A fundamental change of circumstances (see p. 104).
res communis	Land or sea that can be used by any state or is subject to a common regime (see p. 40).
reservation	A unilateral statement, however phrased or named, made by a state when consenting to be bound by a treaty by which it purports to exclude or to modify the legal effect of certain provisions of the treaty in their application to that state (see p. 67).
retorsion	Retaliatory act which is not unlawful (p. 425).
secondary legislation	Legislation by the executive under power given by primary legislation (q.v.).
signatory	An imprecise term best avoided (see p. 65).
soft law	See p. 11.
sovereignty	The right of a state to act independently of other states, subject only to such restrictions as international law imposes.
state	A defined territory with a permanent population and a government (see p. 16).
state responsibility	Responsibility of a state in international law for its wrongful acts (see pp. 407 *et seq.*).
subject of international law	Possessor of rights and obligations in international law, mainly states and international organisations (see p. 13).
subordinate or subsidiary legislation	Secondary legislation (q.v.).
subsidiarity	See p. 483.
terra nullius	Territory belonging to no state (see p. 38).
toilette	The final tidying up of a legal text, especially a treaty.
travaux préparatoires (or *travaux*)	Preparatory work of a treaty (see pp. 94–5).
treaty	See p. 57.
ultra vires	Exceeding legal authority.
uti possidetis	See p. 23.

ABBREVIATIONS

Works cited in the footnotes

Aust	A. Aust, *Modern Treaty Law and Practice*, Cambridge, 2000
B&B Docs.	Birnie and Boyle, *Basic Documents on International Law and the Environment*, Oxford, 1995
BGG	Brownlie and Goodwin-Gill, *Basic Documents on Human Rights*, 4th edn, Oxford, 2002
Birnie and Boyle	Birnie and Boyle, *International Law and the Environment*, 2nd edn, Oxford, 2002
Brownlie	I. Brownlie, *Principles of Public International Law*, 6th edn, Oxford, 2003
Collier and Lowe	Collier and Lowe, *The Settlement of Disputes in International Law*, Oxford, 1999
Denza	E. Denza, *Diplomatic Law*, 2nd edn, Oxford, 1998
Hertslet	Hertslet, *Commercial Treaties* (reprinted in 10 vols., 1970)
Higgins	R. Higgins, *Problems and Process*, Oxford, 1994
O'Connell	D. O'Connell, *International Law*, 2nd edn, London, 1970
Oppenheim	*Oppenheim's International Law*, 9th edn, London, 1992
R&G	Roberts and Guelff, *Documents on the Laws of War*, 3rd edn, Oxford, 2000
Satow	*Satow's Guide to Diplomatic Practice*, 5th edn, London, 1979
Shaw	M. Shaw, *International Law*, 5th edn, Cambridge, 2003
UN Depositary Practice	*Summary of Practice of the Secretary-General as Depositary of Multilateral Treaties*
UN Multilateral Treaties	*Multilateral Treaties Deposited with the Secretary-General*
Whiteman	M. Whiteman, *Digest of International Law*

Other abbreviations

AC	*Appeal Cases* (Law Reports, England and Wales)
AD	*Annual Digest and Reports of International Law Cases* (16 vols.) (now ILR).

AFDI	*Annuaire Français de Droit International*
AJIL	*American Journal of International Law*
AER	*All England Law Reports*
ASA	air services agreement
ASIL	American Society of International Law
A&T	administrative and technical
ATS	*Australian Treaty Series*
AU	African Union (formerly the OAU)
Aust YBIL	*Australian Yearbook of International Law*
BIICL	British Institute of International and Comparative Law
BIT	bilateral investment treaty
BSP	*British and Foreign State Papers*
BYIL	*British Yearbook of International Law*
CCAMLR	Convention on the Conservation of Antarctic Marine Living Resources 1980
CFI	Court of First Instance (EU)
CFSP	Common Foreign and Security Policy (EU)
Ch	*Chancery Division* (Law Reports, England and Wales)
CLJ	*Cambridge Law Journal*
CLP	*Current Legal Problems*
CLR	*Commonwealth Law Reports*
Cm, Cmd, Cmnd	UK Command Papers (official publication)
CMLR	*Common Market Law Reports*
CoE	Council of Europe
CSCE	Conference on Security and Co-operation in Europe (now OSCE)
CTBT	Comprehensive Nuclear Test-Ban Treaty 1996
CTS	*Consolidated Treaty Series*
CWC	Chemical Weapons Convention
DSB	Dispute Settlement Body (WTO)
EC	European Community
ECHR	European Convention on Human Rights
ECJ	European Court of Justice (EU)
ECOSOC	Economic and Social Council (UN)
ECR	*European Court Reports*
ECSC	European Coal and Steel Community
EEA	European Economic Area
EEC	European Economic Community
EEZ	exclusive economic zone
EFTA	European Free Trade Area (not EC or EU)
EJIL	*European Journal of International Law*
ES	Emergency Session of the UN General Assembly
ETS	*European Treaty Series*

EU	European Union
EURATOM	European Atomic Energy Community
EWCA (Civ)	Law Report (England and Wales), Court of Appeal, Civil Division
EWHC (Admin)	Law Report (England and Wales), High Court, Administrative Division
EWHC (Ch.)	Law Report (England and Wales), High Court, Chancery Division
EWHC (QB)	Law Report (England and Wales), High Court, Queens Bench Division
FAO	Food and Agriculture Organization
FCO	Foreign and Commonwealth Office (UK)
FRG	Federal Republic of Germany
FRY	Federal Republic of Yugoslavia (see SFRY)
F.2d	*Federal Reporter* (2nd series) (US)
GAOR	*General Assembly Official Records*
GATS	General Agreement on Trade in Services
GATT	General Agreement on Tariffs and Trade
GDR	German Democratic Republic
GYIL	*German Yearbook of International Law*
Hague Recueil	*Recueil des Cours, Académie de Droit International de la Haye*
Hansard	Official record of UK parliamentary debates (Lords or Commons)
HKSAR	Hong Kong Special Administrative Region
HMSO	Her Majesty's Stationery Office (UK)
IAEA	International Atomic Energy Authority
IASTA	International Air Services Transit Agreement 1944
IATA	International Air Transport Association
ICAO	International Civil Aviation Organization
ICC	International Criminal Court or International Chamber of Commerce
ICCPR	International Covenant on Civil and Political Rights 1966
ICJ	International Court of Justice
ICLQ	*International and Comparative Law Quarterly*
ICRC	International Committee of the Red Cross
ICSID	International Centre for the Settlement of Investment Disputes
ICTR	International Criminal Tribunal for Rwanda
ICTY	International Criminal Tribunal for the Former Yugoslavia
ILA	International Law Association
ILC	International Law Commission
ILM	*International Legal Materials*
ILO	International Labour Organization
ILR	*International Law Reports* (see also AD)
Iran–US CTR	*Iran–US Claims Tribunal Reports*
ITU	International Telecommunications Union

IWC	International Whaling Convention/Commission
KB	*King's Bench Division* (Law Reports, England and Wales)
LL.R	*Lloyds Law Reports*
LNTS	*League of Nations Treaty Series*
LQR	*Law Quarterly Review*
MERCOSUR	Mercado Común del Sur
MFA	Ministry of Foreign Affairs
MLR	*Modern Law Review*
MOU	Memorandum of Understanding (see p. 53)
NAFTA	North American Free Trade Agreement 1992
NATO	North Atlantic Treaty Organization
NGO	non-governmental organisation
NILR	*Netherlands International Law Review*
NLM	national liberation movement
NY	New York
NYIL	*Netherlands Yearbook of International Law*
OAS	Organization of American States
OAU	Organization of African States (now African Union)
OECD	Organization for Economic Co-operation and Development
OJ	*Official Journal of the European Communities*
OSCE	Organization for Security and Co-operation in Europe (previously CSCE)
PCA	Permanent Court of Arbitration
PCIJ	Permanent Court of International Justice (replaced by the ICJ)
PJCCM	Police and Judicial Co-operation in Criminal Matters (EU)
PLO	Palestine Liberation Organization
PRC	People's Republic of China
QB	*Queen's Bench Division* (Law Reports, England and Wales)
QMV	qualified majority voting
RIAA	*Reports of International Arbitral Awards*
RoC	Republic of China (Taiwan)
SCOR	*Official Records of the UN Security Council*
SFRY	Socialist Federal Republic of Yugoslavia (see FRY)
SI	statutory instrument (UK secondary legislation)
SPLOS	document of a meeting of the states parties to UNCLOS
TEU	Treaty on European Union (Maastricht Treaty)
TIAS	*Treaties and other International Agreements* (US)
TLR	*Times Law Reports*
TRIPS	Agreement on Trade-Related Aspects of Intellectual Property Rights
TRNC	Turkish Republic of Northern Cyprus
UAR	United Arab Republic
UK	United Kingdom of Great Britain and Northern Ireland

UKHL	Law Report (UK), House of Lords
UKTS	*United Kingdom Treaty Series*
UN	United Nations
UNCC	UN Compensation Commission
UNCIO	UN Conference on International Organization
UNCITRAL	UN Commission on International Trade Law
UNCLOS	UN Convention on the Law of the Sea 1982
UN Doc.	UN official document
UNESCO	UN Educational, Scientific and Cultural Organization
UNGA	UN General Assembly
UNHCHR	UN High Commissioner for Human Rights
UNHCR	UN High Commissioner for Refugees
UNIDROIT	International Institute for the Unification of Private Law
UNJurYB	*UN Juridical Yearbook*
UNMIK	UN Mission in Kosovo
UNSC	UN Security Council
UNTS	*United Nations Treaty Series*
US	United States of America
UST	*United States Treaties and other International Agreements*
WHO	World Health Organization
WLR	*Weekly Law Reports*
WMO	World Meteorological Organization
WTO	World Trade Organization or World Tourism Organization
YB	Yearbook
YBIL	Yearbook of International Law
YBILC	*Yearbook of the International Law Commission*
ZaöRV	*Zeitschrift für ausländisches öffentliches Recht und Völkerrecht*

International law

> The truth is that international law is neither a myth on the one hand, nor a
> panacea on the other, but just one institution among others which we can
> use for the building of a better international order.[1]

Oppenheim. *Oppenheim's International Law*, 9th edn, London, 1992,
   p. 3–115
Shaw, *International Law*, 5th edn, Cambridge, 2003, pp. 1–246
Higgins, *Problems and Process*, Oxford, 1994, pp. 1–55
Brownlie, *Principles of Public International Law*, 6th edn, Oxford, 2003,
   pp. 3–68
Parry, *The Sources and Evidences of International Law*, Cambridge, 1965

First let us clear away any misunderstandings about private international
law and transnational law.

Private international law/conflict of laws

Private international law is an unfortunate term for what is more properly
and accurately called *conflict of laws*. That is the body of rules of the
domestic law[2] of a state which applies when a legal issue contains a foreign
element, and it has to be decided whether a domestic court should apply
foreign law or cede jurisdiction to a foreign court.[3] Many of the rules are
now found in legislation. Naturally, over time the domestic rules grow
closer as states come to adopt similar solutions to the same problems, but
they remain domestic law. Established in 1893, the Hague Conference on
Private International Law seeks primarily to harmonise domestic rules on

---

[1] J. Brierly, *The Law of Nations*, 5th edn, Oxford, 1955, Preface, reprinted *ibid.* in 6th edn,
   Oxford, 1963.
[2] See p. 12 below, including its relationship to international law.
[3] Dicey and Morris, *Conflict of Laws*, 13th edn, London, 2000, p. 3; Cheshire and North,
   Private International Law, 13th edn, London, 1999, p. 7; J. Collier, *Conflict of Laws*, 3rd edn,
   Cambridge, 2001, pp. 386–94.

conflict of laws, and since 1954 has concluded some thirty-six multilateral treaties.[4] These must be distinguished from treaties that seek to unify or harmonise states' substantive domestic laws, such as on carriage by air or sea, or intellectual property.[5] UNIDROIT is an international organisation with fifty-nine member states that seeks to harmonise domestic laws, especially commercial.[6] Despite its name, it is neither a UN body nor a UN specialised agency. But UNCITRAL *is* a UN body charged with promoting the harmonisation of international trade law.[7]

A legal matter can raise issues of both international law and conflict of laws, particularly on questions of jurisdiction,[8] and today the distinction between international law and conflict of laws can be blurred as more international law, treaties in particular, reaches right down into the internal legal order, as exemplified by the law of the European Union.[9] Nevertheless, it is still vital to appreciate the distinctions between different categories of law, their purpose and how they develop.

Transnational law

This term seems to have been coined to describe the study of any aspect of law that concerns more than one state, in particular conflict of laws, comparative law (the study of how the laws of different states deal with a particular area or issue of domestic law), supranational law (European Union law) and public international law, particularly in the commercial field. It may bring useful insights into the development of law, but one should not be led into believing that we are now living in a world where all laws of whatever type are rapidly converging. Within many states, especially federations and even in the United Kingdom, there are separate systems of domestic law, and this is likely to continue for a very long time.

The nature of international law

International law is sometimes called *public* international law to distinguish it from private international law, though, as already explained, even this can lead to misunderstandings. Whatever the connections international law has with other systems of law, it is clearly distinguished by the fact that it is not the product of any national legal system, but of the states

---

[4] Oppenheim, p. 7. See www.hcch.net.   [5] Oppenheim, p. 6, n. 11.
[6] See www.unidroit.org.   [7] See p. 389 below.   [8] See p. 43 below.
[9] See p. 466 below.

(now over 190) that make up our world. In the past, international law was referred to as the Law of Nations.[10] Although it had been developing over many centuries,[11] international law as we know it today is commonly said to have begun properly with the Dutch jurist and diplomat, Grotius (Hugo de Groot), 1583–1645, and with the Peace of Westphalia 1648.[12] That event marked not only the end of the Thirty Years War but also the end of feudalism (and, with the Reformation, obedience to the Pope) and the establishment of the modern state with central governmental institutions that could enforce control over its inhabitants and defend them against other states. But since those states had to live with each other, there had to be common rules governing their external conduct. Although rudimentary rules had been developing ever since civilised communities had emerged, from the mid-seventeenth century they began to develop into what we now recognise as international law.

But is international law really law?

Unfortunately, this question is still being asked, and not only by students. The answer depends on what is meant by law. Whereas the binding nature of domestic law is not questioned, new students of international law are confronted with the issue: is international law merely a collection of principles that a state is free to ignore when it suits it? Whereas every day newspapers report crimes, it is usually only when a flagrant breach of international law occurs that the media take notice of international law. This can give a distorted impression of the nature of international law. International law has no ready sanction for its breach. Because there is no international police force or army that can immediately step in, international law is often perceived as not really law. Yet the record of even the most developed domestic legal systems in dealing with crime does not bear close scrutiny.

Although it is as invidious as comparing apples and oranges, in comparison with domestic crime states generally do comply rather well with international law. If, as H. L. A. Hart argued,[13] law derives its strength from acceptance by society that its rules are binding, not from its enforceability,

---

[10] See J. Brierly, *The Law of Nations*, 6th edn, Oxford, 1963. See especially pp. 1–40 on the origins of international law.
[11] See Shaw, pp. 13–41; A. Nussbaum, *A Concise History of the Law of Nations*, rev. edn, New York, 1954.
[12] 1 CTS pp. vi, 70, 198 and 319   [13] *The Concept of Law*, Oxford, 1961.

then international law is law. The raison d'être of international law is that relations between states should be governed by common principles and rules. Yet what they are is determined by national interest, which in turn is often driven by domestic concerns. Those matters on which international law developed early on included freedom of the high seas and the immunity of diplomats. Both were vitally important for the increasing international trade, the famous 1654 Treaty of Peace and Commerce between Queen Christina and Oliver Cromwell epitomising this new reality.[14] As we will see when we look at the sources of international law, its binding force does not come from the existence of police, courts and prisons. It is based on the consent (express or implied) of states, and national self-interest: if a state is seen to ignore international law, other states may do the same. The resulting chaos would not be in the interest of any state. While the language of diplomacy has changed over the centuries from Latin to French to English, international law has provided a vitally important and constantly developing bond between states. As this book will show, today in many areas of international law the rules are well settled. As with most domestic law, it is how the rules are to be applied to the particular facts that cause most problems.

To look at the question from a more mundane point of view, international law is all too real for those who have to deal with it daily. Foreign ministries have legal departments. Some are large: the US State Department has some 150 legal advisers; the UK Foreign and Commonwealth Office thirty-five, including some seven posted in Brussels, Geneva, New York and The Hague. Their task is to advise on a host of legal matters that arise in the conduct of foreign affairs. They also have the conduct of cases involving international law in international, foreign and UK courts and tribunals. If international law is not law, then they and their legal colleagues in other foreign ministries are drawing their salaries under false pretences. Which brings one to international lawyers.

International lawyers

Although more students are studying international law, it is not easy for a young lawyer to practise it. Even in large law firms that have international law departments, the bulk of their work is commercial arbitration. The involvement of barristers and advocates in international law is usually

---

[14] 1 BSP 691.

incidental to their normal work. Most of the distinguished practitioners of international law who appear before international courts or tribunals are professors of international law. As a rule, foreign ministry legal departments are staffed by diplomats who have legal training, but who alternate between legal and political posts. Few have legal advisers who during their careers do little other than law, the British Diplomatic Service being a prime exception. There are jobs for international lawyers also in the United Nations and other international organisations.

Sometimes the media will describe a person as an 'international lawyer', yet he may at most have a practice with many foreign clients, and be concerned more with foreign law and conflict of laws. Yet, when the media is full of stories questioning the lawfulness of a state's actions, some domestic lawyers rush to express their opinions, usually critical. They are not always wrong, but usually display a lack of familiarity with international law, apparently believing that the reading of a textbook or an (apparently simple) instrument like the UN Charter is enough. The fact that some textbooks are lucid and make international law accessible, does not mean that a domestic lawyer, however eminent, can become an expert on it overnight. The difficulties that the judges of the House of Lords (the UK's final appeal court) had in grappling with international law in the *Pinochet* case, despite having been addressed by several international law experts, are amply demonstrated by their differing separate opinions.[15] Some domestic lawyers have specialised in particular areas of international law such as aviation, human rights or the environment, without a good grounding in international law generally. A tax law expert will necessarily have a sound knowledge of contract, tort and other basic areas of domestic law, without which it would be difficult to advise effectively.

The sources of international law

International law differs from domestic law in that it is not always that easy to find out what the law is on a particular matter. Domestic law is reasonably certain and found mostly in legislation and judgments of a hierarchy of courts. In contrast, international law is not so accessible, coherent or certain. There is no global legislature (the UN General Assembly does not equate to a national legislature), and no formal hierarchy of international courts and tribunals. As with the (mainly unwritten) British

---

[15] R. v. *Bow Street Stipendiary Magistrate, ex parte Pinochet (No. 3)* [2000] 1 AC 147; [1999] 2 WLR 825; [1999] 2 All ER 97; 119 ILR 135.

Constitution, an initial pointer to the international law on a given topic is often best found in the textbooks. They will explain that international law is derived from various sources, which are authoritatively listed in Article 38(1) of the Statute of the International Court of Justice (annexed to the UN Charter) as:

(a) international conventions, whether general or particular, establishing rules expressly recognised by the contracting states;
(b) international custom, as evidence of a general practice accepted as law;
(c) the general principles of law recognised by civilised nations;
(d) subject to the provisions of Article 59,[16] judicial decisions and the teachings of the most highly qualified publicists of the various nations, as subsidiary means for the determination of rules of law.

Treaties

The reference in (a) to 'international conventions' is to bilateral and multilateral treaties. For the moment it is enough to say that, as with domestic legislation, treaties now play a crucial role in international law, important areas of customary international law having now been codified in widely accepted treaties. In consequence, custom and the other sources of international law are no longer as important as they used to be. But that does not mean that custom is on a lower level than treaties. There is no formal hierarchy of the sources of international law. As between parties to a treaty, the treaty binds them. As between a party to a treaty and a non-party, custom will apply, including custom derived from treaties.[17] General principles of law, judgments and the opinions of writers are of less importance as sources. (The law of treaties is dealt with in some detail in Chapter 5.)

Customary international law

Customary international law – or simply 'custom' – must be distinguished from the customary law that is an important part of some states' domestic law and deals largely with family matters, land and suchlike. In international law a rule of custom evolves from the *practice* of states, and this can

---

[16] Decisions of the Court are binding only on the parties to the case (*res judicata*).
[17] See p. 8 below.

take a considerable or a short time. There must be evidence of substantial uniformity of practice by a substantial number of states. In 1974 the ICJ found that a customary rule (now superseded) that states had the right to exclusive fishing within a twelve nautical mile zone had emerged.[18] State practice can be expressed in various ways, such as governmental actions in relation to other states, legislation, diplomatic notes, ministerial and other official statements, government manuals (as on the law of armed conflict), and certain unanimous or consensus resolutions of the UN General Assembly. The first such resolution was probably Resolution 95(I) of 11 December 1946 which affirmed unanimously the principles of international law recognised by the Charter of the Nürnberg International Military Tribunal and its judgment.

When a state that has an interest in the matter is silent, it will generally be regarded as acquiescing in the practice. But if the new practice is not consistent with an established customary rule, and a state is a *persistent objector* to the new practice, the practice either may not be regarded as evidence of new custom or the persistent objector may be regarded as having established an exception to the new customary rule.

But to amount to a new rule of custom, in addition to practice there must also be a general recognition by states that the practice is settled enough to amount to an obligation binding on states in international law. This is known as *opinio juris* (*not* the opinions of jurists). Sometimes the recognition will be reflected in a court judgment reached after legal argument based on the extensive research and writings of international legal scholars. In themselves, neither judicial pronouncements nor favourable mention in a UN resolution, even when adopted by a large majority, are conclusive as to the emergence of new custom.[19] But in *Nicaragua v. US* (Merits) (1986)[20] the International Court of Justice found that the acceptance by states of the Friendly Relations Declaration of the General Assembly[21] constituted *opinio juris* that the Charter prohibition on the use of force now also represented custom. There is however a growing tendency for international courts and tribunals, without making a rigorous examination of the evidence, to find that a customary rule has emerged. In *Tadić* the International Criminal Tribunal for the Former

---

[18] *Fisheries Jurisdiction (UK v. Iceland; Germany v. Iceland), ICJ Reports* (1974), p. 3, at pp. 23–6; 55 ILR 238. For the present law, see p. 319 below.

[19] See the *Namibia* Advisory Opinion, *ICJ Reports* (1971), p. 6; paras. 87–116; 59 ILR 2; and the *Legality of Nuclear Weapons* Advisory Opinion, *ICJ Reports* (1996), p. 226, paras. 64–73; 110 ILR 163.

[20] *ICJ Reports* (1986), p. 14, paras. 183–94; 76 ILR 1.   [21] ILH (1970) 1292.

Yugoslavia ruled that it had jurisdiction over war crimes committed during an internal armed conflict even though its Statute does not provide for this.[22]

Establishing *opinio juris* can be difficult and everything will depend on the circumstances.[23] It is easiest when the purpose of a new multilateral treaty is expressed to be codification of customary international law. Even if the treaty includes elements of progressive development,[24] if it is widely regarded by states as an authoritative statement of the law, and constantly and widely referred to, it will soon come to be accepted as reflecting the customary rules, sometimes even before it has entered into force. This was certainly the case with the Vienna Convention on the Law of Treaties 1969, which even now has only 101 parties.[25] Although many provisions of the UN Convention on the Law of the Sea 1982 (UNCLOS) went beyond mere codification of customary rules in most respects, the negotiations proceeded on the basis of consensus.[26] It was therefore that much easier during the twelve years before UNCLOS entered into force for most of its provisions to become accepted as representing customary law.

An accumulation of bilateral treaties on the same subject, such as investment treaties, may in certain circumstances also be evidence of a customary rule.[27]

General principles of law recognised by civilized nations[28]

Compared with domestic law, international law is relatively underdeveloped and patchy, though in the last fifty years it has developed several important new specialised areas. International courts and tribunals have always borrowed concepts from domestic law if they can be applied to relations between states, and by this means have developed international law by filling gaps and strengthening weak points. Such concepts are chiefly

---

[22] See the decision of the Appeals Chamber: www.icty.org, Case IT-94-1, paras. 65 et seq; 105 ILR 453.

[23] Shaw, pp. 68–72.   [24] See n. 26 below.

[25] See p. 52 below. See also A. Aust, 'Limping Treaties: Lessons from Multilateral Treaty-making' (2003) NILR 243 at 248–51.

[26] See H. Caminos and M. Molitor, 'Progressive Development of International Law and the Package Deal' (1985) AJIL 871–90.

[27] See p. 373 below.

[28] 'Civilized' should not be seen as a demeaning term; the Statute is merely referring to states that have reached an advanced state of legal development.

legal reasoning and analogies drawn from private law,[29] such as good faith and estoppel.

Good faith

The obligation to act in good faith is a fundamental principle of international law, and includes equity.[30] Article 2(2) of the UN Charter requires all Members to fulfil their Charter obligations in good faith. Similarly, the Vienna Convention on the Law of Treaties 1969 requires parties to a treaty to perform the treaty (Article 26), and to interpret it (Article 31(1)), in good faith.[31] The principle is not restricted to treaties but applies to all international obligations.

Estoppel

Known as preclusion in civil law systems, estoppel has two aspects. A state that has taken a particular position may be under an obligation to act consistently with it on another occasion. And when a state has acted to its detriment in relying on a formal declaration by another state, the latter may be estopped from denying its responsibility for any adverse consequences.[32]

Norms

Sir Robert Jennings, a former President of the International Court of Justice, once famously said that he would not recognise a norm if he met one in the street. But, some international lawyers speak of norms of international law. In English, norm means a standard. Use of the word seems to have been popularised by Professor Hans Kelsen,[33] who saw international law as at the top of the hierarchy of law. The term is used more by civil lawyers than common lawyers. It may be useful in theoretical analysis of certain international law issues.[34] Unfortunately, it is also used loosely to cover not only principles and rules but also *lex ferenda* (see

---

[29] See H. Lauterpacht, 'Private Law Sources and Analogies of International Law', in E. Lauterpacht (ed.), *International Law: Being the Collected Papers of Sir Hersch Lauterpacht*, Cambridge, 1970–8, vol. 2, pp. 173–212; B. Cheng, *General Principles of Law as Applied by International Courts and Tribunals*, Cambridge, 1953, reprinted 1987.

[30] Oppenheim, pp. 38 and 44.   [31] See further pp. 79 and 90 below, respectively.

[32] Oppenheim, pp. 1188–93. See p. 57 below about the possible legal consequences of an MOU.

[33] *General Theory of Law and State*, Harvard, 1945.

[34] See for example D. Shelton, 'International Law and "Relative Normativity"', in M. Evans (ed.), *International Law*, Oxford, 2003, pp. 145–72.

below), but without a clear distinction being made between established law and aspirations.[35] The term is very rarely found in treaties.

Judicial decisions

Although, formally, judgments of courts and tribunals, international and domestic, are a subsidiary source of international law, in practice they may have considerable influence. Because judgments result from careful consideration of particular facts and legal arguments, they carry persuasive authority. There are relatively few international courts and tribunals, but thousands of domestic ones; and most cases involving international law come before domestic courts, often final courts of appeal.[36] The cumulative effect of such decisions on a particular legal point can be evidence of custom, though domestic courts sometimes get international law wrong.

Teachings of the most highly qualified publicists

The role played by writers on international law is also subsidiary. In the formative days of international law their views may have been more influential than they are today. Now their main value depends on the extent to which the books and articles are works of scholarship, that is to say, based on thorough research into what the law is (*lex lata*), or may be, rather than comparing the views of other writers as to what the law ought to be (*lex ferenda*). A work of rigorous scholarship will inevitably have more influence on a court, whether domestic or international.

General international law

One sees this phrase from time to time. It is a rather vague reference to the corpus of international law other than treaty law, and therefore includes those treaty principles or rules that have become accepted as also customary international law.[37]

Obligations erga omnes

In *Barcelona Traction* (Second Phase), the International Court of Justice pointed out that certain obligations on a state are owed to all states,

---

[35] See 'Soft law', p. 11 below.
[36] See the cumulative indexes to *International Law Reports*, published by Cambridge University Press.
[37] See p. 6 above. On Statements of international law, see (2003) BYIL 585–6.

or *erga omnes* (for all the world). These include *jus cogens* and important human rights.[38] Certain treaties have been held to create a status or regime valid *erga omnes*.[39] Examples include those providing for neutralisation or demilitarisation of a certain territory or area, such as Svalbard or outer space; for freedom of navigation in international waterways, such as the Suez Canal, or for a regime for a special area, such as Antarctica.[40]

Jus cogens

Jus cogens (or a peremptory or absolute rule of general international law) is, in the words of Article 53 of the Vienna Convention on the Law of Treaties 1969:

> a norm accepted and recognised by the international community of states as a whole as a norm from which no derogation is permitted and which can be modified only by a subsequent norm of general international law having the same character.

The concept was once controversial.[41] Now it is more its scope and applicability that is unclear.[42] There is no agreement on the criteria for identifying which principles of general international law have a peremptory character: everything depends on the particular nature of the subject matter. Perhaps the only generally accepted examples of *jus cogens* are the prohibitions on the use of force (as laid down in the UN Charter)[43] and on genocide, slavery and torture. This is so even where such acts are prohibited by treaties that parties can withdraw from.[44] It is wrong to assume that all the provisions of human rights treaties, such as due process, are *jus cogens* or even rules of customary international law.[45]

'Soft law'

There is no agreement about what is 'soft law', or indeed if it really exists.[46] Generally, it is used to describe international instruments that their

---

[38] See *Legal Consequences of the Construction of a Wall in the Occupied Palestinian Territory* Advisory Opinion, *ICJ Reports* (2004), paras. 154–9; ILM (2004) 1009.

[39] See M. Ragazzi, *The Concept of International Obligations Erga Omnes*, Oxford, 1997, pp. 24–7; and p. 354 above.

[40] See pp. 354 et seq below for details.

[41] See I. Sinclair, *The Vienna Convention on the Law of Treaties*, 2nd edn, Manchester, 1984, pp. 203–41.

[42] For an in-depth discussion of *jus cogens*, see Sinclair, pp. 203–26.

[43] See p. 224 below.   [44] See p. 101 below.   [45] See p. 245 below.

[46] See Birnie and Boyle, *International Law and the Environment*, 2nd edn, Oxford, 2002, pp. 24–7.

makers recognise are not treaties, even if they employ imperative language such as 'shall', but have as their purpose the promulgation of 'norms' (see above) of general or universal application. Such non-treaty instruments are typically called Guidelines, Principles, Declarations, Codes of Practice, Recommendations or Programmes. They are frequently found in the economic, social and environmental fields. The Rio Declaration on Environment and Development 1992 is one.[47] Because the subject matter is usually not yet well developed, or there is a lack of consensus on the content, it cannot be embodied in a treaty. But the soft law Universal Declaration of Human Rights 1948 has been the source for many universal and regional human rights treaties. Many 'soft law' instruments can be regarded as MOUs in the sense that there is no intention that they should be legally binding.[48]

Comity

In their international relations states also observe certain rules of comity.[49] These are not legally binding, but rules of politeness, convenience and goodwill, such as the reciprocal provision of free, but limited, on-street parking for diplomats.[50] Later some may become binding rules. Courts may also rely upon comity as a reason for not accepting jurisdiction in a case, but this seems to be due to a misunderstanding. The courts are then really applying either a rule of conflict of laws or acting with restraint in exercising their jurisdiction in accordance with principles of international law.[51]

Domestic law

The law that applies within a state is described variously as 'national', 'internal' or 'municipal' law, though most international lawyers now seem to favour 'domestic law'. That term will be used here, even though it can sometimes be confused with family law.

For international lawyers, the most important aspect of domestic law is its relationship (interface) with international law.[52] Most judgments on

---

[47] ILM (1992) 876; B&B Docs. 9; and see p. 330 below.
[48] See pp. 53, 55 below as to the meaning of MOUs.
[49] See Oppenheim, pp. 50–1; Brownlie, p. 28.
[50] See *Parking Privileges for Diplomats* (1971) 70 ILR 396; and E. Denza, *Diplomatic Law*, 2nd edn, Oxford, 1998, pp. 164–5.
[51] See p. 161 below.
[52] See generally Oppenheim, pp. 52–86; E. Denza, in M. Evans (ed.), *International Law*, Oxford, 2003, pp. 415–42.

issues of international law are made by domestic courts, and by this means much of international law has been developed and will continue to do so.[53] Although international law exists on the international plane, much of it is now intended to reach deep into the internal legal order of states and so operate in domestic law. This is most obvious with treaties, many of which have to be implemented in domestic law to be effective. International law does not allow a state to invoke its domestic law to justify its failure to perform a treaty,[54] but this applies equally to the rest of international law.[55] The way in which domestic courts deal with an issue of international law is therefore important. (The place of treaties in domestic law is explained at pp. 79–86 below.)

How customary international law is applied by domestic courts is entirely dependent on the constitution and law of each state. Most treat customary international law as part of domestic law and, therefore, unlike foreign law, does not (as in common law systems) have to be proved by expert evidence, but is usually a matter for legal argument. The chief difference of approach is between those constitutions that provide that customary international law is supreme law (e.g. Germany), and those where it is not. In the latter case, if there is a conflict between customary international law and (1) the constitution, the constitution prevails (e.g. the United States), *or* (2) legislation, the legislation prevails (e.g. the United Kingdom and most Commonwealth states). The latter rule reflects the pure form of dualism.[56]

Subjects of international law

By 'subjects', is not meant topics, but those persons or entities to which international law applies. It obviously applies to states since they have always been a fundamental concept of international law (see the next chapter).[57] But can international law apply also to natural persons (individuals) and legal persons (like corporations)? Such persons are not creations of international law, and are not regarded by most authorities as subjects of international law to whom international rights (and obligations) attach directly.[58] Instead they are generally seen as 'objects' of international law.

---

[53] See the consolidated index to the 126 (and counting) volumes of *International Law Reports* published by Cambridge University Press.

[54] Article 27 of the Vienna Convention on the Law of Treaties (see p. 79 below).

[55] Oppenheim, pp. 82–6.

[56] See further in respect of treaties, at pp. 81–3 below.

[57] Oppenheim, p. 16.

[58] For a thought-provoking view, see Higgins, pp. 38–55.

Although international law increasingly gives rights to, and imposes obligations on, persons, the notion that they therefore enjoy rights under international law goes too far. Such rights can be enforced by or against persons only through action by states. A person with a claim against a foreign state cannot himself take his claim to an international court or tribunal. Either his state has to do it for him,[59] or there must be some mechanism established by the two states (usually a treaty) under which he can himself bring his claim directly before an international tribunal.[60] Likewise, if under international criminal law or the law of armed conflict persons are liable to be prosecuted in domestic or international courts for serious breaches, that can be done only if states have agreed on the establishment of the necessary international or domestic means to do that,[61] and both will need some domestic action by states. In short, international rights and obligations still exist on the international plane.[62]

An important subject of international law is now also the international organisation (see pp. 196 *et seq* below).

National liberation movements

With the development of the law relating to non-self-governing territories and the principle of self-determination, certain rebel movements – now usually referred to as national liberation movements (NLMs) – may be in the process of acquiring the status of a subject of international law,[63] though, with the notable exception of Palestine, most of the peoples represented by NLMs have now obtained statehood for their territories. This process was helped by permanent observer status in the United Nations being accorded to NLMs that were recognised by the Organization of African Unity (now the African Union) or the League of Arab States, so in practice excluding secessionist movements.

NGOs

Even if they operate internationally (like Amnesty or Greenpeace), non-governmental organisations (NGOs) are bodies established under

---

[59] See pp. 183–4 below.
[60] For example, under bilateral investment treaties, see p. 373 below, though enforcement of an award may need to be done in domestic law.
[61] See pp. 263 *et seq* below.
[62] See also pp. 251 *et seq* below on the relationship between international and domestic law.
[63] See Oppenheim, pp. 162–4; Shaw, pp. 220–3; Brownlie, pp. 61–2.

domestic law. Although they have proliferated enormously in the second half of the twentieth century, and been very active and sometimes influential on the international scene, they are not subjects of international law.[64] They are essentially providers of information, lobbyists or pressure groups, and as such may properly be regarded as so-called non-state actors. The International Committee of the Red Cross (ICRC) has a rather special status.[65]

[64] Oppenheim, p. 21.   [65] See pp. 196 and 262 below.

2

States and recognition

States are, at this moment of history,
still at the heart of the international legal system.[1]

Oppenheim. *Oppenheim's International Law*, 9th edn, London, 1992, pp. 119–203

Shaw, *International Law*, 5th edn, Cambridge, 2003, pp. 177–217.

Crawford, *The Creation of States in International Law*, Oxford, 1979

Brownlie, *Principles of Public International Law*, 6th edn, Oxford, 2003, pp. 69–101

Although international organisations, non-governmental organisations and individuals (so-called non-state actors) now participate much more in the international legal order,[2] this is because states have given them parts to play. They still have only supporting roles. Only states have international legal personality to the fullest extent.[3] In this chapter we will therefore look first at states and then at some non-state actors, other than international organisations.

Criteria for statehood

The accepted criteria for statehood is that the entity has to demonstrate that it has '(a) a permanent population; (b) defined territory; (c) a government; and (d) capacity to enter into relations with other states'.[4] Let us take these in turn.

A permanent population. The population does not have to be homogeneous racially, ethnically, tribally, religiously, linguistically or otherwise. But it must be a settled population, though the presence of certain inhabitants who are traditionally nomadic does not matter.

Territory. Size does not matter either. At one time it was thought that countries with a small territory or population ('mini- or micro-states')

[1] Higgins, p. 39.   [2] Higgins, pp. 46–55.   [3] See p. 13 above.
[4] Montevideo Convention 1933, 165 LNTS 19, and see Oppenheim, pp. 120–3.

were not eligible for UN membership. But since 1990, Andorra, Liechtenstein, Monaco, Nauru, San Marino and Tuvalu have joined the United Nations. Although they include some wealthy countries, some are very poor. Nor do the land or maritime boundaries have to be defined definitively.

Government. There must be a central government operating as a political body within the law of the land and in effective control of the territory. But once a state has been established, military occupation by another state or civil war will not affect that statehood.

Independence in external relations. The government must be sovereign and independent, so that within its territory it is not subject to the authority of another state. The corollary is that the state thus has full capacity to enter into relations with other states. The constituent states of a federation, or the overseas territories of a state,[5] are not sovereign and do not have international legal personality. The full title of Switzerland is the Swiss Confederation, but its constitution is that of a federation.[6]

But to become a sovereign state in practice requires recognition by other states.

Recognition of states

There are two competing theories on recognition: either recognition is no more than a formal acceptance of the existing facts (the declaratory theory), or it is the act of recognition that creates the new state as an international legal person (the constitutive theory).[7] But unless an entity is accorded recognition as a state by a sufficiently large number of states, it cannot realistically claim to be a state with all the corresponding rights and obligations. For many years some states refused, for purely political reasons to do with the Cold War, to recognise either North or South Korea,[8] North or South Vietnam[9] or East or West Germany,[10] although all satisfied the criteria for statehood. Their admission to the United Nations

---

[5] See p. 29 below.   [6] See Oppenheim, pp. 246–8 on confederated states.

[7] See Shaw, pp. 368–76 and C. Warbrick in M. Evans (ed.), *International Law*, Oxford, 2003, pp. 205–67.

[8] See Oppenheim, pp. 133–5. Both were admitted to the United Nations only in 1991.

[9] See Oppenheim, pp. 141–3. In 1977, the single state of Vietnam was admitted to the United Nations.

[10] For the special legal status of Germany, the Federal Republic of Germany and the German Democratic Republic, see Oppenheim, pp. 135–41.

was therefore blocked.[11] (As to the quite different question of the *representation*, see p. 197 below.)

The suggestion that there is an obligation to recognise an entity as a new state, on the basis that, on an objective view, it satisfies all the criteria for recognition, has never been widely accepted.[12] Nor were the, scarcely practical and politically naïve, Guidelines on the Recognition of New States in Eastern Europe and in the Soviet Union issued by the European Community on 16 December 1991.[13] Issued without proper consideration of the legal and political consequences, the Guidelines required that in order to be recognised each aspirant state had to give assurances that it would respect the rule of law, democracy and human rights, and guarantee the rights of minorities and the inviolability of all frontiers. Not surprisingly, the assurances were quickly given. The record since suggests that some of the new states, and indeed members of the European Community, saw the exercise as a diplomatic figleaf to cover over-hasty recognition.

Today Taiwan (see below) operates as far as possible like a state, but is recognised by only a few states, mostly small and poor. The reason for its international limbo is political, its government purporting to be the government of all China, albeit in temporary exile. On the other hand, Palestine, although recognised mainly by Arab states, is treated by other states and in the United Nations virtually as if it were a state.[14] This is for good political reasons.

Membership of the United Nations is open only to 'states', although this term is not defined in the Charter, and in the past countries that were not states were Members. Even when they were still republics of the Soviet Union, the Byelorussian SSR (now Belarus) and the Ukrainian SSR (now Ukraine) became original Members as part of a deal under which India, which gained independence only in 1947, also became an original Member. That has now been put right by their independence. Today admission to the United Nations is usually the shortest and quickest route to recognition of statehood. But it amounts to recognition only by those Members supporting admission.[15] Nevertheless, most countries that could be regarded as states are now UN Members.[16] The

---

[11] See pp. 205–6 below.   [12] Shaw, pp. 372–3.
[13] (1991) BYIL 559–60. See also the EC Declaration on Yugoslavia of the same date: (1991) BYIL 560–1.
[14] See p. 26 below.   [15] See UN Doc. S/1466 (1950), and Oppenheim, pp. 177–83.
[16] Several Arab Members have declared formally that they do not recognise Israel.

principal – though so far problematic – exceptions are the Vatican City, Taiwan and Palestine.[17]

Vatican City

As a result of the Lateran Treaty 1929 between the Holy See and Italy,[18] and recognition and acquiescence by states, the Vatican City (albeit tiny in area and with a resident population of papal functionaries) would seem to be a state even though its sole purpose is to support the religious and moral purposes of the Holy See. It has permanent observer status in the United Nations, is a full member of some other international organisations, and is a party to multilateral treaties.[19]

Taiwan

The island of Taiwan (Formosa) was surrendered by Japan to the Republic of China (RoC) in 1945. Following the civil war in China, which left the mainland under the control of the communist forces, the (nationalist) government of the RoC fled to Taiwan. The victorious communists proclaimed the People's Republic of China (PRC) in 1949, and it soon became widely recognised, though not by the United States until 1979. The nationalist government still claims to be the government of all China, and has therefore not claimed statehood for Taiwan. As the purported government of the RoC, Taiwan has diplomatic relations with some small developing states. Rapprochement between Taiwan and the PRC may one day be possible. In 2001 the RoC (under the name 'Chinese Taipei') became a member of the World Trade Organization on the basis that it is a separate customs territory, as has also the European Communities, Hong Kong, China and Macao, China.

Turkish Republic of Northern Cyprus

Unlike the preceding examples, the so-called Turkish Republic of Northern Cyprus (TRNC) is recognised only by one state, Turkey.[20] Following the decision of representatives of the Turkish Cypriot community in 1963 to cease participating in organs of the Republic of Cyprus (ROC) and refusing to recognise its laws, there were serious civil disturbances and

---

[17] See p. 26 below.   [18] 130 BSP 791.   [19] Oppenheim, pp. 325–9; Shaw, pp. 218–19.
[20] See UNGA Res. 541 (1983) and Res. 550 (1984).

UN peacekeeping forces were deployed. Extensive population movements resulted in the majority of the Turkish Cypriots moving to the north of the island. Following the overthrow of the ROC Government in 1974 by a coup d'état inspired by the then military regime in Greece, the Turkish army invaded the north, and continues to occupy it.[21] A buffer zone (the Green Line) separates the occupied north from the south. In separate referendums in April 2004, a UN settlement plan for Cyprus was approved by the Turkish Cypriots but rejected by the Greek Cypriots. The Republic of Cyprus became a member of the EU on 1 May 2004, but for the time being not in respect of those areas in which the ROC Government does not exercise effective control (i.e. the occupied part).

Republics

Most states are republics, and this can lead to misunderstandings. The full title of the Soviet Union was the Union of Soviet Socialist Republics, yet the many republics of the USSR were merely provinces.[22] The Russian Federation[23] now consists of twenty-one (non-independent) republics (including Chechnya, Ingushetia and North Ossetia), forty-nine oblasts, ten autonomous okrugs, six krays, two federal cities and one autonomous oblast. The Republic of *South* Ossetia is not part of Russia, but a renegade province of the state of Georgia, itself a former Soviet republic. Republika Srpska is one of the two entities, the other being the Federation of Bosnia and Herzegovina, constituting the state of Bosnia and Herzegovina.[24] Kosovo is a province of Serbia, itself a constituent part of the state of Serbia and Montenegro (formerly the Federal Republic of Yugoslavia), though since 1999 it has been under UN administration (UNMIK).[25] The fifty states of the United States of America are constituent parts of the federal state of that name, sometimes referred to as the 'nation state'.

Yugoslavia

Even though the Federal Republic of Yugoslavia (FRY) asserted that it was the continuation of the Socialist Federal Republic of Yugoslavia (SFRY),

---

[21] See Oppenheim, pp. 189–90.

[22] See text to n. 15 above on the even more misleading cases of Byelorussia, and Ukraine. Its title, Commonwealth of Independent States, correctly represents the position of its former Soviet republic members (see n. 43 below).

[23] See p. 393 below on the continuation of statehood.

[24] See Article I(3) of the so-called Dayton Agreement, ILM (1996) 75.

[25] See www.unmikonline.org.

the other former republics of the SFRY, as well as most third states, did not accept this or the FRY's claim to the seat of the former Yugoslavia in the United Nations and other international organisations.[26] In September 1992 the UN General Assembly decided that the FRY could not continue automatically the membership of the SFRY; that it should apply for membership; and that it could not take part in the work of the General Assembly.[27] The effect of this ambiguous decision was that the membership of 'Yugoslavia' was not terminated or suspended, but its practical consequence was that FRY representatives could no longer take part in the work of the General Assembly, its subsidiary organs, or conferences or meetings convened by the General Assembly.[28]

Domestic courts and unrecognised states

Nevertheless, domestic courts sometimes adopt the sensible view that, even if the government does not recognise an entity as a state, life has to go on, and so they may give effect to laws and acts of public authorities of unrecognised states when they concern the ordinary but essential day-to-day aspects of life, such as births, marriages, divorces, deaths[29] and certain commercial matters.[30]

Self-determination[31]

One of the purposes of the United Nations is to develop friendly relations among nations based on respect for the principle of equal rights and the principle of self-determination of peoples (Article 1(2) of the UN Charter), and Article 73 of the Charter declares that the interests of the

---

[26] (1992) BYIL 655–8. See also the report of the Badinter Commission, 92 ILR 162 at 166. The ICJ elided the question in *Genocide (Bosnia v. Yugoslavia)* (Provisional Measures), *ICJ Reports* (1993), p. 3, at pp. 20–3; ILM (1993) 888; 95 ILR 1.

[27] See UNSC Res. 757 (1992), 777 (1992), 821 (1993) and 1074 (1996), and UNGA Res. 47/1, 47/229 and 48/88; ILM (1992) 1421. See also the detailed consideration of the status of the FRY between 1992 and 2000 in *Legality of the Use of Force (Serbia and Montenegro v. Belgium)* (Preliminary Objections), *ICJ Reports* (2004), paras. 25 and 54–91.

[28] See UN Doc. A/47/485. For the problems of succession to FRY treaties and property, see pp. 399 and 402 below.

[29] See *Hesperides Hotels v. Aegean Turkish Holidays* [1978] QB 205; 73 ILR 9, *per* Lord Denning *obiter* (the case concerned Turkish-occupied Northern Cyprus); *Caglar v. Bellingham* 108 ILR 510 at 535–40; *Reel v. Holder* [1981] 1 WLR 1226; 74 ILR 105.

[30] *Al-Fin Corporation's Patent* [1970] Ch 160; 52 ILR 68.

[31] See A. Cassese, *Self-Determination of Peoples*, Cambridge, 1995.

inhabitants of non-self-governing territories are 'paramount', and envisages, among other things, the development of their eventual self-government. At that time independence for most territories was not envisaged, but events moved rapidly. Paragraph 2 of the Declaration on the Granting of Independence to Colonial Countries and Peoples of 1960[32] declared that all peoples have the right to self-determination, and thus to determine freely their political status. Article 1(2) of the International Covenant on Civil and Political Rights 1966[33] also provides that all peoples have the right of self-determination, which is now a right *erga omnes*.[34]

Those overseas territories that still remain have freely chosen to stay as they are, at least for the moment. This can be illustrated by the example of Gibraltar (less than 6 sq kms).[35] A 1967 referendum of the inhabitants resulted in 12,138 voting for the status quo and 44 for returning to Spain. Ignoring the referendum, and Article 73 of the UN Charter, UNGA Resolution 2429(XXIII) (1968) called for the end of the 'colonial situation'. The resolution was adopted with sixty-seven votes, with eighteen against and thirty-four abstentions. Although Gibraltar is still an irritant in Anglo-Spanish relations, much has changed since then: Spain is now a democracy, and the two states belong to the European Union. In 2002 a proposal for joint sovereignty was rejected in another referendum by 17,900 to 187. Spain retains two small enclaves on the coast of Morocco: Ceuta and Melilla.

Judgments in delimitation disputes can lead to a significant number of people suddenly finding themselves living under the government of a different state and as their nationals.[36] A negotiated settlement or plebiscite, or the involvement of an impartial organisation like the United Nations, rather than resort to law, can be a better way of handling such politically and emotionally charged matters.[37]

---

[32] UNGA Res. 1514 (XV).

[33] 999 UNTS 171 (No. 14668); ILM (1967) 368: UKTS (1977) 6.

[34] See *Legal Consequences of the Construction of a Wall in the Occupied Palestinian Territory* Advisory Opinion, *ICJ Reports* (2004), para. 87; ILM (2004) 1009. On *erga omnes*, see p. 10 above.

[35] See p. 37 below on the legal title to Gibraltar.

[36] See *Cameroon v. Nigeria* (Merits), *ICJ Reports* (2002); and see Oppenheim, pp. 685–6 on the option found in some cession treaties to retain the previous nationality.

[37] For an account of the dispute over sovereignty of the Falkland Islands, which illustrates some of the complex legal and political factors involved in resolving such disputes, see Shaw, pp. 452–3.

Secession

The principle of self-determination was originally conceived primarily for colonial situations, and so any proposed secession by the people of part of a metropolitan state is likely to be highly contentious. Not only is the notion of a 'people' not easy to apply,[38] but the principle of self-determination is inevitably in tension with those of territorial integrity[39] and *uti possidetis*.[40] Between 1945 and the end of the Cold War there has been only one successful case of secession by force (Bangladesh).[41] But during that period there were several failed attempts at secession, such as those by Biafrans, Eritreans, Katangans, Basque separatists in Spain and the IRA in Northern Ireland.

Most claims to statehood are likely to come either from a former overseas territory (and should pose no problem),[42] or from a part of a state that asserts it has become a new state. Somaliland was a British protectorate until 1960 when, only days after independence, it joined with the former Italian Trust Territory of Somaliland to form the new state of Somalia, now widely seen as a 'failed state'. Since 1991 Somaliland has been effectively independent of Somalia.

Although states are naturally cautious about recognising secession, international law does not prohibit it. The independence of fourteen former republics of the Soviet Union (Armenia, Azerbaijan, Belarus, Georgia, Kazakhstan, Kyrgyzstan, Moldova, Tajikistan, Turkmenistan, Ukraine and Uzbekistan, and the Baltic states of Estonia, Latvia and Lithuania) was quickly achieved by 1991, the predecessor state not having seriously opposed it. The Minsk Agreement of 8 December 1991, establishing the Commonwealth of Independent States, and the Alma Ata Declaration of 21 December 1991, together recognised the end of the Soviet Union and the independence of those former republics.[43] Attempts to secede have generally not been successful if the predecessor state has opposed it.[44] It is also easier if there is no government in effective control of the predecessor state, the state then not being able either to oppose or to agree to secession.

Recognition is also easier if the original state has dissolved, especially if it was a somewhat artificial creation. Other states therefore soon accepted

---

[38] See Cassese, *Self-Determination of Peoples*, Cambridge, 1995.
[39] See p. 41 below.   [40] See p. 42 below.
[41] Singapore seceded from Malaysia in 1965 by consent.
[42] See p. 391 below.   [43] See ILM (1992) 138 or www.cisstat.com/eng/cis.htm.
[44] See J. Crawford, 'State Practice and International Law in Relation to Secession' (1998) BYIL 85–117.

the fact that the Socialist Federal Republic of Yugoslavia had broken into the states of Bosnia and Herzegovina, Croatia, Macedonia and Slovenia, which were then admitted to the United Nations. (The so-termed Federal Republic of Yugoslavia raised difficult questions.)[45] These are good examples of international law reflecting the realities. In contrast, in the United Nations Macedonia is referred to as '*the former* Yugoslav Republic of Macedonia' (emphasis added), Greece having objected vehemently to Macedonia calling itself by the same name as a neighbouring northern Greek province. The lower case 't' and 'f' indicate that it is *not* the name of the state.[46]

Territorial integrity and uti possidetis

The principle of territorial integrity may be seen as an impediment to recognition. But if the particular circumstances merit it, states have shown their willingness to recognise secession. Being a matter of political judgment, recognition is largely dependent on whether secession has become a political and irreversible fact.

The principle of *uti possidetis*[47] is not an obstacle to recognition of secession of part of a state. The principle places no obligation on minority groups to stay part of a unit if it maltreats them. If they establish a separate entity that is shown to have permanence, it will eventually be recognised by the international community: 'international law will recognise new realities'.[48] Eritrea was an Italian colony from 1896, and was occupied by British forces in the Second World War. In 1950 the UN General Assembly decided that it should be an autonomous part of a federation with Ethiopia. That did not work and a long period of strife with the central government ensued. In 1993, a referendum in Eritrea was overwhelmingly in favour of independence, and independence was declared in April 1993, Eritrea becoming a Member of the United Nations the same year.

Recognition of governments

Even though a state and its territory are often seen as synonymous, a state exists only in law. It must therefore act through its government. One must not confuse recognition of states with that of governments. In itself,

---

[45] See p. 20 above and pp. 399 and 402 below.
[46] See M. Wood, 'Participation of the Former Yugoslav States in the United Nations' (1997) YB of UN Law 231.
[47] See p. 42 below.   [48] Higgins, pp. 125–6.

a change of government does not affect the state. Even when the change has been brought about by unconstitutional or violent means, the legal personality of the state is unaffected (as are treaties to which the state is bound).[49] The question of recognition of a government arises only when it has come to power unconstitutionally. Recognition may then be withheld for political reasons, or may be limited to recognition *de facto* (see below). Although the new regime may be all too clearly in effective control of the territory, with a reasonable prospect of permanence and with the obedience of the mass of the population, recognition may be withheld as a sign of political displeasure. But since international law is concerned more with the realities, if the new regime was not at first recognised because of the way it came to power, yet is clearly in effective control and firmly established, in international law it will be regarded as the government.[50]

Numerous unconstitutional changes of government took place in the 1970s, particularly in developing countries. The practice of formally announcing recognition of a usurper regime was often politically embarrassing since recognition was sometimes perceived, albeit wrongly, as political approval of the new regime. This predicament led several states to abandon the practice of formal recognition. Following the adroit French principle of recognising only states, since 1980 the nature of the relations that the United Kingdom has with a new regime must be determined and deduced from the particular circumstances. Where previously the British Government would have accorded formal recognition to a new government, now it will – but only if asked – say that it deals with it on a normal government-to-government basis.[51] US practice appears to be more pragmatic: the Administration may formally recognise an unlawful change of government when it approves of the change, but otherwise leaves its view of the new government to be deduced from the relations it has with it: diplomatic, consular, or none.[52]

Governments in exile

When a foreign invader or local insurgents have occupied a state, its government may flee abroad and, provided the state of refuge agrees,

---

[49] See p. 393 below.

[50] *Tinoco Claims Arbitration* (*United Kingdom* v. *Colombia*), 2 ILR 34.

[51] For the formal statement of the new practice, see (1980) BYIL 367 and C. Warbrick, 'The New British Policy on Recognition of Governments' (1981) ICLQ 568–92. See generally Shaw, pp. 380–2.

[52] M. West and S. Murphy, 'The Impact on US Litigation of Non-Recognition of Foreign Governments' (1990) *Stanford Journal of International Law* 435–78.

operate as a government in exile with the same legal status as it had before. Recognition of a revolutionary government established abroad before it has gained control over the greater part of the territory of the state concerned may well be premature and amount to an interference in the affairs of the state.[53]

De jure and *de facto* recognition

An entity, whether claiming to be a state or a government, may be recognised either *de jure* or *de facto*, which terms qualify the status of the entity, not the nature of the recognition. Recognition *de jure* means that the entity fully satisfies the applicable legal criteria; recognition *de facto* is only of the current position of the entity, and is therefore usually provisional. *De facto* recognition can, however, last a long time. The United Kingdom and other Western states refused to recognise as *de jure* the 1940 annexation by the Soviet Union of the Baltic states (Estonia, Latvia and Lithuania). Instead, they merely recognised that the Soviet Union had *de facto* control over them. This lasted until 1991 when the re-emergence of the three Baltic states was recognised by many states, including the Soviet Union (soon to renamed the Russian Federation).[54]

Palestine[55]

Palestine had been part of the Ottoman Empire. From 1922, it was a League of Nations mandated territory entrusted to the United Kingdom, which formally relinquished the mandate on 15 May 1948, the day the state of Israel was proclaimed. Israel was admitted to the United Nations in 1949. General Assembly Resolution 181 (II) (1947) had recommended the partition of Palestine into two independent states, one Arab, one Jewish, and the creation of a special international regime for Jerusalem, but the plan was never implemented. The Arab population of Palestine and the Arab states rejected this. On the day Israel proclaimed its independence, an armed conflict broke out between Israel and a number of Arab states. Following Security Council Resolution 62 (1948), general armistice agreements were concluded in 1949 between Israel and the neighbouring

---

[53] See Oppenheim, pp. 146–7.   [54] Oppenheim, pp. 193–4.
[55] See www.un.org/Depts/dpa/qpa/; *Legal Consequences of the Construction of a Wall in the Occupied Palestinian Territory* Advisory Opinion, *ICJ Reports* (2004), paras. 70–8; ILM (2004) 1009; Oppenheim, p. 131, n. 2, p. 163, n. 9 and pp. 194–6; and Shaw, pp. 221–2.

states. Articles V and VI of the Agreement between Israel and Jordan fixed the armistice demarcation line (later called the 'Green Line' owing to the colour used for it on maps) separating Israel and the West Bank, then occupied by Jordan. Article VI(8) provided that these provisions would not prejudice any final political settlement, and that the Green Line was without prejudice to future settlements regarding territory or boundary lines.

During the later conflict with Arab states in 1967, Israeli forces occupied all the territories which had constituted Palestine under the League of Nations mandate, including the West Bank and East Jerusalem (from Jordan),[56] as well as the Gaza Strip (from Egypt) and the Golan Heights (from Syria). In Resolution 242 (1967), adopted by unanimity, the Security Council emphasised the inadmissibility of acquisition of territory by war and called for the withdrawal of Israel's armed forces 'from territories occupied in the recent conflict'.

From 1967 Israel took a number of measures aimed at changing the status of Jerusalem, including purporting to make it the capital of Israel. The Security Council condemned those measures, and in Resolution 298 (1971) confirmed that all legislative and administrative actions taken by Israel to change the status of Jerusalem were invalid and could not change that status. Israel does not claim sovereignty over the territories occupied since 1967, and under customary international law in those territories Israel therefore has the status of an occupying power. Subsequent events in the territories have done nothing to alter this situation. The continued occupation by Israel is a military occupation subject to the limitations of the Hague Regulations 1907 (Section III) and the Fourth Geneva Convention.[57]

In November 1988, the Palestine National Council, the Parliamentary Assembly of the Palestine Liberation Organization, declared a state of Palestine. Since 1993, a number of agreements have been signed between Israel and the Palestine Liberation Organization. They required Israel to transfer to Palestinian authorities certain powers and responsibilities exercised in the occupied territories by its military authorities and civil administration. Such transfers have taken place, but, as a result of

---

[56] In 1988, Jordan announced its disengagement from the West Bank, although it did not renounce any claim it had to sovereignty.

[57] See pp. 259–60 below, and *Legal Consequences of the Construction of a Wall in the Occupied Palestinian Territory* Advisory Opinion, *ICJ Reports* (2004), paras. 89–101; ILM (2004) 1009. See also UNSC Res. 252 (1968), 465 (1980), 497 (1981); UNGA Res. 2253 and 2254 (1967) and 2949 (XXVII) (1972).

subsequent events, have remained partial and limited. In 1994, a nascent Palestinian government, the Palestinian Authority,[58] was established.

Given that Palestine lacks control over so much of the territory it claims, as well as the well-known and profound political problems, Palestine has not yet succeeded in being generally recognised as a state. It has not been admitted as a Member of the United Nations, though it does have permanent observer status there,[59] the same as that accorded to non-member states and regional international organisations. At present, any application by Palestine for membership would be vetoed in the Security Council.

Western Sahara

Formerly Spanish Sahara, in 1976 the territory (with a population of about 267,000) was partitioned between Mauritania and Morocco, Morocco taking over the whole when Mauritania withdrew in 1979. The Polisario Front disputes Morocco's sovereignty and fought a guerrilla war with Morocco. It ended in 1991 with a UN-brokered ceasefire. A UN-organised referendum on the final status of the territory has repeatedly been postponed.[60] It is not *terra nullius*.[61]

Means of recognition

Recognition can be express, as in a diplomatic note or formal public announcement. More often it is effected by means of an act that carries the inevitable implication that it would not have been done if the entity were not recognised. Supporting admittance to UN membership is the most obvious example of implied recognition; establishment of diplomatic relations or the conclusion of a bilateral treaty are others. Participation in an international conference in which the entity takes part, or becoming a party to a multilateral treaty to which the entity is also a party, does not amount to recognition.[62] Although legally unnecessary, when ratifying a multilateral treaty which Israel has ratified some

---

[58] For details, see Shaw, pp. 221–2.
[59] See UNGA Res. 3210 and 3237 (XXIX) (1974), 3375 (XXX) (1975) and 43/177 (1988).
[60] See www.un.org/Depts/dpko/missions/minurso/.
[61] See *Western Sahara* Advisory Opinion, *ICJ Reports* (1975), p. 12, paras. 75–83; 59 ILR 14.
[62] For numerous examples of acts that do not amount to recognition, see Oppenheim, pp. 170–4.

states formally declare that their ratification does not imply recognition of Israel.

A visit by a high-level official, or a (publicised) meeting with a senior official of the purported government, should not amount to recognition if the position of the state is well known, though sometimes it may be prudent to make it clear in advance, and perhaps publicly, that nothing should be inferred.

Overseas territories[63]

The term 'overseas territory' describes a territory which is under the sovereignty of a state ('parent state') but which is not governed as part of its metropolitan territory, unlike French Guiana, Guadeloupe, Martinique and Reunion which under the French Constitution are *départments* of France. Previously, overseas territories were known as colonies or dependent territories. Article 73 of the UN Charter describes overseas territories as 'non-self-governing'. Today, most overseas territories that have a permanent population have considerable internal self-government, with mainly defence and foreign affairs remaining the responsibility of the metropolitan state. With the great wave of decolonisation that began after the Second World War, over 100 overseas territories have gained their independence and become Members of the UN, thereby transforming the UN from a smallish club of mostly developed states into a body truly representative of the world. The UN organs concerned with non-self-governing territories are no longer so active.[64]

Today, there is not the great variety in overseas territories that there was only thirty years ago. But Australia, Denmark, France, The Netherlands, New Zealand, Norway, the United Kingdom[65] and the United States still have between them some fifty overseas territories.[66] Quite a few are unlikely ever to be viable as states, having no permanent population or only a very small one. At the last count, Pitcairn had about forty-six inhabitants. On the other hand, larger and more affluent ones like Bermuda and

---

[63] See generally K. Roberts-Wray, *Commonwealth and Colonial Law*, London, 1966.

[64] For details, see Oppenheim, pp. 282–95 or www.un.org.

[65] The full name – United Kingdom of Great Britain and Northern Ireland – derives from the uniting in 1801 of the Kingdoms of Great Britain (England, Wales and Scotland) and of Ireland, the reference to 'Ireland' being changed in 1922 to 'Northern Ireland' on the independence of the rest of the island.

[66] For a list, see Aust, pp. 423–4.

Puerto Rico could well exist as states, but choose to remain as they are. The right of self-determination means only that a people are free to choose how they should be governed, and for an overseas territory independence is not the only option.[67]

British territories

The fourteen remaining British overseas territories are the responsibility of the Foreign and Commonwealth Office, except for the Sovereign Base Areas (see below). There are also three other British territories: the Channel Islands of Guernsey and Jersey and the Isle of Man. They are thought by most people, including most British people, to be part of the United Kingdom since at first sight they appear indistinguishable from the United Kingdom, even if the Channel Islands are geographically much closer to France. But they are not part of the United Kingdom and in British law are known as 'Crown Dependencies', and are the responsibility of the Department of Constitutional Affairs.[68] Although the Crown Dependencies are part of the European Union, not all EC rules apply to them.

There have been several types of overseas territories.

Colonies

Most overseas territories were, and still are, colonies. A colony is a non-metropolitan territory over which the parent state (the colonial power) exercises control. The parent state can determine the extent (if any) to which the colony has control of its internal affairs, though even for the most advanced colonies the parent state will usually retain responsibility for defence and foreign affairs. A colony cannot conclude treaties without the authority of the parent state. Nor can it enter into diplomatic relations, although consular posts may be established in the colony with the permission of the parent state.[69] But some colonies have been given such extensive responsibilities in foreign affairs that some states dealing with them have failed to appreciate that they are not truly independent. The Cook Islands is in 'free association' with New Zealand, its inhabitants retaining New Zealand nationality.[70] This has caused such confusion

---

[67] See pp. 21–2 above.   [68] See www.dca.gov.uk/constitution.htm.   [69] See p. 157 below.
[70] See www.mfat.govt.nz/foreign/regions/pacific/cookislandsdeclaration/ cooksdec.html. As to Puerto Rico and the Netherlands Antilles and Aruba, see Oppenheim, p. 280, nn. 21 and 22.

that the Cook Islands have become a member of some international organisations that are open only to states,[71] and have established diplomatic relations with certain states.

The Sovereign Base Areas in Cyprus (Akrotiri and Dkehelia) are the parts of the former colony that were retained by the United Kingdom when Cyprus became independent. Because of their role as military bases in accordance with special treaty arrangements with Cyprus,[72] they are not administered like a normal colony, being the responsibility of the Ministry of Defence.

Protectorates

This is a term sometimes given to a protected state or colony. It is not a term of art. None are left.

Protected states

A protected state is an entity that has some of the attributes of a state but is under the guardianship of another state. The status is now largely of historic interest.[73] Although Andorra is still cited as a protected state, being under the joint protection of the French President and the Bishop of Urgell in Spain, since it became a Member of the United Nations the protection would seem to be of a somewhat formal nature.[74] Monaco[75] and San Marino[76] have special treaty arrangements with France and Italy, respectively, but are now also UN Members. Bhutan became a UN Member in 1971, but its foreign affairs are supervised by India.[77]

Condominiums

A condominium is a territory over which two or more states exercise sovereignty jointly.[78] It is now largely of historical interest, the last one being the (rather improbable) Anglo-French condominium of the New Hebrides established in 1887,[79] which resulted from naval and other rivalries in the Pacific. The two states each retained jurisdiction over their own

---

[71] The Cook Islands became a party to UNCLOS under the special provisions of Arts. 305 and 306.

[72] 382 UNTS 8 (No. 5476); UKTS (1961) 4.   [73] Oppenheim, pp. 266–74.

[74] See www.andorramania.com/constitution_gb.htm or Oppenheim, pp. 271–2.

[75] Oppenheim, p. 271, n. 1(1).   [76] Oppenheim, p. 272, n. 1(3).

[77] Oppenheim, p. 274.   [78] Oppenheim, pp. 565–7.

[79] 79 BSP 545 and UKTS (1907) 3, (1927) 28 and (1935) 7; and Shaw, pp. 206–7.

nationals. Third states' nationals had on arrival the novel and unenviable experience of having to opt to be either 'British' or 'French' during their stay, though free to eat where they liked. There were native courts and a final appeal court, the Joint Court, consisting of one British and one French judge and a president appointed by the King of Spain. By the end of the Spanish Civil War, the presidency was vacant and remained so for the next forty years, the two national judges always being able to reach an amicable agreement. The territory became independent as Vanuatu in 1980.

Mandated and trust territories

Again, these are of mainly historical interest. Article 22 of the Covenant of the League of Nations provided for overseas territories of Germany and Turkey to be placed under the administration of certain 'mandatory states'.[80] The term derives from the agreements, called 'mandates', between the League and those states entrusted by the League with the administration of the territories on behalf of the League. A mandate did not cede or transfer territory.[81]

Article 75 of the UN Charter replaced mandated territories by trust territories, although the purpose was very similar. Alone of the mandatory states, South Africa refused to place the territory of South West Africa under the trusteeship system (it gained its independence as Namibia eventually in 1990).[82] The system was administered by a principal UN organ, the Trusteeship Council, which suspended operation in 1994 following the independence of the last trust territory, Palau. Although suggestions have been made that certain states or territories might be placed under the Trusteeship Council, Article 75 would not be suitable for this purpose. Instead, action has been taken by the Security Council.[83]

---

[80] Oppenheim, pp. 295–318; Shaw, pp. 201–4.
[81] *International Status of South West Africa*, Advisory Opinion, *ICJ Reports* (1950), p. 132; 17 ILR 47; and *Namibia (South West Africa) Legal Consequences*, *ICJ Reports* (1971), p. 6, paras. 117–27 and 133; 49 ILR 2. See also *Certain Phosphate Lands (Nauru v. Australia)*, *ICJ Reports* (1992), pp. 240 and 256; 97 ILR 1; *Cameroon v. Nigeria*, *ICJ Reports* (2002), para. 212.
[82] For the long, tortuous history of the struggle with South Africa, see Oppenheim, pp. 300–7.
[83] See p. 225 below on Kosovo and UNMIK.

3

Territory

Es ist die letzte territoriale Forderung, die ich Europa zu stellen habe.[1]

Oppenheim, *Oppenheim's International Law*, 9th edn, London, 1992, pp. 661–718

Shaw, *International Law*, 5th edn, Cambridge, 2003, pp. 409–55

Brownlie, *Principles of Public International Law*, 6th edn, Oxford, 2003, pp. 105–69

Crawford, *The Creation of States in International Law*, Oxford, 1979

Jennings, *The Acquisition of Territory in International Law*, Manchester, 1963

Among other things, to be a state there must be a government in effective control of territory.[2] Territorial sovereignty covers all land, internal waters, territorial sea and the airspace above them. A state does *not* have sovereignty over its continental shelf or exclusive economic zone. Instead, it has 'sovereign rights' over the former and sovereign rights and certain other rights and jurisdiction over the latter.[3]

Most of the international law on territory results from disputes between states as to ownership. These days, they tend to be more over land or maritime boundaries, or islands or small areas of land. Although it is not to be found on most maps, Hans Island is a 3 sq km barren, uninhabited island off the northernmost tip of western Greenland in the Kennedy Channel between Greenland and Canada. Both Denmark and Canada claim it. Although the island is ice-covered, the predicted effect of global warming could make the surrounding area more accessible for the exploitation of mineral resources. As assertions of ownership both states have recently stepped up naval visits to the island. Canada also has disputes or

---

[1] 'It is the last territorial claim which I have to make in Europe.' Hitler's speech in Berlin on 26 September 1938, referring to the Sudetenland.

[2] See p. 16 above for the criteria for statehood.

[3] See pp. 308 and 305 below, respectively.

potential disputes with Russia and the United States over much larger Arctic regions.

For a new state – whether previously an overseas territory or part of the metropolitan territory – title to its territory is effectively acknowledged by recognition of its statehood. The new state will inherit any existing disputes as to the extent of the territory or its boundaries. Many of the boundaries of former overseas territories were not well defined, thus giving rise to many disputes and proceedings in international courts and tribunals.[4]

Boundary, border or frontier?

To describe the limits of territory, all three terms are used, but boundary is used more often and is also more suitable for describing maritime limits, and so will be used here.

Delimitation and demarcation

These two terms are often confused, even in treaties. *Delimitation* is the process of determining the land or maritime boundaries of a state, including that of any continental shelf or exclusive economic zone, by means of geographical coordinates of latitude and longitude.[5] The resulting lines are then usually drawn on a map or chart. The process is naturally done for adjacent states, though unilateral delimitation may be necessary for the maritime limits of an isolated territory.[6] The determination may be embodied in a treaty or in the judgment of an international court or tribunal. *Demarcation* is the further and separate procedure of marking a line of delimitation (usually only on land) with physical objects, such as concrete posts, stone cairns etc. In practice, demarcation often involves some degree of delimitation, since a line on map may look rather different on the ground, and sensible adjustments may need to be made. The task of the UN Iraq–Kuwait Boundary Demarcation Commission also

---

[4] See, for example, *Cameroon v. Nigeria* (Merits), *ICJ Reports* (2002); I. Brownlie, *African Boundaries: A Legal and Diplomatic Encyclopaedia*, Oxford, 1969; M. Shaw, *Title to Territory in Africa*, Oxford, 1986.

[5] As to maritime delimitation, see pp. 309–11 below.

[6] And see p. 309 below on the Commission on the Limits of the Continental Shelf.

involved determining certain geographical coordinates, which required new mapping.[7]

Intertemporal principle[8]

In his award in the leading case of the *Island of Palmas*, the single arbitrator, Max Huber, in deciding whether a state has established its claim to territory, stated that one must assess the facts in the light of the international law at the relevant time, not the law at the time the issue falls to be decided.[9] He therefore had to decide whether in the early sixteenth century the mere discovery by Spain of the 2.4 sq km island was sufficient to give it good title then. (See also 'Discovery', p. 36 below.)

Critical date[10]

The resolution of all territorial disputes turns on complex facts extending over many years or centuries. The doctrine of the critical date is by no means easy to apply, and may be something of a chimera. Depending on the circumstances, in essence it is the date by which the rights of the parties to a territorial dispute have so crystallised that what they do afterwards does not affect the legal position. In the *Island of Palmas*, the arbitrator had to decide also if Spain had title to the island in 1898 so that it could by a treaty of that year pass sovereignty to the United States. So 1898 was the critical date, and Huber decided that by that date The Netherlands had acquired a better title than Spain.[11]

Means of acquisition

The traditional classification of the ways in which territory can be validly acquired has been criticised as simplistic, in that it does not take sufficient

---

[7] See UNSC Res. 678 (1991), paras. 2–4, S/25811 (containing the Commission's final report of 20 May 1993) and UNSC Res. 833 (1993).

[8] See R. Higgins, 'Time and the Law: International Perspectives on an Old Problem' (1997) ICLQ 501.

[9] (1928) 2 RIAA 831; 4 AD 103. For a concise description of the case, see J. Brierly, *The Law of Nations*, 6th edn, Oxford, 1963, pp. 163–9. An almost complete text of the award is in H. Briggs (ed.), *The Law of Nations*, 2nd edn, New York, 1952, pp. 239–47.

[10] See Shaw, pp. 431–2; Brownlie, pp. 125–6; Oppenheim, pp. 710–12.

[11] N. 9 above.

account of the interaction of various principles.[12] Nevertheless, the normal method is good enough for present purposes. If the reader is ever lucky enough to advise on a territorial dispute, he or she will soon find that the starting point is an exhaustive collection of all the relevant facts and documents, territorial disputes being very much fact-driven. Examination and assessment of the facts will inevitably suggest which legal arguments best support the client's case. Unlike land disputes in domestic law, there is no detailed set of rules to decide who has ownership. Instead, international courts and tribunals study and weigh up all the evidence to decide which of the parties to the dispute has the better case. Given that so much depends on the particular circumstances, no attempt will be made to repeat here the lengthy treatment of the subject in the leading textbooks. It is sufficient to mention some of the main points.

Discovery

For a time in the fifteenth and sixteenth centuries, the mere sighting of a previously unknown territory may have been enough to give good title to a state, although even this is doubtful. But it soon became established that a symbolic act, such as the planting of a flag or a formal proclamation, was also required to confirm title. And, by the mid-sixteenth century, discovery was seen as conferring no more than an inchoate (provisional) title that needed to be completed by effective occupation (see below).

Conquest and annexation

In the past, conquest (sometimes called subjugation), followed by annexation, was a means of acquiring valid title to territory. Whether annexation now provides good title will therefore depend on (1) the international law at the time (the intertemporal principle), (2) (possibly) whether the annexing state has established effective control over the territory, and (3) whether other states have recognised the annexation. Even in the period between the two World Wars, it was not clear if a state could acquire good title by conquest and annexation. Now Article 2(4) of the UN Charter prohibits the threat or use of force against the territorial integrity of

---

[12] Brownlie, pp. 126–7.

another state or the acquisition of territory by force.[13] The International Court of Justice has found that the building of the wall by Israel in the occupied Palestinian territory, while professed to be a temporary security measure, may prejudge the future boundary between Israel and Palestine in that Israel may seek to integrate into its territory the Israeli settlements, and their means of access. If the wall were to become permanent, it would be tantamount to annexation.[14] The so-called Friendly Relations Declaration 1970[15] confirmed that territory cannot be validly acquired by force or the threat of force, although that does not affect any treaty concluded before the UN Charter and valid under international law (in practice, a treaty of cession). In Resolution 662 (1990), the UN Security Council rejected Iraq's purported annexation of Kuwait.

Cession

Even in the past, it was not simply conquest that conferred title, but a subsequent treaty of cession (sometimes part of a peace treaty). In 1704, Anglo-Dutch forces seized Gibraltar from Spain, the territory then being ceded by Spain to Great Britain[16] by the Treaty of Utrecht of 13 July 1713,[17] although there is a dispute over part of the isthmus linking Gibraltar and Spain. Despite sovereignty having been validly transferred by the Treaty – which obliges the United Kingdom to offer to return the territory to Spain were it ever minded to relinquish sovereignty – from the 1960s Spain pressed for Gibraltar to be returned to it.

Despite the circumstances in which many old treaties of cession were concluded, they remain good roots of title. Many were entered into quite voluntarily, and several involved payment (Alaska by Russia to the United States in 1867 for US$7.2 million, and the Danish West Indies to the United States in 1916 for US$25 million). Territory can also be exchanged, particularly in the realignment of a boundary.

Cession will include all aspects of territorial sovereignty, including airspace and the territorial sea, and sovereign rights over the continental shelf and rights and jurisdiction over the exclusive economic zone.

---

[13] Regarding occupied territory, see *Legal Consequences of the Construction of a Wall in the Occupied Palestinian Territory* Advisory Opinion, *ICJ Reports* (2004), para. 87; ILM (2004) 1009.

[14] *Ibid.*, paras. 119–21.   [15] UNGA Res. 2625 (XXV), Part 1.

[16] See p. 29, n. 65 above for an explanation of the difference between 'Great Britain' and 'United Kingdom'.

[17] 28 CTS 325; 1 BSP 611.

Cession does not affect the rights of third states, such as state servitudes (see below).

Occupation and prescription

These are more conveniently dealt with together, as they have an important common factor: the exercise by a state of effective control.[18]

Terra nullius is vacant land that belongs to no state. The clearest case is the unclaimed sector of Antarctica.[19] There may also be some uninhabited islands and other territories that are still *terrae nullius*. But territory inhabited by peoples with a social or political organisation is not *terra nullius*.[20] *Terra nullius* can be acquired by any state (not by a private person or company, unless acting for the state) that has the intention to claim sovereignty and occupies it by exercising effective and continued control. Occupation is a peaceful means of acquiring territory.

In contrast, prescription is the acquisition of territory that is not *terra nullius*, but was obtained by means that were of doubtful legality or patently illegal. Although international law is not keen to legalise unlawful conduct, the aim of international law is always stability and certainty. Thus, provided territory has been under the effective control of a state, and has been uninterrupted and uncontested for a long time, international law will accept that reality. But timely protests by the 'former' sovereign will usually bar the claim. How long effective control must last depends entirely on the circumstances of each case. Often, there will be sovereign activities (*effectivités*) in relation to the territory by the disputing states. In the case of remote or uninhabited territory, they may be physical (visits by military or government officers) or formal (legislation for the territory).[21]

Of course, if territory was acquired by unlawful use of force, prescription may not help to confer a valid title (see above). Establishing title by prescription usually also involves consideration of matters such as acquiescence, estoppel and recognition.

Acquiescence, estoppel and recognition

In judging whether a territorial claim is good, especially one based on prescription, the acquiescence of the former sovereign would obviously be important, as equally would be protests by that state. A rival claimant

---

[18] Shaw, p. 424.   [19] See p. 355 below.
[20] *Western Sahara* Advisory Opinion, *ICJ Reports* (1975), p. 12, paras. 75–83; 59 ILR 14.
[21] See Shaw, pp. 426–9 and 432–6.

may also be estopped[22] by its previous conduct.[23] Recognition by third states, or the former sovereign, of a claim will also be important. India's seizure in 1961 of Goa, a Portuguese colony on the west coast of India, and its incorporation into India in 1962, was not condemned by the United Nations, there being much bitterness at Portugal's colonial policy. The incorporation was soon recognised by most states, and eventually by Portugal.[24]

Boundary treaties

A treaty that establishes or confirms a boundary creates a regime that all other states must recognise.[25] A party to the treaty cannot invoke a fundamental change of circumstances as a ground for terminating it,[26] except perhaps where the conditions for the legitimate operation of the principle of self-determination exist.[27]

Leases

Although no longer common, a state can by treaty lease part of its territory to another state. During the term of the lease, the territory then comes under the sovereignty of the lessee state. Although the island of Hong Kong, and the lower part of Kowloon on the Chinese mainland, were in the mid-nineteenth century ceded by China to the United Kingdom in perpetuity,[28] the much larger New Territories extending up from Kowloon were leased by China to the United Kingdom in 1898 for 99 years.[29] During that period, the whole of Hong Kong was regarded by the United Kingdom and other states as coming under British sovereignty. All of Hong Kong was restored to China at midnight on 30 June 1997.[30]

The US naval base at Guantanamo Bay was leased by treaty from Cuba in 1903. It gave the United States the right to 'exercise complete

---

[22] See p. 9 above.   [23] *Temple of Preah Vihear, ICJ Reports* (1962), p. 6; 33 ILR 48.

[24] See Oppenheim, p. 196.

[25] See pp. 10 and 354 on objective or *erga omnes* regimes.

[26] Article 62(2)(a) of the VCLT, see p. 104 below.

[27] See the ILC Commentary on draft Article 59 (later Article 62 of the Vienna Convention on the Law of Treaties), para. (11), of the final draft Articles on the Law of Treaties, in A. Watts, *The International Law Commission 1949–1998*, Oxford, 1999, pp. 764–5.

[28] 30 BSP 389 and 50 BSP 10.

[29] 90 BSP 17. See p. 108 below on so-called unequal treaties.

[30] Joint Declaration on the Question of Hong Kong 1984,1399 UNTS 33 (No. 23391); ILM (1984) 1366; UKTS (1985) 26.

jurisdiction and control' over the leased land and waters, but recognised the continuance of the 'ultimate sovereignty of the Republic of Cuba'.[31]

Because such treaties transfer sovereignty, at least *de facto*, they should be distinguished from leases granted to foreign states under the domestic law of the grantor state, such as for military bases,[32] although today the land may be made merely 'available'.[33] Such leases involve no transfer of sovereignty.

Rivers

If a boundary between two states is a river, and unless a treaty provides otherwise, if the river is *not* navigable generally the boundary is the mid-line of the river. If it is navigable, the boundary is generally the mid-line of the *thalweg*, the principal channel, but all depends on the particular facts.[34]

State servitudes[35]

A state servitude is a legal right over the whole or part of territory granted by one state to another, such as a right of passage.[36] The right is *in rem*, in that it is not merely personal to the states by and to which it is granted, but remains in force even if sovereignty over the territory changes.

Res communis

This term refers to territory over which no state has sovereignty *and* which cannot be appropriated by any state (cf. *terra nullius*, p. 38 above).

---

[31] 96 BSP 546–7 and 551–3; (1910) AJIL 4, Suppl. 177; Lazar, '"Cession in Lease" of the Guantanamo Bay Naval Station and Cubais "Ultimate Sovereignty"' (1969) AJIL 116; Whiteman, vol. 2, p. 1216. The text is also on the US Navy website of the base (www. nsgtmo.navy.mil), which explains that 'ultimate sovereignty' means that Cuban sovereignty is 'suspended' during the period of US occupancy. In *Rasul* v. *Bush*, (542 US _ (2004); ILM (2004) 1207) the US Supreme Court held (6–3) that *habeas corpus* extended to aliens in territory over which the US exercises 'plenary exclusive jurisdiction', which included the base.

[32] For example, the so-called Lend-Lease Agreements of 1940–1 between the UK and the US, 203 LNTS 201 and 204 LNTS 15; UKTS (1940) 21 and (1941) 2.

[33] See the UK–US Exchange of Notes of 30 December 1966 concerning the availability for defence purposes of the British Indian Ocean Territory (which includes the island of Diego Garcia), 603 UNTS 273 (No. 8737); UKTS (1967) 15; TIAS 6296; 18 UST 28; as amended in 1976, 1032 UNTS 323 (No. 8737); UKTS (1976) 88; and in 1987, UKTS (1988) 60.

[34] Oppenheim, pp. 664–6.   [35] See Oppenheim, pp. 673–6.

[36] *Right of Passage over Indian Territory*, *ICJ Reports* (1960), p. 6; 31 ILR 23.

A state must respect its use by other states and not do anything that might adversely affect their use of it. Obvious examples include the high seas,[37] outer space and the celestial bodies.[38] But the term may also be used to describe legal regimes established by treaty to administer resources common to two or more states, such as an oilfield,[39] or, perhaps more controversially, a special region like Antarctica.[40]

Common heritage of mankind

The Moon Treaty 1979 provides for the Moon and other celestial bodies to be 'the province of all mankind'.[41] Articles 136 and 137 of the UN Convention on the Law of the Sea 1982 go slightly further and provide that 'the Area' (the deep seabed beyond the limits of national jurisdiction) and its mineral resources is 'the common heritage of mankind', so that no state may claim or exercise sovereignty or sovereign rights over them. The rights in the resources are vested in 'mankind as a whole, on whose behalf the [International Sea-Bed] Authority shall act'.[42] The concept of the common heritage is controversial[43] and has not yet been used in other contexts, although sometimes the concept is used loosely.

Territorial integrity and *uti possidetis*

Article 2(4) of the UN Charter requires all Members to refrain from the threat or use of force against, *inter alia*, the 'territorial integrity' of any state. Although the Charter does not define that term, it is now well established, and reflects the fundamental international objective in the stability of boundaries. It later became prominent during the major period of decolonisation. The boundaries of African territories in particular were drawn with little regard for the inhabitants, so that people of the same ethnic group were often divided by a colonial boundary. But rather than embarking on the immensely difficult and politically hazardous task of

---

[37] See p. 312 below.   [38] See p. 367 below.

[39] The Norway–UK Agreement relating to the Exploitation of the Murchison Field Reservoir of 16 October 1979, 1249 UNTS 174 (No. 20387); UKTS (1981) 39, provides for the Reservoir, which straddles the boundary of the parties' continental shelves, to be exploited as a single unit.

[40] See p. 354 below.

[41] On the Moon Treaty and outer space, see p. 368 below.   [42] See p. 311 below.

[43] See Birnie and Boyle, *International Law and the Environment*, 2nd edn, Oxford, 2002, pp. 143–4.

seeking to redraw numerous boundaries, it was decided to leave them as they were on independence. Paragraph 6 of the Declaration on the Granting of Independence to Colonial Countries and Peoples 1960 declared that any attempt aimed at the partial or total disruption of the territorial integrity of a country is incompatible with the purposes and principles of the United Nations.[44]

The principle of territorial integrity is complemented by the doctrine of *uti possidetis*. It was originally devised so that the administrative divisions of the Spanish Empire would be regarded as the boundaries of the newly independent Latin American states, and so it was hoped would prevent boundary disputes between them.[45] The African Union (previously the Organization of African States) also upholds the doctrine, for the reasons given in the preceding paragraph.[46] In 1986, a chamber of the ICJ considered the principle as one of general international law.[47] It was followed by the so-called Badinter Commission in relation to the former Yugoslav republics: 'whatever the circumstances, the right of self-determination must not involve changes to existing frontiers at the time of independence.'[48]

(The relationship between the two principles and that of self-determination is discussed at pp. 21–2 above.)

---

[44] UNGAR 1514 (XV). For Europe, see the Helsinki Final Act 1975, Questions Relating to Security in Europe, Part 1, IV, ILM (1975) 1293.

[45] Oppenheim, pp. 669–70.

[46] Article 4(b) of the Constitutive Act of the African Union: see www.africa-union.org.

[47] *Burkino Faso* v. *Republic of Mali, ICJ Reports* (1986), p. 554; 80 ILR 459. Paras. 20–6 may have been the work of the Argentine judge, Ruda. See also *Libya* v. *Chad, ICJ Reports* (1994), p. 6; 100 ILR 1.

[48] Opinion No. 2; ILM (1992) 1497; 92 ILR 167. The Commission was referring to the *internal* boundaries of the former Socialist Federal Republic of Yugoslavia.

4

Jurisdiction

The long arm of the law. (Anon.)

Oppenheim. *Oppenheim's International Law*, 9th edn, London, 1992, pp. 456–78
Shaw, *International Law*, 5th edn, Cambridge, 2003, pp. 573–620
Higgins, *Problems and Process*, Oxford, 1994, pp. 56–77
Lowe, 'Jurisdiction', in M. Evans (ed.), *International Law*, Oxford, 2003, pp. 329–55

We are here concerned with the extent to which international law permits a state to exercise its jurisdiction over persons or things in its territory and sometimes abroad. This issue is an aspect of the sovereignty of states, as reflected in the principles of the equality of states and non-interference in another state's domestic affairs. Domestic jurisdiction takes two main forms: prescription (the making of law) and enforcement (implementation of the law by the judiciary and the executive). Having been developed over the years, mostly by judgments of domestic courts, the principles are fairly well established. Conflicts of jurisdiction in civil matters are generally resolved by applying conflict of laws rules.[1] Disputes over jurisdiction occur more often in the enforcement of laws of a regulatory nature. The main problem today is when the assertion of jurisdiction by a state adversely affects the commercial or economic interests of foreign nationals.

International law leaves a fair measure of jurisdictional discretion to states, which can assert jurisdiction if this can be justified by a permissive rule of international law. Although jurisdiction will be discussed according to the traditional principles, it may be that a general principle has now emerged that a state may exercise jurisdiction if there is a sufficiently close connection between the subject matter and the state to override the interests of a competing state.[2]

---

[1] See above.   [2] And see n. 15 below.

Territorial principle

This is the primary basis for jurisdiction. A state is free to legislate and enforce that legislation within its territory, the main exception being when that freedom is restricted by treaty. A state is generally free to apply its legislation to any person within its territory, including foreign nationals; and a constructive presence (a certain degree of contact with the territorial state) may be enough, especially for legal persons like corporations.

A state can also apply its laws to ships flying its flag or aircraft registered with it, and persons on board. Although a state has sovereignty over its airspace, acts committed on board foreign-registered aircraft are primarily subject to the jurisdiction of the state of registration.[3] Jurisdiction in the territorial sea, in the exclusive economic zone or on the high seas is dealt with elsewhere.[4]

Officials of a foreign state cannot take evidence or exercise other jurisdiction without the consent of the territorial state.[5] Such activities may not be done even in the foreign state's embassy since it is not foreign territory.[6] Nor can legal process be served directly in another state, only by means acceptable to the two states, often agreed by treaty. A court must be careful about demanding that a defendant produce documents held in another state.[7] The exercise of criminal or disciplinary jurisdiction over members of the foreign armed forces will depend on agreement with the host state, and this will usually be in a status-of-forces agreement.[8] Only in the most exceptional circumstances could a court of one state sit in another state to try a national of a third state.[9]

The immunity of foreign diplomats and states from the jurisdiction of domestic courts does not mean that there is no territorial jurisdiction over them, just that it cannot be exercised unless immunity is waived.[10]

Nationality principle

A state can legislate to regulate activities of its nationals abroad, whether living there or merely visiting. One of the advantages of nationality is that the tax laws of your state may still apply to you if you live abroad, or if you have foreign investments or conduct business activities. Similarly,

---

[3] See p. 287, n. 17 below on the Tokyo Convention.   [4] See pp. 301 *et seq* below.
[5] See p. 263 below on mutual legal assistance.   [6] See p. 125 below.
[7] On such extra-territorial discovery, particularly in US antitrust cases, see p. 48 below, and Oppenheim, pp. 464–6.
[8] See p. 175 below.   [9] See p. 295 below on the Lockerbie trial.   [10] See p. 152 below.

legislation governing the conduct of government officials will apply to what they do abroad. To varying degrees, states have legislation that provides that their nationals who commit offences abroad may be prosecuted at home,[11] and for this purpose extradition may be available.[12] Unless a treaty allows for it,[13] legislation cannot be enforced within another state.

Passive personality principle

The assertion of jurisdiction by a state over acts committed abroad against its own nationals by foreign nationals ('victim jurisdiction') is contentious. *The Lotus*[14] is often cited as the basis for the principle, but this is doubtful. Its *dictum* that a state can assert jurisdiction unless there is a rule prohibiting it went much too far.[15] Although previously opposed to it, in response to the growing number of terrorist attacks on US nationals abroad, in the 1980s the United States enacted legislation under which such crimes can be tried in the United States.[16] The legislation seems to have been used only to deal with terrorist offences, and the principle is now found in various counter-terrorism conventions.

Protective principle

In certain circumstances, a state may establish its jurisdiction over a foreign national who commits an offence abroad prejudicial to the state's security, even if the act is not an offence under the local law. The scope of this principle is not well defined,[17] but is most clearly seen in some of the treaties that provide for quasi-universal jurisdiction.

Universal and quasi-universal jurisdiction

It is exceptional for states to have jurisdiction under their law over crimes committed abroad by foreign nationals against foreign nationals. But certain crimes – piracy, slavery, torture, war crimes, genocide and other crimes against humanity – are so prejudicial to the interests of all states, that customary international law (in this case, often derived from treaty

---

[11] For example, the Offences Against the Person Act 1861, s. 4 (conspiracy abroad to commit murder).

[12] See p. 264 below.   [13] See p. 175 below on status-of-forces agreements.

[14] 1927 PCIJ Ser. A, No. 10; 4 AD 5.

[15] On this, and the principle in general, see Higgins, pp. 65–9 and Shaw, pp. 589–91.

[16] See p. 48, n. 34 below.   [17] Shaw, pp. 591–2.

law)[18] does not prohibit a state from exercising jurisdiction over them, wherever they take place and whatever the nationality of the alleged offender or victim. This is known as 'universal' jurisdiction, although states have generally been reluctant to exercise it in cases where they have no connection with the persons involved.[19] However, in 2004–5, an Afghan national was tried in London for torture carried out in Afghanistan between 1992 and 1996. The principle has in recent years been embodied in universal treaties[20] dealing with terrorism,[21] drug trafficking[22] and corruption.[23] Since in such cases the principle binds only the treaty parties, it is known as *quasi*-universal jurisdiction.

In the past, it was questioned whether the parties can agree to extradite or put on trial nationals of states that are not parties, since no treaty obligation can be imposed on a third state without its written consent. But application of the principle places no obligation on a third state; the obligation is on the party in whose territory the person is found. Moreover, the conventions were adopted within universal international organisations, either by consensus or by thumping big majorities. This represents a sufficient degree of general acceptance by states that the exercise of such extensive extra-territorial jurisdiction in these circumstances is not contrary to international law. The principle in the ten conventions, and in some other universal treaties,[24] has become so well established that it is now unchallengeable.

Effects doctrine

Some of the principles discussed above clearly have extraterritorial effect in that the state asserts jurisdiction over persons present, or matters

---

[18] See, for example, genocide, p. 270 above.

[19] See paras. 19–65 of the joint separate opinion of Judges Higgins, Kooijmans and Buergenthal in the *Arrest Warrant* case, *ICJ Reports* (2000); ILM (2002) 536; and Reydams, *Universal Jurisdiction*, Oxford, 2004.

[20] Treaties to which all states may become parties.

[21] See p. 287 below.

[22] Vienna Drugs Convention 1988, 1582 UNTS 165 (No. 27627); ILM (1989) 493; UKTS (1992) 26.

[23] See Article 44(11) of the UN Convention Against Corruption 2003, A/RES/58/422; ILM (2004) 37.

[24] See Article 7(1) of the Convention Against Torture 1984, 1465 UNTS 85 (No. 24841); ILM (1984) 1027; UKTS (1991) 107; Article 6(9) of the Vienna Drugs Convention 1988, 1582 UNTS 165 (No. 27627); ILM (1989) 493; UKTS (1992) 26; Article 10(4) of the Convention on the Safety of United Nations and Associated Personnel 1994, 2051 UNTS 363 (No. 35457); ILM (1995) 484; Articles 42–44 of the UN Convention Against Corruption 2003 A/RES/58/422; ILM (2004) 37.

occurring, outside its territory. But in the last half-century, 'extraterritorial' has become synonymous with certain controversial US legislation expressed to apply to persons abroad, including non-US nationals,[25] in respect of acts done abroad that are considered to have a substantial and harmful effect in the United States (the so-called effects doctrine).

The doctrine has been applied especially to overseas subsidiaries of US companies, even when the subsidiary is locally incorporated (here referred to as 'foreign subsidiaries'),[26] on the basis that they are still 'US' companies and should therefore still be subject to such US laws. This might not matter so long as the legal obligations do not conflict with the legal regime of the other state. But legislation that seeks to impose domestic policy constraints on companies incorporated and operating abroad may well infringe the sovereignty of other states. This is particularly so when it is devised to further US national policy by imposing strict regulatory requirements accompanied by severe criminal penalties or penal damages, such as treble damages. In 1979, after the seizure of US embassy staff in Tehran, the United States froze all Iranian assets, including dollar accounts held abroad by foreign subsidiaries. After martial law had been imposed in Poland, in 1982 US legislation prohibited foreign subsidiaries from supplying material for the building of the Siberian pipeline. While COCOM existed to supervise technological exports to the communist bloc, the United States sought to impose its export controls on foreign subsidiaries. More recently, the so-called Helms–Burton and D'Amato legislation of 1996, first, authorised legal proceedings in US courts against foreign companies (not just foreign subsidiaries) 'trafficking' in property of US nationals expropriated by Cuba, and, secondly, imposed sanctions on foreign companies taking part in the development of the oil industries in Iran and Libya.[27]

Many Western states and the European Community opposed these extravagant assertions of jurisdiction. However, the European Court of Justice has adopted an effects doctrine similar to that of the United States, holding that Community competition law applies to anti-competitive agreements reached abroad by foreign companies if they are implemented within the Community.[28]

---

[25] First enunciated in *US* v. *Aluminium Company of America*, 148 F 2d 416 (1945); *American International Law Cases*, vol. 9, p. 13.

[26] See p. 182 below on the nationality of companies.

[27] See ILM (1996) 357 and 1273, respectively.

[28] *ICI* v. *Commission* (Dyestuffs case) [1972] ECR 619; 48 ILR 106; *Ahlstrom* v. *Commission* (Wood Pulp cases) [1988] ECR 5193; 96 ILR 148.

There has also been considerable resentment at attempts to apply US
antitrust legislation, such as the so-called Sherman Act, against foreign
companies operating also in, but not based in, the United States (such as
foreign airlines), and in particular demands for the wide-ranging production of documents held abroad, and awards of treble damages. This has
led to states enacting 'blocking' legislation under which the government
could prohibit the production of documents in the courts of the other
state. The UK legislation also allows a UK national or resident to sue in
the United Kingdom to recover multiple damages awarded by a foreign
court.[29] But the US courts have developed a balancing test that takes into
account various matters in deciding whether they should assert jurisdiction in such cases. They include conflicts with foreign law or policy,
whether the conduct was prohibited in the other state, the availability of a
foreign remedy, the importance of intent to harm US commerce, and the
effect on foreign relations.[30] Happily, such disputes seem to have become
much rarer.

Alien Tort Claims Act 1789[31]

The date *is* correct, though it was only in the 1980s that the Act was res-
urrected as a means of avoiding the limitation in the Foreign Sovereign
Immunities Act that prevents US courts hearing claims based on torts
committed outside US territory. In *Filartiga*,[32] a US Federal Appeals Court
held that, under the Act, a foreign national could sue in the United States
an official of a foreign state (not the state itself)[33] for torture committed
by him in that foreign state. This was on the tenuous basis that he had been
served with the proceedings in the United States and torture was an international crime that all states have the right to prosecute wherever it is committed. This led to rather newer legislation, including an amendment to
the 1789 Act (made by the Anti-Terrorism and Death Penalty Act 1996),[34]
which removed state immunity for murder, or terrorist acts causing

---

[29] Protection of Trading Interests Act 1980. See *British Airways* v. *Laker* [1984] 3 All ER 39;
    74 ILR 65; and *Midland Bank* v. *Laker* [1986] 2 WLR 707; 118 ILR 540.
[30] *Timberlane*, 549 F 2d 597 (1976); 66 ILR 270; *Mannington Mills*, 595 F 2d 1287 (1979); 66
    ILR 487.
[31] See now 28 USC s. 1350 (1982). See generally H. Fox, *The Law of State Immunity*, Oxford,
    2002, pp. 208–12; Shaw, pp. 607–10; Higgins, pp. 211–12.
[32] 77 ILR 169. On universal jurisdiction, see p. 45 above.
[33] On this, see *Argentine Republic* v. *Amerada Hess*, 488 US 428 (1989); 81 ILR
    658.
[34] AJIL (1997) 187.

personal injury or death, done anywhere in the world on behalf of a state that has been designated as a state sponsor of terrorism, unless neither the claimant nor the victim is a US national. In 2004, in *Sosa* v. *Alvarez-Machain*,[35] the US Supreme Court restricted the use of the Act when harm was caused by acts of foreign officials that do not amount to a violation of customary international law. The Act has been used unsuccessfully to bring cases against foreign companies based on historical human rights abuses that have little or no connection with the United States.

Abduction[36]

Abduction is the seizure (kidnapping) of a person for trial abroad, so bypassing any extradition treaty or procedure.[37] (Sometimes it is described as 'rendition', but that term also covers lawful means of obtaining a fugitive from justice.) Abduction clearly breaches local law. And, since the laws of one state cannot be enforced in another state without its permission, it also violates international law, including that on human rights, such as the right to security of the person and due process.[38] Thus the injured state can protest and claim compensation.[39]

The person is usually seized from foreign territory, although occasionally he may be seized on board a foreign ship on the high seas. The most dramatic example is still the abduction by Israeli agents in 1960 from Argentina of Adolf Eichmann for trial in Israel for crimes against humanity committed during the Nazi period.[40] Since then, there have been many other abductions.

The other important issue is whether the courts of the abducting state will accept jurisdiction over the person despite the violation of international law. This matter has so far been left to be decided entirely by domestic courts. Much depends on the particular circumstances, courts having shown themselves more willing to accept jurisdiction if the abduction was not from foreign territory or the offence was an international crime (as in the case of Eichmann). Current US law is that jurisdiction will not be accepted if torture or similar outrageous conduct has been involved.[41] But in 1992, in *US* v. *Alvarez-Machain*, the US Supreme Court

---

[35] 542 US __ (2004).
[36] Oppenheim, vol. 1, pp. 387–9; Higgins, pp. 69–73; Shaw, pp. 604–7.
[37] On extradition, see p. 264 below.   [38] But see p. 226 above on self-defence.
[39] See pp. 407 *et seq* below on state responsibility.
[40] See UNSC Res. 138 (1960); and A. Aust, 'The Security Council and International Criminal Law' (2002) NYIL 23 at 26.
[41] *US* v. *Yunis*, ILM (1991) 403–9.

held that the circumventing of an extradition treaty would not, in itself, prevent jurisdiction being exercised unless abduction was prohibited by the terms of the treaty.[42] In contrast, the UK courts will not accept jurisdiction if the person was brought forcibly into the United Kingdom in violation of international law and in disregard of any extradition treaty or process.[43]

[42] 504 US 655 (1992); 95 ILR 355; ILM (1992) 901.
[43] *Bennett* [1993] 3 WLR 90; 95 ILR 380. See also the South African case of *Ebrahim*, ILM (1992) 888; 95 ILR 417.

5

The law of treaties

Open covenants of peace, openly arrived at . . .[1]

Aust, *Modern Treaty Law and Practice*, Cambridge, 2000
McNair, *The Law of Treaties*, 2nd edn, Oxford, 1961
O'Connell, *International Law*, 2nd edn, London, 1970, pp. 195–280
Sinclair, *The Vienna Convention on the Law of Treaties*, 2nd edn, Manchester, 1984
Blix and Emerson, *The Treaty Maker's Handbook*, Dobbs Ferry, NY, 1973
Summary of Practice of the Secretary-General as Depositary of Multilateral Treaties 1999 (ST/LEG/7/Rev.1) ('*UN Depositary Practice*')
Multilateral Treaties Deposited with the Secretary-General ('*UN Multilateral Treaties*')
UN Treaty Collection: http://untreaty.un.org/english/treaty.asp (which has both of the above)

Anyone interested in international law needs to know the law of treaties. Because the subject is so important, this chapter is the longest, although the author's book on treaties should be consulted for more detail. The Vienna Convention itself is essential reading,[2] in particular the definitions in Article 2, of which the following should be especially noted:

'negotiating state' means a state, which took part in the drawing up and adoption of the text of the treaty;
'contracting state' means a state, which has consented to be bound by the treaty, *whether or not the treaty is in force*;
'party' means a state, which has consented to be bound by the treaty *and for which the treaty is in force*. (Emphasis added)

---

[1] Woodrow Wilson, speech to Congress, 8 January 1918.
[2] 1155 UNTS 331 (No. 18232); ILM (1969) 689; UKTS (1980) 58. See the text in Aust, p. 361.

The Vienna Convention on the Law of Treaties 1969

The Vienna Convention on the Law of Treaties 1969 ('the Convention' or 'the 1969 Convention') codified the law of treaties, i.e. the rules and procedure for making and applying treaties. Unless otherwise indicated, references in this chapter to numbered Articles are to Articles of the Convention. The rights and obligations created by a treaty are more properly known as 'treaty law'.[3]

Although it still has only 101 parties, the Convention is regarded by the International Court of Justice as generally reflecting customary international law, and for most practical purposes the Convention is an authoritative statement of customary international law and so can be applied to most treaties, despite the Convention not having retroactive effect (Article 4).[4]

The Convention does not apply to oral agreements. Nor does it cover succession to treaties,[5] responsibility for breach of treaties[6] or the effect of hostilities on treaties.[7]

What is a treaty?

Article 2(1)(a) of the Convention defines 'treaty' as:

> an international agreement concluded between states in written form and governed by international law, whether embodied in a single instrument or in two or more related instruments and whatever its particular designation.

The Convention uses 'treaty' as a generic term, and so includes treaties that may be described as universal or regional, intergovernmental, inter-ministerial or administrative. A treaty can be made between only two parties (*bilateral*) or three or more (*multilateral*), and most of the Convention applies to both types. A *plurilateral* treaty is one made between a limited number of states with a particular interest in the subject matter.[8] A *constituent* treaty establishes and regulates an international organisation. A *universal* treaty is one intended to apply to all states. A *regional* treaty is self-explanatory.

To be a treaty, the agreement must have an international character. It must therefore be the following.

---

[3] The title of Aust is therefore not that accurate, but sounded better to the publisher.
[4] See further Aust, pp. 10–11.   [5] See p. 393 below.
[6] See p. 414 below.   [7] See p. 105 below.
[8] See the Estonia Agreement, 1890 UNTS 176 (No. 32189); UKTS (1999) 74.

An international agreement concluded between states

An agreement between a state and a multinational company, such as an oil concession, is not a treaty,[9] even if it says that it shall be interpreted by reference to rules of international law.[10] Treaties between states and international organisations or between international organisations are not covered by the Convention (Article 3), but are the subject of the Vienna Convention on the Law of Treaties between States and International Organizations or between International Organizations 1986 ('the 1986 Convention').[11] The 1986 Convention follows the 1969 Convention very closely.

In written form

Even though the original text of a treaty is usually typed or printed, it can be in a telegram, telex, fax message or e-mail, or rather in an exchange of them.

Governed by international law

This means that there must be an intention to create obligations under international law.[12] The intention must be gathered from the terms of the instrument itself and from the circumstances of its conclusion, not from what the parties say afterwards was their intention.[13]

Although a treaty can be in any form, government lawyers may use carefully chosen vocabulary to indicate that, rather than creating a treaty, the participants intend only to record their mutual *understandings*. Such instruments are an important means for doing business between states, and a large number, both bilateral and multilateral, are made every year covering a wide range of subjects.[14] Most are never published. Such instruments have been described by using various terms, including 'gentlemen's agreements' and 'political agreements', but are now most

---

[9] *Anglo-Iranian Oil Company (United Kingdom* v. *Iran)* (Preliminary Objections), *ICJ Reports* (1952), p. 89, at p. 112; 19 ILR 507.

[10] See C. Greenwood, 'The Libyan Oil Arbitrations' (1982) BYIL 27–81. See p. 57 below on agreements between states which are governed by domestic law.

[11] ILM (1986) 543. It is not yet in force. See p. 58 below.

[12] *Aegean Sea Continental Shelf* case, *ICJ Reports* (1978), p. 3, at pp. 39–44; 60 ILR 562.

[13] *Qatar* v. *Bahrain, ICJ Reports* (1994), p. 112, paras. 26–7; ILM (1994) 1461; 102 ILR 1.

[14] For an example, see ILM (1982) 1.

commonly referred to by the abbreviation 'MOU' (see below), which is short for 'Memorandum of Understanding'.

Whether embodied in a single instrument or in two or more related instruments

The classic form of a single instrument treaty has for a long time been joined by treaties drawn in less formal ways, such as exchanges of (diplomatic) notes (or letters), which usually consist of one initiating note and one reply note. They can be on matters of national importance or the mundane. Although they are often self-standing, they can be supplementary to another treaty. A treaty can also consist of several instruments.[15]

Whatever its particular designation

International instruments are not designated (named) systematically, and so the name, in itself, does not determine its legal status. What is decisive is whether the negotiating states intend the instrument to be (or not to be) legally binding. Although it is reasonable to assume that an instrument called a Treaty, Agreement or Convention is a treaty, one should examine the text to make quite sure. Most other names are problematic. Both the UN Charter and the Charter of the Commonwealth of Independent States 1993 (CIS)[16] are treaties, but the OSCE Charter of Paris 1990[17] and the Russia–United States Charter of Partnership and Friendship 1992[18] are MOUs. Calling an instrument a Memorandum of Understanding does not establish its status, since – and most confusingly – some treaties are also given that name.[19] Only by studying the text can one decide its legal status.

An exchange of notes (or letters) also may constitute either a treaty or an MOU. If the exchange is intended to be a treaty, it is customary to provide expressly that it '*shall constitute an agreement between* our two Governments'; if intended as an MOU, it is usual to specify that the exchange '*records the understanding of* our two Governments' (emphasis added).

---

[15] See p. ✳✳✳ below on the establishment of the Iran–US Claims Tribunal.
[16] ILM (1995) 1279.   [17] ILM (1991) 193.
[18] ILM (1992) 782.   [19] See Aust, p. 20.

Treaty names

Treaties have always been given a variety of names, including less common ones like Compact, Solemn Declaration, Protocol of Decisions, Platform, Concordat, Agreed Minute and Terms of Reference. In 1992, a treaty between Lithuania and Russia on the withdrawal of Russian forces from Lithuania was concluded with the simple name 'Timetable'.[20] It is quite common to refer to a treaty by reference to the place where it was negotiated or concluded. For example, the Convention on International Civil Aviation 1944 is usually called 'the Chicago Convention'.

A treaty does not *have to be signed*

The Convention's definition of a treaty does not mention signature because signature is not necessary. A treaty can be constituted by an exchange of third-person diplomatic notes, which are initialled but not signed. An unsigned, and uninitialled, instrument may be preferred for purely political reasons.[21]

MOUs

States indicate their intention to conclude a treaty by consciously employing terminology such as 'shall', 'agree', 'undertake', 'rights', 'obligations' and 'enter into force'. As already indicated, when states intend to conclude an MOU, instead of 'shall' they use a less imperative term, such as 'will'. Terms like 'agree' or 'undertake' are avoided; the instrument is expressed to 'come into operation' or 'come into effect'; and most of the final clauses usually found in treaties and the testimonium (the final, formal wording of a treaty beneath which the diplomatic representatives sign)[22] are omitted. The instrument will normally be called a 'Memorandum of Understanding' or 'Arrangement'. Some MOUs, like the Helsinki Final Act 1975, have an express provision to the effect either that they are not eligible for registration (as a treaty) under Article 102 of the UN Charter[23] or that they are 'politically binding'.[24] Problems can arise when states later

---

[20] Sadly, the name was changed when it was registered: see 1690 UNTS 395 (No. 29146).
[21] For an EU example, see UKTS (1994) 2.   [22] See Aust, pp. 352–3.
[23] ILM (1975) 1293. As to Article 102, and the legal effect of registration or non-registration, see p. 112 below.
[24] ILM (1987) 191, at p. 195, para. 101.

differ on the status of an instrument, chiefly bilateral. It is therefore essential that the status is clearly agreed during the negotiation.

The fifty-three Members of the Commonwealth tend to use MOUs, bilateral or multilateral, even in those cases where other states might employ a treaty. The Commonwealth schemes for mutual legal assistance in criminal matters and extradition are set out only in MOUs.[25] The member states of the European Union use MOUs,[26] as do most other states.

In US practice, use of non-treaty language does not necessarily preclude the instrument from being a treaty. To overcome some of these problems in the defence field, the United Kingdom, Canada and Australia have concluded 'chapeau agreements' with the United States.[27]

Today, MOUs are employed in most areas of international relations – diplomatic, defence, trade, aid, transport etc. In many cases, a treaty could be used, but for the reasons given below an MOU is used instead. Frequently, MOUs supplement treaties.

A common reason for preferring an MOU is confidentiality. Many arrangements, especially in the defence field, must be kept confidential and are therefore found only in MOUs. Often, a defence treaty will be supplemented by numerous MOUs.[28]

MOUs do not need elaborate final clauses or the formalities (international or national) which surround treaty-making. Most often, an MOU will become effective on signature. Not being a treaty, an MOU is generally not subject to any constitutional procedures, such as presentation to parliament, although that will depend on the constitution, laws and practice of each state. The lack of formalities also means that an MOU is much easier to amend.

Are MOUs really treaties?

Some doubt has been expressed as to whether the distinction between MOUs and treaties is valid, since each embodies some sort of agreement.[29] This theory ignores the abundant state practice. A state is free to conclude, or not to conclude, treaties. When they do not wish to conclude a legally

---

[25] See p. 264, n. 5 below.
[26] See EU Doc. PESC/SEC 899 of 9 August 1996. See also the Opinion of the Advocate-General of the European Court of Justice in *France* v. *Commission* [1994] ECR I-3641; 101 ILR 29.
[27] See Aust, p. 34.   [28] See Aust, p. 36.
[29] J. Klabbers, *The Concept of Treaty in International Law*, The Hague, 1996.

binding instrument, they make this clear by a deliberate and careful choice of words.

But can an MOU sometimes have legal consequences? Although this will depend on the circumstances and the precise terms of the MOU, the intention of a state as expressed in an MOU may exceptionally have legal consequences. In general, when a clear statement is made by one state to another, and the latter relies upon that statement to its detriment, the first state is estopped from going back on its statement. Underlying this is the fundamental international law principle of good faith.[30]

Agreements between states governed by domestic law

States also contract with each other under domestic law, if, for example, the subject matter is exclusively commercial, such as the purchase of commodities in bulk. If a state leases land from another state for an embassy, there will be an instrument under domestic law, such as a lease, even though this may be granted pursuant to a treaty.[31]

Capacity to make treaties

Treaties are made between subjects of international law, predominantly states; between states and international organisations; and between international organisations. Every state possesses the capacity to conclude treaties (Article 6). There is no difference in international law between a treaty concluded on behalf of states and one concluded on behalf of governments or their ministries (including other agencies of the state, but generally not public bodies which have legal personality separate from that of the state).[32] A treaty entered into by a government or ministry binds the state, and changes of government will not affect its binding force on the state.[33]

Federations

Federal constitutions vary as to whether their constituent units have the power to enter into treaties. The Australian states, the Canadian provinces

---

[30] On good faith and estoppel, see p. 9 above.   [31] See p. 124, n. 15 below.
[32] See p. 411 below and Oppenheim, pp. 346–8.   [33] See also p. 25 above.

and the states of the United States have no such power.[34] Some federal constitutions authorise their constituent units to enter into agreements on certain matters or to do so if they have the specific consent of the federation,[35] and, given the need for such general or specific federal consent, in international law those agreements will ultimately be the responsibility of the *federal* state.

Overseas territories[36]

Overseas territories do not have the power to conclude treaties in their own right, but they may be authorised by the state to which they belong to enter into treaties either *ad hoc* or generally in certain specific subject areas. The Hong Kong Special Administrative Region is a party to many treaties.[37] But the 'parent' state remains ultimately responsible for the performance of the treaties.

Some multilateral treaties permit territorial entities that are not independent to be parties to the treaty. Article 305 of the UN Convention on the Law of the Sea 1982 permits certain self-governing associated states and internally self-governing territories to become parties, provided they have competence over matters governed by the Convention, including competence to enter into treaties on such matters.[38]

International organisations

An international organisation has the capacity to conclude treaties if this is provided for in its constituent instrument or if it is indispensable for the fulfilment of its purposes.[39] There are now numerous treaties between international organisations and states (e.g. headquarters agreements) and between international organisations. The rules governing such treaties are set out in the Convention on the Law of Treaties between States and International Organizations or between International Organizations 1986.[40] Increasingly, multilateral treaties, especially in fields such as the

---

[34] B. Opeskin, 'Federal States in the International Legal Order' (1996) NILR. 353–86, n. 45 and generally.

[35] Oppenheim, pp. 248–55.   [36] See p. 29 above.   [37] See p. 405 below.

[38] UN Convention on the Law of the Sea 1982, 1833 UNTS 397 (No. 31363); ILM (1982) 1261; UKTS (1999) 81. The Cook Islands is a party (see p. 30 above). See also p. 383 about WTO membership.

[39] *Reparations* advisory opinion, *ICJ Reports* (1949), p. 174; 16 ILR 318.

[40] ILM (1986) 543. It is not yet in force.

environment, trade and commodities, provide for certain international organisations to become parties. The UN Convention on the Law of the Sea 1982 allows this if their member states have transferred competence to the organisation, including the competence to enter into treaties, over matters governed by that Convention.[41]

Credentials and full powers

Credentials

Credentials are issued by a state, usually by the foreign minister, to a delegate to an international conference at which a multilateral treaty is to be negotiated, authorising him to represent that state. It is then presented to the host government or international organisation.[42] But the representative only has authority to negotiate and adopt the text of the treaty and to sign the final act.[43] He will need specific instructions from his government before he can sign the treaty itself, as well full powers if these are required. Credentials and full powers can be combined in one document.

Full powers

Article 2(1)(c) defines 'full powers' as:

> a document emanating from the competent authority of a state designating a person or persons to represent the state for negotiating, adopting or authenticating the text of a treaty, for expressing the consent of the state to be bound by a treaty, or for accomplishing any other act with respect to a treaty.

But it is only those acts that are actually specified in the document that will be authorised. A person is considered as representing a state for the purpose of adopting or authenticating the text of a treaty if he produces appropriate full powers or if it appears from the practice of the states concerned, or from other circumstances, that their intention was to dispense with full powers (Article 7(1)).

Full powers are simply written evidence that the person named in them is authorised to represent the state in performing certain acts in relation to the treaty, but normally only in relation to its signature. Their

---

[41] See Article 305(1)(f) and Annex IX.
[42] See R. Sabel, *Procedure at International Conferences*, Cambridge, 1997, pp. 43–51.
[43] See p. 61 below.

production is a fundamental safeguard for the other representatives, and for the depositary of a multilateral treaty, that they are dealing with a person with the necessary authority. But, before doing any act covered by full powers, the holder must still obtain specific instructions from his government.

The general trend towards rather more informality in treaty-making does not mean that full powers are now seldom needed, although there is a tendency to dispense with them for bilateral treaties and, in practice, full powers are usually dispensed with for an exchange of notes. Full powers are required to sign a multilateral treaty, unless the negotiating states agree to dispense with them. The UN Secretary-General will insist on full powers being produced for the signature of treaties for which he is to be the depositary. Heads of State or government or foreign ministers (the 'Big Three') do *not* need full powers to sign or ratify a treaty (Article 7(2)).

A state may issue its permanent representative to an international organisation, especially the United Nations, with continuing full powers, known as *general full powers*.

(For procedure generally, see Aust, pp. 62–4.)

Adoption and authentication

Adoption

Once the negotiations are complete, it is necessary for the negotiating states to adopt the text. A bilateral treaty is often adopted by initialling the text. The act of adoption does *not* amount to consent to be bound by the treaty. Unanimity for adoption (Article 9(1)) is now restricted to bilateral treaties or treaties drawn up by only a few states (plurilateral treaties). Adoption at an international conference requires a two-thirds vote of the states 'present and voting' (which excludes abstentions) unless, by the same majority, they decide to apply a different rule (Article 9(2)). In practice, consensus, or 'general agreement', is now the norm for adoption of most multilateral treaties.

Consensus

Consensus is often incorporated in the rules of procedure of an international conference.[44] Its three main features are that it is not the same as

---

[44] See generally R. Sabel, *Procedure at International Conferences*, Cambridge, 1997, pp. 303–13.

unanimity, a state can join a consensus even if it could not vote in favour; and it is not incompatible with 'indicative voting' (a straw poll). It has been expressed succinctly as 'the absence of any formal objection'.[45] Even when rules of procedure provide for adoption by a specified majority, it is normal for there first to be an attempt to reach consensus, voting being used only as a last resort.

Authentication

Before a negotiating state can decide whether to consent to be bound by a treaty it needs to have the adopted text, once it has been thoroughly checked and cleaned up (the *toilette finale*), authenticated by a document certifying that it is the definitive and authentic text, and therefore is not susceptible to alteration. Initialling the text of a *bilateral treaty* is normally regarded as amounting to both adoption *and* authentication, at least if the treaty is to be in only one authentic language. However, in practice, each state is free to suggest technical, or even substantive, changes at any time before signature.

The business of negotiating a *multilateral treaty* is often a confused affair, and in the final hectic stages errors and inconsistencies invariably creep into the text. It is not unusual for the basic negotiating text to be only in English, and for some of the language texts to be available in final form only at the end of the conference. There is then a need not only to check the adopted text for typographical inconsistencies and errors, but also to translate it into other authentic languages.[46] It is common for a treaty adopted within an international organisation to be authenticated by the adoption of a resolution by an organ of the organisation, such as the assembly, or by an act of authentication performed by the president of the assembly or the chief executive officer of the organisation.[47]

Final act

A final act is a formal statement or summary of the proceedings of a diplomatic conference. Treaties adopted by the conference and other related documents, such as resolutions and agreed or national interpretative statements, will be attached. It is usual for each negotiating state to sign the

---

[45] Article 161(7)(e) of the UN Convention on the Law of the Sea 1982, 1833 UNTS 397 (No. 31363); ILM (1982) 1261; UKTS (1999) 81.
[46] See also p. 110 below.   [47] See Aust, pp. 72–3 for the UN practice.

final act, although this is optional, and anyway signature does *not* commit the state to sign or ratify any attached treaty. Full powers are not needed to sign a final act, the credentials of the representative being enough. The Convention mentions final acts only in Article 10(b).

The Final Act of the Helsinki Conference on Co-operation and Security in Europe 1975 is an MOU. There is no treaty attached. But, unlike most final acts, it contained lengthy, substantive provisions of great (political) importance.[48]

Consent to be bound

A 'contracting state' is one that has consented to be bound by a treaty, even though it may not yet have entered into force (Article 2(1)(f)). A 'party' is a state that has consented to be bound by a treaty *and* for which the treaty is in force (Article 2(1)(g)). At that point, and only at that point, is the state bound by the treaty (Article 26). To consent to be bound is therefore the most significant act that a state can take in relation to a treaty. Although two steps are necessary to become a party (consent to be bound plus entry into force) sometimes they take place simultaneously.

A state can express its consent by signature, by an exchange of instruments constituting a treaty, by ratification, by acceptance or approval, by accession or by any other agreed means (Article 11). Either the treaty will specify how consent is to be expressed or it will be implicit.

Signature only

This is quite common for a treaty between two or a few states if none need prior parliamentary approval or new legislation.[49] It is normally evident from the terms of the treaty when signature expresses consent to be bound (Article 12(1)(a)), the entry into force clause providing that the treaty shall enter into force on the date of signature, or on the date of second or last signature.

'Open for signature'

Many multilateral treaties, especially UN treaties, provide that they will be 'open for signature' until a specified date, after which signature will no longer be possible. Thereafter, a state may only accede (see below).

---

[48] ILM (1975) 1293. And see pp. 55 above and 196 below.   [49] See Aust, p. 75.

Witnessing

Because of the political importance of some treaties, such as the Camp David Accords 1979 or the Dayton Agreement 1995, the signing may be witnessed by heads of state or government, or foreign ministers, of third states. But the signature of a witness has no legal effect. In itself, it will not make the witness's state a guarantor of the performance of the treaty.

Exchange of instruments

It is the act of exchange that constitutes consent to be bound if the instruments so provide or if the states so agree (Article 13). The exchange usually takes the form of an exchange of notes or letters.

Ratification

Ratification is 'the international act so named whereby a state establishes on the international plane its consent to be bound by a treaty' (Article 2(1)(b)). Although parliamentary approval of a treaty may well be required – and be referred to, most misleadingly, as 'ratification' – it is a quite different, purely *domestic*, process. Ratification is an *international* act. It consists of (1) the execution of an instrument of ratification by or on behalf of the state and (2) either its exchange for the instrument of ratification of the other state (bilateral treaty) or its lodging with the depositary (multilateral treaty).

The normal reason for requiring ratification is that after signature one or more of the negotiating states needs time before it can give its consent to be bound. The treaty may require new implementing legislation, which should be done before the treaty enters into force for the state. Even if no legislation is needed, the constitution may require parliamentary approval of the treaty or some other procedure like publication, before the state can ratify. Or the government may just need time to consider the implications of becoming a party.

It is another common misconception that once a treaty has been ratified it is then legally binding on the ratifying state. However, the situation is quite different from the coming into force of legislation. Ratification does not make the treaty binding on the state *unless and until the treaty has entered into force for that state*. When that happens, the state becomes a 'party' to the treaty (Article 2(1)(g)). Whether ratification will bring the treaty into force for the ratifying state depends entirely on the provisions of the treaty.

Who can sign the instrument of ratification?

An instrument of ratification has to be signed on behalf of the state. Usually the head of state, head of government or foreign minister (the 'Big Three') sign it. Anyone else needs full powers.

Acceptance or approval

Consent to be bound can be expressed by 'acceptance' or 'approval' under similar conditions to those which apply to ratification (Article 14(2)). There is no substantive difference between acceptance or approval and ratification. It is now common for multilateral treaties to provide that signature shall be 'subject to ratification, acceptance or approval'. The rules applicable to ratification apply equally to acceptance or approval, and, unless the treaty provides otherwise, acceptance and approval have the same legal effect as ratification.

Accession

Accession is the primary means for a state to become a party to a multilateral treaty if, for whatever reason, it is unable to sign it. The treaty may restrict signature to certain, or a specified category of, states, or a deadline for signature may simply have passed. No state has a right to accede unless the treaty so provides or the parties agree to it (Article 15)). Multilateral treaties that are subject to ratification – which is most of them – will almost always include an accession clause, and the right to accede will usually be exercisable even *before* the entry into force of the treaty. This is commonly done by making entry into force conditional on the deposit of a certain number of instruments of ratification (or acceptance or approval) *or* accession. The rules on deposit of instruments of ratification apply also to instruments of accession, which has the same legal effect as ratification.

Any other agreed means

Article 11 is a good example of the flexibility of the law of treaties in providing that the consent of a state to be bound may be expressed by 'any other agreed means'. Thus it is possible for a treaty to be adopted, without signature[50] or any other particular procedure, and enter into force *instantly* for all the adopting states. The treaty which established the Preparatory Commission of the Comprehensive Nuclear Test-Ban Treaty 1996 (CTBT) was adopted by a resolution of the states which had signed the CTBT and was binding in international law immediately without any further act by those states.[51]

'Signatory', 'party' and 'adherence'

All too often one reads or hears that a state is a 'signatory' of a treaty, with the implication that it is a party. Signature is only one way of consenting to be bound, and it is often subject to ratification. But, even when a treaty has been ratified, that does not mean that it has entered into force, so making the ratifying state a 'party'. 'Signatory' is therefore a loose and misleading term, and should be avoided except when it is clear from the context that it refers only to the fact that a state has signed, and nothing more. (Similarly, one should avoid the English idiomatic term 'signed up to'.) An acceptable generic alternative may be to say that the state has 'adhered' to the treaty, although this may lead to more misunderstandings, although the term will sometimes be used in this book.

Note that, unless otherwise indicated, in this book the terms 'ratification', 'consent to be bound' and 'adherence' are used to cover also approval, acceptance and accession.

The 'all states' and 'Vienna' formulas

During the Cold War, problems arose over treaties which provided that 'all states' could become parties. There were some entities over which there were disputes as to whether they were states: the German Democratic Republic, North Korea and North Vietnam.[52] So the so-called 'Vienna formula' was included in new treaties. Article 81 of the Convention is typical: a disputed entity was entitled to become a party if it was a member of at least one of a number of specified international organisations. There has been no need for such a formula since 1973.[53] Many older treaties will still have the formula, but in most cases this will, as in the past, cause no

---

[50] See p. 55 above.   [51] UKTS (1999) 46.   [52] See p. 17 above.
[53] See M. Wood, 'The Convention on the Prevention and Punishment of Crimes Against Internationally Protected Persons, Including Diplomatic Agents' (1974) ICLQ 791 at 816–7; UN Juridical YB (1974) 157 and (1976) 186.

problem. 'All states' clauses should therefore now be used for all treaties that are intended to have universal application.

Rights and obligations before entry into force

In the period before the entry into force of a treaty, the acts of adopting, signing and ratifying will create certain rights and obligations for the negotiating states. The most obvious relate to those matters that have to be dealt with so that the treaty can enter into force. As from adoption of the text, the provisions on depositary functions, authentication, consent to be bound, reservations, and other matters arising necessarily before entry into force, will apply (Article 24(4)).

Obligation not to defeat the object and purpose of a treaty before its entry into force

Article 18 requires a state 'to refrain from acts which would defeat the object and purpose of a treaty' before its entry into force for that state. When the treaty is subject to ratification, this obligation lasts until the state has made clear its intention not to become a party. This is what the United States did when it famously 'unsigned' the Statute of the International Criminal Court by sending a note to the UN Secretary-General saying that it did not intend to become a party.[54] When a state has already ratified, the Article 18 obligation continues pending entry into force of the treaty, provided this event is 'not unduly delayed'.

But there is uncertainty as to the extent of the obligation, and one can determine whether the obligation applies only by examining the treaty in the light of all the circumstances. There is virtually no practice, but it is possible to formulate the following propositions.

It is sometimes argued (especially by students) that a state that has not yet ratified a treaty must, in accordance with Article 18, nevertheless comply with it, or at least do nothing inconsistent with its provisions. This is clearly wrong because the act of ratification would then have no purpose since the obligation to perform the treaty would not then be dependent on ratification. All that the signatory state must not do is anything which would affect its *ability* to comply fully with the treaty once it has entered into force; it does not have to abstain from all acts

---

[54] See *UN Multilateral Treaties*, Ch. XVIII.10, note to US entry.

which will be prohibited after entry into force. Thus the state must not do any act that *would* invalidate the basic purpose of the treaty.[55]

Withdrawal of consent to be bound before entry into force

A state which has consented to be bound may nevertheless withdraw its consent before the treaty enters into force. This happens very rarely.[56]

Development of treaties

There is sometimes a need for provisions permitting the development of a legal regime created by a treaty. This can be done in two main ways: by framework treaties and by legally binding measures adopted by organs of international organisations. A *framework treaty* is a multilateral treaty which is no different in its legal effect from other treaties, but which provides a framework for later, and more detailed, treaties (often called Protocols) that elaborate the principles declared in the treaty. The term is used particularly in connection with environmental treaties.[57]

It is not unusual when establishing an international organisation for the constituent instrument to give one of its organs the power to impose on the member states legally binding *measures* by which the object and purpose of the organisation can be more effectively achieved. If the Security Council determines under Chapter VII of the UN Charter that there is a threat to international peace and security, it can impose measures to maintain or restore international peace and security.[58] Article IX of the Antarctic Treaty 1959 provides for the adoption of measures in furtherance of the principles and objectives of the Treaty.[59] Similar provisions are found in fisheries treaties.[60]

Reservations

Article 2(1)(d) defines a reservation as:

> a unilateral statement, however phrased or named, made by a state, when signing, ratifying, accepting, approving or acceding to a treaty, whereby it purports to exclude or modify the legal effect of certain provisions of the treaty in their application to that state.

---

[55] See Aust, pp. 93–5. [56] *UN Depositary Practice*, paras. 157–9.
[57] See Birnie and Boyle, *International Law and the Environment*, 2nd edn, Oxford, 2002, pp. 14 and 25.
[58] See p. 214 below. [59] See p. 356 below. [60] See p. 334 below.

Reservations must be distinguished from 'derogations', which are statements authorised by a treaty by which a party is able to exclude certain provisions in their application to it during a particular period, such as a public emergency.[61]

Bilateral treaties

A reservation cannot be made to a bilateral treaty, all the terms of which must be agreed before it can bind the parties. To make a 'reservation' to a bilateral treaty therefore amounts to a request for a modification. The treaty cannot be binding unless and until the other state accepts. The reservations regime of the Convention is therefore inapplicable. The United States has a long history of making its ratification of bilateral treaties conditional on modifications being made.[62]

Multilateral treaties

A state may, by means of interpretative declarations or reservations, seek to fine-tune or adjust the way in which a multilateral treaty will apply to it. The need for either stems from the nature of the multilateral treaty-making process. The many different constitutions, legal systems, cultures, languages and religions, and different national policies, of negotiating states pose problems for the successful negotiation of even a regional, let alone a multilateral, treaty. Reaching agreement requires many compromises. Now that most multilateral treaties are adopted by consensus,[63] inevitably some of the negotiating states will be dissatisfied with at least some aspects of the text. But a state may, for political reasons, be reluctant to stand in the way of reaching consensus, and may even sign a treaty despite its unhappiness at the result. The option of not becoming a party may be unattractive.

Interpretative declarations

Interpretative declarations are as widely used as reservations. Their purpose is to establish an interpretation of a particular provision of a treaty that makes that provision acceptable to the state concerned. Often, it is used merely to make the provision consistent with existing domestic law. If other parties do not make conflicting declarations or indicate

---

[61] See p. 245 below.   [62] See Aust, pp. 106–7.   [63] See p. 60 above.

their disagreement, they can be regarded as having tacitly accepted it. When acceding to the 1969 Convention, Syria declared that in Article 52 (Coercion) the reference to 'force' included economic and political coercion. Other parties formally rejected this.[64] The vast majority of interpretative declarations do not produce any response.[65]

Disguised reservations

As the definition of reservation makes clear, it does not matter how a declaration is phrased or what name is given to it – one must look at the substance. On ratification of the Chemical Weapons Convention 1992,[66] the United States stated that, for the purposes of the Annex on Implementation and Verification, it would be a 'condition' that no sample collected by an inspection team could be removed from the United States for analysis. The Annex does not envisage any such restriction. The statement went beyond mere interpretation and amounted to a reservation.[67]

Reservations *generally* not *prohibited*

A state may seek to *adjust* certain provisions of a treaty *in their application to itself*. Sometimes its parliament will require adjustments as a condition of its approval of ratification. But, except perhaps for some human rights treaties, reservations are generally not so numerous or so extensive as to jeopardise the effectiveness of a treaty. Despite the impression one may get from the immense amount of writing on the subject in recent decades, most reservations can be dealt with perfectly well by application of the provisions in Articles 19–23.

Nor is there anything inherently wicked or even undesirable in formulating a reservation. It would be quite wrong to think that the world is divided into reserving states and objecting states. Many states make reservations, and most are not objected to. Many states have made reservations to the Convention on the Rights of the Child 1989, only some of which were objected to.[68]

---

[64] *UN Multilateral Treaties*, Ch. XXIII.1.
[65] As to other declarations made on ratification of the Convention, see Sinclair, *The Vienna Convention on the Law of Treaties*, 2nd edn, Manchester, 1984, p. 63–8.
[66] 1974 UNTS 317 (No. 33757); ILM (1982) 800; UKTS (1997) 45.
[67] See *UN Multilateral Treaties*, Ch. XXVI.3. [68] See *UN Multilateral Treaties*, Ch. IV.11.

Article 19 states the basic rule that a state *may* formulate a reservation *unless*:

(a) the reservation is prohibited by the treaty: it is increasingly common for treaties, particularly on human rights, or those that result from a 'package deal', to provide expressly that reservations are not permitted;
(b) the treaty provides that only specified reservations may be made: typically, a reservation may be made in respect of one or more specified Articles, such as an Article providing for the submission of disputes to the International Court of Justice;[69]
(c) exceptions (a) and (b) do not apply, but the reservation is incompatible with the object and purpose of the treaty (the compatibility test).

Although only paragraph (a) expressly uses the term 'prohibited', paragraphs (b) and (c) in effect specify the other situations in which reservations are prohibited. But, whereas it is relatively easy to determine whether a reservation is prohibited under paragraphs (a) or (b), when a treaty is silent about reservations it can be difficult to assess whether a reservation passes the compatibility test.[70] Many differing views have been expressed as to how the test should be applied, especially to human rights treaties,[71] and the practice of states is patchy and uncertain. Today, as treaties become longer and more complex, identifying the object and purpose of a treaty like the UN Convention on the Law of the Sea 1982[72] is virtually impossible, given its 320 Articles and nine annexes, unless for this purpose it is permissible to break down the treaty into various subjects, such as the high seas, straits, the continental shelf etc.

Acceptance of, and objection to, reservations

Even when a reservation is not prohibited under Article 19(a), (b) or (c), other contracting states can still object to it for any reason of law or policy. By formulating a reservation, the reserving state is consenting to be bound subject to a condition. It makes an offer which is subject to acceptance by the other contracting states. It will, therefore, not be

---

[69] See the TIR Convention 1975, 1079 UNTS 89 (No. 16510).
[70] There is a *considerable* literature. See, for example, L. Lijnzaad, *Reservations to UN Human Rights Treaties*, Dordrecht, 1995.
[71] See p. 75 below.   [72] 1833 UNTS 397 (No. 31363); ILM (1982) 1261; UKTS (1995) 81.

legally effective in relation to another contracting state unless that state has accepted it either expressly or by necessary implication. (The only exceptions are where a reservation has been expressly authorised by the treaty (Article 20(1)).) But, in practice, most objections are made on the ground that the reservation is prohibited, and usually because it fails the compatibility test.

'Plurilateral treaties'

This term describes a treaty negotiated between a limited number of states with a particular interest in the subject matter. Article 20(2) provides that if it appears from the object and purpose of the treaty that the application of it in its entirety, and between all the parties, is an essential condition for the consent of each of them to be bound by it, any reservation will require the acceptance of all the parties. Examples might include the Antarctic Treaty 1959, which had only fifteen negotiating states and created a special regime, for which the integrity of the Treaty is vital.[73]

Constituent instrument of an international organisation

Where a treaty forms the constitution of an international organisation, it is also essential to preserve its integrity. Article 20(3) provides that a reservation will require the acceptance of the competent organ of the organisation – usually an assembly of the members – unless the constituent instrument otherwise provides.

All other cases

Before 1951, generally the rule was unanimity: a reservation was only effective if it had been accepted by all the negotiating states, expressly or tacitly, and usually before signature. This changed after the 1951 International Court of Justice advisory opinion on certain reservations which had been made to the Genocide Convention 1948.[74] Article 20(4) sets out the residual rules to be applied when one is not dealing with an expressly authorised reservation, a plurilateral treaty or the constituent instrument of an international organisation. The rules were intended to be a flexible means of accommodating the different needs of the reserving state and the other contracting states:

---

[73] See p. 354 below.   [74] *ICJ Reports* (1951), p. 15; 18 ILR 364.

(a) acceptance by another contracting state of a reservation constitutes the reserving state a party to the treaty in relation to that other state if or when the treaty is in force for those states;

(b) an objection by another contracting state to a reservation does not preclude the entry into force of the treaty as between the objecting and reserving states unless a contrary intention is definitely expressed by the objecting state;

(c) an act expressing a state's consent to be bound by the treaty and containing a reservation is effective as soon as at least one other contracting state has accepted the reservation.

It is rare for a contrary intention to be 'definitely' (explicitly) expressed (paragraph (b)), and Article 20(5) provides that acceptance of a reservation can be *tacit*. The combined effect of Article 20(5) and paragraph (c) is that the reserving state will become a contracting state unless *all* the other contracting states (1) object to the reservation *and* (2) explicitly object to the reserving state becoming a contracting state. This is most unlikely ever to happen. The Convention puts the onus on an objecting state both to express its objection and, if it does not want the treaty to enter into force between it and the reserving state, to say so explicitly. But this did not take sufficiently into account the actual practice of states. Very few states object even when a clearly objectionable reservation has been made.

It is thus possible that not every party to a multilateral treaty will be bound by the treaty to every other party. A reserving state, Utopia, may be a party to a treaty in relation to Ruritania (which raised no objection), but not Freedonia (which did, and expressly said that it precluded the treaty entering into force between it and Utopia), although Ruritania and Freedonia may themselves be mutually bound. However, although such a result is not surprising if the reservation is not prohibited, there is good reason to believe that the scheme of Article 20(4) and (5) does *not* apply when the reservation is prohibited, including when it has been objected to even by one contracting state on the ground that it fails the compatibility test (see below).

The legal effects of reservations and of objections to reservations

Article 21(1) sets out the rules governing the legal effects of a reservation which has been established (i.e. in accordance with the requirements of Articles 19, 20 and 23 (see below)) with regard to another party: that is to say a reservation which is legally effective in relation to another party, not being prohibited under Article 19(a), (b) or (c) or objected to by the other party. Such a reservation:

(a) modifies for the reserving state *in its relations with that other party* the provisions of the treaty to which the reservation relates to the extent of the reservation; and
(b) modifies those provisions to the same extent for *that other party* in its relations with the reserving state.

Thus a party is bound only to the extent to which it has agreed to be bound – so that if a party has made an effective reservation it will operate reciprocally between it and any other party which has not objected to it, modifying the treaty to the extent of the reservation for them both in their mutual relations. But, as between the other parties, the treaty is unaffected (Article 21(2)).

Some unresolved issues

The main unresolved issue is whether the regime constructed by Articles 20 and 21 applies to *all* reservations. Certainly it works satisfactorily with respect to permissible reservations. But severe problems arise if one attempts to apply it to reservations prohibited under Article 19(a), (b) or (c). Nevertheless, there is a view that there is nothing in the scheme that precludes its application to a prohibited reservation; provided it has been accepted under Article 20(4). This could be done under Article 20(5), and (as pointed out) is usually done tacitly, the reserving state becoming a party in relation to those states that do not object. But the argument must necessarily seek to draw a distinction between reservations prohibited by Article 19(a) and (b) and those prohibited by Article 19(c), on the basis that the question whether a reservation passes the compatibility test is a matter for each contracting state. Yet, Article 19 makes no such distinction. It authorises the formulation of reservations subject to three exceptions. It is most unlikely that Articles 20 and 21 were intended to apply to reservations which Article 19 says may not be made. It is not argued that, if a treaty prohibits the making of reservations, or allows only specified ones, a contracting state could nevertheless accept (perhaps even tacitly) a prohibited reservation. The rules in Article 21 on the legal effects of reservations refer to reservations 'established' in accordance with Articles 19, 20 and 23, and it is hard to see how one could validly establish a reservation when it is prohibited.

When a treaty is silent about reservations, the determination whether a reservation passes the compatibility test is not easy, but there is no reason why it should be treated any differently to the other classes of possibly prohibited reservations. The compatibility test should be applied objectively, even if in most cases it has to be applied by states rather than by a court, a situation which is very common in international law. If a reservation has been objected to by even one contracting state for failing the test, the reserving state has an obligation to consider the objection in good faith. If the two states (there may of course be more) cannot agree, the question then becomes a matter of concern to the other contracting states, whether or not they have objected.

There is a related question: if a state has made a prohibited reservation, is it then bound by the treaty but without the benefit of the reservation? In *Belilos*, the European Court of Human Rights held that a declaration by Switzerland to the European Convention on Human Rights (ECHR) was an invalid reservation, but that it could be disregarded, Switzerland remaining bound by the ECHR in full.[75] However, *Belilos* needs to be seen in the light of the particular circumstances. The issue arose within a regional system dedicated to adherence to common social and political values. The ECHR has a special character and must be interpreted in the light of contemporary conditions, its enforcement machinery and its object and purpose.

Objections to reservations show a divergence of views by states on the question of whether a *prohibited* reservation can be disregarded. Some do not say what effect its objection would have. Some say their objections do not preclude the entry into force of the Convention between them and the reserving state, so leaving ambiguous the effect of the reservation on its obligations under the Convention. Some say that, although their objections do not preclude the entry into force of the Convention between them and the reserving state, it would do so without the latter benefiting from the reservation. This ignores the plain fact that the reserving state had made it clear that it was willing to be bound only subject to a condition. The better view is that, if one or more contracting states have objected to the reservation as being prohibited, it is the reserving state that must decide whether or not it is prepared to be a party without the reservation;

---

[75] ECHR Pubs. Series A (Preliminary Objections), Vol. 132 (1988); 88 ILR 635. See also *Loizidou* ECHR Pubs. Series A, Vol. 310 (1995); (1995) 20 EHRR 99; 103 ILR 621; and S. Marks, 'Reservations Unhinged: The Belilos Case before the European Court of Human Rights' (1990) ICLQ 300.

and until it has made its position clear it cannot be regarded as a party. There is an express provision to this effect in the European Agreement concerning the Work of Crews of Vehicles Engaged in International Road Transport 1970 (AETR II Agreement).[76]

Reservations to human rights treaties[77]

In the case of a human rights treaty, there may be weighty political reasons why a state is reluctant to object to the entry into force of the treaty between it and a reserving state, even when it has objected to the reservation. Most objecting states are reluctant to take the position that the treaty will not be in force between it and the reserving state unless and until the reservation is withdrawn. In fact, when faced with a questionable reservation to a human rights treaty, most parties remain silent. And those that do formally express views frequently take differing positions. There have been a variety of responses, particularly by Western European states, to the general reservations to human rights treaties made by the United States to the effect that nothing in the treaty requires or authorises legislation or other action by the United States that would be prohibited by the Constitution of the United States as interpreted by the United States (the 'constitutional reservation'). Another similar general reservation is one that seeks to subordinate a human rights treaty to the domestic law of the reserving state, in particular to Islamic (*Sharia*) law (the 'religious reservation').

Treaty monitoring bodies

The problem of determining whether a reservation is permissible, and in particular whether it passes the compatibility test, is further compounded by the absence in most cases of a standing tribunal or other organ with competence to decide such matters. Although the European Convention on Human Rights and the American Convention on Human Rights[78] each have a permanent court, most modern universal human rights treaties establish no more than a committee of (albeit mostly distinguished) independent experts to monitor the way in which the parties carry out their obligations. The best known is the Human Rights

---

[76] See p. 76, n. 81 below.
[77] There is a *huge* literature. For a recent survey of the subject, see J. Gardner (ed.), *Human Rights as General Norms and a State's Right to Opt Out*, BIICL, London, 1997.
[78] See pp. 246–8 below.

Committee established by the International Covenant on Civil and Political Rights 1966.[79] The Committee is not empowered to give decisions binding on the parties. Nevertheless, in its General Comment No. 24 in 1994,[80] the Committee said that it must necessarily take a view as to the status and effect of a reservation if this is required in order for it to carry out its functions, in particular considering reports from parties. The Committee gave the impression that it could in such circumstances make an authoritative determination. This view has been severely criticised. It, and similar committees, cannot be equated to international courts or tribunals that reach decisions binding on the parties after hearing full legal argument.

Some ways of minimising the problem of reservations

If express provision is made in each new treaty, many of the problems of reservations may be avoided. The European Agreement concerning the Work of Crews of Vehicles Engaged in International Road Transport 1970 (AETR II Agreement) provides that a non-authorised reservation shall be deemed to be accepted if, within six months of being notified of it, *none* of the contracting states has opposed it. Otherwise, the reservation shall not be admitted, and, if it does not withdraw the reservation, the reserving state shall not become a party.[81]

A more recent formulation is found in the FAO Compliance Agreement 1993:[82] reservations shall become effective only upon *unanimous* acceptance by all the parties; parties not having replied within three months from the date of notification shall be deemed to have accepted; failing unanimous acceptance, the reserving state shall not become a party to the Agreement. Of course, the reserving state can always withdraw the reservation or deposit a fresh acceptance without the reservation.

Procedure

A statement made during the negotiation of the treaty or on its adoption, even if recorded formally, must be made again if it is to be effective as a reservation. If it is made on signature of a treaty that is subject to ratification, to be effective it must be formally confirmed by the reserving state when expressing its consent to be bound (Article 23(2)).

---

[79] See p. 248 below.
[80] See ILM (1995) 839; 107 ILR 54. The text, and the observations of France, the United Kingdom and the United States, are in J. Gardner (ed.), *Human Rights as General Norms and a State's Right to Opt Out*, BIICL, London, 1997, pp. 185–207.
[81] 993 UNTS 143 (No. 14533), Article 21(2).   [82] ILM (1994) 968; B&B Docs. 645.

Since a reservation can be withdrawn, it may in certain circumstances also be possible to modify, or even to replace, a reservation, provided the result is to limit its effect. Some treaties make express provision for this.[83]

Late reservations

Although the Convention does not authorise the making of reservations other than when a state consents to be bound, if the UN Secretary-General subsequently receives a reservation he will sometimes circulate the text with a note that, unless he receives an objection within ninety days, the reservations will be deemed to have been accepted. This is only done when the reservation is specifically authorised by the treaty or is the same as one already made by another state.

The International Law Commission study

Since 1993, the International Law Commission has had on its agenda 'Reservations to Treaties', for which Professor Alain Pellet was appointed Special Rapporteur. Since 1995, he has produced nine reports. Instead of proposing amendments to the Convention, the Commission intends to produce a draft set of 'Guidelines' for consideration by the Sixth Committee of the UN General Assembly.[84]

Entry into force

A treaty is not like national legislation which, once in force, applies to all to whom it is directed. A treaty is much closer to a contract: even when it has entered into force it is in force *only for those states that have consented to be bound by it*. Each of them is then a 'party' to the treaty (Article 2(1)(g)), and should never be referred to by the ambiguous term 'signatory'.[85] But, when a state expresses its consent to be bound, that does not necessarily mean that the treaty will enter into force for it at that time; it depends on whether the treaty is already in force or whether further consents are needed to bring it into force.

---

[83] See Article 13(2) of the European Convention on the Suppression of Terrorism 1977, 1137 UNTS 93 (No. 17828); ILM (1976) 1272; UKTS (1978) 93.
[84] See his reports, and those of the ILC, at www.un.org/law/ilc/.   [85] See p. 65 above.

Express provisions

A treaty enters into force in such manner and on such date as provided for in the treaty or as the negotiating states may agree (Article 24(1)). There are various ways:

1. On a date specified in the treaty.
2. On signature by both or all the states. This is common for bilateral treaties that do not have to be approved by parliaments or require new legislation.[86]
3. On ratification by both (or all) states.
4. Conditional on ratification by certain states specified by name or category. The Comprehensive Nuclear Test-Ban Treaty 1996 cannot enter into force until the forty-four states named in Annex 2 to the Treaty have ratified.[87]
5. On ratification by a minimum number of states.
6. As in 4 or 5, but the minimum number of states must also fulfil other conditions, often financial or economic, designed to ensure that the treaty does not enter into force until the states that have a significant interest in the subject matter have ratified.[88]
7. On the exchange of instruments of ratification (bilateral treaties).
8. On notification by each state to the other (or others) of the completion of its constitutional requirements. This is more common for bilateral treaties.
9. In the case of a treaty constituted by an exchange of notes, on the date of the reply note, although a further stage (such as in 8) is frequently added.

Date of entry into force

For *multilateral* treaties, it is usual to provide that entry into force will be after a specified period following the deposit of the last instrument of ratification needed to bring the treaty into force (see Article 84(2) of the Convention itself), the range generally being from thirty days to twelve months.

When a state ratifies after the entry into force of the treaty, it will enter into force for that state on the date of deposit of the instrument of ratification or, more usually, after a specified period which is usually the same period as for the original entry into force of the treaty.

---

[86] See, for example, p. 82, para. (b) below.   [87] ILM (1996) 1443.
[88] See pp. 339–40 below on the Kyoto Protocol.

Provisional application

The subject of Article 25 is sometimes loosely described as provisional 'entry into force', but it is concerned only with the *application* of a treaty on a provisional basis pending its entry into force. The growing need for provisional application clauses is caused by the need to bring into force early those treaties (or at least certain substantive parts) which are subject to ratification and the problem of achieving that objective, especially for treaties which require a substantial number of ratifications for entry into force.[89]

Preparatory commissions

A further approach increasingly employed is to establish a preparatory commission, or 'prepcom'. This is usually a body composed of all the negotiating or signatory states which is entrusted with the task of making the necessary arrangements for when the treaty enters into force. The need for a prepcom is particularly acute when the treaty establishes an international organisation.[90]

Treaties and domestic law[91]

Once a treaty has entered into force for a state, it does not necessarily become part of its law.[92] Treaty law and domestic law[93] operate on different legal levels. Treaty law creates rights and obligations binding on states and other international legal persons. But, when a treaty confers rights or imposes obligations on natural or legal persons, they can be given effect only if they have been made part of the domestic law of a party.

Duty to perform treaties

Article 26 contains the fundamental principle of the law of treaties: every treaty in force is binding upon the parties to it and must be performed in good faith (*pacta sunt servanda*). Article 27 is the corollary: a party may not invoke the provisions of its internal law as justification for its failure to

[89] See Aust, pp. 139–41.
[90] See pp. 141–2, and the example of the International Criminal Court Prepcom, UN Doc. A/CONF.183/C.1/L.76/Add.14.
[91] As to international law and domestic law, see p. 12 above.
[92] Cf. customary international law, p. 13 above.   [93] See p. 12 above.

perform a treaty. Thus, if new legislation or modifications to existing law are necessary in order to comply with a new treaty, the state must ensure this has been done by the time the treaty enters into force for it. Otherwise the state risks being in breach of its treaty obligations and will be liable in international law if, as a result of that omission, another party, or one of its nationals, is harmed.[94] That parliaments are slow to legislate is no excuse. Nor can a state plead in its defence that there has been a change of government, since the treaty binds the *state*, not its government.[95] It is very difficult to plead that a treaty is invalid because its consent to be bound was expressed in violation of its law.[96]

Constitutional provisions

Some treaties, such as treaties of alliance, should not need to have effect in domestic law. For other treaties, it may be necessary to create new criminal offences or other enforcement mechanisms. How this is done depends on the constitution of each state. Although no two constitutions are the same, there are two general approaches: 'dualism' and 'monism'. Both are doctrines developed by scholars to explain the different approaches. Although monism is often presented as the opposite of dualism, this is misleading: many constitutions contain both dualist and monist elements. The United Kingdom has perhaps the purist form of dualism; Switzerland perhaps the most developed form of monism. In between there are many variations.[97]

Monism

The essence of the monist approach is that a treaty may, without legislation, become part of domestic law once it has been concluded in accordance with the constitution and has entered into force for the state. However, in many cases legislation will also be needed. When it is not needed the treaty is commonly described as 'self-executing'. Although there are many variations, there are usually three main common features.

---

[94] See p. 407 below.   [95] See pp. 24–5 above.   [96] See p. 107 below.

[97] See the summaries in Aust, pp.146–9; and the constitutions of several states in Hollis, Blakeslee and Ederington (eds.), *National Treaty Law and Practice*, Leiden, 2005. G. Flanz (ed.), *Blaustein's Constitutions of the World*, Dobbs Ferry, NY (loose-leaf), is an invaluable source for the texts of constitutions. See also Reisenfeld and Abbott (eds.), *Parliamentary Participation in the Making and Operation of Treaties: A Comparative Study*, The Hague, 1994; and F. Jacobs and S. Roberts, *The Effect of Treaties in Domestic Law*, London, 1987.

First, the constitution requires the treaty to be first approved by parliament, although there are exceptions for certain types of treaty or certain circumstances. Secondly, a distinction is made between treaties according to their nature or subject matter, some being regarded as being self-executing, others requiring legislation. Thirdly, a self-executing treaty may constitute supreme law and override any inconsistent domestic legislation, whether existing or future.

Dualism

Under the dualist approach, the constitution accords no special status to treaties; the rights and obligations created by them have no effect in domestic law except in so far as legislation gives effect to them. When legislation is specifically made for this purpose, the rights and obligations are then said to be 'incorporated' into domestic law. This approach reflects, on the one hand, the constitutional power of the executive generally to bind itself to a treaty without the prior consent of the legislature and, on the other hand, the supreme power of the legislature under the constitution. And treaty provisions that have been incorporated then have the status only of *domestic* law and can be amended or repealed by later legislation, even if this would be in beach of the treaty.

United Kingdom

United Kingdom constitutional practice

The UK form of dualism was bequeathed to most of the former overseas territories of the United Kingdom, and so has been followed in almost all the other fifty-two Commonwealth states.[98] The treaty-making power of the United Kingdom is exercised by the Secretary of State for Foreign and Commonwealth Affairs (the foreign minister). Although Parliament does not have to consent to the Government entering into a treaty, under a constitutional practice known as the Ponsonby Rule a treaty which is subject to ratification (or analogous procedure) is communicated to Parliament, with a short explanatory memorandum. Twenty-one sitting days are then allowed for Parliament to decide if it wishes to debate the treaty. This seldom happens unless implementing legislation is needed anyway or the treaty is of major political importance, in which case the Government would normally arrange for a debate.

---

[98] See the detailed account of United Kingdom treaty law and practice in *National Treaty Law and Practice*, n. 97 above, pp. 727–64; Oppenheim, pp. 56–63; and (1992) BYIL 704.

Implementing legislation can take three main forms:

(a) An Act of Parliament (statute). The text of the whole or part of[99] the treaty may be scheduled (annexed) to the Act, which will provide that the scheduled provisions shall have the force of law in the United Kingdom. Alternatively, the Act will merely make such changes to the law as are necessary to give effect to the treaty.[100]

(b) An Act of Parliament conferring all the powers necessary to carry out obligations under *future* treaties. For example, bilateral air services agreements can be concluded without the need for fresh legislation each time since existing legislation, both primary and secondary, is sufficient to implement them.

(c) An Act of Parliament that provides a *framework* within which *secondary legislation* can be made to give effect to a certain category of treaty, usually bilateral. The Act can either:

  • authorise the Crown to make secondary legislation *incorporating the treaties into domestic law*. This is usually done by an Order made by The Queen in Council (an 'Order in Council') to which the text of the treaty is attached. Such legislation is frequently made for bilateral double taxation conventions[101] and social security conventions.[102] Normally the Order does not have to be approved in draft by Parliament, although once made it can be annulled by Parliament (the negative resolution procedure).

  • authorise the Crown to make secondary legislation *to implement obligations imposed by certain categories of treaty*. The treaty is not attached. Instead, its provisions are 'translated' into the language of the Act. Orders in Council made under the International Organizations Act 1968 give effect to treaties conferring privileges and immunities on international organisations and tribunals, and persons connected with them.[103] The Orders have to be approved, in draft, by both Houses of Parliament. This requires a short debate in each House (the affirmative resolution procedure).

---

[99] Compare the Diplomatic Privileges Act 1964 (part of the treaty) with the Consular Relations Act 1968 (whole of the treaty).

[100] See the State Immunity Act 1978, which mainly implements the European Convention on State Immunity 1972: see p. 162 below.

[101] Income and Corporation Taxes Act 1988, section 788(10); SI 1991 No. 2876 (Czechoslovakia).

[102] Social Security Act 1975, section 143; SI 1991 No. 767 (Norway).

[103] See the Tribunal for the Law of the Sea (Immunities and Privileges) Order 1996 (SI 1996 No. 272).

Interpretation and application of treaties by United Kingdom courts

British judges have not always been at their happiest when confronted by a treaty. Admittedly, they are not helped by the strict separation of treaties from domestic law inherent in the dualist approach. The courts have, however, developed certain principles which alleviate some of the strictness of dualism:[104]

- If the language of legislation implementing a treaty is unambiguous, the court will not look behind the legislation at the treaty, but if it is ambiguous the court will examine the treaty.
- Ambiguous legislation will be interpreted in the way which is most consistent with the international obligations of the United Kingdom, including *un*incorporated treaties (such as the European Convention on Human Rights before it was incorporated).
- In so far as a treaty has been incorporated by attaching all or part of it to legislation, the courts should interpret it according to the rules of international law, in particular Articles 31–33 of the Convention, even though the Convention has not been incorporated.[105]

The courts of most other Commonwealth states take a similar approach.

European Community law

Because the United Kingdom is dualist, EC law is enforceable in the United Kingdom only because United Kingdom legislation has so provided. But, when applying EC law, the British courts must construe it as such law, *not* as United Kingdom law, and must follow decisions of the European Court of Justice.[106] However, because decisions taken under the Common Foreign and Security Policy (CFSP) and Police and Judicial Co-operation in Criminal Matters (PJCCM)[107] are not directly applicable in the domestic law of the member states, they need specific legislation.

United States

The way treaties are dealt with under the US Constitution reflects both dualist and monist approaches, and has rightly been described as

---

[104] Oppenheim, pp. 56–63 and p. 1269, n. 2 (significantly, perhaps the longest footnote in that noteworthy work); R. Gardiner, 'Treaty Interpretation in the English Courts since Fothergill v. Monarch Airlines' (1995) ICLQ 620.

[105] *Sidhu* v. *British Airways* [1997] 1 All ER 193, at pp. 201–12.

[106] See section 3 of the European Communities Act 1972.   [107] See p. 478 below.

'remarkably complex'.[108] Any non-American lawyer who has to deal with the effect of a treaty in US law would be well advised to consult a good American law firm. Under Article II, Section 2(2), of the Constitution, the President may ratify a 'Treaty' only with the 'Advice and Consent' of the Senate signified by the affirmative vote of two-thirds of the members present. This is sometimes referred to, misleadingly, as 'ratification', since only the President can do that act. Although the Constitution mentions only one type of international agreement (a 'Treaty'), from the earliest days an alternative form has been employed by the US Government in order to avoid the problems inherent in obtaining Senate approval. These so-called 'executive agreements' are nevertheless regarded by both the US Government and other governments as treaties in international law. Under a federal statute, known as the 'Case Act',[109] all executive agreements have to be notified to Congress within sixty days of entry into force and published annually. (Unless otherwise indicated, a reference in the following paragraphs to a 'treaty' includes an executive agreement; and a reference to a 'Treaty' is to a treaty that needs Senate approval.)

Most treaties entered into by the United States have been, and still are, executive agreements. They can be broken down into four categories:

1. those authorised by a prior Act of Congress;
2. those subsequently approved by Act of Congress;
3. those entered into by the President in exercise of his executive power (a controversial and ill-defined area); and
4. those authorised by a previous Treaty or executive agreement.

'Self-executing' treaties

Under Article VI, Section 2, of the Constitution, all Treaties are the 'supreme law of the land', and the Supreme Court has interpreted this as applying also to executive agreements. The provision is often, and mis-leadingly, described as making treaties 'self-executing'. By this is meant that the treaty, once it has entered into force, is directly applicable as if it were an Act of Congress. But, contrary to what is sometimes asserted, whether it is self-executing does not depend on whether it is a Treaty or

---

[108] J. Jackson, in Jacobs and Roberts (eds.), *The Effect of Treaties in Domestic* Law, London, 1987, vol. 7, pp. 141–69. For a critical commentary on compliance by the United States with treaties, see D. Vogts, 'Taking Treaties Less Seriously' (1998) AJIL 458–62. Unfortunately, the article on US law in *National Treaty Law and Practice*, n. 97 above, is disappointing.

[109] Public Law 92-403, as amended by I USC 112b; ILM (1972) 1117 and ILM (1979) 82.

an executive agreement. The self-executing concept has led inevitably to considerable confusion and uncertainty, since there is no sure method for determining in advance whether a treaty will be self-executing. The matter may ultimately have to be decided by the US courts. There is now considerable jurisprudence, but it is not easy even for American lawyers to advise whether a particular treaty, or part of it, is self-executing. The crucial factor is the intention of the parties. It is usually necessary to consider various factors such as language and purpose, the specific circumstances, the nature of the obligations and the implications of permitting a private right of action without the need for legislation. However, a treaty will not be self-executing if it clearly envisages implementing legislation. In some cases, the non-US party to the treaty may have to intervene in legal proceedings in the United States to protect its position.

Hierarchy of norms

If a treaty is self-executing, it may come into conflict with US domestic law. Whenever possible, the courts will seek to reconcile the two, but that is not always possible. When this happens, the general residuary rules are:

- treaties prevail over common law;
- treaties prevail over state law;
- the Constitution prevails over *all* treaties; this rule may, in part, have led in recent years to the Senate requiring the President to attach a reservation when ratifying certain human rights treaties;[110]
- in the case of a conflict between a Treaty and an Act of Congress, the later in time prevails. However, there is still considerable uncertainty as to whether a later executive agreement prevails. The judicial decisions do not give a clear guide, although it is probably fair to say that generally an executive agreement concluded in exercise only of the executive power of the President will not prevail over a prior Act of Congress.

Interpretation of treaties by US courts

US courts tend to have regard less to the text and more to the intention of the parties and the object and purpose. Where there is more than one reasonable interpretation, the one which is more favourable to private rights will be adopted. The courts do not follow the formal scheme of Articles 31 and 32 of the Convention (to which the United States is anyway not yet a party). The court will give weight to an interpretation given by

---

[110] See, for example, p. 75 above.

the Government in *amicus curiae*[111] briefs and, when applicable, to any understanding expressed by the Senate when giving Advice and Consent.

Implementation by federal states

The performance of treaties by federal states can give rise to problems. Although Article 29 provides that, unless there is a different intention, a treaty is binding upon each party in respect of its entire territory,[112] it may be difficult for a federal government to ensure that a treaty is fully implemented in all the constituent units. Under a federal constitution, certain powers, such as taxation and criminal justice, may be shared with the constituent units, so that if the latter have to legislate there could be delays or even obstruction. When powers have to be exercised in performance of a treaty obligation, the federal constitution may then provide for such matters to be vested exclusively in the federal government, or, under a monist-type constitution, a treaty once ratified may override inconsistent state law. Although, in principle, in the United States executive agreements also override state law, in practice it is not always easy for the federal government to convince state governments and legislatures that they are obliged to comply with them. This happens most frequently with provisions for exemption from taxes.

Territorial application

Some treaties, such as the Outer Space Treaty 1967,[113] apply to the activities of a party or its nationals outside its territory. But all treaties will require *some* action within the territory of the parties, although not always legislation. Territory comprises the metropolitan territory of a state and its overseas territories.[114] Unless it appears otherwise from the treaty, references to territory include the territorial sea, but not the continental shelf or an exclusive economic zone or a fisheries zone.[115]

In most cases a treaty will be silent as to its territorial scope. This is not usually a problem unless a party has overseas territories and the content of the treaty is capable of applying to them. Because of their very nature, treaties like the Charter of the United Nations have to apply to all the

---

[111] In the United States, a written statement filed with the court by someone who is not a party to the case but has an interest in the outcome and wishes to influence the court.

[112] See p. 33 above.   [113] See p. 367 below.

[114] See p. 29 above.   [115] See p. 33 above.

territory of the parties. Article 29 lays down merely a residual rule: a treaty is binding upon each party in respect of its entire territory unless a different intention appears from the treaty or is otherwise established. A different intention can be established in various ways.

Territorial extension clauses

Bilateral treaties

Some bilateral treaties have a provision that they may be extended to such territories for whose international relations the Government of X is responsible, as may be agreed between the parties in an exchange of notes.[116]

Multilateral treaties

Before the era of de-colonisation, it was common to include a similar provision in multilateral treaties.[117] But, from the 1960s, 'colonial clauses' fell out of favour. Other means were therefore established by which states could extend treaties to their overseas territories (see below). The clauses are now more likely to be found in treaties on matters such as customs and extradition.

Declaration on signature or ratification of a multilateral treaty

When a multilateral treaty does not by its nature clearly apply to all the territory of a party, yet is silent as to its territorial scope and lacks a territorial clause, there is a well-established practice by which a state can decide to which, if any, of its overseas territories the treaty will extend. At the time of signature or ratification, the state declares either that the treaty extends only to the metropolitan territory, or that it extends (and may later be extended further) to an overseas territory or territories. The UN Secretary-General views this constant practice of states, and acquiescence by other states, as having established a different intention for the purposes of Article 29.[118] The practice is based on the premise that, unless the treaty has to apply to all overseas territories in order to be effective, it does not

---

[116] See the South Africa–United Kingdom Investment Promotion and Protection Agreement 1994, UKTS (1998) 35.
[117] See Article XII of the Genocide Convention 1948, 878 UNTS 277 (No. 1021); UKTS (1970) 58.
[118] *UN Depositary Practice*, paras. 273–85.

apply to them unless specifically extended to them. Today, many territories are small (some very small), but most have internal self-government. Given their circumstances, they do not necessarily need or want every multilateral treaty to apply to them.

Political sub-divisions of metropolitan territory

Many states, such as federations, have constitutions that divide the metropolitan territory into political sub-divisions. Even when it is only the federation that can be party to treaties, their implementation may require action by the governments and legislatures of the sub-divisions, yet the federation remains responsible in international law for the due performance of all treaties.[119] There are certain methods by which these problems can be reduced: territorial clauses, federal clauses, and federal reservations.[120]

Successive treaties

A particularly difficult problem is posed when a treaty is followed by another one or more treaties that are wholly or partly on the same subject matter. When the treaty is bilateral, or all the parties to two or more multilateral treaties are the same, there should be no particular problem. But the parties to multilateral treaties are seldom all the same, and the issue is growing in importance with the increasing number and complexity of multilateral treaties. The problems (which are related to the rules on amendment of treaties) can be alleviated by an express 'conflict clause'; otherwise the residual rules in Article 30 apply. For examples of such clauses and a discussion of Article 30, see Aust, pp. 173–83.

Interpretation

Treaties represent negotiated compromises reconciling often wide differences. The greater the number of negotiating states, the greater the need for imaginative and subtle drafting to bridge the gap between opposing interests. Inevitably this sometimes produces texts that are unclear or ambiguous. There is no treaty that cannot raise some question

---

[119] See p. 57 above. See generally B. Opeskin, 'Federal States in the International Legal Order' (1996) NILR 353–386. See *Paraguay* v. *US (Breard), ICJ Reports* (1998), p. 248; ILM (1998) 810 (ICJ); ILM (1998) 824 (US Supreme Court); 118 ILR 1.

[120] See Aust, pp. 169–72.

of interpretation, and most disputes submitted to international adjudication involve a problem of interpretation. Although Articles 31 and 32
are concerned with interpretation, they contain much that is of practical value to the treaty-maker or to anyone involved in implementing a
treaty.

Article 31

General rule of interpretation

1. A treaty shall be interpreted in good faith in accordance with the ordinary
   meaning to be given to the terms of the treaty in their context and in
   the light of its object and purpose.
2. The context for the purpose of the interpretation of a treaty shall com-
   prise, in addition to the text, including its preamble and annexes:
   (a) any agreement relating to the treaty which was made between all
       the parties in connection with the conclusion of the treaty;
   (b) any instrument which was made by one or more parties in con-
       nection with the conclusion of the treaty and accepted by the other
       parties as an instrument related to the treaty.
3. There shall be taken into account, together with the context:
   (a) any subsequent agreement between the parties regarding the inter-
       pretation of the treaty or the application of its provisions;
   (b) any subsequent practice in the application of the treaty which estab-
       lishes the agreement of the parties regarding its interpretation;
   (c) any relevant rules of international law applicable in the relations
       between the parties.
4. A special meaning shall be given to a term if it is established that the
   parties so intended.

Paragraph 1

Paragraph 1 gives no greater weight to one particular factor, such as the
text ('textual' or 'literal' approach), or the supposed intentions of the
parties, or the object and purpose of the treaty ('effective' or 'teleological'
approach). Placing undue emphasis on the text, without regard to what
the parties intended; or on what the parties are believed to have intended,
regardless of the text; or on the perceived object and purpose in order to
make the treaty more 'effective', irrespective of the intentions of the parties,
is unlikely to produce a satisfactory result. The International Court of
Justice has held in several cases that the principles embodied in Articles 31
and 32 reflect customary international law.[121]

---

[121] See, for example, *Libya* v. *Chad, ICJ Reports* (1994), p. 4, at para. 41; 100 ILR 438.

The first principle – interpretation *in good faith* – flows directly from the principle of *pacta sunt servanda* (Article 26). Even if the words of the treaty are clear, if applying them would lead to a result which would be manifestly absurd or unreasonable (to adopt the phrase in Article 32(b)), one must seek another interpretation. When in 1991 the Union of Soviet Socialist Republics (mentioned specifically in Article 23(1) of the UN Charter) was renamed the Russian Federation, no UN Member suggested that the Charter would have to be amended before the Russian Federation could occupy the former Soviet seat.[122]

It is important to give a term its *ordinary meaning* since it is reasonable to assume, at least until the contrary is established, that the ordinary meaning is most likely to reflect what the parties intended. As McNair put it, the task of interpretation is:

> the duty of giving effect to the expressed intention of the parties, that is, their intention *as expressed in the words used by them in the light of surrounding circumstances.*[123]

The determination of the ordinary meaning can be done only within the *context* of the treaty and in the light of its *object and purpose*. The latter concept, as we have seen in relation to reservations to treaties,[124] can be elusive. Fortunately, the role it plays in interpreting treaties is less than the search for the ordinary meaning of the words in their context, but an interpretation that is incompatible with the object and purpose may well be wrong.

Paragraph 2 (context)

Paragraph 2 specifies what comprises the context. When a treaty refers to an 'aircraft', does that include all aircraft, civil and military, and what about microlights, hovercraft or balloons? For this purpose, one must look at the treaty as a whole, including the title, preamble and any annexes. For example, Article I of the Comprehensive Nuclear-Test-Ban Treaty[125] prohibits 'any nuclear weapon test explosion *or any other nuclear explosion*'. The thought that this might ban the *use* of nuclear weapons is, however, quickly dispelled by the unambiguous title of the treaty.

Paragraph 2 also provides that, in addition to the text, including the preamble and annexes, the context comprises:

---

[122] See *UN Multilateral Treaties*, Ch. I, nn. 4 and 9.
[123] McNair, *The Law of Treaties*, 2nd edn, Oxford, 1961, p. 365. For once, the emphasis is his.
[124] At p. 70 above.   [125] ILM (1996) 1443.

(a) *any agreement relating to the treaty which was made between all the parties in connexion with the conclusion of the treaty.* The agreement does not have to be part of the treaty, or be itself a treaty; but it must be a clear expression of the intention of the parties. When the ENMOD Convention 1977 was negotiated, a series of 'Understandings' were agreed regarding the interpretation or application of the Convention.[126]

(b) *any instrument made by one or more parties in connexion with the conclusion of the treaty and accepted by the other parties as an instrument related to the treaty.* The Dayton Agreement 1995 included many such instruments,[127] as do EU constituent treaties.

Such agreements and instruments are usually made at the conclusion of the treaty, or soon afterwards.

The explanatory reports approved by the government experts involved in drafting conventions of the Council of Europe, and adopted at the same time as the conventions and published with them, provide an invaluable guide to their interpretation and should be seen as part of the 'context' in which the conventions were concluded.[128] As such, they must be distinguished from 'official' commentaries which are later produced and, depending on the circumstances, may come to be regarded as authoritative, such as the *Handbook on Procedures and Criteria for Determining Refugee Status*, published by the UN High Commissioner for Refugees (UNHCR). The detailed Commentaries of the International Law Commission (ILC) on its draft Articles are especially valuable.[129] Commentaries published by organisations, such as the ICRC on the Geneva Conventions of 1949, are highly persuasive.[130]

Paragraph 3(a) (subsequent agreements)

Sub-paragraph (a) provides that, together with the context, there shall be taken into account any 'subsequent agreement' between the parties

---

[126] 1108 UNTS 151 (No. 17119); ILM (1977) 16; TIAS 9614. See also the Understandings in the UN Convention on State Immunity 2004, p. 160 below.

[127] ILM (1996) 75.   [128] Sinclair, pp. 129–30. For an example, see ILM (1994) 943.

[129] Though they must be used with care, since the final version of an Article may differ materially. See A. Watts, *The International Law Commission 1949–1998*, Oxford, 1999, which includes the full text of draft Articles with their Commentaries and the final adopted text.

[130] J. Pictet (ed.), *The Geneva Conventions 1949: Commentary*, Geneva, 1952–60. But see also S. Rosenne, *Practice and Methods of International Law*, New York, 1984, pp. 50–1.

regarding the interpretation of the treaty or the application of its provisions. There is no need for a further treaty; the paragraph refers deliberately to an 'agreement', not a treaty. The agreement can take various forms,[131] including a decision adopted by a meeting of the parties, provided this is clearly the purpose.[132] Where a treaty needs a small modification that is essentially procedural, it may be possible to embody it in an agreement as to the application of the treaty. This technique is particularly useful if there is a need to fill a lacuna, to update a term or to postpone the operation of a provision. The date for the first election of judges of ITLOS was specified in UNCLOS, but the date turned out to be premature and the election was postponed by a consensus decision of the Meeting of Parties.[133] These techniques are very important for treaty implementation.

Paragraph 3(b) (subsequent practice)

Sub-paragraph (b) provides that, together with the context, there shall be taken into account any subsequent practice in the application of the treaty that establishes the agreement of the parties regarding its interpretation. Reference to practice is well established in the jurisprudence of international tribunals. However precise a text appears to be, the way in which it is actually applied by the parties is usually a good indication of what the parties understood it to mean, provided the practice is consistent, and is common to, or accepted by, all the parties.[134]

Article 37(1) of the Vienna Convention on Diplomatic Relations 1961 refers to the 'members of the family of a diplomatic agent forming part of his household'.[135] The phrase is not defined, and even in 1961 there was doubt as to exactly which persons formed part of a diplomat's household: did it include a thirty-year-old perpetual student child? Given the changes in society since then (and to which even diplomats are not entirely immune), might other persons now be considered members of the family? Does it now include unmarried partners? And, if so, what about partners of the same sex? In interpreting the phrase, great weight

---

[131] See the example given in R. Gardiner, 'Treaties and Treaty Materials: Role, Relevance and Accessibility' (1997) ICLQ 643 at 648–9.
[132] See p. 471 below.   [133] SPLOS/3 of 28 February 1995.
[134] See the US–France Air Services Arbitration, 1963, 38 ILR 182.
[135] 500 UNTS 95 (No. 7310); UKTS (1965) 19.

must necessarily be given to the practice of states, most states having had to face such problems.[136]

Perhaps the most dramatic, and oft-quoted, example of interpretation by subsequent practice is the way in which Members of the United Nations have interpreted and applied Article 27(3) of the Charter in relation to the veto.[137]

Paragraph 3(c) (relevant rules of international law)

Sub-paragraph (c) provides that, together with the context, there shall be taken into account any relevant rules of international law applicable in the relations between the parties. For example, in certain cases, reaching an interpretation which is consistent with the intentions (or perceived intentions) of the parties may require regard to be had not only to international law at the time the treaty was concluded (the 'inter-temporal rule'),[138] but also to contemporary law.[139] In interpreting today a reference to the continental shelf in a treaty of, say, 1961, it would probably be necessary to consider not only the Geneva Convention on the Continental Shelf 1958, but also the United Nations Convention on the Law of the Sea 1982.[140]

Paragraph 4 (special meaning)

A special meaning must be given to a term if it is established that the parties so intended (paragraph 4). Notwithstanding the apparent meaning of a term in its context, it is open to a party to invoke any special meaning, but the burden of proof rests on that party.[141]

Supplementary means of interpretation

Article 32

Supplementary means of interpretation

Recourse may be had to supplementary means of interpretation, including the preparatory work of the treaty and the circumstances of its conclusion,

---

[136] See further p. 147 below.   [137] See p. 213 below.   [138] See p. 35 above.

[139] See R. Higgins, 'Some Observations on the Inter-Temporal Rule in International Law', in J. Makarczyk (ed.), *Theory of International Law at the Threshold of the 21st Century*, The Hague, 1996, pp. 173–81; and R. Higgins, 'Time and the Law: International Perspectives on an Old Problem' (1997) ICLQ 501–20.

[140] See Sinclair, pp. 138–40, and Oppenheim, para. 633(11).   [141] See Sinclair, pp. 126–7.

in order to confirm the meaning resulting from the application of Article 31, or to determine the meaning when the interpretation according to Article 31:

(a) leaves the meaning ambiguous or obscure; or

(b) leads to a result which is manifestly absurd or unreasonable.

The preparatory work (*travaux préparatoires*, or *travaux* for short) of a treaty is an important supplementary means of interpretation. It is by its nature less authentic, often being incomplete and misleading. Nevertheless, in certain circumstances, recourse may be had to *travaux* to 'confirm' the meaning resulting from the application of Article 31, and international tribunals have long done so.[142] In order to understand what the negotiating states intended, recourse to the *travaux* and the circumstances of the conclusion of the treaty may be necessary.[143] In *Lockerbie*, the United Kingdom maintained that it was not intended that the UN Charter should give the International Court of Justice a power of judicial review over Security Council decisions, and that this is clearly supported by the *travaux* of the Charter.[144]

The rest of Article 32 provides that recourse may also be had to the same supplementary means of interpretation when reliance on the primary means produces an interpretation which (a) leaves the meaning 'ambiguous or obscure' or (b) leads to a result which is 'manifestly absurd or unreasonable'. In this case, the purpose is not to confirm, but to determine, the meaning.

When the ordinary meaning appears to be clear, the primary duty to interpret a treaty in good faith means that, if it is evident from the *travaux* that the ordinary meaning does not represent the intention of the parties, a court may 'correct' the ordinary meaning.[145] This is how things work in practice; for example, the parties to a dispute will always refer the tribunal to the *travaux*, and the tribunal will inevitably consider them along with all the other material put before it.

The *travaux* are generally understood to include successive drafts of the treaty, conference records, explanatory statements by an expert

---

[142] See, for example, McNair, p. 413, n. 3, and p. 422, n. 4.   [143] O'Connell, p. 263.

[144] *Libya* v. *United Kingdom* (Preliminary Objections), *ICJ Reports* (1998), p. 9, paras. 4.17–4.18; ILM (1998) 587; 117 ILR 1 and 644; and the submissions of the Lord Advocate (CR 97/17, para. 5.46), and the dissenting opinion of President Schwebel.

[145] S. Schwebel, 'May Preparatory Work Be Used to Correct Rather than Confirm the "Clear" Meaning of a Treaty Provision?' in J. Makarczyk (ed.), *Theory of International Law at the Threshold of the 21st Century*, The Hague, 1996, pp. 541–7.

consultant at a codification conference, uncontested interpretative statements by the chairman of a drafting committee and ILC Commentaries. Their value will depend on several factors, the most important being authenticity, completeness and availability. The summary record of a conference prepared by an independent and experienced secretariat will carry more weight than an unagreed record produced by a host state or a participating state. However, even the records of a conference served by a skilled secretariat will generally not tell the whole story. The most important parts of negotiating and drafting often take place informally, with no agreed record being kept. The reason why a particular compromise formula was adopted, and what it was intended to mean, may be difficult to establish.[146] This will be especially so if the form of words was deliberately chosen to overcome a near irreconcilable difference of substance. The final drafting of new Article 3*bis* (prohibition on use of force against civil aircraft) of the Chicago Convention was done by hectic, highly visible and informal (literally back-of-the-envelope) negotiations during a mayoral reception near the end of a three-week conference.[147]

Other supplementary means of interpretation

It is also legitimate to assume that the parties to a treaty did not intend that the treaty would be incompatible with customary international law.[148] There are several other means of interpretation, though it is not always easy to distinguish them from familiar legal techniques, often based on commonsense or grammatical rules. Many derive from principles of domestic law, especially Roman Law.[149]

Implied terms

Although it is not for an international tribunal to revise a treaty by reading into it provisions that it does not contain by necessary implication, it is sometimes necessary to imply a term, and this has been the approach of the International Court of Justice[150] and the European Court of Human

---

[146] See p. 126 below on whether service of legal process can be made on a diplomatic mission.

[147] ILM (1984) 705; UKTS (1999) 68. A young Danish delegate watched the informal negotiations with much professional amusement, and later married me.

[148] O'Connell, p. 261.   [149] See Aust, p. 200.

[150] The Court will not 'revise' a treaty on the pretext that it has found an omission: see S. Rosenne, *The Law and Practice of the International Court of Justice*, 3rd edn, The Hague, 1997, pp. 172–3.

Rights.[151] At the end of the Falklands conflict, there was not enough accommodation on the islands for the approximately 10,000 prisoners of war captured in the final stages, the ship carrying the tents having been sunk by the enemy. Following consultations with the ICRC, it was decided that the POWs could be kept on merchant ships and warships in Falklands waters until they could be repatriated. Although Article 22 of the Third Geneva Convention[152] prohibits holding on ships POWs who are captured on land, given that its object and purpose is the welfare of POWs, one could properly imply a term that when, for reasons beyond its control, a party to a conflict was unable to comply with Article 22, it may hold POWs on ships if that is preferable to leaving them on land without sufficient protection from the elements. Good interpretation is often no more than the application of commonsense.

Thus one has to look at the treaty as a whole, plus all other relevant materials, assessing their respective weight and value. This is, in fact, what international lawyers and international courts and tribunals do when confronted by a difficult question of interpretation.

Interpretation of treaties in more than one language

Many treaties, bilateral as well as multilateral, are bilingual or plurilingual. The language of one of the negotiating states may not be widely spoken, and to produce a draft and hold the negotiations in that language may be unduly burdensome. Bilateral negotiations are therefore frequently held in the language of only one of the states, or in a third language with which both are comfortable, which these days is often English. This may be reflected in the languages in which a treaty is concluded and in the choice of a language text to prevail in the case of a difference. The Kuwait Regional Marine Environment Convention 1978 was concluded in Arabic, English and Persian, but provides that in the case of divergence the English text prevails.[153] The Convention was almost certainly drafted, and possibly even negotiated, in English.

Multilateral negotiations are more likely to be held in more than one language, although there are notable exceptions. Although the

---

[151] See McNair, *The Law of Treaties*, 2nd edn, Oxford, 1961 Ch. 26; and Merrills, *The Development of International Law by the European Court of Human Rights*, 2nd edn, 1993, pp. 84–90.

[152] 75 UNTS 3 (No. 972); UKTS (1958) 39.

[153] ILM (1978) 511. See also the Japan–Pakistan Cultural Agreement 1957, 325 UNTS 22 (No. 4692).

proceedings of the General Assembly of the United Nations and its committees are conducted in the six official languages, informal meetings (of which there are many) are often held, and drafting done, only in English.

Treaties that have been concluded in more than one language can cause problems of interpretation if there are material differences between the language texts even after the *toilette finale*.[154] But, if there is still a discrepancy, the problem can be overcome if the treaty provides that in the case of inconsistency the text in one language shall prevail.

These treaty practices are reflected in Article 33. But, if the treaty was negotiated and drafted in only one of the authentic languages, it is natural to place more reliance on that text, particularly if it is unambiguous. The Dayton Agreement 1995 was negotiated entirely in English, even though there are supposed to be authentic texts in Bosnian, Croatian and Serbian.[155] Although such texts are equally authentic, in practice they may not carry quite the same weight as the original. This approach is not incompatible with paragraph 4, and the jurisprudence of the International Court of Justice would seem to support this approach in suitable cases.[156]

Third states

A third state is one which is 'not a party to the treaty' (Article 2(1)(h)), and therefore can range from a state which is not eligible to become a party to a state which has ratified but for which the treaty is not yet in force. A treaty does not impose obligations on or create rights for a third state without its consent (Article 34).

Two conditions must be satisfied before a third state can be bound by a treaty obligation: first, the parties must intend the provision to be the means of establishing the obligation of the third state; and, secondly, the third state must have expressly accepted the obligation in writing (Article 35). Conduct consistent with acceptance of the obligation is not enough. But even if a third state has accepted an obligation in a treaty, it does *not* thereby become a party to the treaty.

There is nothing in international law to prevent two or more states creating by treaty a *right* in favour of a third state (a sort of trust). Thus a right arises for a third state (or a group of states to which it belongs) if the parties to the treaty so intend and the third state assents. Since

---

[154] See Aust, p. 203.   [155] ILM (1996) 75.   [156] Sinclair, pp. 147–52.

the third state is not required to do anything, unless the treaty provides otherwise its assent is presumed as long as the contrary is not indicated (Article 36(1)). When exercising a right conferred on it, the third state must comply with the conditions for its exercise (Article 36(2)).

The Convention does not deal with *erga omnes* rights and obligations as such, but the rule in Article 36(1) (by which a right can be accorded to 'all states') furnishes a sufficient legal basis for the establishment of treaty rights and obligations valid *erga omnes*.[157]

Amendment

Amendment needs always to be thought about seriously when drafting and negotiating a treaty; afterwards is just too late. Although amending a bilateral treaty causes no great technical difficulty, amending a multilateral treaty can raise a multitude of problems. It may have as many as 150 or more parties and be of unlimited duration. These factors lead to two basic problems. First, the process of agreeing amendments and then bringing them into force for all the parties can be even more difficult than negotiating and bringing into force the original treaty. Secondly, because of their long life multilateral treaties are often in need of amendment.

Before the Second World War, treaty amendment usually required unanimity. This is generally still the rule for the constituent treaties of regional international organisations like the Council of Europe and the European Union. But in other cases a practice has developed by which an amendment enters into force only for those parties willing to accept it. This means that the *original* treaty still remains in force (1) as between the parties that do *not* accept the amendments and (2) between those parties and the parties that *do* accept them. This results in a dual treaty regime. This highly unsatisfactory result is made much worse when there is a series of amending treaties. The several failed attempts to modernise the Warsaw Convention 1929 has meant that the parties to the various amending and supplementing instruments all vary, thus preventing the implementation of a uniform compensation scheme throughout international civil aviation.[158]

Therefore, today, many treaties, especially multilateral, now have built-in amendment mechanisms.

---

[157] See p. 10 above for more on *erga omnes*.   [158] See p. 350 below.

Bilateral treaties

The parties to a bilateral treaty can always agree to an amendment, the only question is the way in which it is expressed. Often, it is to the effect that any amendments or modifications agreed by the parties shall come into effect when confirmed by an exchange of notes.

Multilateral treaties

It is essential to include in most multilateral treaties an effective amendment mechanism. The constituent instruments of international organisations especially need to have built-in amendment procedures under which, once an amendment has been finally endorsed by a specified percentage of the members, it is then binding on *all* members. Article 108 of the Charter of the United Nations has perhaps the most succinct and elegant procedure:

> Amendments to the present Charter shall come into force for all Members of the United Nations when they have been adopted by a vote of two thirds of the members of the General Assembly and ratified in accordance with their respective constitutional processes by two thirds of the Members of the United Nations, including all the permanent members of the Security Council.

The essential characteristic of this procedure is that once an amendment has entered into force it also binds *those who did not vote for or ratify it.*

Other amendment procedures included in treaties in recent years are often elaborate. No two are the same, each being tailored to suit the particular needs of the organisation or treaty,[159] but they usually provide for:

- the number of parties, or votes in the plenary body or meeting, needed to support an amendment before it has to be put to the vote of the parties;
- the majority needed for adoption of the amendment;
- whether the adopted amendment needs to be ratified or accepted;
- if applicable, the number of parties which need to ratify for the amendment to enter into force;

---

[159] Blix and Emerson, *The Treaty-Maker's Handbook*, Dobbs Ferry, NY, 1973, pp. 225–39, has many examples from before 1966. See also the UN *Handbook of Final Clauses* (http://untreaty.un.org/English/FinalClauses/Handbook.pdf.), pp. 97–105.

- where ratification is not required, whether the amendment can be adopted by tacit agreement; and
- whether the amendment binds those parties that have not accepted it (the crucial issue).

Under Article XIII of the FAO Agreement to Promote Compliance with International Conservation and Management Measures by Fishing Vessels on the High Seas 1993 (Compliance Agreement),[160] a proposed amendment requires the approval of the FAO Conference by two-thirds of the votes cast, and comes into force *for all* after acceptance by two thirds of the parties.[161] However, if an amendment involves new obligations for parties (which is assumed unless the Conference decides otherwise by consensus) it comes into force for each party only when it has been accepted by it. The subject matter of the Agreement is not only important, but also contentious. The amendment procedure reflects the reluctance of states to be bound by amendments they have not agreed to. To be fully effective therefore, any amendments are likely to need at least approval by consensus.

Contrast the Compliance Agreement procedure with Article VII of the Comprehensive Nuclear Test-Ban Treaty 1996.[162] Any party can propose amendments. If a majority of the parties support consideration of the proposal, a conference must be held. An amendment is adopted by the vote of a simple majority of the parties at the conference, provided no party casts a negative vote. The amendment enters into force for *all* parties thirty days after *all those parties that voted for the amendment* have deposited instruments of ratification.[163]

Duration and termination

Denunciation is a unilateral act by which a party seeks to terminate its participation in a treaty. Lawful denunciation of a *bilateral* treaty *terminates* it. Although denunciation is also used sometimes in relation to a multilateral treaty, the better term is *withdrawal*, since if a party leaves a multilateral treaty that will not normally result in its termination.

---

[160] ILM (1994) 968; B&B Docs. 645.
[161] For the FAO acceptance procedure, see Aust, p. 87.
[162] ILM (1996) 1443. Article VII is modelled on Article XV of the Chemical Weapons Convention 1993, 1974 UNTS 317 (No. 33757); ILM (1993) 800; UKTS (1997) 45.
[163] See further, Aust, pp. 218–9.

Express provisions

These days, most treaties contain specific and comprehensive provisions on duration and termination or withdrawal. There are a great variety.[164]

Indefinite duration with *un*conditional right to terminate

Many *bilateral* treaties make no provision for duration but include a termination clause that provides that either party may terminate the treaty by means of written notice to the other, termination taking effect on the expiry of a specified period.[165] Most *multilateral* treaties of unlimited duration will allow a party an unconditional right to withdraw. A UN treaty will usually provide that any party may withdraw by giving twelve months' written notice to the UN Secretary-General.

Indefinite duration with *conditional* right to withdraw

Article XVI of the Chemical Weapons Convention 1993 states that the Convention shall be of unlimited duration,[166] but provides for withdrawal, albeit subject to special conditions based on those in the Nuclear Non-Proliferation Treaty 1968 (NPT):[167]

> Each State Party shall, in exercising its national sovereignty, have the right to withdraw from this Convention *if it decides that extraordinary events, related to the subject matter of this Convention, have jeopardised the supreme interests of its country.* It shall give notice of such withdrawal 90 days in advance to all other States Parties, the Executive Council, the Depositary and the United Nations Security Council. *Such notice shall include a statement of the extraordinary events it regards as having jeopardised its supreme interests.* (Emphasis added)

Given that a treaty must be performed in good faith,[168] even though the above provision gives the withdrawing party a discretion, it must nevertheless have grounds for its decision. Furthermore, the extraordinary events must be 'related to the subject matter' of the Convention. The need

---

[164] See also Blix and Emerson, *The Treaty-Maker's Handbook*, Dobbs Ferry, NY, 1973, pp. 96–113.

[165] UK–US Treaty on Mutual Legal Assistance in Criminal Matters 1994/1997, 1967 UNTS 102 (No. 33632) and 2114 UNTS 392 (No. 36773); UKTS (1997) 14 and UKTS (2002) 8. For the special provision found in air services agreements, see Aust, pp. 225–6.

[166] 1974 UNTS 317 (No. 33757); ILM (1993) 804; UKTS (1997) 45.

[167] 729 UNTS 161 (No. 10485); ILM (1968) 809; UKTS (1970) 88; TIAS 6839 (Article X(1)).

[168] See p. 79 above.

for these elements is reinforced by the requirement to state what are the extraordinary events.[169]

Duration with conditions on termination

Conventions adopted within the International Labour Organization often require a lengthy period of notice and impose strict conditions on when notice can be given, for example that a member state cannot denounce until the convention has been in force for ten years, and, if it does not then denounce it within twelve months, it may not then denounce it until the expiration of a *further* ten-year period, and so on.[170]

Comprehensive clauses

When the parties are not sure how long they envisage the treaty lasting, they will often include a clause which provides for an initial term which can be extended, either expressly or tacitly, as well as for withdrawal. Such flexible provisions enable the parties to keep their options open, and are normally found in bilateral treaties. The Slovenia–United Kingdom Cultural Co-operation Agreement 1996 provides that it

> shall remain in force for a period of five years and *thereafter* shall remain in force until the expiry of six months from the date on which either Contracting Party shall have given written notice of termination to the other through the diplomatic channel.[171] (Emphasis added)

Termination or withdrawal by consent

A treaty may of course be terminated, or a party withdraw from it, at any time with the consent of all the other parties (Article 54(b)). This can be done even if the treaty provides for a minimum period of notice.[172]

No provision for termination or withdrawal

Some general law-making conventions are naturally silent as to their duration, but have provisions for denunciation or withdrawal. One cannot

---

[169] See Aust, pp. 227–8 on North Korea's first attempt to withdraw from the NPT. It announced its final withdrawal on 10 January 2003.

[170] See ILM (1987) 633–67.

[171] UKTS (1996) 14, Article 18. For a discussion of the meaning and effect of 'thereafter', see Aust, pp. 229–30.

[172] See the 1996 Exchange of Notes between Armenia and the United Kingdom to terminate the Soviet Union–United Kingdom Visa Abolition Agreement 1964, UKTS (1998) 57.

imply a right of denunciation or withdrawal unless it is established that the parties intended to admit the possibility of denunciation or withdrawal or a right of denunciation or withdrawal may be implied by the nature of the treaty (Article 56(1)). Since it is now very common to include provisions on withdrawal, when a treaty is silent it may be that much harder for a party to establish the grounds for the exception. The same may apply in the case of some codification conventions. In any event, in many cases the rules of such conventions reflect, or have become accepted as, customary law, and so withdrawal may make little or no legal difference.[173]

A party will not be able to withdraw from a treaty transferring territory or establishing a boundary (cf. Article 62(2)(a)).[174] Other treaties that are unlikely to be capable of withdrawal are treaties of peace or disarmament, and those establishing permanent regimes, such as for the Suez Canal.[175] Most human rights treaties do not provide for withdrawal.[176]

Termination or suspension for breach[177]

Like the violation of any other international obligation, breach of a treaty obligation may entitle another party to terminate or withdraw from the treaty or suspend its operation. If it causes harm to another party, that party may have the right to take reasonable countermeasures, or to present an international claim for compensation or other relief.[178]

Material breach

A 'material' breach of a bilateral treaty by one party entitles the other to invoke the breach as a ground for terminating the treaty or suspending its operation in whole or in part (Article 60(1)). The material breach must be of the treaty itself, not of another treaty or of rules of general international law.[179] Multilateral treaties pose different problems, since a material breach by one party may not affect all other parties, but the interests of the latter must also be taken into account.[180] Determining what is a 'material breach' will depend upon the circumstances of each case. Article 60(3) defines a material breach as a repudiation of the treaty not sanctioned by the Convention; or the violation of a provision 'essential

---

[173] See, p. 8 above.   [174] See Aust, pp. 234 and 307.   [175] See p. 363 below.
[176] See the Human Rights Committee's General Comment No. 26 (61), ILM (1995) 839.
[177] See generally S. Rosenne, *Breach of Treaty*, Cambridge, 1985.
[178] See pp. 407–27 below.
[179] *Gabčikovo*, *ICJ Reports* (1997), p. 7, para. 106; 116 ILR 1.
[180] See Article 60(2); and Aust, pp. 237–8.

to the accomplishment of the object and purpose of the treaty'.[181] This last quoted phrase is not the same as a 'fundamental' breach (see below). It can therefore be a breach of an important ancillary provision. If a party to the Chemical Weapons Convention (CWC) obstructs the conduct on its territory of international inspections to verify that it is complying with the CWC, this could well be a material breach since the inspection regime is an essential means of monitoring the effectiveness of the CWC.[182]

Fundamental breach

A fundamental breach is one that goes to the root of a treaty. Although it is not mentioned expressly in the Convention, the concept is contained within that of a material breach. On 1 September 1983, Soviet forces unlawfully shot down Korean Airlines flight 007. Several states with air services agreements with the Soviet Union unilaterally suspended them, for varying periods and with immediate effect, to prevent Aeroflot from landing in their territory. They were entitled to do so because the Soviet action undermined the fundamental basis of all air services agreements: that each party will ensure the safety of the others' civil aircraft.[183]

Supervening impossibility of performance

If an *object* which is indispensable for the execution of a treaty disappears permanently or is destroyed, thereby making performance of the treaty impossible, a party can invoke this as a ground for terminating or withdrawing from the treaty (Article 61(1)). There are few precedents. In *Gabikovo*, the International Court of Justice rejected this plea.[184] Possible examples of impossibility of performance are the submergence of an island (which global warming may now make a practical possibility) or the permanent drying-up of a river.

Fundamental change of circumstances (rebus sic stantibus)

The principle, recognised by domestic law, that a person may no longer be bound by a contract if there has been a fundamental change in the

---

[181] See the use of 'material breach' by the UNSC in e.g. UNSCR 1441 (2002), paras. 1 and 4.

[182] 1974 UNTS 317 (No. 33757); ILM (1993) 800; UKTS (1997) 45.

[183] See G. Richard, 'KAL 007: The Legal Fallout' (1983) *Annals of Air and Space Law* 146 at 150; K. Chamberlain, 'Collective Suspension of Air Services' (1983) ICLQ 616 at 630–1.

[184] *ICJ Reports* (1997), p. 7, paras. 102–3; ILM (1998) 162.

circumstances which existed at the time it was signed (in English common law, the doctrine of frustration),[185] has been acknowledged to apply also to treaties. Article 62 is in restrictive terms, strictly defining the (cumulative) conditions under which a change of circumstances may be invoked as a ground for terminating a bilateral treaty or withdrawing from a multilateral treaty. The principle has been invoked many times, and is recognised by treaties,[186] but it has not so far been *applied* by an international tribunal.[187] In *Gabčikovo*, the International Court of Justice rejected the argument that profound political changes, diminishing the economic viability of a project, progress in environmental knowledge and the development of new norms of international environmental law constituted a fundamental change of circumstances. The Court emphasised that the stability of treaty relations requires that Article 62 be applied only in exceptional cases.[188] In addition, Article 62(2) provides that the principle cannot be invoked if the treaty establishes a boundary.

Severance of diplomatic or consular relations

The severance of diplomatic or consular relations does not affect the legal relations established by a treaty, except in so far as those relations are indispensable for the application of the treaty (Article 63). This rule applies to both bilateral and multilateral treaties. In fact, the severance of diplomatic relations may not make a substantial difference.[189]

Outbreak of hostilities

The legal effect of the outbreak of hostilities between parties to a treaty is still uncertain,[190] and the only comprehensive treatment of the subject is now out-of-date.[191] The topic is outside the scope of the Convention (Article 73). But, it is clear that there is no presumption that hostilities, however intensive or prolonged, will necessarily have the effect of terminating or suspending the operation of treaties between the parties to the conflict.

---

[185] See *Halsbury's Laws of England*, 4th edn, re-issue, vol. 9(1), 1998, para. 897.
[186] Oppenheim, para. 651, n. 2.   [187] See Oppenheim, para. 651, n. 8.
[188] *ICJ Reports* (1997), p. 7, para. 104; ILM (1998) 162; 116 ILR 1.
[189] See p. 154 below.   [190] Oppenheim, para. 655.
[191] Oppenheim, 7th edn, vol. II, para. 99. See also McNair, pp. 693–728; and O'Connell, pp. 268–71.

The situation is somewhat analogous to that of severance of diplomatic relations, so that treaties may continue to apply except in so far as their operation is not possible during a period of hostilities. Certain commercial treaties, such as air services agreements, may be suspended. Treaties creating special regimes or fixing boundaries will continue in force. As between even the belligerent parties, multilateral treaties whose purpose is to regulate the affairs of belligerents (such as the Geneva Conventions 1949) will of course apply. Once the conflict is over, the parties will need to assess to what extent the hostilities have affected their treaty relations. They may have to go though a joint process similar to that which some states carry out on a succession of states.[192]

Can one validly withdraw from a treaty and immediately become a party again?

Trinidad and Tobago acceded to the International Covenant on Civil and Political Rights 1966 (ICCPR) in 1978, and to the Optional Protocol to it in 1980.[193] Parties to the Protocol agree to individuals communicating with (i.e. petitioning) the Human Rights Committee established by the Covenant. By 1998, Trinidad and Tobago had decided that this procedure was being increasingly 'abused' by prisoners sentenced to death. That year, it withdrew from the Protocol but at the same time deposited an instrument of reaccession. It included a reservation that the Human Rights Committee would not be competent to receive and consider communications from such prisoners. Guyana did the same in 1999. The stratagem may be seen as a single transaction, the only purpose of which was to enter a late (and therefore probably invalid) reservation.[194] Following objections to the reservation,[195] in 2000 Trinidad and Tobago withdrew from the Optional Protocol. Despite some objections, Guyana did nothing.

Desuetude

A treaty may be regarded as no longer in force by virtue of disuse[196] or obsolescence.[197] In 1990, Austria declared that certain provisions

---

[192] See, for example, p. 400 below.
[193] ICCPR and Optional Protocol, 1999 UNTS 171 (No. 14668); ILM (1967) 368; UKTS (1977) 6.
[194] See p. 67 above.
[195] See UN Multilateral Treaties, Ch. IV.5, note to Trinidad and Tobago.
[196] See McNair, pp. 516–18 and 681–91.
[197] But see H. Thirlway, 'The Law and Procedure of the International Court of Justice 1960–1989' (1992) BYIL 94–6.

of the Austrian State Treaty 1955[198] had become obsolete. There were no objections.[199] In Uppsala in April 2004, Sweden and the United Kingdom celebrated the 350th anniversary of the Treaty of Peace and Commerce concluded by Queen Christina and Oliver Cromwell. But, although the treaty was expressed to be of indefinite duration, some subsequent treaties like the Treaty of Rome, the WTO Agreement, etc., may have overtaken it.

Invalidity

This is the least important part of the law of treaties. An invalid treaty is a rarity, there being a natural presumption that a treaty is valid.

The violation of an internal law on competence to conclude treaties is probably the one basis for invalidity that could be of some practical importance. Given the overriding need for certainty in treaty relations, Article 46 provides that:

1. A state may not invoke the fact that its consent to be bound by a treaty has been expressed in violation of a provision of its internal law regarding competence to conclude treaties as invalidating its consent unless that violation was manifest and concerned a rule of its internal law of fundamental importance.
2. A violation is manifest if it would be objectively evident to any state conducting itself in the matter in accordance with normal practice and in good faith.

The negative formulation emphasises the exceptional character of the rule. There are a number of procedures in treaty-making, such as ratification, which enable a state to reflect fully before deciding whether or not to become a party, and to comply with any constitutional requirements. States are entitled to regard other states as having acted in good faith when its representatives express their consent to be bound. A state cannot claim that its consent has been expressed in violation of its internal law regarding competence to conclude treaties if the consent has been expressed by its head of state, head of government or foreign minister, since they each have indisputable authority to express consent (Article 7(2)). If a state seeks

---

[198] 217 UNTS 223 (No. 2249); UKTS (1957) 58; TIAS 3298.
[199] Kennedy and Specht, 'Austrian Membership in the European Communities' (1990) *Harvard International Law Journal* 407.

to invoke constitutional defects after the treaty has entered into force and after it has been carrying it out, it will be estopped (prevented) from asserting the invalidity of its consent.[200]

There could, however, be occasions when an overseas territory has concluded a treaty in its own name and without any authority from the parent state.[201] Whether the territory's lack of competence to conclude the treaty was manifest will depend on the circumstances, but a foreign ministry should be able to distinguish overseas territories from sovereign states.

Article 46 must be distinguished from Article 27, which provides that a party may not invoke the provisions of its internal law as justification for its failure to perform a treaty.[202] That rule will always apply, unless the treaty has been held to be invalid.

Articles 47–53 contain other grounds for invalidity, including error, fraud, corruption, coercion and conflict with a *jus cogens* norm.[203]

'Unequal treaties'

So-called 'unequal' or 'Leonine' treaties are those which are said to have been forced upon a weaker state by a stronger one. The Convention does not mention them, and the idea has never been accepted in international law. In discussing it, most writers have generally relied on certain nineteenth-century treaties, such as the so-called capitulation treaties,[204] and were heavily influenced by the effect of decolonisation, and to some extent by the views of the Soviet Union and other communist regimes of Eastern Europe.[205] It is a cornerstone of international law that all states are equal: that is equal before the law, even if not equal politically, economically or militarily. One has to accept that very few states are ever equal in power. To allow a state to avoid its treaty obligations on the ground of inequality would undermine the stability of treaty relations. The presumption that treaties are valid is not easy to rebut, especially if one cannot find facts to satisfy one of the many specific grounds of

---

[200] See p. 9 above.   [201] As to authority, see p. 58 above.   [202] See p. 79 above.

[203] See further Aust, pp. 253–6. For *jus cogens*, see p. 11 above.

[204] See McNair, pp. 514, 527–31 and 662–4; Chiu, 'Communist China's Attitude towards International Law' (1966) AJIL 239–67.

[205] Brownlie, p. 591, and compare with Oppenheim, pp. 1291–2. See also Koshevnikov, *International Law*, p. 281; Lester, 'Bizerta and the Unequal Treaty Theory' (1962) ICLQ 847; Sinha, 'Perspective of the Newly Independent States on the Binding Quality of International Law' (1965) ICLQ 123; Detter, 'The Problem of Unequal Treaties' (1966) ICLQ 1069; and Caflisch, 'Unequal Treaties' (1992) GYIL 52–80.

invalidity in the Convention, and there are very few examples of those grounds being successfully invoked.

The depositary

The exacting and thankless role of a depositary (*not* depository) is vital to the effective functioning of multilateral treaties, ensuring throughout their life that the necessary formalities and procedures are properly performed, recorded and notified. The rules are in Articles 76–79.

Designation of a depositary

The depositary may be a state or an international organisation. When it is a state, the duties should be carried out only by the foreign ministry, *never* subcontracted to another government department, or public or private agency. Being a depositary neither prevents the state becoming a party, nor obliges it to become one.

Most multilateral treaties are now adopted within an international organisation or at an international conference convened by one, and the chief administrative officer of the organisation will usually be designated the depositary. Other treaties are usually deposited with the state that hosted the conference.

The UN Secretary-General is the depositary of treaties adopted within the United Nations or at conferences convened by it. But just because all treaties have to be *registered* with the United Nations does not mean that the UN Secretary-General is willing to be the depositary of any treaty; registration and depositary functions are quite separate. He will agree to be the depositary of other treaties only if satisfied that they are intended to be open to all states. He is the most experienced depositary, over 500 treaties having been deposited with him. The *Summary of Practice of the Secretary-General as Depositary of Multilateral Treaties* (ST/LEG/7/Rev.1) is an invaluable guide on the depositary practice of the United Nations, and essential reading for any depositary. An up-to-date version is available at http://untreaty.un.org/english/treaty.asp.

Multiple depositaries

During the Cold War, for political reasons[206] certain treaties, such as the Partial Test-Ban Treaty 1963[207] had three depositaries: the Soviet Union,

[206] See p. 17 above.   [207] 480 UNTS 43 (No. 6964); UKTS (1964) 3; TIAS 5433.

the United Kingdom and the United States.[208] A state wishing to sign, ratify or accede to such treaties was (and still is) able to do so with any one of them.

Duty to act impartially

It is a fundamental principle that a depositary must at all times act impartially. A depositary state must keep a clear distinction between its views and national interests as a state and its functions as depositary. When a depositary receives an instrument from an entity which it does not recognise as a state, it must not seek to judge the validity of the instrument. Instead, it must notify interested states without comment. It is for the latter to form a view as to the legal position. But, where it is indisputable that an instrument is unacceptable, the duty of the depositary is simply to refuse it: if, for example, only UN Members are eligible to become parties to the treaty and the entity is obviously not one. The corollary of impartiality is that nothing that a state does as a depositary will prejudice it as a state.

Functions of the depositary

Subject to any provisions in the treaty or as may be agreed by the contracting states, the principal functions are listed in Article 77. Now that depositary functions are so well established and largely codified in the Convention, it is enough simply to designate a depositary on the understanding that the duties will be performed in accordance with the law of treaties and established practice.

Correction of errors

Due to their length and complexity, and the time pressure under which many are negotiated today, it is common for multilateral treaties to have textual errors: typographical, spelling, punctuation, numbering or cross-referencing, or a lack of concordance between the authentic language texts. There may be a simple drafting mistake, such as use of inconsistent terminology. But correcting anything that is more than an obvious 'physical' error or mistake of spelling or numbering may affect the substance.

---

[208] See Schwelb, 'The Nuclear Test Ban Treaty and International Law' (1964) AJIL 642 at 651–3; Oppenheim, vol. I, para. 50, n. 6; (1980) *UN Juridical YB* 207–8.

Attention may be drawn to an error by a state or the depositary. If there is a dispute as to whether there is an error, the problem may have to be decided in accordance with Article 48 (Error),[209] not Article 79 that deals with corrections only where there is no dispute as to the existence of an error. It is more likely, however, that there will be no dispute, merely a difference of view as to how to deal with the matter. Since the subject of corrections is discrete, the reader is referred to the text of Article 79 in which the procedure for correcting errors is set out in detail.

Registration and publication

Registration

Article 102(1) of the UN Charter requires that 'every treaty and every inter-national agreement' entered into by any Member of the United Nations is registered with the Secretariat as soon as possible, and then published by it. By the end of 2004, over 50,000 treaties had been registered, more than 1,000 being registered each year.

The term 'international agreement' embraces unilateral engagements of an international character. Thus declarations under Article 36(2) of the Statute of the International Court of Justice are registered.[210]

Regulations and procedure

Detailed regulations and guidance on registration have been adopted by the UN General Assembly in consultation with the Secretariat, and are explained in detail in the UN *Treaty Handbook*.[211] The main ones are:

- A treaty is not registered until it has *entered into force*. There is no time limit for registration.
- Registration may be done by any party and relieves all other parties of the obligation to register.
- All subsequent actions effecting changes in a treaty, such as amendment or termination, must also be registered.

To register a treaty, one must file certain documents with the Treaty Section of the Office of Legal Affairs of the United Nations. These are described in detail in the *Treaty Handbook*.

---

[209] See p. 108, n. 203 above.   [210] See p. 452 below.
[211] Access: http://untreaty.un.org/English/access.asp.

Associated documents

Provided it meets the basic conditions of the Regulations, any document lodged with the Secretariat for registration will be registered. Protocols, annexes, maps, etc. that are integral to the treaty must be registered and will be published with the treaty in the *United Nations Treaty Series* (UNTS) even if they are ephemeral. Care must be taken with MOUs.[212] Before any MOU referred to in a treaty, or associated with it, is supplied to the Secretariat, it is important that its non-treaty, and non-confidential, status has been confirmed in writing by all the states concerned.

Legal effect of registration or non-registration

Although the vast majority of instruments presented for registration are without doubt treaties, some MOUs are on rare occasions registered.[213] But the act of registration, as such, has no effect on the status of the instrument. It does not confer any status that the instrument does not already have, and a non-registered treaty is still a treaty.[214]

When there is a dispute as to status, the fact that the instrument has (or has not) been submitted for registration may, depending on the circumstances, be evidence of the intention of the states concerned as to its status. Registration by one party (which is usual) is evidence only that that party regards the instrument as a treaty. The lack of any protest about the registration is not necessarily evidence that another party accepts that the instrument is a treaty; states do not routinely monitor registrations. Equally, non-registration is, in itself, not evidence that the instrument is not a treaty. There are many reasons why what are obviously treaties are not registered: ignorance, inertia, lack of staff or simple oversight.

Article 102(2) of the UN Charter provides that no party to a treaty entered into by a UN Member, which has not been registered, may invoke it before any organ of the United Nations. However, the principal judicial organ of the United Nations, the International Court of Justice, does not apply the provision strictly, or perhaps at all. In *Qatar* v. *Bahrain*, the 1987 parallel Exchanges of Notes that the parties agreed constituted a treaty were invoked before the Court, which gave full regard to their terms even though they had not been registered.[215] Other organs of the United

---

[212] See p. 53 above.   [213] See Aust, p. 29.

[214] See generally D. Hutchinson, 'The Significance of the Registration or Non-Registration of an International Agreement in Determining Whether or Not It Is a Treaty' (1993) *Current Legal Problems* 257–90.

[215] *ICJ Reports* (1994), p.112; ILM (1994) 1461; 102 ILR 1.

Nations have on occasion allowed states to invoke an unregistered treaty; and it is unthinkable that the Security Council would ignore a treaty that is relevant to a matter of international peace and security just because it was not registered.

Publication

There is no international rule requiring a state to publish a treaty. Finding its text, especially that of a recent treaty, or even finding proof of a treaty's existence, is not at all easy, although the Internet has made it much easier.[216] The problem affects practitioners as much as scholars and students. Because a treaty cannot be published in the UNTS until it has entered into force and been registered, one has to rely heavily on national or commercial sources. However, the UN Treaty Collection website now has, in order of their deposit, *Texts of Recently Deposited Multilateral Treaties*. Although this is limited to those deposited with the UN Secretary-General, it does allow one to access certain treaties well before they enter into force.

Publication by the United Nations

Article 102 requires the Secretariat of the United Nations to publish treaties registered with it. They are published in the single series of the UNTS, although it no longer publishes in full (1) treaties of assistance and co-operation on financial, commercial, administrative or technical matters, (2) some ephemeral treaties, and (3) treaties that are published by a UN specialised or related agency (e.g. the IAEA). Publication is done in all the authentic languages of the treaties and, if these do not include English and French, with translations into those two languages. By the end of 2004, the UNTS consisted of over 2,100 paper volumes, containing over 50,000 treaties. Publication on paper takes some time, but all treaties that have been registered are available almost immediately at http://untreaty.un.org/English/acces.asp.

The UNTS Cumulative Index is now also available on the website, although it does not cover treaties registered in the last three to four years. Unfortunately, searching for a treaty on the website is not always that easy unless one knows that it has been registered and, if so, the registration number or at least the date of adoption or signature. Whenever

---

[216] R. Gardiner, 'Treaties and Treaty Materials: Role, Relevance and Accessibility' (1997) ICLQ 643–66; S. Rosenne, *Practice and Methods of International Law*, New York, 1984, pp. 48–51.

possible this book gives the registration number. But, if one has the reference to the volume of the UNTS in which the treaty is published, or an ILM reference, it may sometimes be quicker to look up the treaty on paper. Alternatively, a Google search will often produce the text.

The UN Secretary-General is also the depositary of over 500 multilateral treaties. The annual publication, *Multilateral Treaties Deposited with the Secretary-General* (in this book referred to as *UN Multilateral Treaties*), is an authoritative guide to the status of those treaties, containing as it does information on signatures, ratifications, accessions, successions, declarations, reservations and objections. It is published in English and French. Correct as of 31 December each year, it is normally published in March or April of the following year. A more up-to-date English version is available on the website. Access to the UN Treaty Collection website is free, but access to some parts of the collection, such as the UNTS, is by subscription only, but many libraries provide free access.

Publication by states

Whether, or when, a treaty is published by a state is dependent on its constitution, legislation and practice. Publication may be in an official gazette or journal, or in an official treaty series. In the United Kingdom, all treaties which the United Kingdom has concluded, and which are subject to ratification or a similar two-step procedure,[217] are published as Command Papers in the Country, European Communities or Miscellaneous Series. The United Kingdom is party to over 2,400 treaties. Since 1892, every treaty has been published in the *United Kingdom Treaty Series* (UKTS), once it has entered into force for the United Kingdom. The UKTS is not published in volumes, each treaty being published separately. Since 1974, only the English text of *multilateral* treaties has been published. Earlier British treaties dating back centuries can be found in *British and Foreign State Papers* (BSP). In contrast to some (chiefly monist) states, neither laying a treaty before Parliament, nor its publication in the UKTS has legal effect, neither procedure making the treaty part of the law of the United Kingdom.[218] Further information can be obtained by consulting www.fco.gov.uk/treaty/ or by e-mailing treaty.fco@gtnet.gov.uk.

Sources of treaty texts

International Legal Materials (ILM), published by the American Society of International Law six times a year since 1962, is an invaluable source

---

[217] See p. 81 above on the Ponsonby Rule.   [218] See p. 81 above.

of texts of many recently concluded treaties of general interest, whether bilateral or multilateral. It is often the easiest way to find a treaty whose entry into force is considerably delayed.

The Australian Treaties Library (www.lii.edu.au/au/other/dfat/) has the texts of all the treaties Australia has been party to since the early twentieth century, and many recent ones that are not yet in force. Texts of multilateral treaties and related material are also available through the Multilateral Project begun in 1992 at the Fletcher School of Law and Diplomacy at Tufts University, Massachusetts, USA (www.tufts.edu/ fletcher/multilaterals.html). The data includes a list of treaty secretariats with their Internet servers, which is useful for more up-to-date information about the status of treaties, lists of parties etc. Information on developments of interest to the more computer-literate lawyer is given regularly in *What's Online in International Law*, published in the newsletters of the American Society of International Law (www.asil.org). The website of the Lauterpacht Research Centre for International Law at Cambridge, England (www.law.cam.ac.uk/rcil/) has many useful links and is well worth a browse.

For the text of treaties concluded between 1648 (Peace of Westphalia) and 1919, the best source is the 231-volume *Consolidated Treaty Series* (CTS), although not all the treaties have been translated into English or French. For those concluded between 1919 and 1946, one should consult the 205-volume *League of Nations Treaty Series* (LNTS). For US treaties, there is the *Treaties and other International Acts Series* (TIAS) issued in single pamphlets, and the *United States Treaties and other International Agreements* (UST) published in annual volumes since 1950. The currently over 126 volumes of the *International Law Reports* (ILR), with its excellent index, are an important source for the decisions of courts and tribunals, international and national, on, *inter alia*, treaty questions.

Treaty indexes

Apart from the UN treaty publications, there are certain independent treaty indexes. A quite comprehensive listing of treaty indexes and texts of treaties is, rather surprisingly, that of the Los Angeles Public Library (www.lapl.org/guides/find_treaty.html). For the main multilateral treaties since 1856, there is Bowman and Harris, *Multilateral Treaties, Index and Status* and its cumulative supplements (1984–, London, Butterworths), Rohn, *World Treaty Index* (2nd edn, 1984, ABC-Clio), and Parry and Irwin, *Index-Guide to Treaties* (2nd edn, 1984, Dobbs Ferry,

NY, Oceana). The annual index to *Treaties and other International Acts Series* (TIAS) can also be a useful source.

For United Kingdom bilateral and multilateral treaties, there is Parry and Shepherd's four-volume *Index of British Treaties 1101 to 1988* (1970 and 1991, London, HMSO). The *United Kingdom Treaty Series* has annual indexes and quarterly *Supplementary Lists of Ratifications, Accessions, Withdrawals etc.*, that are not limited to acts by the United Kingdom. There is also I. Kavass (ed.), *US Treaty Index 1776–1990* (1988, Buffalo, NY, Hein & Co.)

Further reading on treaties

For succession to treaties, see pp. 393–400 below; and for hints on the drafting of treaties and on final clauses, see Aust, pp. 332–60.

6

Diplomatic privileges and immunities

Never has there been such a big embassy from here . . . I have six pages, four dwarfs, about twenty liveried servants, who will all be splendidly dressed, five trumpeters, musicians, a pastor, surgeons, physicians and a company of well-equipped soldiers.[1]

Denza, *Diplomatic Law: Commentary on the Vienna Convention on Diplomatic Relations*, 2nd edn, Oxford, 1998

Oppenheim. *Oppenheim's International Law*, 9th edn, London, 1992, pp. 1053–131

Satow's Guide to Diplomatic Practice, 5th edn, London, 1979

There are now 183 states parties to the Vienna Convention on Diplomatic Relations 1961 (in this chapter, 'the Convention'). Even for the handful of non-parties, the Convention now represents an authoritative statement of the law, and as such is relied on heavily by the International Court of Justice.[2] Nevertheless, the manner in which the Convention is interpreted and applied can vary to some degree from state to state. All members of diplomatic missions and their local legal advisers therefore need to familiarise themselves with the practice and procedures of the receiving state, which will often publish guidance.

(In this chapter, references to specific Articles are to those of the Convention, unless otherwise indicated.)

Since diplomacy is the means by which a state conducts relations with other states, the Convention plays a crucial role by regulating the establishment of permanent bilateral diplomatic missions to represent the interests of the state and the protection of its nationals, and the privileges and immunities accorded to missions and their staff to give them the

---

[1] Franz Lefort, writing as nominal head of the 1697–8 Russian diplomatic mission to Western Europe in which Peter the Great travelled incognito, quoted in L. Hughes, *Russia in the Age of Peter the Great*, New Haven, 1998, p. 23.

[2] *Case Concerning US Diplomatic and Consular Staff in Tehran (USA v. Iran)*, ICJ Reports (1980), p. 3, paras. 45–55; 61 ILR 502.

necessary freedom and security to carry out their work. Other missions and entities, and persons connected with them, also enjoy certain privileges and immunities. These are described at p. 155 (special missions), p. 156 (consular posts) and p. 199 (international organisations), below.

The establishment of diplomatic relations and permanent diplomatic missions

The establishment of diplomatic relations and permanent diplomatic missions requires the consent of both states (Article 2). They must be sovereign states and must recognise each other as such.[3] Recognition is usually soon followed by the establishment of diplomatic relations, and sometimes the establishment of relations constitutes the act of recognition.

The two states are known by the self-explanatory terms *sending state* and *receiving state*. The term *diplomatic mission* is generic. Most are called embassies, but some have titles such as Libyan People's Bureau. As between the fifty-three Commonwealth states, their diplomatic missions are, for historical reasons,[4] called high commissions, and their ambassadors are high commissioners.

Even when diplomatic relations have been achieved, permanent diplomatic missions do not have to be set up, or at least not in both states. If the two states do not have much in the way of mutual interests, neither may feel the need to have permanent missions, particularly if both states are small with limited resources. Alternatively, only one of the states may set up a permanent mission, provided the other state is content to conduct diplomatic relations mostly via that mission. This is not uncommon for newly independent states. Diplomatic relations can also be conducted by accrediting to the receiving state the head of the sending state's permanent diplomatic mission to a third state, or assigning members of his diplomatic staff to represent the sending state. He or they will then visit the receiving state as necessary (Article 5). This practice has been used even more in recent years because of the large increase in the number of states and their lack of money. Relations can also be conducted by *ad hoc* diplomacy, by special missions,[5] or in contacts between permanent missions to international organisations, in particular between permanent missions to the United Nations.

---

[3] For states and recognition, see p. 17 above.
[4] Satow, paras. 41.26–41.28.   [5] See p. 155 below.

The functions of a diplomatic mission

The main functions of a diplomatic mission are described in Article 3(1): representing the sending state, protecting its interests and those of its nationals, negotiating with the receiving state, reporting what goes on in the receiving state and promoting friendly relations, which includes providing the local population with information about the sending state. The list is not exhaustive, and the customary functions include also cooperation with the receiving state in trade promotion, and financial, economic, scientific, defence and cultural matters and, increasingly, prevention of crime (in particular drug-trafficking and terrorism) – in fact, anything which the two states wish to do together through the means of their respective missions.

These days, performing consular functions is an important role for most diplomatic missions, as expressly recognised both by Article 3(2) of the Convention and by Article 2(2) of the Vienna Convention on Consular Relations 1963 (the 'Vienna Consular Convention'),[6] which provides that the establishment of diplomatic relations implies consent to the establishment of consular relations. When a member of a diplomatic mission performs a consular function, he does so in accordance with the Vienna Consular Convention but retains all his diplomatic privileges and immunities. This is important since consular and diplomatic functions overlap to some extent, particularly in the protection of one's nationals, and consular privileges and immunities are limited. When a member of a diplomatic mission performs consular functions, he should generally deal with the local authorities, police, judicial, etc., rather than central government (Article 70(3) of the Vienna Consular Convention). To avoid misunderstandings as to the nature of his duties, it is desirable that he should be given a consular appointment in addition to his diplomatic post (e.g. First Secretary and Consul), and both appointments be notified to the receiving state.

There are, of course, grey areas. Some missions may get involved in *commercial activities*. Even when these activities can be regarded as proper functions of the mission (buying large quantities of foodstuffs for the sending state), the transactions may not enjoy state immunity.[7] Trading activities, such as selling airline tickets or charging fees for language lessons, are generally not regarded as diplomatic functions. Although the promotion of tourism, in itself, is not outside those functions if done

---

[6] 596 UNTS 261 (No. 8638); UKTS (1973) 14; TIAS 6820.   [7] See pp. 165 *et seq* below.

within the mission as part of its role of providing information about the sending state, a separate tourist office, even if it does not trade, does not perform a diplomatic function and is therefore is not part of the premises of the mission (see below).[8] It is not unusual for a mission to establish a *school* for the children of the members of the mission. Its premises may properly be regarded as part of the mission, and the teachers members of the administrative and technical staff. However, problems can arise if the school also admits children of nationals of the sending state who are not members of the mission, children of members of other missions or children of nationals of the receiving state. Much will depend on the attitude of the receiving state. The more the school becomes a commercial operation, the more the receiving state is likely to question its diplomatic status. However, the receiving state may agree to treat the school as part of the mission: see Article 47(b).[9]

The members of the mission

The members of a diplomatic mission are the head of mission, the diplomatic staff, the administrative and technical staff ('A&T staff') and the service staff. The head of mission and the diplomatic staff are defined in Article 1(e) as 'diplomatic agents', and enjoy the highest scale of privileges and immunities; the other members of the mission are on lower scales of privileges and immunities.

The head of mission has to be expressly accepted by the receiving state before he can take up his post. This is done by obtaining the *agrément* of the receiving state. No form is prescribed, although something in writing is usual and desirable. No reasons have to be given for refusing *agrément*, although if they are given they should relate to the person rather than his government. The receiving state can require its prior approval (not *agrément*) of military, naval or air attachés (Article 7).

The sending state may 'freely appoint' the other members of the mission, who also do not have to be members of the diplomatic service. There is no requirement for prior or subsequent approval by the receiving state. Nor can it require that locally engaged staff be chosen from a list provided

---

[8] See *Diplomatic Immunities and Privileges: Government Report on Review of the Vienna Convention on Diplomatic Relations and Reply to 'The Abuse of Diplomatic Immunities and Privileges'*, published by the British Government in 1985, Cmnd 9497, para. 39. For extracts, see (1985) BYIL 437–53.

[9] See p. 154 below.

by it; nor require that the receiving state employ someone it does not want.[10]

The foreign ministry of the receiving state must be notified, in advance where possible, of all appointments and of the arrivals and departures of members of the mission. The engagement and discharge of local staff must also be notified. Notifications should clearly indicate whether the person is a diplomatic agent, a member of the A&T staff or service staff by describing the post (e.g. first secretary, communications officer, driver). Members of the family and private servants must also be notified. In doing so, a sending state must naturally act in good faith and not abuse the scheme of the Convention by notifying, say, an embassy accountant as a diplomatic agent, since he does not perform duties of a diplomatic nature. In case of abuse, the receiving state could take action under Article 9 to have the member of staff removed (see below). In case of persistent abuse, it could limit the number of mission staff in accordance with Article 11 (see below). In most cases, the foreign ministry will raise the matter informally with the mission. If the mission cannot provide an acceptable explanation, it will either have to withdraw the notification or risk the receiving state using its powers to force withdrawal.

Failure to notify a person entitled to privileges and immunities (and consequent omission from the local diplomatic list) will not affect the person's entitlement, which takes effect automatically on arrival in the receiving state to take up post (unless he is already there, in which case entitlement only begins once the appointment has been notified (Article 39(1))). Nevertheless, since the freedom of a sending state to appoint the members of its mission requires the receiving state to exempt the arriving members from immigration restrictions, failure to notify in advance could result in inconvenience.

But there is no presumption of diplomatic immunity: it must be established in each case, and a diplomatic passport is *not* conclusive evidence of diplomatic status.[11] Whether a person is a member of a mission is essentially a matter of fact. Any problem can usually be resolved by discussions with the receiving state. When the issue is raised in connection with legal proceedings, the courts of the receiving state will often look to its foreign ministry for guidance. Failure to notify a person, or a significant delay in doing so, may make it more difficult to convince a court or the foreign ministry that the person is really a member of the mission. In practice,

[10] See Denza, pp. 50–5.   [11] See p. 141 below.

such difficulties are more likely to arise when the person who has not been notified has been locally engaged, or is involved in an activity which is not obviously a function of a diplomatic mission,[12] or claims to be a member of the family of a member of the mission.[13]

Members of the *diplomatic* staff should be nationals of the sending state, although, exceptionally, they can be nationals of the receiving state if the latter agrees (Article 8). The receiving state can apply the same rule to nationals of third states who are not nationals of the sending state. The rule does not apply to the rest of the staff of the mission, many of whom are likely to be local nationals, for reasons of convenience and cost.

Persona non grata

Article 9 confers on the receiving state the unqualified power to require the removal of any member of the mission. For a diplomatic agent the receiving state notifies the sending state that he is *persona non grata*, and for all other cases that he is 'not acceptable'. The notification can be done at any time, even before the person's arrival in the receiving state. The sending state is then obliged either to recall the person or to terminate his functions with the mission. If it refuses or fails to remove him within a reasonable time, the receiving state can refuse to recognise him as a member of the mission so that he will no longer enjoy any privileges or immunities. These powers are essential, and are no more than a reflection of the fact that diplomatic and A&T staff enjoy complete immunity from the criminal jurisdiction of the receiving state and the inviolability of their person and residence. Under Article 39(2), the person is entitled to have a 'reasonable' time in which to leave, retaining his privileges and immunities until then. Unless the circumstances are quite exceptional, forty-eight hours is the minimum reasonable period, seven to fourteen days being normal.

However, specific use of the Article 9 procedure is rare, and done more for political purposes. In practice, it is usually enough for the receiving state to request the recall of the person within a specified number of days, and this is normally done without trouble. When a serious offence has been committed, the sending state may have the choice of waiving the person's immunity or withdrawing him. Persistent flouting of parking regulations is a good reason for requiring withdrawal.

[12] See p. 119 above.   [13] See p. 147 below.

But no reasons for demanding recall have to be given by the receiving state. There may be no conclusive proof of unacceptable conduct, or there may be a difference between the two states as to its true nature or purpose. In practice, reasons are often given, although sometimes wrapped up in diplomatic obfuscation ('activities incompatible with his status', i.e. spying). Whether the receiving state makes the reasons public depends largely on whether the conduct was purely personal, such as drunken driving, or had been authorised or condoned by the sending state, such as subversion, terrorism or espionage.

Size and composition of the mission staff

In the absence of a specific agreement with the sending state, the receiving state can require that the number of staff of the mission 'be kept within limits considered by [the receiving state] to be reasonable and normal, having regard to circumstances and conditions in the receiving state and to the needs of the particular mission' (Article 11). Similarly, the receiving state can also refuse to accept officials of a particular category, such as defence attachés, provided this is done for all diplomatic missions in the receiving state. Articles 13–20 deal with vital protocol matters such as credentials, precedence and flags, so need not detain us.[14]

The premises of the mission

The 'premises of the mission' are defined in Article 1(i) to include all the buildings and land, irrespective of ownership (they may well be leased), used for the purposes of the mission, including the residence of the head of mission, which today is usually physically separate from the chancery. The Convention does not require missions to be at the seat of government, although they usually are. Some receiving states (e.g. Switzerland) require them to be there. In order to control the location of missions, some states have legislation governing the use of property for the premises of a diplomatic mission. The Diplomatic and Consular Premises Act 1987 requires the consent of the British Government before property can acquire the status of premises of a diplomatic mission. A certificate issued under the Act is conclusive evidence of whether land is or was at any time the premises of a mission. The sending state may establish offices forming

---

[14] See Denza, pp. 86–106 and, where necessary, the references in it to Satow.

part of the mission in another part of the receiving state (including an overseas territory), only with the prior express consent of the receiving state (Article 12).

Facilitating the acquisition of premises for the mission

The receiving state must either 'facilitate the acquisition, in accordance with its laws, by the sending state of premises necessary for its mission or assist the latter in obtaining accommodation in some other way' (Article 21). It must also assist 'where necessary' in obtaining suitable accommodation for the members of the mission. Although the receiving state must therefore provide administrative assistance, it does not have to go as far as actually providing premises. Nor does it have to change its laws, which may prohibit aliens from owning land or restrict the choice of areas in which missions may be located. Sometimes states will conclude a treaty to provide for the reciprocal provision of land for new mission premises and regulate the construction of the premises.[15]

Help with facilities for the mission

There is not much substance to the obligation in Article 25 for the receiving state to accord 'full facilities' for the performance of the functions of the mission. Assistance in obtaining telephone lines, or permits for alterations or extensions to the premises, are examples of the kind of assistance that can be expected. But it is only 'assistance'. Since Article 41 requires all persons enjoying privileges and immunities to respect local laws and regulations, Article 25 cannot be invoked to avoid normal planning controls and licensing requirements. There is certainly no obligation on the receiving state to ensure the provision of public utility services (electricity, gas, telephone, etc.) if the mission has not paid its bills. Article 25 is usually invoked to bolster a request or complaint based on a more specific provision of the Convention.[16]

Also, requests for assistance must be reasonable. It is doubtful if the receiving state is required to provide a certain number of exclusive free parking places in the road outside the mission or residence. Given the traffic problems in cities today, to insist on such a privilege could

---

[15] See the Russia–UK Agreements of 1996, UKTS (1997) 1 and 2.
[16] See Denza, p. 167.

be unreasonable. The provision of parking spaces is a courtesy, not an obligation.[17] Nevertheless, even in cities with a serious traffic problem, a small number can usually be found for each mission; and these days there may be security reasons for the senior staff of some missions to be able to park near to the entrance of the mission and those guarding it. No doubt the provision of parking spaces is also influenced by considerations of reciprocity; the receiving state may have a problem in arranging for the allocation of spaces, but will want to ensure that it has sufficient for its own mission in the sending state.

Inviolability of the premises of the mission

It is sometimes said that a diplomatic mission is 'foreign soil'. This may be correct culturally, but not legally. The land on which the mission premises stand remains part of the territory of the receiving state, and buying or leasing the land has to be done under local law.[18] But Article 22(1) states the fundamental principle that the premises of the mission are inviolable: agents of the receiving state may not enter without the consent of the head of mission. However, if a mission is located in part of a commercial office building (quite common these days), those parts that it shares with non-diplomatic tenants will not enjoy inviolability. The essence of inviolability is freedom from interference, coupled with a special duty to protect (see below). Inviolability is an *absolute* rule, since any exception to it could be abused by a receiving state.[19] In contrast to consular premises,[20] the prohibition on entry applies even in an emergency. If an ambassador would rather his embassy burn down than call in the local fire service, all the receiving state can do is to try to persuade him to let them in.

Diplomatic missions with chanceries and residences in historic buildings in prime locations can now be an obstacle to the building of highways and shopping malls. But ambassadors need not worry. The mission cannot be required to move. Even if negotiations with the receiving state do not resolve the matter, inviolability means that the mission cannot be made to move or to give up part of its land even if suitable alternatives are offered free.

Inviolability has various other consequences.

---

[17] See p. 12 above on comity.
[18] See *Radwan* v. *Radwan* [1972] 3 All ER 1026; 55 ILR 579.
[19] See the examples in Denza, pp. 116 *et seq.*   [20] See pp. 157–8 below.

Police action

Since 1961, there have been examples of police entering diplomatic missions without permission in pursuance of their normal duties, in particular pursuing suspected criminals. But, even if the police were unaware of the status of the premises (unlikely in most cases), the intrusion would amount to a breach of its inviolability. There is, however, a possibility that in very exceptional circumstances police may enter the premises without consent if its occupants, whether diplomats or terrorists, clearly pose a real and immediate danger to human life *outside* the premises.[21] In all other cases, the receiving state has the remedies of *persona non grata* or severing diplomatic relations.

Service of legal process

By legal process is meant writs, summonses and suchlike, which can usually be served either in person or by post. Personal service on the premises of the mission and the residences of members of the mission would be a breach of their inviolability, and therefore ineffective. If service by post is attempted in ignorance of the prohibition, it does not amount to a breach, but it is equally ineffective. In theory, the sending state's consent could be given to effect service on the premises, but this in unlikely. In practice, if a mission wishes to allow service it can, if local law allows, authorise its local lawyers to accept service, if necessary reserving its position on immunity from jurisdiction.

For the purposes of Article 22, it does not matter whether the process is addressed to a member of the mission, the mission itself or the sending state, the attempt to serve will be ineffective. The distinction is, however, important for the legal proceedings. It is important to know if one should bring a claim against a member of the mission or against the sending state.[22] A mistake could be serious.

Immunity from jurisdiction

Article 22(3) makes the premises of the mission, and all property on it, immune from search, requisition, attachment or execution. Now that a state is less able successfully to assert state immunity, the protection given

---

[21] For a discussion of this dilemma in the case of the Libyan Mission siege in London in 1984 and the possibility of justifying entry on the basis of self-defence, see Denza, pp. 124–6.
[22] See p. 138 below.

by this provision is a valuable safeguard. What is unclear is the extent to which local courts can exercise jurisdiction in relation to the premises of the mission without breaching the Convention.[23] Much will depend on whether the law of state immunity of the receiving state allows claims concerning the property of foreign states; and, if it does, to what extent they can be made with respect to the premises of a mission. In principle, the holding of land by a state for the purposes of a diplomatic mission is an act *jure imperii* (performed in a governmental or public, rather than commercial or private, capacity) and should be protected by state immunity. But, under section 16(1)(b) of the (UK) State Immunity Act 1978, a state is accorded immunity from legal actions concerning '*title* to or its *possession* of property used for the purposes of a diplomatic mission' (which wording reflects the immunity from civil jurisdiction for a 'real action' accorded to a diplomatic agent by Article 31(1)(a) of the Convention). Since these terms seem to be directed more to questions of ownership and the right to occupy, it may be that proceedings for more mundane, but nevertheless important, matters such as arrears of rent or breach of covenant are permissible. But even if successful, judgment against the state would not disrupt the working of the mission since the judgment could not be enforced by execution against the premises of the mission or property on them.[24]

Bank account of the mission

This leaves the question of whether a judgment against a sending state can be executed against the bank account of its diplomatic mission. The point is not answered by the Convention, since immunity under Article 22(3) does not extend to property outside the premises of the mission, other than vehicles (see below). However, it is now established from a series of judgments in various countries that the bank account of a diplomatic mission enjoys immunity; to inquire into whether some of the funds represent the proceeds of commercial activity, or were to be used for such activity, would be to interfere in the affairs of the mission.[25]

Protection from intrusion or damage

The inviolability of the mission premises is reinforced by the special duty placed on the receiving state to take 'all appropriate steps' to protect the

---

[23] See Denza, pp. 129–31.   [24] See p. 125 above.
[25] Denza, pp. 131–4 and 166–7. See also p. 173, n. 45 below.

premises against any intrusion or damage (Article 22(2)). If the mission is particularly vulnerable, its protection against intrusion may require a twenty-four-hour police or military guard. It also requires the receiving state to expel intruders if the head of mission so requests. But his consent has not always been sought before action was taken by the receiving state, most conspicuously in the case of the unilateral action by the Peruvian Government to lift the siege of the Japanese ambassador's residence in Lima in 1996. This was a breach of the inviolability of the residence and disregarded the primary responsibility of the ambassador and his government for the well-being of all persons in the building.

Although the duty under Article 22(2) is limited to 'all appropriate steps', when damage has been caused to mission premises, whether from outside or by intruders, in practice the receiving state pays compensation even if it has not admitted any fault or it would not be easy to prove fault. In return, receiving states expect, and sometimes make it a condition of payment, that sending states accord reciprocal treatment. It has been the long-standing UK practice to make an *ex gratia* payment for such damage, although there could be special circumstances when this might not be justified, for example a terrorist attack. Given the nature of such an attack and the near impossibility of preventing it, unless the receiving state had been alerted to the impending attack and had done nothing, it may not be reasonable to expect it to pay compensation. Accordingly, the United Kingdom now advises missions to insure themselves against damage, including from terrorist attacks.

Disturbance of the peace of the mission and impairment of its dignity

Article 22(2) also places a duty on the receiving state to prevent any disturbance of the peace of the mission or the impairment of its dignity. This duty is fraught with difficulty, particularly for a receiving state which is at an advanced stage of democracy where the freedoms of speech and assembly are jealously guarded. Balancing them with the duty under the Convention is not always easy, but there is no requirement to insulate a mission from the free and peaceful expression of views. Some states have quite specific and detailed laws or regulations on what demonstrators may and may not do. Others, including the United Kingdom, deal with demonstrations on a case-by-case basis, leaving it largely to the police to decide what is appropriate in the particular circumstances. Happily, in London the police have a wealth of experience on which to draw. The police must ensure that the work of the mission is not disrupted, that staff are not put in fear, and that both staff and visitors can come and go freely. This will often mean that the demonstrators are kept on the opposite side of the street from the embassy. (A similar policy should also be followed if a demonstration is held outside the foreign ministry, given that members of missions need to have unimpeded physical access to it.) Very noisy demonstrations are frequent today with the use of powerful loudhailers. Allowing them too near to a mission is difficult to reconcile with the duty under the Convention.

Asylum

The Convention does not deal with the question of whether, and in what circumstances, a diplomatic mission may grant diplomatic asylum. All that needs to be said here is that, even if it is wrongly granted, the receiving state must, of course, respect the inviolability of the mission premises. (Diplomatic asylum is dealt with at p. 187 below.)

When inviolability of mission premises begins and ends

Although Article 39 has detailed rules on when the privileges and immunities of members of a mission begin and end, the Convention does not do the same for the premises of the mission. Their mere acquisition will, in itself, not make them 'premises of the mission'. But once the premises are ready to be occupied, they probably then become premises of the mission and will continue so even if later they have to be vacated for refurbishment. They will cease to have their special status once they cease to be used for the purposes of the mission, which is essentially a question of fact, and which in practice is often a matter of negotiation with the receiving state. The receiving state can always agree to treat the site on which new buildings for the mission are being constructed as premises of the mission.[26]

Some states have legislation or administrative rules on the matter. The UK Diplomatic and Consular Premises Act 1987[27] requires express consent before property can be regarded as premises of the mission. Consent can be withdrawn in certain circumstances, in particular if the premises have been abandoned.

---

[26] See the Russia–UK Agreement of 1996, UKTS (1997) 1, Article 6.
[27] For the note about it circulated to all diplomatic missions, see (1987) BYIL 1987 541.

Exemption of mission premises from taxation

It is a basic principle that one state does not tax another, since this would amount to taking property of the latter and anyway would be almost impossible to enforce. Accordingly, the sending state and the head of mission are exempt from all dues and taxes, national, regional or municipal, in respect of the premises of the mission, whether owned or leased, other than such as represent payment for 'specific services rendered' (Article 23). Thus if the sending state owns the mission premises, it is liable to pay only that portion of local taxes which represents payment for such services, that is to say general services which are financed from taxes and which are clearly beneficial to all missions, such as street maintenance, lighting and cleansing, and fire services (the so-called beneficial portion). Services which missions are less likely to benefit from are public education and libraries, and welfare services. Although missions do benefit from the services of the police, since under Article 22 the sending state has a duty to provide protection, the mission is not liable to pay for them. The beneficial portion is not based on the amount of services actually used each year, since given their nature that would be impossible to calculate, but on the amount spent on the beneficial services relative to that spent on the other services. How this is applied in practice will vary from state to state.

The exemption does not, however, apply to dues and taxes payable under the law of the receiving state by persons contracting with the sending state or the head of mission (Article 23(2)). Thus, if a lease provides that property taxes paid by the landlord are added to, or included in, the rent, the sending state cannot claim exemption. But the exemption will apply if under the lease the mission is otherwise liable to pay the taxes direct to the authorities.

Inviolability of mission archives

The 'archives and documents' (documents) of the mission are inviolable at all times wherever they may be (Article 24). The term documents has to be given a wide definition to include at least all items included in the definition of 'consular archives' in Article 1(1)(k) of the Vienna Convention on Consular Relations 1963.[28] Today, it would also include documents held by electronic means, such as those stored on computer hard and floppy

---

[28] 596 UNTS 261 (No. 8638); UKTS (1973) 14; TIAS 6820.

disks, CD-ROMs, memory sticks and whatever other new information-storage methods are invented. The inviolability is extensive. It does not depend on the documents being in the custody of a member of the mission or being readily identifiable as mission documents (no mission stamp is required), even when outside the mission. Inviolability lasts indefinitely. Closure of the mission, severance of diplomatic relations or armed conflict make no difference (see Article 45). The receiving state has an obligation to protect the inviolability of the documents in all circumstances and to return them immediately if they have been lost or stolen. If the documents are disclosed (other than by the sending state) during legal proceedings, it is the duty of the court to respect their inviolability and to ensure they are returned. This would be so even if the sending state is the defendant and state immunity does not apply to the proceedings. If, however, a member of a mission had communicated a document to a third party as part of his functions, it loses its inviolability.

Means of transport

As with property *inside* a mission's premises, its means of transport have immunity from search, requisition, attachment or execution wherever they are (Article 22(3)). This does not amount to inviolability, but stopping and searching by the police of a motor vehicle is prohibited, as is wheel-clamping, which is a breach of immunity from criminal jurisdiction. But the vehicle may be towed away if it is causing a serious obstruction, the driver cannot be traced and it cannot just be moved out of the way. No charges can be imposed, inconvenience being the only penalty. These points apply equally to the personal vehicle of a member of a mission who enjoys immunity from criminal jurisdiction.

Freedom of movement

Subject to its laws and regulations concerning special zones entry into which is prohibited or regulated for reasons of national security, the receiving state must ensure to all members of the mission freedom of movement and travel in its territory (Article 26). Such freedom is essential to enable the members of the mission to report properly on conditions in the receiving state and to protect its nationals. Any zones should therefore not be so extensive as to render freedom of movement and travel illusory.

Freedom of communication

Article 27(1) states the fundamental principle that the receiving state must permit and protect 'free communication' by a diplomatic mission for all official purposes. 'Free' does not mean without payment, but rather unrestricted communication between the mission and the sending state and its other missions, its nationals wherever they are, missions of third states and international organisations. The means by which this can be done is, however, circumscribed by the rest of the provision. Thus the right for the mission to use 'all appropriate means' is limited to communications with its government and its other missions and consulates. For this purpose, the appropriate means include the use of diplomatic couriers and messages in code and cipher. But in communicating with third parties, including their own nationals, missions may not use such means. Wireless transmitters can, and of course do, transmit messages in code and cipher, but they cannot be used for transmissions to third parties. Moreover, the installation and use of a transmitter (but not of telephone lines by which coded faxes and e-mails can be sent) requires the consent of the receiving state, but once this has been given the use of the transmitter is not subject to inspection or other intrusive regulation. However, both sending and receiving states have obligations to the International Telecommunications Union (ITU) to ensure that transmitters do not cause harmful interference with other transmissions. Where the receiving state has laws and regulations regarding compliance with ITU requirements, the mission should therefore comply with them (see Article 41(1) and (3)).

Inviolability of official correspondence

Article 27(1) confers inviolability on 'all correspondence relating to the mission and its functions'. Without the consent of the sending state, it cannot be used in evidence in the local courts or be opened by the receiving state. Unfortunately, this apparently simple formula is unclear as to its scope. All correspondence sent by the mission is covered, but it is not clear if correspondence to the mission from its own government or its other missions is also covered. This has less practical importance today when sensitive messages are either sent by electronic means in code or cipher or by diplomatic bag.

The diplomatic bag

The diplomatic bag used to be the best means of ensuring secure communications between a sending state and its diplomatic missions. Even after secure wireless or telephonic transmissions became widely used for diplomatic communications, the diplomatic bag was still much used for sending lengthy classified documents and sensitive items of equipment. Today, the ability to send even voluminous texts by secure fax or e-mail has not made the diplomatic bag redundant, but it is certainly used less frequently. Nevertheless, problems remain in applying the rules laid down in the Convention. At root is a dilemma: how to balance the interests of the sending state in a secure means of communication, against the concern of the receiving state that the inviolability of bag should not be abused. The problem is complicated by the simple fact that each state is both a sending state and a receiving state.

What is a diplomatic bag?

Most diplomatic bags are still mailbags made of stout woven fabric, although no doubt human rights norms now prevent them being sewn by prisoners. But the bag does not have to be a sack or pouch. Because it can be used for heavy and bulky items, such as communications equipment and computers – even building materials – the bag can be a freight container carried on a lorry, although the vehicle itself would not usually be accepted as a bag.

To have the status of a diplomatic bag, 'the packages constituting the diplomatic bag must bear visible external marks of their character' (Article 27(4)). Although it is for each sending state to inquire into the precise requirements of the receiving state as to the marking of diplomatic bags, international practice normally requires (1) the bag to be sealed with a wax, metal (commonly lead) or plastic official seal of the sending state or its diplomatic mission, and (2) a label (tied or stuck to it) addressed to the mission or the foreign ministry and bearing an official stamp.

The diplomatic bag must be clearly distinguished from packages which, although destined for, or sent from, a mission, do not carry the necessary marks of a diplomatic bag. Such packages come within Article 36(1)(a).[29]

What may the diplomatic bag contain?

Article 27(4) requires the bag to contain 'only diplomatic documents or articles intended for official use'. This is reinforced by Article 41(1) and (2), which places a duty on the members of the mission to respect the

---

[29] See p. 146 below.

laws and regulations of the receiving state and not to allow the mission to be used 'in any manner incompatible with the functions of the mission'. Thus the use of the bag to send narcotic drugs, weapons and explosives is an abuse of the Convention and local law, although some receiving states do permit the use of arms for personal defence. Nevertheless, provided the bag bears the correct marks evidencing that it is a diplomatic bag, the fact that it contains prohibited items will *not* affect its status.

Prohibition on opening or detaining the diplomatic bag

Article 27(3) prohibits the bag from being 'opened or detained'. Although not expressed in terms of inviolability, that is its effect. Except in the exceptional cases described below, a receiving state must never open a bag or impede its passage. Even if it has grounds for suspecting that its inviolability is being abused, the receiving state has no right to open it or to require it to be returned to the sending state or the mission. (Requiring it to be sent back is the formula in Article 35(3) of the Vienna Consular Convention and was one of several suggested formulas in the 1980s to replace Article 27(3), but no agreement could be reached.)[30] There are, however, occasions when a receiving state claims the right to detain, refuse admittance to, or even open, an incoming bag that it claims to be suspect. The reaction of the sending state will depend on the circumstances, but as a last resort the sending state may in practice have no option but to return the bag to its foreign ministry. Before doing so, it should of course firmly remind the receiving state that if it persists in its illegal demand it risks reciprocal action (see Article 47(2)(a)).[31]

There are cases, fortunately extremely rare, where the circumstances are so exceptional that the receiving state may feel compelled, in the genuine interests of protecting human life or its national security, to insist on a bag being opened against the objections of the sending state. Such cases will occur only when there are very strong grounds for believing that the bag contains a human being, a corpse or explosives.[32]

Scanning the diplomatic bag

Scanning by X-rays or by using ultrasound or radioactivity detectors was either not technically possible, or widely practised, in 1961. Today, the

---

[30] See Denza, pp. 199–203.

[31] And see p. 154 below. See also Denza, pp. 187–9, on reservations made by certain Arab states to Article 27 in which they claim the right to reject a suspect bag if the sending state does not agree to it being opened.

[32] For examples, see Denza, pp. 197–9.

safety of aircraft is of paramount importance and a variety of means are used to detect explosives, weapons and drugs. Regrettably, such items are sometimes carried in diplomatic bags. But no airline is obliged to carry any person (including even an ambassador) or any item which it considers illegal or a safety risk. It may therefore require as a condition of carriage that a diplomatic bag be submitted to scanning by the airline or airport security authorities. If the scanning indicates a suspicious item the airline can refuse to take the bag. But, can the receiving state scan a bag *on arrival* in its territory; and if it finds the bag is being abused, what can it do? Depending on the circumstances, the mission may be willing to open the bag in the presence of officials of the sending and receiving states, although it is under no obligation to do so. The practice and views of states on the matter differ, but one may tentatively summarise the position as follows. Scanning is permissible provided it is not so intrusive in nature, or in the way it is carried out, that *details* of the contents could be revealed. Use of a sniffer dog to detect drugs is therefore acceptable, as is a radioactivity detector. On the other hand, certain X-ray and other equipment is capable of 'reading' the contents of documents and electrical equipment. This would be equivalent to opening the bag and inspecting its contents. But, even if the scanning is proper and reveals the presence of items such as guns, the receiving state is not entitled either to open the bag or to delay it. Instead, it should of course inform the mission and seek its comments. If the mission insists on the bag being released forthwith, it should be. If, however, the receiving state insists on the bag being returned to the sending state, despite the fact that this would be a breach of the Convention, since the sending state will itself already be in breach, it is not in a strong position to protest.

If the bag is in transit via a third state, that state must accord it the same inviolability and protection as the receiving state (Article 40(3)).

The protection given by international law to the diplomatic bag applies whether or not it is accompanied by a diplomatic courier (for reasons of cost most bags today are unaccompanied), but for practical purposes a bag is naturally more secure if accompanied.

Diplomatic couriers

The messengers specially entrusted with the delivery of the diplomatic bag are accorded functional immunity – only so much as is necessary for the protection of the bag. Article 27(5)–(7) provides for three categories:

The full-time diplomatic courier Because of the expense this is a dying race. He holds a diplomatic courier's passport indicating his status, and carries a document indicating the number of packages constituting the diplomatic bag, which must bear the visible external marks required by Article 27(4). In view of his function, the receiving state must protect him. He therefore enjoys personal inviolability (see below) and is not liable for any form of arrest or detention even when he has delivered the bag and returns without another one. His personal baggage, however, enjoys no special status and can be inspected or even confiscated. If the courier transits a third state, that state must accord him the same inviolability and protection as the receiving state (Article 40(3)).

The ad hoc courier Also for reasons of cost, these are used increasingly. The *ad hoc* (or 'casual') courier has the same status as a full-time courier, except that his immunities, as a courier, cease once he has delivered the bag. Such couriers are often members of a diplomatic mission who are sent to a neighbouring state to collect a bag delivered there by a full-time courier.

The captain of a commercial aircraft A bag may be entrusted to the captain of a commercial aircraft scheduled to land at an authorised airport in the receiving state. Although he must be provided with a document indicating the number of packages constituting the diplomatic bag, he is not a diplomatic courier. Nevertheless, if the aircraft has to transit a third state, that state must accord the bag the same inviolability and protection as the receiving state (Article 40(3)). Since the captain is not a courier, a member of the diplomatic mission has the right to collect the bag 'directly and freely' from him. A diplomatic bag can also be entrusted to the captain of a state aircraft, including a military aircraft.[33]

Personal inviolability

Since Ancient Greece it has been a fundamental principle that the person of a diplomatic agent is inviolable: he is not liable to any form of arrest or detention, and the receiving state must treat him with due respect and take all appropriate steps to prevent any attack on his person, freedom or dignity (Article 29).

No arrest or detention

Although the prohibition on arrest or detention is self-explanatory, there are certain exceptional circumstances when a diplomat can be detained

---

[33] See p. 172 below on the immunity of state aircraft.

temporarily, either in the interests of protecting others or in his own interest. There have been (a few) cases where a diplomat waving a gun about in the street has been disarmed by police. Similarly, if a diplomat is found by police to be obviously drunk in charge of a motor vehicle he can be stopped and held by police until his mission or family collects him. Nor does inviolability mean that a diplomat can ignore procedures established to ensure general safety. Thus, if he refuses to submit to screening by airport metal detectors or X-ray machines, or to a search of his person or baggage, the airline is not under any obligation to carry him.

Safeguarding from attack

The duty to 'take all appropriate steps' to prevent any attack on the diplomat's person, freedom or dignity rests on the receiving state, even if the sending state also takes steps to protect its diplomats (in which case it must conform to local laws, in particular those on the possession and use of firearms).[34] What is 'appropriate' will depend on the circumstances. There is no need for a permanent guard on the residence of even an ambassador unless there is reason to believe that he may be at risk. The decision on what is reasonable must be left to the receiving state, although it should consult closely with the mission. Similarly, if a diplomat is taken hostage (other than in a mission or residence),[35] what to do, and when is a matter for the *receiving* state; the receiving state is not under any obligation to do what the sending state asks of it, such as giving in to kidnappers' demands.[36] If, however, the receiving state is clearly unable or unwilling to do what is necessary to obtain the release of the hostages, and their lives are in serious danger, the sending state may, in exercise of its inherent right of self-defence, use reasonable force to free them.[37]

Inviolability of the private residence

We have seen that the residence of the head of mission is treated as part of the premises of the mission and thus enjoys inviolability (Articles 1(i) and 22). The private residence of a diplomatic agent enjoys the same inviolability (Article 30(1)). For this purpose, the residence may be temporary,

---

[34] See p. 153 below on Article 41.
[35] See p. 128 above on the Lima hostages.   [36] See Denza, pp. 212–14.
[37] See further p. 227, para. (1), below. On the rescue of Israeli nationals at Entebbe airport, see Oppenheim, para. 131, n. 11.

such as a hotel room occupied on arrival at post. The inviolability is not lost when the residence is temporarily left unoccupied during a holiday or when repairs are being carried out. A second (e.g. vacation) home will be accorded inviolability only while a member of a mission physically occupies it.

Inviolability of private papers, correspondence and property

Although official papers in the possession of the diplomatic agent already enjoy inviolability,[38] Article 30(2) confers inviolability also on his private papers and correspondence. Thus, if he is sued in respect of a private professional or commercial activity for which he has no immunity from jurisdiction,[39] he cannot be compelled by the local courts to produce such papers, although his head of mission could direct him to comply with the demand.

All property in the possession of a diplomatic agent, even if owner-ship is disputed, is inviolable (Article 30(2)). 'Property' includes his bank account and motor car. There are three exceptions: (1) enforcement of a judgment when, in accordance with Article 31(1)(a)–(c), he has no immunity (see below); (2) inspection of his personal baggage (Article 36(2)(b));[40] and (3) since it can have no greater inviolability than those of the mission, his motor car can also be towed away if it causes an obstruction.[41]

The difference between diplomatic immunity and state immunity

Diplomatic immunity and state (or sovereign) immunity (see the next chapter) are often confused. State immunity is the immunity of a state, and its officials and agents, from the jurisdiction of another state. Diplo-matic immunity is accorded to the members of a diplomatic mission, and in the case of diplomatic agents amounts to almost total immunity from jurisdiction. State immunity is not governed by a treaty of universal application (although the United Nations recently adopted a Convention on the Jurisdictional Immunities of States and their Property 2004)[42] and so the extent of the immunity varies from state to state. Keeping a clear distinction between state immunity and diplomatic immunity is there-fore vital. Unfortunately, the difference is not always well understood by

---

[38] See p. 130 above on Article 24.   [39] See p. 140 below on Article 31(1)(c).
[40] See p. 147 below.   [41] See p. 131 above.   [42] See p. 160 below.

courts, private lawyers, or even foreign ministries. Confusing the two can lead to trouble.

Take a simple case: an ambassador contracts with a local decorator for the repainting of the embassy. The ambassador disputes the bill, but the decorator will not reduce it. How is this typical dispute to be resolved? Because the ambassador would in any event have diplomatic immunity, one might think that all the decorator can do is to urge his foreign ministry to put pressure on the ambassador or his government to pay or to negotiate a settlement. But, in this case the ambassador would have signed the contract as part of his official functions, and therefore *on behalf of his state*. It is the state that is the party to the contract, not the ambassador. In fact, the embassy – merely a number of diplomats representing their state – has no legal personality and cannot therefore be sued.[43] So, can the decorator sue the state? Whether a state can be sued in a foreign court will depend on whether under the law of the receiving state a foreign state can claim immunity in the particular circumstances and, if so, whether or not that immunity is then waived.[44]

When considering legal proceedings in a matter in which a diplomat has been directly involved, it is crucial to analyse the situation or transaction to see if he was acting on behalf of his state or personally. Issuing legal proceedings against a diplomat when they should be against his state is pointless and will only cause delay and expense. To help avoid confusion, when a member of a diplomatic mission signs a contract, lease or suchlike as part of his official functions, he should do so expressly on behalf of his state, and only the state should be named as the party.

Diplomatic immunity

A diplomatic agent is wholly immune from the *criminal* jurisdiction of the receiving state (Article 31(1)). This immunity is necessarily linked to the inviolability of his person.

The position regarding *civil and administrative* jurisdiction is slightly different. That jurisdiction includes, in effect, all jurisdiction which is not criminal, although what is classified as criminal will vary from country to country. Parking and other minor traffic offences are often not regarded as criminal offences. The immunity covers all civil and administrative matters, which touch the diplomatic agent, including divorce and child

---

[43] See a 1956 judgment of the Supreme Court of Croatia in 23 ILR 431.
[44] See p. 143 below.

custody. Article 31(1) provides, however, for some exceptions. The legal problems concerning diplomatic immunity are largely about how to deal with the consequences of immunity when it is not waived or the application of these exceptions.[45]

Exception (a): private immovable property in the territory of the receiving state

There is no immunity in respect of civil proceedings concerning title to or possession of land and buildings on the land. It seems that this applies also to the principal private residence of a diplomatic agent. However, even if a court were to order the diplomatic agent to leave, the inviolability of his residence (unless waived) would prevent the order being enforced (Article 30). The practice of states varies as to whether proceedings for recovery of rent or other such obligations also come within the exception.

Exception (b): private involvement in succession proceedings

There is no immunity if the diplomatic agent is involved as a private person, and not on behalf of the sending state, in civil proceedings relating to the estate of a deceased person.

Exception (c): private professional or commercial activity

There is no immunity in respect of civil proceedings relating to any professional or commercial activity carried on by the diplomatic agent outside his official functions. If a diplomat writing a book in his spare time defames someone he will have no immunity from an action for defamation. The activity must generally be continuous, not an isolated act unless it is of some magnitude, like the speculative purchase of land. Investments in shares and suchlike are also likely to fall within the exception. Although Article 42 prohibits a diplomatic agent from practising 'for *personal* profit' any professional or commercial activity, this does not forbid all paid activities. The exception in Article 31(1)(c) is for the benefit of persons doing business with him if he were to embark on profitable work, whether in breach of the prohibition or with the consent of the receiving state.

---

[45] For a full account of the problems, see Denza, pp. 237–53.

The exception is more likely to be relevant to a diplomatic spouse who works.[46]

Proof of diplomatic immunity

Whatever the basis for immunity under the Convention, it is for the person claiming it to establish that he is entitled to it. Immunity can never be presumed. In an attempt to smooth their passage through foreign customs and immigration, some states issue diplomatic passports to government ministers, members of the legislature and sometimes even persons with no public office. But the possession of a diplomatic passport or diplomatic visa is, in itself, never proof of immunity. To prove it requires evidence that (1) the person holds a position in a diplomatic mission which confers immunity *and* (2) that the immunity covers him in the particular circumstances of the case.[47] How these matters are established depends on the law and practice of each state. Obviously, the foreign ministry of the receiving state can help, but it has to be careful not to pre-empt the local courts. Even the apparently simple act by the foreign ministry of confirming that Mr Smith has been notified as a diplomatic agent serving in the Embassy of Ruritania does not prove that the person claiming immunity *is* Mr Smith – that also has to be proved. And, even if he is, as we have already seen – and will see again when we discuss other members of a diplomatic mission – whether his immunity applies in the particular circumstances of the case is a question of law. Some states (e.g. the United States) will sometimes certify to their courts points of fact and law; other states (e.g. the United Kingdom) will certify only matters of fact.[48] A foreign ministry may nevertheless indicate, albeit informally, whether it considers a person a member of a diplomatic mission. In doing so, it is important for the ministry to be even-handed. In responding to any factual enquiries about diplomatic status, the ministry must always remember that a successful claim of immunity could severely affect the rights of others. It must therefore not only consider the matter with great

---

[46] See p. 147 below.

[47] This equally applies to persons claiming immunity as a member of a special mission (p. 155 below), a consular officer (p. 158 below), a head or former head of state (p. 177 below) or a person connected with an international organisation (p. 200 below).

[48] Section 4 of the Diplomatic Privileges Act 1964 provides that a certificate by or on behalf of the Foreign and Commonwealth Secretary is conclusive evidence as to the *facts* in it. The question of immunity is for the court alone.

care, but all information provided to one party should be sent also to the other party or parties concerned.

Immunity from giving evidence

A diplomatic agent is not obliged to give evidence as a witness (Article 31(2)). The sending state may, however, agree to waive his immunity solely to enable him to do so. Whether it will be possible to attach conditions as to the manner in which he gives evidence will depend on the law and practice of the receiving state.

What immunity is not

For so long as a person has immunity it protects him in the receiving state against legal proceedings in respect of all current and past matters, including private matters. In respect of acts performed in exercise of his functions as a member of the mission, the immunity continues indefinitely (Article 39(2)). But the law of the receiving state still applies to the immune person as it does to other persons (Article 41(1)); it is just that it cannot be enforced against him while the immunity lasts and is not waived. Immunity from jurisdiction is therefore not the same as being 'above the law'. The insurer of a person enjoying immunity should therefore always settle a claim against the insured person for the full and proper amount even if immunity has not been waived. Most receiving states now require members of foreign missions to hold third party motor vehicle insurance.

Nor does immunity from the jurisdiction of the receiving state exempt a person from the jurisdiction of his own state (Article 31(4)). In the case of a serious criminal offence, the sending state may be willing to waive immunity (as is increasingly done) or to recall the person and to prosecute or discipline him at home. In practice, much can be achieved by discussions between the mission and the foreign ministry of the receiving state; and if the case is serious and the mission uncooperative, the foreign ministry always has the power to require the person's recall.[49]

Immunity from execution

Even if immunity from jurisdiction has been waived, a judgment cannot be enforced by execution against the person, private residence or private

[49] See p. 122 above.

property of the immune person (Articles 31(3), 29 and 30). This is subject only to the three exceptions in Article 31(1), in which cases his property can be seized provided there is no infringement of the inviolability of the person or his residence. Reliance on immunity and inviolability in order to evade legal obligations is a serious matter and may lead to the receiving state requiring the person to leave.[50]

Waiver of immunity

The purpose of diplomatic immunity is to ensure the efficient performance of the functions of a diplomatic mission; it is not for personal benefit. *Immunity cannot therefore be validly waived by the person enjoying it.* It can be waived only by or on behalf of the sending state (Article 32(1)). The law of the receiving state must determine whether immunity has been waived, and particular care must be taken with criminal proceedings since the accused diplomat might challenge the waiver. Waiver by the head of mission will normally be regarded as valid, unless it purports to be of his own immunity; and most governments require a head of mission to seek authority before waiving the immunity of any of his staff.

Waiver of diplomatic immunity must be express; it cannot be implied (Article 32(2)). Thus, if a person enjoying immunity takes part in civil or criminal proceedings as a defendant, but without an express waiver, the proceedings will be void. Informal or voluntary co-operation with proceedings does not amount to waiver. Whether waiver can be given in advance of the events giving rise to legal proceedings is not clear. However, since state immunity can be waived in advance,[51] an advance waiver for the purpose of at least *civil* proceedings (e.g. disputes under a lease) may be possible. It is most unlikely that advance waiver for criminal proceedings is possible, since, unlike some civil transactions, one cannot predict the circumstances that may give rise to criminal proceedings. Once validly waived in respect of particular proceedings, the immunity is lost for those proceedings, but not otherwise.

On the other hand, if a person enjoying immunity *initiates* civil proceedings, he cannot invoke his immunity in respect of any counter-claim directly connected with his claim (Article 32(3)). But, if he began the proceedings not knowing of his immunity, he will be entitled to have the proceedings dismissed.[52]

---

[50] See p. 122 above.   [51] See p. 165 below.   [52] Denza, pp. 283–4.

In civil proceedings, *waiver of immunity from execution* of the judgment requires a separate waiver (Article 32(4)). It is probable that this does not apply to criminal proceedings because the penalty is inseparable from the finding of guilt, and the practice of states seems to support this.[53]

Social security exemption

Since a diplomatic agent will continue to be subject to the social security legislation of the sending state, he is exempt from local social security obligations (Article 33(1)). A private servant who is in his sole employ is also exempt if he is not a national of or 'permanently resident'[54] in the receiving state and is covered for social security by the sending state or a third state (paragraph 2). But, if that exemption does not apply, the diplomatic agent must carry out the employer's obligations under local social security legislation (paragraph 3). Although the Convention does not provide specifically that a mission must comply with local social security legislation in respect of those of its staff who are *not* exempt (mostly locally engaged), sending states increasingly take the view that they should – as good employers – ensure that local social security contributions for non-exempt staff are paid by the mission. Even when a member of a mission is exempt, he can take part in the local social security scheme if this is permitted by local law (paragraph 4). Nothing in Article 33 affects the provisions of social security agreements past or future (paragraph 5).

Exemption from taxation

Although he remains subject to taxation by his sending state, a diplomatic agent is exempt in the receiving state from 'all dues and taxes, personal or real, national, regional or municipal' (Article 34). This exemption is very broad and includes direct and indirect taxation. But there are important *exceptions* to the general exemption:

(a) '[I]ndirect taxes of a kind which are normally incorporated in the price of goods and services'. The main indirect taxes are value added taxes and sales taxes. The exception is interpreted in two ways. Some states, particularly the United Kingdom, do not grant general exemption for

---

[53] But see Denza, pp. 284–6.   [54] See p. 149 below.

value added tax even when the amount is identifiable at the point of sale. Many states take the contrary view and either provide tax exemption cards or have refund procedures. Other states, including the United Kingdom, allow as a concession certain refunds on high-value goods.

(b) '[D]ues and taxes on private immovable property situated in the territory of the receiving state, *unless* he holds it on behalf of the sending state for the purpose of the mission'. Although the intention as to the scope of this exception is not clear,[55] it would appear from state practice since 1961 that most receiving states now exempt the residence of a diplomatic agent from local property taxes, although sometimes on the basis of reciprocity (see Article 47(2)(b)). Accommodation used for purely private purposes, such as a weekend cottage, is not exempt.

(c) '[E]state, succession or inheritance duties levied by the receiving state, subject to the provisions of paragraph 4 of Article 39'. See the discussion of Article 39.[56]

(d) '[D]ues and taxes on private income having its source in the receiving state and capital taxes on investments made in commercial undertakings in the receiving state'. A diplomat cannot enjoy exemption from taxation on local investments. There are, of course, other ways in which expatriates can lawfully arrange their finances so as to minimise tax.

(e) '[C]harges levied for specific services rendered'. See the discussion of Article 23.[57]

(f) '[R]egistration, court or record fees, mortgage dues and stamp duty, with respect to immovable property, subject to the provisions of Article 23'. The fees, dues and duties referred to all relate only to 'immovable property', i.e. land and buildings. The proviso about Article 23, which exempts the premises of the mission from all taxes except those which represent payment for specific services rendered, means that, for example, if the fee payable for registration of the transfer of legal title to the residence of a diplomatic agent is quite out of proportion to the cost of that service, and therefore amounts to a tax, there is exemption from at least the excess amount.

In calculating the tax due on non-exempt income, any income that is exempt must be disregarded.

---

[55] Denza, pp. 301–6.　　[56] See p. 150 below.　　[57] See p. 130 above.

Exemption from personal services

Article 35 exempts a diplomatic agent from all personal services, from any kind of public service (such as sitting on a jury), and military obligations, including those connected with requisitioning, contributions and billeting of soldiers.

Exemption from customs duties and inspection

These exemptions are of considerable practical importance and can cause problems due to the natural desire of a receiving state to prevent abuse of such valuable privileges and the natural human weaknesses of diplomats.

Exemption from customs duties

Article 36(1) requires the receiving state to permit the import, free from all customs duties, taxes and related charges, other than service charges, of 'articles for the official use of the mission' and 'articles for the personal use of a diplomatic agent or members of his family forming part of his household, including articles intended for his establishment', this latter privilege continuing throughout his posting. It is for the head of mission and the sending state to determine, in good faith, what is covered by these formulas; these days they include even construction materials needed for the premises of the mission. However, the receiving state is not under an obligation to allow the entry of goods the import of which is subject to a general prohibition (cf. Article 41). It may, of course, make exceptions on a concessionary basis. Similarly, since the Convention contains no privileges regarding exports, any prohibition on exporting certain articles, such as antiquities, applies equally to the mission and its staff.

These important import privileges are qualified by the right given to the receiving state to control the exercise of the privileges by means of its laws and regulations in order to prevent abuse. They can prescribe procedural formalities, restrictions on quantities, the period within which duty-free entry of goods will be allowed on first installation (for those staff entitled to that privilege),[58] and regulations on subsequent disposal of goods imported duty-free (a motor vehicle can usually be sold locally only to a buyer entitled to the same import privileges).

---

[58] See p. 148 below (A&T staff).

Exemption from inspection

Article 36(2) generally exempts the *personal baggage* of a diplomatic agent from search, but permits the receiving state to inspect it (including unaccompanied baggage) if there are 'serious grounds' for presuming that it contains articles not covered by the exemptions in Article 36(1), or articles the import or export of which is prohibited by its law or controlled by its quarantine regulations. The inspection must be conducted in the presence of the diplomat or his representative. These conditions do not apply to security searches required by airports or airlines.[59] A package which does not constitute personal baggage is subject to normal inspection, unless it constitutes a diplomatic bag.[60]

Members of the family of a diplomatic agent

The immunities and privileges in Articles 29–36 are also enjoyed by 'the members of the family of a diplomatic agent forming part of his household', unless they are nationals of the receiving state (Article 37(1)). The quoted formula certainly covers the spouse and any minor children, but practice varies from state to state as to which other persons come within it. A student child who has reached majority but lives with the diplomat is usually included, as also is a student who lives with him during the vacations. Increasingly, non-married partners are being accepted; but probably not yet same-sex partners. A widowed parent who lives as part of the diplomat's household may be accepted. Some states will not recognise more than one wife of a polygamous marriage. Difficult cases will be the subject of consultations, but, if these do not result in agreement, in practice the final decision lies with the receiving state.

Working spouses

Increasingly these days, diplomatic spouses of either sex want to work during a posting. Some states make difficulties and refuse work permits, often citing as the reason the immunity of the spouse. Yet the prohibition in Article 42 on a member of a diplomatic mission practising a profession or commercial activity for personal profit does not apply to spouses. And anyway immunity should not be an obstacle. Under Article 31(1)(c) the spouse will have no immunity from civil or administrative jurisdiction in

[59] See p. 137 above.   [60] See p. 133 above.

relation to work *not* undertaken for a diplomatic mission. The work will be subject to tax (Article 34(d)), and the person will have to satisfy any professional requirements. Thus a spouse who works as, for example, a doctor, teacher or computer programmer will have to pay tax and can be sued in respect of the work. Yet some receiving states make it a condition of granting a work permit to a diplomatic spouse that his or her *general* immunity from jurisdiction be waived in advance. This is wrong. Since the spouse will have no civil or administrative immunity in respect of the work, there is no reason for a general waiver. Nevertheless, many states have found it necessary or prudent to conclude bilateral reciprocal arrangements authorising their respective diplomatic spouses to work subject to certain conditions and procedures.[61]

Administrative and technical staff

Article 37(2) provides that a member of the administrative and technical (A&T) staff of the mission (e.g. registry, secretarial, communications and security staff), and members of his family forming part of his household, also enjoy the privileges and immunities in Articles 29–36, subject to certain qualifications.

- The exemption from *civil and administrative jurisdiction* in Article 31(1) is limited to acts performed *in the course of the officer's duties*. Thus, in addition to his official acts, he will be immune in respect of acts incidental to his duties, such as driving to an official appointment. Nevertheless, *full immunity from criminal jurisdiction* and *inviolability of person, residence and property* is the same as that of a diplomatic agent.
- The customs privileges in Article 36(1) are limited to goods imported on *first* arrival in the receiving state, although a period of three to twelve months is usually allowed.

Service staff

Service staff are the members of the staff of the mission in its domestic service (Article 1(g)). They are therefore those employed by the sending state, not by members of the mission. They include drivers, kitchen staff, porters and gardeners. They enjoy immunity only in respect of 'acts performed in the course of their duties'. Evidence of the head of mission

---

[61] Turkey–UK Agreement on Diplomatic Dependants' Employment 2000, UKTS (2000) 98. And see Denza, pp. 325–8.

that a particular act was done in the course of the person's duties will be persuasive, but not conclusive. It is ultimately for the courts to decide. Service staff also are exempt from taxes on their salaries and from social security contributions (Article 37(3)).

Private servants

A private servant is a person in the domestic service of a member of the mission, not one employed by the sending state (Article 1(h)). He enjoys exemption only from taxes on his salary, and from social security contributions provided he is covered by a social security scheme in another state (Article 33(2)). But the receiving state must exercise its jurisdiction 'in such a manner as not to interfere unduly with the performance of the functions of the mission'. This obligation can be discharged by the exercise of administrative discretion.

Nationals and permanent residents of the receiving state

Unless the receiving state grants additional privileges and immunities, a diplomatic agent who is a national of, or is permanently resident in, the receiving state enjoys only immunity from criminal and civil jurisdiction, and inviolability, in respect of 'official acts performed in the exercise of his functions' (Article 38(1)). This immunity is narrower than that of a member of the A&T staff, and amounts, in effect, to state immunity. All other members of the staff, and private servants, who are nationals or permanent residents of the receiving state enjoy privileges and immunities only to the extent allowed by the receiving state, although it must exercise its jurisdiction over them 'in such a manner as not to interfere unduly with the performance of the functions of the mission' (Article 38(2)).

A constant problem is in applying the concept of 'permanently resident'. Certain factors may well point to an intention to permanently reside in the receiving state: having been recruited locally; marriage to a permanent resident of the receiving state; other substantial personal links forged with the receiving state; and little likelihood of being posted after five years' service with the mission. But each case has to be dealt with on its own facts. Determining whether or not a particular person is a permanent resident may have to be discussed by the receiving and sending states, or, if necessary, decided by a court.[62]

---

[62] See generally Denza, pp. 343–9.

Although under Article 37(1) members of the family of a diplomatic agent do not enjoy privileges and immunities if they are local nationals, they do not lose them if they are permanent residents, although such cases are likely to be rare. In contrast, members of the families of A&T staff who are local nationals or permanent residents have no privileges or immunities (Article 37(2)).

Commencement of privileges and immunities

Privileges and immunities are enjoyed from the moment the entitled person enters the receiving state to take up his post or, if already there, when his appointment has been notified to the foreign ministry (Article 39(1)). As indicated earlier,[63] there is no absolute obligation on the sending state to give prior notification of arrival, only 'where possible' (Article 10(2)). Difficult problems can arise when diplomatic status is claimed long after the person has arrived, and often for the purpose of asserting immunity from prosecution for a serious criminal charge. Since diplomatic status cannot be assumed, it has to be established, if necessary to the satisfaction of a court.[64] Therefore, a late notification, especially if it is received after criminal charges against the person have been announced or are imminent, may well be seen as not having been made in good faith. If the foreign ministry, or a court, is not satisfied that the status has been established, they can disregard the notification.

Termination of privileges and immunities

When the functions of an entitled person have come to an end (i.e. he has ceased to be a member of staff of the mission), his privileges and immunities 'normally' cease on his *final* departure from the receiving state (Article 39(1) and (2)). He is allowed a 'reasonable period' in which to leave, during which the privileges and immunities continue, even in the case of an armed conflict. What is a reasonable period will depend on the circumstances, but a month is normal. If the person is dismissed from the diplomatic service *en poste*, he will be entitled to a reasonable period in which to leave. If he is dismissed because of serious criminal charges made against him in the receiving state, the sending state should at the same time waive his immunity. However, even once he has finally left,

[63] See p. 121 above.   [64] See p. 141 above.

his immunity with respect to acts performed 'in exercise of his functions as a member of the mission' will continue. Other acts (private acts) will no longer enjoy immunity.

If a member of a mission dies, the members of his family continue to enjoy their privileges and immunities until the expiry of a reasonable period in which to leave the country (Article 39(3)). But, if a member of the family loses entitlement to privileges and immunities (as a spouse will do as a result of separation or divorce), the entitlement probably ceases with immediate effect.[65]

Third states

Diplomats in transit

When a diplomatic agent is in a third state, he enjoys no privileges and immunities, with two exceptions. We have already dealt with one, the *ad hoc* diplomatic courier.[66] The other is when a diplomatic agent passes through, or is in, a third state, provided he has any necessary visa for it, 'while proceeding to take up or return to his post, or when returning to his own country'. The third state must accord him inviolability and 'such immunities as may be required to ensure his transit or return' (Article 40(1)). The immunities do not extend to exemption from search of personal baggage or from confiscation of prohibited items. (One must also remember that possession of a diplomatic passport is not proof that the person is a diplomatic agent.)[67] Any members of the family of the diplomatic agent who enjoy privileges or immunities and who accompany him, or are travelling separately to join him or to return to their country, must be treated in the same way. In similar circumstances, the third state must 'not hinder' the passage of members of the A&T or service staff, and members of their families (Article 40(2)).

Communications in transit

Third states are also required to accord to official correspondence and other official communications in transit, including messages in code or cipher, the same freedom and protection as is accorded by the receiving state; and to accord diplomatic couriers (provided they have any necessary

---

[65] Denza, p. 361.   [66] See p. 136 above.   [67] See p. 141 above.

visas) and diplomatic bags in transit, the same inviolability and protection as the receiving state is bound to accord (Article 40(3)).

Duties of the mission to the receiving state

Several duties of the mission are set out in Article 41. First, and most importantly, all persons enjoying privileges and immunities have a duty to respect the laws and regulations of the receiving state. Immunity from local law does not mean that one is above the law; it is still applicable to a diplomat (otherwise there would be no point in waiving immunity), even if he cannot be forced to appear before the courts. Enjoyment of immunity therefore carries with it a duty not to abuse it by ignoring the law. If he does, his privileges and immunities will not be affected, although in a serious case his immunity may be waived or he may be required to leave.

Secondly, members of a mission must not interfere in the internal affairs of the receiving state. The scope of this duty is not always well understood. It does not mean that a diplomat cannot, if instructed by his government, express in public views about the domestic policy of the receiving state, even though his government must be careful not to interfere in those affairs. But a diplomat must not express his personal views on such matters.

Thirdly, all official business with the receiving state must be conducted with or through the foreign ministry of the receiving state, or such other ministry as may be agreed. But, in practice these days, much business, and not always of a technical nature, is conducted directly with other ministries without any prior agreement with, or even knowledge of, the foreign ministry. However, if the foreign ministry insists on business on all, or specific, subjects being conducted only with it, the mission must comply. Today, many treaties are negotiated by a mission directly with the other ministries without reference by the mission or those ministries to either foreign ministry. This is a thoroughly bad practice. Treaty-making is not as simple as it may seem. The expertise lies with foreign ministries, who should always be kept informed of progress, and whose approval should always be obtained before any text is finalised. Similarly, if a matter concerns a dispute, both foreign ministries need to be made aware of it at an early stage.

Lastly, the premises of the mission must not be used in any manner incompatible with the functions of the mission, such as for commercial purposes. The granting of diplomatic asylum by the mission is incompatible with its functions, unless it is permitted by customary international law or by a treaty to which both the sending state and the receiving state are parties.[68]

End of the functions of a diplomatic agent

The functions of a diplomatic agent come to an end when his state so informs the receiving state, or when the latter informs the sending state under Article 9(2) that it refuses to recognise him as a member of the mission (see Article 43). But there are other circumstances: death, breach of diplomatic relations, disappearance of the sending state (e.g. the German Democratic Republic) or unconstitutional change of its head of state, so occasioning the need for fresh credentials for its heads of missions.[69] The replacement of the government of the sending state by constitutional means does not affect the functions of its diplomatic agents. And, even if the government is overthrown unconstitutionally, the receiving state will usually continue to regard its diplomatic agents as still functioning pending recognition of the new government. Difficulties can arise when there is an internal conflict in the sending state, and there is a disagreement among the members of the mission as to which party to support. These types of problem can be resolved only in the light of the particular circumstances.[70]

Facilities for departure

If diplomatic relations deteriorate or are broken off, or if an armed conflict breaks out with the receiving state, it must nevertheless grant facilities to enable persons enjoying privileges and immunities, and members of their families, to leave 'at the earliest possible moment'. This includes members of families who are local nationals, but not staff who are local nationals (which would include dual nationals). If the mission needs it, the receiving state must place at its disposal the necessary means of transport for its members and their property (Article 44).

Breach of diplomatic relations and the protection of the interests of the sending state

Diplomatic relations are broken off from time to time, although even an armed conflict between two states does not always result in the severance of all contacts. Discreet contacts are often continued in a third state

---

[68] See p. 187 below.
[69] For details, see Satow, paras. 21.1–21.15.   [70] See further Denza, pp. 386–8.

(sometimes with the help of its government) or between permanent missions to the United Nations or other international organisations. The receiving state is under an obligation, even in the case of an armed conflict, to respect the premises of the mission, its property and its archives (Article 45(a)). The sending state is entitled to entrust custody of the premises of the mission, its property and its archives to a third state acceptable to the receiving state (Article 45(b)). Similarly, the sending state may also entrust the protection of its interests and those of its nationals to a third state ('protecting power') acceptable to the receiving state (Article 45(c)).

Once the mission has been closed down, its premises lose inviolability, unless they house an 'interests section'. There is a growing trend for the interests of the sending state and its nationals to continue to be looked after by a small number of its staff, who for this purpose become members of staff of the mission of the protecting power. In many cases, the interests section is housed in the premises previously occupied by the sending state's mission. So it is, to some degree, business as usual, except that the staff of the interests section must obey the orders of the head of mission of the protecting power, and if the interests section is in its old premises it must fly the flag of the protecting power. To arrive at this situation requires agreed arrangements between the protecting power and the state whose interests it will be protecting. There will also have to be arrangements between the protecting power (acting as surrogate) and the receiving state, since the latter can reserve the right to consent to the appointment to the diplomatic staff of a mission of nationals of a third state who are not also nationals of the sending state (Article 8(3)), and the receiving state will normally want to make reciprocal arrangements for an interests section in the sending state.[71] The protecting power (and the receiving state) may insist that the interests section limits itself to reporting and consular matters.

Non-discrimination and reciprocity

Although Article 47 states that the receiving state must not discriminate between states, it recognises that the receiving state is entitled to depart from this rule (a) if the sending state applies the Convention restrictively, in which case the receiving state can reciprocate; and (b) where by custom or agreement states treat each other more favourably than required by

[71] See Denza, pp. 399–402.

the Convention. Thus, if a receiving state unnecessarily restricts the free movement of members of a mission, the sending state can do likewise. Also, two states may accord on a reciprocal basis greater privileges and immunities to the staff of their respective missions. During the Cold War, some Western states reached mutually beneficial reciprocal agreements with some Soviet Bloc states under which junior staff were also accorded full immunity and inviolability, and some of these agreements may still be in effect.

Special missions

A special mission is 'a temporary mission, representing the state, which is sent by one state to another state with the consent of the latter for the purpose of dealing with it on specific questions or performing in relation to it a specific task'. Since the beginnings of diplomacy, such *ad hoc* missions have been an essential part of diplomatic relations, and pre-date embassies as we know them today. Although the permanent diplomatic mission is still a cornerstone of diplomatic relations, special missions are an essential complement. The vast majority are made up of diplomats and civil servants, but some are led by ministers, and some by foreign ministers, prime ministers or heads of state. Many special missions are sent to negotiate a bilateral or multilateral treaty or to discuss problems related to the implementation or interpretation of a treaty.

The above definition of special mission is taken from Article 1(a) of the Convention on Special Missions 1969.[72] The definition does not cover the situation in which two or more states send temporary missions to meet in a third state, with or without its knowledge. When this is done at head-of-state level, customary international law may accord members of a special mission sufficient immunity, but when it is done at official level there is doubt as to what immunity they enjoy.

Since the rules of customary international law on special missions were not at all clear, the International Law Commission drafted the Special Missions Convention, drawing copiously on the 1961 Convention, so giving special missions privileges and immunities almost identical to those of permanent diplomatic missions. Yet, because members of special missions generally live in hotels, stay for only a few days or weeks and rarely bring their families, they do not have to cope with all the problems of

[72] 1410 UNTS 231 (No. 23431); ILM (1970) 127.

permanent missions; nor do they cause the same problems for the host state as do permanent missions. Therefore, conferring on special missions the same scale of privileges and immunities is not easy to justify. This may be why the 1969 Convention did not enter into force until 1985 when it received the necessary twenty-two ratifications (and even now has only thirty-five) and this only because in the 1990s nine former republics of the Soviet Union and Yugoslavia ratified it in a bout of post-independence enthusiasm.

A few of the non-party states have legislation on special missions; the others rely on customary international law as determined by their courts.[73] It is almost certain that, provided a state has consented to it, a special mission will have immunity from civil and criminal jurisdiction in respect of official acts, but what else it may enjoy seems to depend mostly on domestic law, if any. This may not be satisfactory given the increasing number of special missions. But, the writer has been on numerous special missions, sometimes to dodgy places, but has never felt the need for special legal protection. Indeed, assuming that they are aware of the lack of a clearly defined status of a special mission, that uncertainty may be a good influence on its members.

(As to representatives of states to international organisations, see pp. 199–202 below.)

Consular relations

L. Lee, *Consular Law and Practice*, 2nd edn, Oxford, 1991
Oppenheim, pp. 1132–55

The office of consul goes back a long way, and until 1963 was regulated by customary international law and bilateral consular conventions. The latter are not affected by the Vienna Convention on Consular Relations 1963 (the Convention),[74] and can be supplemented, extended or amplified (Article 73). The Convention followed the pattern of the 1961 Diplomatic Convention, although the substance drew heavily on largely established practice as reflected in consular conventions. The Convention entered into force in 1967 and now has 167 parties. The International Court of Justice

---

[73] See Oppenheim, pp. 1125–6
[74] 596 UNTS 261 (No. 8638); UKTS (1973) 14; TIAS 6820. For the ILC Commentary on the draft Articles of the Convention, see A. Watts, *The International Law Commission 1949–1998*, Oxford, 1999, vol. I. pp. 230 *et seq.*

sees the Convention as an authoritative statement of international law.[75] The provisions of the Convention broadly follow those of the Diplomatic Convention, so only the most important provisions and differences will be mentioned below.

The establishment of diplomatic relations implies consent also to consular relations. Today, most embassies also carry out consular functions in accordance with the Convention, although the staff retain their diplomatic status.[76] But there is still a need for states to establish 'consular posts' (not missions) separate from their diplomatic missions. The establishment of each post requires the consent of the receiving state, including its location and the district (sometimes just a port) that it will cover (Articles 2–4).[77] A consul may not act outside his district.

The functions of a consular post are set out in detail in Article 5 and include protection of, and assistance to, nationals of the sending state; developing commercial, economic, cultural and scientific relations and reporting on developments in those areas; providing information about conditions in the receiving state; issuing passports and visas; performing notarial and similar acts; transmitting legal documents; and supervising and assisting ships and aircraft registered in the sending state.

A consul has freedom of communication with, and access to, a national of the sending state who has been detained by the local authorities, which, if the person so requests, must inform the consul of that fact, and the detained person informed 'without delay' of his rights (Article 36).[78] The consul can help arrange for him to have a local lawyer, giving legal advice *not* being a consular function. A consul has the right to visit any of his nationals who have been imprisoned.

Consular posts are headed by a consul-general, consul, vice-consul or consular agent, usually the first or the second named. The appointment must first be approved by the receiving state by means of an *exequatur*, although the consul may be allowed to exercise his functions on a provisional basis (Articles 8–14). Normally, consuls are subordinate to the head of his state's local diplomatic mission.

The premises of a consular post are inviolable, and the authorities of the receiving state need the consent of the head of post to enter them,

---

[75] *Case Concerning US Diplomatic and Consular Staff in Tehran (USA v. Iran), ICJ Reports* (1980), p. 7, paras. 45–55; 61 ILR 502.

[76] See p. 119 above.

[77] China–UK Exchange of Notes 1999, 2139 UNTS 256 (No. 37305); UKTS (2000) 93.

[78] See *LaGrand (Germany v. USA), ICJ Reports* (2001) p. 9, para. 128; 118 ILR 37.

although, unlike a diplomatic mission, this is assumed 'in case of fire or other disaster requiring prompt protective action' (Article 31).[79] The consular bag is inviolable but, unlike the diplomatic bag,[80] if the receiving state has 'serious reason' to believe that it contains something other than official correspondence, documents or articles intended exclusively for official use, it may request that the bag be opened in the presence of an authorised representative of the sending state. If the request is refused, the bag must be returned to its place of origin (Article 35(3)).[81]

If criminal proceedings are instituted against the head of post and any other consular officer (not 'consular employees', who are support staff), they must appear before the competent judicial authorities, but may not be arrested or detained pending trial, except in the case of a 'grave crime' and pursuant to a judicial order (Article 41). But consular officers and consular employees are immune from both the criminal and the civil jurisdiction of the receiving state 'in respect of acts performed in the exercise of consular functions'.[82] The only exceptions to this are civil actions on a contract concluded by a consular officer or employee who did not expressly or impliedly contract as agent of the sending state, and actions by a third party for damage arising from an accident caused by a vehicle, vessel or aircraft (Article 43). In addition, all members of a consular post can be called by a court to give evidence. If a consular officer should decline, he cannot be forced or penalised, but other members of the post cannot decline to be a witness (except on matters to do with their official functions) or to produce official correspondence or documents (Article 44). All these protections can be waived (Article 45).

Honorary consuls can perform the same duties as career consular officers, but are usually local businessmen (and often local or third state nationals) and unpaid. The Convention generally applies to them as to career consular officers (see Articles 58–68). The most important exceptions are that neither his premises nor his person is inviolable and he must appear before the court if criminal proceedings are instituted against him (Article 63), although he is immune from criminal jurisdiction in respect of official acts even if he is a local national or permanent resident (Articles 58(2) and 1(1)).

---

[79] Cf. diplomatic missions.   [80] See p. 134 above.
[81] See Denza, pp. 199–203.   [82] See Oppenheim, pp. 1144–6 for examples.

7

State immunity

L'état c'est moi.[1]

Fox, *The Law of State Immunity*, Oxford, 2004[2]
Oppenheim. *Oppenheim's International Law*, 9th edn, London, 1992, pp. 341–76
Shaw, *International Law*, 5th edn, Cambridge, 2003, pp. 621–67

State immunity is also known as sovereign immunity, reflecting its origins in the sanctity of kingship. State immunity may be pleaded by a foreign state when a person wishes to make it a party to legal proceedings in the court of another state, usually as the defendant. If successful, the plea prevents the court from exercising jurisdiction over the state, provided of course that it has jurisdiction in the particular case. The dispute can then be disposed of only by the courts of the foreign state itself, by an international court or tribunal or by diplomatic settlement. Originally, state immunity was absolute, and remained so into modern times even though states were then carrying out many commercial transactions abroad. It was not until the second half of the twentieth century that a restrictive approach – removing immunity for commercial matters – came to be generally accepted.

State immunity is a doctrine of customary international law. But unlike the law of state responsibility, which has been developed almost entirely by international courts and tribunals, state immunity is much more the product of judgments of domestic courts. Their approaches to state immunity reflect differences between their legal, political and economic systems. But, in recent decades, there has been more convergence in domestic legislation and judgments, so that it is now easier to describe the law of state

---

[1] Louis XIV, 13 April 1655.
[2] Most unfortunately, it was published before it became clear that there would be a UN convention on the subject. The paperback edition published in 2004 has a new preface on that and other recent developments.

immunity.[3] This is now helped by the UN General Assembly's adoption on 2 December 2004 of the UN Convention on the Jurisdictional Immunities of States and Their Property (in this chapter, the 'UN Convention').[4] The (integral) annex to the Convention contains 'Understandings' with respect to certain of its provisions. The Convention does not apply to questions of immunity involving states or their property arising in proceedings instituted before its entry into force (after thirty ratifications), except insofar as it reflects customary international law.[5] But, even before then, the Convention may well influence domestic courts who will by their judgments still develop the law. Therefore, the best advice one can give to anyone with a claim against a foreign state, or indeed the state itself, is to instruct lawyers who really are expert in the local law on state immunity. But first we must distinguish state immunity from other related subjects.

The relationship of state immunity to other legal doctrines

Diplomatic immunity distinguished

When an embassy is involved in a transaction there is often confusion between diplomatic immunity and state immunity, although legal proceedings should almost always be against the sending state, not the embassy or any member of it (see p. 138 above for a most practical example). As with diplomatic immunity, state immunity does not mean that local law is not applicable to a foreign state, only that it cannot be enforced by legal proceedings unless the immunity is waived. But, given that the purpose of diplomatic immunity is the protection of diplomats, it is, apart from certain minor exceptions, absolute. Because the customary international law on diplomatic immunity was so well developed, it was possible to codify it in 1961 in the Vienna Convention on Diplomatic Relations. That law is as firm and accepted today as in 1961. Unfortunately, that cannot be said of the law of state immunity, even though it has undergone considerable changes in the last forty years, and is no longer absolute.

---

[3] For a perceptive introduction to the basic problems, see Higgins, pp. 78–86.
[4] A/RES/59/38. The Convention is also at www.untreaty.un.org/English/treaty.asp (go to 'Access to Databases', then 'Texts of Recently Deposited Multilateral Treaties'). The text was based on a draft by the ILC: see A. Watts, *The International Law Commission 1949–1995*, Oxford, 1999, vol. III, pp. 1999–2103.
[5] See p. 8 above on the effect of such treaties on customary international law.

Non-justiciability

In contrast to state immunity, the doctrine of non-justiciability applies when a foreign court does have jurisdiction, for example in proceedings between private parties, but declines to exercise it, either at the request of the defendant or on its own initiative. Under the doctrine, a domestic court may decide not to exercise jurisdiction even over private parties if the object of the dispute relates to inter-state matters for which the court considers there to be no judicial or objective standards by which to judge the issues. Non-justiciability can also describe a rule of private international law,[6] under which a court applies the law of the foreign state and recognises the validity of its legislation and acts done according to that law.[7] This can be criticised as an example of judicial timidity, since the legality under international law of many acts of foreign states can be judged by domestic courts. International law provides an objective standard by which the validity of acts can be assessed, and so any adverse effect of the judgment on foreign relations is less likely. The English courts have refused to recognise Nazi laws discriminating against Jews[8] and, more recently, Iraqi legislation violating basic principles of the UN Charter.[9] But there are other cases where the underlying issue is better decided by an international court or tribunal in proceedings to which the state is a party, such as a maritime boundary dispute.[10]

Act of state

Non-justiciability must be distinguished from a substantive defence known as act of state.[11] In English law, this normally refers to a defence to an action for a tort committed abroad whereby in response to a claim by an alien the defendant may plead that he acted under the orders, or with the approval, of the British Government. The term is also used to describe a doctrine developed by the US courts. It is not a rule of international law; rather it is more to do with the respective constitutional roles

---

[6] See p. 1 above.   [7] *Luther* v. *Sagor* [1921] 3 KB 532; 1 AD 49.
[8] *Oppenheimer* v. *Cattermole* [1976] AC 249; 72 ILR 446.
[9] *Kuwait Airways* v. *Iraqi Airways* [2002] 2 AC 883; [2002] 2 WLR 1353; [2002] 3 All ER 209; 125 ILR 602. For a detailed examination of the case and of the English law on non-justiciability, see Fox, *The Law of State Immunity*, Oxford, 2004, pp. 489–502.
[10] See *Buttes Gas and Oil Company* v. *Hammer* [1982] AC 888; [1981] All ER 616; 64 ILR 331.
[11] See Oppenheim, p. 368, n. 15.

of the US judiciary and executive. Under this doctrine, US courts exercise restraint in not questioning the validity of the taking of property abroad by a foreign state, even if it may have been done in breach of international law, unless there is a treaty with the foreign state governing the matter.[12] The approach is similar to that of non-justiciability.

Human rights

In 2002, the European Court of Human Rights ruled that in the present state of international law state immunity is not incompatible with human rights.[13]

Sources of the law on state immunity

It may be some time before the UN Convention enters into force. It is not clear to what extent parts of it reflect customary international law or represent progressive development. Nevertheless, the Convention, being the only universal treaty on the subject, represents a good basis from which to examine what the customary law is or, at least, may be. The Convention will therefore be the focus of the following pages, even though in parts it is rather lacking in clarity and certainty, and the law of state immunity will vary from state to state.

The Convention will be discussed along with the only other treaty on the subject, the European Convention on State Immunity 1972 (in this chapter, the 'European Convention'),[14] since Article 26 of the UN Convention provides that nothing in it shall affect rights and obligations under existing treaties on state immunity. Although the European Convention is much concerned with reciprocal enforcement of judgments by the parties to it (only eight), it has been influential in the formulation of legislation by other states. Two leading pieces of legislation will examined: the State Immunity Act 1978 (in this chapter, the 'UK Act'),[15] which largely follows the European Convention, and the Foreign Sovereign Immunities

---

[12] *Sabbatino*, 35 ILR 1. See Fox, pp. 482–9 and Shaw, pp. 170–2.

[13] *Al-Adsani* v. *UK*, ECHR App. No. 35763/97; 123 ILR 24.

[14] 1495 UNTS 182 (No. 25699); ILM (1972) 470; UKTS (1979) 74.

[15] ILM (1978) 1123. The legislation of Australia, Canada, Malawi, Pakistan, Singapore and South Africa has been modelled on the Act, and the UN Convention has borrowed several of its provisions. The Act does not apply to visiting forces (s. 16(2)) to which only the common law applies: see *Holland* v. *Lampen-Wolfe* [2000] 1 WLR 1573; [2000] 3 All ER 833; 119 ILR 367, and p. 175 below.

Act 1976 (in this chapter, the 'US Act'), as amended.[16] (It is the policy of the US Government not to assert more immunity abroad than a foreign state would enjoy under the Act in the United States.) The courts of states that do not have legislation on state immunity have to rely on customary international law as deduced by examining the practice (mainly legislation and judgments) of other states.[17] They will now also have the UN Convention to consider.

Only a short and very general overview can be given. Advice on an actual situation will always require a close and detailed examination of the facts and the applicable law of the state of the forum (court).

Which entities enjoy immunity?

What is a state has already been discussed.[18] Article 2(1)(b) of the UN Convention defines a state to include:

(i) '[I]ts various organs of government.' That is to say, all branches or emanations of government through which the government acts, including agencies and diplomatic missions. Proceedings against a government are effectively against the state. The legislature and judicial organs are also part of the state, although they are unlikely to have proceedings brought against them as such in a foreign court.

(ii) '[C]onstituent units of a federal state or political subdivisions of the state, which are entitled to perform acts in the exercise of the sovereign authority, and are acting in that capacity.' Entitlement depends on the constitution of the state.

(iii) '[A]gencies or instrumentalities of the state or other entities, to the extent that they are entitled to perform and are actually performing acts in exercise of sovereign authority of the state.' This depends on the constitution and laws of the state. The reference to 'other entities' would not normally include a corporation established by the state which has an independent legal personality, even if its purpose is

---

[16] For the Act as amended, see www.law.nyu.edu/kingsburyb/fall01/intl_law/basicdocs/ foreign%20 sovereign%20imm%20act.htm.

[17] A comparative study of European states' laws on state immunity, done for the Council of Europe, should be published by the British Institute of International and Comparative Law in 2005.

[18] See p. 16 above. See p. 410 below on the attribution of conduct to a state. A state may in certain cases be responsible for acts of private persons who themselves may not enjoy state immunity in respect of the acts.

non-commercial. The BBC and the British Council were both created, and are financed, by the state but are not part of it. Their assets
are therefore not those of the United Kingdom. Most states have
similar, so-called public corporations or parastatals.[19] But they, and
even a purely commercial entity, like a bank, could have immunity
in respect of, say, the processing of requests for exemption from foreign exchange control restrictions or economic sanctions. On the
other hand, a state trading organisation, even if it is part of the state,
would not enjoy immunity in respect of its commercial activities (see
below). (See also Article 27 of the European Convention; section 14
of the UK Act; and section 1603(a) and (b) of the US Act.)

(iv) '[R]epresentatives of the state acting in that capacity.' This covers
all natural persons authorised to represent a state, in its various
manifestations, in respect of acts done by them on behalf of the
state, and includes the head of state acting in his official capacity.[20]
If a public official is sued for something that he did in his official
capacity, this would amount to suing the state, and so he could plead
state immunity.[21] Diplomats also have personal immunity from suit,
and Article 3 of the UN Convention provides that the Convention
is without prejudice to the privileges and immunities enjoyed under
international law by diplomatic missions, consular posts and other
diplomatic missions and delegations, and persons connected with
them. Furthermore, customary international law regulates certain
special areas (such as foreign forces).[22] Being *lex specialis*, it is not
affected by the UN Convention, the fifth preambular paragraph of
which affirms that the rules of customary international law continue
to govern matters not regulated by the Convention.

Exceptions to immunity

The approach taken both in the treaties and in legislation is that acts
or omissions by a state are immune unless they fall within an exception

---

[19] See also p. 411 below.   [20] See also p. 177 below.
[21] *Propend* v. *Sing*, 11 ILR 611; and *Holland* v. *Lampen Wolfe* [2000] 1 WLR 1573; [2000] 3
All ER 833; 119 ILR 367. In *Jones* v. *Saudi Arabia* [2005] 2 WLR 808, the English Court
of Appeal held that, although the defendant state was immune, its officials who allegedly
tortured Mr Jones were not, although whether a claim should lie against them depended
on all relevant factors, including whether the English courts were the proper forum. The
judgment is being appealed to the House of Lords. See also p. 177 below on criminal
prosecutions.
[22] See p. 175 below.

(Article 5 of the UN Convention; Article 15 of the European Convention; section 1 of the UK Act; and section 1602 of the US Act). However, some of the exceptions have exceptions (and there are even some exceptions to those exceptions). None of this makes understanding the subject easier.

Consent

A state can always waive its immunity by consenting to proceedings, and do so in advance. But a contractual clause that the law of another state will govern a contract does not amount to consent to the jurisdiction of that state's courts. A state cannot claim immunity if it initiates or intervenes in proceedings, unless the latter was done in ignorance of the facts entitling it to immunity, and immunity is then claimed as soon as possible. It is not consent if the state intervenes merely to claim immunity, or for the sole purpose of asserting a right in the property at issue, provided the state would have been entitled to immunity if the proceedings had been brought against it. A state instigating or intervening in proceedings does not usually have immunity in respect of a counter-claim.

Article 17 of the UN Convention provides that a state that enters into a written agreement with a foreign national to submit disputes concerning a commercial transaction (which includes investment matters: see the relevant Understanding) to arbitration cannot invoke immunity before a foreign court in a proceeding relating to that agreement, the arbitration procedure or the award, unless the agreement provides otherwise.

The US Act provides for waiver by implication. Many contracts with states provide that disputes will be submitted to arbitration, and this may amount to implied consent to the courts of the state where the arbitration would be held exercising its supervisory powers over the arbitration. Under the UK Act, when a state has agreed in writing (though not with another state) to submit a dispute to arbitration, it is, subject to any contrary provision in the arbitration agreement, not immune from proceedings in the UK courts that relate to the arbitration.

(Articles 7, 8, 9 and 17 of the UN Convention; Articles 1, 2 and 3 of the European Convention; section 2 of the UK Act; and section 1605(a)(1) of the US Act.)

A separate, express waiver of immunity from execution of the judgment is necessary (see below).

Commercial transactions

At the heart of the modern restrictive approach is the principle that a state is not immune in respect of its commercial transactions (Article 10 of the UN Convention; Articles 4 and 7 of the European Convention; section 3 of the UK Act; and section 1605(a)(2) of the US Act). The problem – for which no completely satisfactory solution has yet been found – is how to define 'commercial'.[23] Since we are here concerned with the activities of a state, a distinction has to be drawn between those transactions which anyone can do (*acta jure gestionis*) and those which only a state can do (*acta jure imperii*). One can distinguish between these two types of transaction according to either the *nature* of the transaction or its *purpose*. The purchase by a state of uniforms for its army is obviously commercial in nature, but is done for a public purpose since only states have (real) armies. The main problem with the purpose test is that all acts by a state are necessarily for some public purpose. Thus, in 1963, the *Bundesverfassungsgericht* (the German Federal Constitutional Court), in the leading case of the *Empire of Iran*,[24] preferred to look at the nature rather than the purpose of the transaction.

Article 2(1)(c) of the UN Convention defines a 'commercial transaction' as:

(i) any commercial contract or transaction for the sale of goods or the supply of services;
(ii) any contract for a loan or other transaction of a financial nature, including an obligation of guarantee or of indemnity in respect of any such loan or transaction;
(iii) any other contract or transaction of a commercial, industrial, trading or professional nature, but not including a contract of employment of persons (dealt with in Article 11: see below).

The UN Convention then avoids choosing between the nature and purpose tests by adding in paragraph 2:

> In determining whether a contract or transaction is a 'commercial transaction' under paragraph 1(c), reference should be made *primarily* to the *nature* of the contract or transaction, but its *purpose* should also be taken into account if the parties to the contract or transaction have so agreed, or if, in the *practice of the state of the forum*, that purpose is relevant to determining the non-commercial character of the contract or transaction.[25] [Emphasis added]

---

[23] See the comprehensive comparative survey in Fox, pp. 272–303.
[24] 45 ILR 57, at pp. 80–1.
[25] The formula was originally inserted to help, in particular, developing countries making bulk contracts for food or medicine for humanitarian purposes. It is almost the same

Thus a court should first consider the nature of the contract or transaction. If it is clearly *non*-commercial (e.g. a prohibition on food imports due to a health scare), there should be no need to go further. But if it appears to be commercial, then it is open to the defendant state to argue that its purpose is non-commercial, and this would apply even to contracts for the sale of goods or services, and loans etc. The purpose test would normally have to be carried out by applying the practice of the forum state, and so this takes one back to the jurisprudence of its courts. It has proved impossible for courts to avoid completely inquiring into the purpose of a state's transaction in order to evaluate its nature; they just have to look at the whole context.

Although the commercial exception is already applied by most legal systems, both common law and civil, how this is done varies. The UK and US formulas, as construed and applied by their courts, are not necessarily better or worse than, or even that different from, the one in the UN Convention, which is a compromise between the different approaches taken by states.

Section 3(3) of the UK Act defines 'commercial transaction' as any contract for the supply of goods and services, any financial loan or indemnity and:

> (c) any other transaction or activity (whether of a commercial, industrial, financial, professional or other similar character) into which a state enters or in which it engages *otherwise than in exercise of sovereign authority*.
> [Emphasis added]

Subparagraph (c) covers not only contracts but all other activities that are not essentially of a public character, such as regulatory acts. The English courts have interpreted the italicised words as requiring an examination of the nature of such transactions or activities, not their purpose: has the state acted in exercise of its sovereign authority (in public law) or like a private person (in private law)?[26] But even this approach may well involve some inquiry into purpose.

as in the 1991 draft of the International Law Commission: see its own commentary in Watts, *The International Law Commission 1949–1995*, Oxford, 1999, vol. III, pp. 2017–21.

In paragraph 3, the statement that '[t]he provisions of paragraphs 1 and 2 regarding the use of terms in the present Convention are without prejudice to the use of those terms or to the meanings which may be given to them in other international instruments or in the internal law of any state', means that the definitions are for the purpose of state immunity only and do not affect similar terms in treaties or domestic law on other subjects.

[26] See Lord Wilberforce in *I Congreso del Partido* [1983] AC 244 at 269; 64 ILR 307, at 320. For the facts and a discussion of the case, see Shaw, pp. 635–6.

Section 1603(d) of the US Act provides that the commercial character of an activity

> shall be determined by reference to the nature of the course of conduct or particular transaction or act, *rather than by reference to its purpose.* [Emphasis added]

The italicised words have been relied upon by US courts 'only so far as is absolutely necessary to define the nature of the act',[27] an approach not unlike that of the UK courts. Thus, if a state does something that a private person can do (e.g. issues bonds), it is not immune even when done for a public purpose. If it is something that only a state can do (e.g. regulate a bond market), it is immune. The US Act's commercial exception also requires that in respect of the activity there is a jurisdictional link with the United States (section 1605(a)(2)).

The European Convention is much concerned with the reciprocal enforcement of judgments against state parties. But, although Article 4 is formulated differently to the equivalent provisions in the UK and US Acts, or the UN Convention, the end result may be similar: if an activity is one which only a state can do, it may have immunity.

Contracts of employment

Under Article 11 of the UN Convention, unless the states concerned agree otherwise, a foreign state has *no* immunity from proceedings relating to a contract of employment for work to be performed for it in the forum state. This exception to immunity has itself exceptions that provide *for immunity* in the following cases (and to which there are some exceptions):

(a) The work is 'in the exercise of governmental authority'. It would have to be of a non-commercial nature, and so would include acts of a regulatory nature, such as verifying that certain products are suitable for import into the employer state.
(b) The employee is a diplomatic agent or other person enjoying diplomatic immunity or a consular officer. These are almost always nationals of the employer state and can usually instigate employment proceedings in that state.
(c) Recruitment, renewal or reinstatement issues.

---

[27] *Republic of Argentina v. Weltover*, 504 US 607 (1992); 100 ILR 509. See Fox, pp. 197–202.

(d) Dismissal or termination issues if the head of state, head of government or foreign minister of the employer state has determined that the proceedings 'would interfere with the security interests' of the state. The Understanding on this provision says that this refers primarily to national security and the security of diplomatic missions and consular posts.

(e) The employee is a national of the employer state when the proceeding is instituted, *unless* he has permanent residence[28] in the forum state. Despite the poor drafting of this last exception, the intention would seem to be that there would be no immunity unless one of the (main) exceptions in (a) to (d) or in (f) applies.

(f) The employer state and the employee have otherwise agreed in writing, *unless*, by reason of the subject matter of the proceedings, there are public policy reasons conferring exclusive jurisdiction on the courts of the forum state.

The provisions, with their exceptions to exceptions, mainly reflect the varied state practice, making them complex and lacking in coherence.

Article 5 of the European Convention accords no immunity where the employment is performed in the forum state, unless (a) the employee is a national of the employing state, (b) when the contract was signed he was neither a national of the forum state nor habitually resident there, or (c) the parties to the contract agreed in writing otherwise, unless under the law of the forum state its courts have exclusive jurisdiction by reason of the subject matter. Sections 4 and 16(1)(a) of the UK Act generally follow the European Convention.[29] The US Act has no specific provision for state employment contracts, which for state immunity purposes therefore have to be treated in the same way as other contracts.

Disputes about employment by a diplomatic mission or consular post of a locally engaged person are a particular and constant problem.[30]

Torts (delicts)

Under Article 12 of the UN Convention, there is no immunity in respect of proceedings for pecuniary compensation for death or personal injury, or damage or loss of tangible property, caused by an act or omission

---

[28] See p. 149 above on permanent residence.
[29] However, that Convention has only eight parties, including Belgium and Switzerland, whose courts have not always followed the Convention on employment matters.
[30] See p. 149 above; and (2005) ICLQ 705–8.

attributable to the foreign state, provided the act occurred in the territory of the forum state and the author of it was there at the time. This follows Article 11 of the European Convention and the general trend of state practice. Under the UN Convention, the European Convention and the UK and US Acts, the tort exception applies even when the act was ostensibly performed in exercise of sovereign authority. The exception does not include non-tangible loss, such as economic loss or damage to reputation. Nor does it include loss that is not actionable under the law of the state where the act was committed, which would include acts of foreign armed forces during an armed conflict or any other non-insurable risks.[31] In other words, Article 12 cannot put the claimant in a better position than he would be in if no issue of state immunity arose.

Section 5 of the UK Act goes slightly further in not requiring the author to be in the United Kingdom when the act was committed. Thus proceedings against Libya for compensation for the sabotage of the Pan Am aircraft over Lockerbie in 1988 could be brought in Scotland even though the perpetrator of the crime was not in the United Kingdom at the time. In *Al-Adsani*, a person who claimed to have been tortured abroad by local officials was held not able to sue in the United Kingdom on the basis that he had received medical treatment there for his injuries.[32]

Section 1605(5) of the US Act is similar to the UK Act, but includes also non-tangible loss (except for defamation and similar matters and loss or damage caused by the exercise of a 'discretionary function'). But, if the act is criminal (say, murder), there would be no immunity since there can be no discretion for a state to commit such an act.[33]

Ownership, possession and use of property

Article 13 of the UN Convention provides no immunity from proceedings relating to a foreign state's right or interest in, or possession or use of, or any obligation arising out of (a) immovable property (land) in the forum state; (b) a right or interest in movable or immovable property arising by way of succession, gift or *bona vacantia*; or (c) a right or interest in the administration of property, such as trust property, a bankrupt's estate or a company in liquidation. Articles 9 and 10 of the European Convention

---

[31] See the ILC Commentary to the final draft of Article 12, in Watts, *The International Law Commission 1949–1995*, Oxford, 1999, vol. III, pp. 2068–71, and A/C.6/59/SR13.

[32] [1996] 1 LLR 104; 107 ILR 536.

[33] *Liu v. Republic of China*, 101 ILR 519.

and section 6 of the UK Act provide for similar exceptions to immunity. Section 16(1)(b) of the UK Act accords immunity specifically from proceedings concerning a state's title to or possession of property (not just land) used for the purposes of a diplomatic mission.[34] Although there might seem to be no need to accord such immunity, since diplomatic premises are inviolable and immune from execution,[35] there would be little point in allowing proceedings unless the sending state had consented, and this is reflected in the general saving provisions of Articles 3 and 21(1)(a) of the UN Convention[36] and Article 32 of the European Convention.

Intellectual and industrial property rights

A foreign state will not be immune from proceedings relating to intellectual or industrial property rights (patents, copyright, trademarks, etc.), including infringements of the rights of third persons, that are protected in the forum state (Article 14 of the UN Convention; Article 9 of the European Convention; section 7 of the UK Act).

Ships

Article 32 of the UN Convention on the Law of the Sea 1982[37] confirms the immunity of 'warships and other government ships operated for non-commercial purposes'. The law on shipping is immensely complicated, due partly to differences between common law concepts of Admiralty proceedings and actions *in rem* and civil law procedures. Article 16 of the UN Convention therefore states the immunity in general terms: states can agree otherwise, but, if a court has jurisdiction in proceedings relating to the operation of a ship owned or operated by a foreign state, the ship will have no immunity unless it was, when the cause of action arose, used for 'government non-commercial purposes'.[38] In addition to warships and naval auxiliaries, coastguard, police and customs vessels and other vessels

---

[34] See also p. 123 above.   [35] See p. 125 above.
[36] Article 21(1)(a) makes clear that a bank account of a diplomatic mission cannot be seized: see further p. 127 above.
[37] 1833 UNTS 3 (No. 31363); ILM (1982) 1261; UKTS (1999) 81.
[38] The text of Article 16, apart from the omission of the former paragraph 3, is close to the ILC final draft Articles. The ILC Commentary on the final draft Articles (in A. Watts, *The International Law Commission 1949–1995*, Oxford, 1999, vol. III, pp. 2079–86 or www.un.org/law/ilc/) is therefore very useful.

owned or operated by a foreign state will be immune, provided that, at the time, they were on *only* government non-commercial service. There is no immunity from proceedings relating to the carriage of cargo unless it was carried on an immune ship or is owned by the foreign state and used or intended to be used exclusively for government non-commercial purposes. A certificate, signed by a diplomatic representative or other competent authority of the foreign state, that a ship or cargo is of a governmental and non-commercial character, is evidence of that, but is not conclusive. (See also section 10 of the UK Act and section 1605(b) of the US Act.) The European Convention does not apply to proceedings regarding ships owned or operated by states or to the carriage of cargo by such vessels or to the carriage of cargo owned by a state (Article 30). Instead, the Brussels Convention for the Unification of Certain Rules relating to the Immunity of State Owned Vessels 1926 and its 1934 Protocol apply.[39]

Aircraft and space objects

Article 3(3) of the UN Convention provides that the Convention is without prejudice to the immunities enjoyed by a state under international law with respect to aircraft or space objects owned or operated by it.[40]

Registration of a foreign judgment

Many states have treaties or laws that, on a reciprocal basis, enable the judgment of a foreign court to be registered in their courts and enforced by them as if it were one of theirs. But, if the foreign judgment is given against a foreign state by its *own* courts, registration requires the prior consent of the foreign state, which is rather unlikely to be given.[41]

Criminal jurisdiction

A state cannot be charged with a criminal offence (but see below on heads of state), and none of the above, nor the UN Convention, applies to criminal proceedings.[42]

---

[39] 176 LNTS 199; UKTS (1980) 15.

[40] As to which, see pp. 346 and 367 below, respectively.

[41] *AIC* v. *Nigeria* [2003] EWHC 1357 (QB). See Fox (2004 edn), pp. xxvii–xxx.

[42] The resolution adopting the Convention (A/RES/59/38) agrees with the general understanding of the negotiators that the Convention does not cover criminal proceedings.

Enforcement

Even when there is no immunity, that does not mean that the claimant will be able to enforce a judgment against the property of the defendant state. Consent by a state to the exercise of jurisdiction does not imply consent to measures of constraint. Before embarking on any proceedings, a claimant's lawyers will always assess whether any judgment could be enforced effectively, in terms of both the law of the forum state, and whether at the end of the process there is likely to be enough property available on which the judgment could be executed.

Pre-judgment measures of constraint

Such measures as attachment and arrest (not of persons) before judgment can only be taken if the defendant state has expressly consented to them. This can be done by express provisions in an arbitration agreement, or in a written contract, or by allocating or earmarking property for the satisfaction of the claim (Article 18 of the UN Convention).

Execution of the judgment

No judgment can be executed by attachment, arrest or execution without the consent of the defendant state or by allocating or earmarking property for the satisfaction of the claim.[43] But Article 19(c) of the UN Convention has an exception to this strict rule. Execution can be effected where it has been established:

> that the property is specifically in use or intended for use by the state for other than government non-commercial purposes and is in the territory of the state of the forum, provided that post-judgment measures of constraint may only be taken against property that has a connection with the entity against which the proceeding was directed.

Article 21 of the UN Convention provides that, without consent, the following property shall be considered as specifically in use or intended for use by the state for government non-commercial purposes: (a) the property of diplomatic missions, etc.;[44] (b) property of a military character; (c) the property of a central bank or other monetary authority;[45]

---

[43] As to waiver of immunity from execution of an arbitral award, see Fox, pp. 266–7.
[44] See p. 127 above on the bank accounts of diplomatic missions.
[45] See *AIC* v. *Nigeria* [2003] EWHC 1357 (QB), paras. 53 and 58.

(d) property forming part of the cultural heritage or state archives; or (e) property which is part of an exhibition of scientific, cultural or historical interest and not for sale. The above provisions of the UN Convention represent probably the nearest to generally accepted state practice in this difficult area. But, one must always carefully explore the law of the forum state: see, for example, sections 10 and 13 of the UK Act and sections 1609–1611 of the US Act.[46]

Procedure

Service of process

Some attempts to serve process on a foreign state have been unsuccessful due to mistakes by claimants' lawyers (who sometimes wrongly treat the matter as involving only service out of the jurisdiction) or uncertainty as to the procedure in the *forum* state. Article 22 of the UN Convention provides that service of the writ or other document instituting the proceedings (with a translation if necessary) *shall* be effected by its transmission *through diplomatic channels* to the foreign ministry of the defendant state. Service is deemed to have been effected once *that* foreign ministry has received it. It is not clear if the foreign ministry of the *forum* state has a legal duty to transmit the documents, but a refusal (perhaps for foreign relations reasons) or other failure to transmit them would seem to be a matter for the law of the forum state. Service can also be effected by any other means agreed by the two states or which is acceptable to the defendant state, provided it is not precluded by the law of the state of the forum. Once a state has entered an appearance on the merits of the case (not merely to contest jurisdiction), it is precluded from claiming that service had not been validly effected. (See also Article 16 of the European Convention; section 12 of the UK Act;[47] and section 1608 of the US Act.) Service cannot be validly effected by delivering the documents to a diplomatic mission of the defendant state.[48]

Judgment in default

Article 23 of the UN Convention generally follows established practice. A judgment in default of appearance cannot be rendered against a foreign state unless the court finds that (a) the state has been correctly served,

---

[46] And see Fox, especially, pp. 368–417.
[47] For a detailed account of UK procedure, see Fox, pp. 179–83.
[48] E. Denza, *Diplomatic Law*, 2nd edn, Oxford, 1998, pp. 127–9 and p. 126 above.

(b) at least four months have elapsed from the date of service, and (c) the court is not precluded from exercising jurisdiction, that is, it is satisfied there is no immunity. A copy of any default judgment (with a translation if necessary) must be transmitted to the foreign state by one of the means for service of process on it, and at least four months from its receipt are allowed for an application to have the judgment set aside. (See also Article 16(7) of the European Convention; section 12(4) and (5) of the UK Act; and section 1608(e) of the US Act.)

Visiting forces

Activities of the armed forces of a state, including the procurement of goods, are governed by customary international law. Under such *lex specialis*, property of a military character is immune from execution. But when, in peacetime, its armed forces are physically present in another state with its consent, there is generally a real practical need to provide in some detail as to how civil and criminal jurisdiction over those forces is to be exercised. This can be done by a status-of-forces agreement (SOFA) or *ad hoc*.[49] A SOFA has the effect of modifying the rules on state immunity as between the parties. Perhaps the best known multilateral SOFA is the NATO SOFA 1951,[50] which has served as a model for other multilateral and bilateral SOFAs.[51]

Civil claims

Under Article VIII of the NATO SOFA, claims by the parties against each other for loss or damage to state property are dealt with by mutual waivers or arbitration. Claims by *third parties* are dealt with differently. *Tort* claims concerning *official* acts are dealt with by the host state in the same way as claims against its own armed forces, with the sending state paying a proportion of any compensation. Tort claims in respect of *non-official* acts are either settled *ex gratia* by the host state or are dealt with by the local courts in the normal way.[52] Immunity can be claimed only against the enforcement of a judgment in respect of an official act. Not surprisingly, disputes

[49] If only a very small number of persons are being sent for a short time, it may be sufficient to notify them as members of the A&T staff of the diplomatic mission (see p. 148 above).
[50] 199 UNTS 67 (No. 2678); UKTS (1955) 3. See S. Lazareff, *Status of Military Forces under Current International Law*, Leiden, 1971.
[51] See Oppenheim, pp. 1162–4.
[52] For details of British procedures, contact the Directorate of Claims and Legal (Finance and Secretariat) (DC&L(F&S)), Ministry of Defence, London SWIA 2HB.

can arise as to whether a tortious act was, in the words of the NATO SOFA, 'done in the performance of official duty', and provision is made for these to be resolved by an arbitrator. *Contractual* claims are within the jurisdiction of the courts of the host state, and therefore immunity may be pleaded.

Section 16(2) of the UK Act provides that the Act does not apply to proceedings relating to anything done by foreign armed forces in the United Kingdom which are the subject of the Visiting Forces Act 1952. That Act implements the NATO SOFA and has been applied also to non-NATO visiting forces. Thus, in deciding whether an act is official or unofficial, the UK courts have to the apply the common law restrictive doctrine of state immunity to decide whether the act was public or private in nature, and for this purpose they look at the whole context. In *Holland* v. *Lampen-Wolfe*, it was decided that alleged defamatory remarks about a US national employed by the US forces as a civilian teacher on a US military base in the United Kingdom, and made by her civilian superior (also a US national), were acts done within the sovereign authority of the United States and therefore immune.[53] But, in *Gerber* v. *Gerber*, the use of baby foods on a foreign military base in breach of a registered trademark was held not to have been done in exercise of sovereign authority.[54]

Criminal jurisdiction

SOFAs make provision for the criminal jurisdiction of the sending and host states over members of the visiting force. As with civil proceedings, the details will vary from agreement to agreement, but they follow generally the NATO SOFA. Under that, the sending state has exclusive jurisdiction over offences under its military law, provided they are not also offences under the law of the host state. The host state has exclusive jurisdiction over offences under its law, provided they are not offences under the law of the sending state. Where an act is an offence under the law of both states, so that each has jurisdiction (concurrent jurisdiction), the sending state has primary jurisdiction over those offences that are solely against its property or security, or against another member of the force, or done in performance of official duties. In all other cases, the host state has primary jurisdiction. Jurisdiction can of course be waived by either state.

---

[53] [2000] 1 WLR 1573; [2000] All ER 833; 119 ILR 367. See also *Littrell* v. *USA (No. 2)* [1995] 1 WLR 82; [1994] 4 All ER 203; 100 ILR 438, in which medical treatment of a US airman at a US military hospital by US personnel was held to be an immune matter.

[54] [2002] EWHC 428 (Ch).

Heads of state, heads of government, foreign ministers and other senior officials

This subject had not been considered in depth until a decade ago,[55] but since then it has received prominence due to attempts to pursue some current or former foreign leaders for serious international crimes.

Civil proceedings

The official acts of a head of state are treated as those of the state. But an act done by him in his private capacity (*ratione personae*) is subject to the customary international law applicable to a head of state (Article 3(2) of the UN Convention). States have taken different approaches. Some European courts have held that there is no immunity for private acts.[56] In contrast, section 20 of the UK Act accords a head of state, and members of his family forming part of his household, the same inviolability and immunities as the head of a diplomatic mission, which covers all official and almost all private matters.[57] A head of state cannot be arrested or served with legal process. But, once he leaves office, he can be sued in respect of private matters arising during his time in office. Whether a head of government, foreign minister or other senior official has the same immunity is not clear. But now that many monarchs and presidents have little real power, it being exercised instead by their heads of government, there is a trend to accord heads of government and foreign ministers the same degree of immunity.

Criminal proceedings

In 2002, in the *Arrest Warrant* case, the International Court of Justice held that the issue of a warrant for the arrest of a foreign minister for war crimes and crimes against humanity, and its circulation to other states, were coercive measures that violated his inviolability and absolute immunity from criminal jurisdiction under customary international law for all acts, public or private, committed while in office or before.[58] This decision necessarily applies also to heads of state and heads of government,

---

[55] A. Watts, 'The Legal Position in International Law of Heads of State, Heads of Government and Foreign Ministers' (1994-III) 247 *Hague Recueil* 40.
[56] Fox, pp. 439–40.   [57] See pp. 120 and 139 above.
[58] *The Arrest Warrant of 11 April 2000 (Democratic Republic of Congo v. Belgium)*, *ICJ Reports* (2002); ILM (2002) 536.

and may apply to other senior officials such as defence ministers.[59] But, once such a person has left office, can he be arrested and prosecuted for a crime committed while in office? He would have no continuing immunity for private crimes, but the *Arrest Warrant* judgment suggests that he would have continuing immunity for crimes committed in his *public* capacity.[60] So, could a head of state order the commission of acts of torture yet remain immune from prosecution for it abroad, even after he has left office? In its judgment in *Pinochet (No. 3)*, the House of Lords (the UK's highest court) held that the former Chilean President had no immunity from extradition to Spain to face charges of torture committed while he was in office.[61] Under the Torture Convention, a head of state can be liable for the crime,[62] and it would be inconsistent with the obligation under that Convention (to which Chile, Spain and the United Kingdom are parties) to extradite or prosecute offenders if a former head of state could retain his immunity for such crimes, Chile having, by ratifying the Torture Convention, by implication waived any continuing immunity. But the differing reasoning of the judges makes it difficult to state with any certainty the exact basis on which the court came to its decision, and whether the precedent has wider implications. Although the judgment may be followed for the crimes listed in the Statute of the International Criminal Court (genocide, war crimes and crimes against humanity) or with the authorisation of the UN Security Council, it seems unlikely that it extends to terrorist offences or to simple murder. The international law on this matter is still evolving.[63] The UN Convention does not apply to criminal proceedings.[64]

(As to the position of such persons in relation to international criminal tribunals, see pp. 273–82 below.)

---

[59] See the case of the Israeli Defence Minister, Mofaz, in (2004) ICLQ 771.
[60] And has been so applied by the Belgian, Dutch, German and Spanish supreme courts, at least when there was no jurisdictional connection with the forum state: Fox (2004 edn), pp. xviii–xix; and L. Reydams, *Universal Jurisdiction*, Oxford, 2004, pp. 141 and 165. But see the joint separate opinion in the *Arrest Warrant* case of Judges Higgins, Kooijmans and Buergenthal, paras. 19–65, and (2002) ICLQ 959.
[61] *R. v. Bow Street Metropolitan Magistrate, ex parte Pinochet (No. 3)* [2000] 1 AC 147; [1999] 2 WLR 825; [1999] 2 All ER 97; 119 ILR 135. See also (1999) ICLQ 687.
[62] 1465 UNTS 85 (No. 24841); ILM (1984) 1027; UKTS (1991) 107.
[63] Fox, pp. 421–48.   [64] See A RES/59/38, para. 2.

8

Nationality, aliens and refugees

But in spite of all temptations / To belong to other nations /
He remains an Englishman.[1]

Nationality

Oppenheim. *Oppenheim's International Law*, 9th edn, London, 1992,
pp. 851–96.

Possession by a natural person (an individual) or a legal person (such as a
corporation) of the nationality of a state provides them with a link to that
state for the purposes of international law. The most important aspect of
this link is the right of the state in international law to protect its nationals
as against other states. The law of each state primarily determines who are
its nationals. In certain, and usually exceptional, cases, international law
will not recognise a person as a national of a state even if the state regards
him as its national. Although the nationality (if lawfully obtained) will be
valid in the state of nationality, it may not be recognised for the purposes
of international law. The state of the new nationality may not be entitled
to make an international claim on his behalf unless it can establish that
at the relevant time he had a 'genuine connection' with it.[2]

Dual nationality

A dual national is a person who has the nationality of two (and sometimes
more) states. It can be acquired in various ways, deliberately or acciden-
tally. A child is sometimes born a dual national. The law of one or both
states may require the child, usually when it reaches the age of majority

---

[1] W. S. Gilbert, *HMS Pinafore*, Act I.
[2] See *Nottebohm*, *ICJ Reports* (1955), p. 4, at pp. 22–6; 22 ILR 349. The effectiveness in
international law of the conferring by Iceland in 2005 of its nationality on the chess grand
master, Bobby Fischer, is therefore problematic.

(usually eighteen or twenty-one), to choose which nationality to keep, and allows perhaps a year in which to choose or lose nationality. If a person later acquires a further nationality, whether he retains the nationality of his first state will depend on the law of that state, which may provide for automatic withdrawal of his nationality or require him to choose within a certain period. When a dual national is in one of his states of nationality, he cannot usually seek the protection of the other, although the latter may make representations. However, there is a trend, at least among Western states, to claim the right to protect a dual national when detained in the state of his other nationality if his connection with that state is tenuous (e.g. his only connection is a parent born there). In a third state, a dual national can be protected by either state.[3]

Citizenship

The term 'citizenship' usually denotes entitlement, under the law of a state, to full civil and political rights, and citizenship and nationality normally coincide.

In the law of a state which still has the remnants of a colonial empire, 'citizenship' may be limited to person with close connections with ('belongs to') the metropolitan territory, those belonging to its overseas territories having a separate status. Thus, the British Nationality Act 1981, as amended, distinguishes between three main categories: (1) British citizens – those belonging to the metropolitan territory of the United Kingdom, to the Channel Islands or to the Isle of Man,[4] and now also to all remaining British overseas territories; (2) British Overseas Territories Citizens – persons who belonged to a former overseas territory but did not acquire the citizenship of that country on independence; and (3) British Nationals (Overseas) (former belongers of Hong Kong).[5] Nevertheless, in international law, all those in the various categories are nationals of the United Kingdom, even though only British citizens are free of all UK immigration control.

Under the 1981 Act, there is also the category of 'Commonwealth citizen' enjoyed in the United Kingdom and its overseas territories by all citizens of Commonwealth states, although, in itself, it does not confer the right freely to enter the United Kingdom. However, in recognition of the ties between the United Kingdom and its former territories,

---

[3] See p. 441 below on dual nationality and claims.
[4] See p. 29 above.   [5] See www.passport.gov.uk.

Commonwealth citizens are entitled to stand for election to the British Parliament, to vote in British elections and to sit on juries. Usually, this is not reciprocated by Commonwealth states. For similar reasons, citizens of the Republic of Ireland (which is not in the Commonwealth) have the same entitlements.

The right to leave and return to one's state of nationality

Under Article 12(2) of the International Covenant on Civil and Political Rights 1966,[6] a person is entitled to leave any country, including his own, but this right is probably not yet established in customary international law. With the virtual end of communist regimes, the right to leave is now general in domestic law, and has led to a substantial increase in so-called economic migrants.[7] But, in some cases, financial and other obstacles (e.g. refusal of a passport, restrictions on the states which can be visited or loss of nationality on leaving) may make the right problematic. The right may of course be subject to restrictions to prevent persons accused of crimes from fleeing, and for health and other reasons of public interest.

Article 12(4) guarantees the unrestricted right of a person to return to his own country.[8]

Passports[9]

Even a (genuine) passport raises no more than a presumption that the holder is a national of the state of issue, although the presumption is not easily rebutted. National law governs the issue of passports, and an unjustified refusal of a passport can amount to a severe restriction on the ability to leave or return to one's state of citizenship, and is a possible breach of the state's international obligations.[10]

Statelessness

If a person loses his citizenship, but does not acquire a new one, he becomes stateless. Although the state in which he is living will treat him as an alien

---

[6] 999 UNTS 171 (No. 14688); ILM (1967) 368; UKTS (1977) 6.
[7] See p. 189 below.   [8] But note the UK position, p. 243 below.
[9] D. Turack, *The Passport in International Law*, Lexington, MA, 1972; J. Torpey, *The Invention of the Passport*, Cambridge, 2000.
[10] See Oppenheim, p. 866, n. 7.

(see below), it does not have to recognise the right of any other state to protect him. The stateless person will be covered by such human rights obligations as are binding on his state of residence, but enforcing those rights may not be easy, although if there is a breach of a human rights treaty any other party to it will have the right to complain. In an attempt to reduce statelessness, the United Nations adopted the Convention relating to the Status of Stateless Persons 1954.[11] This gives less favourable treatment than the Refugees Convention (see below), and has only fifty-seven parties. The Convention on the Reduction of Statelessness 1961 has a meagre twenty-nine parties.[12] However, many stateless persons will have a claim to refugee status.

Legal persons

The buildings and employees of a legal person (such as a company) are its physical embodiment, but for legal purposes they are not the company. A company is the most common form of corporation, and is created by law. Given this fundamental distinction from natural persons, determining the nationality of a corporation is not as easy, although it is particularly important for the purpose of the protection under international law of the corporation's assets and activities abroad and the bringing of international claims. The basic principle is that a corporation has the nationality of the state in which it was incorporated or in which it has its registered office or head office. In *Barcelona Traction (Second Phase)*, the International Court of Justice decided that a company incorporated in Canada, and with its head office there, had Canadian nationality even though 88 per cent of the shareholders were Belgian nationals.[13] These days, for tax purposes many companies are incorporated in one state (where the registered office is), but have their headquarters in another state. An international tribunal may therefore look behind the legal veil (or facade) of incorporation to determine in which state the control and ownership of the corporation really lies. The state with which the company has a close, substantial and effective connection, may then be treated as the state of nationality. *Foreign branches* of a company will usually have the same nationality as the company, but if the company incorporates *subsidiary companies* under the law of another state, they will probably have the nationality of that

[11] 360 UNTS 117 (No. 1518); UKTS (1960) 41.
[12] 989 UNTS 175 (No. 14458). See A. Aust, 'Limping Treaties, Lessons from Multilateral Treaty-Making' (2003) NILR 243 at 262–3
[13] *ICJ Reports* (1970), p. 3, paras. 32–101; 46 ILR 178. See Brownlie, pp. 466–71.

state. A multinational company can pose further problems since it may be incorporated in one state, have its headquarters in another, and do most of its business in other states.[14] But all depends on the precise facts and circumstances, including the reason nationality is an issue.

A treaty, especially a bilateral treaty, will often define which companies are to be regarded as covered by it. This is particularly important for bilateral investment treaties (BITs), which provide for compensation in the event of expropriation.[15] The grant of the right to operate scheduled air services is usually restricted to airline companies that are substantially owned and effectively controlled by the parties or their nationals.[16]

The jurisdiction of the Iran–US Claims Tribunal[17] is limited to claims by corporations that are incorporated under either Iranian or US law, provided that 50 per cent or more of the stock is held by Iranian or US nationals. Nationality is presumed if the claimant can establish *prima facie* that there is such a 50 per cent holding and the respondent produces no evidence to the contrary. But the rule should not be seen as reflecting any general principle, being limited to the particular circumstances.[18]

Ships and aircraft

A ship has the nationality of the state whose flag it is entitled to fly irrespective of the nationality of the person(s), or company, which owns it. The flag can be readily changed.[19] The flag state is important for the purpose of jurisdiction over the ship, especially on the high seas.[20] An aircraft has the nationality of the state in which it is registered,[21] but this can also be changed. In both cases, nationality for the purpose of international claims may have to be made in respect of the beneficial owner of the ship or aircraft.[22]

Diplomatic protection

A state has the right to protect its nationals abroad, that is to say, to ensure that another state treats them in accordance with treaties binding on both states and the minimum standards for treatment of aliens

---

[14] See Oppenheim, p. 863, n. 15, on the complexities of multinational company nationality.
[15] See p. 375 below.   [16] See p. 348 below.
[17] See p. 445 below for more about the Tribunal.
[18] See Collier and Lowe, *The Settlement of Disputes in International Law*, Oxford, 1999, pp. 80–1 and 194–5 for more details of how the rule operates.
[19] See further, p. 316 below.   [20] See p. 312 below.
[21] See further, p. 346 below.   [22] See Brownlie, pp. 471–2.

laid down in customary international law. But there is no corresponding duty on a state to protect its nationals.[23] Not surprisingly, this is generally not understood. Whether a state decides to take action to protect one of its nationals (including legal persons) will depend on several factors: whether the national can establish the necessary facts that he has been treated wrongly by the foreign state; whether he can, and has taken, steps to correct the wrong; whether the case is meritorious; whether the state has the means to take effective action with the foreign state.[24] If a state makes a formal claim in respect of one of its nationals, natural or legal, the person must also satisfy the nationality-of-claims rule.[25] Since 1997, the International Law Commission has been studying diplomatic protection, which covers several of the issues outlined in this chapter. The ILC's work will not be finished for a few years yet, and some of its conclusions may well be controversial.[26]

Aliens

Oppenheim. *Oppenheim's International Law*, 9th edn, London, 1992, pp. 896–948.

In relation to a state, an alien is any person who is not one of its nationals (i.e. a non-national). An alien will not have the same rights and obligations as nationals, although some states confer on aliens certain rights otherwise enjoyed only by their nationals. The principal disadvantage of being an alien is that one has no entitlement to enter or stay in a foreign state, unless this is conferred by treaty. Entry and residence can be made subject to presentation of a passport or a national identity card, obtaining a visa and restrictions as to length of stay, place of residence and employment. A national of an EU state enjoys almost unrestricted freedom of entry into other EU states, although permanent residence can be subject to certain restrictions. For certain EU states, the Schengen Agreement 1990 has abolished internal immigration controls for EU and third state citizens.[27] In the case of tourists and short-stay visitors, many states have unilaterally waived the requirement of a visa or have concluded bilateral visa-abolition agreements.[28] For migrant workers and workers who frequently cross a

---

[23] *Barcelona Traction ICJ Reports* (1970), p. 3, at para 78; 46 ILR 178.
[24] See *Abassi* [2002] EWCA Civ 1598.   [25] See p. 441 below.
[26] See www.un.org/law/ilc/.   [27] ILM (1991) 68, and see p. 483 below.
[28] For example, the Poland–UK Agreement 1992, UKTS (1992) 69.

frontier (*fronteliers*), there are many bilateral treaties waiving visa and passport requirements.[29]

Aliens are subject to the law and jurisdiction of the foreign state. Certain of the laws of his own state will continue to apply to him, although they may well not be enforceable while he is abroad; and the jurisdiction of his home state will extend to certain crimes and other acts committed by him while abroad.[30] Unless prevented by its treaty obligations, the foreign state is free to treat aliens less favourably than its own nationals, for example by prohibiting them from owning land (as in Denmark) or doing certain work, especially in the professions. Aliens are usually not allowed to be government officials, to stand for parliament or to vote.[31] But, an alien who takes up residence will normally be subject to local taxation. If he still remains subject to the tax laws of his own state, a double taxation agreement between the two states may lessen his tax burden.[32]

The life of an alien is – or at least should be – better if the foreign state is a party to the International Covenant on Civil and Political Rights 1966.[33] These require that all persons in the territory of a party, regardless of national origin, enjoy certain basic rights. Other human rights treaties will also apply to aliens. Many bilateral treaties afford specific protection to aliens, such as treaties of commerce and friendship, and consular conventions.

Property of aliens[34]

An alien, whether an individual or a corporation, may be subject to special restrictions on the holding of property. But if an alien owns property lawfully, customary international law requires the state to protect his property rights by allowing him access to its courts on an equal footing to its nationals. But a state (by means of governmental or other public bodies) is not prevented from expropriating the property of aliens so long as certain conditions are met. 'Expropriation' means the compulsory deprivation of property against the payment of compensation. 'Nationalisation' usually means *general* expropriation, typically of a whole industry. In contrast, 'confiscation' is the taking of property without compensation.

---

[29] See Oppenheim, pp. 901–3.   [30] See pp. 44–5 above.
[31] But see p. 180 above for a notable exception.
[32] See, for example, the Australia–UK Double Taxation Agreement 2003, UKTS (2004) 5.
[33] 999 UNTS 171 (No. 14668); ILM (1967) 368; UKTS (1977) 6. See pp. 235 *et seq* below.
[34] See the extensive references to cases in Oppenheim, pp. 911–33.

'Sequestration' is the taking possession of property temporarily, the legal title to which remains with the owner. (References below to 'expropriation' generally include also nationalisation, confiscation or sequestration.)

Expropriation can be done by various means. It is rarely effected by sending soldiers to occupy a factory and replacing all the managers with local officials. It can be done by much less obvious means, such as imposing penal rates of taxation on certain types of companies to drive them out of business. One has to examine all the facts and circumstances to determine the *substantive* effect of the act that the alien owner claims has deprived him of his property.[35] An act that causes a significant diminution in the value of the property may well constitute expropriation.

The factors which must be considered in determining whether an expropriation is lawful in international law are (1) whether it was done in accordance with proper legislation or arbitrarily; (2) whether it was done for a public purpose (an environmental concern may not be enough);[36] (3) whether aliens were discriminated against; and (4) whether appropriate compensation has been paid. Whether the compensation is appropriate depends on whether it is adequate and effective, and promptly paid. Whether these criteria are met will depend on the facts of each case. The calculation of the amount of compensation is usually complicated, but compensation for loss of property should reflect its market value immediately before the expropriation was formally announced or had become known. To be effective, the compensation must be paid in a form that is of value to the alien. If paid in money, it must be in a currency that can be transferred abroad and freely exchanged.

Such, or similar, criteria have been included in thousands of bilateral investment treaties (BITs), that are generally concluded between a developed and a developing state.[37] Disputes may also be submitted under other multilateral treaties such as the World Trade Organization Agreement,[38] the North American Free Trade Agreement (NAFTA)[39] or Protocol 1 to the European Convention on Human Rights 1950 (ECHR),[40] provided the states involved are parties to them. Expropriation claims may also fall within the jurisdiction of specially established tribunals, such as the Iran–US Claims Tribunal,[41] or the UN Compensation Commission

---

[35] See *Sporrong and Lönnroth* (1982) 5 EHRR 35; 68 ILR 86, at pp. 104 *et seq.*, and *Starrett Housing Corp.* v. *Iran*, ILM (1984) 1090 at 1107–17; 85 ILR 349.

[36] *Santa Elena* v. *Costa Rica*, ILM (2000) 1317.   [37] See p. 373 below.

[38] See p. 382 below.   [39] See p. 387 below.

[40] See p. 237 below.   [41] See p. 445 below.

established by the UN Security Council by Resolution 687 to compensate those who suffered loss as a result of Iraq's invasion of Kuwait.[42] (On dispute settlement generally, see Chapter 22 below.)

Asylum

A state can let an alien enter and remain in its territory even if his own state objects. This is more correctly called the grant of *asylum* (or *political asylum*), and is conferred by states in their discretion. Aliens have no 'right' of asylum,[43] it is merely the right of the state to grant it. The practice of asylum pre-dates by centuries the Refugee Convention (see below). The concept is wider than refugee status in that it can be granted when the person has no fear of persecution. Persons fleeing from famine or floods and given shelter in a foreign state may often be misdescribed as 'refugees' because they seek refuge, but they are more accurately described as *displaced persons* who have been given asylum, often only for a temporary period. In the same way, persons genuinely seeking refuge from persecution are often confusingly referred to as *asylum-seekers*.

Diplomatic asylum

Diplomatic asylum must be clearly distinguished from the asylum just described. Diplomatic asylum is the giving of protection by a diplomatic mission to a person fleeing from the authorities of the host state (not just from a crowd). The person can be a local national, a national of the sending state or a national of a third state. Except as between some Latin America states, this practice is not favoured since it amounts to the sending state abusing the inviolability of its diplomatic mission[44] by acting in a manner which conflicts with its duty to respect the local laws, and indeed the sovereignty, of the host state.[45] Nevertheless, from time to time persons will enter a mission and claim diplomatic asylum. It may be either physically difficult to eject them (though the mission can authorise the local police to do so) or politically awkward. The intruders may have good grounds for believing that they will be treated severely by the local authorities, and there will be the inevitable media attention. If there is

---

[42] See www.unog.ch/uncc/ and p. 446 below.
[43] The reference to 'asylum' in Article 14 of the Universal Declaration of Human Rights 1948 (see p. 235 below) is to the rights of refugees.
[44] See p. 129 below.   [45] See p. 152 below.

genuine humanitarian case, it will need all the diplomatic skills of the head of the mission, and his foreign minister, to balance their legal duty to the receiving state and their moral duty. That a person wants refuge in the sending state is not a valid reason for protecting him, although the sending state will be in a stronger position, politically and legally, if there are grounds for believing that, if ejected, he would be subjected to 'summary justice', or otherwise dealt with arbitrarily or treated inhumanly.[46]

Refugees

Hathaway, *The Law of Refugee Status*, Toronto, 1991

Office of the UN High Commissioner for Refugees, *Handbook on Procedures and Criteria for Determining Refugee Status*, Geneva, 1992 (www.unhcr.ch)

Weis, *The Refugee Convention 1951: The Travaux Préparatoires Analysed with a Commentary*, Cambridge, 1995

Feller, Türk and Nicholson (eds.), *Refugee Protection in International Law*, Cambridge, 2003

Oppenheim. *Oppenheim's International Law*, 9th edn, London, 1992, pp. 890–6

Definition of refugee

The relevant treaty is the Convention relating to the Status of Refugees 1951, as amended by the 1967 Protocol extending the Convention to cover all refugees, past, present and future. The two instruments are referred to collectively as 'the Refugee Convention' (in this chapter, 'the Convention').[47] Article 1A(2) defines 'refugee' as a person who

> owing to a well-founded fear of being persecuted for reasons of race, religion, nationality, membership of a particular social group or political opinion, is outside the country of his nationality and is unable or, owing to such fear, is unwilling to avail himself of the protection of that country.[48]

[46] See generally Oppenheim, pp. 1082–6; Satow, paras. 14.17–14.23; *R. (B. Children)* v. *Secretary of State for Foreign and Commonwealth Affairs* [2005] 2 WLR 618.

[47] 189 UNTS 137 (No. 2545) and 606 UNTS 267 (No. 8791); UKTS (1954) 39 and UKTS (1969) 15.

[48] See also Article I of the OAU Convention on Specific Aspects of Refugee Problems in Africa, 10 September 1969, 1001 UNTS 60 (No. 14691), which expands on the Convention definition by covering persons who have fled from, in effect, generalised violence. That is very relevant in the African context, although most conflicts in Africa are characterised by inter-ethnic violence and so in many such cases the Convention definition would also apply.

The definition applies also to a stateless person who is outside the country of his 'habitual residence' and is unable or, owing to such fear is unwilling, to return to it.

Some important misunderstandings are caused by misuse or misapplication of basic terms. Refugees must be clearly distinguished from other persons with whom they are constantly confused. Because of war or natural disaster, people have long sought safety in foreign countries, and the last quarter of the twentieth century saw a substantial rise their numbers. It is therefore important to distinguish from refugees such *displaced persons* seeking *asylum* (see above), since persons seeking protection as refugees are frequently referred to, often disparagingly, as 'asylum-seekers'.[49] The same period also saw a large increase in *economic migrants* whose sole purpose in leaving their state is to seek a better life. Then there are *internally displaced persons* (IDPs) who have had to leave their homes for various reasons, but who are still in their own country. The Office of the UN High Commissioner for Refugees (UNHCR) has only a limited mandate for IDPs. It does not have a mandate for the other groups mentioned in this paragraph or for other 'persons of concern', such as former refugees who have been repatriated, stateless persons or persons who have been displaced by war or generalised violence where there is no element of persecution *per se*. This section does not deal with those categories.

Although not all states are parties to the Convention (there are 142 parties), its basic principles, in particular the definition of a refugee and the prohibition on *refoulement*,[50] are now part of customary international law. Unlike asylum, the status of refugee under the Convention is a *right under the Convention*. Once the criteria have been satisfied, states have an obligation to treat the person as a refugee; there is no discretion. However, states have to use their domestic legislation and procedures in dealing with claims to refugee status. One has therefore to consider each refugee application, not only on its own particular facts but also in the light of the law of the state concerned. Although there is some room for varying opinions in interpreting some aspects of the Convention, in applying their legislation states should be guided by the Convention, UNHCR Guidelines, and Conclusions of the UNHCR Executive Committee. Here, one can only outline the most important provisions of the Convention.

---

[49] The media have much to answer for; but are not helped when the Convention is incorporated into UK law by the Asylum (*sic*) and Immigration Appeals Act 1993.
[50] See p. 193 below.

The UNHCR was established in 1951 by General Assembly Resolution 428 (V). Annexed to the resolution was the UNHCR's Statute. The Statute gives it a mandate to protect refugees whether or not the state in which they are is a party to the Convention, provided the state is co-operative. Even if it is unco-operative, the UNHCR still has a mandate in respect of refugees within that state's territory, so that it can still make *démarches* to the authorities on their behalf and publicise their plight.

Application for refugee status

The proposition that a refugee should make his claim in the first country at which he arrives is controversial and not supported by the Convention or other legal instruments. But the determination of refugee status should be made by the first state in whose territory the claim to refugee status is made.[51] Every state is obliged to admit refugee claimants, this duty of admission flowing from the principle of non-*refoulement* (see below), and is a key part of refugee law. The claim is often made at immigration control at an airport or seaport. Since the territory of a state includes its territorial sea, a claim can be made on or from a ship in the territorial sea, or by a lawyer on behalf of the claimant once the ship has entered the territorial sea. Thus, when a ship carrying persons seeking refuge has entered the territorial sea of a state, it should not be turned back. The practice of a state declaring a 'migration zone' within its territory, within which a person can apply for refuge but leaving outlying areas outside the zone in an attempt to avoid the Convention applying there, is not compatible with Convention obligations unless the state makes provision for applications to be properly processed outside the zone, either in its territory or in a third state, and, if they are successful, to admit the refugees into the zone.

Once the claim has been made, the state should not require the claimant to leave while his application is pending, as this might result in a breach of the prohibition on *refoulement*.[52]

A passport is *prima facie* proof of the nationality of the claimant, but is not conclusive.[53] It is not necessary for a person claiming refugee status to have lawfully entered the state where he makes the claim (Article 31(1)). One must therefore be very careful when one reads about

---

[51] See the EU's so-called Dublin Agreement 1990, 2144 UNTS 492 (No. 37439); UKTS (1996) 72.

[52] See section 6 of the (UK) Asylum and Immigration Appeals Act 1993.

[53] See pp. 141 and 181 above.

'illegal immigrants'. Used correctly, this term means only that the persons have entered another state without the necessary visa. Many economic migrants fall into this category. But the term illegal immigrant is often used in a derogatory sense, and it may obscure (and be so intended by politicians) the fact that the person may be a genuine refugee even if, as a matter of domestic law, he has arrived in the state without permission and is there illegally only in that sense. Not surprisingly, most refugees are quite unable to obtain a visa before entering the state of refuge. Embassies and consulates may refuse a visa or be inaccessible, and the Convention does not require states to process refugee applications abroad, although there is a growing trend to do this. Because most airlines will not carry passengers who do not have a passport and any necessary visas, many genuine refugees smuggle themselves into the state of refuge, as do some economic migrants.

Fear of persecution

An applicant's fear of persecution will be well founded (i.e. real) if he establishes to a reasonable degree that if he were to return to his state it is likely he would be persecuted. Fear being largely subjective, the applicant's perception will be important, but it must still be reasonable. So there must be some basis in fact that he, or other persons in his state in a like position, have been or are likely to be persecuted. In addition to a detailed investigation of the background of the individual and his family, the state of refuge will have to assess the conditions in his own state in order to determine whether the fear is reasonable. But persecution of him or others does not have to be the reason he left his state, since circumstances can change for the worse subsequently.

The persecution must be for reasons of race, religion, nationality, membership of a particular social group or political opinion, although a rigid line cannot be drawn between these categories; they often overlap. The Convention does not define persecution, although it must amount to some significant form of ill-treatment, usually involving human rights abuses. The ill-treatment does not have to be physical. Serious discrimination in matters such as education or healthcare, if particularly severe and cumulative, may amount to persecution, but the threshold is high. In itself, fear of punishment for a crime (including for desertion from the armed forces or draft-dodging) will not be enough. The person would have to show that, because of his political opinions etc., the real purpose of a prosecution would be to persecute him or that, for the same reason, he would not get a fair trial or the sentence would be excessive. Persecution for reasons of 'nationality' includes persecution of ethnic or linguistic groups. Being of a different political opinion to that of the government will, in itself, not be enough; the person would have to show that, because of his opinions, he has a real fear of persecution, and this is more likely if he has actively expressed those opinions.

Persecution can also be done by a dominant minority, but states vary on whether fear of persecution by *private* persons is sufficient, and this includes organisations as well as individuals who are not formally tied to the state, for example rebel armed forces and paramilitary groups. Some states regard private persecution as insufficient, and others only if the persecution is known to the authorities and they were unwilling or unable to provide protection.[54] The UNHCR Handbook makes clear that, depending on the circumstances, persecution by non-state agents can fall within the Convention. The majority of states also follow this route (including several Western European). There is also significant jurisprudence to this effect. The purpose of the Convention is to provide surrogate (international) protection where national protection of an individual's fundamental rights has failed. The identity of the persecutor is not therefore particularly relevant. Although the first state the claimant enters should process his claim, a state that takes a narrow view and rejects the claim may, instead of returning him to his state (which could amount to a breach of the non-*refoulement* obligation) do nothing to prevent him entering another state that takes a more liberal approach.

Even where a state may grant diplomatic asylum in one of its diplomatic missions to a local national,[55] since an embassy is *not* part of the territory of the sending state[56] the asylum-seeker cannot claim refugee status while he is still in his own state.

Exceptions to refugee status

Article 1, Sections C to F, of the Convention list four cases where a person coming within the definition of refugee is nevertheless excluded from the protection of the Convention: he no longer needs protection (Section C); he is receiving protection and assistance from UN organs or agencies

---

[54] See the judgment of the House of Lords in *R. v. Home Secretary, ex parte Adan* [2001] 2 AC 477; ILM (2001) 727; and Feller, Türk and Nicholson (eds.), *Refugee Protection in International Law*, Cambridge, 2003, p. 59.
[55] See p. 187 above.   [56] See p. 125 above.

other than the UNHCR, for example the UN Relief and Works Agency for Palestine Refugees in the Near East (UNRWA) (Section D); although not a national of his new state of residence, its authorities treat him as if he were one (Section E). Section F is rather different in that it lists, in the pointed words of the UNHCR Handbook, 'persons not to be deserving of international protection'. A state is required *not* to treat a person as a refugee if there are 'serious reasons for considering'[57] that:

(a) he has committed a crime against peace (aggression), a war crime or a crime against humanity;[58]
(b) he has committed a serious non-political crime outside the country of refuge prior to his admission to that country as a refugee; or
(c) he has been guilty of acts contrary to the purposes and principles of the United Nations.

Category (c) might appear somewhat vague,[59] but it has been applied by domestic courts and is of increasing importance. To make it clear that persons involved in terrorism are not entitled to refugee status, in 1996 the UN General Assembly reaffirmed that terrorism, including knowingly financing, planning and inciting terrorist acts, is 'contrary to the purposes and principles of the United Nations', and that before recognising refugee status, states should ensure that the person has not participated in terrorist acts.[60] All potential Section F cases, including terrorist ones, require the most careful examination by national authorities since difficult issues are often involved.

Non-*refoulement*[61]

A state is *not* obliged to give refuge to a person even if he has established his refugee status. But, in addition to not returning him to his own state, he must not be sent to a third state if his life or freedom would there be threatened on account of his race, religion, nationality, membership of a particular social group or political opinion (Article 33(1)). This is known as the principle of non-*refoulement*. It applies even before a claim to refugee status has been verified, provided there is a *prima facie* claim.

---

[57] It is not necessary to prove that he has been convicted of a relevant criminal offence.
[58] For an explanation of these terms, see p. 271 below.
[59] But see the UNHCR's guidelines on Article 1F on its website, www.unhcr.ch.
[60] Paras. 2 and 3 of the Declaration annexed to A/RES/51/210; ILM (1996) 1188.
[61] From the French 'refouler', to return.

The test is whether his life or freedom 'would' be threatened, and is thus an objective test, the refugee's perception not being so relevant. In the case of a political refugee, it may be necessary to determine whether the third state would be able to protect him from abduction or attack by agents of his own state.

A mass influx of refugees into a state can cause considerable problems, particularly as such movements tend to be into developing countries with limited resources. The 1967 UN General Assembly Declaration on Territorial Asylum[62] states that in order to safeguard the local population such refugees may be refused entry or, if already in the state, returned even if they may be persecuted. But the Declaration is not legally binding and an attempt to convert it into a treaty was unsuccessful. Yet, the Convention was written with mass movements in mind (World War Two refugees) and its limited exceptions to the prohibition on *refoulement* do not include situations of mass influx.[63]

Protection for the state of refuge

The prohibition on *refoulement* does not apply when there are 'reasonable grounds' for regarding the refugee as a danger to the security of the state of refuge or, having been convicted of a 'particularly serious crime' constitutes a danger to the community of that state (Article 33(2)). Similarly, Article 32 permits the expulsion of a refugee on grounds of 'national security or public order'. Expulsion must be done with due process of law, and the refugee must be given a reasonable time in which to seek admission to another state. However, even when the state of refuge would be entitled to send the person to another state, including his own, the state of refuge may be prevented from doing so by its obligations under other human rights treaties. Such obligations are also relevant in the case of those who are excluded from refugee status by virtue of Article 1, Section F (see above). The European Court of Human Rights has decided that Article 3 of the European Convention on Human Rights has extraterritorial effect.[64] This prevents a person, whatever his nationality, being sent to another state if there he might be subject to inhuman or degrading treatment.[65]

---

[62] See A/RES/2312(XXII).
[63] Conclusion No. 22 (1981) of the UNHCR Executive Committee. Hence the need for improved burden-sharing between states, one of UNHCR's current priorities.
[64] For an explanation of this term, see pp. 44–9 above.
[65] *Chahal* v. *UK* (1997) 23 EHRR 413; 108 ILR 385.

Article 3 of the Torture Convention 1984[66] prohibits the return or extradition of a person to another state if there are substantial grounds for believing that he would be in danger of being tortured.

Obligations of the state of refuge to the refugee

The Convention has two dozen Articles on the treatment of refugees by the state of refuge. Generally, these require refugees to be treated no less favourably than other aliens who are there and not to discriminate as between refugees on grounds of race, religion or country of origin. (The Convention counter-balances this with the obligation on refugees to abide by the laws of the host state.) Many of the provisions are now subsumed by other international human rights obligations. There is a (qualified) obligation to issue refugees with travel documents. Before the Convention, these were known as 'Nansen Passports'.[67]

---

[66] 1465 UNTS 85 (No. 24841); ILM (1984) 1027; UKTS (1991) 107; BGG 229.
[67] Oppenheim, p. 892, n. 8; I. Kaprielian-Churchill, 'Rejecting "Misfits": Canada and the Nansen Passport' (1994) *International Migration Review* 281–300.

9

International organisations

I don't want to belong to any club that will accept me as a member.[1]

Schermers and Blokker, *International Institutional Law*, 4th edn, Leiden, 1995

Klabbers, *An Introduction to International Institutions*, Cambridge, 2002

Sands and Klein (eds.), *Bowett's Law of International Institutions*, 5th edn, London, 2001

Shaw, *International Law*, 5th edn, Cambridge, 2003, pp. 1161–215

International organisations grew out of the diplomatic conferences of the nineteenth century as states sought more effective ways to deal with problems caused by the rapid development of international society. The International Telegraphic (later Telecommunications) Union and the Universal Postal Union were founded in the 1860s. There are now countless international organisations, ranging from large ones with global responsibilities and virtually universal membership, such as the United Nations and the UN specialised agencies, to regional or highly specialised organisations, such as the (large) European Union and the (tiny) International Whaling Commission. Although each organisation is different and must be studied separately, they share the following basic characteristics:

- Establishment by treaty (constituent treaty), although there are some exceptions. The Organization for (previously Conference on) Security and Co-operation in Europe (OSCE/CSCE), emerged following the Helsinki Final Act 1975, which was not a treaty.[2] Nor was the Commonwealth or its secretariat established by treaty.[3] The International Committee of the Red Cross (ICRC) is a Swiss corporation, and states are not members of it. However, it has a special place internationally, being regarded with particular respect by governments and referred to in (and sometimes a party to) treaties.[4]

---

[1] G. Marx, *Groucho and Me*, 1959, Ch. 26.   [2] See p. 62 above.
[3] See ILM (1965) 1108.   [4] See further Shaw, pp. 192 and 821.

- Membership limited exclusively or primarily to states. This is reflected in the alternative generic term 'intergovernmental organisation'. Only states can be members of the United Nations, but the European Community has been able to become a member of certain organisations, such as the FAO[5] and the Commission for the Conservation of Antarctic Marine Living Resources,[6] which admit to membership organisations on which their members have conferred exclusive competence for certain matters. Some organisations admit as members *non-state entities* on the basis that they are separate customs territories. Thus China, Hong Kong (the Hong Kong Special Administrative Region (HKSAR))[7] and China, Macau, as well as Chinese Taipei (Taiwan), are full members of the World Trade Organization (WTO). Both China and the HKSAR are members of the International Textiles and Clothing Bureau, the World Tourism Organization (WTO) and the World Meteorological Organization (WMO). Other organisations have a separate category of associate membership for the overseas territories of members. Many organisations allow non-member states and some non-state entities to be observers without the right to vote.
- International legal personality separate from its members (see below).
- Financed by the members.
- Permanent secretariats.

International organisations usually have three main organs: an assembly, in which all the members are entitled to sit (usually with one vote each); an executive body (often with restricted membership); and a secretariat. These organs need to be carefully distinguished from the organisation itself and its members.[8]

Membership and representation

Many international organisations, such as the UN specialised agencies, are open for membership by any state. Others that are limited to particular regions (e.g. Europe) or interests (e.g. Antarctic science) restrict effective membership accordingly.[9] Issues of membership are quite different

---

[5] See the FAO Constitution, Article II(3) at www.fao.org.
[6] See Article XXIX of the CCAMLR Convention, 402 UNTS 71 (No. 22301); ILM (1980) 837; UKTS (1982) 48; TIAS 10240; B&B Docs. 628.
[7] Section VI of Annex I to the Joint Declaration on the Question of Hong Kong, 1399 UNTS 33 (No. 23391); ILM (1984) 1366; UKTS (1985) 26.
[8] See p. 208 below.   [9] See p. 357 below.

from questions of representation. Representation is concerned with which government is entitled to represent a state within an international organisation. A prime example is China. The Republic of China was an original Member of the United Nations. But in 1949 the Nationalist (Kuomintang) Government lost the civil war to the Communists and retreated to the island of Formosa (Taiwan). The victors formed the Government of the People's Republic of China (the 'PRC Government'), which the United Kingdom and other States recognised as the PRC Government in 1950. But opposition, led by the United States, to the PRC Government representing China in the United Nations persisted until 1971, when the General Assembly decided that the PRC Government should represent China.

Credentials

Credentials must be distinguished from representation. Credentials are set out in a formal document issued, by a head of state or government or the foreign minister, to an international organisation (or to the state or body organising a diplomatic conference) stating that the person (or persons) named in the document is (or are) authorised to represent that state. The rules of procedure of the organisation (or conference) will govern the requirements for credentials,[10] and a credentials committee is usually convened to scrutinise them.

Withdrawal[11]

The UN Charter and some other constituent treaties have no provision permitting a member state to withdraw, but the right to do so can probably be implied,[12] although in some cases (such as the European Union) there might be heavy financial consequences.

International legal personality

An international organisation is rather like a company in that it has legal personality separate from its members. This makes the organisation a

---

[10] See Rules 27–29 of the Rules of Procedure of the UN General Assembly and Rules 13–17 of the Provisional (*sic*) Rules of Procedure of the UN Security Council. See also R. Sabel, *Procedure at Diplomatic Conferences*, Cambridge, 1997.

[11] See Klabbers, *An Introduction to International Institutional Law*, Cambridge, 2002, pp. 121–6.

[12] See Aust, pp. 233–4, especially n. 46.

subject of international law, with rights and duties under it.[13] Perhaps the most important aspect of separate international legal personality is that the international organisation can enter into treaties with other subjects of international law, whether member states, non-member states or other international organisations.[14] Its constituent treaty may provide that it shall have international legal personality; otherwise, this may be inferred from its purpose, the powers given to it by its members and its practice.[15]

The constituent treaty will usually provide also that in the territory of each member the organisation shall have the legal capacity it needs to carry out its functions, such as entering into contracts, buying and selling land and taking part in legal proceedings. This means, in effect, that each member must accord it the status of a corporation in its domestic law. Whether this requires legislation will depend on the constitutional law and practice of the member. In the United Kingdom, and possibly in some other states that follow the dualist approach to the status of treaties in domestic law,[16] the fact that the United Kingdom is a party to a treaty establishing an international organisation will, in itself, not accord it legal personality in United Kingdom law. There will usually have to be legislation (either an Act of Parliament or an Order in Council under the International Organisations Act 1968) to accord it corporate status.[17] When legal personality has been conferred on an international organisation by the law of a member state, the law of a non-member state may treat the organisation as having legal personality even in that state.[18]

Immunities and privileges

To ensure that ministers, diplomats and other officials attending meetings of an international organisation, whether at its headquarters or elsewhere, are free from interference in carrying out their duties, they enjoy certain immunities and privileges. They are also accorded to the organisation itself and its staff. The guiding principle is that there must be a functional need for immunity, primarily to ensure independence of the participants and the organisation. Certain fiscal privileges are accorded to

---

[13] On subjects, see p. 13 above.
[14] On treaties with international organisations, see p. 53 above.
[15] *Reparations for Injuries Suffered in the Service of the United Nations, ICJ Reports* (1949), p. 174; 16 ILR 318. Because they were not established by treaty, there may be some doubt whether the Commonwealth or the OSCE have international legal personality.
[16] See p. 81 above.   [17] See generally Shaw, pp. 1187–93, and p. 82 above.
[18] *Arab Monetary Authority* v. *Hashim* [1991] 2 WLR 738; 85 ILR 1.

representatives of members, and to the organisation and its staff. This is justified on the different basis that the host state (the state where the organisation has its headquarters or where it is holding a meeting) should not benefit from taxes and duties paid from the income of the organisation, its staff or representatives of members since the income comes from the members. The host state will anyway benefit in many ways, particularly economic, from having the organisation or conference in its territory.

The constituent treaty, or a protocol to it, will usually provide for the immunities and privileges. Such instruments tend to follow a pattern set initially by the General Convention on the Privileges and Immunities of the United Nations 1946[19] and the Convention on the Privileges and Immunities of the Specialised Agencies 1947, which has a separate annex for each agency.[20] More recent treaties have more detail and exceptions from immunity from jurisdiction.[21] They are normally supplemented by a treaty with the host state (headquarters agreement)[22] elaborating on the immunities and privileges and specifying the necessary procedures.

Although the provisions vary slightly depending on the organisation and how old the treaty is, they generally provide that the organisation, its staff and representatives of members will be immune (to varying degrees) from legal proceedings unless the organisation (or the member state concerned, as the case may be) waives immunity. Immunity is a matter for the domestic courts, but if the organisation has determined that a person has immunity and that the act in question attracts immunity, there is a presumption of immunity. Although the determination is not binding on the courts, it must be given the greatest weight and not set aside by them except for the most compelling reasons.[23]

Some very senior staff of an organisation may be accorded full diplomatic immunity, but otherwise the staff (even when they have left it) and representatives of members will be immune only from legal proceedings for what they say or do in their work, and in more recent treaties there is usually no immunity in respect of motor accidents. Experts on mission for an organisation, such as consultants, are accorded such privileges and immunities as are necessary for the independent exercise of their

---

[19] 1 UNTS 15 (No. 4).   [20] 33 UNTS 261 (No. 521).
[21] See the Agreement on the Privileges and Immunities of the Organization for the Prohibition of Chemical Weapons (OPCW), UKTS (2002) 31.
[22] See p. 359 below on the recent headquarters agreement between the Antarctic Treaty Secretariat and Argentina.
[23] See the *Immunity from Legal Process* Advisory Opinion (Cumaraswamy), *ICJ Reports* (1999), p. 62, paras. 57–65; 121 ILR 405.

functions. These usually include immunity from personal arrest or detention; and immunity in respect of what they do in the course of performing their mission, including what they say and write.[24] The organisation will be exempt from income tax, but the staff will be subject to a notional internal tax.

It is now common for contracts with an organisation to provide for an advance waiver so that any contractual disputes can be referred to arbitration. The immunity of the organisation may also be much less where it has a commercial purpose. The European Bank for Reconstruction and Development has virtually no immunity from legal proceedings and its assets can be seized to pay a judgment debt once all appeals have been exhausted.[25]

A particular problem arises if a staff member of, or representative to, an international organisation is considered by the host state to be a threat to its security. The relationship between the host state and the organisation is different from that between it and a sending state. Constituent treaties emphasie the fundamental principle that the organisation must be able to function freely and independently. Although they require the chief officer to waive the immunity of a staff member or expert on mission in a proper case, there may well be a dispute about this. Furthermore, the representatives of member states are accredited to the organisation, not to the host state. Although a few constituent treaties or headquarters agreements acknowledge the right of the host state to require the removal of a person who is considered by the host state to be a threat to its security, most do not. Nevertheless, even without such an express provision, some host states take the view that they can deport such persons or refuse them admittance.

The Vienna Convention on the Representation of States in their Relations with International Organizations of a Universal Character 1975[26] provides for the relations between states and intergovernmental international organisations of a universal character (those whose membership and responsibilities are on a worldwide scale), and to the representation

---

[24] See the *Applicability of Article VI, Section 22, of the Convention on the Privileges and Immunities of the UN* Advisory Opinion (Mazilu), *ICJ Reports* (1989), p. 177; 85 ILR 322 and Cumaraswamy (n. 23 above), p. 62.

[25] See the 1990 Agreement establishing the EBRD, Articles 46, 47 and 55 (www.ebrd.com/about/basics/index.htm).

[26] See A. Watts, *The International Law Commission 1949–1998*, Oxford, 1999, vol. I, pp. 449 *et seq.*, and A. Aust, 'Limping Treaties: Lessons from Multilateral Treaty-Making' (2003) NILR 256–8.

of states at conferences convened by or under the auspices of such organisations. The Convention lays down a scale of immunities and privileges for permanent missions of states to such organisations, and for delegations to their conferences. The Convention follows closely the 1961 Diplomatic Convention and the 1969 Special Missions Convention (which had been modelled on the Diplomatic Convention).[27] For instance, Article 59(1) of the 1975 Convention provides that the 'private accommodation' of a member of the diplomatic staff of a delegation to a conference enjoys inviolability. This has always been understood to include a hotel room,[28] and is just one example of a scale of privileges and immunities that goes further than that in, for example, the Convention on the Privileges and Immunities of the United Nations[29] and similar treaties of other universal international and regional organisations. Most international organisations of a universal character have their headquarters, and hold most of their meetings, in Western states. The existing treaties on the privileges and immunities of the organisations and of persons connected with them (which treaties are preserved by Article 4(a) of the 1975 Convention) are regarded by those states as sufficient, and good models for future agreements. After thirty years, the 1975 Convention has only thirty-one of the thirty-five parties needed to bring it into force. Apart from some former communist states of Eastern Europe, only one small Western European state is a party, and no state that is host to a major international organisation.

Liability

Since an international organisation has a legal personality separate from its members, in principle the members are not liable for its acts, in either international or domestic law.[30] However, whether in certain circumstances the members could be liable is currently being studied by the International Law Commission under the topic, 'Responsibility of International Organizations', but it will be several years before any conclusions are reached.[31]

---

[27] See p. 117 above.
[28] See para. (3) of the ILC Commentary on the final draft Article in A. Watts, *The International Law Commission 1949–1998*, Oxford, 1999, vol. I, p. 528.
[29] See n. 19 above.
[30] See the International Tin Council case decided by the (UK) House of Lords: *Rayner* v. *Department of Trade and Industry* [1989] 3 All ER 523 at 529; 81 ILR 680.
[31] See further p. 210 below.

Dispute settlement

A dispute between the members of an international organisation, or between the organisation and its members, about the interpretation or application of its constituent instrument can be settled in accordance with the relevant provisions (if any) of the instrument. Certain instruments, such as the treaties governing the World Trade Organization or the European Union, establish a more or less self-contained legal order and within which the member states have to operate. The treaties therefore include elaborate procedures for settling disputes arising within that legal order.[32] Other international organisations have built-in dispute procedures. Articles 26–29 of the International Labour Organization Constitution provide for a commission of inquiry to hear complaints that a member state is not observing an ILO convention.[33] However, as with other disputes involving member states, it would be expected that the members would first consult fully in an attempt to settle the matter. Even if that is unsuccessful, it does not follow that the dispute settlement procedures of the organisation will be activated. There may be various reasons why members will not want to formalise the dispute. There are many disputes within international organisations that remain unresolved, largely because they are not so important (or at least not important to a sufficient number of members) that they have to be resolved.

The United Nations

It may seem surprising, but the United Nations Charter has no built-in procedure specifically for settling legal disputes within the Organization, other than staff disputes. There are differences of view, some long-standing, about the interpretation or application of the Charter, but these are generally dealt with by negotiations, mostly informal and sometimes inconclusive. Some are on major issues (such as the effective exclusion of South Africa during the period of apartheid).[34] Some are resolved, often by a compromise (such as over the question of the arrears of South Africa's contributions when it resumed its seat); others remain unresolved. Some things are better dealt with by a political 'fix'.

The ICJ has given advisory opinions on various UN internal matters.[35] In the *Lockerbie* cases (now discontinued), the ICJ was asked to interpret

---

[32] See p. 383 below (WTO) and p. 475 above (EU).
[33] See www.ilo.org.   [34] Shaw, p. 1089.
[35] See p. 463 below and www.icj-cij.org (click on 'Decisions').

the Charter in order to decide fundamental questions regarding the respective powers of the Security Council and the ICJ.[36]

The UN specialised agencies

Most disputes within the specialised agencies are settled by negotiation, but if there is a need to pursue a more formal procedure the dispute will be referred in most of the agencies to one of the main organs. If the main organ cannot settle it, the dispute may then be referred to arbitration, or to the ICJ for an advisory opinion.

Staff disputes

The constituent instruments of international organisations provide mechanisms by which disputes between the organisation and staff members can be settled.[37] This is essential since most international organisations have immunity from the jurisdiction of domestic courts. The UN has an Administrative Tribunal, and the ILO Administrative Tribunal decides cases referred to it by other UN specialised agencies.

---

[36] *Lockerbie (Libya* v. *UK)* (Provisional Measures), *ICJ Reports* (1992), p. 3; ILM (1992) 662; 94 ILR 478; and *Lockerbie (Libya* v. *UK)* (Preliminary Objections), *ICJ Reports* (1998), p. 9; ILM (1998) 587; 117 ILR 1 and 664.

[37] See C. Amerasinghe, *The Law of the International Civil Service: As Applied by International Administrative Tribunals,* Cambridge, 1994; J. Klabbers, *An Introduction to International Institutional Law,* Cambridge, 2002, pp. 269–73.

10

The United Nations, including the use of force

. . . measures commensurate with the specific
circumstances as may be necessary . . .[1]

Goodrich, Hambro and Simons, *Charter of the United Nations*, 3rd edn,
    New York, 1969
Bailey and Daws, *The Procedure of the United Nations Security Council*, 3rd
    edn, Oxford, 1998
Simma (ed.), *The Charter of the United Nations*, 2nd edn, Oxford, 2002

The United Nations was established by its Charter of 26 June 1945. Membership is open only to states. By the end of 2004, there were 191 Members, virtually all the states of the world.

Membership

The fifty-one original Members did not have to satisfy the criteria for membership (Article 3). They included India, which did not become independent until 1947, and the Byelorussian Soviet Socialist Republic (now Belarus) and the Ukrainian Soviet Socialist Republic (now Ukraine), both of which were only republics of the Union of Soviet Socialist Republics and did not become independent until 1991.[2] The membership of these three was the result of a political deal at the San Francisco Conference.

New applicants for membership have had to satisfy the criteria in Article 4: an applicant must be a state, be peace-loving,[3] accept the obligations in the Charter and, in the judgment of the Organization, be able and willing to carry out the obligations of membership. The first criterion is essentially legal, whereas the other three are more subjective and political,[4]

---

[1] It is 'un-English'.   [2] See p. 20 above on Russian republics.
[3] This prevented former enemy states (e.g. Hungary, Italy and Japan) from becoming Members until the mid-1950s.
[4] See the *Conditions of Admission to Membership in the UN (Article 4)* Advisory Opinion, *ICJ Reports* (1948), p. 57; 15 ILR 333.

and no longer cause problems. The attributes of statehood have been discussed earlier.[5] Thus an overseas territory of a state, or a constituent part of a state (India successfully opposed the admission of the Indian state of Hyderabad), cannot be a Member. Today, admission raises a very strong presumption that the new Member is a state. Since most UN Members do not recognise as states entities such as Taiwan or the Turkish Republic of Northern Cyprus (TRNC),[6] they have not been accepted as either Members or observers. Nor can an international organisation be a Member, although it can be granted observer status. Palestine also has observer status.[7]

To be accepted as a Member, first the Security Council must recommend membership (and the veto applies),[8] and the General Assembly must then agree to admission by a two-thirds majority vote (Articles 4(2) and 18(2)). In the first five years of the United Nations, most applicants (Iceland, Indonesia, Israel, Burma, Pakistan, Sweden, Thailand and Yemen) were admitted without difficulty. But, following the start of the Korean War in 1950, the Cold War led to many problems. The (then dominant) Western group blocked the admission of the communist states of Eastern Europe, and the Soviet Union and its allies blocked the admission of pro-Western states. The logjam was released by a deal in 1955 which led to the admission of sixteen new Members. Later, in the 1990s, it was accepted that micro-states (e.g. Andorra, Liechtenstein, Monaco, Nauru, San Marino and Tuvalu) could become Members. And Switzerland eventually joined in 2002. The two Germanys and the two Koreas posed particular problems. As the result of new political arrangements, the former two were admitted in 1973 and the latter two in 1991.[9]

Withdrawal, suspension and expulsion[10]

The Charter has no provision for a Member to withdraw, but the right to do so can be implied.[11] In January 1965, Indonesia formally announced that it had decided to withdraw, but in September 1966 said that it would resume its participation in UN activities. The other Members appeared not

---

[5] See p. 16 above.   [6] See p. 19 above.   [7] See p. 26 above.
[8] See the *Conditions of Admission to Membership in the UN (Article 4)* Advisory Opinion, *ICJ Reports* (1948), p. 57; 15 ILR 333.
[9] See p. 392 below.
[10] See J. Klabbers, *An Introduction to International Institutional Law*, Cambridge, 2002, pp. 121–6.
[11] See Aust, pp. 233–4, especially n. 46.

to have regarded the first announcement as amounting to withdrawal,[12] and so Indonesia was not required to re-apply for membership.

A Member which has 'persistently violated the Principles' of the Charter can be expelled if the Security Council so recommends and the General Assembly agrees by a two-thirds majority (Articles 6 and 18). In practice, it is considered preferable for the Member to stay so that it can be more effectively subjected to criticism from the other Members. Also, expelling a Member would set an awkward precedent for some Members: who might be next? Thus it is more likely that a Member would at most be suspended from the exercise of certain rights, such as voting. Under Article, 5, the Security Council can recommend to the General Assembly that a Member against which enforcement action[13] has been taken should be suspended. This has not happened, although a similar effect was obtained by the (legally suspect) rejection of the credentials of South Africa's delegation to the General Assembly during the later years of the apartheid regime. Article 19 provides for a Member's right to vote in the General Assembly to be suspended if it is in arrears in paying its contributions by an amount equal to that due from it for the preceding two years. This happens occasionally, and, for reasons unrelated to ability to pay, the United States got close to losing its vote during the 1990s.

Regional groups

The fifty-one original members could be roughly divided up as: three African, two Asian, six Middle Eastern, seven Communist, twenty Latin American and thirteen Western states. The present 191 Members include some 130 developing countries. The membership is now divided into five (informal) groupings that are important for the purpose of co-ordinating policy and nominating candidates for election to UN organs and subsidiary bodies: African (fifty-three), Asian (including the Middle East) (fifty-four), Eastern European (twenty-one), Latin American and Caribbean (thirty-three) and Western European and others (WEOG) (thirty).

The UN's principal organs

The United Nations has six 'principal organs': the General Assembly, the Security Council, the International Court of Justice, the Economic and

---

[12] See (1966) *UN Juridical YB* 222–3.
[13] Meaning a measure under Chapter VII, often sanctions.

Social Council (ECOSOC), the Trusteeship Council (now defunct) and the Secretariat. The workings of the General Assembly and the Security Council will be discussed most, with the emphasis on their contribution to international law and peace and security. (The International Court of Justice is dealt with at p. 448 below.) Of the principal organs, only the Court and the Security Council have the power to make decisions that are legally binding. The General Assembly's power to take such decisions is limited to internal matters, such as elections to UN organs and bodies, and budgetary and staff issues.

Before criticising 'the UN', one should therefore think what one means by that term. Although the United Nations has international legal personality,[14] it is a complex body, and criticism should be directed at that part of it that is really responsible for the particular matter. That might be the Secretariat, one of the UN's own agencies, the General Assembly or the Security Council. In the case of the latter two organs, one should also try to understand why they – or rather the states that are members of them – acted as they did, or failed to act. The UN Secretariat is limited to what the General Assembly or the Security Council ask it to do and the means they give it; it does not have the extensive initiating powers of the European Commission.[15]

The UN's specialised agencies

The UN specialised agencies are *not* part of the United Nations, and in fact some, such as the Universal Postal Union and the International Telecommunications Union, were first established in the 1860s. But they all have 'relationship agreements' with the United Nations and are regarded as part of the 'UN family'. On important political matters, such as recognition of statehood, they generally follow the lead given by the United Nations. Agencies such as UNEP, the UNHCR and UNICEF are *not* specialised agencies, but bodies set up by the UN General Assembly and *without* separate international legal personality.[16]

The General Assembly

The General Assembly consists of all Members of the United Nations, each having one vote. Decisions on 'important' questions (e.g. the budget

---

[14] On international legal personality, see p. 198 above.
[15] See p. 471 below.   [16] On which, see n. 14 above.

and most elections) are taken by a two-thirds majority of those members present and voting (abstentions not being taken into account). All other matters, including whether a question is important, are decided by a simple majority of those voting. In practice, the Assembly can discuss any matter, although it should not discuss a matter of international peace and security while the Security Council is actively seised of it (Article 12). In general, it does not do this, although the International Court of Justice has recognised an increasing tendency for the General Assembly and the Security Council to deal in parallel with certain matters, and that this is accepted practice consistent with Article 12.[17] The General Assembly is essentially a debating chamber, and only in this sense can it be equated to a legislature. Unlike the European Parliament, it has no powers to challenge an executive body, and does not play a role in making 'legislation' as such (but see below on international law-making). Except for decisions on internal issues, its resolutions are no more than recommendations, although over time the substance of certain resolutions may become accepted as reflecting customary international law.[18] In certain cases, they can also have effect legally.[19]

Main Committees of the General Assembly

The General Assembly meets in plenary session for general debates, to discuss particular topics, and to adopt resolutions. Most of its work is done in six Main Committees, which prepare recommendations for the General Assembly. All UN Members are entitled to take part in the plenary sessions of the General Assembly and meetings of the Committees. The Committees are: First (Disarmament and International Security), Second (Economic and Financial), Third (Social, Humanitarian and Cultural), Fourth (Special Political and Decolonisation), Fifth (Administrative and Budgetary) and Sixth (Legal). Each Committee reports to the plenary, where their recommendations are normally adopted without change and with a minimum of (or no) debate.

The General Assembly has been instrumental in developing international law by (1) establishing the International Law Commission (ILC) (see below), (2) adopting multilateral treaties (usually called

---

[17] *Legal Consequences of the Construction of a Wall in the Occupied Palestinian Territory* Advisory Opinion, *ICJ Reports* (2004), 6 paras. 24–8; ILM (2004) 1009.
[18] See p. 6 above.
[19] See *Namibia* Advisory Opinion, *ICJ Reports* (1971), p. 6, paras. 87–116; 59 ILR 2.

'conventions') drafted mainly by the ILC or the Third or Sixth Committees, and (3) convening diplomatic conferences to negotiate conventions, such as the UN Convention on the Law of the Sea 1982 and the Rome Statute of the International Criminal Court.

Sixth Committee[20]

This Committee, like others, meets during the annual autumn session of the General Assembly, and intersessionally in sub-committees and working groups. Although originally intended as an expert committee that the General Assembly could ask for legal advice or for scrutinising draft legal instruments produced by the other Committees, the Sixth Committee's chief role has been to elaborate conventions for adoption by the plenary, such as recent counter-terrorism conventions.[21] It also oversees the work of the ILC by debating its annual report, commenting on its drafts and proposals for new topics, and deciding what form drafts for international instruments should take (convention, guidelines, model legislation, etc.), and whether the final drafting and negotiations should be done by a diplomatic conference or by the Committee itself.

International Law Commission[22]

Established by the General Assembly in 1949, its (now) thirty-four members, elected by the General Assembly for five-year terms, are mostly professors of international law with some current or former foreign ministry legal advisers. It meets for two, five-week sessions each summer in Geneva. For each new topic it decides to study it appoints one of its members as 'Special Rapporteur'. Each year, he will present the Commission with a report on his research, with proposals and draft Articles for a possible convention or other instrument, such as guidelines. Each year the Commission reports to the General Assembly (in practice, the Sixth Committee) on its work, with the drafts and commentaries on them. The ILC has been successful with the adoption at diplomatic conferences or by the General Assembly of conventions originally drafted by it on, for example, the law of treaties and diplomatic relations, but less so on some other subjects.[23]

---

[20] See www.un.org/law.   [21] See p. 288 (Bombings and Financing) below.

[22] See www.un.org/law/ilc. For a short introduction to the work of the ILC, a bibliography, ILC draft conventions and their commentaries, and the resulting final texts, see A. Watts, *The International Law Commission 1949–1998*, Oxford, 1999.

[23] See A. Aust, 'Limping Treaties: Lessons from Multilateral Treaty-Making' (2003) NILR 243–66.

The Security Council

Membership

The Security Council has fifteen members,[24] five being permanent: China, France, Russia, the United Kingdom and the United States (the 'P5'). The ten non-permanent members serve for two years, five being elected each year by the General Assembly, and cannot serve consecutive terms. In practice, the composition of the non-permanent membership is informally distributed on regional lines, the ten seats being allocated as follows: Africa (three), Asia (two), Eastern European (one), Latin America and the Caribbean (two) and WEOG (two).[25] In practice, each regional group nominates a clean slate of candidates for election, although there are sometimes contested elections for WEOG seats. So that there is always an Arab state on the Council, things are so arranged that each year an Arab state is elected to fill, alternately, an Asian or an African seat (unless a North African state is elected). Each month, the presidency of the Council rotates in alphabetical order.

Working methods[26]

Most Council resolutions are adopted by unanimity or without a vote. A glance at the verbatim records of Council meetings in at least the last fifteen years shows that most meetings at which resolutions were adopted lasted only a few minutes, unless members made formal explanations of vote (EOVs). Unlike the early days of the United Nations, and for most of the Cold War, there is now little or no discussion of draft resolutions or procedural debates at meetings of the Council. Indeed, even before the end of the Cold War members of the Council increasingly discussed Council business informally, often, as diplomats tend to do, in the corridors. Some time in the 1970s a small room was constructed near to the Council Chamber in which the members of the Council could meet together informally, but with simultaneous interpretation into all six UN languages, and (albeit very limited) seating. Apart from the Secretary-General, some of his officials and the interpreters, no-one else is allowed

---

[24] A Charter amendment in 1963, coming into force in 1965, increased the membership from eleven from fifteen.

[25] See p. 207 above.

[26] See A. Aust, 'The Procedure and Practice of the Security Council Today', in R.-J. Dupuy (ed.), *The Development of the Role of the Security Council Workshop*, Hague Academy of International Law Publications, 1992, pp. 365–74; and M. Wood, 'Security Council Working Methods and Procedure: Recent Developments' (1996) ICLQ 150–61.

in the room without the agreement of the members. States that are the object of the consultations are not allowed in, although sometimes a UN expert, such as a Special Representative of the Secretary-General, is invited to address the members.

At these informal 'consultations of the whole', the members discuss all matters which are, or may be, put on the Council's agenda; consider drafts of resolutions and statements; discuss procedural questions; and, most importantly, assess whether a proposal is likely to be adopted if put to the vote. A 'decision' taken in these informal consultations has no legal status at all, and no official record is kept of the discussions. But it is only by these means – which are completely normal in diplomacy, or indeed in business and other fields – that the members of the Council can work really effectively. Being in daily and private contact, their deliberations are much more profitable than if they were conducted in public. Views can be expressed more freely than in the Council Chamber, where they usually have to be given in front of the other UN members, the public and the world's media.

Lack of an official record of the informal consultations makes it difficult sometimes to interpret the terms of a resolution. A good recent example is the so-called first resolution (1441 (2002)) that preceded the 2003 Iraq war, especially paragraphs 12 and 13. The only authoritative indication of the intention of members are any EOVs they make in the Council (not later to the media), although they are often worded with diplomatic obscurity.[27]

In addition to these and other informal contacts, there are constant meetings of certain groups of Council members. These are principally the P3 (France, the United Kingdom and the United States); the P5 (the P3 plus China and Russia);[28] the five to seven members belonging to the Non-Aligned Movement (NAM); and the rest, the so-called non-non-aligned members. Other groups are formed *ad hoc*. Within a group, the members can naturally speak even more freely than in the consultations of the whole. The P5 in particular can better assess whether there might be a veto if a draft resolution were to be put to the vote. When a draft resolution is threatened with a veto, and therefore either is not pursued or is redrafted, the threat is referred to as the 'virtual veto'.

---

[27] See S/PV.4644 on the adoption of UNSC Res. 1441 (2002).
[28] See F. Delon, 'Le rôle joué par les membres permanents dans l'action du conseil de sécurité', as in R.-J. Dupuy (ed.), *The Development of the Role of the Security Council Workshop*, Hague Academy of International Law Publications, 1992, pp. 349–64.

Presidential statements

In addition to resolutions, increasingly the Council makes pronounce-ments in statements by its President ('Presidential statements'). These are not voted on and therefore have to be agreed by consensus. They are not provided for in the Charter or in the Council's Provisional Rules of Procedure.[29] Some of them may have certain legal effects.[30]

Voting

Each member of the Council has one vote but, unlike the General Assem-bly, *procedural* matters are decided not by a percentage of votes cast, but by the affirmative vote of nine or more members (Article 27(2)). No veto can be cast. Under Article 2(3), decisions on all other (i.e. *substantive*) matters are also made by the affirmative vote of nine or more members, provided no permanent member has cast a negative vote (the veto). But the abstention, or even absence, of a permanent member does not count as a veto. This rule is contrary to the plain words of Article 27(3) that require 'the concurring votes' of the permanent members. Although this clearly envisages each of the permanent members having to cast an affir-mative vote, the practice of the Council from 1946 has been to interpret 'concurring' as meaning only 'not objecting'. Thus, during the early stages of the Korean War in 1950, by absenting itself from meetings of the Coun-cil the Soviet Union was not able to prevent the Council taking action.[31] The practice was upheld by the International Court of Justice in the *Namibia* case,[32] even though it seems from the *travaux* of the Charter that this result was not what had been originally intended by the future permanent members.[33]

There were 270 vetoes between 1946 and the end of the Cold War in 1990. Since then, there have been only a handful. One of the reasons is

---

[29] Even 'resolutions' are not mentioned in the Charter, merely 'decisions' and 'measures'. Presidential statements from 1994 can be accessed online at www.un.org/ documents/ pstatesc.htm. For a rare reference to them in a resolution, see the first preambular paragraph to UNSC Res. 1441 (2002).

[30] See S. Talmon, 'The Statements by the Presidents of the Security Council' (2003) *Chinese YB of International Law* 419–65.

[31] Bailey and Daws, *The Procedure of the United Nations Security Council*, 3rd edn, Oxford, 1998, p. 257.

[32] *ICJ Reports* (1971), p. 6, at paras. 20–2; 49 ILR 2.

[33] See Goodrich, Hambro *and Simons, Charter of the United Nations*, 3rd edn, New York, 1969, p. 229.

that, when it appears from informal consultations and P5 meetings that a permanent member is likely to cast a veto, a draft resolution is usually either modified to make it acceptable to the permanent member(s) or just not put to the vote (the virtual veto). Furthermore, abstention by *any* seven members will prevent any decision being adopted ($15 - 7 = 8$), and is known as the 'collective veto'.[34]

Whether a matter is procedural or substantive is itself a substantive question. Thus a permanent member can cast a veto both on the proposition that a matter is procedural and on the substantive issue (the so-called double veto). Although Article 27(3) prohibits a member from voting on a question relating to a 'dispute' to which it is a party, this does not apply to Chapter VII action (see below). And in most cases that involve a dispute the issue before the Council is not the dispute itself but the 'situation' arising from it,[35] for example the occupation of Kuwait by Iraq in 1990, even though Iraq (dishonestly) claimed that there was a dispute with Kuwait over sovereignty.

Powers of the Security Council

Article 24 confers on the Security Council primary responsibility for the maintenance of international peace and security. Although a highly political body, the Council has the power to impose legally binding measures on all UN members. Most Council resolutions contain only exhortations or recommendations, and are informally referred to as 'Chapter VI resolutions', since under that chapter the Council cannot impose legally binding measures. That can be done only under Chapter VII, or Chapter VIII when the Council authorises enforcement action by regional bodies. The combined effect of Articles 25 and 48 is to place a legal obligation on all UN Members to carry out the measures. A 'Chapter VII resolution' has therefore become shorthand for a legally binding measure. Ironically, since the main value of a Chapter VI resolution is political, it needs to be adopted unanimously for it to carry any real weight. In contrast, a Chapter VII resolution needs only nine votes in favour, and no veto, for it to be legally binding.

Before the Council can decide to impose a measure, Article 39 requires it to determine first the existence of a threat to the peace, breach of the peace

---

[34] In June 2004, the United States were unable to gather nine votes for the renewal of its draft annual resolution about the International Criminal Court: see p. 280 below.
[35] See Articles 34–36 on disputes and situations.

or act of aggression. This is usually expressed in a less specific statement in a preambular paragraph to a resolution that the Council determines that there is 'a threat to international peace and security'. The Council does not categorise further the nature of the threat, such as aggression. Although UNSC Res. 660 (1990) condemned Iraq's invasion of Kuwait, it did not describe the invasion as aggression. Even though objectively there was no doubt that Iraq's action would fall squarely within any definition of aggression, there is no satisfactory internationally agreed definition.[36] Nor is Article 39, or the other Articles of Chapter VII, mentioned specifically in the resolution. If the whole of the resolution is intended to be legally binding, the final preambular paragraph will state that the Council is 'acting under Chapter VII'. If only part of the resolution is intended to be binding, the reference to Chapter VII will precede only that part.

Unfortunately, the Council is not always consistent in the drafting of its resolutions. Sometimes there is no express Article 39 determination or even reference to Chapter VII. Nevertheless, it can usually be inferred from the rest of the resolution, by a statement by the President of the Council, or from the circumstances, that the determination has been made and that the Council is acting under Chapter VII. When the resolution is one of a series of resolutions on the same subject, and it is clear that the Council considers that the threat to international peace and security remains, if a new resolution is only modifying, elaborating or adding to existing measures, there may be no reference either to the determination or to Chapter VII.

An Article 39 determination is a political act. In considering whether to make the determination, the governments of the members of the Council in practice ask themselves essentially political questions: does something really have to be done? If so, what? Could it really be effective? Even if it would not be effective, do we still have to be seen to be doing something? The best example of a futile gesture was UNSC Res. 836 (1993) establishing the 'safe areas' around certain Bosnian towns, including Srebrenica. If the members believe that something has to be done, or seen to be done, they do not indulge in painstaking legal analysis.

The Council has taken action in what would have been seen in 1945 as essentially internal matters. Although Article 2(7) prohibits the United Nations from intervening in matters that are 'essentially within the domestic jurisdiction' of a state, this does not apply to enforcement measures

---

[36] See p. 272 below.

under Chapter VII. Furthermore, human rights have long been regarded in the United Nations as not 'essentially' an internal matter, but of international concern, as evidenced by the action taken by the Council against the white rebel regime in Southern Rhodesia and the apartheid government of South Africa. In the 1990s, when the Council was considering whether to intervene in situations which could well have been seen as essentially internal, a threat to international peace and security was discerned in factors such as the destabilising effect on neighbouring states of civil wars or other internal disturbances (see Resolutions 713 (1991) (Yugoslavia), 794 (1992) (Somalia) and 841 (1993) and 917 (1994) (Haiti)). This is reflected in the wording of the preambles to these resolutions. But, given that precedents were being set, some of the resolutions emphasise the 'unique character' of the situation requiring 'an immediate and exceptional response' (Somalia), or the 'unique and exceptional circumstances' (Haiti). More recently, the Council has recognised the global threat posed by international terrorism to international peace and security.[37]

Obligations of Members under the Charter (which include the obligation to carry out Chapter VII resolutions) prevail over their obligations under any other treaty (Article 103). Sometimes sanctions resolutions will therefore have the effect of overriding or suspending treaty obligations.[38] The trade embargo imposed on the Federal Republic of Yugoslavia required goods traffic on the Danube to or from the FRY to cease, despite the freedom of navigation obligations of the riparian states under the Danube Convention.[39]

In the forty-four years before the invasion of Kuwait in 1990, there had been only a handful of Chapter VII resolutions (84 (1950) on Korea; 221 (1966), 232 (1966), 253 (1968), 399 (1976) and 409 (1977) on Southern Rhodesia; and 277 (1970) and 418 (1977) on South Africa). The end of the Cold War has meant that since 2 August 1990 there have been numerous Chapter VII resolutions.

Uniting for Peace

If because of disagreement among the permanent members the Council is unable to act to maintain international peace and security, the

---

See p. 294 below.
[38] *Case concerning Questions of Interpretation and Application of the 1971 Montreal Convention arising from the Aerial Incident at Lockerbie (Libya v. United Kingdom)* (Provisional Measures), *ICJ Reports* (1992), p. 3, para. 39; ILM (1992) 662; 94 ILR 478.
[39] UNSC Res. 787 (1992), para. 13 and 820 (1993), paras. 15–17.

General Assembly can make recommendations to the membership as a whole for collective measures, including the use of force.[40] Although this course is occasionally suggested, it has been taken only twice. Following the 1956 illegal Suez adventure by France, Israel and the United Kingdom, and British and French vetoes in the Security Council, the General Assembly established the UN Emergency Force (UNEF) to secure and supervise the ceasefire.[41] In 1960, the General Assembly instructed the Secretary-General to assist the Government of the Congo, which later led to military operations against Katangan secessionists.[42] But the inherent weakness of the procedure is that its effectiveness depends entirely on the voluntary co-operation of all the Members concerned, including the host state.

The Council has the power to *demand, prohibit* or *authorise*. In Resolution 660 (1990) it demanded that Iraq cease its illegal occupation of Kuwait. In itself, the demand cannot make a state comply, and in most cases it will not do so until more pressure is put on it. Resolution 660 (1990) was swiftly followed by Resolution 661 (1990) prohibiting trade with Iraq. Three months later, Resolution 678 (1990) authorised a coalition to use force to liberate Kuwait and to restore peace and security in the area, although the authorisation was not legally necessary for the liberation of Kuwait.[43] Resolution 662 (1990), which declared the annexation of Kuwait without legal validity and so null and void, was also very pertinent to domestic legal proceedings.[44]

There are many variations within these three main categories of measures. We will now examine those prohibiting normal activities, or 'sanctions', although that word is not found in the Charter or used in Council resolutions.

Sanctions

Sanctions require states to stop (or prevent their nationals from doing) what would otherwise be lawful. Article 41 contains examples: the interruption of economic relations and means of communication and the severance of diplomatic relations. Until 1990, the prohibition of imports

---

[40] Uniting for Peace Resolution 1950 (UNGA Res. (V), Part A). See also Shaw, pp. 1151–4 and the *Expenses* Advisory Opinion, *ICJ Reports* (1962), p. 151; 34 ILR 281.
[41] UNGA Res. 1001 (ES-I).   [42] UNGA Res. 1474 (ES-IV).   [43] See p. 229 below.
[44] See *Kuwait Airways* v. *Iraqi Airways* [2002] 2 AC 883; [2002] 2 WLR 1353; [2002] 3 All ER 209; 125 ILR 602.

and exports, and associated financial measures, were the main sanctions imposed. Beginning with Iraq, the Council developed a much wider range.

Trade embargoes

A trade embargo is usually the first sanction to be imposed. It is often limited to a prohibition on supplying arms (Resolution 713 (1991) on Yugoslavia), and may go no further. A full trade embargo will prohibit the export to, and import from, the embargoed state of all goods, with the exception of food and medical supplies, and sometimes other humanitarian goods. The embargo may be partial. That on Libya was limited to a prohibition on the supply of arms, aircraft and aircraft equipment, and oil pipeline and refinery equipment (Resolutions 748 (1992) and 883 (1993)). Imports of oil – Libya's main export – were never prohibited. Services are not usually subject to a general prohibition, but financial sanctions normally make it difficult for the providers of services to get paid lawfully.

A trade embargo, whether full or partial, has a serious effect on existing contracts and licences with the embargoed state and its nationals, since most can no longer be performed lawfully. Each Member must do what is necessary in its law to implement and enforce the embargo – as it may have to do for other sanctions. Some states will have to legislate, usually by secondary legislation.[45] In others, the resolution may be superior law, although there may still be need for legislation, for example to make violations of sanctions a criminal offence and to prescribe penalties.

Financial sanctions

Closely linked to a trade embargo are financial sanctions. Without them, the embargoed state would be much better able to pay for smuggled goods. There may be a comprehensive freeze on all existing funds held by the embargoed state, and a prohibition on making new funds available. Exceptions are made for payments exclusively for strictly medical or humanitarian purposes or foodstuffs (see Resolution 757 (1992) for the FRY). But the sanctions may be more limited, the proceeds of future Libyan oil sales not being affected (Resolution 883 (1993)). The sanctions may apply to the state and its agencies, companies and nationals (Resolution 661 (1990)) or be limited to the state and state entities (Resolution 883 (1993)), which naturally makes sanctions that much easier to evade.

---

[45] For example, under the one-section (UK) United Nations Act 1946.

Sequestration and impounding of assets

Resolution 778 (1992) broke new ground in requiring the taking possession (sequestration, not confiscation) of Iraqi funds representing the proceeds of oil sales and transferring them to the United Nations for the Compensation Commission (see below). The funds were returned to Iraq pursuant to Resolution 1483 (2003). Resolution 820 (1993), paragraph 24, required the impounding of ships controlled by FRY interests and their forfeiture if they were found to be violating sanctions.

Flight restrictions

Aviation sanctions were first used in Resolution 670 (1990) and required flights to Iraq to be searched to ensure that embargoed goods were not being carried. The first comprehensive prohibition on all flights to and from an embargoed state was in respect of Libya (Resolution 748 (1992)). The only exceptions were for significant humanitarian need, subject to the approval of the sanctions committee. The resolution also required the closure of all offices of Libyan Arab Airlines. Later, Resolutions 757 (1992) (FRY) and 1070 (1995) (Sudan) had comprehensive prohibitions on flights.

Diplomatic and similar sanctions

Resolutions 748 (1992) and 883 (1993) (Libya), and Resolution 757 (1992) (FRY), required the scaling-down of diplomatic relations. Resolution 757 (1992) also required participation by FRY sportsmen in international events to be prevented, and the suspension of government-sponsored scientific and cultural exchanges. Some sanctions regimes have required the refusal of visas to certain high-level officials.

Weapons of mass destruction

Resolution 687 (1991) is unique in many ways, not least for its indefinite prohibition on the supply to Iraq of weapons of mass destruction (chemical, biological and nuclear) and long-range missiles, and the means to make them. A Special Commission (later replaced by UNMOVIC) and the IAEA were given the immensely intrusive task of finding any such weapons, destroying them and ensuring that Iraq did not acquire or manufacture them again.

Compensation

Another innovation in Resolution 687 (1991) was the establishment of the UN Compensation Commission with the task of compensating those foreign states, corporations and individuals who had suffered loss or damage as a result of Iraq's invasion of Kuwait. The funds to do this are produced by a levy (initially 30 per cent, later reduced to 25 per cent, and now 5 per cent) on the proceeds of the sale of oil by Iraq.[46]

Border demarcation

Another first in Resolution 687 (1991) was the request to the UN Secretary-General to help Iraq and Kuwait establish a commission of experts to demarcate their common border. This task was speedily achieved.[47]

International criminal tribunals

Having jurisdiction over war crimes and crimes against humanity, the International Criminal Tribunal for the Former Yugoslavia (Resolution 827 (1993)) and the International Criminal Tribunal for Rwanda (Resolution 955 (1994)) are not typical sanctions. The establishment of the tribunals was a necessary consequential measure to help maintain international peace and security in the region and elsewhere, as well as a warning that others who commit such crimes in the future will not escape justice. UN Members are required to co-operate with the tribunals by handing over to them persons suspected of such crimes, as well as evidence.[48]

Sanctions committees

For each sanctions regime, the Council sets up a committee on which the fifteen members of the Council each have a seat. However, the chairmanship of the committees does not rotate each month, the post being held for a year. Also, all decisions are taken by consensus. A committee's functions are to monitor compliance with the relevant sanctions regime and to carry out such tasks as the Council gives it. These will depend on the terms of each regime, but can include authorising, expressly or tacitly, humanitarian supplies or flights. Although only the Council itself can interpret the resolutions,[49] in practice the committees do so as well,

---

[46] See UNSC Res. 833 (1993) and 1483 (2003), and p. 446 below for more details.
[47] See p. 34 above for details.   [48] See p. 274 below for details.
[49] But see pp. 460 and 463 below regarding the role of the ICJ.

although difficult cases may be referred to the Council when a committee cannot agree.

Termination of sanctions

Sanctions are usually terminated, wholly or partly, by another Chapter VII resolution. Those against Libya were 'suspended' automatically on the UN Secretary-General reporting to the Council that the two persons accused of the Lockerbie bombing had arrived in the Netherlands for trial before the Scottish court.[50] There could be a similar provision for automatic termination. Since 2000, there has been a tendency for the Council to provide that some measures will be in force for a fixed period unless the Council decides later to extend it (see Resolution 1306 (2000) (Sierra Leone), paragraph 6, and Resolution 1330 (2000) (Iraq), paragraphs 1 and 4. However, such provisions rather defeat the purpose of sanctions since they may encourage the sanctioned state to wait in the hope that the members of the Council will not be able to agree to continue the measure.

Human rights

One has to be cautious of any argument to the effect that the Security Council cannot, when adopting Chapter VII measures, suspend human rights expressly or by implication.[51] There is no reason in principle why a measure should not suspend certain human rights, although in practice the members of the Council would not agree to this unless they considered it to be absolutely necessary. The members do not act unthinkingly, and within the Council there are checks and balances.[52] It may well be necessary for the Council to suspend certain human rights in emergency situations. Most human rights are not absolute and require a balancing of competing interests. Clearly, the Council cannot validly adopt, even by the use of express words, a measure contrary to *jus cogens*,[53] such as authorising the torture of suspected terrorists. But due process is not *jus cogens* and human rights treaties permit derogations to most of their Articles.[54]

---

[50] See UNSC Res. 1192 (1998), para. 8. Libya having finally accepted responsibility for the crimes and payment of compensation, sanctions were terminated by UNSC Res. 1506 (2003).

[51] See, for example, E. de Wet, *The Chapter VII Powers of the United Nations Security Council*, Oxford, 2004.

[52] See p. 211 above.   [53] See p. 11 above.

[54] Article 4 (derogation) of the International Covenant on Civil and Political Rights 1966 applies to Article 14 (due process), and Article 15 (derogation) of the ECHR applies to Article 6 (due process), and see p. 245 below.

At first sight, Resolution 1373 (2001) may seem remarkable in being the first Security Council measure under Chapter VII to address a global and unspecific threat to international peace and security, all previous resolutions having been directed at a particular state, regime or group. The need for a measure with the broad and general scope of Resolution 1373 was due to the particular nature of international terrorism. Unlike a state that has an aggressive intent towards a neighbour that can be detected by observing troop movements, terrorists work in small units and in great secrecy. In most cases, there will be no warning of an attack. Because the attacks are so difficult to detect, states have to take such preventive measures as they can. This means that, in addition to physical security measures, the focus has to be on catching (if necessary even killing) terrorists before they can commit attacks, or starving them of the means, physical and financial, to commit them.

Those were the reasons behind Resolution 1373. There is no danger that the Council will be encouraged to use its Chapter VII powers to pronounce on international law in the way done by diplomatic conferences or by the General Assembly when it adopts a so-called law-making convention.[55] If anything, the establishment of the ICTY and ICTR are closer to law-making in that their Statutes confirm or assert what the Council, acting on behalf of the whole UN membership, considers to be international crimes. But it is only for the purpose of restoring international peace and security in a region, as well as sending a signal to those who might be tempted to commit such crimes in the future. The adoption in 1998 of the Rome Statute of the International Criminal Court shows that international law-making will continue to be done by the normal means.[56]

Charter amendment

The UN Charter has been amended on only three occasions, the only significant amendment being to Articles 23 and 27 to enlarge the Security Council from eleven to fifteen members, which came into force in 1965. Under Article 108, an amendment comes into force for *all* UN Members when it has been adopted by a vote of two-thirds of the members of the General Assembly *and* ratified by two-thirds of the UN membership,

---

[55] Paul Szasz, 'The Security Council Starts Legislating' (2002) AJIL 901–5, was not concerned at this development, pointing out that earlier UNSC resolutions, such as 1265 (1999), 1291 (2000), 1296 (2000), 1314 (2000) and 1325 (2000) dealt in general terms with matters such as the protection of women and children during armed conflicts, albeit only UNSC Res. 1291 (2000) was made under Chapter VII.

[56] See also p. 277 below.

including all the permanent members of the Security Council. Any talk of Security Council reform must take this reality into account. In practice, there can be no further change to the size or composition of the Council without a consensus that includes the five permanent members, who are all unwilling to see any change to their status or powers. Informal discussions in an *ad hoc* group of UN Members about enlargement of the Council have lasted over ten years. There appears to be general agreement that the Council should not have more than twenty-five members. But agreement on new permanent members (each of the states which believes that it should be a permanent member has at least one rival within its regional group), whether any of the new permanent members should have the veto, or whether there should be new 'rotating members', remains elusive.

Use of force[57]

> England is firmly resolved to employ, with all cunning and ruthlessness, the instrument of war which she possesses in her Fleet, according to the principle 'Might is Right'.[58]

In recent years, the use of force by states has produced a lively, sometimes impassioned, debate in the United Nations, parliaments, universities and the media. The law is expressed in relatively simple terms, the problem being how it applies in particular circumstances; and humanitarian intervention remains controversial. The debate is vigorous because much is at stake, not least the life of possibly thousands of people, military and civilian. For any foreign ministry legal adviser, the legality of any proposed use of force is the most important issue he or she ever has to face. The final decision to use force rests with the executive or parliament. A state contemplating the use of force needs to be satisfied that it would be lawful, not merely that a plausible or colourable case could be made to justify it. International law has been developed to make it possible for states to live together in peace and reasonable harmony. When a state decides to use force without either clear authorisation from the Security Council or a firm basis in customary international law, and with serious doubts being expressed by other states about its legality, it is possible that the policy itself may be wrong.

---

[57] See generally Oppenheim, pp. 417–27; Shaw, pp. 1013–53; T. Franck, *Recourse to Force*, Cambridge, 2002; C. Gray, *International Law and the Use of Force*, 2nd edn, Oxford, 2004.

[58] Captain Siegel reporting from the First Hague Peace Conference of 1899 to Berlin on the views of Admiral Fisher, quoted in R. Mackay, *Fisher of Kilverstone*, Oxford, 1973, p. 221.

It must be emphasised that whether a particular use of force is lawful or not, all those involved in the conflict must still comply with the law of armed conflict (see Chapter 12 below).

Prohibition on the use of force

There is now no use for declarations of war,[59] and none have been made since the belated Soviet declaration of war on Japan on 9 August 1945. Tentative attempts were made after the First World War to make the use of force by states unlawful: Article 10 of the Covenant of the League of Nations[60] and the General Treaty for the Renunciation of War as an Instrument of National Policy 1928 ('Briand–Kellogg Pact').[61] This culminated in Article 2(3) of the UN Charter which requires all disputes to be settled by peaceful means, and Article 2(4), which requires all Members to

> refrain in their international relations from the threat or use of force against the territorial integrity or political independence of any state, or in any other manner inconsistent with the Purposes of the United Nations.

Thus, the use of force *within* a state to maintain or restore peace and security is lawful, provided that it is used in a manner consistent with international human rights obligations and the law of armed conflict. Similarly, a state may send forces to another state at its request to help restore order. (As to the responsibility of a leader of a state for an illegal use of force, see p. 429 below.)

Security Council authorisation for the use of force

When the Council authorises the use of force (although its resolutions do not use that f-word in this context), it is permitting states to do what otherwise might be unlawful.[62] Article 42 empowers the Council to authorise states to use force when it considers that other measures '*would be* inadequate or have proved to be inadequate' (emphasis added). Thus the Council does *not* have to impose economic sanctions, or wait to see if sanctions have been ineffective, before it authorises the use of force. Article 42 is never expressly mentioned in resolutions, and

---

[59] See *Oppenheim's International Law*, 7th edn, London, 1952, vol. II, pp. 293–300. See p. 252 below on the terms 'war' and 'armed conflict'.
[60] 225 CTS 188; UKTS (1919) 4; 112 BSP 113.   [61] 94 LNTS 57; UKTS (1929) 29.
[62] But see p. 229 below on the liberation of Kuwait.

Articles 43–47, concerning the availability of forces to put at the disposal of the United Nations, have always been seen as a dead letter. Although the Council can authorise Members to use force, it does not require them to use it. The actions listed in Article 42 are merely illustrative, force having been authorised for various purposes.

Intervention

In Resolution 678 (1990), the Council authorised a coalition of states (so-called coalition of the willing) to use 'all necessary means' to liberate Kuwait and to restore international peace and security in the area. The same authorisation was relied upon as the legal basis for the second intervention in Iraq by coalition forces in 2003.[63] On several occasions between 1992 and 1998 it was also the legal basis for air strikes by UK and US military aircraft on Iraqi military installations in response to breaches by Iraq of the WMD inspection regime established by Resolution 687 (1991), the Council having authorised such use of force in advance.[64] In Resolution 940 (1994), the Council authorised a coalition to use 'all necessary means' to 'facilitate the departure' from Haiti of the military leadership and the restoration of President Aristide. Sometimes the intervention may have to be longer than originally envisaged if a serious threat to human life remains; and in the case of Kosovo the NATO forces (KFOR) were later joined by a UN administration (UNMIK).

Interdiction

This term is used in the sense of to stop and search shipping, and has effectively replaced blockade (see Article 42). Resolution 665 (1990) authorised states to do this in the Persian Gulf and the Red Sea to check whether merchant ships were carrying embargoed goods to or from Iraq. For this purpose it authorised the use of minimal force, in the coy words of the

---

[63] See 'The Use of Force against Iraq' (2003) ICLQ 811; Lowe, 'The Iraqi Crisis: What Now?' (2003) ICLQ 859; and 'Agora; Future Implications of the Iraqi Conflict' (2003) AJIL 553–642; ICLQ (2005) 767–78 (UK Attorney General's advice).

[64] See, for example, UNSC Res. 1154 (1998), which warns that further obstruction by Iraq of weapons inspectors would be a violation of UNSC Res. 687 (1991) and would have the 'severest consequences' for Iraq. Similar warnings had been made in Presidential statements in earlier years (where the term 'material breach' was used), the members of the Council being well aware that 'serious consequences' meant UK/US air strikes. These statements are referred to in the first preambular paragraph to UNSC Res. 1441 (2002), the resolution repeating the key formulations of the statements that failure by Iraq to co-operate fully would constitute a further 'material breach' and that it would face 'serious consequences', see (2003) BYIL 792–6.

resolution, 'measures commensurate with the specific circumstances as may be necessary'. Similar interdiction regimes were authorised in the cases of the FRY (Resolution 787 (1992), paragraph 13) and Haiti (Resolution 917 (1994), paragraph 10).[65]

Protection of civilians and peacekeeping forces

In several cases, the use of force has been authorised for other, more limited, purposes. Resolution 794 (1992) authorised the US-led coalition of forces to use 'all necessary means' to establish a secure environment for humanitarian relief operations in Somalia. Resolution 908 (1994) authorised Members to take 'all necessary measures' to extend close air support in defence of UNPROFOR personnel in Croatia.[66]

Self-defence

Article 51 provides that:

> Nothing in the present Charter shall impair the inherent right of individual or collective self-defence if an armed attack occurs against a Member of the United Nations, until the Security Council has taken measures necessary to maintain international peace and security.

Although the Article is the last in Chapter VII, it is a saving provision, albeit of vital importance. Written in terms that were soon seen as too restrictive even in 1945, the Article is now regarded as confirmation that the obligations of the Charter do not affect the exercise by a state of its inherent right in customary international law to defend itself, so that the right continues to exist alongside the Charter prohibition on the use of force.[67] Moreover, the right of self-defence has been developed, and continues to develop, to meet new threats. This is recognised by members of the Security Council and other states by their reactions (often mere

---

[65] As for further Council action in 2004, see S/PRST/2004/4 of 26 February 2004 and UNSC Res. 1529 (2004) and 1542 (2004).

[66] UNSC Res. 958 (1994). See also UNSC Res. 1270 (1999) and 1289 (2000) about Sierra Leone. UN peacekeeping forces are known colloquially as the 'blue helmets'. In 1989, Austria seriously proposed that there should be a UN force to protect the environment. Several members of its UN mission were then called Helmut, and the author (then in the UK mission) suggested informally that the proposed force be known as the 'Green Helmuts'. The idea was then quickly dropped. Years later, the suggestion was recalled with much affection by the then members of the Austrian mission.

[67] *Military and Paramilitary Activities (Nicaragua v. US)* (Merits), *ICJ Reports* (1986), p. 14, paras. 172–82; 76 ILR 1.

acquiescence) when faced with justifications of the use of force based on self-defence, although one has to bear in mind that the views of states on such matters may also be influenced by extraneous political considerations.

US Secretary of State Webster made the classic statement of the law on self-defence in 1841 in respect of the *Caroline* incident.[68] British forces had seized and destroyed in US territory a vessel being used by US nationals assisting an armed rebellion by Canadians over the border, Canada then being a British colony. Two of the US nationals were killed. Webster declared that, in order to be lawful, such recourse to force in self-defence required:

> a necessity of self-defence, instant, overwhelming, leaving no choice of means, and no moment for deliberation [and involving] nothing unreasonable or excessive; since the act, justified by the necessity of self-defence, must be limited by that necessity, and kept clearly within it.

Webster's criteria were subsequently developed in order to be more in tune with the realities of international life, where there is usually a choice of means and some time for deliberation. Although everything will depend on the facts and circumstances of each particular case, to be a lawful exercise of the right of self-defence the threat or use of force against another state must be:

(1) *In response to an armed attack* (economic pressure is not enough) on its territory, ships, aircraft, embassies, consulates or nationals. The Israeli commando raid on Entebbe airport in 1976 to release Israeli nationals who had been taken hostage by Palestinians was justified because Uganda was unwilling or unable to do anything. Article 51 does not require that the attack be by a state: force can be used in response to a terrorist attack even if no other state is involved. This was recognised expressly by the UN Security Council in Resolution 1368 (2001), following the 11 September 2001 terrorist attacks on the United States.[69] And it is not necessary to wait to be attacked: force can

---

[68] 29 BSP 1137 and 30 BSP 195. See R. Jennings, 'The *Caroline* and *McLeod* Cases' (1938) AJIL 82–99.

[69] See also p. 294 below. The ICJ recently got this completely wrong: see *Legal Consequences of the Construction of a Wall in the Occupied Palestinian Territory* Advisory Opinion, *ICJ Reports* (2004), para. 139; ILM (2004) 1009; and the separate critical opinions of Judges Higgins (para. 34) and Kooijmans (para. 35), and the declaration of Judge Buergenthal (para. 6).

be used in anticipation of, and to pre-empt, an attack; no state is obliged to wait until the enemy missile actually strikes or the terrorist bomb explodes. This is, however, an area where there is also scope for abuse. The Council condemned the destruction in 1981 by Israel of an Iraqi nuclear reactor that Israel suspected was being used in connection with developing a nuclear weapon.[70] And there have been cases where the justification of self-defence of one's nationals was spurious, such as in the case of the US military interventions in Grenada (1983) and Panama (1989).[71] So-called democratic intervention has also been invoked in another unconvincing attempt to justify the interventions, although more on political grounds.[72]

(2) *Necessary.* There must be no viable alternative.[73] The more imminent the attack, the more cogent will be the resort to force.

(3) *Limited* to the immediate purpose. Reprisals,[74] retribution or exemplary or punitive attacks are not permitted, since by definition they would be disproportionate.

(4) *Reasonable and proportionate* to the threat or the force used against it. The US carried out air raids on Tripoli in 1986 in response to supposed Libyan involvement in a terrorist attack on a Berlin discotheque a few days before in which two US nationals were killed and seventy-nine injured, and to try to prevent further attacks. The raid was considered by many states to be a disproportionate use of force. But, when force is justified, it sometimes means that lives have to be sacrificed in order to prevent even greater loss of life. The obvious example would have been the shooting down of the four hijacked airliners before they could carry out their suicide missions in New York and Washington on 11 September 2001, assuming of course that there had been evidence at the time of their real intention.[75]

In the case of collective self-defence (as under Article V of the North Atlantic Treaty),[76] there must first be a request from the state that has been threatened or attacked. But, if a collective security organisation like

---

[70] UNSC Res. 487 (1981). At the time Israel could not make a convincing case, not being able to foresee what would be discovered later. See also V. Lowe, '"Clear and Present Danger": Responses to Terrorism' (2005) ICLQ 185.

[71] Gray, pp. 126–8.   [72] Gray, pp. 50–1.

[73] In *Oil Platforms (Iran v. US), ICJ Reports* (2003), paras. 74–8, the ICJ held the test of necessity to be strict.

[74] See p. 257 below on reprisals during an armed conflict.

[75] See also p. 352 below on Article 3*bis* of the Chicago Convention.

[76] 34 UNTS 243 (No. 541); UKTS (1949) 56.

NATO 'decides' to use force, that is only an internal decision. It can be carried out lawfully only if there is Security Council authorisation or a basis in customary international law, such as self-defence. Article V has been invoked only once, following the terrorist attack on the United States on 11 September 2001. The subsequent military operation in Afghanistan was actually carried out by an *ad hoc* coalition led by the United States acting in self-defence against international terrorism.[77] UNSC Resolution 1386 (2001) replaced the coalition forces with an International Security Assistance Force (ISAF) which since August 2003 has been led by NATO.

When territory has been occupied illegally, the use of force to retake it will be a lawful exercise of the right of self-defence. Although Resolution 502 (1982) demanded that Argentina end its occupation of the Falkland Islands, it did not authorise (or prohibit) the use of force to retake the islands. This was done by the United Kingdom in exercise of its right of self-defence. Although Resolution 678 (1990) authorised a coalition of states to use 'all necessary means' to liberate Kuwait, this could also have been done by the coalition at the request of the Government of Kuwait in exercise of its right of self-defence, and this was expressly recognised in the preamble to Resolution 661 (1990).

Article 51 requires that any use of force in self-defence must be reported immediately to the Council, and that the state must cease using force once the Council has taken the measures 'necessary' to maintain international peace and security. This does not mean that it must stop using force as soon as the Council adopts measures: the measures have first to be shown to be really effective.

Humanitarian intervention[78]

The Security Council can authorise military intervention for humanitarian purposes (Resolution 794 (1992) on Somalia) provided that the situation is a threat to international peace and security. But here we are concerned with intervention in another state to deal with extreme human distress *without* Council authorisation – a vital distinction that is sometimes overlooked.

The Charter is capable of dealing with any threat to international peace and security and has been interpreted and applied by the Council

---

[77] See p. 227 above.
[78] See the comprehensive views given to the UK Parliament by Brownlie, Chinkin, Greenwood and Lowe in (2000) ICLQ 876–943.

pragmatically; and some interventions done without Council authority have been commended by the Council, or at least been acquiesced in.

In April 1991, British, French and US forces entered northern Iraq to protect thousands of Iraqi Kurds who were under serious threat from Iraqi forces. These internally displaced persons were in a critical physical condition: unless food, water, medicine and shelter could be provided quickly, it was plainly evident from the media that they would begin to die in great numbers. But the Kurds could be helped only if they and the aid workers assisting them could be protected from the Iraqi forces. Due to threatened vetoes in the Council, Resolution 688 (1991) did not authorise force to be used, but it did condemn Iraq for the repression of its civilian population; found that the situation 'threaten[ed] international peace and security in the region';[79] and demanded that Iraq end its repression and allow access to international humanitarian organisations. The armed intervention which followed was not authorised by the resolution, and was therefore justified solely on the ground that it was necessary to deal with a situation of extreme human distress.[80] A so-called 'no-fly zone' was established over northern Iraq in April 1991, and over the south of Iraq in August 1992, by the United Kingdom and the United States in order to monitor compliance by Iraq with the demands of Resolution 688. Up to the 2003 Iraq war, British and US military aircraft patrolled the zones, and when attacked or threatened with attack fired in self-defence, not on the basis of any Council authority. The zones were not criticised by the Security Council or the General Assembly.[81]

In August 1990, the Economic Community of West African States (ECOWAS) deployed a military force (ECOMOG) to intervene in the bloody conflict between rival parties in Liberia where law and order had broken down totally. No authority was sought from the Security Council, which seventeen months later commended the action.[82]

In September 1998, the Council expressed its grave concern at the use of excessive and indiscriminate attacks by Serbian and FRY forces on the majority ethnic Albanian population in the Serbian province of Kosovo, leading to the displacement of over 230,000 people. In Resolution 1199 (1998), the Council demanded that the FRY cease its repression, and

[79] It had been drafted by the present author as a Chapter VII resolution, but was watered down once China had indicated informally that it would veto such a resolution.
[80] See (1992) BYIL 822–8.   [81] See (1993) BYIL 736–40.
[82] S/22133. Later ECOWAS procured a UN arms embargo against Liberia (UNSC Res. 788 (1992)).

warned of an impending humanitarian catastrophe. The situation wors-
ened. A draft resolution to authorise NATO intervention was opposed
by Russia and China, and so was not put to the vote. Nevertheless, in
March 1999, NATO forces mounted a bombing campaign against Serbia
in an attempt to stop the attacks on civilians in Kosovo. The action was
explained as justified as an exceptional measure to prevent an overwhelm-
ing humanitarian catastrophe.[83]

The legal basis for such humanitarian intervention remains controversial, both politically and legally. As with self-defence, the justification of
humanitarian intervention may be used as a cover for other, much less
worthy, purposes. States contemplating using it need to satisfy themselves
that the following criteria are met: (1) there must be a compelling and
urgent situation of extreme humanitarian distress which demands immediate relief; (2) the state most directly involved must either not be willing
or able to deal with it (it may of course be the cause of the distress);
(3) there is no alternative, the Security Council being unable to agree on
authorising intervention; and (4) the action must be limited in scope and
time to what is necessary to relieve the distress.[84]

These criteria may well have been satisfied in the case of Darfur in
2004/5. The purpose is to help defend people against a threat to their life.
The fact that they are foreign nationals is no longer a good reason for
doing nothing. Provided the criteria are fully met, a military intervention
can be justified in international law. There are good grounds for saying
that a limited use of force for the sole purpose of relieving extreme human
distress, to stop genocide or ethnic cleansing or other serious violations of
international law, is not a violation of Article 2(4). Its full text is seldom
quoted: it requires Members to refrain in their international relations
from the threat or use of force against the territorial integrity or political
independence of any state 'or in any other manner inconsistent with the
Purposes of the United Nations'. Those Purposes include the promotion
of human rights and the solving of humanitarian problems (Article 1(3)).
When the upholding of the Purposes comes into acute conflict with the
sovereignty of a state that is the very obstacle to achieving them, respect
for its territorial integrity or political independence has to give way to
the overriding needs of humanity or, as the International Court of Justice

---

[83] See (1998) BYIL 593 and (1999) BYIL 592–3. See also the House of Commons, Foreign
Affairs Select Committee, Report on Kosovo, 23 May 2000; and Gray, *International Law
and the Use of Force*, 2nd edn, Oxford, 2004, pp. 37–49.
[84] See (1998) BYIL 593 and (2001) BYIL 696.

has put it, 'elementary considerations of humanity, even more exacting in peace than in war'.[85] The situation is not affected by failure to get Council authorisation for intervention, since such use of force would not violate the Charter. NATO's intervention in Kosovo in 1999 was neither authorised, nor condemned by the Security Council,[86] although it has been criticised by some states and international lawyers. The most cogent criticism would seem to be the manner in which force was used: air strikes on other parts of Serbia rather than the use of ground forces in Kosovo. If from the beginning force had been used directly in Kosovo, it might well not have been seen as unreasonable and the reaction might have been more like that in 1991.

Alternatively, it is argued that humanitarian intervention without Security Council authorisation is unlawful but, as in domestic law, sometimes an illegal act can be legitimate morally. As such, it may be overlooked by the law-enforcement authorities or treated leniently. This way around the dilemma (some might unkindly call it a cop-out) is inherently unsatisfactory since it only moves the issue from the legal to the moral plane. International law has shown itself able to cope with new challenges.

---

[85] *Corfu Channel* (Merits) *ICJ Reports* (1949), p. 4, at p. 22; 16 ILR 155. And see C. Greenwood, 'Humanitarian Intervention: The Case of Kosovo' (1999) 10 *Finnish YB of International Law* 141–75.

[86] On 29 March 1999, a draft resolution (S/RES/1999/328) condemning it was defeated by 12–3–0: see S/PV.3989.

11

Human rights

... unwilling to witness or permit the slow undoing of those human rights to which this nation has always been committed, and to which we are committed today at home and around the world.[1]

Brownlie and Goodwin-Gill, *Basic Documents on Human Rights*, 4th edn, Oxford, 2002 (BGG)

Joseph, Schultz and Castan, *The International Covenant on Human Rights: Cases, Material and Commentary*, Oxford, 2002

Jacobs and White, *European Convention on Human Rights*, 3rd edn, Oxford, 2002

Reid, *A Practitioner's Guide to the European Convention on Human Rights*, 2nd edn, London, 2004

Van Dijk, van Hoof and Heringa, *The Theory and Practice of the European Convention on Human Rights*, 3rd edn, The Hague, 1998

Tomuschat, *Human Rights: Between Idealism and Realism*, Oxford, 2003

UN High Commissioner for Human Rights, www.unhchr.ch[2]

The terms 'humanitarian law' or 'international humanitarian law' (IHL), if correctly used, refer only to that area of international law concerned with the protection of members of armed forces and civilians during an armed conflict or military occupation of territory (see Chapter 12 below). However, human rights do not cease completely to apply once IHL applies. They continue except in so far as the special rules (*lex specialis*) of IHL apply or human rights treaties have been validly derogated from.[3] Human rights jurisprudence may be relevant also to the interpretation of IHL, such as the meaning of torture, for which there are even more instances in peacetime. In other words, IHL and human rights should not

---

[1] John F. Kennedy's inaugural address, 20 January 1961.

[2] *Not* to be confused with the UN High Commissioner for Refugees (www.unhcr.ch).

[3] *Legal Consequences of the Construction of a Wall in the Occupied Palestinian Territory, ICJ Reports* (2004), paras. 102–13; ILM (2004) 1009.

be seen as entirely separate areas of international law. The term 'civil rights' usually refers to human rights in domestic law, particularly in the United States.

The Nazi period was notorious for massive violations of human rights. The next sixty years were marked by the development of sophisticated international human rights treaties. Although influenced by domestic principles, such as those in the US Bill of Rights, the French Declaration of the Rights of Man or the English common law, human rights are no longer regarded as a purely domestic matter. The United Nations is prohibited by Article 2(7) of its Charter from intervening in 'matters which are essentially within the domestic jurisdiction' of a state, Although the actual promotion and protection of human rights within a state must necessarily be primarily the responsibility of its government, human rights are no longer regarded as a matter 'essentially' within each state's jurisdiction, the United Nations having adopted many human rights treaties, and from its earliest days passed resolutions condemning human rights abuses.

The number of treaties and other instruments on human rights is now so great that it is possible only to describe the main principles and the basic international and regional enforcement mechanisms. The wealth of jurisprudence that has been built up and is constantly developing can be understood only by consulting specialised books.

Who enjoys the rights?

A state is required to protect the human rights of everyone 'within its territory and subject to its jurisdiction' (International Covenant on Civil and Political Rights 1966 (ICCPR))[4] or 'subject to its jurisdiction' (European Convention for the Protection of Human Rights and Fundamental Freedoms 1950 (ECHR)).[5] In practice, there may be little difference between the ICCPR and the ECHR formulations: attempts to apply the ECHR to acts taking place outside the territory of a party have generally been unsuccessful. In *Banković* in 2001, the European Court of Human Rights unanimously held that the ECHR did not protect civilians in the Federal Republic of Yugoslavia who had been killed in attacks there by certain

---

[4] International Covenant on Civil and Political Rights 1966 (ICCPR) and Optional Protocol, 999 UNTS 171 (No. 14668); ILM (1967) 368; UKTS (1977) 6; BGG 182.
[5] European Convention on Human Rights (ECHR) 1950, 213 UNTS 221 (No. 2889); UKTS (1953) 71; BGG 398.

member states of NATO, since under the ECHR jurisdiction is essentially territorial.[6] But the English courts have held recently that the ECHR does apply to the actions of British officials and members of the armed forces abroad in situations where they have effective control, as in diplomatic or consular premises or a military prison.[7]

The rights normally apply only to natural persons, but certain of them (mostly in respect of property) apply to legal persons such as corporations.[8]

Legal nature of a human right and exhaustion of domestic remedies

Human rights treaties require the parties to protect the rights by properly implementing and enforcing them, although too many parties do not take these obligations seriously enough. The rights are against the state, not private persons. An attack by a burglar, however serious and disagreeable, is in itself not a breach of the victim's human rights. But, if a policeman attacks you, your human rights may well have been violated. You may then be entitled to take the matter directly to an international tribunal or body. But, if there are remedies available in domestic law, you must first exhaust them,[9] unless it would be unreasonable to insist on your doing so if, for example, the process would be exceedingly long or the remedy ineffective.[10]

Universal human rights treaties

United Nations

In 1948, the United Nations adopted the Universal Declaration of Human Rights.[11] Although often cited as if it were legally binding, it is not a treaty. But it provided the foundation for the treaties, universal[12] and regional, that were to follow. The same year, the Genocide Convention was adopted.[13] The UN bodies most concerned with drafting human rights

---

[6] App. 52207/99; ILM (2002) 517; 123 ILR 94, paras. 59–8.
[7] See p. 187 above on diplomatic asylum and *R. (B. Children)* v. *Secretary of State for Foreign and Commonwealth Affairs* [2005] 2 WLR 618; and *R. (Al-Skeini)* v. *Secretary of State for Defence* [2004] EWHC 2911.
[8] See p. 243 below.   [9] See, for example, ICCPR, Article 41(1)(c) and ECHR, Article 35.
[10] See Shaw, pp. 254–5.   [11] UNGA Res. 217 (III); BGG, p. 18.   [12] See p. 52 above.
[13] For genocide and other crimes against humanity, see pp. 270–2 below.

treaties for adoption by the General Assembly are ECOSOC, and its subsidiary, the Commission on Human Rights (CHR) (*not* to be confused
with the Human Rights Committee (HRC)[14] established by the ICCPR),
and the Third and Sixth Committees of the General Assembly.

The Universal Declaration was followed by treaties on specific subjects,
such as the Refugee Convention 1951,[15] the Conventions on Statelessness
of 1954 and 1961[16] and the Convention on the Elimination of All Forms of
Racial Discrimination 1966 (CERD).[17] But it was not until 1966 that two
general treaties were adopted: the International Covenant on Civil and
Political Rights (ICCPR)[18] and the International Covenant on Economic,
Social and Cultural Rights (ICESCR).[19] The two Covenants now have 154
and 151 parties respectively. The Covenants cover all the most important
human rights, but of the two the ICCPR has been the more influential
because it covers the 'harder' individual rights enunciated in the Universal
Declaration of Human Rights, and has a monitoring mechanism, the
Human Rights Committee.[20] The ICESCR is concerned with collective
rights, such as the right of peoples to self-determination[21] and to dispose freely of their natural resources, as well as rights which, because they
are broad and require positive action by the state, such as provision of
work, housing, food, health and education, make their implementation
more problematic. They are therefore expressed more in terms of aspirations.[22] But the ICESCR has led to the formulation of more detailed
obligations in treaties such as the Convention on the Rights of the Child
1989.[23] The so-called *right to development* is not included in the ICESCR
and, despite the importance of development, the assertion that it is a
right in international law cannot be sustained.[24] The other UN human
rights treaties of most significance are the Convention on the Elimination
of All Forms of Discrimination against Women 1979 (CEDAW),[25] and
the Convention against Torture and Other Cruel, Inhuman or Degrading
Treatment or Punishment 1989.[26]

---

[14] See p. 248 below.   [15] See p. 188 above.   [16] See p. 181 above.
[17] 660 UNTS 195 (No. 9464); UKTS (1969) 77; BGG, p. 160.
[18] 999 UNTS 171 (No. 14668); ILM (1967) 368; UKTS (1977) 6; BGG 182.
[19] 993 UNTS 3 (No. 14531); UKTS (1977) 6; BGG, p. 172.
[20] See p. 248 below.   [21] The right is found also in the ICCPR: see pp. ** above for details.
[22] For a different view, see Higgins, pp. 99–104.
[23] 1577 UNTS 3 (No. 27531); ILM (1989) 1448; UKTS (1992) 44; BGG, p. 241.
[24] Higgins, pp. 103–4.
[25] 1249 UNTS 13 (No. 20378); ILM (1980) 33; UKTS (1989) 2; BGG, p. 212.
[26] 1465 UNTS 85 (No. 24841); ILM (1984) 1027; UKTS (1991) 107; BGG, p. 229.

ILO

In the field of work, the International Labour Organization has since 1919 produced some 185 treaties (termed conventions) to improve labour standards. In 1946, it became a UN specialised agency. It is unique in that representatives of governments, employers and workers have equal representation in the decision-making bodies.[27]

Regional human rights treaties

European Convention for the Protection of Human Rights and Fundamental Freedoms 1950 (ECHR)

The ECHR is the most important treaty adopted by the Council of Europe (CoE), and therefore *not* an EU instrument. It is a precondition of admission as a member of the CoE that the applicant state becomes party to the ECHR and accepts the compulsory jurisdiction of the European Court of Human Rights, the right of individual application[28] and all the Protocols to the ECHR. The ECHR has fourteen Protocols, although only seven are still relevant: Nos. 1, 4, 6, 7, 13 and 14.[29] The substantive Articles of the Protocols are regarded as additional Articles to the ECHR. Since the United Kingdom enacted the Human Rights Act 1998,[30] Ireland is the only party to the ECHR that has not legislated specifically to implement it.

Several CoE Members still have overseas territories, and the ECHR (Article 56), and each Protocol, enables those Members to extend the instrument to all or any of those territories.

The human rights in the ECHR are not quite as extensive as in the ICCPR, although the rights that are common to both instruments are generally formulated in a similar way, the drafters of the ICPPR having benefited from the experience of the ECHR. The real strength of the ECHR lies in the effectiveness of its enforcement mechanism (the European Court of Human Rights) and the maturity of its jurisprudence.[31] And, if a case before the European Court of Justice involves a question of human rights, the ECJ is likely to apply the ECHR, to which all EU

---

[27] See www. ilo.org.   [28] See p. 248 below.
[29] The CoE Parliamentary Assembly sometimes allows a little delay in ratifying a Protocol when there are special circumstances. The ECHR was amended by Protocol No. 11 to restructure the enforcement mechanism. For the text as amended by Protocol No. 11, see www.echr.coe.int or BGG, p. 398. On reform of the Court's procedures, see p. 246 below.
[30] For a short description of the Act, see Aust, p. 154.
[31] For a very brief overview of the jurisprudence, see Shaw, pp. 330–2.

member states are parties.[32] Article 17 of Protocol No. 14 provides for the EU to accede to the ECHR.

American Convention on Human Rights 1969[33]

This is often referred to as the Inter-American Convention, probably because it created an Inter-American Commission (and Court) of Human Rights. Established by the Organization of American States (OAS) based in Washington DC, it entered into force in 1978. The parties do not include some Caribbean states, Canada or the United States. The Convention follows generally the ECHR.

African Charter on Human and Peoples' Rights 1981[34]

The Charter (which is treaty) entered into force in 1986, and all members of the African Union (formerly the OAU) are parties. The Charter follows generally the ICCPR and the ICESCR, but goes further by providing that 'peoples' shall have certain rights, such as the right to development.[35] It also includes a chapter on the 'duties' of the individual. Although some of these duties are to do with the family, others, such as the duty not to compromise the security of the state, may have a similar purpose to the qualifications to certain Articles of the ICCPR and the ECHR that can have the effect of limiting the extent of a right (see below).

Arab Charter on Human Rights 1994[36]

The Charter (a treaty) lists the usual human rights, but the preamble reaffirms the Cairo Declaration on Human Rights in Islam 1990, which specifies human rights in the context of a state governed according to Islamic *Sharia*,[37] and Article 27 allows for restrictions on the exercise of freedom of belief, thought and opinion if they are imposed by law.

---

[32] See also Shaw, pp. 344–53, who also discusses the role of the OSCE and the CIS in human rights.

[33] 1144 UNTS 144 (No. 17955); ILM (1970) 99; www.oas.org.

[34] See www.africa-union.org; 1520 UNTS 218 (No. 26363); ILM (1982) 58. See Evans and Murray (eds.), *The African Charter of Human and Peoples' Rights*, Cambridge, 2002.

[35] See the text to n. 24 above.

[36] For a translation from the Arabic, see BGG, p. 774 or www.al-bab.com/arab/human.htm. It is not yet in force.

[37] For the text of the Declaration, see BGG, p. 764.

Outline of the principal civil and political rights

It may be helpful to summarise very briefly the more important civil and political rights, comparison being made between the ICCPR, the ICESCR and the ECHR. But, for a more authoritative account reference must be made to specialised works. (The references are to Articles of the ICPPR, the ICESCR and the ECHR and its Protocols, as the case may be.)

Right to life (ECHR Article 2, ICCPR Article 6)

Taking a person's life must be done in accordance with law, not arbitrarily. The ECHR is more specific about the circumstances in which a person can be killed, such as in self-defence or to effect an arrest. Protocol No. 6 to the ECHR abolished the death penalty, except in connection with a war. Since 1994, new members of the Council of Europe have either to become a party to Protocol No. 6 or introduced a moratorium on the carrying out of death sentences. Protocol No. 6 is now binding on all parties to the ECHR, except Russia which has been observing a moratorium since it became a member in 1996. Protocol No. 13 of 2002 abolishes the death penalty in all circumstances. So far it has twenty-nine parties.

The ICCPR does not itself prohibit the death penalty, but requires that it be limited to the most serious crimes, and not be imposed retrospectively or for crimes committed when under the age of eighteen or carried out on a pregnant woman. When ratifying the ICCPR, the United States reserved the right to execute a person (except a pregnant woman) even if at the time of the crime he or she was under eighteen.[38] The Second Optional Protocol to the ICCPR of 1989 requires the abolition of the death penalty, and so far has fifty-four parties, some two-thirds being parties to the ECHR.

Prohibition of torture (ECHR Article 3, ICCPR Article 7)

No one shall be subjected to torture or to inhuman or degrading treatment or punishment. The ICCPR adds 'cruel' treatment or punishment, and that no one shall be subjected to medical or scientific experiments without his free consent. (The definition of torture in Article 1 of the Torture Convention 1984 is designed for the purposes of that treaty, which requires

---

[38] See *UN Multilateral Treaties*, Ch. IV.4. It was held to be unconstitutional by the US Supreme Court on 1 March 2005.

the parties to make torture a criminal offence subject to quasi-universal jurisdiction.)[39] The prohibition is now also customary international law. The European Court of Human Rights decided in *Soering* that the extradition of a person to any (in practice, non-ECHR) state where he is wanted for a crime for which he could be sentenced to death, would, if he would then be likely to spend a lengthy period on death row, be a breach of Article 3.[40] This obstacle can be overcome if the requesting state gives an undertaking that the person will not be executed. But, nevertheless, it has had severe repercussions for ECHR states that wish to extradite or deport a person who may be a threat to its security, but who might suffer ill-treatment by the authorities of the destination state. The prohibition in Article 3 is absolute and not subject to any national security exception, express or implied.[41]

Prohibition of slavery and forced labour (ECHR Article 4, ICCPR Article 8)

The two Articles are identical in substance. Forced or compulsory labour does not include labour as part of a criminal punishment, military service, to deal with emergencies, or normal civil obligations.

Right to liberty and security (ECHR Article 5, ICPPR Article 9)

Although the ECHR is rather more detailed, the two Articles are the same in substance. No one shall be deprived of his liberty except in accordance with law. Anyone arrested or detained shall be told the reason and the charge, and shall be brought promptly before a judge and entitled to trial within a reasonable time. He shall be entitled to challenge without delay the lawfulness of his detention before a court, for example by

[39] '[A]ny act by which severe pain or suffering, whether physical or mental, is intentionally inflicted on a person for such purposes as obtaining from him or a third person information or a confession, punishing him for an act he or a third person has committed or is suspected of having committed, or intimidating or coercing him or a third person, or for any reason based on discrimination of any kind, when such pain or suffering is inflicted by or at the instigation of or with the consent or acquiescence of a public official or other person acting in an official capacity. It does not include pain or suffering arising only from, inherent in or incidental to lawful sanctions.'

[40] *Soering*, App. No. 14038/88; Series A, No. 161, 1989; ILM (1989) 1063; (1989) 11 EHRR 439; 98 ILR 270. See also *Rehman* [2003] 1 AC 153, para. 54.

[41] *Chahal* (1997) 23 EHRR 413; 108 ILR 385.

habeas corpus. A person wrongfully arrested or detained shall be entitled to compensation.

Right to a fair trial (ECHR Article 6 and Protocol No. 7, ICCPR Article 14)

Both treaties provide that for civil and criminal trials there shall be a fair and public hearing by an independent and impartial tribunal. In a criminal trial, the accused shall be presumed innocent until proved guilty and accorded certain minimum rights: to be told, in a language he understands, and in detail, of the case against him; to have adequate time and facilities to prepare his defence; to defend himself or through a lawyer of his choosing, with legal aid where necessary;[42] to examine witnesses against him and to call witnesses in his defence; to have an interpreter free if he cannot understand or speak the language of the court; to have the right to appeal to a higher court against conviction or sentence; and to receive compensation for a miscarriage of justice. No one shall be tried or punished again for an offence for which he has already been convicted or acquitted (the double jeopardy rule or *ne bis in idem*).

No punishment without law (ECHR Article 7, ICPPR Article 15)

No one shall be convicted of an offence on account of an act that did not constitute an offence at the time of the offence (*nullum crimen sine lege*), or be given a heavier penalty than that which applied at the time.

Respect for private and family life (ECHR Article 8, ICCPR Article 17)

This right, being rather nebulous, has been a fruitful source of law-making by the European Court of Human Rights. In *Hatton*, the Court held that, although the ECHR does not include environmental rights as such, nevertheless Article 8 protects family life from unreasonable noise intrusion (in this case aircraft noise). But the Court had to apply a test of 'fair balance', so taking into account the interests of both individuals and the wider community.[43]

---

[42] See *Steel and Morris* v. *UK*, 2005, ECHR App. No. 6841/01.
[43] (2003) 37 EHRR 28, p. 611.

Freedom of thought, conscience and religion (ECHR Article 9, ICCPR Article 18)

This includes the freedom to change one's religion or belief and, either alone or in community, in public or in private, to manifest one's religion or belief in worship, teaching, practice or observance. The ICCPR adds that no one shall be coerced to adopt a religion or belief.

Freedom of expression (ECHR Article 10, ICCPR Article 19)

Everyone has the right to hold opinions and to receive and impart information and ideas without interference by public authority and regardless of frontiers. The right was severely tested in *Garaudy* v. *France*.[44] An author had been convicted of writing a book denying that the Holocaust had happened. In considering the usual restrictions on the right set out in Article 10 paragraph 2, the Court cited Article 17, which provides that nothing in the ECHR 'may be interpreted as implying for any state, group or person any right to engage in any activity or perform any act aimed at the destruction of any of the rights and freedoms [in the Convention] or at their limitation to a greater extent than provided for in the Convention'. The Court, following its previous Holocaust denier decisions, found that the conviction had not breached the author's human rights, the application was manifestly ill-founded and so inadmissible.

Freedom of assembly and association (ECHR Article 11, ICCPR Articles 21–22)

Everyone has the right to peaceful assembly (meeting with others in public or private), freedom to associate with others, and to form and join a trade union. The latter right is elaborated in Article 8 of the ICESCR.

Right to marry (ECHR Article 12, ICCPR Article 23)

Despite the explicit wording of Article 12 of the ECHR ('Men and women...have the right to marry and to found a family'), and its own previous judgments, the European Court of Human Rights held in *Goodwin*

---

[44] App. No. 65831/01. Decision of 24 June 2003; 2003-IX-HUDOC (www.echr.coe.int/Hudoc.htm).

that it was a breach of the Article to bar totally a (male to female) trans-sexual from marrying a man.[45]

Freedom of movement (ECHR Protocol No. 4, ICCPR Article 12)

Everyone lawfully within the territory of the state has liberty of movement and the freedom to choose his residence. He is also free to leave a country, including his own. A national shall not be expelled from his own state or arbitrarily prevented from entering it. The United Kingdom is not a party to the Protocol, and has entered a reservation to the Covenant in effect reserving the right to control immigration in respect of certain UK nationals without close connections with the metropolitan territory.[46]

Right to free elections (ECHR Protocol No. 1 (Article 3), ICCPR Article 25)

Elections must be held by secret ballot to allow every citizen to give free expression to his opinion. In *Hirst (No. 2)*, the European Court of Human Rights held that the United Kingdom was in breach of the Protocol in denying all convicted prisoners the right to vote. Although the national legislature has a wide margin of appreciation as to what would be fair restrictions on that right, the British Parliament had never considered the matter in modern times.[47] This judgment is a good example of the creative approach of the Court, which sees the ECHR as 'a living instrument to be interpreted in the light of present-day conditions'.[48] Consequently, the United Kingdom has requested that the case be referred to the Grand Chamber. The decision of the Grand Chamber is awaited.

Right to property (ECHR Protocol No. 1)

The right not to be deprived of possessions, except in the public interest and in accordance with the law, is also enjoyed by legal persons, such as corporations. Deprivation without compensation would normally be a breach.[49] However, the right of a state 'to enforce such laws as it deems necessary to control the use of property in accordance with the general

---

[45] App. No. 28957/95; (2002) 35 EHRR 18, p. 447; (2003) AJIL 658.
[46] See p. 180 above on British nationality.
[47] App. No. 74025/01; (2004) 38 EHRR 40, p. 825.
[48] *Banković* (n. 6 above), para. 64.   [49] See *Lithgow* v. *UK* (1986) 8 EHRR 329, para. 121.

interest' is not affected and should usually not require compensation.[50] Most complaints are about nationalisation or planning decisions. Neither the ICCPR nor the ICESCR has an equivalent provision, having been adopted when communist states were still fairly numerous and influential.

Right to education (ECHR Protocol No. 1, ICESCR Article 13)

The later provision in the ICESCR is much more detailed.

Prohibition of discrimination (ECHR Article 14; ICCPR Article 26)

The right shall be secured without discrimination on any ground, such as sex, race, colour, language, religion, political or other opinion, national or social origin, association with a national minority, property, birth or other status. No one shall be discriminated against on any such grounds by a public authority (ECHR Protocol No. 12).[51]

General qualifications to rights

It would be a mistake to think that all human rights are expressed as absolute. Although some in the ECHR and the ICCPR are absolute (the right to life, prohibitions on torture and slavery, and punishment not in accordance with law), others either have specific conditions or are qualified in general terms. This seeks to balance the rights of the individual and the broader interests of the community in a democratic society. Depending on the particular right, the qualifications may allow for exceptions for the protection of morals, health, private life, juveniles and the rights and freedoms of others, or in the interests of public order, public safety, crime prevention, national security or justice. Each qualification is carefully formulated, and most provide that any exception must also be in accordance with the law and be necessary in a democratic society. These provisions allow a necessary degree of flexibility in implementation. In addition, the European Court of Human Rights also allows a *margin of appreciation* in complying with the ECHR, which is broader in cases involving personal morality.[52] This sensible approach avoids the danger that the ECHR might have become a one-size-fits-all instrument that could not

---

[50] See *Alconbury* v. *Secretary of State* [2003] 2 AC 295, paras. 72–3.
[51] Adopted in 2000 and not yet in force.   [52] See Shaw, p. 330.

accommodate the varying social and cultural differences to be found in European countries, which to the outsider may appear all alike.

Reservations

The treaties necessarily express human rights in fairly general terms. When ratifying, a state may formulate reservations to modify the effect on it of the obligations.[53]

Derogations

In very similar terms, both the ECHR (Article 15) and the ICCPR (Article 4) enable a party to take measures derogating from its obligations. For this there must be a public emergency threatening the life of the nation. The measures must be taken only 'to the extent strictly required by the exigencies [i.e. urgent needs] of the situation' and must not be inconsistent with other obligations under international law. The ICCPR adds that they must not involve discrimination solely on the ground of race, colour, sex, religion or social origin, and no doubt that is how the European Court of Human Rights would interpret Article 15. No derogation is permitted by the ECHR from the right to life (except in wartime), torture, slavery, punishment not in accordance with law or the complete prohibition on the death penalty imposed by Protocol No. 13. The ICCPR includes some other non-derogatible rights, including the freedom of thought.

Any derogation, and the reasons for it, must be communicated to the Council of Europe or the United Nations, as appropriate. *Numerous* derogations have been made.[54] In the case of the ECHR, it is for the European Court of Human Rights to judge whether the conditions for derogation exist, but the state has a wide 'margin of appreciation' as to whether the life of the nation is threatened.[55] In 2001, the United Kingdom gave notice of derogation from Article 9 of the ICPPR and Article 5(1) of the ECHR due to the public emergency existing in the UK caused by the threat of international terrorism.[56] As a result, the Anti-Terrorism, Crime and Security

---

[53] See p. 239 above on the US reservation to the ICCPR on the right to life. For more on reservations, see p. 67 above.

[54] See *UN Multilateral Treaties*, Ch. IV.4.

[55] See *Lawless v. Ireland* (1979–80) 2 EHRR 1; 31 ILR 290; and *Ireland v. UK* (1979–80) 2 EHRR 153; 58 ILR 190.

[56] In connection with the ECHR derogation, see the Human Rights Act 1998 (Designated Derogation) Order 2001 (SI 2001 No. 3644).

Act 2001 was enacted. This enables foreign nationals to be detained indefinitely (although subject to regular judicial scrutiny) if they are considered
to be a threat to national security and suspected of being an international
terrorist, yet are unwilling to leave the UK and cannot be deported or
extradited because that could breach the person's human rights (the right
to life or not to be subjected to torture etc.: see *Chahal*).[57] The power of
detention is subject to annual renewal by Parliament. In 2004, the House
of Lords held that detaining only foreign nationals under the Act was a
breach of their human rights.[58]

Enforcement

Ratifying human rights conventions is fine, but unless they can be effectively enforced they are worth little. Even the most basic human rights
are constantly being abused in many states. Both the ECHR (Article 13)
and the ICCPR (Article 2(3)) provide for the right to an effective remedy
for a violation of any of the rights. Some states ratify human rights conventions without any real intention to respect them or to put in place the
domestic mechanisms by which the rights could be properly protected.
To be effective, a human rights convention needs not only an international machinery, such as an international court or tribunal to which an
individual can complain of a breach of his rights, but also domestic legal
mechanisms by which judgments of the international court or tribunal can
be properly implemented, either by paying compensation or by changing
the law, or both. In practice, this is more likely in truly democratic states
which have the rule of law with an independent judiciary. It is much better
to have domestic legal systems that protect rights effectively, so making it
unnecessary for people to seek redress from an international tribunal.

European Court of Human Rights[59]

In 1998, the original two institutions created by the ECHR, the European Commission of Human Rights and the European Court of Human
Rights, were replaced by one institution, a revised European Court of

---

[57] (1997) 23 EHRR 413; 108 ILR 385.
[58] *A v. Home Secretary* [2004] UKHL 56. The provisions were replaced by the Prevention of
Terrorism Act 2005, which applies also to British nationals.
[59] For information on the Court, including the text of the ECHR, the Protocols, other basic
documents, judgments and other useful information, see www.echr.coe.int.

Human Rights on which each of the parties to the ECHR is entitled to one judge. The Court's jurisdiction extends to all matters concerning the interpretation or application of the ECHR. An individual, a legal person, an NGO or a group of individuals can make an application to the Court alleging a violation of the Convention. A member state may also allege a breach of the ECHR by another member state (an 'inter-state case'), but this is rare. An application will not be admissible unless all local remedies have first been exhausted.[60] The application must then be made within six months.[61] Applications can be made in any official language of a member state, but if declared admissible, all subsequent documentation must be in an official language of the Court, English or French. The application and pleadings are normally available to the public.

The Court sits either as Committees of three judges, Chambers of seven judges or a Grand Chamber of seventeen judges. An application is first examined by a Rapporteur (one of the judges) who decides whether it should go to a Committee or straight to a Chamber. A Committee, by a unanimous vote, may declare inadmissible or strike out an individual application. Otherwise a Chamber will decide, by majority vote, on the admissibility of the case and, if it is declared admissible but is not settled, on the merits of the application. If the case raises a serious question of interpretation of the ECHR, or might result in a judgment inconsistent with a previous judgment of the Court, the Chamber may, before giving judgment, and provided no party to the case objects, relinquish jurisdiction to the Grand Chamber. A judgment of a Chamber may, in exceptional cases, be referred by a party to the case to the Grand Chamber, but will be heard by the Grand Chamber only if it accepts that it raises a serious question of interpretation or application of the ECHR, or a serious issue of general importance. Because of the huge and increasing backlog of cases, it was suggested that decisions on admissibility should be decided by a single judge with two assessors/rapporteurs, and that manifestly well-founded cases (where the situation is similar to previously decided cases so that no new question of law is involved) should be heard by a three-judge panel. The essence of these reforms has been included in Protocol No. 14, which will enter into force once all parties to the ECHR have ratified it.

Most of the facts and legal arguments are presented in writing. If a Chamber or the Grand Chamber agrees to an oral hearing (only in a minority of cases), this consists mostly of prepared statements rather than

[60] See p. 441 below for the relevant rules of international law.
[61] See P. Leach, *Taking a Case to the European Court of Human Rights*, Oxford, 2001.

a dialogue between judges and counsel. A final judgment of a Chamber or the Grand Chamber is binding on the state that is a party to the case. Execution of the judgment is, if necessary, supervised by the Committee of Ministers of the Council of Europe.

The Court may also give advisory opinions at the request of the Council of Europe's Committee of Ministers on the interpretation of the ECHR or its Protocols, although not on the content or scope of the rights and freedoms, there being a perfectly adequate judicial procedure available to complainants, whether individuals or member states.

Perhaps the greatest single factor that makes the ECHR so effective is the right of individual application (petition) to the Court. Under Article 34, applications no longer need the consent of the state party concerned. But about 9 per cent of applications are held inadmissible. The most common grounds are that they are manifestly ill-founded or out of time, domestic remedies have not been exhausted or the application amounts to an appeal on the merits from a domestic judgment. The following are the figures for 2004: about 45,000 new individual applications; applications held admissible, 830; judgments given, 718. A further 20,348 applications were disposed of, leaving some 78,000 pending. Typically, 30 per cent of applications are not pursued by the applicant.

Other regional treaties

The American Convention on Human Rights 1969 has a Commission and a Court of Human Rights, based in San José, Costa Rica, that were inaugurated in 1979.[62] The 1998 Protocol to the African Charter on Human and Peoples' Rights on the Establishment of an African Court of Human and Peoples' Rights[63] entered into force on 25 January 2004 and has so far fifteen parties. The Arab Charter on Human Rights 1994 is not yet in force and will have no human rights court.[64]

Human Rights Committee[65]

In contrast to the ECHR and the American Convention, there is no court established to enforce the ICCPR. Instead, it has an eighteen-member

---

[62] BGG, p. 671; Harris and Livingstone (eds.), *The Inter-American System of Human Rights,* Oxford, 1998; www.corteidh.or.cr.

[63] ILM (2004) 1; BGG, p.741; www.africa-union.org.　　　[64] BGG, p. 774.

[65] D. McGoldrick, *The Human Rights Committee,* Oxford, 1991; and Higgins (for ten years a member of the HRC), pp. 108–10. For the annual reports of the HRC, and of the Committee against Torture and the CERD Committee, see www.unhchr.ch.

Human Rights Committee (HRC), which is often confused with the (very different) UN Commission on Human Rights (CHR).[66] The HRC is composed of nationals of parties, mostly judges or professors of law elected by secret ballot of the parties to serve in a personal capacity for a four-year, renewable term. The HRC meets three times a year in New York and Geneva. It operates, by consensus, in three ways.

Reports

A state must submit a report on how it is implementing the ICCPR to the HRC within one year of becoming a party, and thereafter every five years, although *ad hoc* reports can also be requested. The HRC also accepts information from NGOs. Representatives of each state are questioned about its report at a public hearing of the HRC. Thereafter the HRC issues to all parties specific 'Observations' on each report. If a state fails to submit a report, the HRC can still consider the matter and give its views.

General Comments

The HRC is empowered to issue 'General Comments' on implementation of the ICPPR. So far it has issued thirty-one. Some have been on controversial issues, such as reservations to the ICCPR (General Comment 24).[67] Although the object of a General Comment is to help the parties and to further the purposes of the ICCPR, the HRC has been strongly criticised for straying into controversial questions of international law and, although it is not a court, making pronouncements that were not based on the facts of a particular case and without the benefit of hearing legal argument from the parties concerned. But such of its General Comments as have received wide support may be regarded as a secondary source of international law.[68]

Individual complaints

The (First) Optional Protocol to the ICCPR[69] enables the HRC to consider a 'communication' (petition) from an individual (not a legal person) who is subject to the jurisdiction of a party to the Protocol and who claims that he is the victim of a violation by that party of the ICCPR. The petitioner must first have exhausted all available domestic remedies, provided those remedies have not been unreasonably prolonged.[70] The state has six months to respond. The HRC will not consider a communication that is already being investigated under another international procedure, such

---

[66] See www.unhchr.ch.   [67] See pp. 75–6 above.   [68] See p. 8 above.
[69] 999 UNTS 171 (No. 14668); ILM (1967) 368; UKTS (1977) 6.   [70] See p. 441 below.

as by the European or Inter-American Courts of Human Rights. A Special Rapporteur of the HRC processes new communications, and the HRC's Working Group on Communications, if it is unanimous, decides if a communication is admissible. The HRC considers the communication in private and then sends its views to the petitioner and the state.

Although the procedure may at first sight seem similar to that of individual applications to the European Court of Human Rights, the HRC's views are not binding and there is no prescribed sanction for ignoring them, the chief weapon of the HRC being publicity. A summary of its activities under the Protocol is published in the HRC's annual report to the UN General Assembly.[71]

The Optional Protocol has 105 parties and a party may withdraw from it.[72] Some states, such as the United Kingdom, which are parties to the ECHR, are not parties to the Protocol since they consider the protection given by the European Court of Human Rights sufficiently effective that there is no need in their case for an alternative procedure. But the United Kingdom is now a party to the CEDAW Protocol (see below). A working group of the CHR is considering a proposal for similar optional protocols to the ICESCR.

Other UN monitoring bodies[73]

There are also committees to monitor the implementation of the Racial Discrimination Convention (CERD), the Convention on the Elimination of All Forms of Discrimination against Women (CEDAW) and the Torture Convention. They operate in a similar fashion to the HRC, and include provisions for individual petitions, subject to the state concerned making a general declaration of acceptance in the case of CERD and the Torture Convention, or ratifying the Optional Protocol to CEDAW. There is also a monitoring committee under the Rights of the Child Convention, but no right of individual petition.

---

[71] For a sample of its work, see ILR, vols. 115 and 118.
[72] See p. 106 above on the Trinidad and Tobago manoeuvre.   [73] See www.unhchr.ch.

12

The law of armed conflict (international humanitarian law)

> Then every soldier kill his prisoners!
> Kill the boys . . . ? 'Tis expressly against the law of arms.[1]

Roberts and Guelff, *Documents on the Laws of War*, 3rd edn, Oxford, 2000

Schindler and Toman, *The Laws of Armed Conflict*, 4th edn, Leiden, 2004 (documents)

UK Ministry of Defence, *The Manual of the Law of Armed Conflict*, Oxford, 2004

Oppenheim, *Oppenheim's International Law*, 7th edn, London, 1952, vol. II

Pictet (ed.), *The Geneva Conventions of 12 August 1949: Commentary*, Geneva, 1953–60, 4 vols.

Green, *The Contemporary Law of Armed Conflict*, 2nd ed, Manchester, 2000

The first quote is of Henry V's supposed reaction at the Battle of Agincourt 1415 to the murder of his army's boy servants. The second is that of his Welsh captain, Fluellen, who clearly had a better understanding of the Law of Arms (later the Laws of War).[2] This chapter is headed 'The law of armed conflict' since that is the more correct term to describe the international law governing the conduct of hostilities, including military occupation. International lawyers also use the Latin term *jus in bello* to distinguish it from *jus ad bellum*, the law on the use of force.[3] But the currently fashionable term used by the United Nations, the International Court of Justice and the International Committee of the Red Cross is 'international humanitarian law' (IHL).[4] This reflects the law's fundamentally humanitarian purpose, but can mislead people into thinking that the subject covers all human rights, or even that it is concerned with

---

[1] W. Shakespeare, *Henry V*, Act IV. scenes 6/7.
[2] For the history of the law, see Green, *The Contemporary Law of Armed Conflict*, 2nd edn, Manchester, 2000, pp. 20–53.
[3] See p. 223 above.
[4] The ICTY has jurisdiction over 'serious violations of International Humanitarian Law'.

humanitarian aid. Yet IHL is a neat abbreviation and so will be used for the rest of this chapter.

Even if a state resorts unlawfully to the use of force, IHL will still apply to all parties involved in the conflict.[5] For this there does not have to be a declaration of war or the recognition of a state of war,[6] the mere existence in fact of an armed conflict being enough.[7] In IHL, the term 'armed conflict' has now replaced 'war'. IHL is very detailed and complex. There are over thirty treaties. It is not possible here to do more than mention the more important treaties and principles. For a much fuller treatment of the subject one must consult specialist books such as those listed above.

Sources

Most IHL is now found in multilateral treaties, though an IHL treaty creates in effect a network of bilateral obligations and so usually enters into force after only two states have ratified. Also, unlike most other treaties, the rights and obligations are not reciprocal: if a treaty is violated by one party to a conflict (e.g. by the murder of POWs) another party is *not* entitled to respond in like form or commit a different breach of IHL.[8]

Broadly speaking, IHL treaties can be divided into two main streams: those stating the rules on how hostilities can be conducted in a lawful manner ('Hague Law') and those governing the treatment of non-combatants ('Geneva Law'). These terms reflect the fact that the modern law was first comprehensively promulgated by the Hague Conventions of 1907[9] and then by the Geneva Conventions, of which the latest are the four of 1949, which have 192 parties.[10] A sub-species of Hague Law are those treaties restricting the use of certain weapons (rather than banning their

---

[5] See the 'Reaffirming' paragraph of the preamble to Additional Protocol I of 1977 (n. 12 below).

[6] See C. Greenwood, 'The Concept of War in Modern International Law' (1987) ICLQ 283.

[7] See common Article 2 of the four Geneva Conventions.

[8] But see p. 257 below on reprisals.

[9] Only the following are still applicable: Hague Conventions IV (War on Land) and its Regulations, V (Neutrality), VII (Conversion of Merchant Ships into Warships), VIII (Automatic Submarine Contact Mines), IX (Naval Bombardment), XI (Right of Capture in Naval Warfare) and XIII (Neutrality in Naval Warfare). For their texts and very useful introductions, see Roberts and Guelff, *Documents on the Laws of War*, 3rd edn, oxford, 2000, pp. 67–137.

[10] I (Wounded and Sick on Land), II (Wounded and Sick at Sea), III (POWs) and IV (Civilians): see Roberts and Guelff, *Documents on the Laws of War*, 3rd edn, Oxford, 2000, pp. 195–369. For an authoritative commentary on them, see Pictet (ed.), *The Geneva Conventions of 12 August 1949, Commentary*, Geneva, 1953–60.

production), the most recent being the Certain Conventional Weapons Convention 1980 (CCWC).[11] Geneva Law has been supplemented by Additional Protocols I and II of 1977.[12] The first supplements the four Geneva Conventions, and applies also to armed conflicts between a state and a national liberation movement. The second deals with internal conflicts. Both have been widely ratified. Additional Protocol I now has 162 parties and Additional Protocol II 157 parties. But it would be a mistake to see Geneva Law and Hague Law as mutually exclusive. There has been a tendency for the two streams to merge. For example, a significant part of Additional Protocol I modernises rules of combat, in particular by emphasising the hugely important principle of proportionality. Additional Protocol II also deals with rules of combat. Similarly, the borderline between IHL and human rights law is becoming rather less distinct.[13]

Even when a state is not party to an IHL treaty it will be bound by those of its rules that now also reflect customary international law.[14] The degree to which IHL treaties reflect, or have come to represent, customary law is controversial.[15] The original Hague Law, and much of Geneva Law, although not yet all of Additional Protocols I and II, are now regarded as reflecting customary law and constitute the main body of IHL.[16] The importance of customary law is emphasised by the principle in the so-called Martens Clause,[17] first enunciated in the Hague Conventions and later in the Geneva Conventions.[18] Article 1(2) of Additional Protocol I reaffirmed the application of the principle in cases not covered by the Protocol or by other treaties, that 'civilians and combatants remain under the protection and authority of the principles of international law derived from established custom, from the principles of humanity and from the dictates of public conscience'.[19]

---

[11] See p. 255 below.
[12] 1125 UNTS 3 (No. 17512); ILM (1977) 1391; UKTS (1999) 29 and 30; Roberts and Guelff, *Documents on the Laws of War*, 3rd edn, Oxford, 2000, pp. 419–512. And see Sandoz *et al.* (eds.), *Commentary on the Additional Protocols 1977 to the Geneva Conventions 1949*, Geneva, 1987.
[13] See also p. 233 above.   [14] See p. 8 above.
[15] Although useful, J.-M. Haenckaerts (ed.), *ICRC Study on Customary Rules of International Humanitarian Law*, Cambridge, 2005, overstates many claims to customary law status.
[16] *Legal Consequences of the Construction of a Wall in the Occupied Palestinian Territory, ICJ Reports* (2004), para. 89; ILM (2004) 1009. There are still significant states that are not yet parties to the two Protocols, Germany and the United States in particular.
[17] See Green, *The Contemporary Law of Armed Conflict*, 2nd edn, Manchester, 2000, pp. 17–18.
[18] E.g. Article 63 of the First Geneva Convention.
[19] The preamble to Additional Protocol II has a simpler version.

International and internal armed conflicts

Most IHL deals with international armed conflicts, that is, those between states. Even when a state sends armed forces to another state at its request to fight insurgents, that does not give the conflict an international character.[20] Common Article 3 of the four Geneva Conventions 1949 has some rather inadequate humanitarian principles applicable to 'armed conflict not of an international character'. So with the increased concern about armed conflicts that are solely or partly internal, such as civil wars, Additional Protocol II developed and supplemented common Article 3 in respect of armed conflicts within a state between its forces and dissident forces or other organised armed groups. But, unlike the rest of the Geneva Conventions, neither Article 3 nor Additional Protocol II has enforcement provisions.

The legal distinction between international and internal armed conflicts is, however, becoming smaller. In *Tadic*, the International Criminal Tribunal for the Former Yugoslavia (ICTY) ruled that it has, albeit by implication, jurisdiction over Article 3 crimes. Its sister court, the International Criminal Tribunal for Rwanda (ICTR), has express jurisdiction over breaches of Article 3 and Additional Protocol II;[21] and the International Criminal Court (ICC) has jurisdiction over crimes committed during an internal armed conflict.[22] The more recent treaties on weaponry, such as the 1996 amended Protocol II to the CCWC (on landmines) and the Landmines Convention 1997,[23] apply also to internal armed conflicts. The ICTY decision suggests that the customary law on internal armed conflicts is essentially the same as for international armed conflicts. Although the two Additional Protocols are significantly different, and many internal armed conflicts do not reach the Additional Protocol I threshold, the *Tadić* ruling is realistic and likely to be followed by other courts and tribunals, international and national. Article 8(2)(c) to (f) of the ICC Statute lists extensively war crimes committed during internal conflicts. The wisest course for a force commander is to treat any military operation as if it is an international armed conflict.

The central principles of IHL are that belligerents do not have an unlimited choice of means to attack the enemy; the distinction between combatants

---

[20] See the decision of the Appeals Chamber in *Tadić* (Jurisdiction), www.icty.org (Case IT-94-1-AR72); 105 ILR 453 at 489 *et seq.*

[21] See p. 253 above.   [22] See p. 277 below.

[23] 2056 UNTS 241 (No. 35597); ILM (1997) 1509; UKTS (2001) 21.

and non-combatants must be respected; non-combatants, whether pris-oners of war, the sick or wounded, or civilians, must be treated with humanity; and attacks must be directed against military, not civilian, objectives. In the two World Wars there were deliberate attacks on civilian objects, widespread plunder and acts of revenge. Today, it is clear that only those acts that are necessary to defeat the enemy are permissible, and so the means (e.g. weapons) and the objects against which they are used are restricted. The basic rules for land warfare apply also to warfare at sea or in the air, subject to the necessary adaptations.

Weaponry

The use of certain types of weapon is prohibited.

Conventional weapons

Article 35 of Additional Protocol I reconfirms that the means of injuring the enemy are not unlimited, and thus it is 'prohibited to employ arms, projectiles and material and methods of warfare of a nature to cause super-fluous injury or unnecessary suffering'. The means are set out in treaties and other instruments that are now regarded as representing customary international law, such as the 1868 St Petersburg Declaration,[24] the 1899 Hague Declarations 2 (Asphyxiating Gases) and 3 (Expanding Bullets)[25] and Hague Convention IV and its annexed Regulations Respecting the Laws and Customs of War on Land.[26] The principal and most detailed modern treaty is the Certain Conventional Weapons Convention (CCWC) 1980, which has complex technical provisions in its three original Proto-cols on (I) Non-Detectable Fragments, (II) Mines, Booby-Traps etc., and (III) Incendiaries.[27] On ratifying, a state has to consent to be bound by at least two of the Protocols. Protocol IV on Laser Weapons was adopted

---

[24] Roberts and Guelff, *Documents on the Laws of War*, 3rd edn, Oxford, 2000, p. 53.
[25] *Ibid.*, pp. 59 and 63 respectively. [26] *Ibid.*, pp. 67 and 73 respectively.
[27] UN Convention on Prohibitions or Restrictions on the Use of Certain Conventional Weapons Which May Be Deemed to Be Excessively Injurious or to Have Indiscriminate Effects 1980, 1342 UNTS 137 (No. 22495); ILM (1980) 1523; UKTS (1996) 105; Roberts and Guelff, *Documents on the Laws of War*, 3rd edn, Oxford, 2000, pp. 515–60. For the status of the Convention and Protocols, see *UN Multilateral Treaties*, Ch. XXVI.2. After twenty-five years, the Convention has only ninety-nine parties, and ratification of the later Protocols is slow. For some of the reasons, see A. Aust, 'Limping Treaties: Lessons from Multilateral Treaty-Making' (2003) NILR 243 at 259–60.

in 1995 and Protocol V on explosive remnants of war in 2003. Although Protocol II prohibits only the *indiscriminate* use of landmines, Amended Protocol II of 1996 applies also to internal armed conflicts and the transfer of landmines, but still not their use, stockpiling or production, which are covered by the Landmines Convention 1997.[28] A general amendment to the CCWC and its Protocols to apply them to all non-international armed conflicts was adopted in 2001.[29]

Nuclear, chemical and biological weapons

Although no treaty specifically prohibits the use of nuclear weapons, it is widely agreed that IHL applies equally to their use. The International Court of Justice has held, unanimously, that IHL applies to the threat or use of nuclear weapons, but decided, although only by the casting vote of its President, that it could not 'conclude definitively whether the threat or use of nuclear weapons would be lawful or unlawful in an extreme circumstance of self-defence, in which the very survival of a state would be at stake'.[30] The Court does not appear to have considered the, admittedly paradoxical, possibility that in certain exceptional situations the threat or even use of nuclear weapons might be done altruistically to support demands by it or the United Nations for the observance of fundamental human rights, such as the prohibitions on genocide or, indeed, the use of other weapons of mass destruction against a third state. The advisory opinion may not weigh that heavily with a state that feels that morally it has no choice but to use a nuclear weapon, however terrible that would be.

The so-called Geneva Gas Protocol 1925[31] prohibited the first use of asphyxiating, poisonous or other gases and bacteriological methods of warfare, and is now generally recognised as representing customary international law. It has been supplemented by the Biological Weapons Convention 1972[32] and the Chemical Weapons Convention 1993.[33] Although they are more in the nature of disarmament treaties, the prohibitions

---

[28] 2056 UNTS 241 (No. 35597); ILM (1997) 1509; UKTS (2001) 21.
[29] See Schindler and Toman, *The Laws of Armed Conflict*, 4th edn, Leiden, 2004 or www.icrc.org/ihl/.
[30] *The Legality of the Threat or Use of Nuclear Weapons* Advisory Opinion, *ICJ Reports* (1996), p. 226; 110 ILR 163.
[31] Roberts and Guelff, *Documents on the Laws of War*, 3rd edn, Oxford, 2000, p. 157.
[32] 1015 UNTS 163 (No. 14860); ILM (1972) 309; UKTS (1976) 11.
[33] 1974 UNTS 317 (No. 33757); ILM (1993) 800; UKTS (1997) 45.

on the possession of such weapons means that their use is also banned. They specifically prohibit their use in retaliation for an attack using them, so casting doubt on whether this would still be possible under the Gas Protocol, as some parties have asserted.

Reprisals

A reprisal in wartime is a form of retaliation, but one which goes further than is normally permitted. When a belligerent commits a breach of IHL, the enemy may, exceptionally, respond by action that would normally be illegal, provided a warning has been ignored and the purpose is to stop the breach, not to wreak vengeance. The reprisal must not target civilians or be disproportionate. Additional Protocol I prohibits certain reprisals.[34]

Prisoners of war

The Third Geneva Convention spells out in great detail how POWs must be treated. To take a simple example, on capture a POW can be hooded and restrained only as a temporary measure of military necessity. The most difficult problem is that of determining under Article 4 if a person is entitled to POW status. The principal category is that of members of the armed forces of a party to the conflict, including militias or volunteer corps that are a part of the forces. There is also the category of members of other militias and other volunteer corps, including 'organised resistance movements' belonging to a party to the conflict if they (a) are commanded by a person responsible for his subordinates; (b) have a fixed distinctive sign recognisable at a distance; (c) carry arms openly; and (d) conduct operations in accordance with IHL. Civilian personnel accompanying a force are also included. If there is doubt as to whether a captured person is a POW, he enjoys the protection of the Convention until a 'competent tribunal' has determined his status (Article 5).

The POW categories were enlarged by Additional Protocol I, Articles 43 and 44, to cover also irregular or resistance forces, such as those often used by national liberation movements, which do not identify themselves

---

[34] See Articles 51(6), 52(1), 53(c), 54(4), 55(2) and 56(4). Some parties to Protocol I, including the UK, have reserved the right in certain very limited situations to take reprisals prohibited by Article 56(4). See the UK Ministry of Defence, *The Manual of the Law of Armed Conflict*, Oxford, 2004, paras. 16.16–16.18.

by distinguishing marks, provided they are under proper command and carry arms openly when attacking or when visible to the enemy while deploying to attack. Thus terrorists are unlikely to be covered.[35]

The legal status of aliens detained by US forces at Guantanamo Bay remains unclear. They include some captured during the international armed conflict in Afghanistan that followed the terrorist attacks in the United States on 11 September 2001; some captured during subsequent hostilities in Afghanistan; and others detained in other countries and suspected of terrorism. What is important is that the lawfulness of their detention, and the conditions under which they are held, should be subjected to impartial legal scrutiny, preferably by courts independent of the executive.[36]

Mercenaries

Because states, both developed and developing, find them useful, mercenaries have always existed, and are now often supplied by so-called private military companies. Latterly, the legal status of civilians employed by armed forces to carry out military or quasi-military tasks has been questioned. Article 47 of Additional Protocol I provides that a mercenary shall not have the right to be a combatant or prisoner of war. The meaning of 'mercenary' is set out in a complex and cumulative definition, the essential elements being that he is:

> *motivated* to take part in the hostilities essentially by the *desire for private gain* and, in fact, is promised, by or on behalf of a Party to the conflict, material compensation *substantially in excess of* that promised or paid to combatants of similar ranks and functions in the armed forces of that Party. (Emphasis added)

The definition was taken over by the Mercenaries Convention 1989,[37] but for the very different purpose of making it a criminal offence to recruit, use, finance or train mercenaries or, being a mercenary, to participate directly in hostilities. The definition may be just adequate for the purpose of Additional Protocol I, but is not precise enough to create a criminal offence, since the prosecution would have to prove all the elements of the definition, in particular the motivation of private gain. The

---

[35] See further pp. 284–5 below.   [36] As to the so-called War on Terror, see p. 283 below.
[37] 2163 UNTS 96 (No. 37789); ILM (1990) 89.

Convention did not enter into force until 2001, and now has twenty-six parties.[38]

Civilians and civilian objects

The treatment of civilians is the subject of the Fourth Geneva Convention, which addresses the treatment of enemy aliens in the territory of a belligerent and the inhabitants of occupied territories. They are also the subject of Additional Protocol I, which adds significantly to the duty to protect civilians and civilian objects during active hostilities. The fundamental rule expressed in Article 48 of the Protocol is that belligerents must distinguish between civilians and combatants, and between civilian and military objectives, and direct their operations only against military objectives. The civilian population and civilian objects must not be attacked deliberately or force be used indiscriminately (Article 51(4)), as was done in the 'carpet bombing' of cities during the Second World War. But the death or injury of civilians or damage to civilian property is not illegal if it is accidental or unavoidable. In assessing such matters, one has to apply the rule of proportionality: whether the effect on civilians would be excessive. 'Military objectives' are those which, at the time, offer a definite military advantage if destroyed, captured or neutralised (Article 52). The bombing of a munitions factory will therefore usually be lawful even though civilian workers will be killed, and even if it is situated in a populated area with people living nearby. This is often described, euphemistically, as 'collateral damage', and can now be lessened by the use of laser-guided, precision missiles. The same considerations apply to strategic targets such as roads, bridges, power stations and airports. More difficult questions are whether, and in what circumstances, civilian officials (e.g. government ministers) or installations (civil radio transmitters) can be legitimate military targets.

Occupied territory

Section III of the Hague Regulations,[39] the Fourth Geneva Convention and Articles 61–78 of Additional Protocol I lay down the rights and duties of

---

[38] See A. Aust, 'Limping Treaties: Lessons from Multilateral Treaty-Making' (2003) NILR 243 at 260–2.

[39] Annexed to Hague Convention IV (1907): see Roberts and Guelff, *Documents on the Laws of War*, 3rd edn, Oxford, 2000, pp. 73–84.

a military occupant of foreign territory. The Convention governs most of the relations between the occupant and the local population and, although it applies only for one year after the end of hostilities, the provisions specifically applicable to occupied territory continue for so long as the occupant governs it (Article 6). An occupant's primary duty is to maintain public order and safety and to ensure the basic needs of the population. Local law can be amended or suspended, but not so that it affects legal rights, and local courts should be allowed to function. Private property must not be confiscated. The occupant may collect taxes, but any new taxes must be for the administration of the territory. Local nationals must not be deported, either individually or collectively.

Although the inhabitants of an occupied territory are not prohibited by IHL from resisting the occupying forces, Article 5 of the Fourth Geneva Convention allows the occupier to try saboteurs and others actively hostile to the occupying forces for any crimes they commit.

Palestine

The claim by Israel that the Fourth Geneva Convention applies to the occupied Palestinian territories only *de facto* has been dismissed by the International Court of Justice,[40] which has advised that they are under military occupation, and so subject to the limitations imposed by the Hague Regulations and the Fourth Geneva Convention.[41] The Court also found that the Israeli settlements in the occupied territory, including East Jerusalem, have been established in breach of international law, and that the wall and its associated regime gravely infringes a number of rights under IHL and international human rights treaties of the Palestinians living in the occupied territory which cannot be justified by military necessity, national security or public order.[42]

Enforcement

Although the four Geneva Conventions and Additional Protocol I all require the parties to penalise 'grave breaches' of them (e.g. Articles 49

---

[40] *Legal Consequences of the Construction of a Wall in the Occupied Palestinian Territory* Advisory Opinion, *ICJ Reports* (2004), paras. 90–101; ILM (2004) 1009.

[41] See also UNSC Res. 242 (1967), 252 (1968), 465 (1980), 497 (1981) and 672 (1990); UNGA Res. 2253 and 2254 (1967) and 2949 (XXVII) (1972).

[42] *Legal Consequences of the Construction of a Wall in the Occupied Palestinian Territory* Advisory Opinion, *ICJ Reports* (2004), paras. 123–37.

and 50 of the First Geneva Convention), they deal with only certain war crimes. But all war crimes are crimes for which there is universal jurisdiction, so that any state can prosecute them.[43] The most authoritative, and convenient, list of war crimes, committed in international or internal armed conflicts, is now to be found in the ICC Statute.[44] The defence that an accused was acting under the order of a superior is available only in very limited circumstances.[45]

Since the end of the Cold War, the UN Security Council has had a considerable role in the enforcement of IHL. Numerous (legally binding) resolutions adopted under Chapter VII of the Charter reaffirmed the duty of belligerents to observe IHL, and authorised the use of force to protect civilians from grave and persistent breaches of IHL.[46] The Security Council also established the International Criminal Tribunal for the Former Yugoslavia and the International Criminal Tribunal for Rwanda to try persons for war crimes and crimes against humanity.[47]

UN forces

The members of the armed forces of a UN Member deployed on a UN peacekeeping mission are entitled to use force in self-defence. If under Chapter VII the Security Council authorises Members to use force against another state (as in Resolution 660 (1990)), their armed forces will be taking part in an international armed conflict and IHL will apply to them. If they are on a UN peace-enforcing mission, IHL will still apply to them. Although the United Nations and other international organisations are not parties to IHL treaties, the armed forces of Members made available for UN missions remain bound by IHL and will benefit from its protection.[48] Problems may, however, arise if a Member is part of a 'coalition' but is not party to a particular IHL treaty, such as one of the Additional Protocols, if other members of the coalition are bound by it and it is not clear if the relevant provision is also customary international law. This problem can be alleviated if the coalition forces operate under common

---

[43] See p. 45 above.   [44] Article 8 and the Elements of Crimes. See also p. 277 below.
[45] See p. 273 below. For the historical background see Oppenheim, 7th edn, vol. II, pp. 568–82.
[46] And see p. 226 above.   [47] See p. 273 below.
[48] See common Article 1(1) of the Geneva Conventions; the UN Secretary-General's Bulletin on Observance by UN Forces of IHL 1999 (in Roberts and Guelff, *Documents on the Laws of War*, 3rd edn, Oxford, 2000, pp. 725–30); and the UK Ministry of Defence, *The Manual of the Law of Armed Conflict*, Oxford 2004, paras. 14.1–14.16.

rules of engagement. Enforcement by means of disciplinary or criminal proceedings against members of such armed forces is a matter for the Member concerned.

International Committee of the Red Cross[49]

The ICRC promoted the 1864 and all subsequent Geneva Conventions and the Additional Protocols. It plays a central role in the practical implementation of IHL, in particular under the Geneva Conventions. The role of the ICRC is particularly important for helping to safeguard the health and welfare of POWs, including tracing them, visiting them and enabling them to correspond with their families,[50] as well as the welfare of civilians in occupied territory. Common Articles 9 and 10 (Articles 10 and 11 in the Fourth Geneva Convention) recognise the humanitarian role of the ICRC and provide that it may, with the consent of the parties to the conflict, act as the Protecting Power of one or both of them, and this is usually done. The role of Protecting Power (which can also be done by states) is to safeguard the interests of the parties to the conflict. The ICRC would therefore act as an impartial go-between, passing messages, making representations and suchlike.

---

[49] See also p. 196 above.
[50] See, in particular, Articles 54, 56, 74–77, 79–81 and 122–126 of the Fourth Geneva Convention. The ICRC headquarters are well worth a visit.

13

International criminal law

> The most serious crimes of concern to the international community as a whole must not go unpunished and . . . their effective prosecution must be ensured by taking measures at the national level and by enhancing international cooperation.[1]

The term 'international criminal law' is merely a useful way of describing those aspects of international law that are concerned with crimes having an international aspect or dimension. We will first look briefly at mutual legal assistance in criminal matters and extradition, and then at international crimes and how international law seeks to deal with them. (Terrorism is dealt with in Chapter 14.)

Mutual legal assistance

Oppenheim. *Oppenheim's International Law*, 9th edn, London, 1992, pp. 484–8

Cameron, 'Mutual Legal Assistance in Criminal Matters' (1989) ICLQ 954–65

'Proceedings of the Harvard Law School Conference on International Co-operation in Criminal Matters' (1990) *Harvard International Law Journal* 1–127

Although only a tiny number of criminal cases have an international element, the few that do are often serious in nature. The greater ease with which people now travel abroad means that the authorities of a state investigating or prosecuting a crime may need the help of other states, who may also have an interest. Depending on the law and procedure of the requested state, assistance may be given on an informal basis. The association established by national police forces to exchange criminal intelligence, Interpol,

---

[1] Preamble to the Rome Statute of the International Criminal Court.

may be used.[2] Within the European Union, the European Police Office (Europol) plays a similar role.[3] Assistance can be provided by a state more formally, yet without a treaty.[4] But, if there is a frequent need for help, bilateral or multilateral treaties or schemes for mutual legal assistance in criminal matters may be desirable.[5] Their principal purpose is to help in tracing persons and the obtaining of evidence, including witnesses. The execution of a request is subject to the law of the requested party. Some of the treaties deal with specific crimes such as drug trafficking.[6]

Extradition

Oppenheim. *Oppenheim's International Law*, 9th edn, London, 1992, pp. 948–72

Gilbert, *Aspects of Extradition Law*, Dordrecht, 1991

Stanbrook and Stanbrook, *Extradition Law and Practice*, Oxford, 2000

Extradition (sometimes called rendition)[7] is the procedure by which a person accused or convicted of a crime (although not usually *in absentia* – in his absence) is formally transferred to a state where he is wanted for trial or to serve his sentence. In the absence of a treaty, a state has no obligation to extradite. But extradition can take place without a treaty if this is acceptable to both states and permissible under their laws. It

---

[2] See www.interpol.int.

[3] For the text of the Europol Convention 1995, see 2156 UNTS 200 (No. 37663); UKTS (2000) 103; OJ C316 of 27 November 1995 or see www.europol.eu.int.

[4] See the (UK) Criminal Justice (International Co-operation) Act 1990.

[5] See the Colombia–UK Mutual Legal Assistance in Criminal Matters Agreement 1997, UKTS (2000) 40; and the European Convention on Mutual Assistance in Criminal Matters 1959 and the Additional Protocol of 1978, 472 UNTS 185 (No. 6841) and 1496 UNTS 350 (No. 6841); UKTS (1992) 24; the EU Convention on Mutual Assistance in Criminal Matters 29 May 2000, OJ 2000 NO. C197/3; the 1990 UN Model Treaty on Mutual Assistance in Criminal Matters, A/RES/45/117; ILM (1990) 1410; the UK–US Treaty on Mutual Assistance in Criminal Matters 1994, as amended 1967, 1967 UNTS 102 (No. 33632) and 2114 UNTS 392 (No. 36773); UKTS (1997) 14 and UKTS (2002) 8. See also the Commonwealth (Harare) Scheme Relating to Mutual Assistance in Criminal Matters, as amended in 1999, at www.thecommonwealth.org (click on 'What we do', then 'Law', then 'Documents'). This and other Commonwealth schemes (nn. 9 and 15 below) are not embodied in treaties and so depend on Commonwealth countries enacting matching legislation to implement them.

[6] Chile–UK Agreement on Mutual Assistance on Drug Trafficking, UKTS (1997) 63.

[7] 'Rendition' is a generic term covering all the means of returning alleged offenders (extradition, deportation, expulsion and exclusion) that are, in principle, lawful. Abduction (p. 49 above) is illegal.

can be done *ad hoc*[8] (although this may require the requesting state to agree to accord reciprocal treatment) or pursuant to a non-treaty scheme implemented by parallel legislation in the participating states.[9]

But most extradition is done under the hundreds of extradition treaties concluded during the last two centuries in response to the enormous increase in international travel following the invention of railways, the steamship, sealed roads, motor vehicles and the aeroplane. Most are bilateral and specify the crimes that are extraditable, usually serious offences such as those punishable by imprisonment for at least one year.[10] They will almost always incorporate the *double criminality* principle (extradition is granted only if the act for which extradition is sought is a crime in both the requesting and the requested states, although it does not have to be called by the same name), and the *principle of speciality* (if extradited, the accused will be tried only for the crime for which he was extradited). Most treaties will also require that the requested state be satisfied that there is at least *prima facie* evidence of the guilt of the accused (but see below on simplified extradition).

The request for extradition is normally made formally through the diplomatic channel, accompanied by the arrest warrant, information about the identity of the accused, and the basic facts of the offence. Often, the request will ask for provisional arrest pending arrival of all the necessary paperwork. In most states, the request will be scrutinised by the courts, where the accused can challenge it. Usually, the final decision will be taken by the executive, to which the domestic law will usually give discretion to refuse the request, subject only to treaty obligations.

The constitutions of many states, including some European states, prohibit the extradition of their own nationals, but their laws enable them to prosecute their nationals for serious crimes committed abroad. Other states, including the United Kingdom, can extradite their own nationals and therefore their laws enable prosecution of their nationals only for a few categories of serious crimes committed abroad. The problems created

---

[8] (UK) Extradition Act 2003, section 194.
[9] See the London Scheme for Extradition within the Commonwealth, as amended in 2002: see www.thecommonwealth.org (click on 'What we do', then 'Law', then 'Documents').
[10] See the Hong Kong SAR–UK Agreement for the Surrender of Fugitive Offenders 1997, UKTS (1998) 30 and the 1990 UN Model Treaty on Extradition, A/RES/45/117; ILM (1991) 1410. See also the (CoE) European Convention on Extradition 1957, 359 UNTS 221 (No. 5146); UKTS (1991) 97, although it is now largely overtaken by the new EU Framework Decision (see the text to n. 19 below).

by the own nationals prohibition can be partly[11] overcome by universal or quasi-universal jurisdiction regimes, although such regimes are limited to 'international crimes'.[12]

The accused may successfully plead that it would be contrary to the human rights obligations of the requested state to extradite him to the requesting state. This is particularly so if there are grounds for believing that the accused may be tortured or subject to other cruel or inhuman treatment.[13]

Extradition should be effected directly between the two states by the police of the extraditing state taking the person in their custody to the requesting state (and if by air or sea, preferably in an aircraft or ship registered in the extraditing state) and there handing him over to its police. A transit stop in a third state should not cause problems if the accused remains on the aircraft or ship. But once he leaves it there is the danger that he may challenge the lawfulness of his custody, and a request for extradition from the third state may then be needed.[14]

There are also treaties providing for prisoners to be transferred from the state where they were convicted to serve their sentence in another state, normally their state of nationality.[15] Such arrangements can be mutually beneficial: the first state gets rid of an undesirable, and the offender is nearer his family.

Political exception[16]

Domestic law and extradition treaties often provide that a 'political offence' is not extraditable. This political exception is not required by international law, and must be clearly distinguished from provisions in domestic law or mutual legal assistance or extradition treaties that

---

[11] But on the *Lockerbie* dilemma, see p. 295 below.   [12] See p. 45 above.

[13] See *Soering*, (19**) 11 EHRR 439; ILM (1989) 1063; 98 ILR 270; and *Chahal* (1997) 23 EHRR 413; 108 ILR 385.

[14] The UN flew the two accused of the Lockerbie bombing to the Netherlands for trial before a Scottish court exercising jurisdiction there with Dutch consent. Once they had landed, they had to be extradited from Dutch jurisdiction to Scottish jurisdiction. Luckily, there was no challenge: see A. Aust, 'Lockerbie: The Other Case' (2000) ICLQ 278–96.

[15] See the European Convention on the Transfer of Sentenced Persons 1983, 1496 UNTS 92 (No. 25703); ILM (1983) 530; UKTS (1985) 51), as amended by an Additional Protocol of 1997, 2138 UNTS 244 (No. 25703); and the London Scheme for the Transfer of Convicted Offenders within the Commonwealth, at www.thecommonwealth.org (click on 'What we do', then 'Law', then 'Documents'). See also the Sri Lanka–UK Agreement on Transfer of Prisoners 2003, UKTS (2004) 31.

[16] For a most detailed account, see Oppenheim, pp. 962–72.

assistance or extradition may be refused if the real purpose of a request is to prosecute or persecute the person for his political opinion rather than for the crime itself.[17] There is no agreement internationally on what constitutes a political offence: whether it is the purpose or motive that is political or the crime is directed at the state, such as the assassination of a head of state. In the past at least, US courts have several times refused extradition to the United Kingdom of members of the Irish Republican Army accused of politically motivated terrorist offences.

The political exception has been excluded in respect of some especially cruel offences, such as genocide and certain terrorist offences.[18]

Simplified extradition

Between states with similar standards of criminal justice it may be possible to replace traditional extradition by simplified procedures. This was done in the EU Framework Decision on the European arrest warrant and surrender procedures between member states of 13 June 2002, which aims to simplify and speed up the extradition ('rendition' in the Decision) of accused or convicted persons.[19] As between EU member states, it does this by radical means. All previous extradition procedures, including Council of Europe extradition treaties and bilateral treaties, are replaced. Each member state must comply with a request from a court or prosecutor of another member state for the execution of an arrest warrant issued by him for a person accused of an offence carrying a minimum sentence of twelve months' imprisonment or who has been convicted and sentenced to a minimum of four months' imprisonment. The arrest warrant need only contain a description of the circumstances in which the offence was committed. The judicial authorities, not the executive, decide on the request, which must be done within ninety days of the arrest. Member states cannot refuse a request to hand over their own nationals. The principles of double criminality and speciality no longer apply, although a member state may list those offences that it will exclude from the new procedure on the ground that it would be contrary to fundamental principles of its legal system. But the double jeopardy rule remains.

---

[17] See p. 291 below.
[18] See p. 270 below on genocide and p. 291 below on the trend to exclude the political exception in terrorist cases.
[19] 2002/584/JHA; OJ L190/1, 18 July 2002. As to the legal status of EU framework decisions, see p. 478 below.

A new UK–US Extradition Treaty was signed on 31 March 2003.[20] It is on largely traditional lines, except that an extradition request by the United Kingdom will still have to make a *prima facie* case, but those by the United States will not, thereby creating a new principle of double standards.[21] On 25 June 2003, EU–US treaties on mutual legal assistance and extradition were signed.[22] These supplement, and will require amendments to, bilateral treaties with individual EU states. Although they should enhance cooperation in tackling serious crime, they are on more traditional lines.

Irregular means[23]

Sometimes a state seeks to bypass extradition procedures by deporting a fugitive ('disguised extradition').[24] A state will sometimes seize (abduct) a wanted person without the consent or acquiescence of the state where he is.[25] But such actions may well be contrary to both national and international law.

International crimes

There is no agreed definition of 'international crime', but it is a convenient term for those crimes that are of concern to every state because of their corrosive effect on international society or their particularly appalling nature. For such crimes, international law does not place criminal responsibility on the state on whose behalf the crime may have been done (although the state may incur international responsibility),[26] but on the individual who committed the crime. In addition, although it is by no means universally agreed, it is likely that international law allows a state to prosecute such crimes regardless of where they were committed or the nationality of the accused (universal jurisdiction).[27] Whether the crime is one which can be

---

[20] Cm 5821. It is not yet in force, although the UK already implements it by means of the Extradition Act 2003.

[21] Contrast Article 8(3)(c) with Article IX of the previous 1972 Treaty, 1049 UNTS 167 (No. 15811); UKTS (1977) 16; TIAS 8468.

[22] ILM (2004) 749.   [23] See Oppenheim, pp. 388–90, n. 16.

[24] See *R. v. Governor of Brixton Prison, ex parte Soblen* [1963] 1 QB 829; [1963] 2 QB 243; and Oppenheim, p. 947, n. 7. See also 'Flight to Torture', *The Times*, 26 March 2005, on the alleged complicity of several states with the US in irregular renditions of suspected terrorists.

[25] See p. 49 above.   [26] See p. 410 below.   [27] See p. 45 above for details.

prosecuted in the domestic courts of a state depends on the laws of that state. Although many international crimes will also amount to ordinary crimes (murder), domestic courts will not necessarily have jurisdiction over them; specific legislation may be needed to confer jurisdiction. The acts that today constitute international crimes are nothing new but, with the notable exception of piracy, it was only in the twentieth century that a concerted effort was made to treat them as international crimes.

The crimes discussed below are not the only ones to be called 'international crimes'. The term is also sometimes used to describe crimes covered by international treaties (various terrorist crimes, drug offences, etc.) which impose obligations on states parties to criminalise the activities concerned and to prosecute or extradite suspected offenders. The crimes are ones that the international community has considered as sufficiently serious in effect internationally to warrant a particular form of international cooperation.

Piracy

Customary international law has for centuries treated pirates as international outlaws subject to the jurisdiction of any state. Piracy is any illegal act of violence or detention committed on the high seas for *private* ends by a *private* ship against another ship. Warships of any state may board a foreign-registered ship on the high seas that is suspected of piracy. If it proves to be a pirate ship, it can be seized and those on board arrested and put on trial in the state of the warship.[28] Despite this, piracy is again a curse in several parts of the world.

Slavery

Slavery is an even older practice, and is still with us today. Although there have been various treaties seeking to combat slavery, and it is now accepted that slavery is prohibited by customary international law, it is still not clear if slavery is subject to universal jurisdiction.[29] However, the 1998 Statute of the International Criminal Court (ICC)[30] includes 'enslavement' in its definition of crimes against humanity, defining it as 'the exercise of any

---

[28] The law is now codified in the UN Convention on the Law of the Sea 1982, 1833 UNTS 397 (No. 31363); ILM (1982) 1261; UKTS (1999) 81 (Articles 101, 105, 107 and 110). For more details, see p. 298 below.
[29] See Oppenheim, pp. 978–82.   [30] For the ICC, see p. 277 below.

or all of the powers attaching to the right of ownership over a person
and includes the exercise of such power in the course of trafficking in
persons, in particular women and children'. Although for the purposes of
the jurisdiction of the ICC slavery is limited to acts committed as part of
a widespread or systematic attack directed against a civilian population,
it is now more probable that national courts would be willing to exercise
universal jurisdiction in respect of isolated acts of slavery.

Genocide

W. Schabas, *Genocide in International Law*, Cambridge, 2000

Genocide has been practised for centuries. But the term was invented
only in 1944 by an historian to describe the Holocaust. In 1946, the UN
General Assembly adopted, unanimously and without debate, Resolution
96 (I) declaring genocide to be an international crime. In 1948, the Convention on the Prevention and Punishment of the Crime of Genocide was
adopted.[31] It defines genocide as:

> any of the following acts committed with intent to destroy, in whole or in
> part, a national, ethnical, racial or religious group, as such:
>
> (a) Killing members of the group;
> (b) Causing serious bodily or mental harm to members of the group;
> (c) Deliberately inflicting on the group conditions of life calculated to
>   bring about its physical destruction in whole or in part;
> (d) Imposing measures intended to prevent births within the group;
> (e) Forcibly transferring children of the group to another group.

Although the Convention has only 137 parties, there can no longer be any
doubt that it is a crime in customary international law. The International
Criminal Tribunals for the Former Yugoslavia and for Rwanda and the
International Criminal Court each have jurisdiction over genocide as
defined in the Convention.

Genocide is sometimes grouped together with crimes against humanity, and, like the latter, can be committed in peacetime as well as during
an armed conflict. But what distinguishes it from crimes against humanity is that the acts must be committed 'with intent to destroy' a group,
so putting it in a class of its own. The definition, and the Elements of
Crime that supplement the ICC Statute,[32] suggest that few, if any, of the

---

[31] 78 UNTS 277 (No. 1021); UKTS (1970) 58.   [32] See p. 278, n. 56 below.

crimes committed in the former Yugoslavia against ethnic groups could be classified as genocide, and that most of the acts described as 'ethnic cleansing' were rather crimes against humanity, such as forcible transfers of population. On the other hand, the mass murder in Rwanda in 1994 of the Hutu by the Tutsi was clearly genocide. If committed today the atrocities committed on the Turkish Armenians in 1915 would amount to genocide if it could be established that there was an intent to destroy, in whole or in part, that population.

The Genocide Convention places criminal responsibility on all individuals, Article IV making no exception for heads of state and public officials. But the enforcement of the Convention is left to the courts of the party in whose territory the crime was committed (Article VI). Article VII provides that genocide shall not be considered a political crime for the purposes of extradition. But the Convention does not establish a regime of universal jurisdiction.[33]

Crimes against humanity

Oppenheim, pp. 995–8

W. Schabas, *The International Criminal Court*, 2nd edn, Cambridge, 2004, pp. 41–51

Here we are concerned with grave offences against life and liberty on an extensive scale, even if they are lawful under national law (as they were in Nazi Germany). Crimes against humanity may be seen as *collective* violations of basic human rights, rather than those of an individual. The Charter of the Nuremberg International Military Tribunal included crimes against humanity, although only in connection with war crimes or crimes against the peace.[34] This link no longer exists; crimes against humanity can be committed in peacetime. Article 7 of the Statute of the International Criminal Court lists the crimes (with some more recent additions). They include murder, extermination, enslavement, deportation or forcible transfer of population (e.g. ethnic cleansing), imprisonment, torture, rape, sexual slavery, enforced prostitution or sterilisation and enforced disappearance of persons. But, to be a crime against humanity, the Statute requires such acts to have been committed as part of a 'widespread or systematic attack directed against any civilian population' and to be done 'pursuant to or in furtherance of a state or organisational

---

[33] See p. 45 above.   [34] See n. 42 below.

policy to commit such attack'; and the policy requires that the state or organisation 'actively promote or encourage' the attack (see the ICC Elements of Crimes).[35] Unlike genocide, there is no requirement that the acts must be committed 'with intent to destroy' a group. It is not clear if national limitation periods for crimes can still apply to them,[36] but the ICC has no such limitation on its jurisdiction (Article 29). The jurisdiction of the International Criminal Tribunals for the Former Yugoslavia (ICTY) and for Rwanda (ICTR) include crimes against humanity, and in *Tadic* the ICTY declared that crimes against humanity are part of customary international law.[37]

War crimes

See pp. 251–62 above.

Aggression

Although the Nuremberg International Military Tribunal established that aggressive war is a crime against the peace, none of the international tribunals set up since the end of the Cold War has jurisdiction over that crime, and the International Criminal Court will be able to exercise jurisdiction over the crime of aggression only if and when a definition can be agreed.[38]

Responsibility of superiors

Article 7(3) of the ICTY Statute provides that a superior is responsible for an act done by a subordinate if the superior knew or had reason to know that the subordinate was about to commit the act, or had done so, and the superior failed to take the necessary and reasonable measures to prevent repetition or to punish the perpetrator.[39] Article 28 of the ICC Statute distinguishes military and other superiors. A military commander is criminally responsible for crimes committed by his forces as a result of his failure to exercise proper control over them, if he knew, or should have known, that crimes were being or were about to be committed by

---

[35] See Schabas, *Genocide in International Law*, Cambridge, 2000, p. 279.
[36] See Oppenheim, p. 997, n. 11.
[37] ILM (1997) 908 at 935, paras. 618–23; 105 ILR 453.   [38] See p. 278 below.
[39] See the ICTY judgment in *Čelebići* (1998), ILM (1999) 677, paras. 370 *et seq.*

them and he failed to take all necessary and reasonable measures within his power to prevent or repress them. Other superiors, such as a head of state or government or minister of defence are criminally responsible for crimes committed by subordinates under their effective authority and control as a result of their failure to exercise proper control over them, if the superiors knew or ignored information about the crimes and failed to do all in their power to prevent or repress them. Although the ICC Statute resulted from lengthy and detailed UN negotiations, Article 28 may not represent the present consensus as to the law on this difficult and important issue.

Superior orders

Article 8 of the Nuremberg Charter[40] provided that acting pursuant to superior orders does not free an accused from responsibility, but 'may be considered in mitigation of punishment if the Tribunal determines that justice so requires'. Following on from that, Article 7(4) of the ICTY Statute provides that a superior order does not relieve the accused of responsibility, but may mitigate the punishment. Article 33 of the ICC Statute confirms that an accused cannot plead in his defence that he was carrying out the orders of his superior, but, as the result of a compromise in the negotiations on the Statute, it provides for a limited defence in the case of, in effect, war crimes: if the accused had been under a legal obligation to obey the order *and* did not know it was unlawful *and* the order was not 'manifestly' unlawful. An order to commit genocide or a crime against humanity is declared to be manifestly unlawful.

International tribunals

Although there were earlier proposals for international criminal tribunals,[41] the first to be established was the Nuremberg International Military Tribunal,[42] followed by the Tokyo Tribunal.[43] Having been established by the leading powers that had fought Germany and Japan, they were not truly international, but the law applied by them was proper and

---

[40] See p. 7 above. [41] See Shaw, p. 234.
[42] See 82 UNTS 279 (No. 251); UKTS (1945) 4. The judgment is in (1947) AJIL 173–332. See also *The Charter and Judgment of the Nuremberg Tribunal, History and Analysis* (UN Doc. 1949 V 7), and Woetzel, *The Nuremberg Trials in International Law*, London, 1962.
[43] See 15 ILR 356.

their procedures fair, suggestions of 'victors' justice' being nonsense.[44] The Charter and Judgment of the Nuremberg Tribunal laid down important principles of international law that were endorsed unanimously by the UN General Assembly in 1946.[45] The most important were that persons are individually responsible for international crimes; aggressive war is a crime against the peace; a head of state and other senior officials can be personally responsible for crimes even if they did not actually carry them out; and the plea of superior orders is not a defence. These principles are now part of customary international law even though their precise scope is still not clear (see above).

International Criminal Tribunal for the Former Yugoslavia (ICTY)

Acting under Chapter VII of the UN Charter, the Security Council established the ICTY by Resolutions 808 (1993) and 827 (1993).[46] Located at The Hague, Netherlands, it has criminal jurisdiction over individuals accused of committing in the former Yugoslavia since 1 January 1991 grave breaches of the Geneva Conventions 1949, war crimes, genocide or crimes against humanity, and has ruled that it has jurisdiction over crimes committed during an internal conflict and listed in common Article 3 of the Geneva Conventions.[47] It has concurrent jurisdiction with national courts, but can request them to relinquish jurisdiction in its favour. Cases are tried in one of three trial Chambers, each composed of three judges. These are drawn from the sixteen permanent judges (elected by the UN General Assembly for four-year, re-electable terms, one of whom serves as President of the ICTY), and from twenty-seven *ad litem* (temporary) judges (elected for four-year, non-re-electable terms). A majority of the judges are experts in criminal law and procedure. The Appeals Chamber (which is also the Appeals Chamber for the ICTR) consists of seven of the permanent judges (five from the ICTY and two from the ICTR). Five judges hear each appeal. The Prosecutor is appointed by the UN Security Council, on the nomination of the Secretary-General, for a four-year, re-electable term, and acts independently of the Council or any government.

---

[44] See *Oppenheim's International Law*, 7th edn, London, 1952, vol. II, pp. 579–82.
[45] UNGA Res. 95 (I). See A. Aust, 'The Security Council and International Criminal Law' (2002) NYIL 23 at 25.
[46] The Statute is not annexed, so see the annex to the UN Secretary-General's Report of 3 May 1993 (S/25704) or ILM (1993) 115. A slightly amended version of the Statute is at www.un.org/icty/.
[47] See p. 254 above.

Article 7 of the Statute provides that a person who planned, instigated, ordered, or otherwise aided and abetted in the planning, preparation or execution of a crime, is individually responsible for it;[48] that former heads of state or government and government officials are not relieved of criminal responsibility;[49] that a superior is responsible in certain circumstances for an act of a subordinate (see above); and that a superior order does not relieve the accused of responsibility (see above).

At first there were doubts whether the ICTY would be effective. Unlike the Nuremberg Tribunal, the suspects were still in their own countries, as were witnesses and physical evidence. Success would therefore depend on the co-operation of governments, especially those in the former Yugoslavia. But, despite the problems created by the Milosevic trial, the ICTY has been successful. Over thirty-five trial judgments,[50] and some twelve appeal judgments, have been given. But the ICTY is very expensive. There are over 1,200 staff and the budget for 2004–5 is US$ 272 million. Together with the ICTR budget, this amounts to some 10 per cent of the total UN budget. Therefore, in Resolution 1534 (2004), the Security Council encouraged the two tribunals to concentrate on the most senior leaders, to consider transferring some cases to national courts, to try to complete all investigations by the end of 2004, to finish all trials by the end of 2008 (although this may not apply to Mr Karadzic and Mr Mladic who are still at large), and to finish all other work in 2010.

International Criminal Tribunal for Rwanda (ICTR)

Following the massacres committed in Rwanda and some neighbouring states in 1994, acting under Chapter VII of the UN Charter the Security Council established the ICTR by Resolution 955 (1994), to which its Statute is annexed.[51] Located in Arusha, Tanzania, and with premises in Kigali, Rwanda, it has criminal jurisdiction over genocide, crimes against humanity, and serious violations of common Article 3 to the Geneva Conventions, and of Additional Protocol II 1977 on non-international armed conflicts, committed in 1994 by individuals in

---

[48] Cf. Article 25 of the ICC Statute, p. 280 below.
[49] The provision was intended also to remove immunity from current heads of state, etc.: see the Report of the UN Secretary-General of 3 May 1993 (S/25704), para. 55, and *Milosevic*, Trial Chamber III, Decision of 8 November 2001, paras. 26–34. See also p. 177 above.
[50] States can agree to hold convicted prisoners; see, for example, the UK–UN Agreement of 11 March 2004, UKTS (2004) 20.
[51] It is also in ILM (1994) 1598, and at www.ictr.org.

Rwanda and by Rwandan citizens in neighbouring states. Its powers, composition and procedure are otherwise closely modelled on those of the ICTY. So far over twenty persons have been convicted, with some appeals pending.

Sierra Leone Special Court[52]

The Court was established by a treaty between Sierra Leone and the United Nations of 16 January 2002,[53] although that does not make it a UN body. The Court, located in Freetown, Sierra Leone, began trials in 2004. It has jurisdiction over persons accused of bearing the greatest responsibility for serious offences committed since 30 November 1996 and contrary to common Article 3 of the Geneva Conventions and Additional Protocol II 1977, over other serious violations of international humanitarian law (such as intentionally directing attacks against civilians and conscripting children under fifteen), and over certain serious crimes under Sierra Leonean law. In most other respects, the Statute of the Court follows that of the ICTR.

The main role of the United Nations is for the Secretary-General to appoint, upon nomination by states (in particular, those of the Economic Commission for West Africa (ECOWAS) and the Commonwealth) two of the three judges of the Trial Chamber and three of the five judges of the Appeals Chamber. He also appoints the Prosecutor after consultation with the Government of Sierra Leone. It was intended that the Court should be financed by voluntary contributions made to a trust fund held by the Secretary-General, but funding for the third year of the Court's operations was provided by a UN subvention.

By comparison with the ICTY and ICTR, the number of indictments will be much more limited; in practice, there is likely to be indictments against a maximum of twenty persons. It is intended that the Court should limit its indictments to those persons bearing the greatest responsibility for the crimes listed above. The Court will also have a much shorter life than the ICTY or the ICTR, and is expected to complete most of its work in three years.

---

[52] See Romano, Nollkaemper and Kleffner (eds.), *Internationalized Criminal Courts*, Oxford, 2004, which also covers courts in Timor Leste, Kosovo and Cambodia.

[53] See www.sc-sl.org. The text of the treaty is also in S/2002/246 and 2178 UNTS 138 (No. 38342). See R. Cryer, 'A "Special Court" for Sierra Leone' (2001) ICLQ 435.

International Criminal Court (ICC)

R. Lee (ed.), *The International Criminal Court: The Making of the Rome Statute: Issues, Negotiations, Results*, The Hague, 1999

W. Schabas, *An Introduction to the International Criminal Court*, 2nd edn, Cambridge, 2004 (the appendices include the ICC Statute, the Elements of Crimes and the Rules of Procedure and Evidence)

www.un.org/law/icc

Unlike the ICTY and the ICTR, the ICC was created by treaty, the Rome Statute, which was adopted at a UN conference on 17 July 1998, and which entered into force on 1 July 2002.[54] It now has nearly 100 parties. It is the first permanent and universal international criminal court. Its main limitation is in the number and importance of the states that are not yet parties, such as China, Egypt, India, Indonesia, Iran, Japan, Pakistan, Russia and the United States.

The seat of the ICC is at The Hague, although it can sit elsewhere. It has eighteen judges elected by the parties to serve nine-year, non-renewable[55] terms. All judges must have practical experience of either criminal law and procedure or international humanitarian law or human rights law. The ICC sits in three divisions: Appeals (five judges), Trial (three judges) and Pre-Trial (one to three judges). The Office of the Prosecutor is a separate organ. The Prosecutor must have extensive practical experience of the prosecution or trial of criminal cases, and is elected by the parties for a nine-year, non-renewable term. The working languages are English and French.

Jurisdiction

It must not be thought that in future all major crimes of international concern will be prosecuted in the ICC. Even for most crimes over which it would have jurisdiction it will not actually exercise that jurisdiction. Because of the 'complementarity' rule (see below), the vast majority of crimes that are within the jurisdiction of the ICC will still be dealt with by domestic criminal courts. Nevertheless, the ICC will be explained in some detail since it is of great legal and political importance. The chief value of the ICC is that, when a domestic legal system cannot or will not

---

[54] 2187 UNTS 91 (No. 38544); ILM (1998) 998; UKTS (2002) 35.
[55] Except for those of the initial judges who serve only three-year terms (Article 36(9)).

278 HANDBOOK OF INTERNATIONAL LAW

deal with an international crime, the ICC may be available to deal with it; there should be no need for the UN Security Council to set up an *ad hoc* international criminal tribunal like the ICTY or the ICTR.

The ICC does not have either general criminal jurisdiction or jurisdiction over terrorism or drug trafficking. For the moment, it can exercise jurisdiction only with respect to genocide, crimes against humanity and war crimes. The crimes in the first three categories are exhaustively defined in Articles 6, 7 and 8 of the Statute, and elaborated in the Elements of Crimes.[56] The ICC will not be able to exercise jurisdiction over the crime of aggression until the Statute has been amended to define that crime and the conditions under which the ICC may exercise jurisdiction over it (Article 5(2)).[57] The UN General Assembly adopted its own definition of aggression in 1974,[58] but this is not in itself suitable for the purpose of a criminal prosecution and there is also disagreement about whether Article 39 of the UN Charter, which gives to the Security Council the – essentially political – responsibility of determining whether aggression has occurred, requires that the Council should act as a filter for the exercise of jurisdiction by the ICC.[59]

Under Article 13, the jurisdiction of the ICC can be invoked by:

(a) a party referring an alleged crime to the Prosecutor;
(b) the UN Security Council, acting under Chapter VII of the UN Charter, referring an alleged crime to the Prosecutor;[60] or
(c) the Prosecutor initiating an investigation into an alleged crime.

But under (a) and (c), the ICC can exercise jurisdiction only if (1) the state on whose territory the conduct occurred (or if the crime was committed on board a vessel or aircraft, the state of registration) or (2) the state of nationality of the accused person, is a party to the Statute. But if neither state is a party, either can accept the jurisdiction of the ICC, voluntarily and *ad hoc* (Article 12).

Thus for the ICC to have jurisdiction the accused does *not* have to be a national of a party if the crime was committed in the territory of a party (or on board one of its registered ships or aircraft), or was referred to the ICC by the Security Council.

---

[56] See K. Dörmann, *Elements of War Crimes under the Rome Statute of the ICC*, Cambridge, 2003.
[57] No amendment can be proposed until 1 July 2009 (Article 121(1)).
[58] UNGA Res. 3314 (XXIX); ILM (1975) 588, text at ILM (1974) 710. [59] See p. 214 above.
[60] This was done for the first time in UNSC Res. 1593 (2005), which referred the situation in Darfur (Sudan) to the Prosecutor, who is now investigating it.

The exercise of jurisdiction by the ICC, including the power of the Prosecutor to invoke the ICC's jurisdiction, is further restricted by the important so-called *complementarity* rule in Article 17, under which the ICC must not exercise jurisdiction if it determines that:

(a) the case is being investigated or prosecuted by a state that has jurisdiction over the crime, unless 'the state is unwilling or unable genuinely to carry out the investigation or prosecution';
(b) the case has been investigated by a state that has jurisdiction over the crime and it has decided not to prosecute, unless this was because of the 'unwillingness or inability of the state genuinely to prosecute';
(c) the accused has already been properly tried; or
(d) the case is not of 'sufficient gravity' to justify action by the ICC.

The unwillingness of a state to prosecute may be indicated where there is evidence that it is shielding the accused, where there is an unjustified delay in bringing the accused to justice which is inconsistent with an intention to bring the accused to justice, or proceedings were not conducted independently or impartially. It may therefore be desirable for parties to revise their domestic criminal laws, procedures and practices so that they will be able themselves fully to deal with the crimes.

There are further limitations on ICC jurisdiction.

- In respect of any party, the crime must have been committed after the entry into force of the Statute for that party (Article 11).
- No person can be tried by the ICC and a national court for the same crime (*ne bis in idem*) (Article 20).
- No person can be tried for an offence committed before the entry into force of the Statute (Article 24).
- The accused must have been eighteen or over when the alleged crime was committed (Article 26).

Surrender of accused persons[61]

A party to the ICC Statute is required to arrest and surrender to the ICC a person for whom a warrant of arrest has been issued by the Pre-Trial Chamber, unless the case is inadmissible on the basis of double jeopardy (Arts 58 and 89). A party cannot refuse to surrender its own

---

[61] See Schabas, *An Introduction to the International Criminal Court*, 2nd edn, Cambridge, 2004, pp. 132–6.

nationals even where its law prohibits their extradition, as is made clear by Article 102.

Personal responsibility

Article 25 sets out rules on the *personal responsibility* of the individual, including accessories, conspirators and those who order, solicit or induce a crime. Heads of state or government, parliamentarians and government officials, past or present, are all within the jurisdiction of the ICC (Article 27). This means that on a request for surrender to the ICC such a person cannot plead immunity, although a party is not obliged to surrender a national of a *third* state if he enjoys state or diplomatic immunity in the territory of the party (Article 98).[62]

United States

The United States is opposed to the ICC and has no present intention of becoming a party. Its concerns are particularly addressed to the fact that the ICC can take jurisdiction in certain circumstances even over the nationals of states that are not parties. The Security Council has adopted two US-sponsored (annual) resolutions (1422 (2002) and 1487 (2003)) which requested, purportedly consistent with Article 16 of the ICC Statute, that, if a case were to arise involving the official acts of officials or personnel of a state contributing to an operation established or authorised by the UN, the ICC should not proceed with any investigation or prosecution of such persons for twelve months, unless the Council were to decide otherwise; and that the Council intended to renew the request indefinitely. There were serious doubts whether Article 16 was ever intended to be used in this way, since it appears to envisage only specific cases where the Security Council has determined that there was a threat to international peace and security, not blanket exclusion.[63] But in June 2004 there were not enough votes in the Council for renewing the resolution.

   The United States has also concluded over ninety bilateral treaties (about thirty-five with parties to the ICC Statute) under which the other party agrees not to surrender US military personnel, government officials,

---

[62] *Ibid.*, pp. 81 and 114–15.
[63] See p. 214 above, and Lee, (ed.), *The International Criminal Court: The Making of the Rome Statute: Issues, Negotiations, Results*, The Hague, 1999, pp. 149–52 and Schabas, *An Introduction to the International Criminal Court*, 2nd edn, Cambridge, 2004, pp. 82–5.

INTERNATIONAL CRIMINAL LAW

or civilian employees or contractors, to the ICC.[64] Such treaties may not be compatible with the ICC Statute since the purpose of Article 98(2), under which the treaties purport to be made, was to preserve status-of-forces and similar agreements,[65] not to shield all nationals of non-parties from ICC jurisdiction.

To meet US concerns, UNSC Res. 1593 (2005) excepts from ICC jurisdiction current or former officials or personnel of a state which contributes to a UN mission but which is not a party to the ICC Statute.

Procedure

Article 21 requires the ICC to apply the following law: first, the Statute, the Elements of Crimes and the Rules of Procedure and Evidence; secondly, treaties and principles and rules of international law, including the established principles of the law of armed conflict; and, thirdly, general principles of law derived from national laws. The application and interpretation of law must be consistent with internationally recognised human rights. Even if a person before the ICC is accused of a crime that is subject to a statute of limitations in force in the place where the crime was committed or in his state of nationality, the ICC is not bound by any such limitation (Article 29).

The procedure of the ICC is influenced by that of the ICTY and the ICTR, but draws less on the common law, consisting as it does of principles, rules and procedures drawn from both the civil and common law legal systems. The trial procedure is rather more adversarial than in civil systems, but the judges have greater powers of intervention and control of procedure, in particular over investigations, than in common law systems.

If, on the basis of the information he has received, the Prosecutor considers there is a reasonable basis to proceed with the investigation, he must first seek the authorisation of the Pre-Trial Chamber (Articles 15 and 53). An effective investigation naturally depends upon the co-operation of states, and usually one in particular. In the case of states that are parties, Articles 86–88 and 93–101 have detailed provisions requiring their co-operation in terms similar to those in treaties on mutual legal assistance.[66] If, as a result of his investigations, the Prosecutor determines

---

[64] For example, the US–Uzbekistan Agreement of 18 September 2002, ILM (2003) 39. See also the EU guidelines, ILM (2003) 241, and Schabas, *An Introduction to the International Criminal Court*, 2nd edn, Cambridge, 2004, p. 22.

[65] See p. 175 above.   [66] See p. 263 above.

that a suspect should be arrested, he may apply to the Pre-Trial Chamber for a warrant of arrest (Article 58), and the party in whose territory the person is present is under an obligation to surrender him (Article 89). Since this procedure is not extradition, the request for surrender cannot be refused on the ground that the person is a national of the requested state (Article 102).[67]

Article 67, based on Article 14(3) of the International Covenant on Civil and Political Rights 1966,[68] accords extensive rights to an accused. There are of course provisions for appeal against conviction and sentence (Articles 81–85). The ICC can impose a sentence of imprisonment for a specified number of years up to thirty, or life imprisonment. Once two-thirds of the sentence has been served (or twenty-five years in the case of life imprisonment), and not before, the ICC must review the sentence and may reduce it. As the ICC has no territory and no prison, sentences of imprisonment are served in the territory of a state (which need not be a party) designated by the ICC from those states that have indicated to the ICC their willingness to accept such prisoners. If no state is designated, the prisoner will be held in a Dutch prison.

[67] See p. 264 above on extradition.   [68] See p. 236 above.

14

Terrorism

Terror is the feeling which arrests the mind.[1]

Aust, *Implementation Kits for the International Counter-Terrorism Conventions*, Commonwealth Secretariat, London, 2002[2]
Lambert, *Terrorism and Hostages in International Law*, Cambridge, 1990[3]
Higgins and Flory (eds.), *International Law and Terrorism*, London, 1997
Shaw, *International Law*, 5th edn, Cambridge, 2003, pp. 1048–53
www.un.org/terrorism/

The so-called War on Terror may have begun on 11 September 2001, but terrorism has been practised for centuries. The international struggle against it started in the early part of the last century, and in 1937 the League of Nations concluded a Convention on the Prevention and Punishment of Terrorism.[4] But a world war intervened and it never entered into force.

Terrorist crimes are ordinary crimes even if they are carried out for political, ideological or religious reasons, and so can be prosecuted where they are committed. However, once a criminal has fled abroad, extraditing him may not be easy,[5] and if he cannot be extradited the state of refuge may not have jurisdiction over the crime.[6] When the crime is committed abroad, the person's state of nationality would have to exercise extra-territorial jurisdiction in order to try him, although that is not usually possible for common law states. Nor do they normally assert criminal jurisdiction on the ground that one of their nationals was a victim.[7] And it is unusual for states to have jurisdiction under their law over crimes committed abroad by foreign nationals against foreign nationals.

[1] James Joyce, *A Portrait of the Artist as a Young Man*, 1916, Ch. 5.
[2] Includes detailed commentaries on the ten universal conventions and model bills by Nalin Abeyesekere: see www.the commonwealth.org (click on 'What we do', then 'Law', then 'Documents'). Copies are also obtainable from the Legal and Constitutional Affairs Division, Marlborough House, London SW1Y 5HX.
[3] The book goes much wider than hostage-taking and examines in detail the previous counter-terrorism conventions.
[4] Hudson (ed.), *International Legislation*, vol. VII, pp. 862 and 878.
[5] See p. 264 above.   [6] See p. 44 above.   [7] See p. 45 above.

However, it is now well established in customary international law that since piracy, slavery, war crimes and crimes against humanity are so terrible and affect the peace and security of all states, any state has the right to try persons for these crimes, irrespective of their nationality or where the crime was committed. This is known as universal jurisdiction.[8] But terrorism is not yet quite in that category, one reason being the lack of international agreement on a comprehensive definition of terrorism. Instead, universal treaties adopted by the United Nations or UN specialised agencies and, more recently, Chapter VII measures of the UN Security Council, have been the means by which international law contributes to the struggle against terrorism.

But first certain terms need explanation.

Definitions

'State terrorism'

This is a term for terrorist acts by one state against another or its nationals, such as the holding hostage of US diplomats in Iran in 1979–81, and done either by the state or commissioned or adopted by it. The term is also used to describe widespread acts of cruelty committed by a state against its own people by Hitler, Stalin, Pol Pot, Saddam Hussein, *et al.*

'State-sponsored terrorism'

This was a particular feature of international life in the last decades of the twentieth century, although perhaps less so now. It consists of a state sheltering, training, financing or supplying arms to enable terrorists, often foreign, to attack another state or its nationals. As surrogate warfare, it is cheap and deniable. As the Friendly Relations Declaration 1970 makes clear, states are prohibited from aiding terrorism in any way.[9]

Universal terrorism conventions

No international definition of terrorism

There is still no internationally agreed comprehensive definition of terrorism.[10] Only the elements of the use or threat of force and seeking to create

---

[8] See p. 45 above.   [9] UNGA Res. 2625 (XXV); ILM (1970) 1292.
[10] See Lambert, *Terrorism and Hostages in International Law*, Cambridge, 1990, pp. 13–23; G. Guillaume, 'Terrorism and International Law' (2004) ICLQ 537–47. Schmid and Jongman, *Political Terrorism*, Amsterdam, 1988, identified merely 109 definitions.

a climate of fear seem to be generally agreed. When acts like hijacking or hostage-taking are done for personal reasons or gain, they are regarded as terrorism because of the fear it produces in those directly or indirectly affected. The victims are not concerned with the motives of the terrorist, just that they might die. Following the murder of Israeli athletes by Black September at the 1972 Munich Olympic Games, UNGA Resolution 3034 (XXVII) established an Ad Hoc Committee on Terrorism. But that and later UNGA resolutions included wording that suggested that national liberation movements (NLMs)[11] might be justified in using terrorism because of the violence and repression of colonial, occupying and racist regimes, and that these 'underlying causes' merited equal attention. Hence the hackneyed saying, 'one person's terrorist is another's freedom fighter'.

The law of armed conflict prohibits members of an armed force deliberately attacking civilians or committing acts of terror. But resistance to occupation is not prohibited by international law, and 'organised resistance movements', belonging to a party to the conflict, are recognised by the Geneva Conventions, provided they fulfil certain conditions and conduct operations in accordance with the law of armed conflict. This category was enlarged by Additional Protocol I to the Geneva Conventions to cover also irregular forces, such as members of NLMs, who do not identify themselves by distinguishing marks, provided they are under proper command and carry arms openly when attacking or when visible to the enemy while deploying to attack.[12] Thus terrorists are unlikely to be covered, their secretive organisation and *modus operandi* (exemplified by the suicide-bomber) being such as not to bring them within the scope of the law of armed conflict, so remaining subject to ordinary criminal law.[13]

In 1987, Syria proposed an international conference to define terrorism, which has never been convened. But a slight advance was made in 1994 with a UN Declaration on Terrorism (UNGA Res. 49/60), which included the following statements:

---

[11] See p. 14 above.   [12] See p. 253 above.

[13] The UK reservation to Articles 1(4) and 96(3) of Additional Protocol I to the Geneva Conventions is to the effect that the UK would only consider itself bound by a declaration of adherence to the Protocol (see Article 96(3)) made by a body that has been expressly recognised by the UK as genuinely representing a people engaged in a liberation conflict: see UKTS (1999) 29. See also p. 286 below on the links between the terrorism conventions and the law of armed conflict, and C. Greenwood, 'War, Terrorism and International Law' (2003) *Current Legal Problems* 505.

- terrorism was unequivocally condemned as 'criminal and unjustifiable, wherever and by whomever committed';
- 'criminal acts intended or calculated to provoke a state of terror in the general public, a group of persons or particular persons for political purposes are in any circumstance unjustifiable whatever political, philosophical, ideological, racial, ethnic, religious or any other nature that may be invoked to justify them'; and
- states must refrain from any association with terrorist acts.

There being no express exception for NLMs, the Declaration recognised that terrorism (not defined) is a criminal act that cannot be justified, whatever the motive, and this is reflected in UNSC Res. 1566 (2004), paragraph 3. For regional conventions, motive is also irrelevant,[14] although there is an express NLM exception in the Arab Convention 1998 (Article 2(a)), the Islamic Conference Convention 1999 (Article 2(a)) and the Organization of African Unity Convention 1999 (Article 3(1)).

The nearest approach to a comprehensive definition of terrorism is to be found in the International Convention for the Suppression of the Financing of Terrorism 1999.[15] Since its purpose is to deal with the financing of terrorism, a definition of terrorism was essential. Article 2 therefore lists the offences defined in the nine previous counter-terrorism conventions, and is followed by a kind of mini-definition of terrorism:

> Any other act *intended to cause death or serious bodily injury to a civilian*, or to any other person not taking an active part in the hostilities in a situation of an armed conflict, *when the purpose of such act, by its nature or context, is to intimidate a population*, or to compel a government or an international organisation to do or to abstain from doing any act. (Emphasis added)

But the definition is only for the purposes of the convention. It does *not* create an international crime of terrorism, and so there is still no universally agreed legal definition of terrorism.[16] Instead, the problem has been approached piecemeal.

---

[14] See n. 28 below

[15] 2178 UNTS 229 (No. 38349); ILM (2000) 268; UKTS (2002) 28; 2002 ATS 23. See A. Aust, 'Counter-Terrorism – A New Approach' (2001) *Max Planck YB of UN Law* 285 at 288–94.

[16] The definition of 'terrorism' in the UK Terrorism Act 2000 is for the purpose of proscribing terrorist organisations, in relation to its provisions on terrorist funding, and in connection with police investigations. The Act does not create an offence of 'terrorism'. See also the complex and uncertain definition in the EU Framework Decision on Combating Terrorism of 13 June 2002, No. 2002/475/JHA.

The sectoral, segmental or incremental approach

All the universal conventions deal with certain categories of terrorism that are so manifestly wicked that, unlike some regional treaties, they have no NLM exception. They apply irrespective of where the crime was committed, the nationality of the accused or the motivation. Ten[17] universal conventions were concluded between 1970 and 1999:[18]

- Convention for the Suppression of Unlawful Seizure of Aircraft 1970 ('Hijacking Convention');[19]
- Convention for the Suppression of Unlawful Acts against the Safety of Civil Aviation 1971 ('Montreal Convention');[20]
- Convention on the Prevention and Punishment of Crimes against Internationally Protected Persons, including Diplomatic Agents 1973 ('Diplomats Convention');[21]
- Convention on the Physical Protection of Nuclear Material 1979 ('Nuclear Convention');[22]
- International Convention against the Taking of Hostages 1979 ('Hostages Convention');[23]
- Protocol for the Suppression of Unlawful Acts of Violence at Airports Serving International Civil Aviation supplementary to the Montreal Convention 1988 ('Montreal Protocol');[24]
- Convention for the Suppression of Unlawful Acts against the Safety of Maritime Navigation 1988 ('Rome Convention') and Protocol for

---

[17] The United Nations regards the Convention on Offences and Certain Other Acts Committed on Board Aircraft 1963 ('Tokyo Convention') (704 UNTS 219 (No. 10106); UKTS (1969) 126) as a terrorism treaty because it includes one Article, albeit ineffective, on hijacking, and parts of the Convention were drawn upon when drafting the later conventions. The United Nations also treats as a terrorism treaty the Convention on the Marking of Plastic Explosives for the Purpose of Detection 1991 (ILM (1991) 726; UKTS (2000) 134) because of its practical importance, but it has no jurisdictional provisions.

[18] The texts of the twelve conventions are at http://untreaty.un.org/English/Terrorism.asp and in *International Instruments Related to the Prevention and Suppression of International Terrorism*, UN, 2001. For detailed commentaries on them, see A. Aust, *Implementation Kits for the International Counter-Terrorism Conventions*, Commonwealth Secretariat, London, 2002.

[19] 860 UNTS 105 (No. 12325); UKTS (1972) 39.

[20] 974 UNTS 177 (No. 14118); ILM (1971) 10; UKTS (1974) 10.

[21] 1035 UNTS 167 (No. 15410); ILM (1974) 41; UKTS (1980) 3.

[22] 1456 UNTS 101 (No. 24631); ILM (1979) 1419; UKTS (1995) 61.

[23] 1316 UNTS 205 (No. 21931); ILM (1979) 1460; UKTS (1983) 81. See also Lambert *Terrorism and Hostages in International Law*, Cambridge, 1990, generally.

[24] ILM (1988) 627; UKTS (1991) 20; 1990 ATS 39.

the Suppression of Unlawful Acts against the Safety of Fixed Platforms Located on the Continental Shelf 1988 ('Rome Protocol');[25]

• International Convention for the Suppression of Terrorist Bombings 1997 ('Bombings Convention');[26]

• International Convention for the Suppression of the Financing of Terrorism 1999 ('Financing Convention').[27]

(For the status of these and the regional treaties,[28] see the UN Secretary-General's annual report on *Measures to Eliminate International Terrorism.*[29]

The ten universal conventions vary in their terms, but generally share certain basic elements.

'International' terrorism

The conventions do not apply to offences that are solely internal. The way this is formulated varies according to the subject, but generally the conventions will not apply if the offence is committed within one state, the alleged offender and any victims are nationals of that state, the alleged offender is found in its territory and no other state has a basis to exercise jurisdiction. But all these conditions have to be met if the convention is not to apply.

---

[25] 1678 UNTS 222 (No. 29004); ILM (1988) 672; UKTS (1995) 64; 1993 ATS 10. See Lambert, *Terrorism and Hostages in International Law*, Cambridge, 1990, pp. 4, 26–7 and 115–16.

[26] 2149 UNTS 284 (No. 37517); ILM (1998) 251; UKTS (2001) 31; 2002 ATS 17.

[27] 2178 UNTS 229 (No. 38349); ILM (2000) 268; UKTS (2002) 28; 2002 ATS 23. For an account of its negotiation and a commentary on it, see A. Aust, 'Counter-Terrorism – A New Approach', (2001) *Max Planck YB of UN Law* 285–306.

[28] Inter-American Convention to Prevent and Punish the Acts of Terrorism Taking the Form of Crimes Against Persons and Related Extortion that are of International Significance 1971, 1438 UNTS 195 (No. 24381); European Convention on the Suppression of Terrorism 1977, 1137 UNTS 93 (No. 17828); ILM (1976) 1272; UKTS (1978) 93 (now updated by a 2003 Protocol); SAARC (South Asian) Regional Convention on Suppression of Terrorism 1987; Arab Convention on the Suppression of Terrorism 1998; Commonwealth of Independent States Treaty on Cooperation in Combating Terrorism 1999; Islamic Conference Convention on Combating Terrorism 1999; OAU Convention on the Prevention and Combating of Terrorism 1999. For all these texts, see http://untreaty.un.org/English/Terrorism.asp, or *International Instruments Related to the Prevention and Suppression of International Terrorism*, UN, 2001.

[29] See www.un.org/terrorism/.

Definition of the offences

Although the conventions require implementation by domestic legislation for the offences formulated by them, since most of the offences will already be crimes under existing law (murder, causing explosions, kidnapping, etc.), the provisions on jurisdiction and cooperation are the most valuable. The offences include attempts and being an accessory. Beginning with the Bombings Convention, the concept of conspiracy was added. The Financing Convention made a clearer distinction between the civil law concept of *association malfaiteur* and the similar common law concept of conspiracy.[30]

The essential principle on which the conventions rest is that an alleged offender should not find safe haven in the territory of any party. This is done by the establishment of quasi-universal jurisdiction[31] and the so-called extradite or prosecute rule.

Quasi-universal jurisdiction

The effect of each convention is to create, as between its parties, a regime of universal jurisdiction. Since not all states are parties – although the Hijacking Convention 1970 now has 178 parties – the regime is described as 'quasi-universal jurisdiction'. Each party has to establish its jurisdiction over the offences, not only if they are committed in its territory or by one of its nationals or have another connection with it (such as having been committed on board a vessel flying the party's flag or an aircraft registered with it). It is enough that an alleged offender is *found* in the territory of the party. Even if neither the crime, nor the alleged offender, has any connection with that party, it must nevertheless be able legally to detain him.

Starting with the Rome Convention 1988, a party is also given discretion to establish its jurisdiction if the offence is committed abroad but against one of its own nationals or the state itself. This power had to be given by treaty since many states do not accept the 'passive personality' or 'protective' principles.[32]

---

[30] See Article 2(5)(c), which was taken from Article 25(3)(a) of the Statute of the International Criminal Court, 2187 UNTS 90 (No. 38544); ILM (1998) 998; UKTS (2002) 35.

[31] See p. 45 above.

[32] See p. 45 above. A similar, but non-discretionary, provision is to be found in Article 5(1)(c) and (d) of the Hostages Convention 1979 (n. 23 above).

'Extradite or prosecute'

The detaining state might not extradite the alleged offender to another party. There can be many reasons: he may be one of its own nationals and its law prohibits their extradition; the state may not have confidence in the fairness of the other legal system; or it may not trust the other state to prosecute diligently.[33] If it does not extradite, it is under an obligation 'without exception whatsoever and whether or not the offence was committed in its territory, to submit the case to its own authorities for the purpose of prosecution'. This principle (worded the same in all ten conventions) of *aut dedere aut judicare* (extradite or prosecute) is essential for the effectiveness of the conventions: there is to be no hiding place in the territory of any of the parties for persons accused of terrorism. The requirement is not to prosecute but 'to submit the case to its own authorities for the purpose of prosecution'. There is no obligation to prosecute whatever the circumstances; there may not be sufficient evidence.

A party must investigate any allegation that there is a person in its territory who has committed the offence and, if the circumstances so warrant, ensure the person's presence for the purpose of extradition or prosecution. There is no provision as to which state has priority of jurisdiction, although in practice the state that has custody of the alleged offender has the first option to prosecute.[34]

Extradition

If the crime was committed in the territory, or on a ship or aircraft, of another party, there is of course an important forensic advantage in sending the alleged offender for trial in the place where many of the witnesses are and the evidence is likely to have been collected. The conventions therefore deem the offences extraditable under existing extradition treaties (including multilateral treaties), and the parties undertake to include the offences in every future extradition treaty. As between parties that do not require a treaty for the purpose of extradition, the conventions provide that, subject to the law of the requested party, the parties shall recognise the offences as extraditable. Data on extraditions pursuant to the conventions is not easy to find, although most

---

[33] See p. 295 below on the exceptional factors in the *Lockerbie* case.
[34] See Lambert, *Terrorism and Hostages in International Law*, Cambridge, 1990, pp. 163–5.

states seem to prefer deportation or expulsion, since they are usually quicker.

The political exception

The 'political exception' must be clearly distinguished from provisions in the conventions that mutual legal assistance or extradition may be refused if it has been requested for the purpose of prosecuting or persecuting the person for his political opinions. The political exception dates from the nineteenth century and is a provision in extradition treaties or domestic law that prohibits extradition for so-called political offences: those committed for political purposes or motives.[35] Given that many terrorist crimes are committed for some political purpose, and the earlier conventions do not prohibit the political exception, this can be an obstacle to extradition for a terrorist offence. However, the more recent Bombings Convention 1997 (Article 11) and the Financing Convention 1999 (Article 14) exclude the political exception, as do some extradition treaties in respect of offences under the conventions.[36]

Fiscal offences

Article 13 of the Financing Convention 1999 provides, in effect for the avoidance of doubt, that for the purposes of requests for extradition or mutual legal assistance none of the financing offences shall be regarded as a fiscal offence; and requests cannot be refused on the sole ground that they concern a fiscal offence. In this context, 'fiscal' means relating to money or public revenue. Tax evasion is a typical fiscal offence, although it cannot usually be the subject of mutual legal assistance or extradition.[37]

Armed conflicts

Article 12 of the Hostages Convention 1979 excludes hostage-taking which is a 'grave breach' of the Geneva Conventions and Additional Protocol I,

---

[35] The matter is complicated: see Oppenheim, pp. 962–72 and p. 266 above.

[36] Article 7 of the European Convention on the Suppression of Terrorism 1977 (n. 28 above) excludes terrorist offences from the political exception. See Lambert, *Terrorism and Hostages in International Law*, Cambridge, 1990, pp. 234–5.

[37] The provision was drawn from Article 1 of the Additional Protocol to the CoE Convention on Mutual Assistance in Criminal Matters, 1496 UNTS 350 (No. 6841); ILM (1978) 801; UKTS (1992) 24.

for which the parties to those conventions have an obligation to prosecute or extradite.[38] The tortuous language of Article 12 has led some writers into wrongly believing that the Article does not apply to NLMs. It does.[39] All the Article means is that a person can be prosecuted for a war crime rather than a terrorist act. Although the Protocol applies to activities of NLMs, that does not legitimise hostage-taking by NLMs, only that it has to be dealt with under the Geneva regime.

Article 19(2) of the Bombings Convention 1997 also contains convoluted language that has the effect of excluding from the scope of the Convention the activities of armed forces during an armed conflict or otherwise on duty (know colloquially by the transatlantic term 'military carve-out'). (Article 2(1)(b) of the Financing Convention 1997 has a similar exclusion.) This is necessary since acts, such as causing explosions, are frequently done during an armed conflict, and any abuse of the law of armed conflict can be dealt with under that law.

Criminal liability of corporations

Article 5 of the Financing Convention 1999 is new to terrorism conventions. Although under the other conventions a responsible official of a legal person, such as a company, could as part of his duties commit an offence, the company itself could not. But that would not have been enough for the Financing Convention, since offences under it are most likely to be committed by banks and other financial institutions. When a transfer of money is done with the help of a bank official who knows it is destined for terrorists, it is important that the bank should also be held accountable. The bank does not have to benefit from the offence, although liability is dependent on a person 'responsible for the management or control' of the entity having 'in that capacity' committed a financing offence.[40] Thus, a relatively senior manager, not a clerk (today every bank clerk is called a manager), must have committed the offence. If he used the bank's computer system to transfer the money, even though he was not authorised to do so, the bank would commit an offence. This is because the convicted person would have done the act by virtue of his employment with the

---

[38] 75 UNTS 3 (Nos. 970–3); UKTS (1958) 39 and 1125 UNTS 3 (No. 17512); ILM (1977) 1391; UKTS (1999) 29–30.

[39] See Lambert, *Terrorism and Hostages in International Law*, Cambridge, 1990, pp. 263–98.

[40] See pp. 410–12 below on a similar point on state responsibility.

bank, which gave him access to the system. It could not be said to be a private act.[41]

In many legal systems, when legislation makes it an offence for a 'person' to do an act, this includes a legal person, unless a contrary intention appears. A contrary intention can be inferred where the nature of the act, such as bigamy, could not be committed by a controlling officer in the course of business. The concept of the vicarious liability of corporations is developing in both common law and civil law systems, but naturally varies from state to state. Some legal systems do not enable legal entities to be made criminally liable at all. Article 5 therefore limits the obligation to legal entities located in the territory of a party or organised under its laws (i.e. carrying on business or incorporated there), and thus makes it clear that making a 'legal entity' liable must be done in accordance with the domestic legal principles of each party. And each party is given discretion as to the nature of the liability – criminal, civil or administrative.

Punishment

The parties must make the defined offences criminal offences in their domestic law and impose penalties that take into account the 'grave nature' of the offences.

Protection of the rights of the alleged offender and cooperation by the parties

The conventions require protection of the human rights of the alleged offender after arrest and during any legal proceedings, and for cooperation and mutual assistance between parties in connection with investigations, the provision of evidence and the prevention of offences.

Refugees

Article 1F(c) of the Refugee Convention 1951[42] provides that, if there are 'serious reasons' for considering that a person is 'guilty of acts contrary to the purposes and principles of the United Nations', he is not entitled to

---

[41] See A. Aust, 'Counter-Terrorism – A New Approach' (2001) *Max Planck YB of UN Law* 285–306.

[42] 189 UNTS 137 (No. 2545) and 606 UNTS 267 (No. 8791); UKTS (1954) 39 and UKTS (1969) 15.

refugee status. On 17 December 1996, the UN General Assembly adopted a Declaration that terrorism is contrary to the purposes and principles of the United Nations.[43]

Nuclear terrorism convention

The scope of the Nuclear Convention 1979 being limited, it was felt this might be remedied by the conclusion of a comprehensive treaty on nuclear terrorism. Although the negotiations in the UN Sixth Committee were almost completed in 1998, they were held up by the reluctance of some states to consider an exemption for the activities of the armed forces of nuclear weapon states. Finally, on 13 April 2005, the UN General Assembly adopted the International Convention for the Suppression of Nuclear Terrorism (A/59/766).

Comprehensive Convention on International Terrorism

This ambitious proposal, discussed at the United Nations since 2001, attempts to consolidate all the previous conventions and to fill in gaps. Progress has been delayed by the insistence of some states on an exemption for NLMs even where their activities would not be lawful under the law of armed conflict, and would thus take them outside both the conventions and the law of armed conflict.

Security Council[44]

For over thirty years the United Nations Security Council has been concerned about terrorism. In the Lockerbie resolutions,[45] and repeatedly later, the Council has determined that terrorism is a threat to international peace and security, most famously in Resolution 1368 (2001) following the 11 September 2001 attacks in the United States.

The first Chapter VII measure[46] on terrorism was directed at Iraq. After its invasion of Kuwait on 2 August 1990, many nationals of Kuwait and other states were held in Kuwait, some later being taken to Baghdad where they were held as 'human shields', that is hostages. Resolution 674 (1990) demanded their release. Following the liberation of Kuwait, the ceasefire

---

[43] A/RES/51/210; ILM (1996) 1188. See also pp. 192–3 above.
[44] A. Aust, 'The Security Council and International Criminal Law' (2002) NYIL 23–46.
[45] See n. 48 below.   [46] On Chapter VII, see p. 214 above.

Resolution 687 (1990) recalled the Hostages Convention, categorised all acts of hostage-taking as manifestations of international terrorism, and deplored the previous threats by Iraq to make use of terrorism abroad. It required Iraq to confirm that it would not commit or support any act of international terrorism, not allow any terrorist organisation to operate within Iraq, and to condemn and renounce all acts of terrorism. Iraq agreed.

Lockerbie

When Pan Am flight 103 was sabotaged over Lockerbie in Scotland on 21 December 1988, Libya, the United Kingdom and the United States were (and still are) parties to the Montreal Convention 1971, which now has 180 parties. But when in 1991 charges of murder were laid against two Libyans, in order to get them to trial the United Kingdom and the United States did not invoke the Convention. Since they had been charged as having acted on behalf of the Libyan intelligence services, the alleged complicity of the Libyan Government (with its long, well-documented involvement in terrorism) meant that trial in a Libyan court was unthinkable. Yet, since Libyan law prohibits extradition of Libyan nationals, if an extradition request had been made to Libya under the Convention it would have been obliged to submit the case to its prosecuting authorities.[47] Therefore, a demand was made for the 'surrender' of the two accused for trial in a Scottish or US court. The Security Council adopted a series of resolutions demanding that Libya hand over the two accused for trial in a Scottish or US court, and imposing sanctions.[48] Following Resolution 1192 (1998), the accused were eventually handed over for trial by a Scottish court, albeit sitting in the Netherlands.[49] In 2001, one of the accused, Megrahi, was convicted and sentenced to life imprisonment in Scotland.[50]

[47] The Libyan pleadings to the International Court of Justice in the proceedings brought by it in 1992 against the UK and the US in a vain attempt to stop the sanctions, claimed that, by their actions in the UN Security Council, the respondent states had denied Libya its right under the Montreal Convention to prosecute the accused. The cases also raised an issue of fundamental importance about the respective powers of the ICJ and the Security Council (see p. 460 below). In September 2003, the cases were withdrawn by consent.
[48] Res. 731 (1992), 748 (1992), 883 (1993) and 1192 (1998).
[49] For the long history of how the accused came to be so tried, see A. Aust, 'Lockerbie: The Other Case' (2001) ICLQ 278 et seq.
[50] See ILM (2001) 581–613 (judgment).

Sudan

Following an attempted assassination of the President of Egypt while visiting Ethiopia by persons who then found refuge in Sudan, the Security Council adopted Resolution 1044 (1996) calling upon Sudan to comply with requests by the OAU to extradite the suspects to Ethiopia and to cease support for terrorism. Sudan did not comply. In Resolutions 1054 (1996) and 1070 (1996), the Council, acting under Chapter VII, demanded that Sudan comply and imposed sanctions. Following requests from the OAU, Egypt and Ethiopia, the sanctions were lifted by Resolution 1372 (2001).

Bin Laden, Al-Qaida and the Taliban[51]

In Resolutions 1267 (1999) and 1333 (2000), the Security Council required the Taliban regime in Afghanistan to surrender Usama bin Laden and, as reiterated and consolidated in Resolution 1390 (2002), imposed sanctions on Bin Laden, members of the Taliban and Al-Qaida, and individuals, groups, undertakings and entities associated with them. Resolution 1452 (2002) provides for exemptions from the financial sanctions imposed by Resolutions 1267 (1999), 1333 (2000) and 1390 (2002). They include payments for food, rent or mortgage, medicines, taxes, insurance premiums, public utility charges and payments exclusively for reasonable professional fees. There is a forty-eight-hour tacit 'no-objection' approval procedure if a relevant state notifies the relevant sanctions committee, the 1267 Committee,[52] of a proposal to make an exempt payment.

For the purpose of implementing the sanctions against individuals, Resolutions 1267 (1999), 1333 (2000) and 1390 (2002) provide for lists of Al-Qaida members to be maintained and updated by the 1267 Committee. The present Guidelines for the conduct of the work of the Committee include a procedure to enable a name to be removed. The individual (or group) petitions his government of residence or citizenship. The government consults the government that originally proposed the listing. A joint or, if necessary, unilateral request for de-listing can then be made by the petitioned government to the Committee, under a 'no-objection' procedure. The Committee takes its decision by consensus, but, if that is not achievable, after consultations by the Chairman the matter can be referred to the Security Council. The procedure is expressed to be without

---

[51] The UN English spelling of the names.
[52] See www.un.org/Docs/sc/committees/1267/1267Template.htm.

prejudice to available procedures – recognition that national legal remedies, like judicial review, may be available.

Following the Al-Qaida attacks on the United States on 11 September 2001, the Security Council adopted Resolution 1373 (2001). Drawing on the Financing Convention, it required all states to criminalise the financing of terrorist acts, to freeze the funds of terrorists and to prohibit the supply of funds to terrorists. The resolution does not define terrorism; it just refers to 'terrorist acts'. The resolution does not provide for lists of terrorist groups or individuals to be maintained. In practice, US and other lists circulate among Members but they are not binding in international law, although in some states they may be binding in domestic law and acts based on a listing may be challengeable in a national court.[53] Resolution 1373 (2001) established a separate committee, the Counter-Terrorism Committee, with a broader remit than the 1267 Committee.[54] Resolution 1526 (2004), paragraph 15, emphasised the need for the two committees to cooperate closely.

[53] There are also a number of pending ECJ cases (e.g. *Kadi* and *Aden*) relating to individuals challenging implementation of financial sanctions – which also raise questions of Community competence.

[54] See www.un.org/Docs/sc/committees/1373.

15

The law of the sea

The sea! The sea![1]

Churchill and Lowe, *The Law of the Sea*, 3rd edn, Manchester, 1999
Burke, *The New International Law of Fisheries*, Oxford, 1994
Birnie and Boyle, *International Law and the Environment*, 2nd edn, Oxford, 2002
www.un.org/Depts/los/
www.imo.org

Because the sea has been an essential means of transport since ancient times, and even today merchant shipping still carries 95 per cent (by weight) of all exports, the rules governing the use of the sea (including its resources and environment) are one of the principal subjects of international law. The law is a mixture of treaty and established or emerging customary international law, the customary law having developed over centuries. The first successful attempt to codify the law was the 1958 UN Conventions on the Law of the Sea, but the most important aspects of the law are now set out in the UN Convention on the Law of the Sea 1982 (in this chapter, 'the Convention' or 'UNCLOS').[2] For those parties to the Convention that were parties to the 1958 Conventions, the 1982 Convention replaces them. Although between thirty-seven and sixty-two states are still listed as parties to the four 1958 Conventions, in many cases they are now bound by the 1982 Convention, which entered into force on 16 November 1994, and now has 148 parties. As most of the Convention's provisions represent customary international law,[3] even non-parties, such

---

[1] Xenophon, c. 430–359 BC.
[2] 1. Territorial Sea and Contiguous Zone; 2. High Seas; 3. Fishing; 4. Continental Shelf. The four Conventions, the ILC drafts and commentaries, and a short historical introduction, are in A. Watts, *The International Law Commission 1949–1998*, Oxford, 1999, vol. I, pp. 23–137. UNCLOS is at 1833 UNTS 397 (No. 31363); ILM (1982) 1261; and UKTS (1999) 81.
[3] For an explanation of the term, see p. 6 above, and, in relation to the Convention, see Churchill and Lowe, *The Law of the Sea*, 3rd edn, Manchester, 1999, pp. 16–22.

as Iran and the United States, are already bound by those provisions albeit as customary international law.[4] In considering a particular situation, such as passage through straits, one must thus consider carefully the legal position of the states involved. This requires an investigation into which general treaties on the subject are binding on them (in particular, the relevant 1958 Convention or UNCLOS); if on the specific matter there are any other relevant multilateral or bilateral treaties; and whether customary international law as represented in the 1982 Convention is applicable.[5] The subject is large and there are many exceptions to the rules and special situations. In the space available here, it is only possible to sketch in the outlines by explaining the terminology and describing the principles.

(Unless otherwise stated, references to numbered Articles are to those of the 1982 Convention.)

Internal waters

Internal waters are all those on the landward side of the baselines from which the breadth of the territorial sea is measured (Article 8). They therefore include bays,[6] estuaries, ports, rivers, canals[7] and lakes, including inland seas like the Caspian Sea.

Right of access by foreign ships

A coastal state has sovereignty over its internal waters and, unlike the territorial sea, there is no right of innocent passage through internal waters for foreign ships. Although a right of access to internal waters, in particular ports, may be granted to foreign ships by treaty (typically in a treaty of friendship, commerce and navigation), there is no general right of access for merchant ships.[8] The only clear right of access is when a ship is in distress and there is a risk to the lives of those on board. States can and do impose many conditions on the entry of ships. It can be refused for, among

---

[4] See n. 3 above.

[5] Even when a treaty has 'entered into force', it is binding only on those states which have consented to be bound by it (e.g. by ratifying it), except in so far as the treaty also represents customary international law. One must also check whether a party has made reservations or interpretative declarations and, if so, whether they affect the matter (see pp. ** above).

[6] See pp. 67 *et seq.* above.

[7] The law of the sea does not govern rivers and canals. For the special cases of the Panama and Suez Canals, see p. 363 below.

[8] See pp. 317 below on warships.

other things, security reasons or to prevent pollution. A state can designate which of its ports are open for international trade or immigration.[9]

By entering a foreign port, a ship comes under the territorial jurisdiction of the coastal state. This has several implications. It is not completely free to leave. It must complete all necessary formalities and may be detained if it is in an unseaworthy condition or otherwise poses a danger to those on board or to the environment.

Of particular importance is the degree to which the criminal and civil laws of the coastal state are enforceable against a foreign ship in port. The basic principle is that the coastal state will not enforce its laws if its interests are not affected and the matter can be dealt with effectively under the laws of the flag state. Thus crew discipline is normally left to the captain and the authorities of the flag state. But, if a local national or a person who is not a member of the crew is involved in a serious crime, such as murder, or the captain or consul of the flag state requests the help of the coastal state, it may decide to exercise jurisdiction. A foreign ship is liable to be arrested in port in the case of an action *in rem* against the ship itself, such as a claim arising out of an incident involving the ship or as security in a civil action against its owner. This latter aspect is an area of law on which local legal advice is always essential.

Baselines

The breadth of the territorial sea, the contiguous zone, the exclusive economic zone (EEZ) and the continental shelf (in certain cases) is measured from baselines, behind which the waters are internal. Baselines are also important in the delimitation of a maritime boundary.[10] The subject is complex and highly technical (see Articles 3–16) and will therefore be described only in broad terms.

The *normal baseline* is the low-water mark along the coast[11] as marked on large-scale charts officially recognised by the coastal state. This will inevitably result in a curving baseline. But if the coastline is deeply indented or cut into, or there is a fringe of islands along the coast in its immediate vicinity (Norway is a prime example), a *straight baseline* can be drawn joining appropriate points. Nevertheless it must not depart to any appreciable extent from the general direction of the coast. *Deltas* are treated as part of the coastline. A *low-tide elevation* (a naturally formed

---

[9] See also Articles 25(2), 211(3) and 255.   [10] See pp. 309–11 below.
[11] Coast is not defined but probably relates to the place from where navigation is possible.

area of land which is surrounded by and is above water at low tide, but submerged at high tide) may be used as a baseline if it is wholly or partly within the territorial sea. *Reefs* that are exposed at high tide can also be used as baselines. *Artificial islands* and other offshore installations are disregarded for the purpose of drawing baselines. When there is a *river* that flows directly into the sea, the baseline is a straight line draw across its mouth. When the river flows indirectly into the sea through an *estuary*, the rules on bays apply. When the distance between the natural entrance points of a *bay*[12] does not exceed twenty-four nautical miles a *closing line* can be drawn between those points, the water enclosed by it being internal. If the entrance is wider, a straight line of twenty-four nautical miles is drawn within the bay so as to enclose the maximum area of water that is possible within a line of that length. Otherwise, no maximum length is prescribed for a straight baseline, and as a result the right to draw straight baselines has been much abused.

So-called *historic bays* do not meet the criteria in the Convention and are governed by customary international law, not the Convention (Article 10(6)). To claim an historic bay as internal waters, the state has to prove that it has claimed the bay as its internal waters for a considerable time and has effectively, openly and continuously exercised its authority there without objection from other states. Most claims to historic bays have been objected to, such as the fifty nautical mile closing line for Hudson Bay claimed by Canada, to which the United States objects. Most extravagant is the Libyan claim to a 296 nautical mile closing line for the Gulf of Sirte (or Sidra), to which several developed countries have objected.[13]

The concept of *vital bays* (vital for the security of the coastal state) has been promoted by some developing countries, but is not recognised by the Convention or in customary law.

Territorial sea

A coastal state's sovereignty extends beyond its land territory and internal waters to an adjacent belt of sea known as the territorial sea, although

---

[12] '[A] well-marked indentation whose penetration is in such proportion to the width of its mouth as to contain land-locked waters and constitute more than a mere curvature of the coast. An indentation shall not, however, be regarded as a bay unless its area is as large as, or larger than, that of the semi-circle whose diameter is a line drawn across the mouth of the indentation' (Article 10(2)).

[13] Churchill and Lowe, *The Law of the Sea*, 3rd edn, Manchester, 1999, pp. 43–5

sometimes referred to as 'territorial waters'. Sovereignty extends also to the bed and subsoil of the territorial sea and the air space above it (Article 2(1)).[14] Since sovereignty over the territorial sea is incidental to the sovereignty over the land, it does not have to be established. However, each coastal state has to specify the breath of its territorial sea, which can be up to a maximum of twelve nautical miles measured from the baselines (Article 3). About six states claim between only three and six nautical miles. Some fifteen states, mostly in Africa and Latin America, claim between twenty and 200 nautical miles, but these are not recognised by states that claim twelve nautical miles or less. The laws and regulations of the coastal state apply to the territorial sea, but can be enforced against foreign ships only to the extent indicated below.

Islands

An island is defined as 'a naturally formed area of land, surrounded by water, which is above water at high tide' (Article 121(1)). An island is treated in the same way as other land territory and can therefore have a territorial sea, contiguous zone, EEZ and a continental shelf. Rocks (not defined as such) which cannot sustain human habitation or economic life of their own' cannot have an EEZ or a continental shelf (Article 121(3)), but can have a territorial sea.[15] Artificial islands and other offshore installations have no territorial sea of their own.

Innocent passage

Given the unique character of the sea and its importance for trade, it has long been recognised that ships of all states have the right of 'innocent passage' through the territorial sea (Article 17). By 'passage' is meant navigation through the territorial sea for the purpose of (a) traversing it without entering internal waters or calling at a port or roadstead[16] outside internal waters or (b) proceeding to or from internal waters or a call at such port or roadstead. The passage must be continuous and expeditious

---

[14] See also Article 2 of the Chicago Convention on International Civil Aviation 1944, 15 UNTS 295 (No. 102); UKTS (1953) 8.

[15] The UK's fishery limits were adjusted before the UK ratified UNCLOS to take account of the fact that under UNCLOS the limits could not be based on Rockall since it cannot sustain human habitation or an economic life of its own. See further Churchill and Lowe, *The Law of the Sea*, 3rd edn, Manchester, 1999, pp. 49–50.

[16] An offshore structure at which ships load, unload or anchor.

(no loitering), except for stopping and anchoring which is incidental to ordinary navigation, or made necessary by *force majeure* or distress or to help persons, ships or aircraft in danger or distress (Article 18).

The inclusion of 'innocent' means that passage must not be prejudicial to the 'peace, good order or security' of the coastal state (Article 19). That Article lists twelve activities which are considered prejudicial, including: weapons exercises or practice; espionage; launching or landing aircraft; loading or unloading of commodities, currencies or persons; wilful and serious pollution; any fishing activities; research or surveying; interference with coastal communications; any threat or use of force in violation of the UN Charter; and 'any activity not having a direct bearing on passage'. If passage is not innocent, the coastal state can take the necessary steps within its territorial sea to prevent it (Article 25(1)), usually by requiring the ship to leave, or arresting it if it has breached its laws. The coastal state may also, without discriminating between foreign ships, temporarily suspend innocent passage when this is essential to protect its security (Article 25(3)).

Article 23 recognises that nuclear-powered ships can exercise the right of innocent passage, as well as ships carrying nuclear or 'other inherently dangerous or noxious substances'; provided they carry appropriate documents and observe special precautionary measures established by international agreements. Although Article 22(2) allows coastal states to require such ships (as well as tankers) to confine their passage to certain sea lanes, some states go further and wrongly assert the right to require prior authorisation for such passage. Many parties assert the right to regulate or even prohibit passage through the territorial sea (and sometimes archipelagic waters, contiguous zones to EEZs) for security reasons: see the various reservations and declarations made on ratification.

Rights of the coastal state over ships in innocent passage

The right of innocent passage has to be balanced with the right of the coastal state to protect its legitimate interests. It can therefore make laws and regulations relating to innocent passage in the following areas: protection of navigational aids and of cables and pipelines; conservation of marine living resources (principally fish); environmental protection; scientific research; the prevention of infringement of customs, fiscal, immigration and sanitary laws; and the safety of navigation (Article 21). Charges cannot be levied on foreign ships by reason only of their innocent passage. Such charges may only be made for specific services rendered to them and levied on a non-discriminatory basis (Article 26).

In applying its laws and regulations, the coastal state must not impose requirements or enforce its laws and regulations in a way which would have the effect of denying or impairing the right of innocent passage, or which are discriminatory (Article 24). Thus, the coastal state should[17] not arrest a person on board a foreign ship, or investigate a crime committed on it, if the crime was committed before the ship entered the territorial sea, unless it entered from the internal waters of the coastal state. Nor should the coastal state exercise criminal jurisdiction if the crime was committed during the passage of the ship through the territorial sea unless the ship has just left the internal waters, the crime has an effect on the coastal state, local help has been requested or drug trafficking is involved. In such cases, the master of the ship can require the coastal state to inform a diplomatic or consular representative of the flag state of the action to be taken (Article 27). Similarly, the coastal state must not arrest a foreign ship for the purpose of civil proceedings when it is passing through its territorial waters unless the matter relates to obligations undertaken or liabilities incurred by the ship itself or is related to the passage (Article 28(2)).

The coastal state has a duty to warn all shipping of any known danger to navigation within the territorial sea (Article 24(2)).[18] This applies to man-made and natural dangers, such as volcanic eruptions.

For the position of warships and other state ships, see p. 317 below.

Contiguous zone

The term 'contiguous zone' is less well known. It can extend beyond the territorial sea, but not further than twenty-four nautical miles from the baselines from which the territorial sea is measured (Article 33). Only about one-third of coastal states have established a contiguous zone. Within the zone the coastal state is entitled to exercise the control necessary to prevent and punish infringements of its customs, fiscal, immigration and sanitary laws and regulations when committed within its territory or territorial sea.

Exclusive economic zone

The exclusive economic zone (EEZ) is an area adjacent to the territorial sea and extending up to 200 nautical miles from the baselines from which

---

[17] The rule is one of comity (see p. 12 above).
[18] See also *Corfu Channel* (*UK* v. *Albania*) (Merits), *ICJ Reports* (1949), p. 4; 16 ILR 155.

the territorial sea is measured (Articles 55 and 57). Previously, most of the area would have been high seas, and so the EEZ, not being under the sovereignty of the coastal state, does not have the same legal character as the territorial sea. Instead, it is a zone in which the coastal state enjoys only *sovereign rights* for certain purposes.

Unlike the continental shelf, the rights to which are inherent, an EEZ has to be formally established by the coastal state, and most have done so. A few, such as the United Kingdom, have limited themselves to establishing an exclusive fisheries zone (EFZ). Nearly all states which previously claimed a 200 nautical mile territorial sea (especially South American) have now replaced them with EEZs. Because of their breadth, two or more EEZs may well overlap, and so there may well be a need to delimit the boundary between them.

The EEZ is a recent development. It is particularly important for developing countries since it gives them substantial rights over natural resources within the EEZ. The vast majority of fish stocks are found within 200 nautical miles from the coast. Most overseas territories have also had EEZs established for them.

Rights, jurisdiction and duties of the coastal state in the EEZ

In the EEZ the coastal state has sovereign rights for the purpose of exploring, exploiting, conserving and managing the natural resources, whether living (e.g. fish) or non-living (e.g. oil) of the superjacent waters (above) the seabed and of the seabed and its subsoil (Article 56(1)(a)). Thus, the coastal state has the exclusive right to exploit oil and gas deposits within its EEZ, that right being exercised in accordance with the rules governing the regime of the continental shelf (see below). (Regulation of fishing is discussed at pp. 316 and 319–22 below.)

In addition, the coastal state enjoys limited jurisdiction[19] within the EEZ with regard to certain matters (Article 56(1)(b)):

(a) The construction of artificial islands, installations and structures (e.g. oil platforms). The coastal state has the exclusive right to authorise and regulate the construction, operation and use of such structures and to establish safety zones (normally no more than 500 metres in breadth) around them (Article 60).[20]

(b) Marine scientific research. The coastal state should normally give consent for pure science, but can withhold it if the research is of direct

---

[19] This is less than sovereign rights.   [20] And see p. 309 below.

significance for the exploration and exploitation of natural resources (Article 246(5)). Consent is normally implied if the application contains all the necessary information and, within four months of its receipt, the coastal state has not indicated otherwise or asked for more details (Article 252).

(c) The protection and preservation of the environment, chiefly from pollution by ships and oil platforms (see pp. 341–3 below).

Rights and duties of other states in the EEZ

Although the EEZ is no longer part of the high seas, certain important high seas freedoms can still be exercised in an EEZ (Article 58), the first being *freedom of navigation* by foreign ships, subject to the coastal state's powers in respect of pollution. However, a number of developing countries have legislated or proposed legislation that purports to restrict this basic freedom for shipping in the EEZ.[21] And in 2002, following the *Prestige* disaster that caused serious oil pollution of Spanish beaches, France, Portugal and Spain proposed the banning from their EEZs of elderly, single-hulled foreign oil tankers. Since this would infringe the freedom of navigation, the measure would first have to be agreed with other states through an international organisation such as the IMO, and then fifteen months' notice given. Secondly, all foreign aircraft enjoy the *freedom of overflight* of the EEZ, to which the ICAO Rules of the Air apply, not the laws and regulations of the coastal state. Thirdly, states enjoy the *freedom to lay submarine cables and pipelines* in the EEZ, although the course taken by a pipeline is subject to the consent of the coastal state (Article 79(3)).

International straits

An international strait is a passage used for international navigation that connects one part of the high seas or an EEZ with another part of the high seas or an EEZ (Article 37). It has to be wider than twenty-four nautical miles; otherwise it could consist of territorial sea only. The Convention regime does not apply if (i) the strait has a high seas or an EEZ route through it of similar convenience; (ii) the strait is formed by an island bordering the strait and the mainland; (iii) the strait connects part of the

---

[21] See Churchill and Lowe, *The Law of the Sea*, 3rd edn, Manchester, 1999, pp. 170–3.

high seas or an EEZ with the territorial sea of a third state; or (iv) the legal regime of the strait is regulated by a long-standing treaty.[22] In the first three cases, navigation of the strait will be governed by the rules on innocent passage through the territorial sea or freedom of navigation through the EEZ or the high seas, as appropriate.

In all other cases, the regime of the Convention creates a right of *transit passage* through international straits. This right is greater than innocent passage through the territorial sea, but is less than freedom of navigation on the high seas. Transit passage means navigation (and overflight) solely for the purpose of 'continuous and expeditious' transit from one part of the high seas or an EEZ to another part of the high seas or an EEZ, including passage for the purpose of entering, leaving or returning to a state bordering the strait (Article 38(2)). If an activity is not in accordance with these conditions, such as anchoring, the passage will be subject to the regime of the territorial sea or the EEZ, as the case may be, unless it is rendered necessary by distress or *force majeure* (Article 39(1)(c)).

Archipelagos

Articles 46–54 make special provision for archipelagos. An archipelagic state may draw straight archipelagic baselines joining the outermost points of the outermost islands of the archipelago (Article 47). For this purpose an archipelagic state is one constituted *wholly* by one or more archipelagos and perhaps other islands. An archipelago is a group of islands, interconnecting waters and other natural features which are so closely interrelated that they form an 'intrinsic geographical, economic and political entity', or which historically have been so regarded (Article 46). Fiji, Indonesia, the Philippines and Tonga are prime examples; the Færoes are not because Denmark is a state with a mainland, and therefore not constituted wholly by one or more archipelagos or islands. Nevertheless, the straight baselines (see below) drawn around the Færoes have been recognised by several states. If the archipelagic state is constituted by more than one archipelago, the straight baselines are drawn around each archipelago.

The waters *inside* the baselines, other than internal waters, are archipelagic waters over which the state has sovereignty (Article 49).

---

[22] Such as the Montreux Convention 1936 regulating the Bosphorus and the Dardanelles, 173 LNTS 213; UKTS (1937) 30.

The territorial sea is measured from those baselines in the usual way. Since the drawing of the baselines will cut off large areas of sea, the archipelagic state must respect the traditional fishing rights of neighbouring states. Although foreign ships have the right of innocent passage through archipelagic waters, they, and foreign aircraft, enjoy the more extensive right of 'archipelagic sea lanes passage', which is similar to transit passage through straits (Articles 52–54).

Continental shelf

The continental shelf took on enormous economic importance in the second half of the twentieth century with the exploitation of offshore oil and gas reserves. It comprises the seabed and subsoil of the submarine areas that extend beyond the territorial sea of a coastal state throughout the natural prolongation of the land territory to either (1) the outer edge of the *continental margin* or (2) 200 nautical miles from the baselines from which the breadth of the territorial sea is measured, whichever is the greater (Article 76(1)). The *continental margin* is defined in geophysical terms as comprising (a) what is more properly called the *continental shelf*, that is, that section of the seabed that gradually slopes from the low-water mark to an average depth of 130 metres, from where it descends more steeply, (b) the *slope*, that is, the following section which descends more steeply, and (c) the *rise*, if any, where the sea-bed falls away more gradually to a depth of about 3,500 to 5,500 metres. Beyond that is the deep ocean floor (see Article 76(3).[23] Article 77(4)–(7) contains an exceptionally complex, technical formula for establishing the outer edge of the continental margin.

A coastal state exercises *sovereign rights* (not sovereignty) over its continental shelf for the purposes of exploring it and exploiting its natural resources. These rights are inherent; unlike an EEZ, they do not have to be proclaimed and do not depend on occupation. They are also exclusive; if the coastal state chooses not to explore or exploit the natural resources, no other state may do so without its express consent. The natural resources are mineral or other non-living resources of the seabed and subsoil, as well as living organisms belonging to sedentary species, such as molluscs (Article 77(4)).

---

[23] See Churchill and Lowe, *The Law of the Sea*, 3rd edn, Manchester, 1999, p. 30.

A state that wishes to establish an outer limit of its continental shelf beyond the 200 nautical mile limit is required to submit information to the Commission on the Limits of the Continental Shelf (CLCS)[24] within ten years of becoming a party to UNCLOS (see Article 76 and Annex II, Article 4).[25] The CLCS will then make 'recommendations' to coastal states, and limits established by a coastal state on the basis of the recommendations are 'final and binding' (Article 76(8)). In October 2004, Denmark announced that it would carry out a hydrographic survey of Greenland's northern continental shelf, which may extend as far as the North Pole. If so, this could lead to difficult delimitation problems with other states with territory in the area.[26]

Construction of artificial islands and other installations in the EEZ or on the continental shelf

The coastal state has the exclusive right to authorise and regulate the construction, operation and use of artificial islands, installations and structures (such as oil drilling rigs) in its EEZ or on its continental shelf (Articles 60 and 80). It also has exclusive jurisdiction over them. Notice must be given of construction, and various safety measures must be taken. Safety zones up to 500 metres in extent may be established. Artificial islands, installations and structures do not possess the status of islands, have no territorial sea and their presence does not affect delimitation.

Delimitation

A delimitation[27] problem arises only when the claims to territorial seas, EEZs or continental shelves of two or more states overlap. The delimitation of maritime boundaries is a fertile ground for disputes between states. Many are resolved by negotiation,[28] others by referring the dispute to an international court or arbitral tribunal. The cases raise complex issues of law and fact, the facts naturally being unique in each case. This is therefore not the place to attempt a detailed survey of the principles. Any

[24] See Annex II to the Convention, and the CLCS website, www.un.org/Depts/los/clcs/.
[25] In 2001, a meeting of the states parties decided to extend the ten-year period for those states (mostly developing) for which the Convention entered into force before 13 May 1999. For them the period begins on that date: SPLOS/72 (www.un.org/Depts/los/).
[26] See p. 361 below on the Arctic.   [27] See p. 34 above as to the meaning.
[28] See the Denmark–UK Agreement on the Maritime Delimitation of the Area between the Færoes and the United Kingdom, UKTS (1999) 76.

state that has a delimitation problem will have to take advice from the legal advisers in its foreign ministry, and they will probably need the help of hydrographers and outside public international lawyers with expertise in this arcane subject. We will therefore merely outline the main points.

Territorial sea

In the case of *opposite* states (i.e facing each other), the usual practice is to draw a median line – a line equidistant from the shores of each state. When the states are *adjacent* (next to each other), the land boundary may be extended outwards in the same direction, or, where the land boundary meets the sea, a line may be drawn perpendicular to the general direction of the coast, or the line of latitude at that point may be continued outwards. But these are only general indicators of possible solutions; and offshore islands and other special features may require special treatment (see Article 15). In practice, states, and international courts and tribunals, seek an equitable solution, the matter typically being complex and with no 'legally correct' answer.

EEZ and continental shelf

Articles 74 and 83 lay down identical rules for the delimitation of the EEZ and the continental shelf between states with opposite or adjacent coasts. First, the states must seek to agree the delimitation, which should represent an equitable solution, and most delimitations have been done this way. Secondly, pending agreement, the states should enter into provisional arrangements of a practical nature. Sometimes, these are long lasting and provide for co-operation between states in the exploitation of oil and gas reserves or fish stocks off their coasts in an area that straddles the likely boundary. Such co-operative arrangements (unitisation agreements)[29] can also be made where the boundary has been delimited. Thirdly, if agreement cannot be reached within a reasonable time, the states must resort to the dispute settlement procedure of the Convention.[30] Given that the rules contain only one substantive principle, equity, the way in which this is applied will depend on state practice, judicial and arbitral decisions, and the particular facts of the case. There is a distinct trend

---

[29] See the Australia–Timor Leste Unitisation Agreement of 6 March 2003. www. timorseaoffice.gov.tp/iua.htm
[30] See p. 323 below.

for the same boundary line to be drawn for the continental shelf and the EEZ, deviations from a common line being made only to take account of special circumstances.

Delimitation is a lengthy and complex process. One normally starts by drawing a median line. One then considers whether there are (largely geographical) circumstances which suggest that to delimit on the basis of the median line would be inequitable. Such circumstances include a coast with an exceptional configuration (shape) or offshore islands. If an offshore island is small it will not be taken fully into account in any modification to the median line. However, if the opposite coasts of two states are considerably different in length, a median line drawn between them is likely to produce a substantial disparity between the ratio of the coastlines to each other and the ratio of the continental shelves attaching to each coast. The boundary will then be adjusted so that the ratio between each state's coastline and its continental shelf is not unreasonably disproportionate. But, when a small island is a state in itself, or an overseas territory, it will usually be regarded as generating its own, full continental shelf.

The Area

Whereas most of UNCLOS is based on the 1958 Geneva Conventions on the Law of the Sea and established or emerging customary international law, Part XI, on the 'Area', created entirely new law. It was effectively amended in 1994 by the Agreement on the Implementation of Part XI of UNCLOS ('Implementation Agreement').[31] The term 'Area' was chosen to describe the sea-bed and ocean floor and its subsoil that is not part of the continental shelf of any state. In simple terms, the Area is the *deep* seabed. It is important because parts of it (mostly in the Pacific and Indian Oceans) are rich in mineral nodules (lumps), manganese in particular. The Area and its resources are declared by the Convention to be the 'common heritage of mankind'. They are therefore not subject to any claims to, or exercise of, sovereignty or sovereign rights, although that does not affect the status of the waters (or the airspace above them) that lie over the Area. All rights in its mineral resources (including oil and gas) are vested in mankind as a whole, on whose behalf the International Sea-Bed Authority acts. The Authority organises and controls the exploitation of the mineral resources in the Area.

---

[31] 1836 UNTS 42 (No. 31364); ILM (1994) 1309; UKTS (1999) 82.

All parties to the Convention are members of the Authority, which is based in Jamaica. The Assembly of the Authority consists of representatives of all the Convention parties, who elect the 36 members of the executive organ of the Authority, the Council. Within the general policies established by the Assembly, the Council establishes the specific policies of the Authority. The Enterprise is the organ of the Authority empowered to engage in mining in the Area, but only by means of joint ventures with companies. Since commercial exploitation of the Area is unlikely in the foreseeable future, such limited functions of the Enterprise that need to be carried out at present are done by the Secretariat of the Authority.[32]

The high seas

The high seas are all parts of the sea that are not within an EEZ, the territorial sea, internal waters or archipelagic waters (Article 86). No state may subject any part of the high seas to its sovereignty (Article 89). All states, including land-locked states, enjoy the freedoms of the high seas, of which six are listed in the Convention. They are not absolute, but must be exercised with due regard for the interests of other states in their exercise of the same freedoms (Article 87).

Freedom of navigation

The right for ships flying the flag of a state[33] to sail on the high seas (Article 90) is a cardinal principle of international law. The flag state has *exclusive* jurisdiction over ships on the high seas flying its flag (Article 92(1)), subject to some limited exceptions.

Piracy

Piracy is also a modern, and growing, phenomenon. The Piracy Reporting Centre of the International Maritime Bureau (IMB) of the International Chamber of Commerce recorded 325 pirate attacks in 2004, 30 per cent in Indonesian waters, especially the Strait of Malacca through which a quarter of the world's shipping passes. Murders were up from twenty-one in 2003 to thirty in 2004.[34] International law has for centuries treated

---

[32] For details of the regime once commercial exploitation begins, see Churchill and Lowe, *The Law of the Sea*, 3rd edn, Manchester, 1999, pp. 238–53.

[33] As to the nationality of ships, see p. 316 below.

[34] See www.icc-ccs.org/prc/services.php. The IMB should not be confused with the IMO.

pirates as international outlaws subject to the jurisdiction of any state.[35] Piracy is now defined as any illegal act of violence or detention committed, for *private* ends, by the crew or passengers of a *private* ship or aircraft on the high seas against *another* ship or aircraft, or against persons or property on board it (Article 101).[36] The crew of any warship may board any ship if there are reasonable grounds to suspect that it is engaged in piracy (the so-called right of visit) and, if that proves to be so, they may seize the ship and arrest the pirates. They can then be tried in the courts of the warship's state (Articles 105, 107 and 110).

Slave trading

Similarly, the crew of any warship can board any ship if there are reasonable grounds to suspect that it is engaged in the slave trade (Article 110(1)(b)). However, the flag state of the warship can only report its findings to the flag state of the ship; it cannot seize the ship or prosecute the crew.

Unauthorised broadcasting

This consists of radio or television broadcasting to the general public from a ship on the high seas contrary to international regulations. Any person engaged in it may be prosecuted by the flag state of the ship concerned, the state of which the person is a national, any state where the transmissions can be received, or any state where authorised transmissions are being interfered with. Any such state may seize the ship and its broadcasting apparatus on the high seas and arrest the persons concerned (Articles 109 and 110(1)(c)).

Drug trafficking

Drug trafficking is *not* yet an exception. Although Article 108 requires states to co-operate in the suppression of the illicit carriage of narcotic drugs by ships on the high seas, it does not authorise states to take action against foreign ships. However, it does permit a state which believes that a ship flying its flag is engaged in such traffic to request the help of other states. Such a request naturally signifies the consent of the requesting state to the action requested. The request can be made *ad hoc* or under a treaty. A UK–US treaty of 2000[37] authorises the reciprocal interdiction

---

[35] See p. 269 above.
[36] These criteria mean that in most cases the act cannot be regarded as, for example, ship-jacking (see p. 287 above (Rome Convention)).
[37] UKTS (2001) 2.

(stop and search) in the Caribbean, the Gulf of Mexico and Bermuda of their respective flag vessels suspected of being engaged in drug trafficking, and ultimately their seizure. Other states have concluded similar bilateral treaties.

It is not only drug trafficking for which consent can be given by the flag state for its ships to be interdicted on the high seas; it can consent in respect of any matter, arms smuggling being an obvious example. On 21 December 2001, British forces stopped, boarded and searched a merchant ship, the *Nisha*, registered in St Vincent and the Grenadines, while it was on the high seas. Intelligence had indicated that it might have weapons of mass destruction (WMD) on board, although nothing was found. The action had been authorised in advance by the flag state.

Proliferation Security Initiative

In March 2003, in response to the threat from the proliferation of WMD, certain states agreed to participate under US leadership in the Proliferation Security Initiative (PSI). There are now over sixty states participating. The PSI is not a treaty-based scheme, although it builds upon the Statement of the President of the UN Security Council of 31 January 1992[38] that the proliferation of WMD is a threat to international peace and security. The aim is to impede and stop the trafficking of WMD, their delivery systems and related materials by states or non-state actors engaged in or supporting WMD proliferation programmes. The principal means is the stopping and searching by a participant state or states of shipping suspected of carrying WMD cargoes, but only when this would be consistent with international law, for example, of own flag vessels anywhere and of foreign flag vessels in the participant's ports, territorial sea or contiguous zone (if any), or otherwise with the consent of the foreign state. So far Ship Boarding Agreements have been signed by the United States with Liberia, the Marshall Islands and Panama.[39]

Special zones

Although the high seas are reserved for peaceful purposes (Article 88), this does not mean that force cannot be used on the high seas, provided it is lawful under rules of general international law.[40] Practice firings or

---

[38] S/23500. See also UNSC Res. 1540 (2004).
[39] See generally www.state.gov/t/np/c10390.html and www.warshipsifr.com/pages/huntForWMD.html. Liberia and Panama have numerous ships flying their flags.
[40] See p. 10 above.

naval exercises may also be conducted on the high seas. For this purpose, the state or states involved may issue warnings to shipping generally not to enter the zone where the activity will be carried out. The Convention does not authorise or prohibit such warnings, but, provided they are not too extensive or prolonged, they are in most cases accepted.

Hot pursuit

The right of hot pursuit of a foreign ship by a ship or aircraft for the purpose of arresting it is not a real exception to the freedom of navigation. It is rather an extension of the rights of the coastal state, provided it has 'good reason to believe' that the ship has violated its laws or regulations. So long as the pursuit is begun when the ship is still within internal waters, archipelagic waters, territorial sea or contiguous zone of the coastal state, it can be continued outside so long as the pursuit has not been interrupted (Article 111). It will probably not be interrupted merely by another ship taking over the pursuit. If the order to stop is received when the suspect ship is within the territorial sea or the contiguous zone, the pursuing ship does not also have to be in the territorial sea or the contiguous zone. But if the foreign ship is within the contiguous zone, it may not be pursued unless there has been a violation of the rights for the protection of which the zone was established. The right of hot pursuit applies equally to violations in the EEZ or on the continental shelf, including in safety zones around continental shelf installations, of the laws or regulations of the coastal state applicable in those areas.

The order to stop must be given by a visual or auditory (including radio) signal that can be seen or heard by the foreign ship. Only such force as is necessary and reasonable may be used to effect an arrest. The right of hot pursuit ceases as soon as the ship enters the territorial sea of its own state or a third state. Hot pursuit may only be exercised by warships or military aircraft, or other ships or aircraft clearly marked and identifiable as being on government service and authorised to that effect. The right of hot pursuit is developing to meet the dangers posed by drug trafficking and other modern scourges.[41]

Other high seas freedoms

The other freedoms of the high seas are listed in Article 87(1).

---

[41] See Churchill and Lowe, pp. 214–15.

Freedom of overflight

The aircraft, civil and military, of all states are free to fly in the airspace above the high seas and EEZs, subject only to such rules as are imposed by international law. In the case of civil aircraft, the governing treaty is the Chicago Convention 1944 and the rules promulgated under it by the International Civil Aviation Organization (ICAO).[42]

Freedom to lay submarine cables and pipelines

Like the other freedoms, this so-called right of immersion must be exercised 'with due regard for the interests of other states' in their exercise of the freedoms, and also with due regard for rights under the Convention with respect to activities in the Area. Thus, when laying a cable or pipeline, due regard must be had to existing cables and pipelines and to the need for them to be repaired (Article 79(5)). There are provisions regarding damage to cables or pipelines by ships or submarines, and damage to cables or pipelines by the laying or repairing of other cables and pipelines (Articles 113–114).

Freedom of fishing

This freedom (Article 116) is now subject to various constraints in the interests of the conservation and management of the marine living resources (see pp. 319–22 below).

Freedom of scientific research

There is a general right to conduct scientific research in the high seas, except that in the Area it must be done in conformity with the rules governing the Area (Articles 256–257).

Nationality of ships

Apart from certain exceptions,[43] on the high seas a state can exercise jurisdiction only over ships of its own nationality; no other state may arrest or detain its ships, even for the purpose of investigation (Article 97). Therefore, if a ship is involved in a collision or other navigational incident on the high seas, only its flag state, or the state of nationality of the master or other person in the service of the ship, may exercise criminal or disciplinary jurisdiction over them.

---

[42] See further p. 345 below.   [43] See pp. 312 *et seq* above.

Most states have a register of ships entitled to fly their flag. A ship has the nationality of the state whose flag it is entitled to fly. There must be a 'genuine link' between the ship and the state (Article 91). Unfortunately, such a link is often tenuous (flag of convenience), and thus the amount of actual control that the state exercises may be slight. A ship must not sail under more than one flag, or change its flag during a voyage or while in a port of call, unless it is the result of a real transfer of ownership or registry. A ship that sails under more than one flag is assimilated to a ship without nationality (Article 92). If there are reasonable grounds for suspecting that a ship on the high seas has no nationality, it may be boarded by any warship (Article 110(1)(d)). If the ship is found to be carrying narcotic drugs destined for the state of the warship, it can probably be arrested and persons on board prosecuted in that state. If a ship is flying a foreign flag, or refusing to show its flag, and there are reasonable grounds for suspecting that it is of the same nationality as the warship, the warship may board it (Article 110(1)(e)). If it is found to be wrongly flying the same flag as the warship, it may be seized and taken to a port of the flag state for prosecution.

Warships and ships used only on government non-commercial service

The following paragraphs deal only with the law applicable in peacetime Under Article 29, a warship is:

> a ship belonging to the armed forces of a state bearing the external marks distinguishing such ships of its nationality, under command of an officer duly commissioned by the government of the state and whose name appears in the appropriate service list or its equivalent, and manned by a crew which is under regular armed forces discipline.

The ship does not have to be owned by the flag state (note 'belonging'), provided it fulfils all the criteria; ships chartered for the purpose of transporting troops and under naval command are warships.

In peacetime, a warship may carry out various civil duties in support of the government of the flag state, including enforcing fisheries and anti-pollution laws. On the *high seas*, a warship is comparable to a floating piece of territory of the flag state, since it has complete immunity from the jurisdiction of any other state (Article 95).[44] This applies also in a

---

[44] State immunity in other cases is not usually absolute: see p. 159 above. State immunity should not be confused with diplomatic immunity, or 'diplomatic' clearance (see p. 318 below).

foreign EEZ, although whether a warship may test weapons or conduct manoeuvres there is disputed.[45] Where there is a right of transit passage through *international straits*,[46] this is enjoyed by all ships, and thus includes warships. In such straits, submarines do not have to navigate on the surface. But, when in the *territorial sea* of another state, submarines and other underwater vehicles must navigate on the surface and show their flag (Article 20). Whether a warship enjoys the right of innocent passage through the territorial sea is not agreed. Although Russia, the United Kingdom, the United States and other significant naval powers assert that warships do have that right, some forty states require prior authorisation. In such cases, this is generally sought and normally granted. If a warship does not comply with the laws and regulations of the coastal state concerning passage, it can be required to leave the territorial sea immediately (Article 30). If it does not do so, the coastal state can use reasonable force to remove it.

Since a state can refuse entry to its *ports* to a foreign warship, clearance must be sought by the flag state. This is known as 'diplomatic' clearance since it is done through the diplomatic channel. But, once in the port or other internal waters of the foreign state, the warship continues to enjoy *complete* immunity from the jurisdiction of that state. The vessel remains under the exclusive control of its commander; it may not be entered or persons or property removed from it without his permission. No criminal or civil proceedings may be taken against the vessel or persons on board.[47] Subject to any contrary provisions of an applicable visiting forces agreement,[48] members of the crew who are on shore on *official* business are under the exclusive jurisdiction of the flag state, although they can be forcibly removed to the ship by the local authorities. If ashore on personal business, they can be arrested, prosecuted or sued like anyone else.[49]

As with warships, *foreign governmental ships operated for non-commercial* purposes enjoy state immunity, but determining whether the purpose is non-commercial may not be easy to do. As with any question of state immunity, the position will depend to a large extent on the precise circumstances and the law of the state where the question has arisen.[50]

---

[45] See Churchill and Lowe, pp. 426–7.
[46] See p. 306 above. Other straits are governed either by the rules applicable to the territorial sea or by special treaty regimes.
[47] Cf. p. 300 above.   [48] See p. 174 above.
[49] See generally Oppenheim, pp. 1167–70.   [50] See pp. 171–2 above.

Land-locked and geographically disadvantaged states

A state with no sea coast is land-locked. There are forty-two such states, varying from the small but rich (Switzerland), to the large but poor (Ethiopia). But both have fleets of merchant ships, which enjoy the same rights in the territorial waters, contiguous zones and EEZs of other states, and freedom of navigation on the high seas as all other states. Land-locked states may also exercise the freedom to fish, conduct scientific research, overfly outside territorial waters, and lay cables and pipelines, but not construct artificial islands or other offshore installations (Article 87). Land-locked states do have freedom of transit through states that lie between them and the sea for the passage of persons, goods and means of transport, subject to agreements with the transit states (Article 125). Special, complex and somewhat limited provisions are made for land-locked states, and geographically disadvantaged states, to have access to marine resources.[51]

Fishing

Fishing is a large and vitally important industry. The rules governing it vary depending on whether the fishing takes place in internal waters or the territorial sea, in an EEZ or an exclusive fishing zone (EFZ), or on the high seas.

In internal waters and the territorial sea

Since both the internal waters and the territorial sea of a state are part of its territory, fishing vessels of other states have no right to fish there without the agreement of the coastal state. Such agreements are rare, the most celebrated being the Common Fisheries Policy of the European Community. Under this scheme, fishing vessels registered in one member state have, subject to the detailed rules laid down by the Community, the right to fish in the territorial seas of the other member states. This right does *not* extend to the overseas territories of member states.

In EEZs (and EFZs)[52]

Although within its EEZ a coastal state has sovereign rights over the fish stocks, it has an international duty to conserve those stocks. The coastal

---

[51] Churchill and Lowe, pp. 435–40.
[52] If a state does not wish to declare an EEZ as such, it may establish an exclusive fishing zone (EFZ) for the regulation of fishing up to 200 nautical miles from its coast, as the UK has done.

state will therefore determine, usually on a seasonal or annual basis, how much of each species may be caught in its EEZ (in fisheries jargon, the total allowable catch, or TAC). When its own fishermen cannot take all the TAC, the coastal state has a duty to allow other states to fish for it in its EEZ. But the coastal state has a large degree of discretion in calculating the TAC and as to who should be given access to any surplus. Many bilateral agreements have been concluded to allow for access, subject to reciprocal treatment, payments or licence conditions. Since the member states of the European Community, having transferred competence to it with regard to the conservation and management of sea fishing resources, the relevant rules are adopted by the Community – although enforced by the member states – and it is the Community which negotiates (by means of the European Commission) and concludes agreements on fishing in the EEZs of third states or within competent international organisations.[53]

If a foreign fishing vessel is suspected of breaching the regulations of the coastal state governing fishing in its EEZ, the state may enforce them by boarding, inspecting and arresting the vessel and subsequent prosecution (Article 73). The flag state must be promptly notified of an arrest, and the vessel and crew released promptly once a reasonable bond or other security has been lodged. Penalties for breaches of regulations must not include imprisonment. If there is a dispute between the detaining state and the flag state about the detention, it can be submitted to an international court or tribunal (Article 292).[54] Force may be used against a fishing vessel only if in the particular circumstances it is reasonable and proportionate.[55]

On the high seas

The Convention has little to say about fishing on the high seas. Article 116 states that all states have the right for their nationals to fish on the high

---

[53] Statement by the EC on signature of UNCLOS: see *UN Multilateral Treaties*, Ch. XXI.6, 'Declarations'; UKTS (1999) 179.

[54] See Case No. 2, *The M/V Saiga (No. 2) (St. Vincent and the Grenadines v. Guinea)*, decided by the International Tribunal for the Law of the Sea, ILM (1998) 364 and 1202; 110 ILR 736; www.itlos.org; and Case No. 8, *The Grand Prince (Belize v. France)*, 125 ILR 272. In Case No. 11, *The Volga (Russia v. Australia)*, ITLOS decided in 2002 that Articles 73(2) and 292 did not permit the inclusion of non-financial conditions in a security to obtain release of the vessel.

[55] See *The I'm Alone*, 1935 (7 ILR 203), *The Red Crusader*, 1962 (35 ILR 485), *The M/V Saiga (No. 2)* (Note 55 above), para. 156, and Article 22(1)(f) of the Fish Stocks Agreement (n. 58 below).

seas, subject to (a) treaty obligations, (b) the rights of coastal states in respect of straddling stocks and highly migratory species (see below), and (c) the duty to take measures, either nationally or in co-operation with other states, to conserve fish stocks. This duty is elaborated somewhat by the general principles in Articles 118–119, but co-operation depends on the effectiveness of regional fisheries commissions for the conservation and management of marine living resources.

Shared and straddling stocks and highly migratory species

Fish are notorious for not respecting territorial limits. A species will often migrate between two EEZs ('shared stocks') or between one or more EEZs and the high seas ('straddling stocks'). When two or more EEZs share the same stock or an associated stock, the states have an obligation to seek agreement on measures to ensure the conservation and development of the stock (Article 63(1)). There are several agreements for this purpose under which TACs are agreed annually on a bilateral or a multilateral (regional fisheries commission) basis.[56]

The most important highly migratory species of fish is tuna. Article 64 of the Convention and the Straddling and Highly Migratory Fish Stocks Agreement 1995[57] together provide that, where the species is found in an EEZ, the coastal state and other states fishing in the EEZ or on the high seas beyond it have a duty to co-operate in the conservation and management of the species.

Other highly migratory species include *anadromous species*, such as salmon, which spawn in fresh water before migrating to the sea (Article 66), and *catadromous species*, such as eels, which do the opposite (Article 67), and *marine mammals*.

Sedentary species

Sedentary species, as defined in Article 77(4), include molluscs, such as oysters, but there is doubt whether lobsters and crabs are included.[58] Sedentary species are part of the natural resources of the continental

---

[56] See pp. 333–6 below.
[57] 2167 UNTS 3 (No. 37924); ILM (1995) 1542; UKTS (2004) 19. Its *full* title is thirty-seven words long. It is more usually known as the Fish Stocks Agreement or the Straddling Stocks Agreement. It entered into force on 11 December 2001.
[58] See Churchill and Lowe, pp. 285 and 320.

shelf and the coastal state has no duty to conserve them or allow foreign fishermen to harvest them.

Whales and other marine mammals

A coastal state is allowed by Article 65 to prohibit, limit or regulate the exploitation of marine mammals, such as whales and seals, in its EEZ more strictly than the Convention provides for other living resources. The International Whaling Commission (IWC) regulates whaling in all waters, but its measures apply only to its members, who can opt out of them. (For details on fisheries commissions and the IWC, see pp. 333–6 below.)

Wrecks

There is a lack of control over wrecks outside the territorial sea, although a wreck in the contiguous zone is assimilated to one found in the territorial sea, and the coastal state can require its approval to remove it. The rights of the owners of the wreck and the law of salvage[59] are unaffected (Article 303). But the coastal state has no jurisdiction over wrecked ships of foreign states or their nationals in the EEZ or on the continental shelf. The IMO is currently developing a convention on the removal of wrecks for consideration at a diplomatic conference, perhaps in 2006 but quite possibly later.

Underwater cultural heritage

Concern has been expressed at the need to protect certain prominent wrecks and their contents lying on the seabed. The liner *Titanic* is the most prominent example. The ferry *Estonia*, which sank in the Baltic Sea in 1994, is the subject of a treaty between Estonia, Finland and Sweden (to which other states can accede)[60] to protect the wreck, in particular

---

[59] When compensation is payable for assisting a ship in danger or saving it or its cargo. See now the IMO International Convention on Salvage 1989 (www.imo.org or UKTS (1996) 93), which entered into force in 1996 and now has forty-seven parties representing 36.33 per cent of world tonnage. It is intended to replace the Brussels Convention 1910 (UKTS (1913) 4; 212 CTS 187). The 1989 Convention goes further in providing that a salvager can be paid for preventing or minimising pollution even if it was unable to save the ship.

[60] 1890 UNTS 176 (No. 32189); with Additional Protocol 1996, UKTS (1999) 74, the United Kingdom having acceded.

victims' remains. On 2 November 2001, UNESCO adopted a Convention on the Protection of the Underwater Cultural Heritage.[61] It requires twenty ratifications to enter into force, and so far three states have ratified. It has been criticised by major maritime states, particularly over the exercise of jurisdiction, and so was not adopted by consensus but by eighty-five to four with fifteen abstentions, including the United Kingdom.

Protection of the marine environment

This topic, including pollution by wrecks, is covered at pp. 341–3 below.

Dispute settlement under the Convention

The International Tribunal for the Law of the Sea

Following the entry into force of the Convention in 1994, the International Tribunal for the Law of the Sea (ITLOS, or 'the Tribunal') was established in 1996 at Hamburg, Germany. The provisions on its composition and procedure are in Annex VI (also referred to as the Statute) to the Convention. It has no less than twenty-one judges serving nine-year, re-electable terms. Disputes may be submitted to the full Tribunal or to one of its chambers. The Tribunal has established two chambers of seven for fisheries and marine environmental disputes, respectively; a seabed disputes chamber of eleven; and a summary procedure chamber of five. The Tribunal may also form an *ad hoc* chamber to deal with a particular dispute if the parties so request. The Tribunal generally follows the procedure of the International Court of Justice, English and French being its official languages. As with the ICJ, the fount of all knowledge on the procedure and practice of the Tribunal is the Registrar, who should be consulted by any prospective litigant. In addition to Annex VI, the Tribunal has adopted detailed procedural Rules, as well as Guidelines on the preparation and presentation of cases.[62]

The Tribunal is open to all states parties to the Convention and entities referred to in Article 305(1)(c) to (f) of the Convention. These include international organisations that have become parties to the Convention in respect of matters on which competence has been transferred to them

---

[61] ILM (2002) 37 or see www.unesco.org. See Garabello and Scovazzi (eds.), *The Protection of the Underwater Cultural Heritage* (Leiden, 2003).

[62] See the Tribunal's excellent website, at www.itlos.org, for the Convention, basic documents and judgments.

by their member states, such as the European Community (see Annex IX). It has jurisdiction over any legal disputes concerning the interpretation or application of the Convention (Article 288(1) and Annex VI, Article 21) and the Implementation Agreement 1994.[63] It also has jurisdiction over any dispute under a treaty related to the purposes of the Convention submitted to it in accordance with that treaty (Article 288(2)), and for this purpose the parties to the dispute do not have to be parties to the Convention. For example, the Fish Stocks Agreement 1995 allows the parties to it to submit their disputes under it to the Tribunal.[64]

Means of dispute settlement

The provisions on the settlement of disputes in Articles 279–299 of the Convention and in Annexes V–VIII are hideously complex. The basic rules are:

(1) Any dispute between the parties about the Convention should be resolved by any peaceful means of their choice.
(2) A party to a dispute relating to the Convention may invoke any bilateral, regional or general settlement mechanism to which the parties are already bound and which applies to the dispute, the procedures of the Convention applying only if no settlement has been reached and the mechanism does not exclude recourse to Convention procedures.
(3) Parties may agree to conciliation under Annex V.
(4) If no settlement can be reached by any of these means, any party to the dispute may submit it to a compulsory procedure entailing binding decisions. For this purpose, a party to the Convention may at any time make a general declaration (which can be replaced or revoked) that it chooses one or more of the following means of settlement:
   (a) the Tribunal;
   (b) the International Court of Justice;
   (c) an arbitral tribunal constituted under Annex VII;
   (d) a special arbitral tribunal, constituted under Annex VIII, for disputes about fisheries, the marine environment, scientific research or navigation, including pollution.

---

[63] See n. 31 above.   [64] See Article 30, and n. 57 above.

If the parties to the dispute have both accepted the same procedure, it must be used, unless they agree otherwise; if the parties have not accepted the same procedure, the dispute may be submitted only to arbitration under Annex VII, unless they agree otherwise.

(5) A party to a dispute which is not covered by a declaration is deemed to have accepted arbitration under Annex VII.

(6) There are special provisions for disputes about activities in the Area to be decided by the Sea-Bed Disputes Chamber (Articles 186–191), to which not only states parties to the Convention, but also state enterprises, natural and legal persons, the International Sea-Bed Authority and the Enterprise, have access (Article 153(2)(b)).

The Tribunal can order legally binding provisional measures of protection. When a dispute is submitted to arbitration under Annex VII, any party to the dispute may request the Tribunal to prescribe provisional measures pending the constitution of the arbitral tribunal pursuant to Article 290(5) of the Convention. Four cases have been submitted to the Tribunal under this provision. There is also a special provision under which the Tribunal can order the prompt release of a vessel (Article 292).[65] Seven such cases have so far been dealt with. The Tribunal can also give advisory opinions (Convention, Articles 139(1), 159(10) and 191; Rules, Article 138).

In Resolution 55/7 of 2000, the UN General Assembly established a Trust Fund administered by the Secretary-General to help parties to the Convention to settle disputes through the Tribunal. The Fund is like that established for ICJ cases,[66] being financed by voluntary contributions from states. Applications for assistance from the Fund are considered by a panel of independent experts who make recommendations to the Secretary-General.[67]

The Tribunal began work only in 1996. Despite being relatively unknown and with a jurisdiction that competes with the ICJ and other established means of settlement, it has so far had fourteen cases. All but four were concerned with fisheries, two being about provisional measures in connection with maritime environmental disputes, the other two on

---

[65] Only available when the detaining state has not complied with specific provisions of UNCLOS for prompt release or upon the posting of a bond: see Articles 73, 220(7) and 226(1)(b) or (c).

[66] See p. 449, n. 83 below.

[67] Further information should be sought from the Office of the UN Legal Counsel or the Registrar of the Tribunal.

issues relating to the bunkering of vessels at sea, the nationality of ships, hot pursuit, the use of force at sea and claims for reparation. The Tribunal has delivered seven judgments and made twenty-six orders. Seventeen states parties have been involved.

Increasingly, Annex VII arbitrations (particularly maritime delimitation cases) are being held under the auspices of the PCA.[68]

---

[68] See p. 444 below.

16

International environmental law

Let it be borne in mind how infinitely complex and close-fitting are the
mutual relations of all organic beings to each other and to their physical
conditions of life.[1]

Birnie and Boyle, *International Law and the Environment*, 2nd edn, Oxford,
2002
Birnie and Boyle, *Basic Documents on International Law and the Environ-
ment*, Oxford, 1995 ('B&B Docs.')
Churchill and Lowe, *The Law of the Sea*, 3rd edn, Manchester, 1999
Burke, *The New International Law of Fisheries*, Oxford, 1994

The poet Philip Larkin famously said that sexual intercourse began in
1963.[2] He could have said something similar about the environment and
the 1970s. Although it has always been with us, only in that decade did
the environment truly emerge as an important issue, and international
environmental law (IEL) as a specialised subject of international law.
This chapter is headed '*International* environmental law' since much of
domestic environmental law is not enacted merely to implement treaties,
and indeed may be more advanced than IEL, which is almost entirely
derived from treaties. The subject matter can be controversial and an
area where NGOs, have been especially energetic.[3] But, because of the
sometimes widely differing views of states on what should be done to
protect the environment, the degree to which NGOs influence policy-
making at the international level can be exaggerated.

Environmental protection and the conservation of natural resources
necessarily compete with commercial interests, and a commercial element

---

[1] Charles Darwin, *On the Origin of Species*, London, 1859, Ch. IV, p. 80.
[2] Philip Larkin, *High Windows*, 1974, 'Annus Mirabilis'.
[3] The (ECE) Aarhus Convention 1998, 2161 UNTS 450 (No. 37770); ILM (1998) 999, requires
parties to provide to individuals and NGOs rights of access to information, participation
in decision-making and access to justice in environmental matters. It entered into force in
2001 and has thirty-six parties, including most large EC states.

is almost invariably present in any environmental dispute. The dispute between Ireland and the United Kingdom about the nuclear reprocessing plant at Sellafield in northwest England involves Irish environmental fears and British concern to protect a valuable industrial asset.[4] Neither industry nor commerce is *ipso facto* a threat to the environment. Since we live in an industrialised world, multilateral environmental treaties represent a compromise between the interests of industry and commerce and the protection of the environment, and therefore never entirely satisfy everyone. What is important is that the treaties are properly implemented, not only in law but also in fact. As with human rights treaties, implementation can vary greatly in practice.

The development of the subject has produced certain new concepts, such as the 'precautionary principle', 'polluter pays', and 'sustainable development'. Some of these phrases have entered everyday speech, 'sustainability' in particular being a mantra much loved by politicians. One must be careful to distinguish such concepts from principles of international law, such as the binding nature of treaties. Whether the concepts represent legal obligations depends on the extent to which they have been translated into treaty rules or applied by international courts and tribunals. At the moment they are for the most part no more than 'soft law'.[5] They are discussed below.

Like other specialised areas of international law, IEL is not self-contained. To understand IEL properly, one needs to see it as the application of international law to environmental problems. This requires a basic knowledge of general international law, and the law of treaties in particular. Although there are many treaties whose subject matter is clearly environmental, unlike several areas of international law there is no one multilateral treaty that forms either the basis of the subject, like the Chicago Convention on International Civil Aviation 1944, or contains the basic rules, like the UN Convention on the Law of the Sea 1982. To find IEL on any particular area one may have to examine several treaties, including some that may not immediately seem relevant to the environment. A treaty on any subject may include provisions that are concerned with the environment or are relevant to environmental issues. The parameters of the subject are therefore not well-defined.

A particular feature of IEL is the use of 'framework' treaties: multilateral treaties that provide a structure of principles that are elaborated by the

---

[4] See Churchill and Scott, 'The MOX Plant Litigation: The First Half-Life' (2004) ICLQ 643–76.
[5] See p. 11 above.

adoption later of detailed annexes, schedules or protocols or by national action. The Conventions on Climate Change and Biological Diversity of 1992 are prime examples (see below).

International organisations, in particular the UN and the UN specialised agencies, have played a major part in developing IEL and in promoting the use of consensus[6] as the basis for reaching agreement in international treaty negotiations. Given the need when negotiating an environmental treaty to balance competing interests to achieve a text that has a chance of being widely ratified, reaching consensus is vital to the effectiveness of the treaty. International organisations also play an important role in monitoring the implementation of the treaties.

What is the environment?

We all have our own concept of the environment, which can range from the weather to our next-door neighbours. Since IEL has developed quickly and without a coherent structure, there is no one definition. In each case, what is meant by 'the environment' must be gathered from the treaty concerned. Sometimes, a definition raises more questions than it answers. In the Protocol to the Antarctic Treaty on Environmental Protection 1991[7] the environment is defined to include 'the intrinsic value of Antarctica, including its wilderness and aesthetic values' – whatever that may mean in legal terms.[8]

There now follows a brief outline of the development of IEL, some of its more important concepts, and certain environmental treaties.

The development of international environmental law

IEL could be said to have begun in a small way with the *Trail Smelter* arbitral award in 1938.[9] Although there were a few environmental treaties in the 1940s and 1950s, mostly about fauna (whales, fish, birds and seals) and oil pollution, the start of the IEL era proper began with the Stockholm Declaration of Principles 1972, adopted by the UN Conference on the Human Environment (UNCHE).[10] Principle 21 largely reflects the *Trail*

---

[6] See p. 60 above on consensus.
[7] ILM (1991) 1460; UKTS (1999) 6; ATS (1998) 6; B&B Docs. 468. The title is clumsy: it is the Protocol that deals with the environment, not the Antarctic Treaty.
[8] An ILC draft shows the problem in defining the environment as including 'the characteristics of landscape' (ILC Report 2004, A/59/10, p. 148 or www.un.org/law/ilc/).
[9] 9 AD 315; (1939) AJIL 182 and (1941) AJIL 684. And see p. 344 below.
[10] B&B Docs. 1.

Smelter arbitration in confirming the sovereign right of a state to exploit its own resources pursuant to its environmental policies, but subject to its responsibility not to cause damage to other states.

Following UNCHE, the UN General Assembly established in 1972 the UN Environment Programme (UNEP), with its headquarters in Nairobi.[11] Although not a UN specialised agency, it has been effective in the adoption of environmental treaties and the development of IEL generally. The role of the Environmental Management Group (EMG), chaired by the UNEP Executive Director, is to enhance cooperation in environmental matters both within and beyond the UN system including the specialised agencies and the secretariats of multilateral environmental treaties. The EMG Secretariat is in Geneva.[12]

The Stockholm Declaration is not a treaty, and its other Principles are no more than general objectives to be followed up by the negotiation of treaties, several of which were concluded in the 1970s. Principle 11 states that environmental policies should not adversely affect the development potential of developing countries, so reflecting the fact that the developed world had become so only by despoiling its own environment. This was followed by UN declarations emphasising the freedom of developing countries to decide how to develop their economies. Only with the 'Brundtland Report' in 1987 did sustainable development become the new maxim.[13]

The UN Conference on Environment and Development (UNCED) produced the Rio Declaration on Environment and Development 1992.[14] Its twenty-seven principles on sustainable development attempt to balance the interests of developed and developing countries. Agenda 21 (a forty-chapter programme of action), and the Conventions on Climate Change and Biological Diversity (see below) were also adopted.

Concepts

The precautionary approach

Principle 15 of the Rio Declaration states:

> In order to protect the environment, the precautionary approach shall be applied by states according to their capabilities. Where there are threats of serious or irreversible damage, lack of full scientific certainty shall not be used as a reason for postponing cost-effective measures to prevent environmental degradation.

[11] www.unep.org.
[12] See www.unep.org (go to 'about UNEP', then 'UN Inter-Agency Cooperation').
[13] WCED, *Our Common Future*, Oxford, 1987.   [14] ILM (1992) 876; B&B Docs. 9.

It is also described as the 'precautionary *principle*'. Despite the use of mandatory language ('shall'), Principle 15 does not represent a principle of customary international law. Its scope and application are still unclear and it has not yet been endorsed as such by an international court or tribunal. It can be seen as an application of the principle of state responsibility in the context of *potential* environmental harm, and not only in the case of transboundary activities. But there are still many uncertainties. The possibility of harm must be foreseeable: but how foreseeable? And what is the degree of harm and how should a state respond? Nevertheless, it may be seen as a general principle that is relevant to interpreting and applying the customary law on state responsibility and risk prevention.[15] The precautionary approach has been followed in certain treaties. The Vienna Convention for the Protection of the Ozone Layer 1985, and its Montreal Protocol 1987, require the parties to limit the use of CFCs even before it had been proved conclusively that they cause damage to the ozone layer.[16] It is also included in the Fish Stocks Agreement 1995, Article 6 and Annex II,[17] and the Cartagena Protocol.[18]

The polluter pays

One constantly hears this principle misrepresented and referred to as if it were a widely accepted customary rule applicable in all circumstances. Principle 16 of the Rio Declaration states:

> National authorities should endeavour to promote the internalisation of environmental costs and the use of economic instruments, taking into account the approach that the polluter should, in principle, bear the cost of pollution, with due regard to the public interest and without distorting international trade and investment.

'Internalisation' is an economic term, defined by the OECD as the incorporation of costs as part of the internal economic structure, especially social costs resulting from the manufacture or use of a product. The qualified wording of Principle 16 shows that it is no more than a suggestion as to the economic policy that a state may follow when apportioning the cost of remedying pollution or other environmental damage so that the state does not have to bear an unfair share. Generally, each state has been left to

---

[15] See p. 410 below. [16] See further Birnie and Boyle, pp. 115–24 and p. 338 below.
[17] 2167 UNTS 3 (No. 37924); ILM (1995) 1542; UKTS (2004) 19. See also Churchill and Lowe, p. 309.
[18] See p. 338 below.

decide what policy to follow.[19] A fundamental problem is deciding who caused the pollution. When maritime pollution is caused by the escape of a cargo of oil, it could be the shipowner, the owner of the oil, a pilot or a navigation authority. There are therefore treaties where the costs of marine pollution have been allocated in advance.[20] The *Rhine Arbitration (Netherlands/France)* (2004) held that the principle is not part of international law.[21] It may, however, be influential in the development of environmental treaties.

Sustainable development

Sustainable development is at present a leading concept of IEL, yet its nature is such that it cannot be usefully defined.[22] It is like 'reasonable': only meaningful when applied to the facts of a particular case. The basic concept is that development (industrial, agricultural, communications, etc.) is not inherently bad, but that one should take account of its effect on the environment. Industry should exploit (using the word non-pejoratively) a natural resource in a way that allows the resource to regenerate, not to be destroyed. Fish are a good example. Over-fishing has become so bad that in some areas what was once a common fish has now become a scarce delicacy. This has various implications for consumers, human health and the fishing industry. The dangers were appreciated long ago in the 1958 Convention on Fishing and Conservation of the Living Resources of the High Seas, which defined fish conservation as 'the aggregate of the measures rendering possible the *optimum* sustainable yield'.[23] Later, with decolonisation and the acknowledgment that developing countries also need to be able to exploit their natural resources and develop industry, there came a tension between developed and developing countries as to what is sustainable. The UN Convention on the Law of the Sea 1982 speaks of '*maximum* sustainable yield'.[24] ECOSOC established the Commission on Sustainable Development in 1993, but it is largely ineffective.[25]

Environmental impact assessment (EIA)

EIA began in 1969 as a requirement of US federal law, and has been followed in the laws of many states. Its purpose is to discover at an early stage

---

[19] See Birnie and Boyle, pp. 92–5.   [20] See p. 342 below.
[21] See www.pca-cpa.org (go to 'Arbitrations – recent').
[22] Birnie and Boyle, pp. 40–7 and Ch. 3.
[23] 559 UNTS 285 (No. 8164); UKTS (1966) 39. See Article 2.
[24] Article 61(3).   [25] See Birnie and Boyle, pp. 51–2.

whether a proposed activity may have an adverse effect on the environment and, if so, whether it should be authorised. Principle 17 of the Rio Declaration states:

> Environmental impact assessment, as a national instrument, shall be undertaken for proposed activities that are likely to have significant adverse impact on the environment and are subject to a decision of a competent national authority.

Thus, EIA is a national procedure. There is no general obligation in international law to undertake EIA, except possibly when there may be a risk to the environment of other states or to the marine environment. Internationally, EIA is required (though as a national process) mainly in treaties dealing with pollution of the marine environment from sea – or land-based sources.[26] Perhaps the broadest and most comprehensive provisions are in the Protocol to the Antarctic Treaty on Environmental Protection 1991.[27] Although the wording varies from treaty to treaty, generally the two main requirements are that there must be a proposed 'activity' (or 'project'), not merely general plans, and it must be foreseeable that the activity could have a 'significant' impact (not a minor or transitory impact). There is obviously much scope for a state to argue that a significant impact was not foreseeable; and to prove that a state has acted in bad faith may be difficult. In 1991, the UN Economic Commission for Europe (ECE) adopted the Convention on Environmental Impact Assessment in a Transboundary Context (the Espoo Convention).[28]

Whaling

Given that there are now some 200 multilateral treaties on, or touching on, the environment, only the most significant can be mentioned here. The first of these concerns whaling. The International Convention for the Regulation of Whaling (IWC) was adopted in 1946 and amended by a Protocol in 1956.[29] Its purpose was never to ban the hunting of whales. It was merely to reverse the process of the depletion of whale stocks by the establishment of a regime that would, in the words of the preamble to the IWC, 'provide for the proper conservation of whale stocks and thus make possible the orderly development of the whaling industry'. The IWC

---

[26] Birnie and Boyle, p. 132 and n. 394.   [27] See n. 7 above.
[28] 1989 UNTS 309 (No. 34028); ILM (1971) 802; B&B Docs. 31. It entered into force in 1997 and now has forty parties.
[29] See the consolidated text on the IWC Secretariat website, www.iwcoffice.org.

applies worldwide and now has sixty-six parties. The IWC Commission, whose members represent all the IWC parties, has a Secretariat, situated in Cambridge, England. The Commission meets at least once a year. It can by a three-quarters vote of the members (excluding abstentions and absences), adopt regulations for the conservation and utilisation of whale resources. A regulation becomes binding on all parties after ninety days. If a party objects to a regulation within that period, another period, of up to ninety days, is allowed for any other party also to object. Thereafter, the regulation becomes binding on all parties except those which objected.

The IWC allows a party to authorise its nationals to conduct whaling for scientific research, although the scale of such whaling by Japan has been criticised by other parties. In 1982, the Commission imposed a general moratorium on commercial whaling. It is not binding on Norway which lodged objections. At present, the Commission is almost evenly split between those who support the moratorium and those who do not. This may change as many more small states become parties, thus possibly making it easier to obtain a three-quarters majority to lift or modify the moratorium. Iceland withdrew from the IWC soon after the moratorium was established. When in 2001 it sought to become a party again, though with a reservation that would have enabled it to conduct commercial whaling, its accession was opposed by the moratorium states on dubious legal grounds. By a bare majority, it became a party again at a Special Commission Meeting in 2002 with a modified reservation.

Other fishing

The treatment of whales, considered majestic mammals by many, these days raises great emotion. It is not so for fish (or cows). The several regional regimes for the conservation of other marine living resources have the objective of preventing overfishing so that commercial fishing can continue for the benefit of both the fisherman and the consumer. They include the Northwest Atlantic Fisheries Organization (NAFO),[30] the Commission on the Conservation of Antarctic Marine Living Resources (CCAMLR),[31] and, more recently, the South East Atlantic Fisheries Organization.[32] Each attempts to manage and conserve stocks by adopting various measures that are legally binding on the member states, but has to rely upon them for their enforcement. They set annual total allowable

---

[30] See the NAFO Convention 1978 at www.nafo.ca.
[31] See p. 360 below.   [32] ILM (2002) 257 or www.mfmr.gov.na/seafo/seafo.htm.

catches (TACs) and close the fishing seasons or areas when the TACs have been reached, or allocate quotas; close the fisheries or areas for a whole season; specify minimum fishing net sizes; prohibit or regulate certain fishing methods, such as driftnets or long-lines; and co-ordinate scientific research. A member state can opt out of a particular measure. Despite enforcement being essentially national, it is helped by schemes for international observation and inspection under which fishing vessels of member states can carry an observer, or be boarded by an inspector, of another member state. Observers also have the ancillary function of collecting information, but do not usually have regulatory powers.

The main weakness of the commissions is that some member states do not take their obligations seriously enough or simply do not act in good faith.[33] The commissions have no legal power over non-member states and their fishermen; and decisions are often taken on political, rather than scientific, grounds. Fishing in the EEZs of EC states is subject to the EC Common Fisheries Policy, but some fish stocks are near to collapse due to serious over-fishing caused mainly by decisions taken for political reasons.[34]

A particularly damaging development is for members to ignore the practice of their nationals who avoid the measures by operating vessels flying the flag of non-members.[35] Measures to combat such problems include member states agreeing to prevent the landing or import of certain species, or species caught by prohibited methods (whether or not the fishing vessel flew the flag of a member state) and economic sanctions against non-members (retorsion).[36] In 1993, the FAO adopted the Agreement to Promote Compliance with International Conservation and Management Measures by Fishing Vessels on the High Seas (usually referred to as the Compliance Agreement).[37] Article III places responsibility on the parties to ensure that their flag vessels do not do anything that undermines international conservation and management measures. In particular, the

---

[33] See R. Rayfuse. 'The United Nations Agreement on Straddling and Highly Migratory Fish Stocks: A Case of Wishful Thinking?' (1999) *Australian YBIL* 253–78; R. Rayfuse, 'Enforcement of High Seas Fisheries Agreements: Observation and Inspection under the Convention on the Conservation of Antarctic Marine Living Resources' (2000) *International Journal of Marine and Coastal Law* 579–605; E. Molenaar, 'CCAMLR and Southern Ocean Fisheries' (2001) *International Journal of Marine and Coastal Law* 465–99.

[34] See Birnie and Boyle, pp. 661–3.

[35] See p. 316 above on flags of convenience.

[36] For an explanation of the term, see p. 425 below.

[37] ILM (1994) 968; B&B Docs. 645. It entered into force on 24 April 2003. The twenty-nine parties so far include Argentina, Chile, the EC, Japan, South Korea and the United States.

parties must not allow their flag vessels to fish on the high seas without their authorisation, and before granting it the flag state must be satisfied that, given the links between it and the vessel, it is able to exercise effective control over the vessel. The latter may, for example, be done by tracking the vessel by a satellite vessel monitoring system (VMS) and by robust enforcement methods such as speedy prosecution of violations of fishing licences and the confiscation of catches and gear. The effectiveness of the Agreement will depend largely on whether flags-of-convenience states become parties, and whether they then take their obligations seriously. The problems are still very much with us.

The North-East Atlantic Fisheries Commission (NEAFC) and NAFO have become largely redundant due to the declaration of EEZs in their areas, their regulatory powers now being limited to high seas fisheries. Effective co-operation between the coastal states in respect of stocks that straddle their EEZs is poor.

The Fish Stocks Agreement (or Straddling Stocks Agreement) 1995[38] has detailed provisions designed to deal with the problem of straddling stocks. It only came into force on 11 December 2001, and now has fifty-two parties, but so far this does not include some important fishing states such as Japan and South Korea. The two most effective regional fisheries commissions for this purpose are the relatively new Commissions for the Conservation of Southern Bluefin Tuna (CCSBT)[39] and for the Indian Ocean Tuna (IOTC).[40]

Wildlife

Other treaties have as their aim the protection of nature (including other wildlife which is a source of food) for other reasons, including aesthetic.

The (Ramsar) Convention on Wetlands of International Importance 1971[41] is concerned with the preservation of wetlands. Parties designate wetlands within their territory for inclusion in a 'List of Wetlands of

[38] Agreement for the Implementation of the Provisions of UNCLOS relating to the Conservation and Management of Straddling Fish Stocks and Highly Migratory Fish Stocks 1995, 2167 UNTS 3 (No. 37924); ILM (1995) 1542; UKTS (2004) 19.
[39] See www.ccsbt.org. The CCSBT was adopted by Australia, Japan and New Zealand on 10 May 1993 and entered into force in 1994, 1819 UNTS 359 (No. 31155). South Korea is now also a member.
[40] See www.iotc.org.
[41] 996 UNTS 245 (No. 14583); ILM (1972) 963; UKTS (1976) 34; TIAS 11084; B&B Docs. 447. For the current amended text, see www.ramsar.org.

International Importance' on account of their international significance in terms of ecology, botany, zoology, limnology (study of freshwater phenomena) or hydrology. Each party is required to promote the conservation of wetlands and waterfowl by establishing nature reserves. The parties meet regularly to consult. There are 143 parties.

The Convention on International Trade in Endangered Species of Wild Flora and Fauna 1973 (CITES)[42] is much better known from media reports on the seizure of illegal imports of elephant tusks, etc. It prohibits or regulates trade in endangered species and, to a certain extent, trade with non-parties. For this purpose, the Convention lists the endangered species in three appendices, which are amended from time to time: Appendix I lists species threatened with extinction, trade in which can be authorised only in exceptional circumstances; Appendix II lists species which, although not necessarily now threatened with extinction, may become so unless trade in them is subjected to strict regulation; and Appendix III lists all species that any party identifies as being subject to its regulation to prevent or restrict exploitation, but for which it needs the co-operation of other parties in the control of trade. Permits are required for any trade in any species included in Appendices I, II or III, although the terms vary according to the Appendix. Trade sanctions imposed by CITES parties have proved effective in enforcing the Convention against parties and non-parties. It has 167 parties.

Biological diversity

The United Nations Convention on Biological Diversity 1992[43] echoes the words of Darwin at the start of this chapter, although in more prosaic language, by defining 'biodiversity' as:

> the variability among living organisms from all sources including, *inter alia*, terrestrial, marine and other aquatic ecosystems and the ecological complexes of which they are part; this includes diversity within species, between species and of ecosystems.

'ecosystem' is defined as:

> a dynamic complex of plant, animal and micro-organism communities and their non-living environment interacting as a functional unit.

---

[42] 993 UNTS 243 (No. 14537); ILM (1973) 1085; UKTS (1976) 101; 27 UST 1087; TIAS 82249. For the current amended text, see www.cites.org.
[43] 1760 UNTS 9 (No. 30619); ILM (1992) 818; UKTS (1995) 51; B&B Docs. 390.

Previously, treaties had adopted a piecemeal approach, dealing with endangered species that are valuable for their own sake. The basic principle underlying the Convention is the recognition that, although conserving biodiversity is important for the survival of mankind, sustainable use of biological resources is permissible.

The Convention entered into force after eighteen months, and only two and a half years after it was adopted it already had 100 parties. By the end of 2004, it had no less that 188, although neither Timor Leste nor the United States are parties. Nevertheless, this remarkable achievement (on a par with the Rights of the Child Convention 1989)[44] was possible only because, like childhood, no state can today be seen to be against biodiversity and the Convention needed no (or only minimal) legislation. The Convention itself may therefore not be such a success. It does not place onerous legal obligations on the parties. The numerous compromises that had to be made resulted in requirements that are broad and vague, or carefully qualified. The Convention stresses that states remain in control of their biological resources and, where it calls for domestic action, a party's obligations are qualified at least eight times by the formula 'as far as possible and as appropriate'. The hard work of devising specific binding rules on all parties is left to the negotiation of protocols. The only protocol so far agreed, the Cartagena Protocol on Biosafety 2000, entered into force in 2003 and so far has 124 parties.[45] It is concerned with the possible damage that genetically modified organisms might do to biological diversity, particularly in transboundary movements. The United States considers that WTO rules must prevail over the Protocol and is not a party.[46]

The ozone layer and climate change

By the 1980s, states had become acutely aware of the damage that had been done to the ozone layer in the stratosphere by, in particular, the chlorofluorocarbons (CFCs) in aerosols and coolants. The Vienna Convention for the Protection of the Ozone Layer 1985[47] has few specific obligations, and was followed by the much more substantial Montreal Protocol on Substances that Deplete the Ozone Layer 1987,[48] which entered into force

---

[44] See p. 236, n. 23 above.
[45] 1760 UNTS 79 (No. 30619); ILM (2000) 1027; UKTS (2004) 17.
[46] See Birnie and Boyle, pp. 580–1 and 737–9.
[47] 1531 UNTS 324 (No. 26164); ILM (1987) 1529; UKTS (1990) 1.
[48] 1522 UNTS 3 (No. 26369); ILM (1987) 1541 and ILM (1989) 1301; UKTS (1990) 19.

two years later and now has 189 parties, including Brazil, China, the European Community, India, Russia and the United States. It requires the parties to reduce, and ultimately to eliminate, the production and consumption of certain ozone-depleting substances according to a timetable. Since developing states have so far not contributed much to ozone depletion, they are given more time to comply. The Protocol also bans the import from, or export to, non-parties of such substances. The terms of the Protocol and its annexes are extremely detailed and have been amended several; times.[49] European Community Regulation 91/594 prohibited the production of CFCs after 30 June 1997. The Protocol has so far been largely successful, and, if it continues to make progress, only forty years from now the hole in the ozone layer over Antarctica could be closed.

The UN Framework Convention on Climate Change 1992[50] now has 189 parties, including the United States. It deals with the much more intractable problem of the warming of the atmosphere (global warming) caused by 'greenhouse gases', being gases, such as carbon dioxide (CO_2), produced by the use of fossil fuels and released into the atmosphere, for example by motor vehicle exhausts. The 'ultimate objective' of the Convention is the 'stabilization of greenhouse gas concentrations in the atmosphere at a level that would prevent dangerous anthropogenic (of human origin) interference with the climate'. Unlike the Montreal Protocol, it does not seek to reverse a process that is intimately bound up with modern industrial and commercial development, but to stop it causing further unacceptable warming of the climate. The Convention, rather like the Ozone Layer Convention, lays down broad principles on which future measures should be based, in particular that developed states should take the lead.

So far, the only specific measure that has been adopted is the Kyoto Protocol 1997,[51] which sets individual emission limits and timetables for certain developed parties in respect of six greenhouse gases. A state can set off against its emissions those changes in land use or forestry activities that result in the removal of greenhouse gases (a forest can amount to a 'sink' by removing a greenhouse gas from the atmosphere). Furthermore, the Protocol enables two or more parties, by joint action, to fulfil their obligations by innovative means: aggregation of combined emissions; credit

---

[49] For an up-to-date version, see www.unep.org/ozone/pdfs/Montreal-Protocol2000.pdf.
[50] 1771 UNTS 1907 (No. 30822); ILM (1992) 849; UKTS (1995) 28. See www.unfccc.int/resource/convkp.html.
[51] UNTS (No. 30822); ILM (1998) 22.

against emissions for supporting projects to reduce emissions by another party; trade in emissions permits; and credits for funding projects of another party. The Protocol had been ratified by 151 states and the European Community. To enter into force, it needed fifty-five ratifications, including at least 55 per cent of the states whose aggregate carbon dioxide emissions for 1990 amount to 55 per cent of total emissions. Since emissions from Russia and the United States are such a large proportion of the total, in practice this needed at least one of them to ratify, which Russia did in 2004. The Protocol then entered into force on 16 February 2005. Without the United States, the Protocol's effectiveness will be that much less, though its approach remains controversial.

Nuclear material

The International Atomic Energy Agency (IAEA),[52] with headquarters in Vienna, is not a UN specialised agency, although it is part of the 'UN family' and has close links with the United Nations.

The new use of nuclear power was an early candidate for international action. The OECD Convention on Third Party Liability in the Field of Nuclear Energy 1960 (Paris Convention) is limited to the metropolitan territory of OECD members or associate countries which have always had the biggest concentration of nuclear installations. Its purpose is to harmonise the parties' legislation on liability for nuclear accidents, placing on the operator of a nuclear installation (reactor, factory, storage plant) absolute (but limited) liability, and establishes a common scheme for compensation. The 1960 Brussels Agreement Supplementary to the Paris Convention provides for state-funded compensation for a loss that exceeds the limited liability of the operator under the Paris Convention. Both Conventions have been extensively amended, most recently by a Protocol of 12 February 2004.[53]

The (Vienna) Convention on Civil Liability for Nuclear Damage 1963, concluded within the IAEA, closely follows the Paris Convention but was replaced by the (Vienna) Protocol on Civil Liability for Nuclear Damage 1997.[54] The Convention on Early Notification of a Nuclear Accident 1986[55] was adopted following the Chernobyl disaster. It requires a party

---

[52] www.iaea.org.
[53] For a consolidated text, see www.nea.fr/html/law/legal-documents.html.
[54] ILM (1997) 1462.
[55] 1457 UNTS 133 (No. 24643); ILM (1986) 1377; UKTS (1998) 1; B&B Docs. 300.

to notify immediately any state (not necessarily a party) which is or might be physically affected by a nuclear accident in its territory, or on a ship or aircraft on its register, from which a release of radioactive material occurs, or is likely to occur, if the material has entered, or may enter, the territory of another state and cause significant radiological safety concern. The Convention entered into force in 1986 and now has ninety-two parties, including most nuclear energy states. The Convention on Nuclear Safety 1994[56] does not materially add to the powers of the IAEA.

The marine environment

The forty-six Articles of UNCLOS devoted to this subject demonstrate the importance given to preventing pollution of the marine environment. As with other environmental matters, the rules are detailed and complex, and here one can only sketch in the principal points.[57] Most of the law is to be found in general provisions of UNCLOS and detailed provisions in numerous general, regional and bilateral treaties dating from the 1960s onwards. The most important general treaty is the International Convention for the Prevention of Pollution from Ships (MARPOL) adopted by IMO in 1973. It now has 130 parties representing 97 per cent of the world's shipping tonnage. This covers all types of intentional pollution of the sea by ships, except dumping of waste. The all-important annexes to it are frequently amended.[58] Regional treaties follow MARPOL.

UNCLOS lays down the rules under which such international standards can be enforced. Flag states have a duty to enact laws applicable to their flag ships for the prevention, reduction and control of pollution. These must embody at least generally accepted international rules and standards, such as those laid down by MARPOL Annexes I and II. Flag states have a duty to enforce the legislation wherever the infringement occurs (Article 217). Coastal states have certain powers to legislate for foreign ships in their territorial sea or EEZ. A coastal state has the right to arrest foreign ships for certain breaches of its anti-pollution laws in its territorial sea and EEZ (Article 220); otherwise the flag state can effect the arrest. A

---

[56] ILM (1994) 1518; UKTS (1999) 49; B&B Docs. 307. See Birnie and Boyle, pp. 461–3.
[57] For a detailed, but not exhaustive, account, see Churchill and Lowe, pp. 328–99. See also Birnie and Boyle, pp. 347–403.
[58] ILM (1973) 1319; UKTS (1983) 27; B&B Docs. 189. Given the frequent amendments to MARPOL, particularly its annexes, the best source is the regularly reprinted text of the treaty published by the IMO, available on its website, www.imo.org/imo/links/lnkstart.htm.

port state has wider powers over a foreign ship: when it is in its ports, the state can arrest and prosecute the ship for violation of its anti-pollution laws committed while in its territorial sea or EEZ (Article 220). It can also do so in respect of pollution of the high seas (Article 218). Moreover, if it is unseaworthy and therefore a threat to the marine environment, the port state can prevent it sailing (Article 219).

None of the above applies to warships or other state vessels on government, non-commercial service (Article 236).

Emergencies

If as the result of an incident at sea (collision, stranding etc.) a foreign ship is causing or is threatening to cause, major pollution a coastal state may in its territorial sea or EEZ, or even on the high seas, take such direct measures as may be necessary to prevent, mitigate or eliminate an imminent danger to its coastline.[59] In 1967, the oil tanker *Torrey Canyon* was stranded on the high seas off the United Kingdom spilling all its 120,000 tons of crude oil. The Royal Air Force bombed it. The International Convention on Oil Pollution Preparedness, Response and Co-operation 1990 provides for co-operation to deal with oil pollution incidents, including the sharing of costs.[60]

Liability

The International Convention on Civil Liability for Oil Pollution Damage 1969[61] was replaced in 1992 by a Convention bearing the same title.[62] It imposes liability on a shipowner if oil from his ship damages the territory, territorial sea or EEZ of a party. The liability is generally limited. The International Convention on the Establishment of an International Fund for Compensation for Oil Pollution Damage 1971[63] supplemented the 1969 Convention, but was replaced in 1992 by a Convention, again of

[59] See Article 221 and the International Convention relating to Intervention on the High Seas in Cases of Oil Pollution 1969, 970 UNTS 212 (No. 14049); ILM (1970) 25; UKTS (1975) 77, which also applies to the EEZ.
[60] 1891 UNTS 78 (No. 32194).
[61] 973 UNTS 3 (No. 14097); ILM (1970) 45; UKTS (1975) 106
[62] B & B Docs. 91; but see www.imo.org/imo/links/lnkstart.htm for the up-to-date text.
[63] 1110 UNTS 57 (No. 17146); ILM (1972) 284; UKTS (1978) 95.

the same name.[64] If the shipowner is not liable or is unable to pay in full, or the limit of liability is exceeded, compensation may be payable by the Fund. There are also treaties imposing strict liability for damage to the marine environment by hazardous and noxious substances and by radioactive material.[65]

Dumping

The Convention on the Prevention of Marine Pollution by the Dumping of Wastes and Other Matter 1972 (previously known as the 'London Dumping Convention', and now, as amended by a 1996 Protocol, known as the 'London Convention')[66] prohibits the dumping of waste at sea. The main exceptions are dredged materials, sewage sludge, fish-processing wastes, ships, and continental shelf oil and gas installations. Incineration of waste at sea is also prohibited

Hazardous wastes

The (Basel) Convention on the Control of Transboundary Movements of Hazardous Wastes and their Disposal 1989[67] is particularly successful, now having 165 parties, but not yet Afghanistan, Haiti or the United States. It covers most waste, with the exception of radioactive waste. If a party prohibits the import of hazardous waste, another party must not permit its export to that party. Even if a party has not prohibited the import, other parties must not permit export of the waste to that party if the latter has not given written consent to the specific import or if it does not have the capacity to dispose of the waste in an environmentally friendly manner. Illegal traffic in hazardous wastes is made a criminal offence. If wastes are illegally exported, the state of export must ensure that the wastes are taken back. If this is impracticable, the state of *export* must ensure that the wastes are disposed of properly.

---

[64] UKTS (1996) 87; B&B Docs. 107, but see www.imo.org/imo/links/lnkstart.htm for the up-to-date text.

[65] See Churchill and Lowe, pp. 361–3.

[66] ILM (1972) 1294 and ILM (1997) 7, but see www.imo.org/imo/links/lnkstart.htm for the up-to-date text.

[67] 1673 UNTS 126 (No. 28911); ILM (1989) 657; UKTS (1995) 100; B&B Docs. 322 or www.basel.int.

Liability for environmental damage

In the *Trail Smelter* case, Canada was held liable for damage in the United States caused by the fumes from a Canadian smelter.[68] This was only an application of the long-established international law principle of state responsibility.[69] Most treaties do not include anything about liability, the general principle being enough. However, in the case of international environmental damage, some treaties have attempted to set out expressly what constitutes damage and how it is to be assessed, what sort of liability should apply (absolute, strict or fault), and what remedy should be available (compensation, remedial work or restoration). The issues are highly charged, not least because a lot of money may be at stake. Success has been limited because damage to the environment is a much more complex matter than, say, loss of business or personal injury. Attempts to agree general principles of liability have met with only limited success (for example, with respect to Antarctica)[70] or have led to treaties that will never enter into force or will have few parties. Although the treaties on liability for maritime pollution and nuclear accidents (see above) are quite successful, devising and agreeing on liability regimes for other environmental damage has been much more difficult.[71] The Council of Europe's Convention on Civil Liability for Damage Resulting from Activities Dangerous to the Environment 1993[72] needs only three ratifications to bring it into force. By the end of 2004, it had received only nine signatures and no ratifications. In view of developments in the last ten years, it is most unlikely ever to enter into force. By the end of 2004, the 1999 Protocol to the Basel Convention on Liability and Compensation for Damage Resulting from the Transboundary Movement of Hazardous Wastes[73] had been signed by only thirteen states, and six (all developing countries) had ratified, twenty being needed to bring it into force. The 2001 ILC draft Articles on the Prevention of Transboundary Harm from Hazardous Activities are controversial and have not been adopted as a treaty.[74]

---

[68] See p. 329 above.   [69] See p. 410 below.   [70] See p. 358 below.
[71] See generally Birnie and Boyle, pp. 279–82.   [72] B&B Docs. 132; ILM (1993) 1228.
[73] See www.basel.int.   [74] Birnie and Boyle, pp. 106–7.

17

International civil aviation

An airline ticket to romantic places; and still my heart has wings.[1]

Cheng, *The Law of International Air Transport*, London, 1962
Matte, *Treatise on Air-Aeronautical Law*, Montreal, 1981
Gardiner, *International Law*, London, 2003, Ch. 10
Shawcross and Beaumont, *Air Law*, London, 1977 (includes the texts of
many treaties and legislation)
www.icao.int (includes the current status of most multilateral aviation
treaties)
www.iasl.mcgill.ca/airlaw/index.htm (for a specific collection of air law
instruments)

International civil aviation is not regulated in the same way as shipping. As
well as being quite different in character, air travel is a much newer form of
transport and has been regulated by treaty almost from the beginning. The
Chicago Convention on International Civil Aviation 1944 (in this chapter,
'the Convention')[2] provides the essential framework and established the
International Civil Aviation Organization (ICAO). The Convention has
188 parties.

(References to numbered Articles and annexes are to those of the Convention, unless otherwise indicated.)

International Civil Aviation Organization

The International Civil Aviation Organization (ICAO) is a UN Specialised
agency with headquarters in Montreal, Canada. Its general purpose is the
planning and development of international air navigation. It has wide and
comprehensive regulatory functions, especially with regard to the safety

---

[1] Holt Marvell, *These Foolish Things* (song, 1935).
[2] 15 UNTS (1948) 295 (No. 102); UKTS (1953) 8. The Convention has been amended
several times: see Shawcross and Beaumont, Vol. 2 or the (hard-to-navigate) ICAO, website,
www.icao.int.

of aircraft, although their implementation is for national aviation authorities. The ICAO Council adopts, by a two-thirds majority, International
Standards and Recommended Practices and Procedures. These are contained in eighteen detailed Annexes to the Convention, which take effect
unless a simple majority of states reject them within three months (Article 90).[3] The Standards are regarded as legally binding on the parties to
the Convention, although a party can depart from a Standard by notifying
ICAO.

Civil and state aircraft

The Convention governs only civil aircraft, that is, all aircraft other than
'state aircraft', which are defined as 'aircraft used in military, customs
and police services' (Article 3). State aircraft need special authorisation
(known as 'diplomatic clearance') to fly in the airspace over, or land in,
the territory of another state. An 'aircraft' is defined in Annex 7 to the
Convention as 'any machine that can derive support in the atmosphere
from the reactions of the air other than the reactions of the air against the
earth's surface'. They include balloons, dirigibles (airships) and gliders,
but not hovercraft, rockets, missiles or orbiting satellites.

National airspace

The Convention recognises that 'every state has complete and exclusive
sovereignty over the airspace above its territory',[4] and that the territory of
a state is the land and territorial sea (but not the contiguous or exclusive
economic zones) under the sovereignty, suzerainty, protection or mandate
of the state (Articles 1 and 2). Article 6 thus provides that no scheduled
international air service may be operated over or into the territory of
another state except with its permission or authorisation, although there
is a right of transit over archipelagic waters and some straits.[5] These
provisions are fundamental to the regulation of international air services.
Permission can be given in three ways:

(1) If the two states are parties to the International Air Services Transit
    Agreement 1944 (IASTA).[6] (IASTA must not be confused with IATA

---

[3] Published by the ICAO. See the ICAO website, www.icao.int, for a list of Depositary
Libraries.
[4] As to the distinction from outer space, see p. 367 below.
[5] See pp. 306 and 308 above.   [6] I71 UNTS 387 (No. 502); UKTS (1953) 8.

(the International Air Transport Association), which is an association of airlines, and which itself must not be confused with the ICAO.) Under IASTA, the 121 parties grant to each others' airlines operating scheduled international services the 'First and Second Freedoms' of the air: the right to fly across their respective territories without landing, and to land there for 'non-traffic purposes', such as refuelling or repairs (known also as 'technical stops'), but *not* to set down or take on board passengers or cargo. Although these provisions are habitually repeated in bilateral air services agreements, IASTA can be valuable when there is no such agreement.

(2) By a bilateral air services agreement under which traffic rights are granted (see below).

(3) *Ad hoc.*

International air services, scheduled and non-scheduled

It is important to distinguish between 'scheduled' and 'non-scheduled' international air services, since they are governed by different rules. Scheduled services are commercial services open to the public and operating to a published timetable (schedule). Non-scheduled services are all the rest, predominantly charter flights. Both types of services can carry passengers and/or freight, including mail. Although Article 5 provides a more liberal regime for charter flights, because of the enormous growth in them, especially for tourism, for many years states have in practice required prior permission for them.

Domestic air services

Article 7 reserves to each state the right to operate air services within its territory (including between it and any of its overseas territories). This is known as 'cabotage'. A state can also grant cabotage rights to foreign airlines, usually only in return for similar or other valuable rights.

International airspace

The airspace that is not above a state's territory, including its territorial sea, is open to the aircraft of all states. Nevertheless, for reasons of safety, Article 12 and the annexes have detailed provisions to promote safety in international airspace. For this purpose, international airspace is divided into flight information regions (FIRs) for which a state is responsible and with whose aeronautical authorities all foreign civil aircraft are required to co-operate. However, on occasion a state will purport to close part of international airspace adjacent to its territory. The legal justification may be self-defence,[7] as was the case with the 200-mile Total Exclusion Zone around the Falkland Islands declared by the United Kingdom during the 1982 conflict with Argentina for the purpose of protecting British armed forces. States also declare safety zones when carrying out practice firings or naval exercises outside the territorial sea, and issue general warnings to shipping and aircraft not to enter when the activity is being carried out. If anything, international law requires such warnings,[8] and, provided they are not too extensive or prolonged, they are in most cases complied with without complaint.[9] For many years, the United States and Canada have had air defence identification zones (ADIZ and CADIZ respectively) and require all aircraft when entering them and intending to land in their territory to identify themselves and conform to the directions of ground control, even when over the high seas (the zones reach half way across both the Atlantic and Pacific Oceans). This requirement is loosely based on Article 11 and is apparently acquiesced in by other states.

Civil aircraft and airlines

An aircraft has the nationality of the state where it is registered. Registration can be changed, but dual registration is not allowed (Articles 17 and 18). Although the Convention does not require any connection between the state of registration and the owners of the aircraft, domestic law usually does. An international air service therefore usually operates on the basis of the 'nationality' of each airline, *not* on the nationality of the aircraft. With the exception of the liberalised regime within the European Union, a state will usually grant rights to another state only in respect of airlines over which nationals of that state have 'substantial ownership or control', the criterion normally found in air services agreements. The Report of the ICAO World Wide Air Traffic Conference, held in Montreal in March 2003 with the theme 'Challenges and Opportunities of Liberalisation', recommended that states should consider using a model designation clause under which the state receiving a designation would issue an operating permit provided that, *inter alia*, the designated airline has its principal place of business in the territory of the designating

---

[7] See p. 226 above.
[8] See the *Corfu Channel, ICJ Reports* (1949), p. 4, at p. 22; 16 ILR 155.
[9] See also p. 314 above.

state and that state has and maintains effective regulatory control over the airline.[10]

It is common practice for airlines to charter (lease) foreign-registered aircraft. A so-called wet-lease is of the aircraft and crew; a dry-lease is of the aircraft only.

Air services agreements

Because an airline needs prior permission to put down or take on board passengers or cargo in another state and, unless IASTA applies, even to overfly or make a technical stop, there has developed an extensive network of bilateral treaties known as air services agreements (ASAs). Under them the airlines of the parties are granted rights to operate scheduled services (charter services are usually not included) between, and sometimes beyond, the territory of the two states.[11] They may have separate provision for scheduled freight services, although freight carried in the hold of a passenger aircraft ('bellyhold cargo') is not usually subject to special provisions. Although today many airlines are no longer state-owned, it is the governments which negotiate ASAs. But, since it is very much a commercial negotiation, in effect the governments act for their respective airlines.

Although each ASA is unique, most follow the basic formula set by the UK–US ASA of 1946, now known as 'Bermuda 1'.[12] Among other things, a typical ASA[13] provides for IASTA rights ('First and Second Freedoms'); permits airlines of each party to operate services (the 'agreed services') on a route or routes between the two states and to pick up and set down traffic ('Third and Fourth Freedoms'), and often to pick up and set down traffic to and from third states on a route, or at 'points beyond' the end of a route (although exercise of such 'Fifth Freedom' rights will also require the consent of the third state); designation of the airlines to operate the agreed services, provided the designating party or its nationals have 'substantial ownership and effective control' of them; 'fair and equal opportunity' for the designated airlines to compete; the capacity that can be operated (size

---

[10] ICAO Doc. 9819 at Conf/5 (31/3/03, rev. 10/7/03), pp. 16–23, or see the ICAO website, www.icao.int.

[11] See A. Aust, 'Air Services Agreements: Current United Kingdom Procedures and Policy' (1985) *Air Law* 189–202, which is still largely relevant.

[12] 3 UNTS 253 (No. 36); UKTS (1946) 3. It was replaced on 23 July 1977 by 'Bermuda 2' (1079 UNTS 21 (No. 16509); UKTS (1977) 76) which has been amended several times and has caused numerous disputes. A liberal replacement has been under negotiation for *many* years.

[13] See the Grenada–UK ASA 2002, UKTS (2002) 52.

and type of aircraft and frequency of flights); a mechanism for approval of tariffs (fares); exemption from customs and other duties and taxes on fuel and certain equipment introduced by the airlines into the other state; freedom to convert and remit each airline's net earnings to its home state;[14] the right to bring in airline staff and establish sales offices; and an arbitration procedure. Disputes arise frequently under ASAs and some have gone to arbitration.[15] It is usual to provide for termination of an ASA on twelve months' notice.

Most ASAs – except those with the United States – are supplemented by MOUs.[16] Typically the MOUs specify the names of the airlines that can be designated; elaborate on the route rights and capacity; and may go into more detail about tariffs. Since MOUs contain commercially sensitive information, they are generally regarded by the two states as confidential to them and those of their airlines involved in the services. Given the great changes in international air services in recent decades, the MOUs often have to be modified or replaced, and are sometimes renegotiated annually or seasonally.

In addition to the liberalised regime for air services within the European Union under which EU airlines can carry traffic anywhere within the Union, including (since 1997) cabotage within another EU state, since 1992 the United States has concluded over sixty liberal (so-called Open Skies) ASAs.[17] But, after eight years, such a treaty between the European Union (that shares competence for air services with its member states) and the United States appears to be as far away as ever.[18] A particular obstacle is the European Union's reasonable demand that EU airlines should enjoy cabotage rights within the United States to match US airlines' valuable Fifth Freedom rights within the European Union, which if the European Union ever became a federal state would amount to cabotage.

Warsaw and Rome Conventions

Passengers' luggage gets damaged or lost, and aircraft crash. The purpose of the Warsaw Convention for the Unification of Certain Rules relating to Carriage by Air 1929[19] was to create one liability regime, the key elements

---

[14] Reciprocal exemption from direct taxes is usually provided either in a double taxation convention or in a specific exchange of notes.

[15] See *US* v. *France* (1963), 38 ILR 182; *US* v. *France* (1978), 54 ILR 303; *US* v. *Italy* (1965), 45 ILR 393; *US* v. *UK* (1993), 102 ILR 215.

[16] For an explanation of this shy but ubiquitous animal, see pp. 53–7 above.

[17] See www.state.gov/e/eb/tra/c661.htm.

[18] See www.eubusiness.com (*not* an EU website).   [19] 137 LNTS 11; UKTS (1933) 11.

being uniform documentation, liability without proof of negligence, limits on compensation (but breakable if wilful misconduct is proved), and specified jurisdictions at the choice of the claimant. It has no amendment clause.[20] Further treaties amending or supplementing the Convention were concluded in 1955, 1961, 1971 and 1975. The parties to the original Convention and to each of the further treaties all differ, resulting in a lack of uniformity in the scheme.[21] This was only partly alleviated by airlines adopting special contracts offering higher compensation and the unilateral imposition by the European Community (Regulation 2027/97, as amended by Regulation 889/2002), and by the United States, of higher compensation limits for airlines operating to and from their territory.

The Montreal Convention for the Unification of Certain Rules for International Carriage by Air 1999[22] is intended to replace the whole Warsaw regime. Under Article 17, compensation of up to 100,000 SDRs (about US$120,000) for death or injury resulting from an 'accident' while on the aircraft or on embarkation or disembarkation, is payable without proof of negligence.[23] Above that limit, the carrier is not liable if *it* can prove that the damage was *not* caused by its negligence or wrongful act or omission, or was solely due to a third party. Compensation for loss or damage to luggage is mostly limited to 1,000 SDRs (about US$1,200) for each passenger. The Convention entered into force in 2003 and now has sixty-five parties, including the European Community, all but one of its member states and the United States.

The Rome Convention on Damage caused by Foreign Aircraft to Third Parties on the Surface 1952, as amended by a 1978 Protocol,[24] provides for the absolute liability of operators of foreign-registered aircraft for damage caused by them to persons on the ground.

Jurisdiction over aircraft

Since a state has sovereignty over the airspace above its territory, aircraft on an international route may pass through the airspace of several

---

[20] See p. 98 above on the problem of amending treaties.
[21] For more detail and references, see Aust, pp. 212–13.
[22] See Shawcross and Beaumont, *Air Law*, London, 1977, or UKTS (2004) 44; and B. Cheng, 'A New Era in the Law of International Carriage by Air' (2004) *ICLQ* 833–59.
[23] Thus the problem of whether contracting deep vein thrombosis (DVT) from flying is an 'accident' for this purpose may still be with us: see *Deep Vein Thrombosis and Air Travel Group Litigation* [2003] 3 WLR 956; [2003] 1 AER 935, and cases therein cited from other jurisdictions. But see also Tompkins, 'DVT Litigation Update' (2004) *Air and Space Law* 312 about the failure to give a DVT warning.
[24] Both are in force, but the Convention has only forty-seven parties and the Protocol nine.

foreign states as well as international airspace. The Tokyo Convention on Offences and Certain other Acts Committed on Board Aircraft 1963 lays down jurisdictional rules for criminal offences committed on board during flight, and for acts which jeopardise the safety of the aircraft or persons or discipline on board.[25] It has 178 parties. The state of registration of the aircraft has the right to exercise jurisdiction over such offences and acts (Article 3), although the jurisdiction of other states is not excluded. If a serious assault were to take place, the state of nationality of the attacker or victim, or a state where the aircraft lands, may, depending on its legislation, choose to exercise jurisdiction (such options being important given the increase in 'air rage' incidents). But a state that is not the state of registration must not for this purpose interfere with an aircraft in flight, except in the cases set out in Article 4. But at the 33rd (2001) Session of the ICAO Assembly, Resolution A33-4 encouraged prosecution by the state of first landing for offences on board foreign aircraft if they disturbed public order.[26] (See p. 287 above on aviation terrorism.)

Use of force against aircraft

Article 3*bis* of the Chicago Convention[27] recognises the right of a state to require a civil aircraft to land if it is overflying its territory without permission. But it also recognises that weapons must not be used 'against civil aircraft in flight and that, in case of interception, the lives of persons on board and the safety of aircraft must not be endangered'. Since it is very difficult to force an uncooperative pilot to land without putting the aircraft or its occupants in danger, in practice any landing would have to be voluntary.[28] However, the prohibition on using force is expressed to be without prejudice to the rights and obligations of states set out in the UN Charter. This is an oblique reference to the inherent right of a state to use force in self-defence, as confirmed by Article 51 of the Charter.[29] Thus, in truly exceptional circumstances, a state would be entitled to shoot down a civil aircraft if that is the only way to avoid an anticipated greater loss

---

[25] 704 UNTS 219 (No. 10106); UKTS (1969) 126.

[26] See the ICAO website, www.icao.int. This had already been done by the United Kingdom: see the Civil Aviation (Amendment) Act 1996, section 1.

[27] ILM (1984) 705; UKTS (1999) 68. The Article is an amendment to the Convention prompted by the shooting down by the Soviet Union of Korean Airlines flight KAL007 on 1 September 1983.

[28] See Annex 2 to the Convention for the standard interception rules.

[29] See p. 226 above.

of life. If at the time the US Government knew, or had good grounds for believing that it knew, the real intentions of the hijackers of the four US airliners on 11 September 2001, it could have authorised their shooting-down over less populated areas. During the negotiation of Article 3*bis*, certain Central American states had argued that they should be entitled to shoot down civil aircraft suspected of drug trafficking. This was rejected. Yet, on 20 April 2001, as part of an anti-drug-smuggling campaign assisted by the US Government, Peru shot down a light aircraft, killing two. It was found to be carrying only Christian missionaries.[30] In October 2004, Brazil announced that a domestic law had now come into effect to enable it to shoot down suspected drug trafficking aircraft.[31]

Although in force, the Protocol containing Article 3 *bis* has only 128 parties. Nevertheless, the preamble states that it 'reaffirm[s] the principle of non-use of weapons against civilian aircraft in flight'.

---

[30] See *The Times*, 21 April 2001, and www.cnn.com/2001/US/04/22/ peru.plane.03/.
[31] See http://americas.org/item_15285/.

18

Special regimes

The Pole ... Great God! This is an awful place.[1]

Parts of our globe (the polar regions), particularly important resources (international waterways), and outer space have required special treatment to preserve their unique features, to deal with their unusual characteristics or to protect the interests of states generally. Such special areas are often declared to be demilitarised. In some cases, a regime created by a treaty between only certain states is regarded as an 'objective regime', created not just for the benefit of those states, but also for the benefit of all (*erga omnes*).[2]

Antarctica

Watts, *International Law and the Antarctic Treaty System*, Cambridge, 1992
Birnie and Boyle, *Basic Documents on International Law and the Environment*, Oxford, 1995 (B&B Docs.)
www.ats.org.ar

Antarctica has been primarily a theatre for exploration and science; from the beginning expeditions to explore the continent included scientists. Over the years, many bases have been established in Antarctica for the purpose of conducting research, both the better to understand the continent itself and, more recently, to monitor changes in the global environment. The Antarctic continent is vast and empty. The Antarctic Treaty 1959 (in this section, 'the Treaty')[3] applies to an even larger area: all land,

---

[1] Captain Scott, Diary, 1 January 1912.   [2] See p. 10 above, and Aust, pp. 208–11.
[3] 402 UNTS 71 (No. 5778); UKTS (1961) 97. The official website of the Antarctic Treaty Secretariat is www.ats.org.ar. Another useful site is that of the Australian Antarctic Division, www.antdiv.gov.au, which includes the *Antarctic Treaty Handbook*.

ice shelves[4] and water south of latitude 60° south. That is even larger than the area within the Antarctic Circle, an imaginary line drawn at latitude 66° 33′ South (latitude 60° North runs through the Shetland Islands, Scotland's most northerly islands). There is no permanent population in the Antarctic Treaty area.

The legal status of Antarctica is unique. Seven states claim sovereignty over parts of it (Argentina, Australia, Chile, France, New Zealand, Norway and the United Kingdom). The claims are for sectors (often termed 'pie slices'), consisting of areas bounded by lines of longitude converging at the South Pole, although Norway has not clearly made a claim going as far as the Pole. Russia and the United States have not made claims but each asserts that it has a 'basis of claim'. There is also a large sector (90° to 150° West) that is unclaimed.[5] However, most states, including other parties to the Treaty, do not accept the existence of any territorial sovereignty in Antarctica. Although sovereignty questions have been put on ice (see below), the problems of jurisdiction they raise are only partially resolved by the Treaty. For example, the Treaty provides for the parties to designate observers to carry out inspections in Antarctica to ensure observance of the Treaty, the observers remaining under the jurisdiction of the party of which they are nationals.

The Antarctic Treaty System (ATS)

The governance of Antarctica is provided, albeit imperfectly, by a system of treaties – the Antarctic Treaty and its Environmental Protocol 1991,[6] the Convention on the Conservation of Antarctic Marine Living Resources 1980 (CCAMLR),[7] the Convention for the Conservation of Antarctic Seals 1972,[8] and measures adopted under them. Although there have been attempts in the UN General Assembly to make Antarctica a UN responsibility, these have not come to anything. There are powerful arguments that the ATS is an objective regime.[9]

---

[4] For a pictorial description, see Watts, *International Law and the Antarctic Treaty System*, Cambridge, 1992, p. 116.
[5] For a map showing this and the claims, see Watts, *International Law and the Antarctic Treaty System*, Cambridge, 1992, p. 117.
[6] ILM (1991) 1460; UKTS (1999) 6; ATS (1998) 6; B&B Docs. 468.
[7] 402 UNTS 71 (No. 22301); ILM (1980) 837; UKTS (1982) 48; TIAS 10240; B&B Docs. 628.
[8] 1080 UNTS 175 (No. 16529); ILM (1972) 837; UKTS (1978) 45.
[9] Watts, *International Law and the Antarctic Treaty System*, Cambridge, 1992, pp. 295–8.

The Antarctic Treaty

The preamble to the Treaty recognises the need for Antarctica to be used exclusively for peaceful purposes and not to become the scene or object of international discord. Accordingly, the Treaty provides for Antarctica's demilitarisation and prohibits any nuclear explosions or the disposal of nuclear waste. The Treaty acknowledges Antarctica's substantial contribution to scientific knowledge resulting from international cooperation in scientific investigation, and provides for freedom of scientific investigation in Antarctica and for cooperation to that end, including the exchange of scientific personnel in Antarctica.

Sovereignty clause

Article IV of the Treaty is worth quoting in full, not only for its importance to the operation of the Treaty, but because it has proved a useful precedent for other difficult situations.[10]

> 1. Nothing contained in the present Treaty shall be interpreted as:
>   (a) a renunciation by any contracting party of previously asserted rights of or claims to territorial sovereignty in Antarctica;
>   (b) a renunciation or diminution by any contracting party of any basis of claim to territorial sovereignty in Antarctica which it may have whether as a result of its activities or those of its nationals in Antarctica, or otherwise;
>   (c) prejudicing the position of any contracting party as regards its recognition or non-recognition of any other state's rights of or claim or basis of claim to territorial sovereignty in Antarctica.
> 2. No acts or activities taking place while the present Treaty is in force shall constitute a basis for asserting, supporting or denying a claim to territorial sovereignty in Antarctica or create any rights of sovereignty in Antarctica. No new claim, or enlargement of an existing claim, to territorial sovereignty in Antarctica shall be asserted while the present Treaty is in force.

Article IV thus preserves the differing legal positions of the parties.

Measures

The provisions of the Treaty are contained in eight quite short Articles. Because of their brevity and generality, there was a need for the

---

[10] See, for example, the Argentina–United Kingdom Joint Declarations 1989 and 1996 (ILM (1990) 129 and (1996) ILM 304) regarding co-operation over the Falkland Islands since the 1982 conflict.

Treaty to include a dynamic element. Accordingly, Article IX provides for two classes of parties: (1) the twenty-nine Antarctic Treaty Consultative Parties (ATCPs), being the twelve original parties and those which later acceded and established, to the satisfaction of the then ATCPs, that they conduct substantial scientific research activity in Antarctica; and (2) the rest (currently sixteen), who have acceded only and are effectively observers. The ATCPs are so described because Article IX(1) provides that they shall meet from time to time for the purpose of, among other things, *consulting* together and *recommending* to their governments *measures* in furtherance of the principles and objectives of the Treaty. They now meet annually at an Antarctic Treaty Consultative Meeting (ATCM) hosted each year by a different ATCP. Between 1961 and 1995, ATCMs recommended to the governments of the ATCPs 209 measures on a variety of subjects, including the exchange of scientific personnel and data, the protection of fauna and flora and historic sites, specially protected areas, air safety, telecommunications, tourism, minerals exploration and the disposal of nuclear waste. Article IX(4) provides that measures adopted at an ATCM become 'effective' when they have been approved by all the ATCPs, which then regard them as legally binding.

However, there had been a long-standing misunderstanding, and consequent misapplication, of Article IX(1). From the very beginning, all texts adopted by ATCMs were mistakenly called 'Recommendations' and subjected to the unanimous approval procedure of Article IX(4). Yet a great number of the Recommendations were merely exhortations to do or not to do something, with no intention of creating any legal obligations. Many others were ephemeral or of a procedural nature, for example requests to other bodies. This resulted in many Recommendations not becoming 'effective' until many years after their adoption, if at all, even though they created no obligations, had been overtaken by events, or were ephemeral. This unsatisfactory situation was corrected at the 1995 ATCM which agreed, in Decision 1 (1995),[11] to adopt three basic categories of instrument for embodying decisions taken by an ATCM: (1) a Measure adopted expressly under Article IX(1), if it is intended to be legally binding; (2) a Decision, if it concerns only internal organisational matters; and (3) a Resolution, if the text is no more than recommendatory. Decisions and Resolutions are therefore not adopted under a specific provision of the Treaty.

[11] ILM (1996) 1165.

The Environmental Protocol

In 1991, the ATCPs adopted the Protocol on Environmental Protection to the Antarctic Treaty (the 'Protocol').[12] Since the entry into force of the Protocol in 1998, a party to the Treaty cannot become an ATCP unless it first becomes a party to the Protocol (Article 22(4)). The purpose of the Protocol is to create a comprehensive regime for the protection of the Antarctic environment. It established a new body, the Committee for Environmental Protection (CEP) (see below). Although Article 3 sets out general principles governing the protection of the Antarctic environment, the key provisions are:

• Prohibition on mining for minerals, except for scientific research (Article 7). Article 25(2) and (5) provides that the prohibition shall continue for at least fifty years, unless before then a binding legal regime on mining is in force. A Convention on the Regulation of Antarctic Mineral Resource Activities (CRAMRA) had been concluded in 1988.[13] Opposition to it by Australia and France on environmental or national interest grounds meant that it would not be able to enter into force.
• Environmental impact assessment (EIA)[14] of proposed activities in Antarctica. This is elaborated in Annex I to the Protocol. In addition to preliminary and initial EIAs, a comprehensive EIA must be prepared for any activity which is likely to have 'more than a minor or transitory' impact on the environment. This has to be publicised and later discussed by the CEP. However, the decision whether to proceed with the activity rests with the ATCP concerned.
• The scheme of Annexes to the Protocol. In addition to Annex I on EIA, there are currently three others: Annex II on the Conservation of Antarctic Fauna and Flora; Annex III on Waste Control and Management; Annex IV on the Prevention of Marine Pollution; and Annex V on Area Protection and Management. Additional Annexes may be adopted by a Measure. An Annex to deal with legal liability for damage arising from environmental emergencies was eventually adopted in 2005. Amendments to an Annex can also be made by a Measure, but an Annex may provide for amendments to it to become effective on an accelerated basis; and each of the Annexes provides that an amending Measure

---

[12] See n. 6 above.
[13] ILM (1988) 859. The text is also annexed to Watts, *International Law and the Antarctic Treaty System*, Cambridge, 1992, which has a detailed analysis of that Convention.
[14] See p. 332 above.

shall be deemed to have been approved, and shall become effective, one year after the ATCM at which it was adopted, unless an ATCP requires an extension of the period or says that it does not approve the Measure.

- The CEP. Its sole function is to advise the ATCM on the implementation of the Protocol and to formulate draft Measures for consideration by the ATCM. Each party to the Protocol is a member. It adopts its report to the ATCM by consensus.

- A quite complex procedure for the settlement of disputes, with a choice between the International Court of Justice or arbitration according to the Schedule to the Protocol.

Amendment of the Treaty and the Protocol and its Annexes

Article XII(1) of the Treaty provides that it may be modified or amended by the unanimous agreement of the ATCPs, the instrument entering into force when all the ATCPs have ratified. This is not the simple amendment mechanism found in many later treaties: a further treaty is required, and there is no provision that it should enter into force for all ATCPs once a certain number of them have ratified it.[15] In short, the procedure is cumbersome and has not been used except for the Environmental Protocol. In practice, extensive use of Article IX measures has allowed the ATCPs to develop the Treaty without amending it.

Secretariat

The 2001 ATCM agreed that, instead of the host state of each ATCM providing a temporary secretariat, the Treaty should have a permanent secretariat located in Buenos Aires, Argentina. Measure 1 (2003) provides for the Secretariat to be an organ of the ATCM. Under a headquarters agreement with Argentina, the Secretariat will have, although only in Argentina, legal capacity,[16] and the Secretariat and its staff the usual privileges and immunities.[17] Because it will be some years before the Measure (and the headquarters agreement, which is dependent on the Measure) will enter into force, it will be applied provisionally, and contributions of the ATCPs to the budget of the Secretariat will be voluntary. The Secretariat began work in September 2004.[18]

---

[15] See p. 98 above on amendment problems.
[16] This is exceptional. Normally, it would be the organisation (a new Antarctic Treaty Organization or even the ATCM) on which capacity would be conferred: see p. 198 above.
[17] See p. 199 above.   [18] See its website: www.ats.org.ar.

CCAMLR

The Convention on the Conservation of Antarctic Marine Living Resources (CCAMLR) 1980[19] was established to deal with the problem of conserving fish stocks in the (cold and therefore rich) fishing grounds of the Southern Ocean by promoting rational harvesting from an ecosystem and precautionary perspective,[20] so distinguishing CCAMLR from other fisheries agreements concluded before UNCLOS 1982 or the Fish Stocks Agreement 1995.[21] The Southern Ocean is the sea around Antarctica up as far as the Antarctic Convergence (now termed the Antarctic Polar Front) where the cold Antarctic waters meet the warmer northern waters. Since the Convergence is not a geographic limit, and its position changes with the seasons, the area to which the Convention applies is defined in the Convention by a line which ranges between 45° and 60° South, roughly corresponding to the Convergence.

The Convention has thirty-one parties. Of these, twenty-four are members of the governing Commission, and include Western European states (including Spain and the United Kingdom), the European Community, Russia, Japan, South Korea, Argentina, Chile, the United States, South Africa, Australia and New Zealand. The other seven are observers. The small but expert CCAMLR Secretariat is based in Hobart, Tasmania, where each (Southern) spring the Commission meets to adopt conservation measures binding on the members.

In common with other commissions regulating fishing, the work of the CCAMLR Commission is bedevilled by illegal, unregulated and unreported fishing (IUU). The Commission has taken a leading role in tackling these problems.[22] Since 2000, it has operated a Catch Documentation Scheme for *Dissostichus spp* (a high-value fish known also as toothfish, or sea bass as it often appears on menus) by which landing and trade in the species can be tracked. But, the area covered by CCAMLR is vast and mostly high sea. So far, action by Australia, France and the United Kingdom, in exercise of their coastal state jurisdiction in the EEZs or fishing zones around their sub-Antarctic territories, has been the most effective in ensuring compliance with the conservation measures. Islands within the Convention area 'over which the existence of state sovereignty

---

[19] 402 UNTS 71 (No. 22301); ILM (1980) 837; UKTS (1982) 48; TIAS 10240; B&B Docs. 628. See www.ccamlr.org for the text and other documentation.
[20] See p. 330 above.   [21] See p. 321 above.
[22] See pp. 319 *et seq* above on the general problems and how they are being tackled.

is recognised by all contracting parties' can be taken out of the normal application of the Convention, so enabling coastal state jurisdiction – rather than only that of the flag state of the vessel – to be used to enforce conservation measures.[23] In contrast, the lack of an enforcement capability has led to severe depletion of the *Dissostichus* stock around South Africa's Prince Edward Island.

The Arctic

The North Polar Region, known more usually as the Arctic, is physically and legally quite unlike Antarctica. The Arctic is not a continent: nuclear-powered submarines have travelled under the ice at the North Pole. Nor is the Arctic defined. The Arctic Council deals with the 'Arctic region'. But it is reasonable to regard the Arctic as at least the area lying within the Arctic Circle, an imaginary line drawn at latitude 66° 33' North. This area represents over one-sixth of the surface of the Earth, and, unlike Antarctica, has a population of some four million, including many Inuit and other indigenous peoples. The Arctic Council, established by the Ottawa Declaration of 19 September 1996, is not an international organisation, but rather a forum where the states with territory in the area can discuss matters of mutual concern and supervise projects, mostly to do with environmental protection and the well-being of the indigenous peoples.[24] The representatives of these peoples are 'permanent participants' in the Council. So far, the Council has not adopted any treaties, the Ottawa Declaration and subsequent declarations being no more than MOUs.[25]

Within the area is territory of the members of the Council (Canada, Denmark (Greenland), Finland, Iceland, Norway, Russia, Sweden and the United States (Alaska)). Canada and Russia have potentially the largest territorial claims. Their claims to sovereignty of uninhabited territory have relied on the sector principle, rather than actual occupation.[26] Not being an accepted basis for establishing sovereignty, sectoral claims have not been made by other members.[27] Any claim to sovereignty over the

---

[23] See Aust, pp. 189–90 and 196. On enforcement problems generally, see pp. 334–6 above.
[24] The Secretariat is located in the Icelandic MFA: see www.arctic-council.org.
[25] On which, see pp. 53–7 above. [26] See p. 355 above on sector claims for Antarctica.
[27] See Oppenheim, pp. 692–3, and p. 38 above on occupation.

ice covering the high seas could not in any event be sustained.[28] Even where territorial sovereignty could be established, there would be difficult delimitation issues concerning continental shelves and EEZs.[29] These could assume great importance given the potentially rich natural resources in the area and its continuing strategic importance.

Svalbard

This is the name by which Spitsbergen is now officially known. It is an archipelago of islands lying roughly between latitudes 74° and 81° North and longitudes 10° to 35° East. In the early years of the twentieth century it was regarded as *terra nullius*,[30] but the Treaty of Spitsbergen 1920[31] recognized Norwegian sovereignty over it. The Soviet Union recognised Norway's sovereignty in February 1924 and became a party to the treaty in 1935, although Russia disputes fishing rights with Norway. The treaty now has forty parties, including Albania and Venezuela. Article 9 states that neither naval bases nor fortifications may be established on Svalbard and that the islands may not be used for 'warlike purposes'. The parties' nationals are entitled, subject to Norwegian conservation measures, to have free access to Svalbard's waters and ports, to own property and to hunt and fish on the basis of equal treatment.[32]

Canals

Baxter, *The Law of International Waterways*, Cambridge, MA, 1964

International straits have already been discussed.[33] We are here concerned with waterways, typically canals, that have been dug in the territory of a *single* state, but because they join two parts of the high seas are sometimes subject to a special legal regime for the benefit of all.

---

[28] See p. 312 above on the high seas.
[29] See p. 33 above on possible Danish claims relating to Greenland's continental shelf.
[30] See p. 38 above.
[31] 2 LNTS 8; UKTS (1924) 18; ATS (1925) 10; or http://en.wikipedia.org/wiki/Svalbard/ (also includes general information). See also G. Ulfstein, *The Svalbard Treaty*, Oslo, 1995.
[32] In 1998, the annual *Antarctic* meeting was held at Tromsø, in northern Norway, and Svalbard, to the puzzlement of some local people.
[33] See p. 306 above.

Suez Canal[34]

Opened in 1869, the Suez Canal joins the Mediterranean Sea and the Red Sea. Its status was defined by the Convention of Constantinople 1888.[35] Although the Canal lies entirely within Egypt, Article 1 provides that it 'shall always be free and open, in time of war as in time of peace, to every vessel of commerce or of war, without distinction of flag'. Other Articles provide in detail for its neutralisation. The original parties to the Convention were the then leading European Powers: Austria-Hungary, France, Germany, Italy, The Netherlands, Russia, Spain, Turkey and Great Britain. In 1956, Egypt nationalised the Anglo-French Suez Canal Company that had operated the Canal. Following the aggression by France, Israel and the United Kingdom and the withdrawal of their forces, in 1957 Egypt made a unilateral declaration reaffirming that it would apply the provisions of the Convention.[36] Given its clearly expressed purpose, the Convention has for long been regarded as having created an objective regime, according to the vessels (including warships) of every state freedom of navigation through the Canal at any time. In 1923, in *The Wimbledon*, the Permanent Court of International Justice (the ICJ's predecessor), in upholding the provision granting freedom of navigation through the Kiel Canal at the time (see below), saw the Suez and Panama Canal treaties as illustrations of the permanent dedication of an artificial waterway connecting two open seas to the use of the whole world.[37] In Article V(1) of the Egypt–Israel Peace Treaty of 1979, Egypt confirmed that Israeli flag vessels, as well as cargoes destined for or coming from Israel, would enjoy the same rights of freedom of navigation through the Canal as other states.[38] Despite a few minor hiccups, those rights have been respected ever since.[39]

Panama Canal[40]

The Panama Canal runs between Colón and the city of Panama, joining the Atlantic and Pacific Oceans. Under a 1903 treaty between the newly

[34] For a detailed account and numerous references, see Oppenheim, pp. 592–5.
[35] 171 CTS 241; 79 BSP 18. See also Whiteman, vol. 3, pp. 1076–130 (the text of the Convention is at p. 1081).
[36] 265 UNTS 299 (No. 3821).
[37] PCIJ, Ser. A, No. 1; 2 AD 99. See Brownlie, pp. 264–7, on the various possible bases for international status.
[38] 1136 UNTS 116 (No. 17813) and 1138 UNTS 72 (No. 17855); ILM (1979) 362.
[39] Recent information from the Israeli Foreign Ministry.
[40] For details and references, see Oppenheim, pp. 595–9.

independent Panama and the United States, the latter was granted land for the construction and operation of the Canal in perpetuity. Article 18 provided, in similar terms to that for the Suez Canal, for the Canal to be neutralised and open at all times to the vessels of all states, as had previously been provided in a UK–US treaty of 1901.[41] The Canal opened in 1914. The Panama–US Panama Canal Treaties 1977[42] revised the arrangements pending the Canal coming under the sole control of Panama on 1 January 2000, and confirmed the neutralised status of the Canal and freedom of navigation through it.

Kiel Canal[43]

The Kiel Canal (Nord-Ostsee Kanal) was opened in 1895 and extends for 96 kms through Germany from Kiel to Brunsbüttel, connecting the Baltic Sea with the North Sea. No treaty or unilateral declaration by Germany had accorded it any international status, but Article 380 of the (Versailles) Treaty of Peace with Germany 1919[44] provided for freedom of navigation for all vessels of all states not at war with Germany. Germany's denunciation of this provision in 1936 appears to have been acquiesced in by the other parties to the Treaty of Peace.

International rivers[45]

Freedom of navigation

We have dealt with sovereignty over rivers that are the boundary of two or more states.[46] International rivers that are navigable from the sea are usually an important means of international transport. Although the principle of freedom of navigation on them was declared by the Final Act of the Congress of Vienna 1815, this is still not customary international law,[47] and the Barcelona Convention and Statute on the Regime of Navigable Waterways of International Concern of 1921 has failed to obtain wide adherence.[48] But, over the years, various treaties granting

---

[41] UKTS (1902) 6.
[42] ILM (1977) 1021–98. See also ILM (1975) 1285 and ILM (1978) 817.
[43] See Oppenheim, p. 595.   [44] 225 CTS 188; UKTS (1919) 4.
[45] A detailed account of international watercourses, albeit more from an environmental perspective, is in Birnie and Boyle, *International Law and the Environment*, 2nd edn, Oxford, 2002, pp. 298–331.
[46] See p. 40 above.   [47] Oppenheim. p. 582, text to n. 7.
[48] 7 LNTS 35; UKTS (1923) 28. Oppenheim, pp. 580–2.

freedom of navigation for particular international rivers have been concluded.[49]

The Rhine

The Rhine is the most important Western European river, passing as it does from the North Sea through The Netherlands to Switzerland. Since 1815, it has been recognised as an international river with freedom of navigation, and is currently managed by the Central Commission for Navigation on the Rhine (CCNR), established by the Mannheim Convention, as revised on 17 October 1963,[50] the members of which are Belgium, France, Germany, The Netherlands and Switzerland.

The Danube

The previous regime for freedom of navigation on the Danube and its administration by an international commission[51] was replaced by the so-called Belgrade Convention of 18 August 1948[52] to which only communist states of Eastern Europe were original parties, although (fittingly) Austria also acceded in 1960. It repeats the provisions of earlier treaties that guaranteed freedom of navigation on the Danube on a basis of equality for the commercial vessels and goods of all states. The Danube River Protection Convention of 29 June 1994 (DRPC) aims to achieve sustainable and equitable water management in the Danube Basin, in particular to deal with pollution. The parties are eleven of the Danube's riparian states and the European Community. The International Commission for the Protection of the Danube River (ICPDR) administers the Convention.[53]

Other uses of watercourses

In the past, treaties about the use of international rivers (or more correctly 'watercourses', since 'river' may imply that all of it is navigable) were mainly concerned with navigation. In more recent years, concern about other uses of their waters, that are often vital to the states through which the watercourses or their tributaries flow, have led to various treaties dealing with the way water is extracted and other important economic and

---

[49] For references to such treaties for non-European rivers, see Oppenheim, p. 576, n. 6.
[50] For the text and the five subsequent Protocols, see www.ccr-zkr.org.
[51] See Oppenheim, pp. 575–80.   [52] 33 UNTS 181 (No. 518).
[53] www.icpdr.org/danubis/.

environmental matters. The problems of balancing the opposing interests of upstream and downstream states, including issues raised by human intervention, such as building dams, have been especially acute.

Convention on the Law of the Non-Navigational Uses of International Watercourses[54]

Based on a draft prepared by the ILC, the Convention was adopted by the UN General Assembly in 1997.[55] It covers non-navigational uses of, and measures of protection, preservation and management related to, international watercourses and their waters. The Convention defines 'watercourse' as 'a system of surface waters and groundwaters constituting by virtue of their physical relationship a unitary whole [so including rivers, lakes, aquifers, glaciers, reservoirs and canals that are interrelated with one another], and normally flowing into a common terminus', and 'international watercourse' as 'a watercourse, parts of which are situated in different states'. Since the problems are specific to each watercourse, the Convention does not affect existing treaties.[56] The parties can conclude treaties which apply or adjust the provisions of the Convention to the characteristics and uses of a particular watercourse, provided it does not adversely affect to a significant extent the use by another party without its express consent (Article 3). An international watercourse must be used in an equitable and reasonable manner. The aim is to attain optimal and sustainable utilisation, taking into account the interests of the watercourse states concerned, consistent with adequate protection of the watercourse (Article 5). The Convention is therefore a framework of general and residual principles within which the parties can work to produce a regime suited to a particular watercourse. The ICJ has already endorsed the basic principles of the Convention.[57]

So far, only fourteen states have ratified the Convention. Since it will enter into force only when thirty-five states have ratified, it is not likely to do so for many years, if ever. But a state concerned with a particular watercourse, whether or not it is a party to the Convention, may prefer

---

[54] See S. McCaffrey, *The Law of International Watercourses*, Oxford, 2001.

[55] ILM (1997) 719. For the text, the ILC final draft Articles and commentary, and a useful introduction, see A. Watts, *The International Law Commission 1949–1998*, Oxford, 1999, vol. II, pp. 1331–446.

[56] As to which, see Birnie and Boyle, *International Law and the Environment*, 2nd edn, Oxford, 2002, pp. 323–9.

[57] *Case concerning the Gabčíkovo-Nagymaros Project (Hungary/Slovakia), ICJ Reports* (1997), p. 7, para. 85; ILM (1998) 162; 116 ILR 1.

merely to draw upon it when devising or amending a regime. A recent treaty was the Revised Protocol on Shared Watercourses in the Southern African Development Community 2000.[58]

Outer space

Christol, *The Modern International Law of Outer Space*, New York, 1982
Christol, *Space Law*, Deventer, 1991
Cheng, *Studies in International Space Law*, Oxford, 1997
Oppenheim. *Oppenheim's International Law*, 9th edn, London, 1992, pp. 826–45
Gardiner, *International Law*, London, 2003, pp. 394, 400–1, 406 and 424–9
www.spacelawstation.com

Outer space begins where airspace ends, although exactly where that is cannot be determined. But a commonsense definition might be: anywhere above the earth where aircraft cannot fly because they cannot 'derive support in the atmosphere from the reactions of the air',[59] although that may now be too simple given that the Space Shuttle depends at different times of its journey on rocket propulsion and aerodynamic lift.

Outer space treaties[60]

The Treaty on Principles Governing the Activities of States in the Exploration and Use of Outer Space 1967 (Outer Space Treaty),[61] represented a deal between the Soviet Union and the United States. It now has some 100 parties, including all those states that are directly involved in a significant way in outer space activities. The Treaty's basic principles repeat the terms of earlier UN General Assembly resolutions,[62] and they can now be regarded as representing customary international law.[63]

The principles, which draw in part from principles relating to the freedom of navigation and the provisions of the Antarctic Treaty, are: (1) outer space (defined as including the Moon and other celestial bodies – except of course the Earth) is the province of all mankind, and its exploration

---

[58] ILM (2001) 317.   [59] See p. 346 above on the definition of national airspace.
[60] See also the website of the UN Committee on the Peaceful Uses of Outer Space (COPUOS) and its Legal Sub-committee, www.oosa.unvienna.org/COPUOS/.
[61] 610 UNTS 205 (No. 8843); ILM (1967) 386; UKTS (1968) 10; TIAS 6347. Russia, the UK and the US are joint depositaries (see p. 109 above) of this Cold War treaty, as well as the Astronauts Agreement and the Liability Convention.
[62] 1721 (XVI), 1884 (XVIII) and 1962 (XVII).   [63] See p. 6 above and Shaw, p. 481.

must be carried out for the benefit of all states in accordance with international law; (2) outer space cannot be appropriated by claim of sovereignty, means of use or occupation, or any other means; (3) outer space is free for scientific investigation; (4) no weapons of mass destruction may be put in orbit around the earth or installed on celestial bodies or stationed in outer space; (5) the moon and other celestial bodies must be used exclusively for peaceful purposes, and military equipment or activities of any kind are prohibited, although military personnel may be used for peaceful purposes;[64] (6) when in outer space astronauts must help other astronauts in distress, and states must help astronauts of other states who land in their territory or on the high seas (elaborated in the Agreement on the Rescue of Astronauts, the Return of Astronauts and the Return of Objects Launched into Outer Space 1968 (Astronauts Agreement);[65] (7) a state is internationally responsible for all activities in outer space carried out by it or its nationals, public or private, and the state which launches or procures the launching of a space object, or from whose territory or facility a space object is launched, is liable for any damage caused whether on Earth, in the air or in outer space (elaborated in the Convention on International Liability for Damage caused by Space Objects 1972 (Liability Convention) with provisions for absolute and fault liability);[66] and (8) a state retains jurisdiction and control over any object on its registry which is launched into outer space, registration with the UN Secretary-General being required by the Convention on Registration of Objects Launched into Outer Space 1975 (Registration Convention).[67]

The Moon Treaty 1979[68] declares the moon and its natural resources to be the 'common heritage of mankind', and that the parties will establish an international regime to govern exploitation of the moon once this 'is about to become feasible' (Article 11(5)). The Treaty, which also covers all other celestial bodies (except the Earth), was controversial from the start, and those states that have invested heavily in space exploration have been wary of it. Consequently, although the Treaty entered into force in 1984, it has only eleven parties, none of which are significant actors in space. When exploitation does become feasible, one can expect the major space players to promote another treaty better suited to the needs of that time.

---

[64] The Nuclear Test-Ban Treaty 1963, 480 UNTS 43 (No. 6964); UKTS (1964) 3; TIAS 544, prohibits tests also in outer space.

[65] 672 UNTS 119 (No. 9574); ILM (1968) 149. It has been widely ratified.

[66] 961 UNTS 187 (No. 13810); ILM (1971) 965; UKTS (194) 16; TIAS 7762.

[67] 1023 UNTS 15 (No. 15020); ILM (1975) 43. It has forty-five parties.

[68] 1363 UNTS 3 (No. 23002); ILM (1979) 1434.

The geostationary orbit

The main use of space is for satellites used for navigation, meteorology, broadcasting and remote sensing (the observation of the earth for civil or military purposes). UNGA Resolution 41/65 of 1986 affirmed that outer space can be used for remote sensing by all, no prior permission being needed.[69] Most satellites need to move in an orbit at about 35,900 kms above the Earth, and at a speed that will allow them to remain above the same point on the earth's surface (geostationary orbit). For maximum effectiveness, that point needs to be over the equator so that the satellite can receive from, and transmit to, most populated areas. The geostationary orbit can accommodate only a limited number of satellites, so it is a valuable resource. Since 1976, eight equatorial states have asserted that it is a natural resource belonging to them since it is exclusively the gravitational phenomena generated by *their* part of the earth that lies beneath the orbit that creates the geostationary orbit. This wildly unscientific argument has not been successful: the gravitational pull depends on the *whole* Earth, and the geostationary orbit depends also on the speed of the satellite. Moreover, since the orbit is clearly part of outer space, it cannot be appropriated by any state.[70]

The International Space Station

The International Space Station is governed by an Agreement of 1998 between Canada, member states of the European Space Agency, Japan, Russia and the United States.[71] It provides a framework for long-term international collaboration in the design, development, operation and utilisation of the station under the leadership of the United States. The provisions in Articles 21 and 22 on intellectual property and criminal jurisdiction are particularly interesting.

International space organisations

The five universal outer space treaties all take account of the fact that space activities are often carried out in collaboration with other states or within the framework of an international organisation. In particular,

---

[69] See Oppenheim, pp. 844–5.
[70] See further Gardiner, *International Law*, London, 2003, pp. 424–5.
[71] See www.spacelawstation.com/international.html.

Article XXII of the Liability Convention provides that, if an international organisation is liable for damage, those states parties to the Convention which are members of the organisation are jointly and severally liable with the organisation for the damage, and, if the organisation does not pay compensation as agreed or determined, those states parties are then liable to pay. This is contrary to the usual legal position.[72]

INTELSAT

UNGA Res. 41/65 of 1986 adopted the principle that global satellite communications should be made available on a non-discriminatory basis. The purpose of the International Telecommunications Satellite Organization (INTELSAT) is to establish and operate such a system. INTELSAT grew out of a consortium and in 1964 was established as an international organisation by a treaty and related Operating Agreement, to which the member states or their public or private telecommunications entities are parties. Membership is open to all ITU members. INTELSAT has its headquarters in Washington.[73]

INMARSAT

The International Maritime Satellite Organization (INMARSAT) was established by treaty in 1976[74] to provide mobile satellite communications, initially for shipping. As with INTELSAT, there was a related Operating Agreement to which the member states or their public or private telecommunications entities are parties. Since 1999, INMARSAT has been a limited company operating geostationary satellites. Its headquarters are in London.[75]

European Space Agency

The European Space Agency is the main regional organisation devoted to the launch of satellites, space science and other space activities.[76] It is *not* an EU body.

---

[72] See p. 407 below.   [73] www.intelsat.com.
[74] 1143 UNTS 105 (No. 17948); ILM (1976) 1051; UKTS (1979) 94; TIAS 9605. See ILM (1988) 691 for the 1988 amendment.
[75] www.inmarsat.org.
[76] For the ESA Convention, see 1297 UNTS 161 (No. 21524); ILM (1975) 864; UKTS (1981) 30. The website is www.esa.int.

International Telecommunications Union[77]

The International Telecommunications Union (ITU), with its headquarters in Geneva, has been a UN specialised agency since 1947, but dates from 1932 and is the direct successor to the nineteenth-century International Telegraph Union, which grew out of the International Telegraph Convention 1865.[78] Despite the enormous advances in technology its basic aims have not changed. Its purpose is to maintain and extend international co-operation for the improvement and rational use of global telecommunications of all kinds, involving both governments and the private sector. Almost all states are members. It allocates radio frequencies, and is thus intimately involved in regulating satellite communications. Since it registers frequencies in relation to particular locations, in effect it assigns locations of satellites in the geostationary orbit.

---

[77] See its excellent website, www.itu.int.   [78] 130 CTS 123, 198 and 148 CTS 416.

19

International economic law

The forgotten man at the bottom of the economic pyramid.[1]

Lowenfeld, *International Economic Law*, Oxford, 2003
Sornarajah, *The International Law of Foreign Investment*, 2nd edn, Cambridge, 2004
Collier and Lowe, *The Settlement of Disputes in International Law*, Oxford, 1999

International economic law is a convenient term to cover mainly the multitude of bilateral and multilateral treaties made since the Second World War on trade, commerce and investment. That does not mean that it is a new subject. There are numerous bilateral treaties on trade from earlier centuries, an Anglo/Portuguese treaty of 1353 providing for mercantile intercourse.[2] In the nineteenth and twentieth centuries there were many treaties on trade, customs, establishment and navigation. The last fifty years has seen important multilateral treaty-making in these areas and the conclusion of numerous bilateral investment treaties (BITs). A detailed description of the various new international and regional economic organisations is beyond the scope of this chapter. One can give only a brief overview of the subject, principally BITs and the WTO and similar organisations, concentrating more on the settlement of economic disputes. Dispute settlement in general is dealt with in Chapter 22 below.

Most countries that achieved their independence after the Second World War were developing, and most remain so. During the colonial era, the imperial powers controlled trade and investment between their colonies and themselves and third states. With independence, the new states could have more control over trade and the activities of foreign investors, but they also needed to encourage foreign investment. Initially, the considerable problems caused by the expropriation of foreign businesses had discouraged investors.

---

[1] Franklin D. Roosevelt, broadcast, 7 April 1932.   [2] 1(2) Dumont 286.

Most businessmen are not that aware of treaties, which they may see as the concern only of governments. Even when a treaty is seen as relevant to business, it may appear too difficult to enforce. Many treaties have dispute settlement clauses, but such clauses usually require diplomatic negotiations and, if that fails, international arbitration or recourse to an international tribunal such as the International Court of Justice (ICJ). Such settlement procedures may also depend on a further agreement between both parties. Even on the relatively rare occasions that a dispute goes to international arbitration or the ICJ, it can take many years, and action will remain in the hands of ministers, diplomats and other officials. Some businesses may therefore regard treaties as largely irrelevant to finding quick, practical solutions to commercial problems. They are wrong.

Bilateral investment treaties

One of the answers to a problem of lack of foreign investment was for a developing state to enter into a bilateral investment treaty (BIT) which, because it guarantees protection of foreign investments, also promotes such investments.[3] The Federal Republic of Germany and Pakistan concluded the first BIT in 1959. In the 1970s, concern by foreign investors for the need to establish and maintain a stable climate for investment grew. Expropriation and nationalisation by countries as diverse as Chile, Iran, Jamaica and Libya demonstrated the need for more effective protection and led to a growing number of BITs. Capital-exporting nations like France, Japan, The Netherlands, the United Kingdom and the United States have entered into many BITs. There are now over 2,000, compared with around 300 in 1990. More recently, the World Bank has been organising fresh rounds of BIT-making, so bringing into being what is rapidly becoming a homogeneous (but not yet common) set of rules to govern the global investment market.

A BIT has at least seven distinct advantages for the foreign investor. The *first*, and most obvious, is that it avoids interminable and often inconclusive disputes as to what rules of customary international law govern investment, how the rules should be applied, and how an unresolved dispute between an investor and the host state can be resolved. (For this

---

[3] This is reflected in the name by which the treaties are called by the United Kingdom, for example the Turkmenistan–UK Investment Promotion and Protection Agreement (IPPA) 1995, UKTS (2003) 47.

purpose, 'host state' includes the various executive, legislative and judicial organs of the state, right down to local authorities and local courts.) Without a BIT, an investor in a dispute with a host state would normally first have to exhaust his local remedies – using local law and going through the local courts up to the final court of appeal – before his own state could pursue his rights in international law, such as they may be.[4] Without a BIT, there are no relatively easy (or indeed any) means of resolving the dispute.

The *second advantage* is that, if the host state is alleged to be in breach of the BIT, the investor does not have to ask his own government to take up the claim. Although investors are not parties to BITs, the treaties give foreign investors the right to take host states to international arbitration, and they do not have to exhaust local remedies first. In fact, the investor does not have to involve his own government at all. Nor does the host state have to agree to the arbitration; the process is compulsory once the investor invokes it. This means that it is quicker and surer, the disgruntled investor keeping control of the procedure. Nor is there any risk of the dispute becoming just one on the list of bilateral disputes (including other commercial issues) between the two states. If it were, it might have to take its turn, or might not be pursued at all by the investor's state.

If the dispute is decided in favour of the investor, the BIT requires the award to be enforceable in the courts of the host state. If a host state were not to legislate for this, or if it were interfere in the enforcement process, not only would this give rise to a separate claim by the investor's state,[5] but it would badly affect the host state's standing in the eyes of other states and their investors. The fact that BITs have such an effective dispute settlement mechanism means that the initiation, or mere threat, of the arbitration process may well persuade the host state to resolve the dispute without the need for it to go to trial.

A typical BIT[6]

Most investor states have model BITs which they follow to varying degrees, depending on the negotiating strength of the other state. Although the obligations are expressed as reciprocal, in practice the two parties are a developed state and a developing state, the first representing the investor, the other the state hosting the investment. No two BITs are identical,

[4] See p. 441 below.   [5] See Chapter 21 on state responsibility.
[6] See Dolzer and Stevens, *Bilateral Investment Treaties*, The Hague, 1995. See also http://ita.law.uvic.ca.

but they normally have fairly similar definitions of 'investor' and 'territory' and provisions on fair and equitable treatment; national or most-favoured-nation treatment (MFN) with regard to taxes, repatriation of investments, payments, income, profits etc.; expropriation; national or MFN treatment for losses due to war, revolution, insurrection etc.; the settlement of disputes; and the duration of the BIT and its continued application to investments made before termination.

The entities protected

BITs protect investments made by nationals of one state in the territory of the host state. Nationals are defined as natural persons having the nationality of the investor's state, and legal persons as corporations, partnerships, firms or associations incorporated under its laws.[7] A *third advantage* of BITs is that they often provide that investor companies include also those incorporated under the law of the *host* state, but controlled, directly or indirectly, by a company incorporated under the law of the *investor's* state. An investment made in the Philippines by a local company controlled by a company incorporated in The Netherlands would be protected under the Netherlands–Philippines BIT 1985.[8]

Investments are often made through companies incorporated in the most favourable jurisdiction for protection ('strategic incorporation'), although other important factors must also be considered, including tax advantages. Thus investments can be made abroad through companies incorporated in *third* states. Protection will be further increased when the state of incorporation of the investor company and the host state are parties to a BIT. A German investment made through a Luxembourg company would be protected if the host state has a BIT with Luxembourg. Companies also make investments through subsidiary companies incorporated in the overseas territories of their own or another state. It is therefore important that the relevant BIT also protects investments made by companies incorporated in such territories.

Types of investment protected

BITs define investment in broad terms. For example, the UK–Venezuela BIT 1995[9] defines 'investment' as 'every kind of asset held and in

---

[7] See p. 182 above on the customary international law problems of determining the nationality of corporations.
[8] 1488 UNTS 304 (No. 25565).   [9] UKTS (1996) 83.

particular, though not exclusively, includes' movable and immovable property, shares, contractual rights, intellectual property rights, and business concessions, including 'concessions to search for, cultivate, extract or exploit natural resources' (the latter being commonly included).

Two approaches are used to determine which investments will be protected. The more usual is to protect all aspects of an activity that meet the definition of 'investment'. The other, although much less often found, is to add a requirement that the investment must be approved in writing by the other state in order to qualify for protection.

Contractual disputes, whether with a company in the host state or with the host state itself, are not covered by the BIT, except in so far as the host state has done something that goes beyond a mere breach of contract, such as operating the contract in a way that benefits local company rivals to the detriment of the foreign investor.

Treatment of investments

Since BITs have two basic purposes – to encourage investments and to protect them – they require the host state to accord 'fair and equitable treatment' to inward investment. This is a basic and general standard recognised in customary international law and is not related to the domestic law of the host state. To give substance to the concept of fair and equitable treatment, certain BITs list the activities that are to be protected against injurious measures. This could be said to be the *fourth advantage* of BITs.

In addition, investments enjoy most-favoured-nation or national treatment. MFN treatment gives the foreign investor the same rights as those granted by the host state to investors from the most-favoured third state. Under national treatment, the investor is granted treatment equal to that accorded to local nationals. Often, a BIT provides for the standard to be whatever is most favourable to the investor, which is not necessarily national treatment.

BITs also encourage investment by providing for the free transfer abroad of earnings and capital: this is the *fifth advantage* of BITs.

Expropriation and compensation

There are, even now, controversial issues in customary international law relating to the expropriation of foreign investments. These include even such basic questions as: to what extent does international law, rather than the legislation of the host state, govern expropriation? Do the rules of international law prohibit expropriation which is discriminatory or which is not done for a public purpose? How is compensation to be determined? A BIT resolves these issues as between the parties by regulating the conditions under which expropriation may be carried out and compensation awarded (the *sixth advantage*). Expropriation is prohibited if it is done in a discriminatory way or is not done for a public purpose, some specifying that the purpose must be related to internal needs. But payment of compensation for expropriation is required in any event. Because BITs are quite tightly drafted, some host states have tried to get around the restrictions on expropriation by indirect means. Naked expropriation is now unusual: physically taking over an oil field is just too crude. But discriminatory treatment, or expropriation by indirect means, is still a problem, even in some developed economies.[10] Onerous environmental requirements or discriminatory or penal tax regimes can also amount to expropriation. Some governments have imposed new taxes which in practice apply only to foreign investments, or which bear more heavily on foreign investors than on local businesses and which significantly affect the value of the foreign investment. Arbitral awards have found such methods amount to expropriation.[11]

But the tables have been turned. Originally, BITs were seen as protecting investors from the developed world from the governments of the third world. Now some developed countries, in particular the United States, are being challenged by developing country investors over the imposition of taxes or other unfair treatment of their investments. And they are using BITs to do this.

BITs establish in broad terms the basis on which compensation is assessed. The UK–Venezuela BIT 1995 (Article 5(1))[12] requires that compensation be 'prompt, adequate and effective', and amount to the 'genuine value' of the investment 'immediately before the expropriation or before the impending expropriation became public knowledge, whichever is the earlier', and include interest at 'a normal commercial rate'. The reference to the value immediately before the expropriation became public knowledge is most important since the very fact of expropriation may well affect the value of an investment, and there may be no formal announcement, or there may be 'creeping' expropriation. This will also complicate the determination of the value of the investment.

---

[10] See Reisman and Sloane, 'Indirect Expropriation and Its Valuation in the BIT Generation' (2003) BYIL 115.

[11] See, for example, *Metalclad* v. *Mexico*, ILM (2001) 35; 119 ILR 615.   [12] See n. 9 above.

The date when compensation must be paid is another issue. BITs also provide that payment must be made without delay, and be effectively realisable and freely transferable. Some BITs permit transfer payments by instalment if the compensation is large.

Civil disturbance etc.

BITs also prescribe a standard of treatment if investments are harmed by war, revolution, a state of national emergency, revolt, insurgency or riot. If compensation has to be paid, the investor will be treated in accordance with the standard laid down in the BIT. In some BITs, this will be MFN or national treatment, or whichever is more favourable.

Dispute settlement

However well drafted, the interpretation and application of the provisions of a BIT may not be easy. With so much at stake, it is vital that the investor has a sure and effective way of resolving any dispute. A valuable aspect of BITs is that they provide that, if a dispute between the investor and the host state cannot be settled within a specified period, the foreign investor has the *right* to submit the dispute to international mixed arbitration:[13] the *seventh advantage*. A number of arbitration fora may be available, the BIT sometimes specifying two or more. The International Centre for the Settlement of Investment Disputes (ICSID)[14] is the obvious choice if both states are parties to the ICSID Convention. Other fora include the Stockholm Chamber of Commerce, *ad hoc* tribunals operating under the UN Commission on International Trade Law (UNCITRAL)[15] or the International Chamber of Commerce.[16] Where a BIT gives the investor a choice of forum, in selecting it the investor will consider the expertise of the administering institution and, among other factors, its independence, impartiality and confidentiality. However, many BITs specify only one forum.

Duration of BITs

The initial term of a BIT tends to be ten to fifteen years. When that expires, the BIT either continues in force indefinitely until terminated by notice

---

[13] See p. 445 below on mixed arbitrations.   [14] See p. 379 below.
[15] www.uncitral.org.   [16] www.iccwbo.org.

(usually twelve months), or is renewed tacitly for specified periods, unless notice is given before the end of each (usually ten-year) period. But, even when a BIT has been terminated, it will continue in force, for a period that can range from ten to twenty years, with respect to investments made before the actual date of termination.

ICSID

The International Centre for the Settlement of Investment Disputes (ICSID) was established by the (Washington) Convention on the Settlement of Investment Disputes between States and Nationals of Other States 1965,[17] which entered into force in 1966. Although a separate international organisation, ICSID, has close links to the World Bank, collaborating with it in meeting requests by states for advice on investment and arbitration law. The ICSID Secretary-General also acts as the appointing authority of arbitrators for *ad hoc* arbitrations. ICSID's publications include a multi-volume and periodically updated collection of *Investment Laws of the World, Investment Treaties*, the bi-annual *ICSID Review-Foreign Investment Law Journal* (which has the full texts of ICSID awards),[18] and the *ICSID Annual Report*. The expenses of the ICSID Secretariat are financed out of the World Bank budget, although the costs of individual proceedings are borne by the parties.

ICSID was specially designed to facilitate the settlement of certain investment disputes but, like the Permanent Court of Arbitration,[19] it is not a tribunal. ICSID merely provides facilities and procedures for arbitration between a member state and an investor who is a national of another member state. The Convention does not define an individual's nationality, which is, in principle, determined by the law of the state of nationality, and a person who is also a national of the host state (dual national) cannot therefore invoke the ICSID procedure.[20] Nor does the Convention define the nationality of an investor which is

---

[17] The best source of basic documents and of up-to-date information is at www.worldbank.org/icsid/. See also C. Schreuer, *The ICSID Convention: A Commentary*, Cambridge, 2001, and Collier and Lowe, *The Settlement of Disputes in International Law*, Oxford, 1999. Each has the text of the Convention, which is also in 575 UNTS 159 (No. 8359); ILM (1965) 524; UKTS (1967) 25.

[18] The text of awards from 1991 onwards are available on the ICSID website, www.worldbank.org/icsid/. See also the ongoing comprehensive collection in *International Convention on the Settlement of Investment Disputes Reports*, Cambridge, 1993–.

[19] See p. 444 below. [20] On dual nationality, see p. 179 above.

a legal person, although this will often be determined in the agreement under which the two states have consented to ICSID jurisdiction. But, where the investor is a legal person with the nationality of the host state, but controlled by nationals of another member state (typically share-holders), the investor is not regarded as a national of the host state (Article 25(2)(b)).[21]

Recourse to ICSID arbitration is entirely voluntary, but once a member state and a foreign investor have given their written consent to ICSID arbitration, neither can unilaterally withdraw it (Article 25(1)). Consent to ICSID arbitration is commonly found in investment *contracts* between member states and foreign investors, and ICSID has produced *Model Clauses* for this purpose.[22] Member states can also give prior consent in their own investment laws (only some twenty have done so) or, most importantly, in BITs. Consent excludes resort to any other remedies, including domestic, unless otherwise agreed by the parties to the dispute.[23] Consent may be made subject to the investor exhausting local remedies, but this is unusual for BITs.[24] When adhering to the Convention, or afterwards, a state may inform ICSID that it would not consider submitting certain classes of disputes (Article 25(4)).[25] China has accepted only disputes about compensation for expropriation or nationalisation. Saudi Arabia excludes disputes about oil or acts of sovereignty, and Turkey excludes disputes about land. But such exclusions should not have the effect of taking disputes on those matters out of ICSID jurisdiction if they are otherwise clearly within the scope of the dispute settlement clause of a contract or a BIT.[26]

Where an investor and a member state have consented to a dispute being submitted to ICSID, the state of nationality of the investor is prohibited from giving diplomatic protection to, or bringing an international claim in respect of, the investor unless the other member state fails to comply with the award (Article 27). ICSID arbitration is also one of the main mechanisms for the settlement of investment disputes under four recent multilateral trade and investment treaties: NAFTA, the Energy Charter

---

[21] This reflects a common provision in BITs: see p. 375 above and Collier and Lowe, *The Settlement of Disputes in International Law*, Oxford, 1999, pp. 65–8.

[22] See www.worldbank.org/icsid/.

[23] As to the problems this can cause, see C. Schreuer, *The ICSID Convention: A Commentary*, Cambridge, 2001, pp. 345–96.

[24] See p. 374 above.

[25] See www.worldbank.org/icsid/pubs/icsid-8/icsid-8-d.htm.

[26] Collier and Lowe, *The Settlement of Disputes in International Law*, Oxford, 1999, p. 62.

Treaty, the Cartagena Free Trade Agreement and the Colonia Protocol of MERCOSUR (see below).

Rules of Procedure for the Institution of Conciliation and Arbitration Proceedings ('Institution Rules') govern the early stages of the proceedings. After that, the Rules of Procedure for Conciliation or for Arbitration take over and apply, subject to any changes agreed by the parties to the dispute.[27] Either party to a dispute can invoke the procedure, although it is usually the investor. An ICSID arbitration can be held anywhere the parties agree, not just at ICSID's headquarters. ICSID arbitral tribunals usually have three arbitrators (see the complex provisions of Articles 37–40). A tribunal applies either such law as is agreed by the parties or, in the absence of agreement, the law of the member state party (including its conflict of law rules) and the applicable rules of international law (Article 42). Failure of a party to appear or present his case is not regarded as an admission of liability, so the tribunal may proceed with the case and make an award (Article 45).

There is no appeal against an award, but the tribunal may be asked to interpret or revise it (Articles 50–51). Under Article 52, an application to annul an award on the ground of procedural irregularities is heard by an *ad hoc* committee of three. Two awards have been annulled on the ground that the tribunal had manifestly exceeded its powers, although in both cases the committee has been criticised for going beyond procedural matters and deciding points of law.[28] All ICSID member states, even if they are not parties to the dispute, are required by the Convention to recognise and enforce an ICSID award as if it were a final judgment of their own courts, but state immunity from execution is not affected.[29] In that event, the matter would have to be dealt with under the law of state responsibility. The number of ICSID cases has increased significantly in recent years. By the end of 2004, eighty-six cases had been concluded, with a similar number pending.

In 1978, ICSID promulgated the Additional Facility Rules authorising the Secretariat to administer certain types of proceedings between states and foreign nationals that fall outside the scope of the Convention. The Facility is also available for cases where the dispute is not about investment, provided it relates to a transaction which has 'features that distinguish it

---

[27] For both sets of rules, see www.worldbank.org/icsid/.
[28] Collier and Lowe, *The Settlement of Disputes in International Law*, Oxford, 1999, pp 70–3; Schreuer, *The ICSID Convention: A Commentary*, Cambridge, 2001, pp. 881–1075.
[29] See p. 173 above.

from an ordinary commercial transaction'. The Facility has rarely been used.

Energy Charter Treaty[30]

The Energy Charter Treaty 1994 entered into force in 1998 and now has forty-seven parties, including developing states such as Kazakhstan, Mongolia and Uzbekistan. Russia applies the Treaty provisionally. Although Japan is a member, the Treaty is Eurocentric. It applies to investments that are associated with an 'economic activity in the energy sector'. This covers exploitation, extraction, refining, production, storage, land transport, transmission, distribution, trade, marketing or sale of energy materials and products. It also includes such services as the construction of energy facilities, management and design, and activities aimed at economic efficiency.

Its provisions on investment promotion and protection and the settlement of disputes provide a legally binding framework for co-operation between the parties in the field of energy. Although multilateral, the Treaty is equivalent to a network of BITs. Article 16 gives energy investors the best of both worlds: in so far as a previous or future BIT gives better protection than the Treaty, the BIT will apply, and *vice versa*. The other investment protection clauses are on similar lines to contemporary BITs, although they go into much more detail and generally give better protection. An aggrieved investor has the right, but not the duty, to seek local remedies, but even if he does he can still invoke compulsory international arbitration (under ICSID, *ad hoc* under UNCITRAL rules or under the Stockholm Chamber of Commerce), and he does not have to wait until local remedies have been exhausted.

World Trade Organization

The 1994 Marrakesh Agreement established the World Trade Organization (WTO), as from 1 January 1995.[31] The Agreement incorporates several existing multilateral trade agreements, and four important new

---

[30] 2080 UNTS 100 (No. 36116); ILM (1995) 373; UKTS (2000) 78 and www.encharter.org; T. Walde (ed.), *The Energy Charter Treaty*, London, 1996.

[31] ILM (1994) 1144. The Agreement, including all the agreements making up the WTO, and all other relevant documents are on the WTO website, www.wto.org. See also Matsushita, Schoenbaum and Mavroidis, *The World Trade Organization: Law, Practice and Policy*, Oxford, 2003.

agreements: (1) the General Agreement on Tariffs and Trade 1994 (GATT 1994), which effectively replaced GATT 1947; (2) the General Agreement on Trade in Services (GATS); (3) the Agreement on Trade-Related Aspects of Intellectual Property Rights (TRIPS); and (4) the (vital) Understanding on Rules and Procedures Governing the Settlement of Disputes. The purpose of the WTO is to eliminate or reduce barriers to trade. This required bringing existing and new multilateral trade agreements into a comprehensive system with an effective dispute settlement mechanism. The WTO is also a permanent forum for the negotiation of further reductions in trade barriers. Decisions are taken as far as possible by consensus. If this is not possible, it is taken by a simple majority, unless otherwise provided in the Agreement or another agreement (Article IX).

In contrast to GATT 1947, to become a WTO member one has to accept all the agreements and understandings that make up the WTO. Any state, or separate customs territory,[32] can apply to be a member, the terms of accession being agreed with the existing members. At the end of 2004, there were 148 members, each with one vote. They include all the significant economies, except Russia and Saudi Arabia.

Dispute Settlement[33]

A means of dealing effectively with disputes between WTO members was essential for the credibility of the WTO. The Understanding on Settlement of Disputes is in Annex 2 to the WTO Agreement.[34] Despite its grossly misleading name, the Understanding is an integral part of the WTO Agreement and binding on all WTO members. It applies to most WTO disputes. A Dispute Settlement Body (DSB), on which all WTO members sit, administers the system, establishing panels and adopting panel and Appellate Body reports, monitoring implementation of rulings and recommendations, and authorising countermeasures.

The purpose of the DSB is to provide security and predictability to the multilateral trading system. It therefore seeks settlement of disputes as they arise, not years later, although in practice the process is complex and slow. Members seeking redress for a violation of obligations

---

[32] The European Communities, Hong Kong (China), Macao (China) and Chinese Taipei (Taiwan) are each full members.
[33] See the WTO's own *A Handbook on the WTO Dispute Settlement System*, Cambridge, 2004; Palmeter and Mavroidis, *Dispute Settlement in the World Trade Organization*, 2nd edn, Cambridge, 2004; and *The WTO Dispute Settlement Reports*, Cambridge, 1996–.
[34] ILM (1994) 1226.

or other nullification or impairment of benefits under the 'covered agreements'[35] must have recourse to the Understanding, not to other means.[36] At all stages of any dispute settlement procedure involving a least-developed country member, particular consideration must be given to the latter's special situation.

The DSB began operations in 1995. By the end of 2004, over 300 complaints had been filed, and there are now about thirty new ones each year. Over 100 panels have been established, the other complaints having been resolved by consultations. In the first ten years, some seventy-five panel reports and fifty Appellate Body reports were adopted by the DSB, although the number of appeals is decreasing. The system is complex, and only a brief overview can be given here.

Although the DSB applies the 'customary rules of interpretation of public international law', instead of considering breaches of rights the DSB looks more at whether the 'benefits' that a member expects to derive from a covered agreement have been 'impaired' by measures taken by another member. By its recommendations and rulings, the DSB seeks to produce positive, workable and mutually acceptable solutions.

The objective of the system is first to secure the withdrawal of any unlawful measures. Compensation is to be resorted to only if immediate withdrawal is impracticable, it then being a temporary measure pending withdrawal. The system therefore more resembles conciliation, although it is not left just to economists; lawyers are also intimately involved. But, as a last resort, the member invoking the dispute settlement procedure has, subject to authorisation by the DSB, the option of 'suspending the application of concessions or other obligations under the covered agreements on a discriminatory basis vis-à-vis the other Member' (a long-winded way of referring to the imposition of countermeasures).[37] The Understanding sets strict time limits, although the DSB can extend them, and the parties are always encouraged to reach a solution by any means they can

---

[35] Those agreements listed in Appendix 1 to the Understanding: the WTO Agreement: the Understanding, the Multilateral Trade Agreements (Multilateral Agreements on Trade in Goods, GATS and TRIPS) and the Plurilateral Trade Agreements (the Agreements on Trade in Civil Aircraft and on Government Procurement, the International Dairy Agreement and the International Bovine Meat Agreement). Appendix 2 lists special or additional rules and procedures for covered agreements.

[36] Article 23; and *United States – Sections 301–310 of the Trade Act of 1974*, Report of the Panel, 22 December 1999, WT/DS152/R, paras. 7.35–7.46. The EC also has it own, self-contained system of enforcement: see Case C-5/94, *R. v. MAFF, ex parte Hedley Lomas* [1996] ECR I-2553.

[37] See p. 425 below on countermeasures in general.

agree on. There is no need for nationals of the complainant member who are affected by measures taken by another Member first to exhaust local remedies.[38]

Panels

If the parties to a dispute have not resolved it by consultations, the complaining party may ask that a panel be established. The panel's role is to make findings to help the DSB in formulating recommendations or giving rulings provided for under the covered agreements. A panel has three members unless the parties agree to have five. The Secretariat maintains a list of possible members and proposes nominations. A party can oppose a nomination only for compelling reasons. Should there be no agreement on the appointment of members, the WTO Director-General will at the request of either party make the appointments. Third parties that have notified the DSB of a substantial interest in the matter may make written submissions to, and be heard by, the panel. The panel's deliberations are confidential. It consults regularly with the parties, giving them adequate opportunity to develop a mutually satisfactory solution. But if they fail the panel submits a report to the DSB, which is circulated to all Members. The report is then adopted by the DSB within sixty days, unless a party notifies the DSB that it will appeal, or the DSB decides, by consensus, not to adopt the report (so-called negative consensus).

Appellate Body

The DSB appoints seven persons to serve on the Appellate Body for four-year terms, renewable only once. Three of them sit on any one case. Appeals from panel cases are limited to issues of law covered in the panel report. The power to adopt interpretations of the WTO Agreement and other covered agreements is vested exclusively in the WTO Ministerial Conference and General Council (Article IX(2)). But this does prevent the panels or the Appellate Body interpreting any of the agreements, subject always to such adopted interpretations, which may themselves have to be interpreted.

Only the parties to the dispute may appeal, although third parties which have notified the DSB of a substantial interest in the matter may make

---

[38] See p. 441 below.

written submissions to, and be heard by, the Appellate Body. The proceedings are confidential, and continue for no more than ninety days. The Appellate Body may uphold, modify or reverse the legal findings and conclusions of the panel. The DSB then adopts the report of the Appellate Body (which is binding on the parties) unless the DSB decides, by consensus, not to adopt the report.

Recommendations

When a panel or the Appellate Body concludes that a measure is inconsistent with a covered agreement, it 'recommends' that the member bring the measure into conformity with the covered agreement, and may 'suggest' ways in which the member could implement the recommendation. The findings and recommendation of the panel or Appellate Body cannot add to or diminish rights and obligations under the covered agreements. Within thirty days of the adoption of a panel or Appellate Body report, the member must tell the DSB of its intentions as regards the implementation of the recommendation.

Compensation and countermeasures

Compensation and countermeasures are 'temporary' measures available in the event that recommendations or rulings are not implemented, neither being preferable to full implementation. Compensation is voluntary. If the member fails to comply with recommendations and rulings within the reasonable period it must, if so requested, enter into negotiations with the other party with a view to agreeing compensation. If that cannot be agreed, any complaining party may ask the DSB to authorise it to take countermeasures (Articles 3(7) and 22).

In considering what countermeasures to seek, Article 22(3) requires the complaining party to follow certain general principles: (a) countermeasures should be with respect to the same sector(s) as that in which the panel or Appellate Body has found a violation or other nullification or impairment; (b) if that is not practicable or effective, countermeasures may be sought in other sectors of the same agreement; (c) and if that is not practicable or effective, and the circumstances are serious enough, the complaining party may seek countermeasures in respect of another covered agreement. In applying these principles, account should be taken of (i) the trade in the sector or under the agreement under which the panel or Appellate Body has found a violation or other nullification or impairment, and the importance of such trade to the complaining party and

(ii) the broader economic elements related to the nullification or impairment and the broader economic consequences of countermeasures. The DSB authorises countermeasures unless it decides, by consensus, to reject the request. The level of the authorised countermeasures must be proportionate to the nullification or impairment, and the DSB cannot authorise countermeasures if they are prohibited by a relevant covered agreement. However, the question of countermeasures is referred to arbitration if the respondent member (1) objects that the authorised countermeasures are disproportionate or (2) claims that the principles and procedures set forth in Article 22(3) were not followed when the complaining party had requested authorisation for countermeasures pursuant to subparagraphs (b) or (c) above. The arbitration is carried out by the original panel or by one or more arbitrators appointed by the Director-General. Meanwhile, countermeasures must not be taken. The arbitral award is final. If the countermeasures are approved, the DSB must then, upon request, authorise them, unless it decides, by consensus, to reject the request.

In September 2000, the DSB adopted an Appellate Body report in favour of the EC that the United States had not brought its Antidumping Act 1916 into conformity with its WTO obligations. In January 2002, the EC asked the DSB to authorise countermeasures. The United States objected to their proposed level, and the matter went to arbitration. In February 2004, the arbitration award decided that the EC could impose countermeasures (suspension of its obligations under GATT 1994 and the Anti-Dumping Agreement) within certain parameters.[39] When last heard, the US Senate was considering repeal of the Act.

Rather than going through the panel/Appellate Body procedure, an alternative means of dispute settlement for issues that have been clearly defined by both parties is simple binding and expeditious arbitration within the WTO, and this is encouraged. It is of course subject to the agreement of the parties.

NAFTA

The North American Free Trade Agreement 1992 between Canada, Mexico and the United States entered into force in 1994.[40] NAFTA aims to remove trade barriers and promote fair competition and investment. A Free Trade

---

[39] WT/DS136; ILM (2004) 931.
[40] ILM (1993) 289. The website is the best primary source of texts and other information: www.nafta-sec-alena.org. Collier and Lowe, *The Settlement of Disputes in International Law*, Oxford, 1999, pp. 111–15, has a useful summary of the dispute mechanism.

Commission oversees its implementation and can also give interpretations of the Agreement to domestic courts, although these are not binding in domestic law.

Chapter 20 of NAFTA provides that when there is a dispute between two member states about a trade measure which comes also within the scope of the WTO, the complaining party has discretion as to which forum to use. Under NAFTA, the dispute is subject to consultations and, ultimately, a report by a five-person arbitral panel. If a third NAFTA member has a substantial interest in the subject matter, it may join in as a complaining party. If the panel reports that a measure is inconsistent with NAFTA obligations, yet the member responsible does not remedy this inconsistency, the complaining member can take countermeasures similar to those under the WTO Agreement. But a member state may not provide in its domestic law for any right of action based on a claim that a measure taken by another member state is inconsistent with NAFTA.

Chapter 11 of NAFTA has detailed provisions for the protection of investments similar to those commonly found in BITs, and for investment disputes to be decided by international arbitration under ICSID, the ICSID Additional Facility Rules or the UNCITRAL Rules.[41] Recourse to arbitration bars the investor from pursuing domestic remedies. Arbitrations that have a question of fact or law in common may be consolidated. An award may be enforced under ICSID, the New York Convention[42] or the Inter-American Convention on International Commercial Arbitration 1975 (Panama Convention).[43]

MERCOSUR

The Mercado Común del Sur (MERCOSUR) was established in 1991 by the Treaty of Asunción,[44] and the Ouro Preto Protocol 1994.[45] Its purpose

---

[41] For examples of recent cases, see *Feldman* v. *United Mexican States*, 126 ILR 1 and 536; *Myers* v. *Canada*, ILM (2001) 1408; 126 ILR 161; and *Pope & Talbot Inc.* v. *Canada*, ILM (2002) 1347; 126 ILR 127.

[42] 330 UNTS 3 (No. 4739); UKTS (1976) 26; TIAS 6997. See Collier and Lowe, *The Settlement of Disputes in International Law*, Oxford, 1999, pp. 266–70.

[43] 1438 UNTS 249 (No. 24384); ILM (1975) 336.

[44] ILM (1991) 1041. For this and the other Mercosur treaties and information generally, see www.mercosur.org.uy (Spanish and Brazilian Portuguese only). See also M. Haines-Ferrari, *The MERCOSUR Codes*, London, 2000; Haines-Ferrari, 'Mercosur: Individual Access and the Dispute Settlement Mechanism', in Cameron and Campbell (eds.), *Dispute Resolution in WTO*, London, 1999, p. 270; and Haines-Ferrari, 'Mercosur: A New Model of Latin American Economic Integration?' (1993) *Case Western Journal of International Law* 413.

[45] ILM (1995) 1244. See also (1998) ICLQ 149.

is to develop a common market and customs union. Based in Uruguay, its members are Argentina, Brazil, Colombia, Ecuador, Paraguay, Peru, Uruguay and Venezuela. Bolivia and Chile are associate members. The Protocol of Brasilia 1991 (to be replaced by the Protocol of Olivos 1992, once ratified) has a system for dealing with disputes between the member states, including on behalf of their nationals. First there are direct negotiations, then internal MERCOSUR mechanisms and ultimately an *ad hoc* arbitration panel. The Protocol of Colonia 1993 provides for NAFTA-type mixed arbitration of investment disputes. In 1995, MERCOSUR concluded a framework co-operation agreement with the EU.[46]

MERCOSUR has not been very effective. In late 2004, it was reported that South American states were considering replacing it with a larger and more comprehensive South American Community (Comunidad Sudamericana de Naciones).

International commercial arbitration[47]

It is beyond the scope of this book to go into detail about international commercial arbitration. It is enough to say that there are sets of rules, quite similar in content, for the conduct of commercial arbitrations between (mainly) corporations or, to a much smaller extent, between corporations and states. Unless the parties to a dispute are bound by contract or treaty to accept particular rules, they can agree to use any of these sets of rules. If the latter, they will almost certainly use one of the ready-made sets of rules as a basis, there being no point in reinventing the wheel. Those rules most used are the arbitration rules of the International Chamber of Commerce (ICC)[48] and the UN Commission on International Trade Law (UNCITRAL).[49] Although the parties can agree changes to the rules, if one of the institutions is asked to conduct the arbitration it generally does not look with favour on any messing about with its tried and tested rules. The ICC, based in Paris, was established in 1919. But arbitrations under its rules, or the UNCITRAL rules, can be held anywhere, although they are often held in London or Geneva.

---

[46] See http://europa.eu.int/comm/external_relations/mercosur/intro/.
[47] For the various rules, see Smit and Pechota, *Arbitration Rules – International Institutions*, London, 1997; or for links to the main websites, see www.internationaladr.com/iir/.
[48] See www.iccwbo.org/tribunal/english/arbitration/rules.asp.
[49] See www.uncitral.org/en-index/.

20

Succession of states

Kingdoms are clay.[1]

Shaw, *International Law*, 5th edn, Cambridge, 2003, pp. 861–913
Brownlie, *Principles of Public International Law*, 6th edn, Oxford, 2003, pp. 621–43
Oppenheim. *Oppenheim's International Law*, 9th edn, London, 1992, pp. 204–44
Aust, *Modern Treaty Law and Practice*, Cambridge, 2000, pp. 305–51

A state may change its name, constitution or government by revolution or constitutionally, but it will retain its international legal personality[2] and remain bound by its international obligations. If some of its territory becomes a new state it has to be determined which rights and obligations of the (predecessor) state become those of the new (successor) state. Succession to treaties, to state property, archives and debts, and to membership of international organisations, are the main topics discussed below. The value of state practice before the Second World War as a guide to today's problems of succession is questionable. The post-war era of decolonisation and the end of the Cold War led to the total number of states increasing nearly fourfold and has given us a useful body of modern state practice.

The law is complex, and is especially dependent on the particular circumstances of each case. The two Vienna Conventions on succession (see below) are of some help, but must be approached with caution. One has entered into force, but has very few parties; the other is not in force and is unlikely ever to be so. Neither applies to a succession that occurs before their entry into force. International courts and bodies have endorsed some of their provisions, yet there are substantial doubts as to the extent to which they reflect customary international law. In considering any succession question, one must therefore examine the relevant Vienna

---

[1] W. Shakespeare, *Antony and Cleopatra*, 1.i.12.   [2] See p. 16 above.

Convention and the leading general and specialist works and precedents, always having regard to the particular facts of the case. Succession can happen in many ways.

Independence of an overseas territory

Those states in existence at the end of the Second World War stayed mostly unchanged until the Cold War ended. But, during that period, over 100 overseas territories[3] gained their independence, mostly during the main era of decolonisation from 1945 to 1980. This produced a valuable body of state practice and influenced, although not necessarily helpfully, attempts to codify the law on succession.

Secession

This mainly concerns the metropolitan territory of a state: Singapore seceded from Malaysia (1965), Bangladesh from Pakistan (1971), Eritrea from Ethiopia (1993) and Timor Leste (East Timor) from Indonesia (2002). The most dramatic example was the secession of fourteen republics of the Soviet Union.[4] It was done with the agreement of the predecessor state, which continued in existence under the name of the Russian Federation.[5]

Dissolution

At the end of the First World War the Hapsburg Empire was dismembered, producing several new states, including Yugoslavia. After the Second World War, Yugoslavia became the Socialist Federal Republic of Yugoslavia (SFRY). The end of the Cold War led to the break-up of the SFRY. By 1992 or 1993, the constituent republics of the SFRY (Bosnia and Herzegovina, Croatia, Macedonia, Serbia and Montenegro, and Slovenia) had become independent states. But Serbia and Montenegro, which had re-labelled itself the Federal Republic of Yugoslavia (FRY), wrongly claimed that it was the continuation of the SFRY, and this delayed its recognition.[6]

Czechoslovakia was a product of the dissolution of the Hapsburg Empire. It emerged from the Second World War as a communist state,

---

[3] See p. 29 above.   [4] See p. 20 above about the present Russian republics.
[5] See p. 393 below.   [6] See p. 20 above.

but the end of the Cold War, and the political ambitions of Slovak leaders, led to the so-called velvet divorce. By agreement, at midnight on 31 December 1992, the state of Czechoslovakia was dissolved and succeeded by two states, the Czech Republic and Slovakia.

At the end of the Second World War, Germany was occupied by France, the Soviet Union, the United Kingdom and the United States, who together assumed 'supreme authority' over it. They did not annex Germany, but its international personality was suspended. In due course, two German states, the Federal Republic of Germany (FRG or West Germany) and the German Democratic Republic (GDR or East Germany), were established.[7] Until the reunification of Germany (see below), Berlin had a very special and complex status.[8]

Merger

On 2 July 1976, the two states of the Democratic Republic of Viet Nam (North Vietnam) and the Republic of Viet Nam (South Vietnam) joined together as one state, the Socialist Republic of Viet Nam.[9] On 22 May 1990, the People's Democratic Republic of Yemen (South Yemen) and the Republic of Yemen (North Yemen) merged into a single state, the Republic of Yemen. In 1964, Tanganyika and Zanzibar joined to form one state, the United Republic of Tanzania.

There has been at least one, short-lived merger of two states to form a single state. In 1958, Egypt and Syria joined together as one state, the United Arab Republic (UAR). It was dissolved in 1961, but Egypt retained the name UAR until 1971. In 1982, Gambia and Senegal established the Senegambia Confederation, each state retaining its sovereignty and independence. It was therefore not a union, but a true confederation, and was dissolved in 1989. (The Swiss Confederation is a federal state.)[10]

Absorption and extinction

The Germany that emerged on 3 October 1990 resulted from the Unification Treaty by which the GDR willingly agreed to be absorbed into the FRG, the GDR Länder (states after GDR) becoming Länder of the

---

[7] Oppenheim, pp. 135–9 and 699–700.
[8] Oppenheim, pp. 139–41; and Hendry and Wood, *The Legal Status of Berlin*, Cambridge, 1987.
[9] Oppenheim, pp. 141–3.   [10] See p. 57 above.

FRG. The name of the reunified Germany therefore remained the Federal Republic of Germany.[11]

Recovery of sovereignty

The most recent example is the three Baltic states of Estonia, Latvia and Lithuania. Having gained their independence from Russia after the First World War, in 1940 they were occupied and then unlawfully annexed by the Soviet Union. They regained their sovereignty in 1991 and joined the European Union in 2004.

Transfer of territory

The transfer of part of the metropolitan territory of a state to another state will not usually involve succession, the 'moving boundary' principle applying,[12] as when Alsace-Lorraine was returned to France at the end of the First World War. Although it is a question of degree, the boundary between the two states is simply moved so that the territory transferred becomes part of the transferee's territory, with no succession issues arising.

Continuity of statehood

In 1947, on the partition of India into India and Pakistan, India was regarded by the UN General Assembly as the continuation of the previous state, and Pakistan as a new state. The dramatic changes to the Union of Soviet Socialist Republics in 1991 led fourteen of its republics to break away to become new states, yet the state which had exercised sovereignty over them continued despite the large loss of territory and population, and the change of name to that of its principal constituent part, the Russian Federation.

Succession to treaties

The Vienna Convention on the Law of Treaties does not cover succession (Article 73). One would therefore be forgiven for thinking that the Vienna

---

[11] Oppenheim, pp. 138–9; Shaw, pp. 868–70; see (1997) BYIL 520–9.
[12] See p. 395 below.

Convention on Succession of States in respect of Treaties 1978[13] (the '1978 Convention') provides the answers to all treaty succession problems, but it does not. The Convention entered into force only in 1996 when it achieved the necessary fifteen ratifications. This was only made possible by the adherence of the new states of Bosnia and Herzegovina, Croatia, Estonia, Slovakia, Slovenia, Macedonia and Ukraine. Unless a successor state agrees otherwise, the Convention does not apply to a succession that occurs before entry into force of the Convention for the states concerned.

The International Law Commission (ILC) had prepared the draft of the 1978 Convention. The ILC had noted that state practice indicated no general doctrine which resolved the various problems of succession to treaties, and that the number of different theories of succession did not make the task any easier. The Convention therefore contains much that is a progressive development of international law, and therefore much of it cannot be regarded as reflecting customary international law, the most recent state practice relating to former overseas territories not being consistent. The rules of the Convention concerned with such new states are also excessively complex. They give undue prominence to the so-called clean slate principle, and insufficient weight to the abundant state practice of concluding devolution agreements or, even more importantly, of making declarations of succession. Moreover, the Convention rules about the break-up of metropolitan states did not reflect modern state practice, there then being little practice to draw on. Although parts of the Convention may have been relied upon in drafting certain bilateral succession agreements,[14] its influence and practical value is considerably less than that of the Vienna Convention on the Law of Treaties 1969. Overall, the 1978 Convention is not a reliable guide to such rules of customary law on treaty succession as there are.

The customary law principles[15]

The rules of customary international law on the subject are not easy to state, the circumstances varying widely and the subject being politically charged. The interests and perception of a successor state may differ significantly from those of the predecessor state (assuming it still exists)

---

[13] 1946 UNTS 3 (No. 33356); ILM (1978) 1488. For the treaty, the ILC draft and commentary, and an introduction, see A. Watts, *The International Law Commission 1949–1998*, Oxford, 1999, vol. II, pp. 987–1208. See also A. Aust, 'Limping Treaties: Lessons from Multilateral Treaty-Making' (2003) NILR 243 at 252–3. Oppenheim has a summary of the Convention at pp. 237–40.
[14] See, for example (1995) AJIL 761–2. [15] For more details, see Aust, pp. 307–22.

and of third states. As far as bilateral treaties are concerned, in practice much depends on what can be agreed, expressly or tacitly, between
the successor state and *third* states. When it is possible for the successor
state and its predecessor to reach agreement on treaty succession this will
be important to third states, although they will not be bound by the
agreement. It is therefore a particularly uncertain and controversial area.
Although recent state practice may prove to be valuable, for the moment
it is safer to say that there are only certain customary law principles;
for the rest, there is evolving state practice. Indeed, almost all problems
(particularly with bilateral treaties) are resolved on the basis of agreement between the successor state and third states. Such residual rules of
customary international law as exist play a relatively minor role.

Certain general principles can be deduced with reasonable confidence.
They apply whether a treaty is bilateral or multilateral:

- A new state does not succeed automatically to a treaty if the subject
  matter is closely linked to the relations of the predecessor state with
  the other party or parties. Examples include 'political treaties' such as
  treaties of alliance or defence.
- Without any action by it, a new state will succeed to treaties (or rather
  to the legal situation created by them) relating to matters such as the
  status of territory, boundaries or navigation of rivers.[16] Although this
  principle is well established, its exact extent is not.[17]
- When a state has been absorbed by another (for example, the GDR by
  the FRG), almost all treaties entered into by the absorbed state will either
  simply lapse or their fate will need to be discussed with the other parties.
  Under the 'moving-boundary principle', treaties of the absorbing state
  will extend to the absorbed state, those of the predecessor state ceasing
  to apply. But when there is a true union of states (for example, Yemen),
  most existing treaties will continue to bind the successor state, at least
  as regards that part of its territory for which the treaties were in force
  before the union.[18] This is also the approach of Article 31 of the 1978
  Convention.
- Normally, a new state will not succeed automatically to multilateral treaties. Some writers consider that treaties which embody or
  reflect generally accepted rules of international law (in particular, those
  concerned with human rights or international humanitarian law) bind

---

[16] See *Gabčikovo-Nagymaros* case, p. 401, text to n. 40, below.
[17] See Articles 11 and 12 of the 1978 Convention; Oppenheim, p. 213; Shaw, pp. 871–5. See
Aust, p. 30 on the succession by former Yugoslav republics to the Austrian State Treaty.
[18] And see the entry for Yemen in *UN Multilateral Treaties*, 'Historical Introduction'.

a successor state by virtue of the concept of the acquired rights of the inhabitants of the state.[19] There is little authority for this view. But, in so far as a human rights treaty represents rules of customary international law, a successor state will be bound, but by those customary rules, not by the treaty.[20]

• A new state does not succeed automatically to bilateral treaties, other than to territorial treaties and suchlike (as above).

These general principles do not take one very far, but may be better understood by an examination of some of the more recent state practice.

Former colonies and other dependent territories

Although over 100 overseas territories have attained independence since the Second World War, their practice has not been consistent. It is therefore not possible to promulgate a set of rules of customary law applicable to such situations. The most one can do is to summarise the main approaches which have been taken.

There are two *theoretical* starting points. The first is the nineteenth-century theory of universal succession, which persisted up to the 1960s. According to this, a new state inherited all the treaty rights and obligations of the former colonial power in so far as they had been applicable to the territory before independence. This approach was reflected in the *devolution agreements* entered into by Iraq in 1931 and by some former Asian colonies in the 1940s and 1950s.[21] From 1955, all former British colonies in West Africa, except for The Gambia, concluded devolution agreements with the United Kingdom. These provided that, as from the date of independence, all treaty obligations and responsibilities of the United Kingdom would be assumed by the new state in so far as they could apply to it. Although these agreements created a presumption that a treaty which could have application to the new state would apply to it, they naturally left many questions unanswered.[22] A devolution agreement cannot bind a third state unless it consents, although this might be

---

[19] See R. Mullerson, 'The Continuity and Succession of States, by Reference to the Former USSR and Yugoslavia' (1993) ICLQ 473 at 490–2; M. Shaw, 'State Succession Revisited' (1994) *Finnish Yearbook of International Law* 34; and M. Kamminga, 'State Succession in Respect of Human Rights Treaties' (1995) EJIL 469–84.

[20] See p. 8 above; and Aust, p. 308.

[21] UKTS (1931) 15 (Iraq); Indonesia, 1949 (69 UNTS 266); Vietnam, 1954 (161 BSP 649); Malaya, 1957 (279 UNTS 287 (No. 4046)).

[22] T. Maluwa, 'Succession to Treaties in Post-Independence Africa' (1992) *African Journal of International and Comparative Law* 804.

signified by conduct. Nevertheless, devolution agreements have been useful in serving as formal and public statement of the general attitude of the new state.

The other starting point is the so-called *clean slate* doctrine, under which the new state is free to pick and choose which treaties to succeed to. This approach was followed most famously by the United States when it gained its independence. However, even when the doctrine is applied, treaties that concern territorial rights, like boundary treaties and those granting rights of navigation or passage, will usually bind the new state in any case.[23] The doctrine has been applied in different ways. Following the so-called Nyerere Doctrine, a number of former British territories made unilateral declarations in which they undertook that, for a specified period, they would continue to apply all bilateral treaties validly concluded by the United Kingdom, unless abrogated or modified by agreement. After that period, the new state would 'regard such of these treaties which could not by application of the rules of customary international law be regarded as otherwise surviving, as having terminated'.[24]

Unilateral statements do not bind third states unless they have consented in some way, and so in the longer term such declarations do not resolve all succession problems. Once the time limit has been reached, the effect of the declaration is uncertain unless by then the position of the new state in respect of all bilateral and multilateral treaties which might apply to the new state has been clarified. This is particularly so for treaties entered into expressly for the territory by the former colonial power, although the International Court of Justice has held that the latter bind the new state.[25] Another clean slate approach, adopted by Zambia in 1964, was to avoid any general commitment to confirm or deny the continuing applicability of treaties within any specific period.

Germany

The Unification Treaty entered into by the Federal Republic of Germany (FRG) and the German Democratic Republic (GDR)[26] provided that in principle most treaties entered into by the FRG would apply to the whole

---

[23] See p. 39 above.

[24] See the Declaration by Malawi on 24 November 1964 in the ILA study, *The Effect of Independence on Treaties*, London, 1965, p. 388; T. Maluwa, 'Succession to Treaties in Post-Independence Africa' (1992) *African Journal of International and Comparative Law* 804 at 806–7; Oppenheim, p. 231, n. 21.

[25] *US Nationals in Morocco, ICJ Reports* (1952), pp. 176, 193–4; 19 ILR 255.

[26] See p. 392 above.

of the reunified state (the moving-boundary principle), and for consultations with the other parties regarding treaties to which only the former GDR had been a party.[27] Although the treaty did not bind other parties, most accepted what had been agreed, that most of the GDR's bilateral treaties had lapsed. Germany became party to only a few multilateral treaties to which the GDR alone had been a party.[28] Thus the arrangements did not follow Article 31(2) of the 1978 Convention since it deals with a true merger of states to form a third state.[29]

Russia

Although it declared itself the continuation of the Soviet Union,[30] Russia declared unnecessarily that it would continue to comply with all the international obligations entered into by the Soviet Union.[31] It also sought to agree with some states a list of the bilateral treaties which would continue to apply as between them, since there were treaties entered into by the Soviet Union which in practice concerned only a part or parts of the Soviet Union which had now become independent. The approach taken by Russia and the other states is consistent with Article 35 of the 1978 Convention.

Former Soviet republics

The practice of Armenia, Azerbaijan, Belarus, Georgia, Kazakhstan, Kyrgyzstan, Moldova, Tajikistan, Turkmenistan, Ukraine and Uzbekistan regarding treaties is instructive, although not consistent or entirely clear.[32]

The Baltic states

Since Estonia, Latvia and Lithuania had been independent states until 1940, when they regained their independence in 1991 they did not regard themselves as successor states to the Soviet Union.[33] Instead, they

---

[27] ILM (1991) 457, Arts. 11 and 12.

[28] See the entry for Germany in *UN Multilateral Treaties*, 'Historical Information'; (1992) AJIL 152–73; D. Papenfuss, 'The Fate of the International Treaties of the German Democratic Republic within the Framework of German Unification' (1998) AJIL 469.

[29] Shaw, pp. 875–7.   [30] See p. 393 above.

[31] See the entry for the Russian Federation in *UN Multilateral Treaties*, 'Historical Information'.

[32] See Aust, pp. 312–14.

[33] See their entries in *UN Multilateral Treaties*, 'Historical Information'.

acceded[34] to many multilateral treaties to which the Soviet Union had been (and to which Russia continues to be) a party. There was, however, a problem with bilateral treaties entered into by the Soviet Union during the period of unlawful annexation; to maintain that they had no relevance would have been to ignore the reality of fifty years. With admirable pragmatism, agreement was therefore reached with some neighbouring states to regard certain of those treaties as in force, at least for the time being. Some bilateral treaties entered into in the period between the two World Wars, when the three Baltic states were independent, were agreed to be still applicable, the rest being obsolete or irrelevant by the 1990s. In principle, multilateral treaties entered into during that period will therefore be in force again.

Former Yugoslav republics

The dissolution of the SFRY[35] was anything but amicable, but it created similar succession questions as the break-up of Czechoslovakia (see below), although the attitude of the FRY (Serbia and Montenegro) was a complication.[36]

Bosnia and Herzegovina, Croatia, Macedonia and Slovenia each informed the UN Secretary-General that they considered themselves bound by virtue of state succession to multilateral treaties to which the SFRY had been bound. The SFRY had been a party to the 1978 Convention, and those four new states each deposited instruments of succession to it and to other multilateral treaties. They were apparently guided by Article 9(1) of the 1978 Convention which provides that making a *unilateral* declaration of succession is not enough to make the successor a party to a treaty.[37] The former republics have also entered into bilateral treaty succession arrangements with various states.

The new state of the Federal Republic of Yugoslavia (FRY) asserted, by analogy with Russia, that it was the continuation of the SFRY. The other former republics of the SFRY, as well as most third states, did not accept this.[38] The FRY's assertion of continuation was reflected in its

---

[34] See p. 64 above.   [35] See p. 391 above.

[36] See Wood, Participation of the Former Yugoslav States in the United Nations' (1997) *YB of UN Law* 231; and ILM (1992) 1488.

[37] But cf. Article 34.

[38] (1992) BYIL 655–8. See also the report of the Badinter Commission, 92 ILR 162 at 166. The ICJ elided the question in *Genocide (Bosnia v. Yugoslavia)* (Provisional Measures), *ICJ Reports* (1993), p. 3, at pp. 20–3; ILM (1993) 888; 95 ILR 1.

attitude to treaties. The FRY formally declared that as the continuation of the SFRY it would strictly abide by the SFRY's treaty obligations. This accorded with the wishes of other states that the FRY should abide by those obligations, albeit as one of the successor states of the SFRY. Other states were therefore faced with a dilemma: they wanted the FRY to respect the treaties, especially human rights conventions, to which the SFRY had been a party, but they could not accept the FRY as a party on the basis of continuation of statehood. It was not only a matter of principle: acceptance of the FRY's assertion of continuation could have had an effect on the important question of succession to other rights and obligations of the SFRY, especially with regard to property and debts (see below). In 2000, the FRY accepted that it was not the continuation of the SFRY, and in 2003 changed its name to Serbia and Montenegro.

Czechoslovakia

At midnight on 31 December 1992, the state of Czechoslovakia was dissolved and was succeeded by two states, the Czech Republic and Slovakia. Both declared themselves to be successors to Czechoslovakia and committed to fulfilling its treaty and other obligations.[39] In this they consciously applied the rules in Article 34 of the 1978 Convention. There was no suggestion that the Czech Republic, although the larger of the two new states, was the continuation of Czechoslovakia. The policy adopted by both states with regard to all *multilateral* treaties to which Czechoslovakia had been a party was that they would continue to bind each of the new states. In addition, each state regarded itself as a signatory of all those multilateral treaties that had been signed, but not ratified, before the dissolution.

Bilateral treaties entered into by Czechoslovakia were regarded by the two new states as continuing to apply, except in so far as this would not be appropriate. For example, the application of certain treaties had always been limited to the territory of Slovakia, in particular the 1977 Czechoslovakia–Hungary Treaty regarding the Danube Dam Project. In *Gabčikovo-Nagymaros* case, the International Court of Justice decided that Article 12 of the 1978 Convention (succession does not, as such, affect territorial regimes) reflected a rule of customary international law and applied to the 1977 Treaty; thus the dissolution of Czechoslovakia did not

---

[39] See the entries for the Czech Republic and Slovakia in *UN Multilateral Treaties*, 'Historical Information'; V. Mikulka, 'The Dissolution of Czechoslovakia and Succession in Respect of Treaties', on (1996) *Development and International Co-operation* 45–63.

affect the application of the 1977 treaty to Slovakia, it becoming binding on Slovakia alone on the dissolution.[40]

The Czech Republic and Slovakia each had discussions with certain states which had had bilateral treaties with Czechoslovakia, seeking confirmation that, unless there was a special reason, all the treaties would continue to apply to the two new states. The discussions were also an opportunity to consider whether some treaties might be terminated or be replaced by new ones, particularly taking into account the political changes that had taken place since the end of the communist regime.

Hong Kong and Macau

The circumstances of the handover of Hong Kong to China at midnight on 30 June 1997 were unique and do not provide much in the way of insight into the more usual treaty succession problems. Elaborate arrangements were made by China and the United Kingdom to enable treaty continuity after the return of Hong Kong to China, and to leave the Hong Kong Special Administrative Region (HKSAR) a large degree of autonomy in the conclusion of treaties in its own right. For details, see Aust, pp. 322–31 and www.justice.gov.hk/choice.htm.

Similar provisions were made for Macau.[41]

Succession to state property, archives and debts

As with the 1978 Vienna Convention, the Vienna Convention on the Succession of States in respect of State Property, Archives and Debts 1983[42] ('the 1983 Convention') does not provide the answers to all the myriad problems raised by the topic. Now twenty-two years old, it has received only six of the fifteen ratifications needed for it to enter into force. They are those of the new states of Croatia, Estonia, Georgia, Macedonia, Slovenia and Ukraine, which not unreasonably believed that the Convention would help with the settlement of their own succession issues. The Convention

---

[40] *Gabčíkovo-Nagymaros Project (Hungary* v. *Slovakia), ICJ Reports* (1997), p. 7, paras. 116–24; ILM (1998) 162; 116 ILR 1.

[41] See the statement by China recorded in *UN Multilateral Treaties*, 'Historical Information', and www.macau.gov.mo/constitution/constitution_en.phtml.

[42] ILM (1983) 298. For the treaty, the ILC draft and commentary, and an introduction, see A. Watts, *The International Law Commission 1949–1998*, Oxford, 1999, vol. II, pp. 1209–329. See also A. Aust, 'Limping Treaties: Lessons from Multilateral Treaty-Making' (2003) NILR 243 at 254–5. Oppenheim has a summary of the Convention at Oppenheim, pp. 237–40.

began as an ILC draft, and contains many provisions representing the progressive development of international law. It neither reflects customary law, nor makes new law that would be generally acceptable. It may be that the subject is just not amenable to prescriptive treatment. As with succession to bilateral treaties, it may be something that can only be dealt with on a mainly case-by-case basis.

One of the main flaws of the Convention is the heavy reliance throughout on equity as a guiding, but supplementary, principle for the distribution and apportionment of tangible property. This was entirely understandable as a matter of principle, but it contributed to the Convention's general lack of effectiveness, making it just too vague for application to specific situations. States have to agree on the distribution of assets, yet the Convention gives them no clear or precise guidance on how to do this. It also gives undue emphasis to the simpler case of former overseas territories, yet decolonisation was almost over by 1983.

Former Yugoslav republics

Ironically, the Convention was not a useful guide for the negotiations between the former Yugoslav republics on the complex problems of succession to state property, archives and debts, although the lengthy and difficult negotiations are instructive in understanding the problems and how they can best be met. The principle of equity was of little practical help.[43]

Until the fall of the Milosevic regime, the negotiations dragged on, largely because the FRY maintained the attitude that it was not a successor state to the SFRY.[44] The Convention also gave further scope for delaying tactics. Article 8 provides that the 'state property' of the predecessor state is the property owned by it according to its internal law. The SFRY had claimed to be the most purist of all communist states in believing that the people owned all property. Under the SFRY Constitution, property was in 'social ownership', so replacing ownership by the state with ownership by society as a whole. It was therefore argued, Jesuitically, that either all property (including private property) was state property or that there was

---

[43] For an authoritative account of the problems experienced in the negotiations, see A. Watts, 'State Succession: Some Recent Practical Problems', in V. Goetz, P. Selmer and R. Wolfrum (eds.), *Liber Amicorum Günther Jaenicke*, Berlin, 1998, pp. 405–26.

[44] See p. 399 above.

no state property that could be the subject of state succession. Eventually, on 29 June 2001, the five successor states concluded the Agreement on Succession Issues,[45] which entered into force in 2004. The Agreement does not mention the Convention. Although its Articles on state archives were helpful, the rest were not of much assistance, the settlement of the issue of state debts being done by horse-trading, as graphically illustrated by the fifty pages of detailed annexes.

Membership of international organisations[46]

A new state will not succeed to membership of the United Nations or other international organisations if the predecessor state still exists. In 1947, India (an original Member of the United Nations) was partitioned into India and Pakistan. Since India was regarded by the General Assembly to be the continuation of India, the new state of Pakistan had to apply for membership. If, however, a new state is the result of the union of two states, at least one of which was a UN Member before the union, the new state will usually be accepted as a Member under its new name, without having to apply for membership. When the two Yemens joined together as one state, they retained a seat in the United Nations under the name of Yemen, no application for membership being required. Egypt and Syria were original Members, but had only one UN seat after they joined together in 1958 as the United Arab Republic. When they separated in 1961, Egypt continued as a Member under the name of the United Arab Republic (changing to the Arab Republic of Egypt in 1971), and Syria resumed its UN membership.[47]

When the Soviet Union broke up in 1991, following the precedent of India the Russian Federation was accepted by the UN membership as the continuation of the Soviet Union and so did not have to apply for membership of the United Nations or other international organisations.[48] By contrast, twelve of the former Soviet republics had each to apply for

---

[45] See UNTS No. 40296; ILM (2002) 3 or www.ohr.int/succession.html.
[46] See Schermers and Blokker, *International Institutional Law*, 4th edn, Leiden, 2003, pp. 51 *et seq.*; D. O'Connell, *State Succession in Municipal Law and International Law*, Cambridge, 1967, vol. II, pp. 183 *et seq.*
[47] See the entry for United Arab Republic in *UN Multilateral Treaties*, 'Historical Information', 'UAR'.
[48] Y. Blum, 'Russia takes over the Soviet Union's Seat at the United Nations' (1992) EJIL 354.

UN membership, Belarus (previously the Byelorussian SSR) and Ukraine (previously the Ukrainian SSR) already being members in their own right.[49]

Since neither the Czech Republic nor Slovakia claimed to be the continuation of Czechoslovakia, they had each to apply for membership of international organisations, becoming Members of the United Nations in 1993.

Between 1991 and 1992, the Socialist Federal Republic of Yugoslavia (SFRY) broke up into five states: Bosnia and Herzegovina, Croatia, Macedonia, Slovenia and the Federal Republic of Yugoslavia (Serbia and Montenegro) (FRY). The first four applied for UN membership and were admitted between 1992 and 1993.[50] But the FRY's claim to be the continuation of the SFRY was rejected by the UN membership. In September 1992 the UN General Assembly decided that the FRY could not automatically continue the membership of the SFRY; it should apply for membership, and meanwhile could not take part in the work of the General Assembly.[51] For some years the FRY was in something of a legal limbo.[52] The consistent advice from successive UN Legal Counsel was that the effect of the General Assembly's decision was that the membership of 'Yugoslavia' was not terminated or suspended. But its practical consequence was that FRY representatives could no longer take part in the work of the General Assembly and its subsidiary organs, or in conferences or meetings convened by the General Assembly. It was therefore not allowed to be seated in the United Nations, although, as the result of a pragmatic arrangement, it was allowed to keep open its diplomatic mission to the United Nations and to receive UN documents, and the Yugoslav flag was still flown on the UN building.[53] Following the fall of Milosevic,

---

[49] See p. 205 above.

[50] Because of Greece's objections to the name 'Macedonia' (which is also the name of a northern Greek province), Macedonia was not admitted until 1993, and then only under the cumbersome title of '*the former* Yugoslavia Republic of Macedonia' (emphasis added).

[51] See UNSC Res. 757, 777, 821 and 1074, and UNGA Res. 47/1. 47/229 and 48/88; ILM (1992) 1421.

[52] (1992) *BYIL* 655–8. See also the report of the Badinter Commission, 92 ILR 162 at 166. The ICJ elided the issue in *Genocide (Bosnia* v. *Yugoslavia)* (Provisional Measures), *ICJ Reports* (1993), p. 3, at pp. 20–3; 95 ILR 1, but the full history of UN/FRY relations can be found in its judgment on the *Application for Revision of the 1996 Judgment, ICJ Reports* (2003), paras. 24–64. See also n. 54 below.

[53] For the details, see UN Doc. A/47/485. For a full account, see M. Wood, 'Participation of the Former Yugoslav States in the United Nations' (1997) *YB of UN Law* 231.

the FRY dropped its claim of continuation and applied for membership, being admitted in 2000, changing its name to Serbia and Montenegro in 2003.[54]

Representation in international organisations

It must be remembered that the question of who is entitled to represent a state in an international organisation is a quite different matter from whether a state is a member.[55]

Hong Kong Special Administrative Region

Section VI of Annex I to the Joint Declaration on the Question of Hong Kong[56] provides that the Hong Kong Special Administrative Region (HKSAR) shall be a separate customs territory, and may participate in relevant international trade agreements and organisations (including preferential trade arrangements). For this purpose, the HKSAR does not need authorisation from the Chinese Government. The HKSAR became a member of the World Trade Organization (WTO), as did China some years later. Both China and the HKSAR are members of the International Textiles and Clothing Bureau, the World Tourist Organization, and the World Meteorological Organization (WMO). As a member, the HKSAR has a vote in its own right.

Similar arrangements were made for Macau when it became the Macau Special Administrative Region in 1999.[57]

Nationality of natural persons

A problem that can arise when a new state emerges is that some of the inhabitants who had been nationals of the predecessor state do not necessarily acquire the nationality of the successor state. In UNGA Res. 55/153 of 2000, the General Assembly recognised that the ILC's draft Articles on the nationality of natural persons in relation to the succession of states would provide a useful guide for practice, and invited governments to take

---

[54] See the detailed consideration of the status of the FRY between 1992 and 2000 in *Legality of the Use of Force (Serbia and Montenegro v. Belgium)* (Preliminary Objections), *ICJ Reports* (2004), paras. 25 and 54–91; and C. Gray, (2005) ICLQ 787–94.
[55] See p. 197 above.   [56] 1399 UNTS 33 (No. 23391); ILM (1984) 1366; UKTS (1985) 26.
[57] See www.macau.gov.mo.

its provisions into account, as appropriate, in dealing with this issue. The basic principle of the draft Articles is that no national of a successor state should as a result of succession become stateless. In 2004, the General Assembly invited Members to submit comments on the advisability of elaborating a legal instrument and postponed further consideration until 2008.[58]

[58] A/RES/59/34.

21

State responsibility

It is one thing to define a rule and the content of the obligation it imposes, and another to determine whether that obligation has been violated and what should be the consequences.[1]

Crawford, *The International Law Commission's Articles on State Responsibility*, Cambridge, 2002[2]

Gray, *Judicial Remedies in International Law*, Oxford, 1987

Higgins, *Problems and Process*, Oxford, 1994, pp. 146–68

Oppenheim. *Oppenheim's International Law*, 9th edn, London, 1992, pp. 499–511 and 528–54

Shaw, *International Law*, 5th edn, Cambridge, 2003, pp. 694–721

A state is responsible in international law for conduct in breach of its international obligations. Although the International Law Commission (ILC) began studying the subject in 1956, it was not until 2001 that it produced its final draft Articles ('the Articles') on the Responsibility of States for Internationally Wrongful Acts.[3] The UN General Assembly circulated them in 2001. In A/RES/59/35 (2004), the General Assembly commended the draft Articles without prejudice to the question of any further action on them (such as adopting the Articles as a treaty), invited Members to comment on future action, and decided to consider the matter again in 2007.

The law of state responsibility is customary international law. Unlike state immunity, which has been developed largely by domestic legislation and domestic courts, state responsibility is pre-eminently an area of international law developed by state practice and international judgments, of which numerous examples are referred to in the ILC's Commentary on

---

[1] Roberto Ago, *ILC Yearbook*, 1970, vol. II, p. 306, para. 66(c).

[2] A very useful book by the very last ILC Special Rapporteur on the subject, containing the text of the final draft Articles, the ILC's detailed Commentary on them, background documents and a sixty-page introduction.

[3] The final draft Articles and the ILC Commentary are also in the ILC's 2001 report (A/56/10) and at www.un.org/law/ilc/.

the Articles.[4] The ILC's work has been followed closely by states, and their comments taken into account by the ILC. The ILC adopted the Articles without a vote, and with consensus on virtually all points.[5] The Articles inevitably include some elements of progressive development, such as that on the procedural aspects of countermeasures. But, being essentially a codification of customary international law, they are a good indication of what it is. International courts and tribunals have over the years cited with approval previous ILC drafts.[6] Even if the final draft Articles are never turned into a new convention, they are certain to continue to be very influential with international courts and tribunals.

The Articles will not be quoted in full, but will be described in the light of the ILC Commentary. Inevitably, this is only a general introduction; each new issue will require a thorough consideration of the particular facts, the Articles, the ILC Commentary, relevant judgments and other sources.

Terminology

Some of the words and phrases as used by the ILC and in this chapter have the following meanings:

'international obligation': an obligation owed under international law by one state to another state (therefore 'primary obligation');

'primary rules': the rules of international law which determine whether there has been a breach of a primary obligation;[7]

'secondary rules': the rules of international law which determine whether a breach of a primary obligation is attributable to a state and the legal consequences (i.e. the law of state responsibility);

'internationally wrongful act': a breach of a primary obligation which is attributable to a state;

'injury': the effect of an internationally wrongful act on another state or its nationals, including any damage, material or moral;

'injured state': the state harmed by the injury;

---

[4] See the list of some 400 (almost entirely international) cases in Crawford, *The International Law Commission's Articles on State Responsibility*, Cambridge, 2002, pp. xv–xxxiii.

[5] *Ibid.*, p. 60.

[6] See, for example, *Gabčíkovo-Nagymaros Project (Hungary v. Slovakia), ICJ Reports* (1997), p. 7, para. 47; 116 ILR 1.

[7] See Shaw, pp. 698–700.

'responsible state': the state which caused, or is believed to have caused, the injury;

'act': includes on omission;

'person': includes a legal person, such as a corporation and other legal entities.

(Unless otherwise indicated, references to numbered Articles or to the Commentary are to the ILC's final draft Articles and the related paragraphs of its Commentary.)

General matters

Three general points need to be made. First, Article 55 makes it clear that the Articles are residual in the sense that they do not apply 'where and to the extent that the conditions for the existence of an internationally wrongful act, or the content or implementation of the international responsibility of a state, are governed by special rules of international law'. Such *lex specialis* includes treaty provisions that: make certain conduct lawful; provide how responsibility is to be apportioned for certain aspects of reparation (Article IV of the Convention on the International Liability for Damage Caused by Space Objects 1972 provides for joint and several liability for damage to a third state caused by a collision between space objects launched by two states, and for strict and fault liability);[8] or provide a specific mechanism to settle questions of responsibility and reparation, the WTO system making special provision for the consequences of breaches of its rules.[9]

Secondly, Article 56 makes it clear also that customary international law will continue to apply to matters not covered by the Articles, so leaving open the development of the law of state responsibility, such as liability for the injurious consequences of acts not prohibited by international law.[10] It also has the effect of preserving those legal effects of a breach covered by the law of treaties or another area of international law.

Thirdly, the Articles are without prejudice to the UN Charter, Article 103 of which provides that obligations under it prevail over any other

---

[8] 961 UNTS 187 (No. 13810); ILM (1971) 965; UKTS (1974) 16; TIAS 7762. For a list of other treaties providing for absolute or strict liability, see Oppenheim, pp. 510–11. See also Article 41 on just satisfaction in the (amended) European Convention for Human Rights (www.echr.coe.int).

[9] See pp. 382 *et seq* above.

[10] For current ILC work on this topic, see www.un.org/law/ilc/.

treaty obligations.[11] The purpose of Article 59 is to make it clear that the Articles will not prejudice any action by the United Nations concerning compensation by a state.[12]

The internationally wrongful act of a state

This part of the Articles defines the general conditions necessary for state responsibility to arise.

General principles

Articles 1, 2 and 3 provide that every internationally wrongful act of a state entails its international responsibility. The act is wrongful only when conduct (a) is *attributable* to that state under international law and (b) constitutes a *breach* of an international obligation of that state (Article 2). The Articles do not define when a state will be in breach of international law (see the quote at the start of the chapter). That has to be determined by applying the primary rules (the law of treaties, customary international law and other sources of international law) to the facts of each case. Whether a degree of fault, such as wilfulness or negligence, is necessary is determined in each case by those primary rules. Actual damage is not necessary unless the particular rule so provides. It is irrelevant that the conduct is lawful (or, for that matter, unlawful) in the responsible state's internal law.[13] *The Articles are therefore secondary rules as to when wrongful conduct will be attributable to a state and the legal consequences.* The Articles do not deal with the responsibility of international organisations or individuals.[14]

Attribution of conduct to a state

Organs of the state

For a state to be responsible, the conduct in question must be attributable to the state. The general rule is that only the conduct of a state's organs of government or its agents (persons or entities acting under the direction, instigation or control of those organs) can be attributable to the state.

---

[11] See p. 216 above.
[12] Such as the provisions concerning compensation to be paid by Iraq: see p. 220 above.
[13] See p. 79 above on Article 27 of the Vienna Convention on the Law of Treaties 1969.
[14] On which, see pp. 428–9 below.

The organ can be legislative, executive or judicial, or of any other nature, including one carrying out commercial functions. (Although a breach of contract will not entail a breach of international law, a denial of justice by the courts of the state in enforcing, or failing to enforce, the contact would.) Organs include those of national, regional or local government, and persons or entities whatever their level (Article 4(1)), and any person or entity having that status under the internal law of the state (Article 4(2)). It also includes persons or entities that in fact act as organs, even if they are not classified as such by internal law. Police forces outside London are not treated in UK law as state organs,[15] but are regarded as such in international law since their task, the maintenance of law and order, is a fundamental function of the state.

Purely personal acts cannot be attributed to a state, even if committed by someone who is clearly an agent of the state, such as an assault by a policewoman on a foreign national she catches in bed with her husband, even if the assailant has not yet taken off her uniform.[16] The conduct of persons or entities that are not organs, but are empowered by internal law to exercise 'elements of governmental authority', will be considered as an act of the state if in the particular instance the person or entity acts in that capacity (Article 5). The rule covers the relatively new phenomenon of parastatals and privatised state corporations. And even private persons or entities can be included if they are specifically empowered by internal law to carry out governmental functions, such as administering government regulations or guarding prisons. The degree to which the state may be involved in an entity, such as owning or funding it, is not decisive.[17] But in all cases the internal law must specifically authorise the conduct as involving the exercise of governmental authority. The rule is thus unlikely to apply to such public corporations as the BBC or the British Council.[18]

If an organ of state A is 'placed at the disposal' of state B to exercise elements of governmental authority of state B, its conduct is considered an act of state B (Article 6). The organ must be acting with the consent, and under the authority and direction and control, of the other state and for its purposes. The rule would apply to the armed forces of one state

<hr>

[15] *Halsbury's Laws of England*, 4th edn, 1999, vol. 36(1), para. 205.
[16] See *Mallén*, RIAA, vol. V, p. 516 (1929), at p. 531. The example, unfortunately, is not taken from the case cited, but shows the delicate line that sometimes has to be drawn.
[17] *Hyatt International Corporation* v. *Iran* (1985) 9 Iran–US CTR 72 at 88–94.
[18] See also pp. 163–4 above on similar issues in state immunity.

sent to help another state if, and only if, those forces are placed under the exclusive command and control of the latter state.

Unauthorised or ultra vires conduct

The conduct of state organs, or persons or entities empowered to exercise elements of governmental authority, are considered acts of the state if those organs, persons or entities act in that capacity, and even if they exceed their authority or contravene instructions (Article 7). This is a strict rule, states having sought to evade responsibility by claiming that the conduct was unauthorised. We are here concerned not with purely personal acts (see previous page), but with conduct done in a government capacity, even if it is unauthorised or in excess of authority (*ultra vires*), torture being an all too typical example. The act must have been purportedly or apparently done while carrying out official functions ('cloaked with governmental authority').[19] In the leading case of *Caire*, two Mexican officers, having failed to extort money from a French national, took him to their barracks and murdered him. Mexico was held liable.[20] A Libyan was convicted of having committed the Lockerbie murders as a member of the Libyan intelligence services, but even if he acted without authority Libya would still be responsible for his conduct. In applying this rule, one is concerned only with the question of attribution, not with whether the conduct itself was a breach of international law, which is a separate matter. Where the conduct was unlawful under local law and there are local remedies available, generally those remedies must first be sought by the national of the injured state.[21]

Other conduct attributable to the state

Articles 8 to 11 deal with conduct that is not that of a state organ etc., but is nevertheless attributable to the state.

The conduct of a person or group of persons is considered an act of a state if in fact that person is acting on the state's instructions or under its direction or control (Article 8). They can be private persons and the conduct does not have to involve governmental activity. Thus a state is responsible for the acts of private groups that carry out, say, terrorist

---

[19] *Petrolane Inc.* v. *Iran* (1991) 27 Iran–US CTR 64 at 92; 95 ILR 146.
[20] RIAA, vol. V, p. 516 (1929), at p. 531; 5 ILR 146.
[21] On exhaustion of local remedies, see p. 441 below.

attacks on its instructions. Conduct will be attributable to the state if it was an integral part of a specific operation directed or controlled by it. In the case of the Nicaraguan *contras*, only those activities which the United States actually participated in or directed were held attributable to it.[22] When the conduct is under the effective control of the state, acts going beyond what was authorised will still be attributed to the state.

In exceptional circumstances (for example, during or in the immediate aftermath of revolution, war or foreign occupation), the conduct of private persons is attributable to the state only if three conditions are met: (1) they are in fact exercising elements of governmental authority, even if this is on their own initiative; (2) they do so in the absence or default of the official authorities, which may be due to the total or partial collapse of state institutions; and (3) the circumstances 'call for' the exercise of those elements of governmental authority, in that there is a need for the functions to be carried on (Article 9).[23]

Article 10 concerns another exceptional case, that of an insurrectional movement.[24] If it becomes the new government of a state, so that there is real and substantial continuity between the former movement and the new government, the movement's previous conduct during the struggle is attributable to the state,[25] as well as acts of the previous government. (Whereas a government can be overthrown, the state generally remains in being, and it is the state to which international obligations attach.)[26] If an insurrectional or other movement succeeds in establishing a *new* state, either by decolonisation or secession, the previous conduct of the movement is attributable to the new state. In any event, some conduct of the previous government in relation to a movement, whether or not the movement was successful, will also be attributed to the state, such as failure to protect an embassy from an attack by insurgents.

Even if conduct is not attributable to a state under Articles 4–10, it will be attributable to the extent that the state acknowledges and adopts the conduct as its own (Article 11). Mere (non-tangible) support or endorsement is not enough. The conduct will usually be that of private persons.

---

[22] *ICJ Reports* (1986), p. 14, paras. 75–125, 215–20 and 254–6; 76 ILR 1. Although in *Tadić* (Case IT-94-1; 105 ILR 453) the ICTY Appeals Chamber appeared to go further, it was dealing with questions of individual criminal responsibility.

[23] See *Yeager* v. *Iran* (1987) 17 Iran–US CTR 92 at 104, para. 43; 82 ILR 178.

[24] See for example p. 14 above.

[25] See *Pinson*, RIAA, vol. V, p. 327 (1928), at p. 353; 4 ILR 9; *Short*, 82 ILR 148; *Yeager*, 82 ILR 178; *Rankin*, 82 ILR 204.

[26] See p. 390 above.

When the acknowledgment and adoption is unequivocal and unqualified, attribution may well be given retrospective effect. In the *Tehran Hostages* case, the International Court of Justice found that the seizure of the US embassy and the detention of its staff by militant students was attributable to Iran. By subsequently endorsing the actions and perpetuating them, organs of the Iranian state had made those actions into acts of the state.[27]

Breach of an international obligation

But, even if conduct is attributable to the state, it must still be established that the conduct was in breach of the state's international obligations. That will be the case if the act is 'not in conformity with what is required of [the state] by that obligation', and regardless of the origin or character of the obligation (Article 12). Articles 13–15 set out ancillary rules in general terms. To determine whether there has actually been a breach of an international obligation, one has to examine the facts of each case in the light of the primary rules, whether contained in a treaty or in customary international law. International law does not draw the distinction found in domestic law between contractual and tortious responsibility, and therefore, in deciding whether there has been a breach of a treaty, one may have to interpret its provisions in the light of relevant customary international law. An international obligation can exist in respect of any matter. The enactment of legislation that is in conflict with an international obligation will not necessarily amount to a breach: it depends how the legislation is given effect.[28]

Intertemporal rule[29]

The rule in Article 13 is critical: 'An act of a state does not constitute a breach of an international obligation unless the state is bound by the obligation in question at the time the act occurs.' This is a general principle of international law: an act must be judged according to the applicable international law at the time, not the law when a dispute about it arises, which could be many years later.[30] The corollary is that, even if the obligation

---

[27] *US Diplomatic and Consular Staff in Tehran*, *ICJ Reports* (1980), p. 3, para. 74; 61 ILR 502.

[28] See Commentary on Article 12, para. (12).

[29] As to territorial disputes and the evolutionary interpretation of treaties, see pp. 35 and 93 above, respectively.

[30] *Island of Palmas*, 4 AD 3.

were to cease (for example, by termination of a treaty), any responsibility that had already accrued would be unaffected. The principle applies equally to a new *jus cogens* (peremptory norm).[31]

Extension in time of breach of an international obligation

Identifying when an internationally wrongful act begins, and how long it continues, is a problem that often arises. Article 14(1) provides that the breach of an international obligation by an act that itself does not have a 'continuing character' occurs at the moment the act is performed, even if its effects continue. When a wrongful act has been completed but its effects continue (for example, pain from torture), this prolongation is relevant to the amount of compensation. A breach by an act that does have a continuing character extends over the entire period the wrongful act continues, such as unlawful occupation of territory or an embassy (Article 14(2)). The same rule applies to a breach of an obligation to prevent a given act occurring. The concept of a wrongful act having a continuing character is particularly important if a court did not have jurisdiction in respect of the act when it began, but acquires jurisdiction later.[32] When the wrongful act actually occurs depends on the nature of the international obligation that is alleged to have been breached and on the facts. Conduct of a preparatory character will not normally be enough.[33]

Breach consisting of a composite act

The breach of an international obligation through a series of acts 'defined in the aggregate as wrongful' occurs when conduct occurs which, taken with other acts, is sufficient to constitute the wrongful act. The breach then extends over the entire period the acts are repeated and are still wrongful (Article 15). Genocide or systematic acts of discrimination prohibited by a trade agreement would fall into this category.

Articles 16–19 deal with the responsibility of a state that aids, assists, directs, controls or coerces another state to commit an internationally wrongful act.

---

[31] See p. 11 above.
[32] Such as when property is seized before the Court had competence for the matter: *Loizidou* v. *Turkey* (Merits), (1997) EHRR 513, paras. 41–7 and 63–4; 108 ILR 443.
[33] *Gabčíkovo-Nagymaros Project, ICJ Reports* (1997), p. 7, para. 79; ILM (1998) 162; 116 ILR 1.

Circumstances precluding wrongfulness

Although they do not affect the international obligation, certain circumstances can justify an act in breach of that obligation, thus precluding the wrongfulness of the act. The circumstances are therefore in the nature of a defence, the onus of establishing it lying with the state seeking to avoid responsibility.

The first obvious case is when *consent* is given by a state to the commission of an act by another state that would otherwise be wrongful (Article 20). Consent to foreign military aircraft entering sovereign airspace is a simple and obvious example.[34]

The wrongfulness of an act is precluded if it constitutes a 'lawful' measure of *self-defence* done in conformity with the UN Charter (Article 21). The act must therefore be within the limits placed on acts of self-defence. This is judged according to the law on the use of force (*jus ad bellum*).[35] But, even when the use of force is lawful, responsibility will remain for any breaches of the law of armed conflict (*jus in bello*)[36] or of non-derogable human rights.[37] Nor are *countermeasures* wrongful, provided they are lawful (Article 22) (see below).

There are some exceptional defences. An act is not wrongful if it was done because of *force majeure*, although this is difficult to establish. *Force majeure* is defined as 'the occurrence of an irresistible force or of an unforeseen event, beyond the control of the state, making it materially impossible in the circumstances to perform the [international] obligation' (Article 23).[38] *Force majeure* will not be a defence if the situation is due to the conduct of the state or if it has unequivocally assumed the risk of the situation arising. Severe weather or a military attack may make it materially impossible to avoid a breach of the obligation. It is not enough that it has become more difficult to perform the obligation.[39]

Similarly, an act is not wrongful if its author has no other reasonable way, in a situation of *distress*, of saving his life or that of others entrusted to his care. The defence does not apply if the situation of distress is due to the conduct of the state or if the act is likely to create a comparable or greater peril (Article 24). Here we are concerned with the immediate

---

[34] See p. 346 above.   [35] As to self-defence generally, see pp. 226–9 above.
[36] See p. 251 above.   [37] See p. 245 above.
[38] See the *Rainbow Warrior*, 82 ILR 499 at 553.
[39] The conditions for termination of a treaty on the ground of supervening impossibility are even stricter (see p. 104 above).

need to save human life, usually when a ship or aircraft is in distress due to weather or mechanical failure.[40]

More general cases of emergencies come within the defence of *necessity*. Since the plea arises only when there is an irreconcilable conflict between an essential interest of a state and its international obligations, it can be open to abuse, and so Article 25 circumscribes it severely. Necessity may not be invoked to excuse an act in breach of an international obligation unless the act (a) is the 'only way' to safeguard 'an essential interest' against a 'grave and imminent peril' and (b) does not seriously impair an essential interest of a state owed the obligation or the international community as a whole.[41] Moreover, it cannot be raised if the international obligation excludes the possibility of invoking necessity (as in the law of armed conflict) or the state contributed to the situation of necessity. The defence has often been invoked, but will be successful only in exceptional circumstances, and usually not when financial or economic circumstances are cited.[42]

Nothing in Articles 20–25 permits a state to breach a peremptory norm (*jus cogens*) of international law, such as the prohibitions on genocide, slavery, aggression or crimes against humanity (Article 26).[43] Even when wrongfulness is precluded by one of the defences, once the circumstances precluding wrongfulness no longer exist, the state must comply with the international obligation, unless the obligation has by then been terminated (Article 27(a)). And, even where the wrongfulness of an act is precluded, compensation may be due if 'material loss' has been suffered, although such loss would not be determined in accordance with the latter Articles but by agreement (Article 27(b)).[44]

Content of the international responsibility of a state

When an internationally wrongful act has been committed, a new legal relationship arises between the states involved, in particular the obligation to make reparation. This constitutes the substance of the responsibility of

---

[40] See also Article 18(2) of UNCLOS.
[41] See *M/V Saiga (No. 2)*, 120 ILR 143 at 191–2.
[42] See *Gabčíkovo-Nagymaros Project, ICJ Reports* (1997), p. 7, paras. 51–2; ILM (1998) 162; 116 ILR 1. And compare Article 62 of the Vienna Convention on the Law of Treaties 1969 (pp. 104–5 above).
[43] See pp. 268–72 above, and Articles 40 and 41 below.
[44] See the ILC Commentary on Article 27, paras. (4)–(6).

the state.[45] Article 28 repeats the principle in Article 1 that an internationally wrongful act of a state entails its international responsibility, and links it with the corollary that such responsibility involves legal consequences, which are then set out in Articles 29–33. The legal consequences of an internationally wrongful act do not affect any continuing duty to comply with the obligation that has been breached; the breach does not, as such, terminate the obligation (Article 29).

Cessation and non-repetition

The state responsible for the internationally wrongful act is under an obligation (a) to cease the act, if it is continuing,[46] and (b) to offer appropriate assurances and guarantees of non-repetition, if circumstances so require (Article 30). Since wrongful acts of a continuing character are quite common, cessation – and thus a resumption of compliance with the obligation – is often the main demand by the injured state, reparation being a secondary consideration. In some cases, cessation may shade into restitution (see below), such as the return of stolen objects. An assurance or guarantee of non-repetition, with perhaps a promise to repeal objectionable legislation, may overlap with satisfaction (see below).

Reparation

The principle of reparation in Article 31 is central. The responsible state is under an obligation to 'make full reparation for the injury caused by the internationally wrongful act'. 'Injury' includes 'any damage, material or moral', caused by the act.[47] It is not necessary for there to be material damage. 'Moral' damage includes pain and suffering, loss of loved ones and affronts to honour, dignity or prestige.[48] The obligation to 'make full reparation' is used in the most general sense of making amends by wiping out the consequences of the wrongful act,[49] and consists of restitution, compensation or satisfaction. The obligation arises automatically on the commission of the wrongful act. It does not require a demand from the injured state, although the form of reparation will usually be dependent on

---

[45] See also Article 36(2)(c) and (d) of the Statute of the ICJ.
[46] See p. 383 above on the WTO dispute settlement mechanism.
[47] See Crawford, *The International Law Commission's Articles on State Responsibility*, Cambridge, 2002, p. 31.
[48] *Rainbow Warrior*, 74 ILR 499.
[49] See the leading case of the *Factory at Chorzów*, 4 AD 258.

that state's response. There must of course be a causal link between the act and the injury, and questions of remoteness of damage may arise. Failure by the injured state to take reasonable steps to mitigate the damage will not affect the right to reparation, although it may be taken into account in calculating any compensation.

Article 32 echoes Article 3: the responsible state cannot rely on provisions of its internal law to justify a failure to comply with its obligations of cessation and reparation. The obligations of the responsible state may be owed to more than one state, or to the international community as a whole; and any right arising from the international responsibility of a state may accrue directly to a person or entity other than a state (Article 33). For example, a person whose human rights have been violated may have a procedure by which he can obtain reparation without his state of nationality being involved.[50]

Forms of reparation

Articles 34–39 elaborate the general principle in Article 31 of full reparation by describing its three forms, the relationship between them, interest and the effect of any contribution to the injury made by the injured state. The three forms of reparation (restitution, compensation and satisfaction) are not mutually exclusive; an injury may be such that more than one form, even all three, will be needed (Article 34). The invasion and occupation of Kuwait by Iraq required all three: the return of people and property, compensation for bodily injury and property loss or damage, and an acknowledgement by Iraq of its wrongful acts.[51] Each form of reparation must be proportionate to the injury.[52] Reparation for the illegal seizure of property may well require both its restitution and compensation for loss of use and material damage, although in most cases an injured state can choose to receive compensation in place of restitution (Article 43(2)(b)).

Restitution

The responsible state is under an obligation to re-establish the situation that existed before the wrongful act, in so far as this is 'not materially

---

[50] See pp. 246 *et seq* above.
[51] See UNSC Res. 687 (1991), the so-called ceasefire resolution or 'the Mother of all Resolutions'.
[52] See Shaw, pp. 714–20 for a useful summary of some of the case law.

impossible' or 'does not involve a burden out of all proportion to the benefit deriving from restitution instead of compensation' (Article 35). The release of a detainee, the return of property or the repeal of legislation are simple examples.[53] Restitution is the re-establishment of the *status quo ante* only, any further damage being a matter for compensation. Restitution will not be required if property has been lost or destroyed or has become valueless, but mere legal or practical difficulties to restitution are generally no excuse. Third party rights may have to be taken into account if, for instance, illegally seized property has since been acquired in good faith by a third party.

Compensation

Not surprisingly, compensation is the most common form of reparation, either alone or together with restitution or satisfaction, or both. The responsible state is under an obligation to compensate for damage caused by its wrongful act insofar as it has not been made good by restitution (Article 36). This includes damage suffered by the state itself, its property and personnel, and damage suffered by the state's nationals, whether natural or legal persons.[54] Compensation also covers any 'financially assessable' damage, including loss of profits insofar as that can be established. Although Article 31 defines damage as including 'moral' damage, the term 'financially assessable' excludes compensation for moral damage to a state, for which it has to be content with satisfaction. Compensation can be awarded for damage to the environment of a state, such as by pollution.[55]

Compensation is for actual loss: unlike some domestic laws, international law has no settled concept of penal or exemplary compensation.[56] How the amount of compensation is assessed will depend on the content of the relevant *primary rules* and the behaviour of the states concerned, the aim being to reach an equitable and acceptable outcome.[57] The valuation of capital is a particular problem.[58] Expropriation of assets gives rise to special difficulties.[59]

---

[53] For more specific examples, see the Commentary on Article 35, para. (5).
[54] See p. 182 above.   [55] See p. 344 above.
[56] See Article 41 below; Oppenheim, p. 533; and Crawford, *The International Law Commission's Articles on State Responsibility*, Cambridge, 2002, p. 36.
[57] See the ILC Commentary on Article 36, paras. (7) to (34).
[58] *Ibid.*, paras. (22) to (34).   [59] *Ibid.*, para. (20), n. 582; and pp. 185–7 above.

An international court or tribunal can award compensation even if it is not specifically claimed.[60] An arbitration tribunal may already be provided for by a treaty[61] or established *ad hoc*. Compensation can of course be agreed as part of a settlement, often on a without prejudice or *ex gratia* basis.

Satisfaction

Insofar as an injury cannot be made good by restitution or compensation, the responsible state must give satisfaction. This may be an acknowledgment of the breach, an expression of regret, a formal apology or 'another appropriate modality'. Satisfaction must not be out of proportion to the injury or be humiliating (Article 37). An injured state cannot insist on satisfaction if full reparation can be given by other means. Normally, moral damage can be remedied by compensation, so only an injury that is not financially assessable can be made good by satisfaction. Such injuries would have to amount to an affront or other non-material injury to a state, and are often of a symbolic character arising from the very fact of the breach. Examples include insults to state symbols like the flag, violations of sovereignty, or ill-treatment of ministers or diplomats. The form of satisfaction will depend on the circumstances. It may consist in the taking of disciplinary or criminal proceedings or in paying symbolic damages. An apology, verbal or written, is common and can be required by an international court or tribunal or be made voluntarily.

Interest

Interest is payable on the principal sum of any compensation 'when this is necessary to ensure full reparation', the rate and the method of calculation being set so as to achieve that result. Interest runs from when the compensation 'should have been paid' (Article 38). If compensation is assessed as at the date of the injury, interest will generally run from then. Alternatively, it may run from the date of the claim, the award or the settlement. There is no established rule or practice, the matter being left to courts and tribunals to decide in the light of all the circumstances. The award of interest is not automatic, but payment of interest is now normal. It can be awarded by an international court or tribunal (which, unless

---

[60] *The Factory at Chorzów*, 1927, 4 AD 258.   [61] See Chapter 21 below.

there are express provisions to the contrary, have an inherent power to do so), or be agreed as part of a settlement. Traditionally, compound interest has not been awarded unless there were special circumstances,[62] although this might change.[63] Interest is not usually included where compensation for loss of profits is awarded.

Contribution to the injury

In determining reparation, account must be taken of any contribution to the injury by a wilful or negligent act of the injured state, or by any person or entity in relation to whom reparation is sought (Article 39). This reflects a common, basic principle of domestic law.[64]

Serious breaches of obligations under peremptory norms of general international law

Articles 40 and 41 concern the international responsibility of a state for a 'serious' breach of an obligation arising under a peremptory norm of general international law (*jus cogens*).[65] To be 'serious', the breach must involve a 'gross or systematic' failure to fulfil the obligation. The particular consequences are, first, states must cooperate to bring, through lawful means, the serious breach to an end, irrespective of whether or not an individual state is actually affected by the breach. (Unlike most of the provisions of the Articles, this particular requirement almost certainly represents progressive development.) Secondly, states must not recognise as lawful a situation created by a serious breach, nor give aid or assistance to maintain that situation.[66] Thirdly, a serious breach will have all the consequences of an internationally wrongful act and to such further consequences that the breach may entail under international law, and,

---

[62] *Compañía des Desarrollo de Santa Elena SA* v. *Republic of Costa Rica*, ICSID Case No. ARB/95/1, February 2000, paras. 103–5; ILM (2000) 1317 or www.worldbank.org/icsid/.

[63] See F. Mann, 'Compound Interest as an Item of Damage in International Law', in F. Mann, *Further Studies in International Law*, Oxford, 1990, p. 377, at p. 383.

[64] For references to examples, see the Commentary, para. (4), n. 658.

[65] See p. 11 above and the discussion above of Article 26, p. 417.

[66] See UNSC Res. 662 (1990) regarding the purported annexation of Kuwait. In its the *Legal Consequences of the Construction of a Wall in the Occupied Palestinian Territory* Advisory Opinion, *ICJ Reports* (2004), paras. 154–60; ILM (2004) 1009, the ICJ appears, somewhat rashly, to have endorsed draft Article 41 and adopted its wording, even though the matter had not been thoroughly argued in the written or oral submissions.

possibly, punitive damages. All states are entitled to invoke the responsibility of a state for breaches of such obligations (Article 48).

The implementation of the international responsibility of a state

Invocation of responsibility by an injured state

Article 42 defines the injured state entitled to invoke the responsibility of another state by reference to which the obligation is owed.[67] First, it is owed to a state to which the obligation is owed individually. This is the most usual situation, and it would arise in the case of breach of a bilateral treaty. Secondly, it is owed to one of a group of states, or the international community as a whole, but the breach affects a state 'specially'. The group may be all the parties to a multilateral treaty, but only one or some are affected by the breach by another party. Thirdly, it is owed to all states of the group, or of the international community, when the breach is 'of such a character as radically to change the position of all other states to which the obligation is owed'. This is likely to apply to breach of a disarmament treaty or of a plurilateral treaty,[68] if the breach affects them all. Invocation of responsibility by a state, other than the injured state, acting in the collective interest is dealt with by Article 48 (see above).

Notice of claim by an injured state (Article 43)

Although state responsibility arises without any need for the injured state to invoke it, in practice an injured state has to give notice to the responsible state of its claim. No special form is required, but a protest is insufficient. A formal notice of claim must be made either to the responsible state or to an international court or tribunal. Since the injured state can only require the responsible state to comply with its obligations, it cannot stipulate what the responsible state must do. But it may specify the conduct that the state should take in order to cease the wrongful act, if it is continuing, and what form reparation should take. The form in which the claim should be presented is not specified, although in practice it should be written, and if it is made to an international court or tribunal it must conform to its rules and practice.

---

[67] Based on Article 60(2) of the Vienna Convention on the Law of Treaties 1969.
[68] See p. 71 above.

Admissibility of claims

Article 44 restates two fundamental rules that a state may not invoke the responsibility of another state in respect of injury to its nationals if the claim (a) does not satisfy the nationality of claims rule[69] or (b) is one to which the rule of the exhaustion of local remedies applies,[70] and any available and effective local remedy has not been exhausted.

Loss of right to invoke responsibility

An injured state cannot invoke state responsibility if it (a) has validly waived any claim or (b) is to be considered as having, by reason of its conduct, validly acquiesced in the lapse of the claim (Article 45). Waiver must be clear and unequivocal. An unreasonable delay in puruing the claim could amount to acquiescence. This will depend on all the circumstances, including whether the responsible state has been severely disadvantaged. This is more likely if the original notification of the claim was unduly delayed, rather than if there was merely a leisurely prosecution of the claim.

Plurality of injured or responsible states

Where several states are *injured* by the same internationally wrongful act (see Article 42(b)), each injured state may separately invoke the responsibility of the responsible state (Article 46). Where several states are *responsible* for the same internationally wrongful act (by a joint operation, acting through a common organ, or one or more acting under the direction and control of another), the separate responsibility of each state may be invoked for conduct attributable to it. But this does not permit an injured state to recover more compensation than the damage it suffered, and is without prejudice to any right of recourse by a responsible state against the other responsible states for a contribution (Article 47). Whether each will be liable for the whole damage (so-called joint and several liability) or for a proportion will depend on all the circumstances.[71]

---

[69] See p. 441 below.   [70] See pp. 441–2 below.
[71] See *Certain Phosphate Lands in Nauru, ICJ Reports* (1992), p. 240, paras. 48 and 56; 97 ILR 1. The case was settled (*ICJ Reports* (1993), p. 322) on terms whereby Australia met the claim and New Zealand and the UK contributed (1770 UNTS 379 (No. 30807)).

Countermeasures[72]

The ability to take countermeasures is a most important means by which a state can respond effectively to breaches of its international rights rather than relying solely on methods of peaceful settlement. Even if such methods are readily available, they may take years to produce a result (an international interim measure of protection (injunction) not being that easy to get or to enforce),[73] and compensation (even if full and paid promptly) often not being a real substitute for performance of the broken obligation. Given that enforcement of international law is not done within a legal system with a hierarchy of courts supported by sophisticated enforcement mechanisms, a state sometimes has to resort to such self-help measures to protect effectively its rights and those of its nationals. The right to take countermeasures is well established. But by taking them a state takes the risk that the action of the other state may be held to be lawful, thereby making the countermeasures themselves unlawful.

Countermeasures must be distinguished from reprisals (a term now properly used only in the context of the law of armed conflict),[74] retorsion (a response not involving any breach),[75] sanctions, as generally understood,[76] or suspension or termination of a treaty.

Countermeasures consist in the injured state not performing certain of its international obligations towards the responsible state, but only for the purpose of inducing the responsible state to cease acting wrongfully and make full reparation (Article 49). Lawful countermeasures are not wrongful (Article 22). The issue of countermeasures normally arises in a bilateral context. The classic example involves obligations under a treaty, especially an air services agreement.[77] The agreement between Ruritania and Freedonia allows one airline of each state to operate a daily return flight between the two capitals using jumbo jets. Ruritania Air decides to fly with a smaller aircraft, but Freedonia Air continues to fly jumbos. Although that is Freedonia Air's right under the agreement, Ruritania Air asks its government to deny Freedonia Air permission to land jumbos, and the Ruritanian Government does so. Rightly incensed, Freedonia Air asks its government to deny Ruritania Air permission to land more than

---

[72] See O. Elagab, *The Legality of Non-Forcible Counter-Measures in International Law*, Oxford, 1998.

[73] See p. 459 below. [74] See p. 257 above. [75] See Shaw, pp. 1022–3.

[76] See p. 217 above. [77] See p. 349 above.

three times a week until the Ruritanian Government withdraws its action, and the Freedonia Government does so.[78] That is a counter measure.

Objects and limits of countermeasures

Article 49(1) emphasises that countermeasures are exceptional and limited; in particular they must be necessary and not a punishment. Countermeasures do *not* have to be reciprocal, in the sense of being limited to suspension of the performance of the same or a closely related obligation. In the above example, Freedonia cannot reply precisely in kind, although the countermeasure is directly related to an obligation under the air services agreement. Sometimes taking countermeasures in an unrelated field of activity may be unavoidable. A state cannot respond by breaching certain sacrosanct obligations (see below). As with other Articles, the rules on countermeasures are residual.[79] Occasionally, a treaty may prohibit countermeasures, or require their prior authorisation.[80] Countermeasures must cease once they have had the desired effect (Article 49(2)) and must, as far as possible, be taken in such a way as to permit the resumption of performance of the responsible state's obligations, i.e. be reversible (Article 49(3)).

Proportionality

Countermeasures must be 'commensurate with' (proportionate to) the injury suffered, taking into account 'the gravity of the wrongful act' and 'the rights in question' (being those of both states) (Article 51). Proportionality is an essential requirement. If the countermeasures are excessive, the injured state will itself have committed an internationally wrongful act. In many cases, there will be no exact equivalence between the acts of the responsible state and the countermeasures. But the more closely countermeasures are related to the breach, the more likely they are to be proportionate. It will usually be sufficient if there is a rough approximation. So, the suspension by the United States of all Air France flights between Paris and Los Angeles, in response to France's refusal to allow US airlines flying between Los Angeles and Paris to change to smaller aircraft for the section between London and Paris, was held to be not 'clearly

---

[78] For air services examples, see *Air Services Agreement of 27 March 1946 (US v. France)*, (1963) 38 ILR 182 and (1978) 54 ILR 303. See also *US v. Italy* (1965) 45 ILR 393.
[79] On Article 55, see p. 409 above.   [80] See p. 386 above.

disproportionate'.[81] But everything depends on the particular facts and circumstances.

Procedural conditions

Resort to countermeasures is an exceptional action. Therefore, before embarking on that course, the injured state should take the procedural steps set out in Article 52. However, since they may well *not* represent customary international law, we use the conditional tense ('should', rather than 'shall' or 'must'). First, the injured state should call upon the responsible state to cease its wrongful act and to make reparation. In practice, it is likely that this requirement will have already been met by discussions – albeit brief – between the two states. Secondly, the injured state should notify the responsible state of its decision to take countermeasures, and offer to negotiate. Thirdly, since in many situations these two requirements may take too long, paragraph 2 recognises that the injured state may take 'such urgent countermeasures as are necessary to preserve its rights', such as freezing bank accounts held in the injured state. The 'rights' referred to are both the right to take countermeasures and the primary rights that are the subject matter of the dispute. Fourthly, the countermeasures should be suspended 'without undue delay' if the wrongful act has ceased or the dispute is 'pending' before an international court or tribunal that has jurisdiction to make decisions on the parties. The dispute will be 'pending' only once the court or tribunal is in a position to deal with the case. If it is an *ad hoc* tribunal set up pursuant to a treaty, the dispute will be pending only when the tribunal is actually constituted, and this can take months.[82] This latter provision presupposes that the court or tribunal will have the power to order interim measures of protection.[83] If the dispute has been referred by a national of the injured state to a tribunal,[84] countermeasures would not be justified except in exceptional cases. Fifthly, countermeasures may be taken or continued if the responsible state fails to implement the dispute settlement procedures in good faith, such as non-cooperation in the establishment or procedure of a tribunal, non-compliance with an interim measures order or a refusal to accept the final decision. Countermeasures must of course be

---

[81] *Air Services Agreement of 27 March 1946 (US v. France)*, (1978) 54 ILR 303, para. 83. See also *Gabčíkovo-Nagymaros Project (Hungary v. Slovakia)*, *ICJ Reports* (1997), p. 7, at paras. 85 and 87; ILM (1998) 162; 116 ILR 1.
[82] See p. 442 below.   [83] See p. 459 below.   [84] See p. 374 above.

terminated as soon as the responsible state has complied with its obligations of cessation and reparation (Article 53).

It is possible that a state may lose its right to take countermeasures if it delays doing so for so long that it must be deemed to have waived its right to take them.

Obligations not affected by countermeasures

Article 50 lists four obligations which must never be affected by countermeasures: (a) to refrain from the threat or use of force; (b) to protect fundamental human rights; (c) the prohibition in international humanitarian law of reprisals; (d) peremptory norms of general international law. Paragraph 2 lists two other obligations which have important functions in relation to the resolution of the dispute that has given rise to the threat or use of countermeasures, and which must therefore also be respected: (a) obligations under any dispute settlement procedure applicable between the two states; and (b) obligations to respect the inviolability of diplomatic or consular agents, premises, archives and documents.

Responsibility of an international organisation

Article 57 makes it clear that the Articles do not affect any question of the responsibility of an international organisation, or of any state for the conduct of an international organisation. An international organisation has international legal personality separate from its member states[85] and there can no longer be any doubt that the organisation is responsible in international law for its own acts.[86] The ILC began consideration of the topic of the responsibility of international organisations only in 2002. It seems very likely that, in producing draft Articles on this topic, it will use those on state responsibility as a model.[87]

There are various problems that will have to be addressed. First, whose conduct can be attributable to the organisation? In most cases, there will be no problem, but what if a person is injured (in the broadest sense) by the conduct of an official of a state implementing a decision of

---

[85] See p. 198 above.
[86] See *Difference Relating to Immunity (Cumaraswamy)* Advisory Opinion, *ICJ Reports* (1999), p. 62 at para. 66; 121 ILR 405; and Article 60 of the Vienna Convention on the Law of Treaties between States and International Organisations and between International Organisations 1986 (ILM (1986) 543), although it is not yet in force.
[87] See the ILC Report for 2003, para. 44, and the current state of play at www.un.org/law/ilc/.

the organisation, such as sanctions? Is the organisation liable? Secondly, whereas an organisation can be liable to a state that is not a member of it, can it be liable to its member states? There would seem no reason in principle why not. Although one must be careful of pushing the analogy with companies too far, a company that injures a person is liable even if he is a shareholder or employee. Thirdly, are the member states liable collectively for the conduct of the organisation? This is the most controversial issue.[88] Article 3(4) of the Agreement establishing the International Fund for Agricultural Development 1976 provides expressly that no member shall be liable by reason of its membership for acts or obligations of the Fund.[89] If this represents the position in international law, a subsidiary question is whether there could be circumstances in which one could 'lift the corporate veil' to expose the member states to liability? Although it is not directly related to these issues, it may be relevant that most international organisations have more or less total immunity from jurisdiction conferred on them, so that *domestic* legal remedies are generally not available,[90] and that international dispute settlement mechanisms generally do not have jurisdiction over international organisations.[91]

Individual responsibility

Article 59 makes it clear that the Articles do not affect any question of the individual responsibility under international law of any person acting on behalf of a state. Although a state is responsible for a wrongful act of its officials or agents, they may also have individual criminal responsibility for the same acts. This is especially so for violations of the law of armed conflict and other international crimes.[92] The Article leaves open the issue of possible individual *civil* responsibility for such crimes.[93]

---

[88] See the helpful summary of how the English courts wrestled with this problem in the International Tin Council legislation in J. Klabbers, *An Introduction to International Institutional Law*, Cambridge, 2002, pp. 303–6, and pp. 300–19 on this particular topic generally.

[89] 1059 UNTS 191 (No. 16041); ILM (1976) 922; UKTS (1978) 41.

[90] See p. 199 above.

[91] Klabbers, J. Klabbers, *An Introduction to International Institutional Law*, Cambridge, 2002, pp. 254–5.

[92] See p. 177 above.

[93] See Article 14 of the Torture Convention, 1465 UNTS 85 (No. 24841); ILM (1984) 1027; UKTS (1991) 107; BGG, p. 229.

22

Settlement of disputes

the law's delay . . .[1]

Collier and Lowe, *The Settlement of Disputes in International Law*, Oxford, 1999

Brownlie, *Principles of Public International Law*, 6th edn, Oxford, 2003, pp. 671–94

Merrills, *International Dispute Settlement*, 3rd edn, Cambridge, 1998

Handbook on the Peaceful Settlement of Disputes between States, UN, New York, 1992

Any respectable domestic legal system has a hierarchy of tribunals ending with a final court of appeal. International law has no such system. Since each state is sovereign, it cannot be required to submit to the jurisdiction of an international tribunal (which term includes international courts) unless it has consented to its jurisdiction. And there is no hierarchy of tribunals, but rather an unsystematic patchwork.[2] Even though judgments of the International Court of Justice (ICJ) are very influential, it is not at the apex of the international legal system. In this chapter, we look at some international tribunals. (See p. 246 above for the European Court of Human Rights, p. 273 above for international criminal tribunals, p. 382 above for the World Trade Organization and p. 475 below for the European Court of Justice.)

Many disputes are settled quickly and informally; others can take many years to resolve; some are never resolved; and with some it is better to manage them than attempt a resolution.[3] A dispute is usually between only two parties. There is no one method of dispute settlement, or even

---

[1] W. Shakespeare, *Hamlet*, II.i.56.

[2] For a chart showing the main universal and regional international courts and tribunals, see www.pict-pcti.org.

[3] See R. Jennings, 'The Role of the International Court of Justice' (1997) BYIL 1 at 51, n. 100, where he cites as an example the Antarctic Treaty 1959 (402 UNTS 71 (No. 5778); UKTS (1961) 97) in which the parties have effectively frozen their sovereignty dispute.

one that is generally used. Nor is the method necessarily dictated either by the importance or magnitude of the dispute or how long it has lasted. There are treaty disputes that are never settled even when a method is provided in the treaty itself. (The term 'settle' is used here in the more general sense of 'resolve', and not in its narrow sense of agreeing terms upon which pending litigation is discontinued.)

In the UN Charter, Article 33 elaborates the basic principle enunciated in Article 2(3), that all Members shall settle their international disputes by peaceful means, and lists the most usual ones: negotiation, mediation, conciliation, arbitration and judicial settlement. The methods can be broadly divided into voluntary and compulsory, depending on whether or not the parties to a dispute are under a treaty obligation to enter into a particular means of settlement. But this does not mean that under a voluntary process the parties will never be bound by the result; nor that under a compulsory process the result will always be binding: it depends entirely on the terms that have been agreed.

Informal means

We will first look at methods of resolving legal disputes that do not involve an international tribunal, although the parties should still need lawyers.

Negotiations and consultations

There is of course nothing to prevent the parties seeking to resolve a dispute by direct negotiations, and this is normally the first step in every dispute. Even if the dispute is to be referred to arbitration or judicial settlement, it is desirable that the points at issue should be better defined by negotiations. Held in decent privacy, they may also make it easier to reach a settlement. Once a dispute is elevated to a more formal or public level, it can be more difficult, at least politically, to settle. Positions become entrenched and public 'face' may require that neither side should be seen to compromise.

Negotiating procedures are infinitely flexible, the process being completely under the control of the parties. Once a third party is brought in, the negotiations may gain a momentum of their own which the parties (at least individually) may not be able to stop or influence effectively. This may be one reason why most disputes are settled by bilateral negotiations; although it may also be true that most disputes are not so intractable that the parties have to resort to more formal methods. One should treat with great caution any proposal for a new general treaty on dispute settlement.[4] There are already quite enough of them and, although formal methods of dispute settlement have an important role to play, they are often no substitute for, or no better than, a carefully negotiated settlement.

Negotiations can last as long as the parties wish, and may be stopped and resumed at any time, although some dispute settlement clauses in treaties prescribe a time limit after which either party is free to invoke whatever third-party means of settlement is provided for in the treaty.

There is no significant difference between consultations and negotiations, although consultations are often made a formal pre-condition for moving to a third-party settlement procedure. The UK/US Air Services Agreement 1977 ('Bermuda 2') provides for a dispute to be the subject of a 'first round of consultations' before it can be submitted to third-party settlement,[5] and 'first *round*' means at least two meetings with a break in between for reflection. Some treaties require the parties to do no more than enter into consultations or negotiations with a view to reaching a settlement or to agreeing on another method of settlement. These have to be implemented in good faith, so they must be conducted purposefully.

If negotiations are successful, it is essential that the parties record what has been agreed. The form will depend on the circumstances. It may involve an amendment to a treaty or a public statement. If the parties do not want publicity, they may record the terms of settlement in an unpublished MOU.[6] Although not itself legally binding, an MOU may nevertheless have legal consequences, as was demonstrated in the award in the *UK/US User Charges Arbitration*.[7]

If the negotiations are not successful, one of the parties to a treaty dispute may decide to terminate the treaty. This could be described as 'the other way of settling a dispute'. Since 1945, the United Kingdom has terminated at least four air services agreements: Philippines (1953 and 1984); United States (1976); and Lebanon (1981).[8] Sometimes a dispute becomes so bad that termination and starting afresh is the only sensible way out of the impasse. It does not mean, of course, that the dispute may not still be settled by reference to a third party if the treaty so provides

---

[4] See A. Aust, 'Limping Treaties: Lessons from Multilateral Treaty-Making' (2003) NILR 243 at 247–8.

[5] 1079 UNTS 21 (No. 16509); UKTS (1977) 76.

[6] See pp. 53–7 above on MOUs.   [7] 102 ILR 215, especially 561–4.

[8] A. Aust, 'Air Services Agreements: Current United Kingdom Procedures and Policies' (1985) *Air Law* 189 at 198–9.

(a dispute settlement clause usually remains in force in relation to matters occurring before termination of the treaty),[9] or the parties may agree to this. Termination can have the advantage of effectively drawing a line under the dispute, so enabling the parties to negotiate a new treaty.

Involvement of third parties

It may be necessary to seek the help of a third party. Whether this will be successful – even whether it will be possible – will depend on various factors. One will be the degree of cooperation from the other party to the dispute. Despite the existence of several general treaties on the settlement of disputes, in many cases there will be no agreement binding the parties to any means of third-party settlement applicable to the particular dispute. It would then be necessary to negotiate – probably in unfavourable circumstances – an *ad hoc* agreement on a method of settlement. If the method is mediation or conciliation, unless the agreement provides for the parties to accept the recommendations of the third party (which is not usual), neither party is legally bound to accept them.

Conciliation

Conciliation may be provided for in the treaty that is the subject of the dispute or in a general treaty on the settlement of disputes to which the parties in dispute are both bound,[10] or it may be agreed *ad hoc*. The nature of conciliation is neatly expressed in the Annex to the Vienna Convention on the Law of Treaties 1969, which provides for conciliation of disputes between parties to the Convention in certain limited circumstances. The Annex provides in part that:

4. The [Conciliation] Commission may draw the attention of the parties to the dispute to any measures that might facilitate an amicable settlement.

5. The Commission shall hear the parties, examine the claims and objections, and make proposals to the parties with a view to reaching an amicable settlement of the dispute.

---

[9] See pp. 246–7 above.
[10] The ambitious, but so far unused, OSCE Convention on Conciliation and Arbitration 1992 (ILM (1993) 557) provides for *compulsory* conciliation, although the outcome is not binding. See Bloed (ed.), *The Conference on Security and Co-operation in Europe*, Dordrecht, 1993, p. 870.

This formula became a model for multilateral treaties, in particular for the UN Convention on the Law of the Sea 1982.[11]

A conciliation commission is usually composed of three to five members, one national member being appointed by each party and the other one or three neutral members chosen jointly by the national members. A neutral member serves as chairman. If a party fails to appoint its member, or there is no agreement on the choice of the neutral member(s), it is essential for the treaty to provide for the necessary appointment to be made by an eminent independent person, such as the President of the International Court of Justice or the Secretary-General of the Permanent Court of Arbitration. It is therefore also essential to set time limits for all appointments to avoid one party obstructing the process. The Annex to the Vienna Convention provides a useful model for multilateral treaties, and was a model for provisions which, by providing for a permanent list of conciliators, largely avoid the problem of leaving the appointment of conciliators solely in the hands of the parties.[12]

Conciliation is inevitably more expensive than negotiation, since each party will not only have to pay its own expenses, including the fees of any outside lawyers or experts it engages, but also half of the costs of the conciliators, their accommodation and staff.

The results of conciliation are almost invariably non-binding. Once again, the matter is well expressed in the Annex to the Vienna Convention:

> 6. . . . . The report of the Commission, including any conclusions stated therein regarding the facts or questions of law, shall not be binding upon the parties and it shall have no other character than that of recommendations submitted for the consideration of the parties in order to facilitate an amicable settlement of the dispute.

Thus, conciliation is, from one point of view, usually less effective than arbitration or judicial settlement, the results of which are legally binding, yet it can be just as expensive and time-consuming. If conciliation has not led to a settlement, unless the parties can then agree to take the dispute to arbitration or judicial settlement, there may be no formal means of resolving it.

---

[11] 1833 UNTS 397 (No. 31363); ILM (1982) 1261; UKTS (1999) 81 (Annex V, Articles 5 and 6).

[12] For a bilateral precedent, see the Swiss–United Kingdom Treaty for Conciliation, Judicial Settlement and Arbitration 1965, 605 UNTS 205 (No. 8765); ILM (1965) 943; UKTS (1967) 42.

Mediation and good offices

Mediation is usually an *ad hoc* method involving the agreed intervention of a third person in an attempt to reconcile the claims of the parties by advancing his own ideas for a compromise. It is more of a political process and, as such, it may not be suitable for the resolution of a legal dispute. Good offices are very similar in nature, indeed the terms are almost interchangeable, and consist in a third person (these days often the UN Secretary-General, or rather his special representative) offering his impartial assistance. The process therefore suffers from the same weaknesses as mediation, at least as far as legal disputes are concerned.

Compulsory binding settlement

The real value of a compulsory binding settlement procedure is that a party to a dispute should not have to resort to it. A party which really knows it is in the wrong should be well aware that if it persists in its unlawful action it risks all the trouble and expense of international legal proceedings, and eventual judgment against it. Of course, states do not always act rationally, and some will take a risk or view legal proceedings as a useful way of buying time. Nevertheless, even though one cannot know to what extent the threat, or simply the possibility, of compulsory settlement influences the decisions of states, from the experience of domestic legal disputes it is reasonable to assume that the deterrent factor is significant. But, of course, in many cases there will be a genuine legal dispute.

The settlement of a dispute by compulsory means requires mutual consent. Whether a party is legally bound to submit the dispute to a particular method of dispute settlement depends entirely on whether it has agreed to do so, either in advance of the dispute arising or subsequently.

The two principal characteristics of compulsory binding settlement are (1) a prior agreement to submit disputes to a third party and (2) a provision in the agreement that the decision of the third party will be binding. These two matters may be provided for (a) in a general treaty on the settlement of disputes to which the parties in dispute are bound, (b) if, as is often the case, the dispute is about a treaty, in the treaty itself, or (c) in an *ad hoc* agreement. But, even if a treaty provides for a method of compulsory third-party settlement, unless the provision is tightly drafted one party may, in practice, be able to delay, or even avoid, the process (see below). We will look at the three basic methods in the context of international arbitration and the ICJ.

But first we must consider some essential preliminary matters.

Jurisdiction and admissibility

Before it judges the merits of a case, an international tribunal must decide both that it has jurisdiction (legal competence to hear the case) and that the claim is admissible. Although jurisdiction and admissibility are separate legal issues, the respondent[13] frequently raises them both at an early stage as *preliminary objections* to the tribunal dealing with the dispute, although raising them together can sometimes have the effect of blurring the distinction between them in tribunal decisions. The proceedings on the merits are suspended until these preliminary issues have been decided, although when an issue of admissibility is closely related to the merits of the case the tribunal may postpone dealing with the issue until the merits stage.

Jurisdiction

For an international tribunal to have jurisdiction, the states in dispute must have consented to conferring jurisdiction on the tribunal to hear the dispute. Whether it has jurisdiction is decided by the tribunal itself, this inherent power being sometimes rather grandly referred to as *la compétence de la compétence*.[14] A plea that active negotiations between the parties are still proceeding will not prevent the tribunal from exercising jurisdiction,[15] unless perhaps such negotiations are required by a compromissory clause (see below) and the tribunal is satisfied that the required negotiations have not yet been completed.

Jurisdiction can be conferred in various ways.

- A clause in a treaty (known as a *compromissory clause*) under which the parties agree to submit all or some of their disputes regarding the interpretation or application of the treaty to arbitration or judicial settlement. The two (parallel) *Lockerbie* cases were brought by Libya against the United Kingdom and the United States to the ICJ under the compromissory clause of the Montreal Convention for the Suppression of Unlawful Acts against the Safety of Civilian Aviation 1971.[16] Clauses providing for arbitration are often drawn in general terms and leave many important details to be worked out only when the clause has been

---

[13] Respondent = defendant; applicant = plaintiff.
[14] See *Prosecutor* v. *Tadic*, 1995 (ICTY Appeals Chamber), Case IT-94-1; 105 ILR 419 and 453.
[15] *Cameroon* v. *Nigeria* (Preliminary Objections), *ICJ Reports* (1998), p. 275, para. 56.
[16] 974 UNTS 177 (No. 14118); ILM (1971) 10; UKTS (1974) 10 (Article 14).

invoked – the worst possible time. It is therefore better to put into the clause as much detail as possible, omitting only that which cannot easily be decided until a dispute has arisen. This will avoid some of the considerable delays that will ensue if crucial matters, such as the method of appointment of arbitrators, are not set out in sufficient detail. The arbitration clause of the UK/US Air Services Agreement 1977 (known as 'Bermuda 2'),[17] which was invoked by the United States in 1988 in the dispute concerning the aircraft user charges at London (Heathrow) Airport,[18] contains the minimum necessary provisions. They were soon found to be inadequate for what turned out to be a very long and complicated arbitration, the rules of procedure of the arbitral tribunal having to be modified several times.[19]

- A *bilateral* treaty under which the parties agree to submit future disputes (not just disputes about treaties) to arbitration or judicial settlement. The treaty can be bilateral or multilateral. The so-called Jay Treaty of 1794,[20] between Great Britain (as it then was) and the United States, led to a series of arbitrations. A more recent bilateral treaty is the UK/Swiss Treaty for Conciliation, Judicial Settlement and Arbitration 1965.[21] Iran successfully invoked the Iran/United States Treaty of Amity 1955[22] as the basis for the ICJ's jurisdiction to hear the dispute it had with the United States over attacks on its oil platforms.[23] Earlier, Nicaragua successfully invoked before the ICJ its 1956 Treaty of Friendship, Commerce and Navigation with the United States.[24] The first *multilateral* treaties concerning dispute settlement were the Hague Conventions for the Pacific Settlement of International Disputes 1899 and 1907 which established the Permanent Court of Arbitration (PCA).[25] The (grandly named) General Act for the Pacific Settlement of Disputes 1928, as revised in 1949,[26] has but eight parties, and its status is somewhat problematic.[27] Other such general treaties followed them, although they have been little used.[28]

---

[17] 1079 UNTS 21 (No. 16509); UKTS (1977) 6.   [18] 102 ILR 215.
[19] For the text, see 102 ILR 551–61.
[20] 52 CTS 243. See T. Bingham, 'The Alabama Claims Arbitration' (2005) ICLQ 1.
[21] See n. 12 above.   [22] Article XXI(2). See 284 UNTS 93 (No. 4132); TIAS 3853.
[23] *ICJ Reports* (1996), p. 803, at p. 820.
[24] Article XXIV. See 367 UNTS 3 (No. 5224). See *ICJ Reports* (1984), p. 392; 76 ILR 104.
[25] See p. 444 below.
[26] 93 LNTS 343; UKTS (1931) 32 and 71 UNTS 101 (No. 912). See also A. Aust, 'Limping Treaties: Lessons from Multilateral Treaty-Making' (2003) NILR 243 at 247–8.
[27] See Collier and Lowe, *Settlement of Disputes in International Law*, Oxford, 1999, pp. 137–8.
[28] European Convention for the Peaceful Settlement of Disputes 1957, 320 UNTS 423 (No. 4646); UKTS (1961) 10. See also p. 433, n. 10, above. See A. Aust, 'Limping Treaties: Lessons from Multilateral Treaty-Making' (2003) NILR 243 at 247–8.

- Adherence to an *optional protocol* to a treaty that is the subject of the dispute. Such a protocol is essentially a compromissory clause but, being a separate treaty, a party to the principal treaty will need to adhere to the protocol in order to accept the jurisdiction of the tribunal. A good example is the Optional Protocol to the Vienna Convention on Diplomatic Relations 1961,[29] which the United States invoked successfully in its dispute with Iran over the Tehran hostages;[30] and the Optional Protocol to the Vienna Convention on Consular Relations 1963,[31] which Paraguay invoked in its dispute with the United States in 1998.[32]
- A *compromis*. If there is no existing agreement, or if such an agreement does not contain enough detail, it will be necessary for the parties to the dispute to conclude a new treaty called a *compromis* (sometimes called in English a 'special agreement', even though at least the British prefer the term *compromis*). The *compromis* sets out all the details of the establishment and procedure of the arbitral tribunal, and usually covers:

  the composition of the tribunal;
  the appointment of its members, including the filling of vacancies;
  the appointment of agents of the parties;
  the precise question(s) to be decided;
  the rules of procedure and methods of work;
  languages;
  the applicable law;
  the seat of the tribunal;
  the appointment of the secretary of the tribunal and his staff;
  costs; and
  the binding nature of the award.

  It may not be necessary to cover all these points if, for example, the *compromis* provides that the working methods of the tribunal will be determined by the tribunal itself. For an example of a *compromis*, see the 1996 Special Agreement between Botswana and Namibia for reference to the ICJ on the determination of part of their common boundary.[33]
- *Reciprocal declarations* under Article 36(2) of the Statute of the ICJ (see p. 452 below).

---

[29] 500 UNTS 241 (No. 7310); UKTS (1965) 19.
[30] *ICJ Reports* (1980), p. 3; 61 ILR 502.   [31] 596 UNTS 487 (No. 8638); UKTS (1973) 14.
[32] *ICJ Reports* (1998), p. 248; ILM (1998) 810 and 824 (Supreme Court); 118 ILR 1.
[33] ILM (2000) 314.

- Consent to jurisdiction being implied from some action in connection with proceedings taken by a state that has not accepted the jurisdiction expressly, known as *forum prorogatum*.[34]

When a treaty provides for the establishment of an arbitral tribunal, it is vital to provide for a third party to make the appointment of a national or neutral arbitrator, should that appointment not have been made within the time specified. There should, however, be no need to include such a provision if the reference to arbitration is 'friendly'. Giving the President of the ICJ or the Secretary-General of the PCA the power to make such appointments normally has a good effect: they have seldom had to exercise the power.[35]

What is a legal dispute?

In addition to the states in dispute having consented to its jurisdiction, for an international tribunal to have jurisdiction, there must be a *dispute* between the parties and the dispute must be *legal*. We are not concerned with a dispute about a matter regulated by domestic law, such as over a lease governed by the land law of one of them, unless there is also an international law aspect.[36]

What constitutes a dispute? In *Lockerbie*, the UK and US respondents argued there was no dispute. To no one's surprise, the ICJ decided that there was a dispute as to whether the Montreal Convention 1971 (on aircraft sabotage and to which the three states were and remain parties) applied in the circumstances of the case.[37] In so deciding, the ICJ referred to the statement of its predecessor, the Permanent Court of International Justice (PCIJ), in *Mavrommatis*: 'A dispute is a disagreement over a point of law or fact, a conflict of legal views or interests between two persons.'[38] The

[34] See Brownlie, pp. 689–90; Collier and Lowe, *Settlement of Disputes in International Law*, Oxford, 1999, p. 136; Schreuer, *The ICSID Convention: A Commentary*, Cambridge, 2001, pp. 228–34; Merrills, *International Dispute Settlement*, 3rd edn, Cambridge, 1998, pp. 123–4.

[35] See *US* v. *France (Air Services)* (1963) 38 ILR 182.

[36] If, for example, the lease was entered into pursuant to a treaty between the two states and one claims that the other is in breach of the treaty. See also p. 124, n. 15 above.

[37] *Case concerning Questions of Interpretation and Application of the 1971 Montreal Convention Arising from the Aerial Incident at Lockerbie (Libya v. United Kingdom)* (Preliminary Objections), *ICJ Reports* (1998), p. 9, para. 53(3); ILM (1998) 587; 117 ILR 1. There was a parallel case against the United States. Since the issues raised by both cases were the same, the Court dealt with them in parallel, although they were never joined. Both cases were withdrawn by consent in September 2003.

[38] PCIJ, Series A, No. 2 (1924), p. 11; 2 ILR 27.

ICJ also quoted from *South West Africa* (Preliminary Objections) ('It must be shown that the claim of one party is positively opposed by the other')[39] and from the *Interpretation of Peace Treaties with Bulgaria, Hungary and Romania*, First Phase, Advisory Opinion ('Whether there exists an international dispute is a matter for objective determination').[40] It is not enough that one party says there is a dispute and the other denies it; though when parties dispute that there is a dispute, there usually is.

The concept of a *legal* dispute is best explained by reference to Article 36(2) of the Statute of the ICJ. This defines legal disputes as those concerning:

> (i) the interpretation of a treaty;
> (j) any question of international law;
> (k) the existence of any fact which, if established, would constitute a breach of an international obligation;
> (l) the nature or extent of the reparation to be made for the breach of an international obligation.

This is a comprehensive definition. Other tribunals, permanent or *ad hoc*, will have jurisdiction over a specified range of disputes. The European Court of Human Rights has jurisdiction only over disputes arising under the European Convention on Human Rights, although in exercising its jurisdiction it may have to consider any of the four matters listed above.[41]

As with disputes between neighbours over a boundary fence, territorial – as well as other – disputes between states are often politically or emotionally charged, such as the long-standing dispute between Argentina and the United Kingdom over sovereignty of the Falkland Islands. But to an international tribunal it is – or at least should be – irrelevant that there is a political dimension to a claim or that the applicant state may have a political motive in bringing it.

Jurisdiction ratio temporis

In deciding whether it has jurisdiction, the tribunal has to consider the provisions of the relevant agreement conferring jurisdiction, whether it was constituted by treaty or reciprocal declarations under Article 36(2) of the ICJ Statute. Either may limit jurisdiction to disputes arising after,

---

[39] *ICJ Reports* (1962), p. 328; 37 ILR 3.
[40] *ICJ Reports* (1950), p. 74; 17 ILR 318.   [41] See p. 246 above.

or facts or situations subsequent to, the date the agreement entered into force, or another date, which could be earlier.[42]

If the tribunal decides that it has no jurisdiction, that ends the proceedings.

Admissibility

Even if the tribunal is satisfied that it has jurisdiction, if the claim is nevertheless inadmissible it will not proceed to the merits. The ICJ has wisely not sought to define the concept of admissibility or to determine the precise distinction between it and jurisdiction. The two claims of inadmissibility most frequently asserted are that the applicant has no legal interest and that local remedies have not been exhausted.

No legal interest

This plea normally arises when the claim is about loss or harm to one of the applicant's nationals, and the respondent asserts that the person (natural or legal) is not a national of the applicant state, and thus the respondent has no responsibility towards the applicant (*nationality of claims rule*). The generally accepted rule is that the person must have had, continuously and without interruption from the time of the loss or harm until judgment, the nationality of the applicant state, and not be a national of the respondent state.[43] The principle of continuity means that assignment of a claim to another national of the same state will not affect the claim. The nationality of the claim must also be assessed by reference to the nationality of the holder of the beneficial interest, not that of a trustee or other nominal holder. On the other hand, if an insurer has a subrogated claim, that should not affect an international claim provided the insured still satisfies the continuity principle. The nationality of corporations can be more difficult.[44]

Exhaustion of local remedies[45]

A state may not exercise its diplomatic protection, or resort to any international procedure to seek redress for one of its nationals, unless the national has exhausted the legal remedies available to him in the state

---

[42] See *Case concerning Certain Property (Liechtenstein v. Germany), ICJ Reports* (2005), paras. 28–52, and the cases therein mentioned.

[43] Oppenheim, pp. 512–15. On dual nationality, see p. 179 above.   [44] See p. 182 above.

[45] See C. Amerasinghe, *Local Remedies in International* Law, 2nd edn, Cambridge, 2003.

of whose action he complains.[46] To establish this defence the respondent must show that an effective remedy is available and that it would not be futile to seek it. When Soviet fighters shot down a Korean airliner in 1983,[47] the United Kingdom was able immediately to demand compensation in respect of the UK nationals who had been killed since there would have been no point in the relatives going to the Soviet courts which at that time were clearly not independent of government. The rule is applied by most international tribunals, including the European Court of Human Rights, but there are important exceptions: bilateral investment treaties (where the rule generally does not apply),[48] in contracts with states under which disputes may be submitted to international arbitration, and the Iran–US Claims Tribunal.[49] In the past, some contracts, especially with South American governments, included the so-called *Calvo Clause*. This required the foreign party to rely exclusively on local remedies and not seek any diplomatic protection. Although not seen much today, the clause did bolster the local remedies rule.[50]

Non liquet

Although this is an obsolete juristic doctrine, it is sometimes contemplated. According to this doctrine an international tribunal should decline to decide a case where rules are not available for its determination because of a lacuna in international law.[51] Scholars have dismissed the notion that because international law was not complete a tribunal could abdicate its responsibility.[52] Article 42(2) of the ICSID Convention expressly prohibits a finding of *non liquet* on the ground of 'silence or obscurity of the law'.[53] This would not seem to imply that the doctrine could in certain circumstances be available, but rather is intended to be a dismissal of the doctrine.

International arbitration[54]

Arbitration is the submission of a dispute to a judge or judges, in principle chosen by the parties, who agree to accept and respect the judgment. The

[46] *Interhandel* (Preliminary Objections), *ICJ Reports* (1959), p. 6, at p. 46; 27 ILR 475.
[47] For details, see Shaw, p. 474.   [48] On this and ICSID, see p. 379 above.
[49] See p. 445 below.   [50] See *North American Dredging Company* (1926) 3 ILR 4.
[51] Parry and Grant, *Encyclopaedic Dictionary of International Law*, New York, 1986, p. 259.
[52] See, for example, E. Lauterpacht (ed.), *International Law: Being the Collected Papers of Sir Hersch Lauterpacht*, Cambridge, 1970–8, vol. 2, pp. 213–36.
[53] See C. Schreuer, *The ICSID Convention: A Commentary*, Cambridge, 2001, pp. 632–3.
[54] See Collier and Lowe, *Settlement of Disputes in International Law*, Oxford, 1999, pp. 189–273, for a useful survey of arbitral procedure.

judges are called 'arbitrators' and their judgment an 'award'. Although some arbitrations are conducted by a single arbitrator, this is really only suitable for a relatively simple case involving a narrow, essentially factual, point. It is normally better to have one arbitrator appointed by each party and one (or, even better, three) neutral arbitrators, the appointments being made as for a conciliation commission.[55] Those appointed by each party be able to explain further their state's position, and be able to share what may be a considerable workload. Although it may be more common to have only three arbitrators (as in the Iran–US Claims Tribunal) this is not ideal since the chairman then needs the support of one of the two national arbitrators in order to reach a decision. He may therefore have to compromise, whereas three neutral arbitrators should be better able to reach an impartial decision.[56]

Many multilateral and bilateral treaties contain arbitration clauses and, apart perhaps from a regional specialist tribunal like the European Court of Justice, rather more treaty disputes are decided by arbitration than by judicial settlement.

Arbitration is not necessarily cheaper or less complicated than judicial settlement. But the parties are better able to control the process (choice of arbitrators, language(s) and confidentiality). If they want a quick decision they can more easily direct the tribunal to finish by a specific date. This is helped by the fact that, even with five arbitrators, reaching a decision should be that much easier than with, say, the fifteen judges of the ICJ. But, such advantages have to be weighed against the fact that all the costs of the arbitrators, the registrar, other staff and accommodation have to be borne by the parties (normally in equal shares whatever the outcome), in addition to their own legal costs. And, since an arbitral tribunal has to be constituted for each case and its rules of procedure may well have to be agreed, the mere setting up of the tribunal can take many months. As we shall see, judicial settlement has certain other distinct advantages over arbitration. In 1998, in *The M/V Saiga (No. 2)*, the parties, Saint Vincent and the Grenadines and Guinea, after beginning arbitration proceedings, agreed to take their dispute to the International Tribunal for the Law of the Sea.[57]

It is often said that the nature of the arbitration process is such that the result is usually a compromise. That may be so, but it would seem from

---

[55] See, for example, the Swiss–United Kingdom Treaty (n. 12 above), Article 16.
[56] D. Bowett (ed.), *The International Court of Justice: Process, Practice and Procedure*, London, 1997, p. 9.
[57] ILM (1998) 360 and 1202; 120 ILR 143. For ITLOS, see p. 323 above.

some of their recent judgments that the ICJ judges, not surprisingly, also reach compromises.

Permanent Court of Arbitration

The Hague Convention for the Pacific Settlement of International Disputes 1899[58] established the Permanent Court of Arbitration (PCA) at The Hague, and for which the Peace Palace, now also home of the ICJ, was opened in 1913.[59] These days, the PCA secretariat (the International Bureau) is very active. The PCA's name is misleading. It is not a court, but a permanent facility (including a courtroom, chambers, offices, library, secretariat services and a list of potential arbitrators) available to states and international organisations to help them conduct arbitrations, whether under the 1899 or 1907 Hague Conventions, or otherwise. The cost of its services are met by the parties in dispute, although they are less than those of other arbitrations because the basic running costs of the International Bureau are met by the (approximately 103) parties to one or both Conventions. Since 1902, the PCA has provided various types of services to many arbitrations. More recent examples include the *US* v. *UK Heathrow User Charges Arbitration* 1988–93[60] and the *Eritrea–Yemen Arbitration* 1996–2002.[61] The PCA has developed model clauses and procedural rules for fact-finding, conciliation and various types of arbitration.[62] Whatever the nature of the dispute, the parties are free to determine most aspects of the procedure and to decide the extent to which the International Bureau should be involved. It is increasingly involved with international commercial arbitrations (such as ICSID) between states or international organisations and private persons or entities, with the PCA Secretary-General being called upon to designate arbitrators in default of their appointment by the parties. He is also the appointing authority in commercial arbitrations conducted under the UNCITRAL Arbitration Rules.[63] At the end of 2004, the PCA had thirteen pending cases, four involving states and non-state entities.

---

[58] 205 CTS 233; UKTS (1901) 9 or www.pca-cpa.org (go to 'Basic Documents').
[59] Its address is Peace Palace, 2517 KJ, The Hague (tel: ++ (31) (70) 302 4242; fax: ++ (31) (70) 302 4167; pca@euronet.nl; and see its excellent website, www.pca-cpa.org.
[60] 102 ILR 215.   [61] 114 ILR 1 and 119 ILR 417.
[62] For example, the Optional Rules for Arbitrating Disputes between Two States 1992 (ILM (1993) 575).
[63] See p. 389 above. The International Bureau also services arbitrations under those Rules.

Mixed arbitral tribunals[64]

A mixed arbitral tribunal is so-called because it is established to deal with disputes that are not between two states, but between a corporation (and sometimes a natural person) and a foreign state (hence 'mixed'). Their most distinguishing feature is that the state of nationality and the other state have agreed that a claim can be brought *direct* to the tribunal; thus there is no need for the state of nationality of the claimant to be involved. And, generally, local remedies do not have to be exhausted.[65] ICSID and other tribunals dealing with investment disputes are the best known.[66]

Two important standing mixed tribunals were set up in the last quarter of the twentieth century to deal with the aftermath of very grave international situations. Both are still in business.

Iran–United States Claims Tribunal[67]

Between 1979 and 1981, Iran held fifty-two US nationals hostage[68] and expropriated US property. The United States responded by freezing Iranian assets, many of which had already been attached by US courts. Iran also had claims against the United States. The Tribunal was established by the so-called Algiers Accords 1981,[69] consisting of a General Declaration by Algeria setting out the commitments made to it by Iran and the United States and Undertakings by the two states, which altogether constituted a treaty.[70] Each state had to terminate all pending litigation between its nationals and the other state that arose out of the crisis, and prohibit further such litigation. The claims would then be dealt with solely by the Tribunal. The United States nullified attachments of Iranian assets. Assets frozen by the United States were transferred to the Netherlands Central Bank to be held in escrow, all but US$1 billion being released to Iran on the safe departure of the hostages. The sum retained was to satisfy awards by the Tribunal to US nationals, being topped up by Iran when it fell below US$500 million, which has been done many times. (The United States

---

[64] See S. Troope, *Mixed International Arbitration*, Cambridge, 1990.
[65] See p. 441 above.   [66] See p. 379 above.
[67] See www.iusct.org. The address is Parkweg 13, 2585 JH, The Hague, Netherlands. See G. Aldrich, *The Jurisprudence of the Iran–United States Claims Tribunal*, Oxford, 1996; the over thirty-three volumes of the *Iran–US Claims Tribunal Reports* (Iran–US CTR), from 1981 onwards, and now published by Cambridge University Press; and Collier and Lowe, *Settlement of Disputes in International Law*, Oxford, 1999, pp. 73–83, for a concise but very useful overview.
[68] See the *US Consular and Diplomatic Staff in Tehran, ICJ Reports* (1980), p. 1; 61 ILR 502.
[69] See www.iusct.org; 1 Iran–US CTR 3; or ILM (1981) 223.   [70] See p. 54 above.

did not have to deposit money.) The United States revoked all trade sanctions and prohibited the pursuit of all prior or future claims against Iran which were not attributable to it.[71]

The Tribunal has jurisdiction over claims (1) by Iranian nationals against the United States and US nationals against Iran arising out of the consequences of the hostage crisis, most claims being by corporations; (2) certain inter-state contractual claims of Iran and the United States; and (3) interpretation of the General Declaration. The jurisdiction is limited to claims about debt, contracts, expropriation and other property rights. Personal injury and property losses directly arising from the hostage-taking are excluded.

The Tribunal has nine judges, three appointed each by Iran and the United States and three by those six. In practice, it has been necessary for the PCA Secretary-General, as the Appointing Authority, to make some of the appointments. The Tribunal usually sits in chambers of three. It applies public international law and private international law, as appropriate.[72] It follows the procedure set out in the UNCITRAL Arbitration Rules,[73] modified to deal with a standing arbitration body handling a large number of claims. The Tribunal's awards are enforceable in the courts of any state.

Claims are presented by the nationals themselves, except that those under US$250,000 are presented by the state of nationality, even though the claim remains that of the national. Some 3,800 claims were filed by the 1982 deadline, about 1,000 being for more than US$250,000. By the end of 2004, there had been 600 final awards, totalling over US$2 billion for US claimants, and over US$1 billion for Iranian claimants.

UN Compensation Commission[74]

Following the end of the (first) Iraq conflict, Security Council Resolution 687 (1991), paragraph 16, reaffirmed Iraq's liability under international law for any direct loss, damage or injury to other states, nationals and corporations as a result of its invasion and occupation of Kuwait. Paragraph 19 directed the Secretary-General to report on the establishment of a compensation fund and a commission to administer it.[75] By Resolution 692 (1991), the Council accepted his report and established the Fund and the UN Compensation Commission, located in Geneva. This was the first

[71] Such as certain acts by the revolutionary students. See pp. 412–13 above on attribution.
[72] See p. 1 above for an explanation of the difference.   [73] See p. 389 above.
[74] See www.unog.ch/uncc/ for the basic documents, Rules, Decisions and facts and figures. See also 109 ILR (all), and Collier and Lowe, *Settlement of Disputes in International Law*, Oxford, 1999, pp. 41–4.
[75] See S/22559, and ILM (1991) 1703.

time the United Nations had set up such a body. Financing for the Fund is provided by a levy on the annual value of exports of oil by Iraq. Resolution 706 (1991) set this at a maximum of 30 per cent, later reduced to 25 per cent by Resolution 1330 (2000) and, following the second Iraq conflict, Resolution 1483 (2003) reduced it to 5 per cent. The money is paid into a UN escrow account.

The Commission is a subsidiary body of the Security Council and is administered by a Governing Council of fifteen, representing the current members of the Security Council, and has its own secretariat. Experts in law, accountancy, insurance etc., nominated by UN Secretary-General, are appointed by the Governing Council as commissioners. Acting in their personal capacity, they sit on three-member panels to examine the claims. If there is no specific guideline in the Decisions of the Governing Council,[76] questions of international law are decided by the panels.[77]

The Commission is unlike the Iran–US Claims Tribunal in that the Commission's procedures differ from those of an arbitration, the basic question of liability having already been decided by the Security Council. The Commission is 'a political organ that performs an essentially fact-finding function of examining the claims, verifying their validity, evaluating losses, assessing payments and resolving disputed claims'.[78] It is therefore more like a national claims commission administering compensation received from another state responsible for an international wrong done to the nationals of the injured state,[79] except that the amount available is not fixed.

Claims are usually submitted by states on behalf of their nationals. After a preliminary assessment by the secretariat, they are considered in private by the panels on the basis of the papers. There are formal hearings only in large or complex cases. The Governing Council then reviews the recommendations of the panels and can modify the compensation. There is no appeal from the decisions of the Governing Council. Payment is in instalments, although the smaller claims have often been paid in full.

The most innovative aspect is the division of claims into six categories. Category 'A' claims are those by individuals who had to leave Iraq or Kuwait between 2 August 1990 and the ceasefire on 2 March 1991,

---

[76] See the website for Decisions, or 109 ILR 553–65 for Decisions 1–40.
[77] See, for example, *Egyptian Workers' Claim*, 117 ILR 195.
[78] Report of the UN Secretary-General, 2 May 1991 (S/22559), para. 20, and reproduced, with Guidelines, in ILM (1991) 1703.
[79] See p. 183 above.

compensation being fixed at US$2,500 per individual and US$5,000 for families; category 'B' claims are those by individuals for serious personal injury or death of a spouse, children or parents, with compensation set at US$2,500 for individuals and up to US$10,000 for families; category 'C' claims are those by individuals for up to US$100,000; category 'D' are those by individuals for over US$100,000; category 'E' are those by private or public corporations; and category 'F' are those by governments and international organisations. Category A and C claims were the largest in number and category F claims the largest in amount. Over 2.6 million claims (including those of about one million Egyptian workers) from some 100 states were submitted amounting to some US$300 billion. Claims in categories 'A' to 'C' were generally dealt with first and paid as a priority. By June 2005 over 2.68 million claims had been resolved, about US$52.5 billion awarded and about US$19 billion paid out.[80] After 12 years the work of the panels is over.

International Court of Justice[81]

The International Court of Justice is a principal organ of the United Nations, and the Statute of the Court is in an integral part of the UN Charter (Article 92 of the Charter). (References in this section to articles are to those of the ICJ Statute, unless otherwise indicated.) The Court sits at the Peace Palace at The Hague, although it can sit elsewhere, and has undertaken one site visit abroad.[82] These days, there is much confusion among the public who, not surprisingly, confuse the ICJ with the ICC or even the ICTY (both of which, to the delight of the Dutch, are also situated in The Hague).

Being a permanent body, the Court has certain distinct advantages over arbitral tribunals. It is always available to hear cases, and the parties do not have to pay anything towards the costs of the Court, apart from what they pay anyway as part of their annual contribution to the UN budget. Although the Court has been criticised for being leisurely, it probably takes

---

[80] See www.unog.ch/uncc/ for up-to-date reports on the Commission's activities.
[81] Most of the material mentioned in this part can be found on the Court's excellent website, www.icj-cij.org. See also S. Rosenne, *The Law and Practice of the ICJ*, 3rd edn, The Hague, 1997; Collier and Lowe, *Settlement of Disputes in International Law*, Oxford, 1999, pp. 124–85; Brownlie, pp. 677–94; Bowett *et al.*, *The International Tribunal Justice: Process, Practice and Procedure*, London, 1997; R. Jennings, 'The Internal Judicial Practice of the ICJ' (1988) BYIL 31; Lowe and Fitzmaurice (eds.), *Fifty Years of the International Tribunal of Justice*, Cambridge, 1996.
[82] See *Gabčíkovo-Nagymaros Project*, *ICJ Reports* (1997), p. 3; ILM (1998) 162; 116 ILR 1.

no more time to dispose of a complex case (and most cases coming before the Court are complex) than would an arbitral tribunal, yet at much less direct cost to the parties. Developing country litigants may also be able to have part of their legal costs met from a trust fund administered by the UN Secretary-General, if the dispute is submitted to the Court by *compromis*.[83] The scope of the jurisdictional competence of the Court should be known in advance, as well as its procedure and practice. Moreover, since the Court has built up a huge body of jurisprudence, and the judges serve for nine year, renewable terms, states and their advisers may be somewhat better able to predict how it may deal with a case.

All these factors should enable the proceedings to take place more quickly, with less trouble to the parties and more cheaply, if that is what the parties want. In the two *Lockerbie* cases (begun in 1992), none of the three parties was keen to have an early trial on the merits, although for different reasons. Nor were some of the judges that keen. The Court therefore agreed to generous deadlines. Before a date was fixed for the trial on the merits, the cases were discontinued by consent in 2003, to the great relief of the parties (and no doubt to the other permanent members), but most disappointing for the onlookers (and some of the judges) in view of the fundamental legal issue involved.[84]

Despite the number of new international or regional courts and tribunals established in recent years, the Court has never been busier. In July 1971, the Court had no cases pending; at the end of 2004 there were thirteen.[85]

Composition of the Court

Each of the fifteen judges sits for a nine-year term or, if he replaces a judge who dies or resigns before the end of his term, for the remainder of that term. A judge may be re-elected more than once. The seats are filled in accordance with an informal regional arrangement that ensures that the Court represents all the main legal systems of the world. There are usually five Western, three African (one each representing common law, civil law and Islamic law), three Asian, two East European and two Latin American judges. In practice, there is always a judge of the nationality of each permanent member of the Security Council. Most of the judges have been either professors of law, appeal judges or foreign ministry legal

---

[83] See www.un.org/law/trustfund.htm.   [84] See p. 460 below.

[85] For this purpose, the eight identical cases brought by the Federal Republic of Yugoslavia against certain NATO member states over the use of force during the Kosovo crisis have been counted as one.

advisers. Some have not been specialists in international law, but that is not a requirement for election, or necessarily always desirable.

Elections for five seats are held every three years at the autumn meeting of the General Assembly, the next being in 2005, the new judges taking office on 6 February of the following year. Elections for casual vacancies are held as necessary. Candidates are nominated usually by the national groups of each UN Member. To be elected, a candidate needs to have an *absolute* majority of votes in both the General Assembly (ninety-six votes at present) *and* in the Security Council (eight votes), the veto not applying (Article 10). The two bodies vote simultaneously but separately. If not all places are filled by the first round of voting, further rounds are held. There is a special procedure that may be invoked if a seat is still unfilled after a third round (Articles 11 and 12), but this has never been used. The Court elects its President and Vice-President for three-year, re-electable, terms.

A judge who is a national of a party to a case can still hear the case (Article 31(1)). If the Court hearing the case does not include a judge of the nationality of a party, that party (often both parties) has the right to choose a judge *ad hoc*, who has all the powers of a substantive judge (Article 31(2), (3) and (6)). Since it would be improper for a judge to sit on a case if, for instance, he had advised on the dispute before he joined the Court, he must therefore excuse (or recuse) himself (Article 24(1)). So, when Judge Rosalyn Higgins (a UK national) joined the Court, she had to excuse herself from sitting on the *Lockerbie* cases, as well as several others. From 1997, the United Kingdom therefore had a judge *ad hoc* in the *Lockerbie* cases.[86] Since Libya did not have a judge of its nationality on the Court, it also had a judge *ad hoc*.

Chambers

The Court can also sit in Chambers (Articles 26–28), the hearings also being in public. A Chamber has all the powers of the full Court, there being no 'appeal' from its decisions to the full Court.[87] The Court can form Chambers of three or more of its judges to deal with particular categories of cases (Article 26(1)). In 1993, the first (and so far only) such Chamber, consisting of seven judges, was formed to hear environmental cases. At the time it was fashionable in some circles to talk of the need for an

---

[86] See the preamble to the judgment on preliminary objections, *ICJ Reports* (1998), p. 9; ILM (1998) 587; 117 ILR 1.

[87] *Land and Maritime Frontier (El Salvador v. Honduras), ICJ Reports* (1990), p. 3, at p. 4. Cf. the European Court of Justice and the Court of First Instance, p. 475 below.

international environmental court. Yet all international environmental disputes involve several areas of international law, and so are better heard by the full Court, which has judges with wide knowledge and experience of international law in general, rather than be treated as special subjects to be sent to a judicial ghetto. This was well demonstrated in the *Gabcikovo-Nagymaros Project (Hungary/Slovakia)*[88] and *Fisheries Jurisdiction (Spain v. Canada)*[89] cases. In practice, most environmental disputes are not referred to international adjudication, most multilateral environment treaties providing at most for the parties to opt in to dispute settlement by the Court or international arbitration.[90] It is therefore not surprising that so far the environmental Chamber has heard no cases.[91]

The Court can also form Chambers *ad hoc* to deal with a particular case, the Court determining the number of judges with the approval of the parties (Article 26(2)). The first *ad hoc* Chamber, of five judges, was formed in 1984 for the *Gulf of Maine (Canada/United States)* case. Although neither the Statute nor the Rules of Court appear to give the parties the right to choose which of the judges should sit, that is what happened.[92] Three other cases have been heard by *ad hoc* Chambers. Chambers have no apparent advantage over the full Court, and are no cheaper for the parties.

Jurisdiction

Although the Court receives on average over 1,000 applications per year from individuals, neither they, corporations or even international organisations can be parties to cases before the Court. The Court can request an international organisation to provide it with information relevant to a case before it, and must receive such information sent to it by an international organisation on its own initiative. And, whenever the interpretation of the constituent instrument of an international organisation, or of a convention adopted under it, is in question before the Court, it must notify the organisation and sent it all the written pleadings (Article 34). Only states can be parties.

---

[88] *ICJ Reports* (1997), p. 7; ILM (1998) 162; 116 ILR 1.
[89] *ICJ Reports* (1998), p. 432; 123 ILR 189.
[90] Although see p. 328, text to n. 4, above on the MOX litigation.
[91] See Birnie and Boyle, *International Law and the Environment*, 2nd edn, Oxford, 2002, pp. 224–6, and p. 323 above.
[92] Collier and Lowe, *Settlement of Disputes in International Law*, Oxford, 1999, pp. 127–8.

Basis for jurisdiction

The Court has plenary subject matter jurisdiction in that, under Article 36(1), its jurisdiction 'comprises all cases which the parties refer to it and all matters specially provided for in the Charter of the United Nations or in treaties or conventions in force'. It is therefore not restricted to handling particular categories or types of disputes. All UN Members are *ipso facto* parties to the Statute of the Court. But that does *not* mean that they have agreed to the Court deciding any dispute between them and other UN Members. As with any other international tribunal, the Court can exercise jurisdiction only if that has been conferred on it by the parties.[93] This can be done by one of the several means described at pp. 436 *et seq* above, and which are encapsulated in Article 36(1). In practice, its jurisdiction has been founded roughly equally on compromissory clauses, *compromis* and reciprocal declarations. In the 1980s, most cases decided on their merits were brought under *compromis*. In the 1990s, more cases were bought unilaterally under compromissory clauses.[94]

Reciprocal declarations

The Statute has a provision special to it: parties to the Statute have the option of making a declaration under Article 36(2) accepting, in relation to any other state accepting the same obligation, the compulsory jurisdiction of the Court in all legal disputes. No *compromis* is needed. At present only sixty-four declarations have been made, although these constitute a wide geographical spread of states, half being by developing countries.[95] From the date a declaration is deposited it creates obligations between the state making it and other states that make such declarations.[96] Once a state has deposited its declaration, it is said to have accepted the compulsory jurisdiction of the Court; although whether the

---

[93] See the separate joint declaration by seven of the judges criticising the Court's reasoning (though not its decision) in finding that it had no jurisdiction in *Legality of the Use of Force (Serbia and Montenegro v. Belgium)* (Preliminary Objections), *ICJ* Reports (2004).

[94] For details, see Collier and Lowe, *Settlement of Disputes in International Law*, Oxford, 1999, p. 133, n. 36. Article 36(1) also gives the Tribunal jurisdiction in 'all matters specially provided for in the Charter', although this is effectively a dead letter.

[95] Merrills, *International Dispute Settlement*, 3rd edn, Cambridge, 1998, pp. 121–9; J. Merrills, 'The Optional Clause Revisited' (1993) BYIL 197.

[96] Although a declaration is a unilateral act, since the effect is to create bilateral agreements between the states, the declarations are registered by the United Nations under Article 102 of the Charter, as to which see p. 111 above.

Court has jurisdiction in a particular case depends on various factors. In practice, most disputes have been referred to the Court under compromissory clauses or by *compromis*.

Meaning of reciprocity

For the Court to have jurisdiction on the basis of two declarations under Article 36(2), a declaration by one state requires that the other accept 'the same obligation'. Thus the essence of the Court's jurisdiction on this basis is reciprocity: a state can rely not only on its own reservations (see below)) but also on any made by the other state. So, if two states have a dispute that arose in, say, 1990, and the declaration of one of them excludes disputes arising before 1995, the Court will not have jurisdiction.[97] In essence, therefore, jurisdiction amounts to the lowest common denominator of the two reservations.

Reservations

Although Article 36 does not provide for reservations to be attached to declarations, this is implicit in the unilateral nature of the declarations. In fact, most declarations have been made subject to reservations.[98] But, if the Court does not have jurisdiction because of a reservation, it may still have jurisdiction on another basis.[99] A limitation on the Court's jurisdiction under a compromissory clause, but not in a declaration, does not affect the declaration.[100]

The United Kingdom is the only permanent member of the Security Council to maintain a declaration. France and the United States withdrew theirs in 1974 and 1985, respectively. China, as represented by the PRC Government, did not recognise the declaration made previously by the Republic of China (Taiwan). The USSR/Russia has never made a declaration.

The previous UK declaration of 1 January 1969 illustrates some of the reservations that can be made. The declaration accepted, as compulsory *ipso facto* and without special agreement, on condition of reciprocity, until such time as notice might be given to terminate the acceptance, the jurisdiction of the Court

---

[97] *Interhandel*, *ICJ Reports* (1959), p. 6, at p. 23; 27 ILR 475.
[98] For the text of the current declarations, see *UN Multilateral Treaties*, C. I.4, at http://untreaty.un.org.
[99] *Nicaragua* v. *US*, *ICJ Reports* (1984), p. 392, paras. 77–83; 76 ILR 104; and *Arbitral Award (Guinea-Bissau* v. *Senegal)*, *ICJ Reports* (1991), p. 53, paras. 22–9; 92 ILR 1.
[100] *Cameroon* v. *Nigeria* (Preliminary Objections), *ICJ Reports* (1998), p. 275, paras. 61–73.

over all disputes arising after the 24th of October 1945, with regard to situations or facts subsequent to the same date, *other than*:

(i)   any dispute which the United Kingdom
   (a) has agreed with the other party or parties thereto to settle by some other method of peaceful settlement; or
   (b) has already submitted to arbitration by agreement with any state, which had not at the time of submission accepted the compulsory jurisdiction of the International Court of Justice.

(ii) disputes with the government of any other country that is a Member of the Commonwealth with regard to situations or facts existing before the 1st of January 1969.

(iii) disputes in respect of which any other party to the dispute has accepted the compulsory jurisdiction of the International Court of Justice only in relation to or for the purpose of the dispute; or where the acceptance of the Court's compulsory jurisdiction on behalf of any other party to the dispute was deposited or ratified less than twelve months prior to the filing of the application bringing the dispute before the Court. (Emphasis added)

The declaration also reserved the right at any time either to add to, amend or withdraw any of the reservations, or any that might later be added. On 5 July 2004, the UK declaration was replaced by a new one accepting the jurisdiction of the Court as before, but only in respect of

disputes arising after *1 January 1974*, with regard to situations or facts subsequent to the same date, *other than*:

(i)   any dispute which the United Kingdom has agreed with the other party or parties thereto to settle by some other method of peaceful settlement;

(ii) any dispute with the government of any other country that is *or has been* a Member of the Commonwealth;

(iii) [as before]. (Emphasis added.)

The new declaration broadens the scope of the Commonwealth exclusion to cover also former Commonwealth countries.[101] The immediate reason was that Mauritius had said that it was considering taking to the Court its dispute with the United Kingdom over the Chagos Archipelago.[102] But,

---

[101] The 1974 Declaration by India is to the same effect. In *Aerial Incident (Pakistan v. India)*, *ICJ Reports* (2000), p. 12, paras. 30–46, the Court held it was effective to prevent it from having jurisdiction on the basis of Article 36(2).

[102] Formerly part of Mauritius when it was still a colony, but detached from Mauritius in 1965 to form, with some islands that had been part of the colony of the Seychelles, the British Indian Ocean Territory.

since the Court would not have jurisdiction (because of the first part of paragraph (ii) of the 1969 declaration), Mauritius was considering first leaving the Commonwealth. The new cut-off date for disputes (1 January 1974) replaced that of the entry into force of the UN Charter, so excluding all claims arising before 1974.[103]

We will now look at the main types of reservation.

Exclusion of certain categories of dispute

Canada's declaration excludes disputes concerning certain fishing conservation measures taken by Canada, and their enforcement.[104] New Zealand excludes disputes about its rights in respect of the marine living resources within its EEZ. These represent just one general category of exclusions; a trawl through all the declarations will show other categories.

Resort to other means of settlement

A common reservation is on the lines of paragraphs (i) of the (two) UK declarations to ensure that another state does not go 'forum-shopping'. But reliance on such a reservation has so far not been successful.[105]

Exclusions by reference to time

It is common to restrict the declaration to disputes arising, or facts or situations, subsequent to a certain date.[106] The effect of the chapeau and paragraph (ii) of the UK's 1969 Declaration was effectively to preclude the Court having jurisdiction in most disputes between the United Kingdom and former British territories concerning the colonial period. The UK's 2004 declaration withdrew its consent to jurisdiction over any dispute arising before 1 January 1974.

Self-judging reservations

The US declaration of 1946 (withdrawn in 1985) included the so-called Connally amendment that purported to exclude from the Court's jurisdiction disputes that were essentially within US domestic jurisdiction 'as

---

[103] *Hansard* (HC) 6 July 2004, WS 32, and (HL) 7 July 2004, WS 35.

[104] See *Fisheries Jurisdiction (Spain v. Canada), ICJ Reports* (1998), p. 432, para. 14; 123 ILR 189.

[105] See *Certain Phosphate Lands in Nauru, ICJ Reports* (1992), p. 240; 97 ILR 1.

[106] See *Interhandel, ICJ Reports* (1959), p. 6, at pp. 10–11; 27 ILR 475, and the other cases described in Collier and Lowe, *Settlement of Disputes in International Law*, Oxford, 1999, pp. 146–8.

determined by the United States'.[107] Other states have made similar reservations. Their validity has been considered in a few cases, but the Court has not yet ruled definitively whether they are invalid and, if so, what the consequences are.[108] The second question raises a problem similar to certain reservations to treaties: whether (1) the Court could sever the invalid reservation from the declaration, or (2) the whole declaration is tainted by it, and therefore is invalid and provides no basis for jurisdiction.[109] The latter alternative is instinctively unattractive to any court, but is probably correct. Although a declaration creates bilateral obligations, it is a unilateral act. The state has said it will accept the jurisdiction subject to that reservation. If it is held to be invalid, but the state refuses to withdraw it, then an essential condition for the state's acceptance of the Court's jurisdiction has not been met.

Vandenberg amendment

The US declaration also included the so-called Vandenberg amendment concerning disputes arising under a multilateral treaty: the Court would not have jurisdiction 'unless (1) all parties to the treaty affected by the decision are also parties to the case before the Court or (2) the United States of America specially agrees to jurisdiction'. The United States invoked this reservation in the *Nicaragua* case, arguing that, since Nicaragua argued that the US was in breach of the UN Charter, all UN Members would have to be parties to the case. The Court held that the reservation applied only to states whose rights and obligations would be affected by its judgment. As El Salvador would be affected, yet was not a party to the proceedings, the Court decided that it could not exercise jurisdiction on the basis of the Charter, but nevertheless could do so on another basis.[110]

Variation of declarations

A state can vary the terms of its declaration only if it has reserved the right to do so (as in the UK declarations).[111] If it has not reserved the right to vary, it would have to withdraw the whole declaration and replace it

[107] On similar, and more recent, US so-called constitutional reservations to treaties, see p. 75 above.
[108] See Collier and Lowe, *Settlement of Disputes in International Law*, Oxford, 1999, pp. 143–6.
[109] See p. 74 above.
[110] *ICJ Reports* (1986), p. 392, paras. 36–56; 76 ILR 1.
[111] See *Right of Passage, ICJ Reports* (1957), p. 125; 24 ILR 840; and *Nicaragua* v. *US, ICJ Reports* (1984), p. 392; 76 ILR 104.

with a modified one. If a declaration is for an indefinite period, it can be withdrawn either in accordance with a reservation to that effect in the declaration or, if not, by analogy with a treaty,[112] only after the expiry of a reasonable notice period.[113] If a declaration is withdrawn or lapses[114] after the Court has been seised of a case, this will not affect the Court's jurisdiction.[115]

Admissibility

This topic has been dealt with at p. 441 above. Respondents often plead that a claim is inadmissible, but the argument rarely succeeds. There are a few cases where the Court decided that it could not exercise its evident jurisdiction. The jurisprudence of the Court shows that it will reject claims that are hypothetical and lacking any real purpose,[116] those which have become moot[117] or those in which the applicant state has no legal interest.[118]

It will also decline to exercise jurisdiction if a state that is not a party to the proceedings has a legal interest that would put it at the centre of the case. The *Monetary Gold* case concerned the ownership of gold removed by Italy from Albania in 1943, but Albania was not a party to the proceedings. Since Albania's legal interest would be the 'very subject matter' of the decision the Court was being asked to make, the Court refused to exercise jurisdiction.[119] In the case of *East Timor* (then a Portuguese colony annexed unlawfully by Indonesia), Portugal brought proceedings against Australia concerning the latter's treaty with Indonesia purporting to delimit the continental shelf between Timor and Australia. Applying the *Monetary Gold* judgment, in 1995 the Court refused to exercise jurisdiction as the 'very subject matter' of its judgment would have been to determine whether Indonesia could have concluded the treaty, yet Indonesia was not a party.[120] But, in the *Certain Phosphate Lands* case, the Court did

---

[112] But see *Fisheries Jurisdiction (Spain v. Canada), ICJ Reports* (1998), p. 432; 123 ILR 189.
[113] See *Nicaragua v. US, ICJ Reports* (1984), p. 392, at p. 420, paras. 52–66; 76 ILR 104.
[114] Article 36(3) allows declarations to be made for a certain time (duration).
[115] *Nottebohm, ICJ Reports* (1953), p. 121, at p. 123; 20 ILR 567.
[116] *Northern Cameroons, ICJ Reports* (1963), p. 15; 35 ILR 353.
[117] *Nuclear Tests, ICJ Reports* (1974), (Australia) p. 253, paras. 21 *et seq.*, and (New Zealand), p. 457, paras. 21 *et seq.*; 57 ILR 348.
[118] *South West Africa, ICJ Reports* (1966), p. 6; 37 ILR 243.
[119] *ICJ Reports* (1954), p. 32; 21 ILR 399.
[120] *ICJ Reports* (1995), p. 90, paras. 33–6; 105 ILR 226.

not find that the interests of non-parties (New Zealand and the United Kingdom), that might well be affected by its judgment, were the 'very subject matter' of the case. In that event, a third party has the option of intervening.

Intervention by third parties

Article 62 gives the Court discretion to allow a third state to intervene in proceedings if it has 'an interest of a legal nature which may be affected by the decision in the case'. Article 81(2) of the Rules of Court requires the third state to specify the interest, the precise object of the intervention, and any basis of jurisdiction that is claimed to exist between the third state and the parties, even though this last stipulation is not required by Article 62. The legal interest must be specific to the applicant, not merely general. So far, the Court has agreed to an intervention only twice. In 1990, in the *Land, Island and Maritime Frontiers* case,[121] a Chamber allowed Nicaragua to intervene on one of the five matters it had raised in respect of which it had demonstrated a legal interest that might be affected by the judgment. In particular, and despite what the Rule says, the Chamber did not require the applicant to show any jurisdictional link with the parties, such a link not being necessary since an intervener does not become a party to the case. It has only the right to be heard, and in any event decisions of the Court bind only the parties and in respect of the particular case (*res judicata*) (Article 59). In 1999, the Court authorised Equatorial Guinea to intervene in the *Land and Maritime Boundary between Cameroon and Nigeria* case,[122] but in 2001 it refused the request by the Philippines to intervene in *Sovereignty over Pulau Litigan and Pulau Sipadan (Indonesia/Malaysia)*, as it had not demonstrated a legal interest.[123]

The applicable law

Article 38(1) requires the Court to decide cases in accordance with international law, and lists the sources.[124] Article 38(2) allows the Court to decide a case *ex aequo et bono*, if the parties agree. This is not the same as

---

[121] *ICJ Reports* (1990), p. 92; 97 ILR 154.   [122] *ICJ Reports* (1999), p. 1029.
[123] *ICJ Reports* (2001), p. 579.   [124] See p. 5 above.

following equitable principles, but involves compromise and conciliation. So far, the Court has not been asked to decide on this basis.[125]

Non-appearance

If one of the parties fails to appear before the Court,[126] or to defend its case, the other party may call upon the Court to decide in its favour (Article 53). When this has happened – five times so far – the Court has always given judgment. But it must first be satisfied that it has jurisdiction (or not merely *prima facie* jurisdiction), and that the claim is well founded in fact and law.[127]

Provisional measures/interim measures of protection[128]

The Statute uses the term 'provisional measures', but the two expressions are interchangeable. The purpose of such measures is similar to an injunction in domestic law: to prevent the respondent from doing something that might render any eventual judgment futile. Article 41 gives the Court power 'to indicate any provisional measures which ought to be taken to preserve the respective rights of either party'. The applicant may seek such measures urgently at the start of the proceedings, and they can be granted so long as the Court considers that *prima facie* it has jurisdiction.[129] Even when there is no clear need for such measures, given that the hearing of the next stage could be two or more years away an applicant may find it a useful way of publicising its complaint early. Requests for provisional measures have proliferated in recent years. In the ten years between 1974 and 1983, only one request was made; in the twenty years between 1984 and 2004, there were fourteen, although this partly reflects the increasing number of cases before the Court.

The Court is willing to order provisional measures if there is a real possibility that without them the rights of the applicant would be affected. In *Genocide Convention (Bosnia v. Serbia and Montenegro)*, the Court ordered the respondent to take all measures within its power to prevent

---

[125] See Brownlie, pp. 25–6 and 690.

[126] 'Appearance' is the term for a formal act acknowledging the application made to the Court. The party can still challenge the jurisdiction of the Court.

[127] See further Collier and Lowe, *Settlement of Disputes in International Law*, Oxford, 1999, pp. 180–2.

[128] See S. Rosenne, *Provisional Measures in International Law*, Oxford, 2004.

[129] See *Cameroon v. Nigeria, ICJ Reports* (1996), p. 13 at p. 21, paras. 30–1.

genocide.[130] In contrast, in *Lockerbie*, the Court (by eleven to five) declined to order provisional measures. Libya had asked for them in order to prevent the United Kingdom and the United States from seeking a Security Council resolution requiring Libya to surrender the two accused of the sabotage and imposing sanctions until it did. Three days after the hearing of the application, and before the Court could give its decision, the Security Council adopted just such a resolution (Resolution 748 (1992)). The Court found that, in view of Articles 25 and 103 of the UN Charter, all the parties were bound by the resolution and that *prima facie* it prevailed over the parties' obligations under the Montreal Convention (the subject of the case), and so the rights claimed by Libya under the Convention could not now be regarded as appropriate for protection.[131]

Previously, it was not clear if the Court's indication of interim measures was legally binding, several having been ignored. In the *La Grand* case, the Court declared that it is binding.[132] This is particularly important since Article 41(2) requires the Court to inform the Security Council of the measures. Now that it is clear that they are binding, the Council may wish in suitable cases to adopt its own measures to reinforce those ordered by the Court.

Judicial review?

The two *Lockerbie* cases[133] raised the issue of whether the Court could judicially review the substance of decisions of the UN Security Council, in particular legally binding measures adopted under Chapter VII, and hold them *ultra vires* the Charter. Although the cases had begun in February 1992, they were discontinued by consent in September 2003, and so the matter was never decided. Nevertheless, despite the enormous amount of academic speculation,[134] all the indications are against the Court having this power. Neither the Charter nor the Statute suggests that it has such a power, and the San Francisco Conference rejected a Belgian proposal

---

[130] *ICJ Reports* (1993), p. 3; ILM (1993) 888; 95 ILR 1.
[131] *ICJ Reports* (1992), p. 3, at paras. 30–43; ILM (1992) 662; 94 ILR 478. The decision in the parallel proceedings brought against the US was identical.
[132] *ICJ Reports* (2001), p. 9, para. 101–2; ILM (2001) 1069; 118 ILR 37. See also (2002) ICLQ 449 and (2002) *Law Quarterly Review* 35. Under Article 290 of the UN Convention on the Law of the Sea 1982, provisional measures prescribed by ITLOS are clearly binding (see p. 325 above).
[133] See n. 37 above.   [134] See the references in Shaw, p. 1148, n. 322.

to give such a power to the Court.[135] The Court has already denied that it has such a power.[136] If it had the power, it could severely hamper the effectiveness of the Security Council; one would never know if and when the substance of a resolution might be questioned before the Court.

Procedure and practice

The Registrar of the Court is the source of all knowledge on procedure and practice and should be consulted at all important stages of the proceedings. But any state contemplating proceedings should also study carefully the Court's Statute, Rules of Court (which set out the procedure in detail) and, most importantly, the current Practice Directions.[137] In recent years, the Court has tightened its procedure and practice to deal with the inordinate length of many written and oral pleading, and so speed up its work.

The applicant must lodge with the Registrar a concise written application outlining the facts and the legal basis for the proceedings. A joint application is made if the case comes by means of a *compromis*. The parties must each appoint Agents. In practice, the Agent is often more of a formal figure, the day-to-day running of the case being done by the deputy-agent, and the pleadings often being drafted by outside counsel.[138] (The international bar has a coterie of mainly Anglophone and Francophone international jurists who appear in most of the cases.) The applicant will then submit a memorial, to which the respondent responds with a counter-memorial. These are followed by a reply and a rejoinder. But, preliminary objections to the jurisdiction or admissibility are frequently raised by the respondent following receipt of the applicant's memorial, and can be lodged at any time before the filing of the counter-memorial. After receiving the response of the applicant, the Court will

---

[135] France, the Soviet Union, the UK and the US were all opposed. See Doc. 2, G/7(k)(l), 3 UNCIO Doc. 335, 336 (1945); Doc. 433, III/2/15, 12 UNCIO, Docs. 47 (1945), at p. 49 and Doc. 498, III/2/19, 12 UNCIO, Docs. 65 (1945), at pp. 65–6.

[136] *Certain Expenses, ICJ Reports* (1962), p. 5; 34 ILR 281; and *Namibia, ICJ Reports* (1971), p. 6; 49 ILR 2. Both were advisory proceedings where an UNSC resolution was in issue, so suggesting that there would be no grounds for a power of judicial review in contentious proceedings.

[137] All this material, judgments, and much else about the Tribunal, are on the Court's excellent website, www.icj-cij.org, under 'Basic Documents'. On working methods, see D. Bowett (ed.), *The International Court of Justice: Process, Practice and Procedure*, London, 1997; and R. Higgins, 'Running a Tight Courtroom' (2001) ICLQ 123–32.

[138] See also D. Bowett, *ibid.*, pp. 12–18.

hear oral arguments on the preliminary objections and take a decision, although sometimes it will leave those oral arguments for the merits stage. Although simultaneous written pleadings may appear to save time, the procedure is generally not efficient, as each side has to anticipate as best it can the arguments of the other, and so another round of pleadings is usually necessary anyway. Although simultaneous written pleadings have been used in proceedings brought under a *compromis*, the Court strongly discourages them in all cases.

Oral pleadings will be held on the merits. Unless there is oral evidence (not usual), the hearings consist of set speeches. It is very rare for any of the judges to ask a question during the oral pleadings. Any questions are generally read out by the judges only at the completion of oral arguments, the parties being then given a couple of weeks to reply in writing. Judgment is given at a further public hearing. Each judge can, and often does, also make a separate declaration or give a separate concurring or dissenting opinion.

The official languages of the Court are English and French, and each party can use whichever language it prefers. The Court can, at the request of a party, authorise the use of another language (Article 39), but any text in that language must be accompanied by a translation into English or French. If oral pleadings or evidence are given in an unofficial language, the party concerned must arrange, at its own expense, for interpretation into one of the two official languages.

Judgments

Effect, interpretation and revision

Article 60 provides that a judgment of the Court is 'final and without appeal'. If there is a dispute between the parties as to its meaning, either can ask the Court to construe it, but it will only do so in respect of questions decided in the judgment.[139] It will revise the judgment only if there is a new fact that was not discoverable at the time of the case, and is of such a nature as to be a decisive factor that would mean revision of at least part of the judgment.[140]

The Court has been criticised for not providing sufficiently reasoned arguments for its decisions.[141] This has been due mainly to the civil law

---

[139] *Asylum, ICJ Reports* (1950), p. 395, at p. 402; 17 ILR 339.
[140] *Tunisia/Libya Continental Shelf, ICJ Reports* (1985), p. 192. paras. 11–40; 84 ILR 419.
[141] A. Aust, 'The Future of the Judicial Function' (1998) *Finnish YB of International Law* 81.

approach of some of the judges who felt that the role of the Court was to make decisions, not to develop the law. That is now changing, although, as the 2004 Advisory Opinion on *Legal Consequences of the Construction of a Wall in the Occupied Palestinian Territory*[142] shows, sometimes the reasoning can be rather brief (although in practice this may reflect deep disagreements on politically-charged issues).[143]

Compliance and enforcement[144]

Each UN Member is obliged to comply with a judgment of the Court in any case in which it is a party. If it fails to comply, the other party may ask the Security Council to take action (Article 94). If the Council determines that the non-compliance is a threat to international peace and security, it can adopt a binding measure under Chapter VII requiring compliance and, if necessary, imposing sanctions.[145] The Council has not yet exercised this power. In 1986, the United States twice vetoed draft resolutions calling on it to comply with the Court's judgment in *Nicaragua v. United States*.[146] Security Council Resolution 915 (1994) established an observer group to monitor Libyan withdrawal from a previously disputed area in accordance with an agreement by the parties on implementation of the Court's judgment in *Libya v. Chad (Territorial Dispute)*.[147]

Advisory opinions

Article 65 authorises the Court to give 'an advisory opinion on any legal question' at the request of whatever body may be authorised by, or in accordance with, the Charter to make such a request. If the matter is urgent the Court can give an opinion quickly, even within a couple of months as in the PLO case (see below).

Under Article 96 of the Charter, the General Assembly and the Security Council may request advisory opinions. Other UN organs and specialised agencies, if so authorised by the General Assembly, may also request advisory opinions 'on legal questions arising within the scope of their

---

[142] *ICJ Reports* (2004), paras. 13–65; ILM (2004) 1009.
[143] See p. 227, n. 69 above on the mishandling of the self-defence issue.
[144] See C. Schulte, *Compliance with Decisions of the International Court of Justice*, Oxford, 2004.
[145] See further p. 214 above.   [146] See S/18250 and records of meetings 2704 and 2718.
[147] *ICJ Reports* (1994), p. 4; 100 ILR 1.

activities'. The request of the World Health Organization for an opinion on the legality of the use by a state of nuclear weapons, because of the effects on the environment and health, was declined by the Court since the WHO was not authorised to deal with matters of legality, only with the effects, of the use of such weapons.[148] But the Court did accept and advise on a similar request from the General Assembly.[149] The Court has so far given twenty-five advisory opinions.

A state cannot ask for an advisory opinion, but all states are entitled to address the Court in writing or orally about a request, and any international organisation considered by the Court as likely to be able to furnish information on the question is notified of the request. They can then file with the Court written statements or make oral statements at a public hearing of the Court. They may also comment, in writing or orally, on the statements of others (see Article 66).

Requests for opinions may concern disputes between states or between a state and an international organisation. The Court's approach to requests was discussed comprehensively in the 2004 Advisory Opinion on the *Legal Consequences of the Construction of a Wall in the Occupied Palestinian Territory*.[150]

Article 68 provides that in exercising its advisory functions the Court shall further be guided by the provisions of the Statute which apply in contentious cases to the extent that it recognises them to be applicable. Article 102(2) of the Rules of Court requires the Court to 'above all consider whether the request . . . relates to a legal question actually pending between two or more states'. But the Court has not refused to give an opinion even when the rights of a state were in issue. Provided the request is about a legal question, the political context in which the request is made is relevant only to the 'propriety' of giving the opinion.[151] An opinion given to the United Nations is to help it in its work, so there must be 'compelling reasons' to decline a request.[152] But the fact that in the *Legality of Nuclear Weapons* Advisory Opinion the Court split evenly on the most difficult question (which was then decided only by the casting vote of the President)[153] illustrates the

---

[148] *ICJ Reports* (1996), p. 66, para. 20; 110 ILR 1.   [149] See p. 203 above.

[150] *ICJ Reports* (2004), paras. 13–65; ILM (2004) 1009.

[151] *Western Sahara*, *ICJ Reports* (1975), p. 12, paras. 23–74; 59 ILR 14.

[152] *Legality of Nuclear Weapons*, *ICJ Reports* (1996), p. 226, para. 14; 110 ILR 163; *Legal Consequences of the Construction of a Wall in the Occupied Palestinian Territory*, *ICJ Reports* (2004), paras. 43–65; ILM (2004) 1009.

[153] *Ibid.*, para. 105(2) E.

difficulties inherent in asking the Court to advise on matters which are unlikely to be resolved by any formal legal process. The legal issue may well be only one aspect of a multifaceted dispute, and the question may lack balance. The fact that it requires only a simple majority of those voting in the UN General Assembly (abstentions not counting) means that the question will often not reflect a consensus of the membership.[154]

Unless the basis for the request provides otherwise,[155] an advisory opinion is not binding, but is usually influential with the states that are directly affected by it, as was the case with the PLO opinion.[156] It may also result in steps being taken by the General Assembly or the Security Council.

Although there are other permanent universal international courts or tribunals, in contrast to the ICJ their jurisdiction is restricted by their constituent instruments to more specific areas of international law.

---

[154] See UNGA Res. ES-10/14 of 8 December 2003.

[155] See *Difference relating to Immunity from Legal Process, ICJ Reports* Cumaraswamy (1999), p. 62; 121 ILR 405. The request was under section 30 of the General Convention on the Privileges and Immunities of the UN 1946, which provides that if the Tribunal is asked to give an advisory opinion on a dispute between the UN and a Member, the opinion 'shall be accepted as decisive'.

[156] *ICJ Reports* (1988), p. 12; 82 ILR 225; ILM (1988) 808.

23

The European Union

The immense popularity of American movies abroad demonstrates that Europe is the unfinished negative of which America is the proof.[1]

Wyatt and Dashwood's European Union Law, 4th edn, London, 2000
Hartley, *The Foundations of European Community Law*, 5th edn, Oxford, 2003
Lasok and Lasok, *Law and Institutions of the European* Communities, 7th edn, London, 2001
Barnard, *The Substantive Law of the EU*, Oxford, 2004
European Communities Legislation: Current Status, Butterworths, London, 3 vols., looseleaf
www.europa.eu.int

Beginning in 1958 with only six member states, the European Union had by 2004 developed into a partnership of twenty-five. In 2003, the then fifteen member states had a total population of 380 million and a total gross domestic product (GDP) of US$10.5 trillion. The equivalent figures for the United States in 2003 were a population of 280 million and a GDP of US$11 trillion. By 2004, the GDP of the previous fifteen member states had just overtaken the US GDP, and the (now twenty-five) member states had a combined population of 456 million.[2] Just as a basic knowledge of the complexities of the US Constitution and how it works is necessary for anyone concerned with international relations, so an understanding of the EU and its procedures is important. Any company exporting to, or selling within, the EU must comply with EU law. Many non-EU states and some of their regions have offices in Brussels, as do many large, non-EU companies. Given the population of the EU, and the collective economic power wielded by its member states, the EU has been for some time an important player in international relations. Having established itself as an international organisation worthy of being a party

---

[1] Mary McCarthy, *New York Times*, 16 February 1980, p. 12.
[2] Figures from the EU Statistical Office, Eurostat (www.europa.eu.int/comm/eurostat/).

in its own right to certain universal treaties, it is of particular interest as a subject of international law.

A brief history

The EU has grown relentlessly from the modest proposal in 1950 of the French Foreign Minister, Robert Schumann, for a fusion of the French and German coal and steel industries as a first step in building (as he envisaged it) an eventual European federation that would make a future war between France and Germany impossible. The first governing treaty, to create the European Coal and Steel Community (ECSC) and to establish a common market in coal and steel, came into being in 1952 with France, Germany, Italy and the Benelux countries (Belgium, Luxembourg and the Netherlands) as the initial members. On 25 March 1957, the so-called Treaty of Rome, establishing the European Economic Community (EEC), and a treaty establishing the European Atomic Energy Community (Euratom), were signed, both entering into force the following year. The Treaty establishing a Single Council and a Single Commission of the European Communities 1965 (Merger Treaty) resulted in the three[3] European Communities being served by the same institutions.

The (Maastricht) Treaty on European Union 1992 (TEU) entered into force in 1993. It created a new overarching entity, the European Union, and clumsily expressed it to be 'founded on the European Communities, supplemented by the policies and forms of co-operation established by' the TEU, that is Title V, Common Foreign and Security Policy (CFSP), and Title VI, Police and Judicial Co-operation in Criminal Matters (PJCCM).[4] The Treaty of Amsterdam 1997 entered into force in 1999, its main successes being reform of the legislative process and the consolidation and renumbering of the separate texts of the EC Treaty and the TEU.

A Treaty establishing a Constitution for Europe ('the Constitution') was formally adopted on 29 October 2004. *If* it should enter into force, it will affect what follows, including the numbering of Articles. (See the end of the chapter for a summary of the main changes.)

---

[3] With the expiry of the ECSC Treaty in 2002, the EC Treaty now applies also to coal and steel.
[4] Previously described as co-operation in the fields of justice and home affairs (JHA), but the Treaty of Amsterdam transferred visas, immigration, refugees and judicial co-operation in civil matters to Title IV of the EC Treaty.

Member states

Denmark, Ireland and the United Kingdom[5] joined the original six members of the European Communities in 1973, Greece in 1981, Portugal and Spain in 1986, Austria, Finland and Sweden in 1995, and Cyprus,[6] the Czech Republic, Estonia, Hungary, Latvia, Lithuania, Malta, Poland, Slovakia and Slovenia in 2004.[7] Bulgaria and Romania are due to join on 1 January 2007. Croatia and Turkey are possible applicants. An applicant state must conclude a treaty of accession with the existing members, which all the states must then ratify before the applicant can become a member. The treaty of accession makes necessary institutional changes and certain agreed modifications, including transitional provisions, to the obligations of the new member to accommodate its particular needs and situation.[8]

European Communities, European Community or European Union?

Given the complex arrangements outlined above, it is small wonder that there is some confusion as to what to call this European organisation. It began as three separate organisations: the ECSC, EEC and Euratom (the three then being referred to collectively as the European Communities). Following the Merger Treaty 1965, the ECSC and Euratom became much less important as separate organisations. The TEU 1992 reflected this by renaming the EEC the European Community (EC). The TEU also established the superior entity, the European Union (EU), but it did not replace the European Communities. Rather, it supplemented them by two new processes: the Common Foreign and Security Policy (CFSP) and the Police and Judicial Co-operation in Criminal Matters (PJCCM). It has generally been the EC that has been party to treaties with third states.[9]

The structure created by the TEU has been likened to a (rather badly designed) Ancient Greek temple having only three pillars surmounted by a pediment. The middle pillar (and certainly the fattest) represents

---

[5] French President de Gaulle had previously vetoed the UK's accession in 1963 and 1967.

[6] Since the northern part of Cyprus is still under Turkish occupation (see p. 19 above), at present only the southern part, controlled by the Government of the Republic of Cyprus, is in fact within the EU.

[7] Apart from Iceland, Liechtenstein, Norway and Switzerland, all the other members of the European Free Trade Area (EFTA) established in 1960 (Austria, Denmark, Finland, Sweden, Portugal and the United Kingdom) have left it and joined the EU.

[8] For example, Denmark was exceptionally allowed to keep its important prohibition on ownership of land by foreign nationals, including EU nationals.

[9] Although see p. 265, n. 22 above for a recent exception.

the European Community (EC), flanked by rather thin second and third pillars representing the CFSP and the PJCCM respectively.[10] The pediment contains the common institutions, political values, objectives, and amendment and accession procedures. However, this deceptively simple image hides the fact that the common institutions operate with different powers, procedures and legal consequences, depending on the substance of the matter, so the image of a Gothic cathedral might be closer to the complex reality.

But the heart of the EU remains the first pillar, the European Community, without which the edifice would collapse. Unlike the CFSP and the PJCCM, the work of the EC covers several large subject areas, and the resulting acts by the Council of Ministers are subject to the sophisticated legal order created by the EC Treaty and the judgments of the European Court of Justice, in particular the primacy of EC law and its direct effect.

But should the new Constitution for Europe ever enter into force, the correct term will then be the European Union, or simply, the Union. Therefore, in a spirit of optimism, the rest of this book refers primarily to the EU, even though, as a matter of law and in contrast to the EC, the EU is not yet generally accepted as having international legal personality.[11] The EC is referred to when dealing with a treaty to which the EC is a party or to legislation which only the EC can make.

(Article numbers are of the Nice consolidated versions of either the amended EC Treaty or the Treaty on European Union (TEU) prepared after the Nice Treaty 2001 by the European Commission for illustrative purposes (see www.europa.eu.int, go to 'The EU at a glance', and then 'Treaties and law'). Unless otherwise indicated, Articles cited are of the EC Treaty.)

The fundamental aim of the EU is to bring its member states closer together economically, socially and politically. The EU has become an extraordinarily complex regional organisation, in terms of the treaties governing it, its procedures and its legislation. But, although it has a certain degree of supranational power, it is *not* a federation. This chapter will outline the structure of the EU and how it works. It will not attempt to describe the substantive law developed by the EU over nearly fifty years in the areas of, for example, a customs union, the single market,

[10] For an unforgettable image, see *Wyatt and Dashwood's European Union Law*, 4th edn, London, 2000, p. 172.

[11] See n. 9 above.

competition, the common agricultural policy, free movement of persons, the right of establishment and social policy. For that, one must consult books such as those mentioned above.

Institutions

Five institutions serve the EU: the Council of Ministers, the Commission, the European Parliament, the Court of Justice and the Court of Auditors. The Council and the Commission are located in Brussels; the Court of Justice and the Court of Auditors in Luxembourg. The Parliament commutes expensively between Strasbourg and Brussels. The powers of each institution are limited to those conferred on it expressly or impliedly by the governing treaties.

Council of Ministers

The Council is composed of ministers from each of the twenty-five member states, the Presidency rotating every six months, beginning on 1 January. The General Affairs Council is composed of foreign ministers, and the Economic and Financial Affairs (Ecofin) of finance ministers. The Council also meets regularly to deal with agriculture, the environment, the internal market and transport, the relevant national ministers attending. The Council (*not* the Commission or the European Parliament) has the final power of decision on primary legislation, such as regulations and directives. Unlike many international organisations, seeking consensus is not normal practice. A few decisions requite unanimity, which means only the absence of negative votes, abstentions not being counted.[12] Most decisions are taken by qualified majority vote (QMV).[13] These days, the so-called *Luxembourg compromise*[14] is rarely invoked. In practice, its effectiveness depends on a member, which claims that a proposed decision subject to QMV would adversely affect one of its vital interests, persuading enough members constituting a blocking minority to abstain from voting.[15]

The Committee of Permanent Representatives (COREPER) prepares the work of the Council, the groundwork being done by specialist working groups. The Council, COREPER and the working groups are assisted by

[12] Cf. UNSC voting, p. 213 above.   [13] See p. 482 below.
[14] *EEC Bulletin*, March 1966, pp. 8–10.
[15] *Wyatt and Dashwood's European Union Law*, 4th edn, London, 2000, pp. 50–1.

a General Secretariat, headed by the Deputy Secretary-General. The staff of the Secretariat are employed by the Council and have their own legal service.

The Council of Ministers must not be confused with the *European Council*. The latter consists of the heads of state or government of the twenty-five member states, and is chaired by the member state holding the Presidency of the Council of Ministers (Article 4 of the TEU). The European Council meets at least once during each half-year. Its role is essentially political, providing strategic direction, and occasionally resolving major disagreements. It can also take important decisions having legal effect. The EC Treaty, as amended, refers to the 'ECU'(European Currency Unit). When in 1995 the member states decided to replace the ECU with the euro, instead of amending the EC Treaty, which would have involved a lengthy ratification procedure and national parliamentary scrutiny, the European Council formally decided that instead of the generic term ECU, the specific name euro would be used. This effective amendment of the Treaty was possible under the law of treaties, since the members of the Council represented, and were acting on behalf of, all the parties to the treaty.[16]

Commission

The nominee for President of the Commission is agreed by the member states by 'common accord', in effect by consensus. His appointment is subject to the approval of the Parliament. The other twenty-four Commissioners are nominated by their member states, and are subject to the approval of the governments of the other member states and the President-designate, who therefore has a veto over any nominee. The agreed nominees are then subject to the approval of the Parliament (Article 216). The Commissioners serve a five-year term, but can be reappointed. Although the Commission acts as one body, the President assigns each Commissioner a portfolio, such as transport, competition or trade. The staff of the Commission is headed by the Secretary-General and are organised into Directorates-General and other services, including the Commission Legal Service.

The Commission, like the secretariat of any international organisation, is independent of the member states. But, in contrast to other international

---

[16] Conclusions of the Madrid European Council 1995 (*Bulletin of the EC*, 12-1995, p. 10). On the law of treaties point, see pp. 91–2 above.

secretariats, most decisions taken by the Council under the EC Treaty are the result of an initiative by the Commission. Almost all legislation enacted by the Council has been proposed and drafted by the Commission (hence the accusation by Europhobes that Europeans are ruled by faceless, unaccountable bureaucrats in Brussels). But, under the TEU, the Commission has no exclusive right of initiative but shares it with the member states. The Commission also implements legislation when given this power by the EC Treaty or by the Council (Articles 7(1) and 202). The Council may also authorise the Commission to make subordinate legislation, such as for the common agricultural policy, or exercise coercive powers in relation to competition policy.

On matters for which the Community has exclusive competence, the Commission represents it internationally (see Article 300).

Parliament

Although it does not have all the powers of a democratic national parliament, and is not close to those who elect them, the Parliament has grown from a talking shop (until 1987 it was called the Assembly) to something more like a real parliament with actual power over the Council and the Commission. The parliamentary term is fixed at five years.

The Parliament currently has 732 members (MEPs), being since 1979 directly elected by universal suffrage in accordance with national electoral laws. The member states currently have the following number of seats: Germany (99), France, Italy and the United Kingdom (78), Poland and Spain (54), Netherlands (27), Belgium, Greece, Portugal, Hungary and the Czech Republic (24), Sweden (19), Austria (18), Denmark, Finland and Slovakia (14), Ireland and Lithuania (13), Latvia (9), Slovenia (7), Luxembourg, Estonia and Cyprus (6) and Malta (5).

The increase in the powers of the Parliament relates to three main areas. It now participates actively in the legislative process (see below); it exercises political supervision over the performance of the Commission, whose members attend parliamentary sessions and committees and are required to respond to written or oral questions (Article 197); and it constitutes the budgetary authority, in which role it is an equal partner with the Council.[17] Although the Parliament has no right of initiative, in practice it can bring varying degrees of pressure on the Council and the

---

[17] See *Wyatt and Dashwood's European Union Law*, 4th edn, London, 2000, pp. 34–6.

Commission. Ultimately, the Parliament can by a censure motion (carried by a two-thirds majority of votes cast and representing a majority of the MEPs) force the resignation of the Commissioners (Article 201). Although not yet used, it probably would have been if the Santer Commission had not resigned in March 1999 in response to pressure from the Parliament following a report by the Court of Auditors on fraud, mismanagement and nepotism within the Commission.

Court of Auditors

The Court is governed by Articles 246–248. Its structure and status are in some ways similar to the Court of Justice, and it also sits in Luxembourg. Its twenty-five members, one for each member state, are chosen generally from persons who are or were members of national audit bodies. The Court examines the accounts of EC revenue and expenditure, and takes its decisions by a simple majority. The Court has no disciplinary powers, but can withhold approval of the accounts, as it has done for the last several years.

(The Court of Justice is dealt with at p. 475 below.)

Legislative procedure

Given the areas covered by the EC Treaty, the Community has produced an enormous amount of legislation. The legislative process is elaborate and involves the Council, Commission and Parliament. The procedure is specified in the provisions in the EC Treaty that authorise action in particular areas, and is known as the 'legal basis'. Action usually requires an initial formal proposal by the Commission, which will then draft a text. But the final decision lies with the Council. Although the Parliament has no role to play in legislation relating to the common commercial policy (Article 133), in other areas it either has a consultative role or exercises a power of 'co-decision' with the Council.

Consultative procedure

Although this procedure has been largely superseded by co-decision, it still applies to legislation on, for example, the common agricultural policy, indirect tax harmonisation, aspects of environmental protection and certain European Monetary Union matters. Although the Council can consider the proposal by the Commission while the Parliament is also studying it, the Council cannot take a final decision until it has received the Opinion of the Parliament (even if that is delayed), unless it first invokes the emergency procedure (Article 196) or requests an extraordinary session of Parliament.[18] If the Commission later amends the substance of its proposal, or the Council intends to amend the text, the Parliament must again be consulted, unless the change is to accommodate a wish of Parliament. There is also a procedure whereby the Parliament can request a meeting of a Conciliation Committee at which the Council and Parliament can discuss proposed Council amendments.[19]

Co-decision procedure

Under this procedure (which is not described as 'co-decision' in the EC Treaty), the Commission submits its proposal to the Council and Parliament at the same time. There then follows an elaborate procedure, which may involve compulsory conciliation. If the process is eventually successful, the final text is signed by the Presidents of the Council and the Parliament (Articles 251–254).[20] But, since 1999, most legislation has been adopted by qualified majority voting[21] in co-decision with the Parliament.

Community law

Community law consists principally of the EC Treaty and related treaties between the member states, including accession treaties; Community legislation (for example, regulations and directives); judgments of the Court of Justice and the Court of First Instance; general principles of law, including fundamental human rights; treaties between the Community and third states; and treaties with third states binding on all the member states where the responsibilities of the latter have been assumed by the Community.

The EC Treaty and legislation

The member states have a legal obligation to comply with the obligations in the EC Treaty and with legislation made under it. The distinctive feature

---

[18] *Ibid.*, pp. 41–2.   [19] *Ibid.*, pp. 42–3.
[20] The complex procedure is described in detail in *ibid.*, pp. 43–7, together with a helpful chart.
[21] See p. 482 below.

of Community law is that it is *directly applicable* in the member states, and in many cases it has *direct effect* (Article 249(2)). *Direct applicability* means that, if a provision in the EC Treaty or in legislation made under it is capable of being applied in member states without further action by them, it becomes part of the law of the member states without the need for it to be incorporated.[22] *Direct effect* means that a provision that gives rise to rights for natural or legal persons can be enforced against member states in their courts,[23] and sometimes against other natural or legal persons.[24] Whether a provision has direct effect is a matter of interpretation. Although a regulation is directly applicable and member states need do nothing to incorporate it, they have a duty to implement directives by legislation, the form and method being a matter for each member state. But, until this is done, the directive will still have direct effect.[25] Member states must also enact supplementary domestic legislation if this is necessary to give full effect to Community legislation, including the creation of criminal offences for breaches of it.

Supremacy of Community law

It has long been established that Community law prevails over any inconsistent national law, present or future. A member state cannot plead its national law to excuse a failure to comply with an obligation under Community law.[26]

Court of Justice

The Court of Justice sits in Luxembourg. It has twenty-five judges (in practice one from each member state) assisted by eight advocates-general. All serve six-year terms, renewable for up to two terms of three years. They have not necessarily held judicial office before, some having been practising lawyers or academics. The Court sits either as a Grand Chamber of eleven judges, if a member state or a Community institution so requests,

---

[22] Because of its dualist approach to treaties (see p. 81 above), section 2(1) of the UK's European Communities Act 1972 provides that Community law is enforceable in the United Kingdom without further action by Parliament.

[23] *Van Gend & Loos*, Case 26/62 [1963] ECR 1 at 12.

[24] *Walrave & Koch*, Case 36/4 [1974] ECR 1405.

[25] See S. Prechal, *Directives in European Community Law*, Oxford, 2005.

[26] *Commission v. Italy*, Case 39/72 [1973] ECR 101; *Costa v. ENEL*, Case 6/64 [1964] ECR 585. And cf. Article 27 of the Vienna Convention on the Law of Treaties 1969, p. 79 above.

or in chambers of three or five depending on the importance or difficulty of the case. The full Court of twenty-five sits only for certain disciplinary matters or in cases of exceptional importance (Article 16 of the Statute of the Court).

The role of the advocate-general is taken from the civil law system. He is treated as a member of the Court, but does not take part in the judgment stage. Once the parties to the case have concluded their written and oral submissions, the advocate-general prepares and presents to the Court an independent and impartial Opinion analysing the facts and the law, identifying the issues and recommending a decision. Often the Court's judgment will closely follow the advocate-general's Opinion, sometimes adopting its reasoning completely. The Court seeks a consensus, but if this is not possible its judgment is decided by a simple majority. There are neither dissenting nor separate judgments.[27]

The jurisdiction of the Court is threefold: (a) to hear claims by the Commission or a member state that a member state has failed to comply with a Community obligation, or for compensation for non-contractual liability (Articles 226–228 and 235); (b) claims by Community institutions or natural or legal persons that an act of an institution is invalid (Article 230); and (c) preliminary rulings on a reference from a national court.

When interpreting Community law, the Court looks more to the object and purpose (teleological approach) of a provision and its context.[28] This is partly because the text in each Community language is equally authentic, and partly because of poor drafting and translation.[29] *Travaux préparatoires*[30] are seldom considered. When a case raises a matter of Community-wide importance, the Court may do a comparative analysis of the laws of the member states.

The Court will usually follow its previous judgments (precedents), but is not required to do so. This means that even statements of law that are not necessary for the judgment can be equally persuasive.[31]

Court of First Instance

Since 1989, the Court of Justice has had attached to it a Court of First Instance (CFI), which also sits in Luxembourg. It has twenty-five judges,

---

[27] Cf. the ICJ, p. 462 above.
[28] Cf. the approach of international tribunals, pp. 88 *et seq* above.
[29] See *R. v. Bouchereau*, Case 30/77 [1977] ECR 1999, paras. 13–14.   [30] See p. 94 above.
[31] On the Courts methods of working, see *Wyatt and Dashwood's European Union Law*, 4th edn, London, 2000, pp. 197–202.

one from each member state. Their terms of appointment are as for the judges of the Court of Justice. The CFI seldom sits in plenary session, most of its business being conducted in Chambers of three or five judges giving, like the Court of Justice, a single judgment. Since 1999, a single judge can deal with simple cases. There are no advocates-general, although any of the judges (apart from the President) can be asked to perform the functions of an advocate-general, although this is rare. There is an appeal from a judgment of the CFI to the Court of Justice on a point of law only, and therefore preliminary rulings under Article 234 cannot be sought from the CFI (Article 225). The appeal can concern only the operative part of the judgment, not the reasoning.

The CFI has jurisdiction in all cases brought by natural or legal persons against the Community or its institutions, and all such actions must be begun in the CFI. The CFI was created to relieve the Court of Justice of some of the burden of the increasing number of pending cases and so shorten the time it takes the Court to give judgment. In 1988, pending cases had nearly doubled as compared to 1980 (605, up from 328). Even at the end of 2004 there were some 1,000 cases pending before the Court and a similar number before the CFI; and it still takes the Court some two years to dispose of a case, and the CFI somewhat less. The CFI was also intended to engage in a more detailed investigation of the facts than the Court is able to do, and this the CFI has done.

The Court and the CFI can exercise only very limited jurisdiction over CFSP and PJCCM matters (Articles 35 and 46 of the TEU).

Preliminary rulings

Since most questions of Community law will be raised in the courts or tribunals of member states, it is vital for the proper functioning of the Community legal order that there should be uniform interpretations. Article 234 provides a means whereby any court or tribunal (which is interpreted liberally)[32] may seek a 'preliminary ruling' from the Court of Justice (not the CFI) concerning (a) the interpretation of the EC Treaty, (b) the validity and interpretation of acts of Community institutions (regulations, directives, etc.) and the European Central Bank (ECB), and (c) the interpretation of the statutes of bodies established by an act of the Council where the statutes so provide. The ruling is binding on the

---

[32] *Vaassen v. Beamtenfonds Mijnbedriff,* Case 61/65 [1966] ECR 261.

national court or tribunal and may require it not to apply even a subsequent national law. 'Preliminary' refers only to the fact that the court or tribunal must apply the ruling to the facts of the case when giving judgment, *not* that the ruling is provisional.

The request (or reference) can be made only while proceedings are pending. Where a question of Community law is raised by a party to the case or by a court or tribunal, and the court or tribunal considers that a decision on it is necessary to enable it to give judgment, it may request a preliminary ruling. Although a court or tribunal therefore has a discretion, unless it has complete confidence that it can deal with the issue of Community law itself, it should make a reference.[33] But, where the question is raised before a court or tribunal against which there is no judicial remedy (*inter alia*, a final court of appeal), that court or tribunal *must* request a preliminary ruling. The reference by the national court or tribunal should be self-contained and self-explanatory, setting out the basic facts of the case and posing a general question of Community law, not the issue as it needs to be decided on the particular facts. It should plausibly explain why a ruling is needed or run the risk of the Court refusing to give one.[34] The parties, any member states and the Commission may submit written and oral observations to the Court, as can the Council, the Parliament or the ECB if an act for which they are responsible is in issue.

Common Foreign and Security Policy and Police and Judicial Co-operation in Criminal Matters

The Council plays a much more dominant role in CFSP and PJCCM. Although the Commission can take initiatives in those areas, in practice it is the member states, in particular the Presidency, which take the lead. The Parliament has to be consulted, but is not directly involved in the decision-making. The member states play a larger role due to the very different range of instruments available under these two pillars. Under the CFSP, the Council adopts 'common strategies', 'joint actions' and 'common positions' (Article 12 of the TEU). These are not legally binding, merely agreed policy positions. Under the PJCCM, the Council adopts

---

[33] See Bingham MR in *R. v. Stock Exchange, ex parte Else (1982) Ltd* [1993] 1 All ER 420 at 426.

[34] See the Note for Guidance on References by National Courts for Preliminary Rulings 1996, [1997] All ER (EC) 1.

'framework decisions' and 'conventions' (Article 34(2)). The former are rather like directives in that they are binding on member states, but leave it to each member state how to implement them. The latter are multilateral treaties to which member states are free to become, or not become, parties.

Furthermore, CFSP decisions on common strategies require unanimity (abstentions are ignored), although when *implementing* a common strategy, or adopting a joint action or common position, a qualified majority is all that is needed, unless the decision has military or defence implications. If a member state declares that for 'important and stated reasons of national policy' it intends to oppose adoption of a decision by qualified majority, a vote must not be taken, although the Council can, again by a qualified majority, ask the European Council to take a decision by unanimity (Article 23 of the TEU). Under the PJCCM, the Council must act unanimously when adopting framework decisions and conventions. Unless it provides otherwise, a convention enters into force (for the ratifying states only)[35] once at least half of the member states have ratified. Measures implementing conventions are adopted within the Council by a majority of two-thirds of the parties.

Legal personality and treaties

The EC and Euratom each has legal personality in the law of each member state (Articles 281 and 282). It is also now clearly accepted by non-member states that the EC and Euratom also have *international* legal personality.[36] Each can therefore conclude treaties with states on subjects for which it has competence, and they have done so on many occasions.[37] Where the EC has *exclusive* competence, the member states can no longer conclude treaties that deal only with those subjects.[38] It is now for the EC alone to enter into such treaties, provided of course that the other negotiating states agree to this. But, where competence is shared between the EC and its member states, or where the area of application of a treaty includes overseas territories of member states,[39] both the EC and the member states

---

[35] See p. 77 above.   [36] See pp. 198–9 above.
[37] See generally Chapter 9 of MacLeod, Hendry and Hyett, *The External Relations of the European Communities*, Oxford, 1996; P. Eeckert, *External Relations of the European Union*, Oxford, 2004.
[38] See p. 481 below.
[39] For example, the Convention on the Conservation of Antarctic Marine Living Resources 1980 (CCAMLR), 402 UNTS 71 (No. 22301); ILM (1980) 837; UKTS (1982) 48; TIAS 10240; B&B Docs. 628.

can become parties. Such a treaty is known as a 'mixed agreement'. There are some treaties, such as ILO conventions, to which member states are parties, but which do not allow for the EC to be a party even if it has exclusive competence for the subject matter. In those cases, the member states that are parties to the treaty have an obligation to protect the interests of the EC. But these internal matters are of no direct concern to the other parties.

Where there is shared competence, such as for social security matters, the member states can still conclude bilateral treaties with third states or with each other, although in doing so they must ensure that the treaty is consistent with Community law. To protect member states' rights when the EC alone concludes a treaty on a subject of shared competence, the member states will usually insist on the inclusion of what is known as a 'Canada Clause', which declares that the member states retain power to enter into treaties on the subject.[40] Some treaties contain a provision under which the EC can make a 'declaration of competence' about the respective competences of itself and its member states with regard to the matters covered by the treaty.[41]

But the TEU does not confer international legal personality on the EU. This was for political reasons, some member states not having wished to enhance the status of the EU in this way. So, when the member states wish to conclude a treaty with a third party within the CFSP and PJCCM fields, the Council concludes it. This will change if the Constitution enters into force.[42]

Human rights

Article 6 of the TEU confirms, what the Court of Justice had previously held, that the EU must respect, as general principles of Community law, the fundamental rights guaranteed by the European Convention on Human Rights 1950 (ECHR). This is hardly surprising given that all member states are also bound by the ECHR. Article 46(d) of the TEU gives the

---

[40] See MacLeod, Hendry and Hyett, *The External Relations of the European Communities*, Oxford, 1996, pp. 234–5. The name of the clause has nothing to do with Canadian federalism, but because the clause was first used in a Canada–EC treaty of 1976, OJ 1976 L260/1.

[41] See Article 5 of Annex IX to the UN Convention on the Law of the Sea 1982 (n. ** above) and Article 47 of the Fish Stocks Agreement 1995, 2167 UNTS 3 (No. 37924); ILM (1995) 1542; UKTS (2004) 19.

[42] See p. 484 below.

Court jurisdiction over human rights questions with regard to action by the institutions insofar as the Court has jurisdiction in respect of the EC, Euratom or the EU. Naturally, human rights must also be respected by member states when implementing Community measures.[43] At present, the EU is not a party to the ECHR, and therefore the European Court of Human Rights has no jurisdiction over EU institutions. However, Article 17 of Protocol No. 14 to the ECHR provides for the EU to accede to the ECHR, although this cannot happen until all the parties to the ECHR have ratified the Protocol.

The Charter of Fundamental Rights was proclaimed on 7 December 2000 by the European Council.[44] Its fifty Articles do not yet have legal status, but reflect and confirm human rights that are already binding on member states as parties to the ECHR, or are taken from Council of Europe conventions or Community directives. Because the Charter includes certain social and economic rights, the scope of which may still not be clear, it remains somewhat controversial.

Acquis communautaire

This fancy phrase means only what the Community has achieved and built upon: constituent treaties, legislation, general principles, judgments of the Court of Justice, treaties with non-member states, etc. An applicant for membership therefore has to accept the *acquis*, subject only to those detailed modifications that are acceptable to the existing members and included in the accession treaty.[45]

Competence

This is shorthand for where power and responsibility for a particular matter lies: with the Community or member states, or shared (Article 5). The Constitution would make this rather clearer than it is now.

Comitology

Comitology means implementation of Community legislation by the Commission with the help of a specialist committee.[46]

---

[43] *Wachauf*, Case 5/88 [1989] ECR 2609, para. 19.
[44] ILM (2001) 266.   [45] See the text to n. 8 above.
[46] See J. Klabbers, *An Introduction to International Institutional Law*, Cambridge, 2002, pp. 178–80.

European Economic Area

This confusing name was created by a 1992 agreement between the EC and the remaining members of the European Free Trade Area (EFTA),[47] under which the latter enjoy the benefits of the single market but without the full privileges and responsibilities of EC membership. The EEA agreement now applies only to Iceland, Norway and Liechtenstein. Switzerland, a member of EFTA, has not ratified the 1992 agreement.

Languages

The EC has twenty-one official languages: Czech, Danish, Dutch, English, Estonian, Finnish, French, German, Greek, Hungarian, Irish,[48] Italian, Latvian, Lithuanian, Maltese, Polish, Portuguese, Slovakian, Slovenian, Spanish and Swedish. Community legislation is issued in all the languages and, in principle, meetings are interpreted into all the languages. Working groups and other informal meetings are conducted in English and French.

Qualified majority voting

As from 1 November 2004, adoption by the Council by qualified majority voting (QMV) of a proposal from the Commission has required at least 232 votes cast in its support, provided they are cast by at least a simple majority of the members (i.e. thirteen). In other cases, the 232 votes must be cast by at least two-thirds of the members (i.e. seventeen). In addition, when a decision is to be adopted by QMV, any member may request verification that the members constituting the majority represent at least 62 per cent of the total population of the Community. If they do not, the decision is not adopted.

The 321 votes in the Council are allocated as follows: France, Germany, Italy and the United Kingdom (29), Poland and Spain (27), the Netherlands (13), Belgium, the Czech Republic, Greece, Hungary and Portugal (12), Austria, Sweden (10), Denmark, Finland, Ireland, Lithuania and Slovakia (7), Cyprus, Estonia, Latvia, Luxembourg and Slovenia (4) and Malta (3). Thus any of the four largest states can use their combined 112–116 votes to block a proposal (e.g. 321 − 112 = 209). The Constitution would change this (see below).

---

[47] See p. 468, n. 7, above.   [48] Irish is used only in the governing treaties.

Schengen

This is shorthand for the 1990 Agreement[49] (signed in the Luxembourg town of that name) abolishing all (internal) immigration checks on travellers between the member states (and now also Iceland and Norway), except Ireland, the United Kingdom and, for the moment, the ten new members who joined in 2004. Under the Agreement, internal checks are allowed only for a limited period when they are necessary for national security or public order reasons. The Schengen countries have a common visa policy for third-state nationals, who once they have entered a Schengen country with a visa issued by that country are then free to travel anywhere within the Schengen area.

Subsidiarity

This contrived term means merely that EC decisions should be taken as closely as possible to the citizen. Unless a matter is one for which the EC has exclusive competence, the EC should not act unless that would be more effective than action at the national, regional or local level (Article 5).

Treaty establishing a Constitution for Europe

A Treaty establishing a Constitution for Europe ('the Constitution') was adopted by an Intergovernmental Conference (IGC) of the member states on 18 June 2004 and signed by all member states on 29 October 2004.[50] It is intended to enter into force on 1 November 2006, provided by then all twenty-five have ratified it. Several member states will first have referendums, and two referendums have already rejected the Constitution.

Although it makes some important changes, the Constitution should not be seen as as radical a development as some eurosceptics would have us believe. It will not give primacy to EU law, since that principle was established long ago. Nor will it make the Union a state. It will not give the Union competence in many new areas; decisions on tax harmonisation will still require unanimity. Rather, the Constitution makes it clearer that the Union is the creation of the member states who, by coming together in the Union, can pursue their common goals more effectively. The main changes would be:

---

[49] ILM (1991) 68.   [50] See www.europa.eu.int/constitution/.

- merging of the EC and the EU (but not Euratom) into one organisation, the Union, with only one governing treaty, the Constitution, yet retaining special procedures for foreign policy, security and defence;
- conferring legal personality on the Union alone;
- integrating the Charter of Fundamental Rights into the Constitution;
- clarifying how the competences are distributed; the Union would have exclusive competence for monetary policy for the euro member states, common commercial policy, the customs union and the common fisheries policy; and the Union would share competence with member states on, for example, the internal market, security and justice, agriculture, transport, energy, social policy, the environment and public health;
- simplifying the legal instruments and procedures available to the institutions;
- clarifying the respective roles of the Council, the Parliament and the Commission;
- extending the co-decision procedure so that some 95 per cent of Union legislation would be adopted jointly by the Council and the Parliament;
- creating a Union Minister of Foreign Affairs (although a Commissioner, he would operate according to a mandate determined by the Council and would be able to conclude treaties between the Union and third states);
- distinguishing the European Council more clearly from the Council of Ministers, and appointing a President of the European Council for a two-and-a-half-year term with limited powers;
- limiting the Parliament to a maximum of 750 seats, with a minimum of six, and a maximum of ninety-nine, seats per member;
- keeping one Commissioner per member state until 2014, after which the number would correspond to two-thirds of the member states, the Commissioners being chosen according to a system based on equal rotation among the member states;
- changing the qualified majority. Adoption of a proposal would require the support of at least 55 per cent of the member states (fourteen out of twenty-five) representing at least 65 per cent of the population of the Union. For a minority to prevent adoption of a decision, it would therefore have to include *at least* four large member states, so making it that much more difficult for such member states to block adoption. Also, Council members representing at least three-quarters of a blocking minority, whether at the level of member states or population, could require a vote to be postponed so that discussions can continue for a reasonable time in an attempt to reach a broader basis for consensus.

Documentation

Given the mass of documents, legal instruments and judgments, finding the one you want is not always easy. Perhaps the first port of call should be the official website, www.europa.eu.int. Regulations have the number first and then the year of publication (e.g. 423/2004, on recovery of cod stocks). Directives have the year of publication first and then the number (e.g. 2003/48/EC, on taxation of savings interest). Each case before the Court of Justice is given a number, preceded by C and followed by the year (e.g. C30/77, *R. v. Bouchereau*). A CFI case number is preceded by T (e.g. T264/97, *D. v. Council*). An appeal is marked with a P (e.g. C310/97P, *Commission v. AssiDoman*). All judgments are published in the official *European Court Reports* (ECR). The *Common Market Law Reports* (CMLR) publishes the most important judgments of the Court and judgments on EC law by courts of member states.

INDEX